P9-CCZ-799

An Experience of Women

An Experience of Women

PATTERN AND CHANGE
IN NINETEENTH-CENTURY EUROPE

Priscilla Robertson

with an Appendix by Steve Hochstadt

DISCARDED

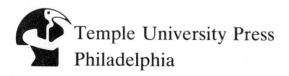
Temple University Press
Philadelphia

LIBRARY
FORSYTH TECHNICAL COMMUNITY COLLEGE
2100 SILAS CREEK PARKWAY
WINSTON SALEM, N.C. 27103

Temple University Press
© 1982 by Temple University. All rights reserved
Published 1982
Printed in the United States of America

Publication of this book has been assisted by a
grant from the Publication Program of the
National Endowment for the Humanities.

Library of Congress Cataloging in Publication Data

Robertson, Priscilla Smith.
   An experience of women.

   Bibliography: p.
   Includes index.
   1. Women—Europe—History—19th century.
2. Feminism—Europe—History—19th century.
I. Title.
HQ1588.R6   305.4'2'094   81-9315
ISBN 0-87722-234-7   AACR2

385.92 R88 f78z

Gift $4.95

VITÂ
CARIORIBUS
FILIIS
SACRUM

Charlotte   Harry   Cary

∽ And yet, there really is a mountain. Only the observer does not get to know it by looking at postcards, any more than the historian can master an event or an era by pondering the outlines of great overarching interpretations. To those familiar with its ridged and wrinkled flanks, with its spread of jagged stone, and with the immense variety of its restless streams, the mountain is far from displaying a clear, conical shape. It offers, rather, the sum of many particular visual impressions—slopes of wood and stone and grass, lines of rock and water, huddled buildings, gaps of sky—which merge in the mind of the viewer endowed with patience and imagination. As do the numerous scraps of evidence hoarded by the historian. All those problems about objectivity and point of view that trouble historians dissolve in the mountain atmosphere.

Oscar Handlin
"Living in a Valley," 1977

ᗡContents

ᴏ Acknowledgments

I began this book when I was a Fellow of the Radcliffe Institute in 1965, before women's studies had become a separate discipline. I do not believe there was another place in the world where comparable freedom and scholarly riches were combined. Ever since that time I have received great courtesy from the Harvard libraries, where the major part of my research was done.

This book could not have been written if the community of scholars had not turned out to be also a community of friends. The British Museum, the Bibliothèque Nationale, the Staatsbibliothek in Munich, all received me with kindness and served me with efficiency. I owe a special debt of gratitude to the Louisville Free Public Library and its inter-library loan officer, Eleanor Narkis, who performed several outstanding feats of detection in locating books. The Kornhauser Health Sciences Library of the University of Louisville was likewise obliging.

The following people have read all or part of the manuscript, and each one of them added something valuable, in substance or in suggestions about the style and readability, or, most often, both: Steve Hochstadt, Charlotte Maneikis, Caroline Krebs, Jim Wayne Miller, John Combs, Donald Symons, Helen Mulvey, who first gave me the idea for this book, and Charlotte Symons, my daughter.

I have been exceptionally lucky in the intelligence and concern of those young people who were involved more intimately in the preparation of the manuscript. My niece, Sharon Tisher, worked at my side in the Bibliothèque Nationale; Jeanne Drennan and Cynthia Bestoso Rettig burrowed successively in the stacks of Widener to elucidate difficult points concerning names, dates, and sources; the latter also checked the Bibliography. Edith Nitch-Smith and Elizabeth Garrott contributed their good taste and sense of order to editing the text, while Janet Levy makes typing into an art form even in a text with a double set of notes and many quotations. I am much obliged to Steve Hochstadt for his expert and original work on the Appendix. Daryll Anderson worked on the Index. I also owe a debt hard to repay to Emma Taylor and Viola Trowel.

I should like to thank Oscar Handlin for permission to use a paragraph from his essay "Living in a Valley" as the epigraph to this volume, and Messrs. Chatto and Windus for permission to use several long quotations from *A Book With Seven Seals*, by Agnes Maud Davies, to which they hold the copyright.

xi

I am enormously grateful to Jane Barry, and to the editorial staff of the Temple University Press for the generosity which has made getting this book to press a pleasure. They have handled the manuscript with meticulous care in large things and in small.

All of these people, the ones mentioned by name and also those who manned the desks of the institutions, made the book better than it would otherwise have been. For the deficiencies, I alone am responsible.

Translations from foreign language titles listed in the Bibliography are by me unless otherwise credited.

An Experience of Women

∽Introduction

> Besides many small and painful things [in past times for women] there
> is also so much of greatness and beauty that we often sigh—where has
> all the depth, interest, devotion, enthusiasm, willingness to sacrifice,
> self-forgetfulness emerged in our shallow, realistic times?
>
> Luise Otto-Peters, 1876

What were women doing in the nineteenth century? How much responsibility did they take? And how was authority exercised by them and over them?

And what did people think about women's role? What was it that made the "woman question" suddenly seem new and important, all across Europe?

This book will try to answer both questions. The nineteenth century was a time when what women could or should do seemed newly perplexing; to some it seemed a problem, to others a cause, but in either case a subject for animated discussion.

∽ I have limited this social-intellectual history to the middle and upper segments of society for three reasons: first, from this group comes most of the direct evidence, for few records of the views of the illiterate exist or are yet discovered, and those that exist are usually filtered through some writing by a member of another class; then, this was the group which had some real choice, for whom the discussion could lead to genuine alternatives, while poverty, overwork, and lack of education kept the working classes from enjoying such opportunity; and lastly, these classes provided the pioneers who broke down the barriers, who supplied new ideas, and who organized a women's movement.

Women of the lower social strata do enter the picture from time to time in several ways. First, there were always some who by character and determination moved into positions where they worked with and influenced the women's movement; women like Suzanne Voilquin and Annie Kenney. Secondly, some of the upper-middle-class leaders of the movement usually felt committed to their sex as a whole and were interested in improving the lot of prostitutes, domestic servants, or factory workers. Lastly, the socialists who organized masses of working-class women interacted with the middle-class feminists in a love-hate relationship that probably held back both movements for reasons that I shall explore at the end of the book.

Yet social class matters less in the study of women than in other areas of social history. Women in the last century faced certain common problems, whether they were duchesses or tradesmen's wives. Law and custom placed them all under their husbands' domination, financially and sexually.

I have included material from four countries and hope to make comparisons among them. In the nineteenth century itself, many writers assumed that there was a special kinship between the racially aligned "Teutonic" English and Germans, and again between the "Latin" French and Italians. Though I have quoted some interesting contemporary generalizations along this line, my material has developed into much more diverse patterns. For this reason I follow no regular order for dealing with the different countries. For each aspect I have tried to pick that nation in which it was most coherent or dramatic, and then contrast this one with the others.

    As for the time span, it runs roughly from 1815 to 1914, from the defeat of Napoleon until the outbreak of the First World War. Through many vicissitudes, this was the century during which women came together for the first time *as women*, to demand that they be recognized as equal human beings, and though they did not get the vote in any of the four countries, they won significant rights over property, children, and their own minds and bodies.

In the eighteenth century there had been less emphasis on sexual roles. Doubtless women were not encouraged to advance in the same way as men, but when they wished to they were not forbidden simply by reason of their sex. Thus they were teaching in Italian universities up until the 1820s; women property owners had occasionally been allowed to vote (in England until the First Reform Act of 1832; in France for the last Estates General of 1789; in Austria and some German states for their provincial assemblies). Some women were licensed to practice medicine. And when they joined in protest against social conditions, as during the French Revolution and up through the 1819 Peterloo massacre in England, they commonly united with their men to fight for universal, not sexual, privileges.

Shortly after the nineteenth century began, however, new philosophies and new social conditions caused a period of hibernation. While men's work increasingly took them out into the world, women were perceived as having their major role within the home. This was not meant to be enslavement, but the answer to genuine social problems, notably the high infant mortality rate, which proper motherly care might abate, and the need to give the young a better start within the home, part of the new interest in children. Many women did find this a fulfilling role, and others were able to use the more serious education it offered as a stepping stone to wider spheres.

In general, women could be summoned outside the home to meet various kinds of practical emergencies, and in Germany, and even more in Italy, they contribute heavily to the wars for national liberation. Meanwhile, in all the continental countries, men were theorizing about new, "liberal" laws and constitutions; when these came into being, women, so recently praised for their devotion, found they were left out of the privileges of citizenship, much to their surprise. All three of the French republics (1792, 1848, 1871) set them back on their heels, and likewise the Civil Codes of the emergent unified nations of Italy (1866) and Germany (1896). It was largely in response to such maneuvers that the women's movement was organized, not just against age-old repressions and habits. In every country women pushed for admission to universities and professions, for the right to handle their own money, for certain civil rights, and especially for guardianship of their children. It is this pattern, with its national variations, its crosscurrents, its sudden supernova-like bursts of energy, its cyclical turnabouts, that this volume attempts to analyze.

ꭞ The book is in two parts. The first half describes the pattern that women's lives were expected to follow; the second presents breakers of that pattern, the rebels. In describing what ordinary life was like, I have tried to explain not only the laws and customs, but the psychological and social assumptions that lay under them. It is impossible to interpret the history of past time exclusively in terms of today's motivations and expectations. I have also tried to indicate what handholds the traditional pattern offered for those who wanted to break out of it.

It is natural to describe the way of life of the majority in terms of generalizations, of rather abstract figures, but the rebels, of course, are sharply individual. And yet even they followed certain typical paths. If one George Sand went to Italy with her lover, it turns out that this was quite a habit among lesser-known women writers of the period, and not just because they were copying her. The women who fell out of step with the majority were very seldom really alone; they usually found a group of comrades marching to the same drum, and the discovery of such patterns has made this book easier to write. I think of such groups as the activist unmarried English women, the members of the German teachers' union, and the heroines of the Italian Risorgimento.

ꭞ As for sources, all kinds of material have been grist for my mill. Philosophic discussions and academic lectures were often reflected, though simplified, in homely books of advice, and their insights confirmed in fiction. Second-rate fiction, I noticed, was often more revealing of the unconscious assumptions of a period than great works of genius, which tend to transcend ordinary thinking. Travelers often observed features of life in a foreign country that escaped the notice of the natives, and occasionally it is possible to get a crossruffing of such views across a national boundary. Then, of course, the expressions of women in diaries and letters and reminiscences are of paramount value, and most valuable of all was the testament of their lives. I have also felt free to share with my readers certain informal material. Conversations with Victorian survivors have helped me to understand what was going on during the period I am studying, and I agree with Luise Otto-Peters, the founder of the German feminist movement, who said,

> We hope to be fair and not to hurt feelings about the good old days; we are not writing a satire, but we welcome humor when it comes by itself, for we possess enough freedom of spirit to enjoy its effect, in life as in social history, and that we can make clear and understand—and conquer—the world better through it than by any other means.[1]

While fully aware of the many useful, imaginative, and revealing uses to which statistical material has been put in the deciphering of history, I have not been able to use it for my purposes.* Some of the difficulties are explained by Steve Hochstadt in the Appendix to this volume. He has surveyed the census material to see if it can confirm or contradict the subjective feelings of my literacy informants. In general he came to the conclusion that because of the absence of class differentiation in most censuses and other statistical data, these data are of rather little use in backing the hypotheses that derive from literary sources, but the few cases that seem to apply do confirm, and none contradict, my conclusions. When I find six observers reporting a certain phenomenon, and nobody denying it, I have a choice of interpretations. Perhaps it is mere chance: six other writers might all be on the other side. Or it may be that the authors are copying clichés from each other (a habit Bacon complained of in the seventeenth century). Or perhaps the six are reporting something real. It is a matter of guessing, since I do not have six thousand witnesses, but I have tried to use judgment in assessing the probabilities and at the same time let my readers know on what sorts of testimony the conclusions are based in each case.

⋘ Names present a problem in view of the fact that most women changed theirs during the course of their lives, many of them several times. I have usually called my characters by whatever appellation seemed easiest for the reader to remember at the moment, and have tried to make connections clear in the Index between, say, Aurore Dudevant

---

*Topology is the branch of mathematics which deals with shapes rather than numbers. If history must be cast into mathematical form, perhaps this is the branch some of us are adopting.

and George Sand (née Dupin). The modern practice of calling women by their current surname does not seem to fit these women, who would never so have referred to themselves. Though I plead guilty to occasional inconsistency, I hope it is clear that I respect many of these women far too much to believe that calling them by their given names from time to time will denigrate their achievements.

Finally, let me list here some of the motifs that will recur during the course of the book.

A major theme is the increasing individualism of women as education and work differentiate their personalities. This made for stronger interest in a personal and unique relationship in marriage, and when this was missing, it led to widespread demands for divorce.

Women's wishes in sexual matters were conflicting, sometimes to have freedom and fulfillment in love "like a man," and at other times to surmount "coarse" physicality and put life on a higher plane, and drag men up there too.

How authority was exercised within the family and how decisions were made, whether by a single individual or by a group process, differed sharply among the different countries, and eventually affected the way in which the women's movements grew.

I have mentioned the continuing but ambivalent relationship between the women's movement and socialism. Socialists stood for equality between the sexes, as between the classes, but they also believed in free love (or so it was believed), communal living, confiscation of capital (on which middle-class women often built their careers), and strict party discipline, which affronted the hard-won individualization of the bourgeois feminists. These differences kept an alliance that might have been fruitful from solidifying.

I am always interested in how individual women asserted themselves, and so this book is full of accounts of particular women. In giving thumbnail sketches of their lives, I have tried to call attention to the ways in which the general conditions surrounding women affected their accomplishment, as well as to give some sense of what it would feel like to be in their shoes.

It is clear that the process of growth moves in no straight line. Women used their home assignment, their need for jobs, their interest in ideas—all sorts of things—to give them one handhold after another. Some of the trends proved retrogressive; some conflicted with others. But if the final picture were totally neat, it would certainly be false. I hope, on the contrary, to show the immense diversity of women with all their courage, their imagination, their determination, and their sense of life.

PART I

The Pattern

The extraordinary woman depends on the ordinary woman. It is only when we know what were the conditions of the average woman's life—the number of her children, whether she had money of her own, if she had a room to herself, whether she had help in bringing up her family, if she had servants, whether part of the housework was her task—it is only when we can measure the way of life and the experience of life made possible to the ordinary woman that we can account for the success or failure of the extraordinary woman. . . .

Virginia Woolf, 1929

∽ I.

The New Domesticity

He sings to the wide world
And she to her nest,
In the nice ear of Nature
Which song is the best?
                    [Origin unknown]

In the eighteenth century domestic life was rather out of fashion in middle- and upper-class circles of Europe. Houses were still centers of production, not just of consumption, as they were to become between 1800 and 1900. Pleasures too were notably taken in public places. The eighteenth century was the great age of pleasure gardens, of public drinking on the part of both sexes, of public balls. Lenore Davidoff points out that the last big public ball in London was held in 1818.[1] The emphasis in girls' education was to produce women of social brilliance who could run salons or help their husbands' careers by other visible success. The relationship to those husbands was often a formal one, but at the same time one of social equality, while children were seen as an inconvenience that should be kept from interfering with the pleasures and intrigues of their mothers. Thus, home life as we think of it today did not flourish.

As the new century opened, a different sentiment began to spread. One of the observers who defined the change—in fact, predicted it—was Maria Edgeworth, who in collaboration with her father, Richard Lovell Edgeworth, published in 1798 a treatise on the pleasures of educating young children. She explained that this work was intended to anticipate the likely fashion of twenty years in the future. By that time, she thought, the ideal of "domestic happiness" would have supplanted the eighteenth century's stress on "success in the world."[2] It is hard to say exactly what led Maria to forecast this change of style, but it turned out to be accurate; in the first years of the nineteenth century, the whole concept of family life was turned around, and the "rather stunted sentiments of motherhood" of the previous period gave way to the widespread feeling that women not only belonged in the home but also had exceedingly important duties to attend to there. To fulfill them would not be a confinement so much as a liberation into a new sphere of importance.

Maria Edgeworth (1767–1849) had ample chance to explore both sorts of life. The daughter of an Irish landowner from County Longford, and a close friend of the Duchess of Wellington, she received such acclaim for her novels that (after Mme de Staël) she might well have been considered the leading woman of letters of her time. Sir Walter Scott wrote that he conceived the idea of the Waverley novels from her. And when her father took her to Paris in 1802, she was received with all the honors of a literary lioness. At that time she had her only love affair: a handsome and honorable Swede asked her to marry him, but though it cost her considerable suffering, she reflected on how much her own family, including fifteen younger brothers and sisters, would miss her, and decided to return to the form of "domestic happiness" with which she was familiar.

The new sentiment was identified in most people's minds with Jean Jacques Rousseau (1712–1778), prophet of a new morality, and, as it happened, a personal friend of Richard Edgeworth. Although Rousseau's advice that mothers should nurse their own babies and that children should be objects of much closer attention than had been customary seemed austere to his early readers, his later disciples explained that this was not really so. "It is a family fête which he celebrates; it is a mother which he presents to the adoration of the world, seated near a cradle, a beautiful child on her bosom, her countenance beaming with joy beneath the tender looks of her husband."[3] Women were to work a universal regeneration, in effect, based on the happiness of children and leading ultimately to freedom for the whole human race.

The first barrage of propaganda addressed to women at the turn of the nineteenth century concerned the duty of staying home, to be followed a few years later by fuller exploration of the possibilities of a life there based on affection and usefulness to menfolk and children. Later still came a perception that the domestic sphere could expand as more and more was demanded in the way of marital companionship and guidance of the young, until finally it seemed, to patriotic orators at least, that mothers were actually the pillars of the new national state.

Rousseau cannot be credited with an ardent interest in women's rights, but two of his principles—romantic love and simplicity in social relationships—came to seem prophetic for natural family life and for the new patriotism. All along, his admirers said, while he seemed only to be thinking of giving mothers to their children, his real aim was to give citizens to the country: "The mother's milk shall be the milk of liberty!"[4] By the twentieth century, such sentiments had become common: "Oh, dear little Frenchwomen, how well you have deserved *of your country* if, by love and good management, you succeed in making your home into a warm comfortable nest from which none goes out except to work" (emphasis added).[5]

There were various ways to embroider on this new emphasis on how women could exert influence from their homes. While French social thinkers were inclined to turn the commitment into a means of increasing their country's military glory, John Ruskin in England specifically declared that women ought to use their position to forbid unjust wars and deal with suffering people.[6] It is true he gave no directions for accomplishing these ends. Women were to order, comfort, and adorn the state, but certainly never to vote. By the turn of the next century, the Swedish feminist Ellen Key was stating firmly that the most important job of adults is to rear a healthy new generation; this was the central work of society.[7]

cṣ Social conditions after the Napoleonic Wars encouraged a retreat into private life all across the continent, but perhaps Germany offered the most dramatic example of a country where "family life," almost lost in the eighteenth century, was revived. In 1806–1807, as French armies overran most German-speaking lands and brought in a set of ideals based on social equality and efficiency, most Germans reacted by trying to preserve their own institutions (such as schools) from French influence, but with very little success. What it finally came down to, in many cases, was each family saving itself, so that children grew up in those years with the feeling that family was the whole of life, not just part of it. Families had to forage for their own food, settle their own disputes, and educate their own children. Out of this experience grew a great national strength, a strength sufficient to drive the French out after a few years and to create a new, fervent patriotism. This brief but heroic period was also ideally suited to future nostalgia. Only in Germany, mused the novelist Karl Immermann in 1839, did the family reach its highest potential—actually, he reasoned, a continuation of the ancient Teutonic notion that woman was holy, combined with the idea that the family was an organic entity.[8] While the Italians had babies by mere instinct, he went on, and the French were noted for cherishing their old people, only in Germany could you find households capable of absorbing all the ages of man and supporting all his varied emotions, egoism as well as sacrifice, opposition as well as dependency.

Unfortunately, it seemed, as governments and other social institutions began the work of restoration after the war years, the German family lost this primary character, and disillusionment crept in. Immermann was able to diagnose this trouble as the result of a shift from love to reason.[9] Oh fatal French influence! The notion of constitutionalism, or of "rights," was having its chilling effect within the home as well as in other institutions of society, Immermann continued, so that parents became afraid to discipline and began acting like old friends with their children, as "equals" in fact.

A few years later a German sociologist, Dr. W. H. Riehl, began a counteroffensive. In 1853 he brought out a treatise, *Die Familie*. Its influence was extraordinary. When an Englishwoman, Mrs. Alfred Sidgwick, tried to find out in 1912 why German women occupied such a low place in society, she was told by a professor that anyone who would speak with authority on the German family must read Riehl's book. Hunting for the volume in question, Mrs. Sidgwick was surprised to find that it had been written almost sixty years before, but throughout that long period there are clear traces of its influence on all sorts of people who were hoping for the regeneration of old German life.

A few words here may give an idea of its flavor. Riehl deplored French political ideas as much as any German, but he also called attention to the dangers of capitalism, which in his opinion had a doubly evil effect. While the new industrial system tended to separate each nuclear family from the organic roots that Riehl believed gave vitality to home life, at the same time capitalistic internationalism worked against patriotism and the organic quality of the nation as a whole.* Unless the family could win back both its autonomy and its hierarchical organization, the whole society would perish either in a police state or in socialist classlessness. In either case, all individuals would be treated as equal and interchangeable. Proper independence for a German, Riehl stated, should not be individual but mediated through a corporate body, and of corporate bodies the family was the first and most important.[10]

In this view of life, the only contact between most family members and the world outside would be through the husband and father. This vision was naturally gratifying to German men, such as Lorenz von Stein, who undertook to discuss woman's place in the national economy in 1880, and who explained just how he wanted his own life to run. When he went out in the morning, he declared, he left his own household and belonged to the world, but when he went back at evening, he expected the soft hand of his wife to smooth his forehead and her friendly words to fall like dew on the cares of the day. At that time he did not wish the world of work to have any claims on him.[11]

In France, different social conditions led to a somewhat similar result, and the valuation of home life increased perceptibly. In the eighteenth century almost all city infants had been sent out to the land to be nursed for several years. This was true for all classes of society; only 20 percent of the babies born in Paris in 1780 had been nursed there, according to the Chief of Police at that time, and these might have come from families rich enough to import a wet nurse. Middle-class babies were regularly exported, while a system of foundling hospitals took infants left on their doorsteps and arranged for their transportation to the

*Compare Sir Henry Maine's study of primitive law: "The unit of an ancient society was the family, of a modern society the individual" (1863). But also compare Levin Schücking's idea, at variance with Riehl's, that "the bourgeoisie's most outstanding achievement is the transformation of the family into a real community" (Schücking, 181). Neither Schücking nor Riehl would have agreed with Marx, though for different reasons. Marx thought that capitalism indeed destroyed the family, but that that was rather a good thing.

country with relays of wet nurses to keep them alive on the way. The mortality rate was nevertheless frightful and was a subject of great concern to the doctors of the day. As the children, rich or poor, grew older, they were often kept in convents for their education and frequently were brought home to their parents' houses for the first time as adolescents, nearly as strangers.

The Revolution of 1789 abolished many of the religious houses which had made this way of life possible, and when the Reign of Terror made activity outside the home dangerous, there was a conspicuous revival of private life,[12] which was to a certain extent consolidated by Napoleon. Although his Civil Code of 1804 limited women's legal freedom, he was much in favor of *mothers* and encouraged girls' education for domestic duties. By the time of the Restoration, in 1815, domesticity had become so fashionable that husbands and wives could often be found at home together in the evening, which was a clear change from the etiquette of the *ancien régime*. Even though the convents were reopened at this time, many girls were now kept at home for their education, and those who were sent away found a much more practical curriculum than had been available for their grandmothers, with more emphasis on domestic skills and less on social accomplishments. It seemed important for women to have something useful inside their heads, and not the least compelling reason given was that it would enable them to teach their children at home.

During the years after Napoleon too, home began to seem a refuge, in a way that it had not previously, for the increasing number of men whose work took them daily out to office jobs. Philarète Chasles, a literary critic, felt that industrial society, far from destroying family life as Riehl had feared, actually created a need for intimacy and a place of retreat from the inexorability of life outside. Such feelings were only intensified by periods of political change, of which France had a great number, so that lay prophets from Jules Michelet on called for renovation of family life as the only possible salvation for society. Men like him, in great numbers, begged women to remain unpolluted by keeping out of public life. If they took on public functions, or even liberal professions, it would taint the nest.

Women's central position in the home, of course, was tied to a new regard for the child. When the long wars were over and children were no longer seen as potential cannon fodder, they began to live at home with their mothers and came to be objects of devotion and individualized attention in a way that had not been previously possible.

It was perhaps easier to love children in this new time, partly because there were now fewer of them, and this too was related to a revolutionary principle. A law of 1790, passed in the time when the Rights of Man were still a flaming ideal, gave equal inheritance to all the children in a family, girls as well as boys. Frenchmen quickly figured out that this rule made it very difficult to leave a fortune to each child unless the number of children was kept small; at least, nearly every French theorizer from mid-century on attributed the noticeable decline in the birth rate to this law,* though the cause-and-effect relationship has been questioned by modern scholars. (In her book about the image of Victorian women in French eyes, Sylvaine Marandon puts the average number of children in a French family at 2.2, while the comparable English figure was 5.5.[13] These are not the same as the census figures, but perhaps reflect the experience of the literate classes whose lives are being explored here, and certainly they agree with the common perception on both sides of the Channel.)

These few children became the object of unprecedented interest to their parents. The practice of sending children out to nurse was almost totally abandoned, and by 1880 it was confined to those small tradesmen and artisans who needed the wife's help in the shop. The moral of a charming and enormously popular book entitled *Monsieur, madame et bébé* (1866) was that French fathers should become *papas sérieux*, and while it concentrated on a single child, the hope seemed to be that this kind of family care would build a nation and turn the young into good citizens, and, as the century wore on, soldiers. Philippe Ariès calls what happened a veritable changed state of consciousness, a new idea of how life could be lived within a family. The Parisian bourgeois was *l'homme d'une famille* even before he was an individual.[14]

But this ideal was quite different from Riehl's for Germany. In 1856 a French professor openly responded to Riehl in a series of lectures given at Strasbourg to an audience of both sexes and all ages.[15] Edouard Janet explained that although he was by profession a philosopher, he wrote in what he hoped would be a popular and domestic style, neither baffling nor elementary. Paying tribute to Riehl's intelligence, he refused to follow him into the patriarchal past, and naturally he attacked Riehl's anti-French bias.

To Janet, what created the family was not authority but affection of a nature that embraced senses and soul, imagination, intelligence, and heart. The most important thing in life, he thought, was not passion (in spite of all our romances) but the establishment of a family. The difference from the German family was that instead of having the father "out front," as Riehl had dictated, each member of the French family was to find within the home his own highest development. Neither slavery for women nor tyranny on the part of men, but a bridle for men's vanity and gross appetites and a protection for women's dignity were his objectives.[16]

In Italy, where the French armies of occupation remained from 1796 through 1815, the striking improvement in family relations owed

---

*One might point out that Frédéric Le Play, the originator of the theory relating the inheritance law to the French birth rate, himself favored rescinding the law, a step which he hoped might revive the patriarchal family. His vision becomes very much like Riehl's.

something to their revolutionary influence, and something to Napoleon's interest in family regeneration, and, something, of course, to the general changes in styles of life. The *cicisbeo*, the permitted lover who formerly acted as an escort to many upper-class ladies, and likewise the family confessor, who often combined his religious duties with tutoring the children and had proved a disruptive force in so doing, started to disappear. A new sort of united family came into existence. Italian mothers began to devote themselves to the care of their own children, as French ones were learning to do. When the French armies left Italian soil and the Austrians came back to dominate the peninsula under the provisions of the Treaty of Vienna, Italians found in their family life a new strength to resist.

It is true that when Lady Sydney Morgan, an Irishwoman, visited Italy in 1820, she was struck by the persisting indifference of Italian mothers, which she attributed to lack of education. She was comparing conditions with those in England, but she roused furious controversy in Italy. An Italian response of 1825 insisted that Italian women could boast of teaching their own children, of taking them out walking, of playing with them at home with toys and dolls, and later on of escorting their daughters personally to balls and theaters.[17] The moral reconstitution of the family was held to be a prime demand of the century. Some years later, in a series of lectures on the Italian woman, Giacomo Oddo explained that women were to be trained to help men, not just for pleasure (as Rousseau had carelessly hoped) but for men's deeper needs. By 1869 Malvina Frank, a Venetian, while asking for equal rights for women, wanted them to be transformed from mere nursemaids into educators, so that womanly advice would prove useful, not just to their families, but once again, *to the state*.[18]

Even though English homes had not been terrorized by revolution or by war on their own territory, the movement toward intense family life occurred there also.* It was strengthened by the emergent industrial system, more potent there than on the continent, and by an evangelical religious revival, which apparently followed the hardships of war spontaneously, but which conveniently served to bridle the demands of potential rebels. The group most likely to produce such rebels was that of the workingmen; but women too might have chosen to follow the militant Mary Wollstonecraft rather than the didactic Hannah More had they not believed very strongly that domesticity was the Christian way of life.

*I do not want to deny that the concept of domesticity has deep roots in England, well documented in English literature. Levin Schücking, in his study of the Puritan family, has traced it through Milton's Eve to the Vicar of Wakefield, who, he says, acts like the president of a small republic. But by the nineteenth century, the privatization of life had led to an underemphasis on the political and social concerns which moved all the great poets before that time and since. See the *Oxford Book of English Verse* and Palgrave's *Golden Treasury*.

The capitalist revolution, we are told by Max Weber, was largely fueled by a sense of vocation and a devotion to the ethic of work arising from Protestant evangelicalism. It seems clear that the feeling that women's mission lay within the home provided them with a set of ideals corresponding to the work ethic for men. E. P. Thompson may be right in saying that among the working class in England the sense of submission was even stronger than the sense of calling,[19] but in women's lives both aspects were evidenced. In a certain manner home could compensate for the mechanization of life outside; on the other hand, women were to be given important new jobs to perform that were to match those done by men outside the home.

Hannah More, whose long life straddled the eighteenth and nineteenth centuries, exemplifies the difference which the new century brought. In her first, or eighteenth-century, career, after having run a successful girls' school, she turned to writing plays and frequented the most brilliant intellectual society of London. In middle life she underwent a religious conversion which made her feel that the theater was evil and led her to dedicate the "fascination" of her style to recommending to the rising generation a life of the strictest denial. Perhaps her most popular work was *Coelebs in Search of a Wife* (1809), which recounted the adventures of a young man who took a tour among several young ladies to pick the right companion for life. Each girl he looked at exemplified what Miss More considered common female faults, until at last he met Lucilla Stanley, pious, well-mannered, docile, although intelligent about the good works she performed in the village and the sober intellectual hobbies, like botany, she was allowed to pursue. A Harvard professor's wife, writing in 1866, remembered how in her youth *everyone* was reading *Coelebs*, and how they admired the author all the more because her own life demonstrated the virtues (although not the marital success) of her heroine Lucilla.[20]

Hannah More had a host of imitators who tried to persuade women that no woman entirely "of the world" could be happy; that even though a mother must repress a taste for intellectual pursuits she could take satisfaction when she regarded her well-ordered nursery; that women should no longer be either pleasure-seekers or breadwinners,[21] although both roles had been permissible in the eighteenth century. As Mrs. Anna Letitia Barbauld , who won a reputation as an educational theorist, put it, men may have varied duties, but "women have but one, and all women have the same."[22]

Edward Bulwer-Lytton, the novelist, in a book entitled *England and the English* (1833), called the new mood "that passion for the Unsocial which we dignify with the milder epithet of Domestic."[23] He found that Englishmen could no longer afford their former habits of outside amusements, and so sought comfort and pleasure at home instead of public places. Surely many observers felt that English homes, on their individual piece of land with their private hedged gardens, and their closed front doors, were the epitome of comfort, at a level unapproached by continental residences.

What home could mean to one of the new breed of Englishmen was demonstrated by Dr. Thomas Arnold, famed headmaster of Rugby. He was described by J. B. Mozley as "domestic from top to toe; his school a family—his family a school. . . . A family was a temple and a church with Arnold, —a living sanctuary and focus of religious joy, —a paradise, a heaven upon earth. . . . He thought and he taught, and he worked and he played, and he looked at sun, and earth, and sky with a domestic heart."[24] And again, Arnold's life "is too full to want our sympathy, too happy to be interesting. . . ."[25]

For an interesting and surprising sidelight on how far the notion of a secondary role for women spread, there is a letter from John Stuart Mill to Harriet Taylor, written just after he had fallen in love with her in 1832, in which he declared that the happiest way for both sexes was for women not to support the family, but "adorn & beautify it. . . . The great occupation of women shall be to beautify it: to cultivate, for her own sake & that of those who surround her, all her faculties of mind, soul and body; all her powers of enjoyment, & powers of giving enjoyment; & to diffuse beauty, elegance, & grace everywhere."[26] If she happened to be energetic, she could work with the man she loved at *his* occupations (emphasis his), but she was not to carry on independently.

ᴄʌʌ In every country, as masculine work was carried out less in private homes and more in industrial plants or offices, the great majority of middle-class men lost their freedom of decision making. They lost control of their own time, the tempo and the choice of their work. For the first time an antithesis developed between home and workplace. Therefore, all the more important became the surcease that they could experience at home, a place for physical relaxation but also one where they did not have to think about money or competition or politics.[27] So they attempted to keep women, the guardians of the home, from thinking about these things, and they managed to do so partly by cultivating the romantic view of women as fragile and unsullied—not entirely a mode of selfishness or domination, but one of chivalry, protection, and the effort to spare them certain sorts of pains.

It was only natural that a home where men could be free and uninhibited did not always turn out to mean the same thing for the women there. Men soon began to feel that women *ought* to stay home, not just that it was a privilege for them to do so, as was shown by the fact that when vacuum cleaners and other household appliances came along in the early twentieth century, these were perceived by some men as a threat to home life rather than as an opportunity for women's liberation. It is interesting and ironical that when women sought freedom from the oppressiveness of home confinement, they sought it precisely in the world of work that men were eager to escape, preferring the discipline of outside employers to the internal and personal pressures of their husbands.

For the time being, in the early half of the nineteenth century, women could feel that they had gained as well as lost. They had won an increase in domestic affection, a new respect for their sex, satisfaction from the management of their households and education of their children, and a feeling that they were above the sordid routines toward which masculine lives were tending. It is important to realize that men were being measured by a new yardstick, and the decision not to measure women by the same represented a privilege for women in one way, though it could be made to seem an evasion in another. Women were very important in the "interiors" that John Lukacs calls the hallmark of the modern bourgeois intelligence, meaning interiors both in the newly privatized homes and thoughts and introspection.[28]

There were certainly losses for women too.* They surrendered independence and contact with public affairs (sordid or not), and there was more than a chance of overdoing the role of motherliness. "I don't much fancy men often understand women; they don't know how restless and weary they get," murmured Anne Jemima Clough in 1849.[29]

At the time retreat into the home seemed to offer a chance of fulfillment. Succeeding generations of females often saw it as a trap.

---

*The regressive features of their changing position were discerned by Frances Wright, a feminist pioneer (1795–1852): "I know not a circumstance which more clearly marks in England the retrograde movement of the national morals than the shackles now forged for the rising generation of women. Perhaps these are as yet more exclusively laid upon what are termed the highest class, but I apprehend that thousands of our countrywomen in the middle ranks, whose mothers, or certainly whose grandmothers, could ride unattended from the Land's End to the border and walk abroad alone . . . I apprehend that the children and grandchildren of these matrons are now condemned to walk in leading strings from the cradle to the altar . . ."(A. Jones, 39f). See also the writings of the poet Arthur Hugh Clough.

ℤ2.

"Only a Girl"

> Some have felt that women's blundering lives are due to the inconvenient indefiniteness with which the Supreme Power has fashioned the natures of women: if there were one level of feminine incompetence as strict as the ability to count to three and no more, the social lot of women might be treated with scientific certitude.
>
> George Eliot, *Middlemarch*, 1873

To justify women's functioning mainly at home, rationalizations were quickly adduced. These were regularly based on an appeal to "nature," sometimes the nature of social organization, more usually the nature of woman herself.

If an average middle-class woman had consulted learned men to find out the latest in nineteenth-century scientific opinion, or if she had picked up books of popular advice based on such sources, she would have been forced to the conclusion that, for one reason or another, women were simply not men's equals. The reasons alleged often overlapped, but it may be convenient here to group them by the main kinds of argument. First there were the sociologists, who tended to stress the hierarchical nature of society and the principles that someone had to be on top and that men were called to this leadership. Then there were those who relied on new biological information about the human ovum and the role of menstruation, who liked to point out that women's brains and bodies were at war with each other in a way that men's were not. A bit later came the psychologists, who were pleased to notice that women had smaller brains and that, even if this did not matter (the weight of some male brains was embarrassingly low), at any rate women lacked the power of "abstraction," although this assertion was sometimes gallantly compensated for by flattering notices of their "intuition."

ℂ To show how the principle of hierarchy was supposed to work in a family, let us go back to Dr. Riehl, who lectured on political economy at the University of Munich from 1854 on. In politics Riehl was almost medieval—or perhaps pre-fascist—in his espousal of corporative ideals, and he felt so deeply about a return to the patriarchal system that he imagined that some of his readers would think part of his book had been given him in his sleep.[1] (It is interesting that Hitler said the same thing about *Mein Kampf*.) Riehl attributed this somnambulistic quality to his deep consonance with the roots of German life. Although he wanted the family to take precedence over the state, which must not encroach on its prerogatives, he wanted the state itself to be penetrated by a family spirit, grounded in the moral participation of its male citizens. He called attention to the fact that as society became more bourgeois with the growth of capitalism, it also became more masculine because women had less importance in the new middle classes than they traditionally had in aristocratic circles or among the peasantry.

The father, he thought, should know how to "march in front," leading not only a retinue of women and children, but a host of unmarried brothers, bachelor uncles, as well as servants, who were to be an integral part of the household. He was to rule this group by loving kindness and a strict sense of justice, though without consultation with other members. Riehl noted with approval the old Germanic law which permitted a man to punish the women in his family without recourse to law courts, but at the same time, he believed so strongly in developing close emotional ties through art and music that, with the collaboration of Ludwig Richter, painter *par excellence* of idyllic childhood, he composed a songbook entitled *Hausmusik*, which he modestly hoped would do its bit to hold German families together.

Only if human beings were sexless, he declared, might they be "free and equal" in the French fashion, but since dependence and inequality proved to be the two "natural" principles on which all societies were organized, hard work and subordination must be laid down as the law, as they were in Genesis. Sexual differentiation, he found, increased with civilization. This was why old-time portraits of women often look mannish in their character and determination, but by mid-nineteenth century there was a demand for more appropriately soft features. At the same time, differences in clothing had reached their ultimate at the time he was writing—and even biological changes had followed suit he believed, so that deep alto voices had disappeared among women, while one had to go to a less civilized country, like Hungary, to find high tenors.*

The hierarchical principle never took quite such a hold in France, where there had been a strong devotion to the ideal of equality since before the Revolution. Count Pellegrino Rossi, an exiled Italian, gave lectures on political economy at the University of Paris during the 1830s, in which he discussed the family as an element in social and political life. Although he felt that someone had to be the head of a family, and it quite suitably was the man, he did not gloat, like Riehl, over feminine dependency, but stated instead that women had brains as powerful as men's and that the state should limit husbandly authority to what was strictly

---

*In 1940 Stefan Zweig commented on the difference in style between the 1890s, when the sexes were distinguished by dress, hair style, and beards, and the time when he was writing, when both sexes appeared tall, slim, beardless, and short-haired (Zweig, 73).

necessary to ensure the prevention of anarchy. Woman was not to be a slave, but at the domestic hearth a queen, and outside it an honored companion. As man was the producer, so woman had the equally important office of conserver of the world's goods. He saw civilization as a process which brought successive reductions in marital, as in paternal, power. While he admitted that he was not enthusiastic about liberated women, he disliked enslaved ones even more.

As we saw in Chapter I, Edouard Janet carried on this tradition, envisaging France as a nation of nuclear families: father, mother, and a very limited number of children, all of whom would interact on a basis of frankness and an approach to equality. True, there would be division of labor, and the wife's role was standarized within the home, but there she would enjoy a real chance to make decisions and to run the domestic show. Janet even raised the question whether *any* authority was needed. He granted that the man was formally considered the head and that his power rested on the potentiality of force, but he did not want modern families to be governed by force. Still, for children at least, some authority was needed, and he concluded that masculine reason was best for this, since it was usually more experienced, more logical, and more impartial than the feminine. Add to this the facts that in civilized states women needed protection and that they consumed more than they could produce by themselves, and one could justify, he concluded, the existing constitution of the family.

A certain national difference is obvious here, the German writer favoring far more subordination of women, and the French tending toward an ideal of equality. This reflected, I believe, what each man saw when he looked about him, because French women were actually far less subordinate than German.*

It should be clear, however, that, especially in the northern countries, many women welcomed their fixed position. Hannah More had written that perhaps no animal was so much indebted to subordination for its good behavior as woman. The English sisters Maria Grey and Emily Shirreff, in 1851, deplored the independence and social equality demanded by Harriet Martineau, arguing that that formidable journalist did not recognize "the indelible law of nature placing women in a subordinate position." They later did become ardent supporters of higher education for women, however. Even Charlotte Brontë, in *Shirley*, had two bright and energetic girls discuss whether women were men's equals and one of them remark that she loved to feel the presence of a superior being.† In Germany, an unmarried Lutheran woman, Amelia Sieveking,

*Hippolyte Taine related it to racial differences. In the north, he explained, the man had to command because he was cold by temperament and needed domestic peace, and the influence of women was less. But in the south, in which he included France as a Latin country, women rose higher, even to superiority, because there sensibility and emotion were more valued.

†Miss Martineau is on record as disapproving of the sort of liberation Miss Brontë's characters derived from falling in love and expressing it.

well known for her work in starting schools, longed for auricular confession in her church so that she might have some source of manly will "to which I could feel myself in every respect subordinate."

∽ Dr. Karl von Baer's discovery of the human ovum in 1827, and the subsequent demonstration that the egg ripened each month and ruptured its envelope, led to a more biological justification for popular opinion about the worth of women. Generalizing from the new knowledge, that public oracle Jules Michelet was moved to a remarkable outpouring of sympathy in a book which he entitled simply *L'Amour*. Woman, he concluded from his reading of the physiologists, suffered from a monthly wound. "She takes flight each month, our beloved sibyl, and each month nature prevents her, by suffering, and by a painful crisis puts her back in the hands of love."[2] Since for a week beforehand she was already troubled, and since the actual event hit her like an underground torrent, and since it took a week to recover from each onslaught, women were in an abnormal state at least three quarters of the time. It is true that in the end she was rejuvenated and brought back to love, but only at the price of pain that should induce in men constant solicitude and protection. Michelet advised husbands never to frighten women. Since a wife could not be expected to work steadily at anything, the husband must be prepared to work for both of them, his job being to create a civil society in which she could live in peace and justice. (Both the existing church and the civil government were hostile to women, he noted.) Above all, the husband should realize that women did not do *anything* in the same way as men, even breathe. Men breathed from the bottom part of the lung, women from the top—another supposedly scientific revelation that was in fact related to the tight corset that prevented full expansion of the lungs and may also have interfered with digestion. But the difference in breathing caused that "beautiful undulation of the bosom" which all men admired so much.[3] Another French writer declared that this fact placed the sex at the very source of the celestial element, with the result that they did not need to eat as much as men.*[4]

The idea that women were ruled by animal impulses, that only men were truly human, affected certain other literary Frenchmen. The Goncourt brothers, without Michelet's trappings of science, related women's brainlessness to their bodies. "All the physical beauty, all the strength, all the development of women is concentrated in . . . the pelvis, the buttocks, the thighs; the beauty of a man is to be found in the upper, nobler parts, the pectoral muscles, the broad shoulders, the high forehead.[5] They

---

*Michelet did not like English and American girls who traveled alone and dared to have wishes and to express them. His sympathy for women is very much in key with James Agee's for the American sharecroppers (in *Let Us Now Praise Famous Men*). Both writers tried to imagine how they would have felt with an agony not their own, and along with flashes of insight, they came up with masses of misplaced sentiment.

concluded that women were incapable of dreaming, thinking, or loving. (This might lead one to inquire whether the brothers themselves had any talent for love—none shows up in their *Journal*, unless it be for each other.) Men like themselves, they went on, needed woman as "an agreeable animal, to which we may become quite attached," but if she tried to *talk* she soon became as unbearable as a piano out of tune.*[6]

The thoroughly misogynic philosopher Arthur Schopenhauer explained that just a look at a woman's shape would indicate that she was not intended for much mental or physical labor, that she paid the debt of life by suffering.[7] And at the London meeting of the Anthropological Society in 1869, James MacGregor Allen reasoned that being disqualified from thought or action for two days a month would prevent women from competing with men, whose thought processes were free from interruption.[8] Herbert Spencer's contribution to the debate was the assertion that sex differences arose out of the somewhat earlier arrest of the processes of evolution in women, presumably because their bodies needed strength to reproduce, while men, genetically, could develop the potential for abstract thought. When Winwood Reade wrote *The Martyrdom of Man* in 1872, he enthusiastically applied evolution (then, of course, a new and fashionable doctrine) to the production of human character as well as to human bodies. The curves of women, but also their reserve, their modesty and their "sublime unselfishness" were attributed to natural selection.

Even so vigorous and adventurous a woman as Lou Andreas-Salomé, when thinking about her sex in relation to the species in 1899, related the active male sperm cell to progress, change, and idealism, while the passive ovum caused its bearer to stick within her house like a snail. She concluded that no woman fully "individualizes," although she thought girls should be given more freedom so that they could learn to be mistresses of themselves. Frau Lou claimed she was building on the scientific theories of the German pathologist Rudolf Virchow, who contended that glands were what created woman's tenderness and loyalty along with her rounded limbs and swelling breasts.†

*Their simple brains were supposed to be incapable of complex disturbances. (Hysteria was an affliction arising from the womb.) It is interesting that when the novelist Sarah Grand (pseudonym of Frances McFall) represented in fiction a sort of institution for psychiatric counseling, it was open only to male patients because it had never occurred to its head that women might need his services. He assumed that nature must have fixed things so that women had no sufferings other than physical ones. Thus Durkheim believed that their lower suicide rate was due to their less complex nature (Hartman and Banner, 78).

†Virchow's views were expressed in a brochure called *Die Zelle und das Weib* (*The Cell and the Woman*). I have been unable to locate a copy in the United States. Patrick Geddes and Arthur Thomson, authors of *The Evolution of Sex* (1889), felt that many so-called secondary characteristics were an expression of "exhuberant [sic] maleness." These views seem to find their twentieth-century development in studies like those popularized by Lionel Tiger and Robin Fox about the effects on young men at puberty of a greater internal shot of testosterone than girls get; by Erik Erikson with his views on women's "inner spaces"; and by Konrad Lorenz through his work on animal behavior.

Though women have long since demonstrated the ability to think abstractly and to work steadily, at that time the well-nigh unanimous opinion of doctors that brain tension had grave repercussions on the feminine organism weighed heavily on every conscientious parent. "To educate the girl is to weaken the future mother" was a respected medical view.[9] In Catherine Winkworth's family, for example, there was a debate on whether her two prolonged "periods of delicacy" (at the ages of ten and twenty) were caused by overstudy. Catherine herself always stoutly maintained that study improved her health, and it was finally decided in her case to blame the trouble on "overwalking." But many families reached the opposite conclusion, and it made it very hard for affectionate parents to agree to set up schools or to send their daughters to them.

It was made to seem as if a woman's brain and her reproductive system played a zero-sum game with each other. If her brain was developed, her power to love would have just that much subtracted from it. Any "woman of genius," mused Henry Wikoff in an aside that he assumed would command general assent, must make a "cruel choice" because cultivating her talent would demand abdication of her "true destiny."[10] This idea was at the root of the famous debate between Dumas and George Sand. Dumas maintained that George Sand had never really loved anybody, but only the *ideas* of her heroes.[11] She countered with the assertion that not only was she herself a great lover, but that all the most famous woman intellectuals of her day were too, naming Mme de Staël, Mme d'Agoult, Mme de Girardin. The idea of brains versus body persisted, however. Speculating on H. G. Wells's advocacy of free love, Beatrice Webb concluded that the reason women could not practice it was precisely that they would then have "no brains left to think with."[12] Of herself she stated that her physical nature had dried up in thirty-five years of brain work and no sex.

Herbert Spencer treated it as a truism when he talked of his father's disappointment with his wife, "the greater because he was not aware that intellectual activity in women is liable to be diminished after marriage by that antagonism between individuation and reproduction everywhere operative throughout the organic world. . . ."[13]

∽ There were those who believed, however, not that woman's physiology somehow interfered with her brain function, but that her mind itself was of inferior quality. The specific deficiency was often named as the lack of a power of abstraction, and it was the most widely held rationalization for denying women a role in larger affairs than those of the home. Auguste Comte, called the father of sociology, had concluded that woman's mental capacity was permanently childish, and even a liberal like Thomas Huxley could tell Kate Amberley (Bertrand Russell's mother) that women would never equal men in power or capacity, though he believed that they were coming out of their "doll state."[14] Likewise

Janet quoted a writer who said he had never met a woman who could follow an abstract argument for a quarter of an hour, though with true French gallantry, Janet softened the blow by adding that even when one could (like Voltaire's friend Mme Duchatelet, who translated Newton), didn't everyone much *prefer* Mme de Sévigné? So Taine, advising his sisters on their reading, tells "the dear girls" not to trouble about exact facts, but to have enough ideas about everything to listen intelligently. "The only examination which a woman has to pass is on the subjects of dress, manners, dancing and music."[15] He discouraged their painting, urging them instead to go to parties—even though he himself would not be caught dead at one of these social gatherings.

Even successful women often shared this view. Fanny Kemble, the actress, declared that it was nonsense to say that intellect was of no sex: woman's nature as well as her training kept her from writing such works of genius as Shakespeare's.[16] Sarah Stickney Ellis, who wrote in the 1840s an enormously popular series of books of advice to English daughters, wives, mothers, and women in general, stressed the need to differentiate between the sexes in education because God had fitted the masculine brain with qualities to match its career in the world; women must be content with mental as well as physical inferiority, and even in the rare case where a woman had higher attainments than her husband, her position must still be inferior. Possession of talent was thus a dangerous thing, like owning a pearl that cannot be worn, nothing being more fatal to the happiness of the couple, and to the social structure as a whole, than exhibition of these gifts.

Another discouraging case (a much later one, which shows how the notion held on) was that of Gina Lombroso, who in *The Soul of Woman* told readers that she had undertaken anthropological study only to please her father, the distinguished criminologist Cesare Lombroso, but dropped it later when she realized that women are not meant to think abstractly and that to do so made her unhappy.

One of the most all-encompassing attacks on women's capabilities came from Pierre Joseph Proudhon (1809–1865), a French socialist. It is true that his views caused a break between him and most other men who called themselves socialist at mid-century, and produced a notable feminine response as well, but as an *enfant terrible* he was widely read and still more widely quoted, and his opinion had the false appearance of mathematical rigor. In a volume called *De la justice*, he modestly averred that he would delve "chastely" into a subject that many considered erotic. His enemies, he said, accused him of monklike continence, to which he responded that he was chaste by nature and that his marriage, though not contracted in church, was the freest and most disinterested act of his life, and that he had studied women's intellect more objectively than most people. As an example of his observations, he recorded the vocabulary of his three-year-old granddaughter, who called the corkscrew the "key" to the bottle, and the lampshade the "hat" of the lamp.[17] He concluded that she had all the force of intellect that she ever would have, and that her mind was irrevocably concrete and incapable of abstract generalization, or of moral principle. Arduous study had convinced him, he went on, that woman's physical inferiority to man's was as two to three, even when she was not menstruating or pregnant, and this fact alone made him the master—a hard law, but the law just the same. When you add the fact that her intellect was in the same proportion, two to three, because she lacked reasoning power, and furthermore that her moral inferiority was in the same proportion because while she understood *love*, the concept of *justice* was forever beyond her, and she also lacked *shame*, the highest virtue for the other sex—simple mathematics demonstrated that two times two times two equals eight, while three times three times three equals twenty-seven.[18] Therefore, woman's overall value was as eight to man's twenty-seven. This turned out to be a good thing for society because between equals competition always developed, but the unequal ratio allowed cooperation instead, even though communication between the sexes was as difficult as that between two species of animals. The proper way to treat women was to shut them up in the house, since if let out, they invariably turned into courtesans.*

When asked about woman suffrage, Proudhon's answer was that the fact that women had organs intended to nourish the young made them unfit for the polls. He is not known to have responded when Jeanne Déroin demanded that he show her the organ which qualified him as an elector.[19]

Herbert Spencer, in a letter to John Stuart Mill, took up the debate by remarking that the deficiency in the female mind was just at the point where complex faculties are needed for political action.[20] By this time it had been discovered that the female brain was not only smaller than the male, but smaller in proportion to the rest of the body. It was also believed by some medical men that mental powers declined faster in the female, though when a German professor was lecturing on this particular point to a mixed audience, a fifty-year-old woman rose to announce that she personally had not felt any falling off. The lecturer was furious, and told his audience that no medical student would be so "subjective," and that this episode alone proved that women could never become doctors.[21]

Even the things at which women were acknowledged to be good were turned against them. For a young girl to be able to play with a baby merely proved that she was childish herself, in the opinion of Schopenhauer, who was proud that no young man *could* perform this duty even if his intentions were of the best.†

*Contemporary gossip had it that Proudhon's wife was just what he deserved: neither pretty nor good-natured nor bright. She was said to be always at her post like a galley slave, and when Michelet once inquired about her health, Proudhon replied that she lacked the leisure to convalesce slowly from her toothaches and headaches (Thibert, Le Féminisme, 182).

†Compare Heinrich von Sybel, who quite simply stated that though women were brainy enough to do men's work, men simply could not do women's; and therefore it was important for society to keep women at it.

The ultimate in the denigration of womanly capacities was reached by Otto Weininger, in *Sex and Character* (1903), although his fanaticism made him suspect and he was probably insane. In his mad view, women had no individuality—proved by the fact that they did not mind changing their names; they were soulless, non-logical, and non-moral. They remembered nothing in life except the sexual moments, they lacked any relation to the truth, and a sensible male would have nothing to do with them.

There were, of course, opinions on the other side. In a famous essay in the *Edinburgh Review* for 1810, Sidney Smith found no intellectual difference between the sexes which could not be accounted for by difference of circumstance. For one thing, women's time was considered of no value and they were kept busy at the lesser and obscure duties of life which "of necessity" fell on the female sex. Let us also notice the early view of a philosophy professor at Edinburgh, Dugald Stewart (Maria Edgeworth's host when she visited Scotland), writing before 1820. The intellectual and moral differences between the sexes, he insisted, were *entirely* the result of education in the broad sense of the term.[22] If women seemed timid, it was because they lacked familiarity with the outside world; if they were especially sympathetic, it was because of their close familiarity with others' distress; if irrational, it was because they lacked the strict study of Latin grammar which stiffens up the masculine brain. From that time on, women never lacked defenders of their intellects, even though the defenders were in the minority for many years.

There was, however, a way of coming to the defense of women that seemed to equalize the odds without challenging the cliché that they lacked the power of abstraction: namely, to maintain that they made up for this lack by the power of intuition. Indeed, it is likely that when a woman, all untrained as she was, came up with a new idea, it would have to be attributed to intuition. To be sure, the assertion could be made with a smile or with a sneer, and the sneerers could still judge that this faculty was not a suitable basis for decisions at the polls.

But even men like John Stuart Mill, who defended women's capacities and argued powerfully for their equal treatment, showed subtle bias against the value of "intuition." "Nobody," declared Mill, "ever perceived a scientific law of nature by intuition, nor arrived at a general rule of duty or prudence by it."[23] This view is in striking contrast with what modern psychologists believe about even the highest scientific abstractions, which usually come to a well-prepared mind in a moment of inspiration, or of a welling up from the unconscious.*

Jürgen Meyer in 1875 challenged the stereotype by pointing out that *men* often had instinctive gifts, that in fact success in teaching depended upon such powers, and that women were often strikingly

---

*Compare George Eliot's put-down, as reported by Frances Power Cobbe: "The masculine brain is always *so* superior,—*what there is of it.*"

logical and depended very much on exact calculations in managing their affairs.[24]

Moreover, this claim to superior access to "reasons of the heart," difficult as it may be to accept today, was turned to good advantage then and proved to be one of the rungs of the ladder by which women climbed up from their low status. Particularly in France, women themselves asserted the claim. Looking around her in the Napoleonic period, Mme de Staël believed that women, at least for the moment, were the superior sex for the very reason that they were attached to life by emotional ties, while men had for the time being lost the chance to exercise such civic and military virtues as would have created *their* path to excellence. Mme d'Agoult made the same point even more directly. The experience of childbirth, she reasoned, gave women immediate access to divine truth, which men could only reach by going the long way round.

The earliest true defender of women's rights in Germany, Theodor von Hippel, felt that the nature of women's minds could save them from the common masculine fault of putting things too easily into words, and he chalked it up as rather a proud mark for the sex that women were not great admirers of Hegel. Though by mid-century they had fewer male supporters than in France, German women such as Luise Büchner, writing in 1856, could make the point that while men were stuck in their narrow roles of lawyer, doctor, professor, women were the true *Menschen*—human beings—and she added that since they stood above party (not being voters), they could become defenders of freedom and, paradoxically, abstract justice.[25] Twenty years later, Hedwig Dohm, the most impatient of the German feminists, declared that it was ridiculous for men to say that they spent all day doing mental work that women could not do. Nursing a sick child or sorrowing at its loss, she felt, was the toughest kind of "mental labor."

Still, the idea that women had something special and different to give to the world, something precious to be treasured, was voiced by Rainer Maria Rilke in 1904:

> Girls and women in their new, their own unfolding will but in passing be imitators of masculine vices and virtues and repeaters of masculine professions. After the uncertainty of such transitions it will become apparent that women only went through the whole range and variety of those (often ridiculous) disguises in order to clean their own most characteristic nature of the distorting influences of the other sex. Women, in whom life lingers and dwells more immediately, more fruitfully and more confidently, must naturally have become fundamentally riper people, more human people, than man who is easy-going, by the weight of no fruit in his body pulled down below the surface of life, and who, presumptuous and hasty, undervalues what he thinks he loves.[26]

As the argument developed in England, it seemed that there was more emphasis on women's improving men than on fulfilling their own existence. Back in 1766 James Fordyce, in his ever-popular *Sermons to*

Young Women, had recommended close association between the sexes so that women could make men more civilized, and a hundred years later it was a commonplace that the rise in the valuation of women was the best measuring stick of the advance of civilization. For example, Henry Thomas Buckle, in a lecture at the Royal Institution in 1858, stated that it was women's influence alone that kept men from being practical and selfish, cruel and violent.*[27]

The extreme of this view was uttered by John Ruskin in *Of Queens' Gardens*. Here he lays down the character of the two sexes: man active, progressive, a doer, a creator; woman designed "for sweet ordering." She does not compete, but she awards the prize. Man can fail, but he protects woman from failure. The happiness and perfection of both sexes, Ruskin assures us, is in asking and receiving from the other what only the other can give.†

Ruskin as an art critic presumably judged woman as a work of art, but Sir Patrick Geddes as a scientist discovered in his studies of sex (or so he claimed) that the dichotomy between the sexes was part of a grand design leading to romantic passion, defined by him as the highest product of the evolutionary process.[28]

Charles Kingsley describes a woman in *Yeast* (1850):

> She was matched, for the first time, with a man who was her own equal in intellect and knowledge. . . . Her mind was beside his as the vase of cut flowers by the side of the rugged tree, whose roots are feeding deep into the mother earth. [But] on all points which touched the heart he looked up to her as infallible and inspired . . . and thus . . . he taught her where her true kingdom lay—that the heart, and not the brain, enshrines the priceless pearl of womanhood.[29]

Auguste Comte described himself as one who had actually been purified by the moral influence of the other sex. (In his case the agent was a lady named Clotilde de Vaux.) Only women, he concluded, and they only by reason of their exclusion from political action, could put society

---

*The *Edinburgh Review* felt that women performed this service through their weakness rather than their strength, and that if women began to compete with men, such chivalry would cease. On the other hand, it was this point of view against which Kipling reacted, hoping to shock his readers with the assertion that the female of the species was more deadly than the male (Kipling, *Female of the Species*). Still, she remained illogical in her fury:

> So it comes that Man, the coward, when he gathers to confer
> With his fellow-braves in council, dare not leave a place for her
> Where, at war with Life and Conscience, he uplifts his erring hands
> To some God of Abstract Justice—*which no woman understands*. [Emphasis added]

†It is interesting to follow these sentiments into books of etiquette. For instance, *Das Buch vom guten geselligen Tone* (*The Book of Correct Social Etiquette*) in 1834 advised its German readers always to talk to women superficially, but to dress well because they were sharp-eyed. By 1900 the tone had changed, as shown in the *Lexicon der feine Sitte* (*The Dictionary of Fine Manners*), which describes the lady as a priestess of good morals who needed to be addressed with sharp ideas (Gert Richter).

on a moral basis. Every woman must be supported by some man—if not a member of her family, then by a taxpayer—because it degraded women to earn their own living. Though economically dependent on men, women were to be somehow free of sexual dependence, and he foresaw a world in which women could create children without male cooperation.[30] The purification of marriage by such startling means would be as great an advance as when polygamy gave way to monogamy, he asserted. (Given these views, it is hard to understand why Comte is billed as the "father" of anything, even sociology.)

ꙮ Many of the same arguments appeared in fiction, where the intellectual "new woman" quickly became a stock character. If the story is to have a happy ending, the heroine is represented as being softened, usually by love, and typically she abandons her career for deeper satisfactions. If there is to be a more bitter conclusion, she is shown as destructive in her relationships, unsuccessful in her work, and finally unhappy.

In a satirical novel, *The Revolt of Man* (1882), Walter Besant created an imaginary world of the future in which women as the "higher sex" have at last taken over all governmental, university, and priestly functions. Young men are the ones who now need chaperonage (by girl grooms), and they can only marry much older women because only such are able to support them. The trouble is that civilization regresses because it turns out that women cannot *create*, cannot do science or art, cannot organize production, so that factories are abandoned and cloth is once more made on hand looms. The book ends happily with the revolt of the male sex and the setting up of a new king. The work is satire, indeed, but it is hard to tell if it shows how monstrous the regiment of women, or how ridiculous nineteenth-century sexual customs.

In 1887 the French novelist Th. Bentzon (a *nom de plume* for Thérèse Blanc) published *Emancipée*, whose hero, a poet, falls in love with a girl medical student. Failing to seduce her, and astonished that she should turn out to be virtuous, he asks her hand in marriage, and as soon as she discovers in herself the capacity for emotional response, she renounces her doctorate, "not believing in the necessity, in housework, of an intellectual accomplishment so profound." When her baby arrives, she feels vindicated: "*Celui-ci me donne raison.*"

I should like to go into another novel, *Only a Girl* by Wilhelmine von Hillern, at greater length because it offers several feminine types and addresses itself squarely to the question of whether brains can make a woman happy. It appeared in 1867, before the question of women's admission to German universities had been seriously broached, and yet it accurately foreshadows every argument that would be used in debates on the subject thirty years later. The author was the daughter of a well-known actress and playwright, Charlotte Birch-Pffeiffer, and was herself a women of many parts. Besides writing potboiling fiction for women's magazines, she was a devoted mother, a horsewoman, and the ruler of a salon where everything from current theater to new theories of physiology was discussed. (When asked if motherhood had interfered with her work, she answered that she had found that an intellectual calling is easy to mesh with family life if a woman knows how to plan her time.) Obviously *Only a Girl* is not based on her own life but on the expectations of her large readership. She flattered their limitations while at the same time enlarging their horizons a bit. Its heroine, Ernestine, is greeted at birth by her father's remark, "It's only a girl." As she grows up, she comes to the conclusion that she is unloved because she belongs to the wrong sex, and so she tries to become as much like a boy as she can. Thus at a child's party she beats the little boys at their own game by shattering a glass bowl with a rock, but unfortunately she cuts a small child, is reprimanded, and so is made to feel a failure again. It is also noticed that she begins to ask "deep" questions as boys do, such as "How did the first people get here?" At this point her uncle, the villain of the piece, thinks she might like to read Darwin, and the plot begins to thicken.

The trouble is that she is to inherit a large fortune with this uncle as guardian, but he will become the heir if she dies a spinster and so he has a strong motive to keep her unmarried. Noting her intellect, he concludes that the surest way to his success if to encourage her interest in science. Carefully sequestering his own daughter in a safe boarding school for ladylike accomplishments, he takes the brilliant niece to a remote valley in Austria, surrounds her with a laboratory, an observatory, books, and tutors, subtly discouraging her faith in Christianity with the argument that no man of science believes in God. Her researches go famously, and at the age of twenty-two she wins a prize—anonymously, of course—at a famous German university, for a paper on the physiology of the eye. The faculty of the institution are stunned to find that the recipient is a woman and further dismayed when they receive a letter of application begging them to allow her to complete her studies for the doctorate under their direction. The professors' discussion of the question is long and full, rambling over whether it is right to refuse admission to an individual of undoubted talent; whether it would be safe to make an exception to the general rule that stemmed from the supposed lower capacities of women's brains (one devil's advocate asking slyly if they aren't really afraid of the competition); and whether the admission of women would disturb the rational ordering of society. The vote is tied, until a certain young professor casts a negative ballot. "Why, I thought you were in love with the girl," remarks one of his colleagues. "And so I am," is the reply. "*That* is why I voted as I did."

The young professor might have been expected to choose someone more like his sister, a rosy, cheerful, good little mother whose husband, another professor, boasts that he makes all the decisions in his family. Her apricot cream is famous, and her interest in the dogs that are to be vivisected is compassionate rather than scientific. Ernestine, meanwhile, is shown as lacking small talk and having such poor housewifely skills that she cannot even cut up beans without slicing her fingers. (This is the woman who has dissected the eye!) However, love being what it is, and Ernestine being presented as ravishingly beautiful, the young professor sets out to seek her affection, with the corollary of weaning her away from science. (If they were married, he explains, he will let her talk to him about science but never contribute anything on her own.) He also wants her to regain her faith in God. The obstacle at this point in the narrative is her pride. Her heart is beginning to soften, but she does not know how to admit it, particularly since her health is starting to break down under a severe regime of study (an inevitable outcome, according to the views of the day), and worse than that, her uncle has lost her fortune by imprudent and criminal investment. Faced with poverty, she finds that she cannot even earn her own living because no one will hire an atheist governess and there is no other work for educated women to do. Just then the cousin emerges from boarding school. Having had a more practical education, she is able to earn money for the two of them, and they share a tiny apartment. Left at home to fix dinner, Ernestine can only make deplorable messes each day. She has always assumed that cooking is a sordid activity until it is explained to her gently by her *Hausfrau* acquaintances that it can be an act of love, and that housekeeping can consist of weaving a web of life to help a husband get out and do his work in the world. Her lover, though momentarily distracted by an "emancipated countess," returns to Ernestine wondering how to salve her pride and winds up with a masterly plan. He obtains the offer of a job for her at the University of Saint Petersburg, where the attitude about women is far less constricted. (The novelist points out, however, that the German attitude of sexual differentiation represents a higher degree of civilization, and reinforces the idea by making the emancipated countess Russian too.) Now that Ernestine is free to choose and is not dependent on the professor for support, she gives in to her feelings and submits her life to his. The final scene, a year later, shows her in bed after childbirth. When she is told that it is "only a girl," she smiles beatifically. All she hopes for her little daughter is that she will find the same happiness in being a woman that she herself has.

The subtitle of this tale is *Physician for the Soul*, and it is quite clear that brains in a woman are felt to be something like a disease. It is also interesting that Ernestine is never won over by sensuality. She is never touched or kissed or made aware of the demands of the body: apparently the literary insistence on virgin purity was too strong. So she is "cured" by an intellectual decision that being a housewife represents a desirable societal role as well as a happy personal choice. But although Frau von Hillern had to weight her story in her housewife readers' favor, Ernestine is given several chances to voice rather eloquently the case for developing her mind, and various forms of unfairness are shown and deplored, at least momentarily. The point is made that girls are treated unfairly from the cradle, and later have little chance to earn their own living, let alone develop their mental powers.

∽ In this chapter I have tried to exhibit certain widely held beliefs about women's potentialities. However irrational such views seem to us, they had a magical attraction for both men and women over a long period of time. They framed people's expectations regarding feminine achievement and thus formed a formidable psychological barrier.

Outstanding women, naturally, were constantly beating against the stereotype. Some women were ultimately led to violence in order to destroy the whole ideology, while others used the accepted philosophy to implement a gentler approach based on the qualities of intuition and motherliness that no one seemed to deny them (even though Harriet Martineau believed that to call certain virtues peculiarly feminine merely held women back). The issue was never fully resolved, and the two approaches toward feminism will be seen in debate throughout the rest of this book.

3.

The *Jeune Fille* and Her Dowry

*La femme est faîte spécialment pour
plaire à l'homme.*
                    Jean Jacques Rousseau

A problem that faced girls of every country was that the course of their lives was usually controlled by a single decision, and that decision often had to be taken before the age of twenty. Men's lives had a different tempo; they had more time to think about choosing a wife, and it was only one of many decisions involving their careers that could be taken one at a time.

Another condition to which girls in the classes we are considering had to adapt was the extreme value placed on their purity. The rationale was that the wife would belong to her husband and that he must be sure that all the children were legitimate. But because the effort to keep the lid on sexual drives always involves irrational processes, a mystique grew up around chastity—female chastity, that is—so strong that Matthew Arnold called this virtue the best single index of any given nation's civilization. Certainly no writer of comparable stature could make such a claim today.

In the sections that follow, I shall study the ways in which marriage decisions were made and chastity was safeguarded in France, England, Germany, and Italy. The differences had, I think, a profound effect on the women's movements in those countries and the way in which various other public problems were considered.

If things are different now, it is due in part to the growing individualism of women during the course of the nineteenth century. This fact was sharply observed by the sociologist Georg Simmel, who believed that the development of women's personalities was a special achievement of the years after 1850. As evidence he cited the increased ability of women to form close friendships like men,* and, by extension, close

---
*Georg Simmel on friendships between women:

Now, women are the less individualized sex; variation of individual women from the general class type is less great than is true, in general, of men. This explains the very personal sexual relationships.[1] So we find that the almost impersonal methods of wife selection that obtained in the early years changed with women's education and independence, and the expectations and the nature of marriage changed likewise. This new view of a more personal and mutual kind of union is observable in every country, but again with special nuances to fit each national scene.

ɔ Both the English and the French considered the way parents across the Channel treated their girls as cruel. The English felt that the French forced their daughters into unwelcome marriages, while to the French, the Anglo-Saxon way of leaving girls to find husbands for themselves— without even a dowry—was utterly heartless. The national difference was basic. The English demonstrated here their strong tendency to rely on the inner resources of an individual and to trust their daughters' characters to keep them out of trouble, and so they gave them considerable personal freedom—even though today we would find the amount of chaperonage oppressive. The French, on the other hand, found their strength within the family as a collective unit; they counted on the wisdom of the older generations to find the mate who could both suit the young person and enhance the well-being of the whole family, and to this end they felt justified in constantly supervising their girls to protect them from the consequences of following their own whims.*

There was no French word for "courtship" simply because there was no such activity in France.†[2] In their book on eighteenth-century Frenchwomen, the Goncourt brothers pictured the girls of the *ancien régime* as having been educated in a convent while the mothers took part in the social whirl. Then, when the moment of marriage came, the girl was extracted from her sheltered life, her husband was presented to her, and she was married forthwith. In the nineteenth century this pattern showed some change. After what seems to have been a flurry of greater

---

widespread opinion that, ordinarily, women are less susceptible to friendship than men. For, friendship is a relation entirely based on the individualities of its elements, more so perhaps even than marriage: because of its traditional forms, its social rules, its real interests, marriage contains many super-individual elements that are independent of the specific characters of the personalities involved. The fundamental differentiation on which marriage is based, as over against friendship, is in itself not an individual, but a species differentiation. It is therefore understandable that real and lasting friendships are rare at the stage of low personality development; and that, on the other hand, the modern, highly differentiated woman shows a strikingly increased capacity for friendship and an inclination toward it, both with men and with women. Individual differentiation here has overwhelmed species differentiation. [*Sociology of Georg Simmel*, 138]

*It was another facet of this national trait which allowed a great deal of personal liberty to English schoolboys, while French masters never let the boys out of their sight.

†Edouard Chantepie, for example, wished that he could hear courtship again spoken of as a French activity, so that "*Faire sa cour redeviendra un mot français* (Chantepie, 276).

opportunities at the turn of the century (whether from revolutionary ideas or the effect of the Enlightenment), a routine set in which girls more often lived at home, educated by mothers who devoted a great deal of personal attention to their upbringing in line with the new idealization of domesticity. A family still chose the husband, however, and it was not until well along toward the end of the century that it became common for a girl to meet men before marriage and to have a voice in the selection of her husband.

It worried Mrs. Frances Trollope, an Englishwoman who traveled in France in the 1830s, that French girls did not go to balls, or, if they did, they danced only with courtly old gentlemen while the young blades sought out young married women as partners. She noted the assembly's astonishment at some Englishmen who took the young girls to dance, following the English idea that balls were for the express purpose of introducing unmarried girls to possible husbands. It was ironical, she thought, that both countries explained their custom by an appeal to "good morals."[3] Even forty years later young ladies were often forbidden parties of private theatricals, such as were common in Germany and England, and there is a report that at a girls' party in Picardy the hostess sent away her twenty-two-year-old son and let the guests dance with each other, half of them being assigned men's parts by wearing a blue rosette.[4] In Paris, to be sure, girls had more chance to meet their parents' friends, and even young men, in the bosom of their families.

The Picardy party is recounted for us by Philip Hamerton, an Englishman who married a French wife and lived in that province for many years (from 1863 until 1890) and wrote several charming books about his friends and neighbors. He was amused to observe that being in love was considered to be in bad taste and that people carefully avoided any appearance of interest in their future mates. Once a young Frenchman requested Hamerton to ask on his behalf for the hand of a girl whom he had never seen but who was represented as having the requisite qualifications. If Hamerton had invited the couple to this house together, both families would have been outraged, so instead he went off with his proposal to the young lady's parents and was told they did not plan to let her marry for another two years. The upshot was that the young man found a readier wife and was married within a month. On another occasion it happened that a mother and her marriageable daughter were spending the day at the Hamertons' house when a young man called fortuitously and was shown by a clumsy servant into the very room where the ladies were sitting. The mother was greatly upset and supposed that Hamerton had planned it that way.*

---

*A word about Hamerton's own courtship illustrates a Scot's adaptation to the French system. He had made friends with his wife's father in Paris and was often invited to spend evenings at the home when she was about sixteen. At that time the idea of an international marriage had never occurred to him, but a few years later he remembered the bright young person who had talked in his presence far more artlessly than *jeunes filles* were accustomed to do, so he went back and asked her father for her hand (Hamerton, *Auto-biography*, 180).

A German girl visiting France in the 1870s heard of a father who wrecked his daughter's chance of a good marriage by taking her to Venice and Rome for six months.[5] No one could be sure what she had been doing there or whom she might have met.*

Such restrictive mores were certainly common, but not quite universal. The rules appear to have been more important to the middle class then to the aristocracy, where social life was more intense for everybody and young people would have more chance to meet; more important for Catholics than for Protestants—witness the very free choice made by the Protestants Charles and Elisa Lemmonier in a college town, where Elisa's parents mingled socially with teachers and professors; and certainly more important at the beginning than at the end of the century, when a new way of life involving longer schooling, more job opportunities, and fashionable sports made it harder to keep young people confined. Some of the new pressures were reflected after 1880 in books of advice, warning mothers of the dangers of cycling or even tennis, which could cause young girls to fall "dangerously in love."[6] (They might even have to shake hands with men their parents knew nothing of!)†[7]

Still, even after 1900, according to Miss Matilda Betham-Edwards,‡ an engaged couple would never be permitted to take half an hour's train trip together to visit relatives in the country. When girls began to go out to offices and jobs, they might come and go unaccompanied, but their parents kept count of the minutes elapsed on the way, and woe to the girl who seemed to have dallied.[8]

A delicate balance of the old and the new is shown in the stories of a Colonel Moll in 1909 and of a certain French bride of 1919. A few years before World War I, the love letters of Colonel Henry Moll were published, after that officer had been killed in the African campaign. He had just become engaged when the call to active duty in July, 1909 interrupted the plans for marriage, and so until his death in November, 1910 he kept in touch with the girl by almost daily letters. He told her, with a freedom that would have been unacceptable fifty years before, how much he loved her and counted on her for intellectual understanding, and he described the sense of potency which her sympathy gave him. "It will be so good to live one for the other, 'at home' [English in the original], where when I work I shall perceive your coming and going, will hear like caressing

---

*One of the difficulties in planning a wedding, according to Baronne Staffe, the authority on etiquette, was to make sure that none of the bridesmaids had to ride to church with a man who was not related to her. It was not safe for young girls to do so, even if a group of them rode together.

†As early as 1855 a French journalist, Alphonse Karr, recorded his shock when he saw some girls actually shaking hands with young men. It used to be, he remarked, that girls would never be touched—nor did they want to talk or laugh aloud.

‡Matilda Betham-Edwards was not only the first woman to write for *Punch* (in a rather female chauvinist style), but, in a completely different capacity, was an officer of public instruction in France under the Third Republic. Her knowledge of French life was extensive, and she had opportunities to investigate French institutions which often gave depth to her descriptions.

music the rustle of your dress."[9] He valued her individuality so much that he believed companionship with her would enrich all cultural activities which they would share.

The second story is of a war bride, the daughter of a post office official in western France.[10] Her father's duties kept him in close touch with certain American officers at the end of World War I, and one of them became a habitué of the house, where there were two grown girls. One day it chanced that this officer met one of the daughters in the square in front of the post office, and as he greeted her they exchanged a few words on the street. When she arrived at her own door, her father met her with a box on the ear that almost knocked her down, claiming that she had endangered her reputation by such palavering. That same evening, conversant with French ways, the American came to call on her parents to ask if he could marry her. Her father went up to her room, told her of the offer, and said the choice was up to her. Although this man had never said a private word to her, she knew that he was well educated and must love her, and so she decided to take her chance. She never regretted the decision.

ᝌ The word "love" in a romantic context can mean sexual passion, or it can mean warm family affection. Michelet explained that the reason he wrote a book on the subject, *L'Amour* (1859), was that he felt France was sick with too much drink and narcotics, and everywhere marriages were failing from lack of love. Yet for him, as for most French people, love was something that grew *after* marriage;[11] the common French opinion of the English condition of "being in love" was that it could not last, whereas their own sort of love could be counted upon for the long haul. "You have to be a bit crazy to believe in a lifetime of passionate love," declared Charles Turgéon in 1902, in his book on feminism.[12]

As has been noted, there seems to have been a time right after the Revolution of 1789 and on into the early Napoleonic period when girls had more independence, and love a different valuation. For example, George Sand's father, a young officer serving in the Italian campaign, fell in love with a French girl who had come there as a rich man's mistress. In letters to his mother (published by his daughter) he vainly tried to convince the old lady that the girl was noble in spirit, that she had loved him enough to follow him to France and to work to support herself, not at first daring to hope for marriage, while her lover was torn between his genuine passion and his sense of duty to his cherished mother.[13] After four years and several failed pregnancies, the couple were married secretly just in time to legitimize George Sand.

Marriages for love, such as this, became extremely rare in the middle decades of the century as a pall of conventionality descended. Most French parents left no liberty of action to a young couple.[14] They were treated (as *Blackwood's Magazine* complained) as though incompetent, and the girls obeyed out of duty, vanity, or eagerness to get the freedoms of a married woman, or at least to fulfill the only destiny they could imagine.[15] Sometimes it was considered a slur to hint that a couple had married for love; thus Hamerton tells of the indignation with which one French wife denied this slander, perhaps attached to her because of her beauty,[16] repeating that she and her husband had only met once, quite formally, before their betrothal. (The implication of the suggestion that she had been married for her beauty was that her dowry might be thought to have been insufficient.)

And so Dumas's statement that no French girl could declare with certainty that she loved her fiancé seems reasonable. And no husband could feel, as an Englishman might, that his wife had chosen him from out of the whole world.

Greville Murray, in the *Westminister Review*, elaborates:

> Everybody knows that when a vessel of hot water having been saturated with saltpetre . . . is allowed to cool, there comes a moment when some of the saltpetre previously accepted by the water is rejected. . . . Something similar to this takes place in the minds of young people at the approach of that interesting period which nature has appointed for love and love-making. The rationale of French education consists in so secluding and guarding the solution, that the crystallisation may not take place before the bit of glass selected by the parents is dropped in. . . . The girl's mind has been filled . . . with ideas of marriage. . . . But at the same time . . . her thoughts . . . have not been allowed to settle on any marriage in particular. She ripens—she grows impatient—the solution is ready to crystallise.[17]

Even though in practice love was not given much of a chance, the idea of marriage for love was tinged with sentimental approval. The Comtesse d'Agoult explained in her memoirs of 1854 that in her youth (in the early 1820s), it was usual to pretend a sudden passion for the recently introduced fiancé, and that the old ladies who made matches liked to believe this.[18] Edmond About in the 1850s wrote a whole book of short stories about couples who had fallen in love and subsequently tricked their parents into arranging marriages for them.* Delphine de Girardin rhapsodized in her newspaper column about the wedding at the Madeleine of Mlle de Ségur in 1844: "How happy the young bride and groom were. The girl was not yet twenty, but they have been in love for six years. There is nothing sweeter than a marriage of inclination." And even if their passion passes, she goes on, they will continue to please each other because their harmony of taste and ideas is lasting.[19] (Of course, the

---

*The opposite twist was satirized by Alfred de Musset in his 1829 play *A quoi rêvent les jeunes filles? (What Do Young Girls Dream About?)*, in which the parents, who have chosen the suitor, get him to pretend to be a romantic hero by coming in through the window at night, singing serenades, and snatching kisses.

Ségurs were not middle class; the image, though, may have pleased middle-class readers.)*

The girls themselves are rarely heard from, but when the Harvard professor's wife, Mrs. Eliza Farrar, took her young sister to an art lesson in Paris, the French students used a momentary absence of the teacher to crowd around and ask if it was true that in England one married for love. Mrs. Farrar was unwilling to stir up discontent, and so she tried to explain that in England they had large country houses with horses and many activities like fishing, boating, and balls. The poor girls listened as if their lives depended on it, and one of them voiced the common sentiment that it would not be hard to be a good wife if you were allowed to choose your own husband.[20] It seemed no wonder to them that Englishwomen were held up as models of virtue.

Karl Hillebrand, a German hot-blood who fled to France at nineteen and subsequently became known for his essays on that country (published in 1881), assures us that, however wistful their hopes, *mésalliances* as a result of passion never occurred in France. He never heard of a young man there who married his sister's governess, or a girl who eloped with her tutor—events which he thought were common among the Germanic race, while in England, he hinted, even greater aberrations occurred.[21]

∽ The procedure of betrothal in France went something like this. A young man who wanted to get married would inform his mother, and she would start looking around among her friends. One such lady happened to tell Hamerton that her son was going to be married. "Who is the young lady?" was the natural response. "Oh," she answered, "I only mean that my son has *decided* to marry, he has not yet fixed upon any young lady."[22] Or the young man himself might have heard of an eligible girl, and he would ask around to find out what she was like, or even try to catch a glimpse of her at church. (Sometimes the wrong girl was pointed out.) But Hamerton tells us that, at least in his province, it was better form not to try to find out for oneself. He tells of a young Frenchman who was engaged to one of two sisters. Since he had never seen either, when he was presented to them he had to ask his mother which was to be his wife. In the more up-to-date cities, or perhaps later in the period, it was common to arrange meetings between a couple for whom marriage was being considered, but the arbiter of etiquette Baroness Staffe (the Emily Post of her era, writing in 1889) is firm that these meetings should seem to be casual.[23] They could meet at a museum, for example, or the young man could call on the girl's mother in a theater box, but though the mother

---

*Delphine herself had had a fairly wild youth. Her mother, Sophie Gay, wrote to a friend in 1823 that Delphine's infatuation with Alfred de Vigny worried her because the couple could not be happy with no money on either side. Later on, when Delphine married "the wild Girardin," his defects of character were partly made up for by his secure establishment position (Page, 160–61).

would try to see what effect was created, the girl was never to be told a thing, even if she became suspicious. As the baroness works out her scenario, once the suitor hears that the girl liked him, he immediately gets his father or some older man to call on her father, in full dress. The girl should never be officially consulted until the father has agreed, at which point the suitor calls on the parents. To a young woman it could mean only one thing when she was asked to come down to the parlor at such a moment. Dressed with negligent elegance, she descended the stairs to sit with her mother, sewing so as to keep her head down. The young man was shown in, they greeted each other, he tried to think of something to say, she remained silent. He was already an expert in women, but her life had been lived like a sleepwalker's. Such was the scene represented again and again on the comic boards, but it surely bore close resemblance to many episodes in real life.

Mme Staffe explained to her readers that the French do not like long engagements, which only give the couple time to get tired of each other.[24] We often hear of three weeks as the period between the signing of the betrothal papers and the wedding—long enough, said one cynic, for the bride to collect her trousseau and the man to dismiss his mistress. During that period the fiancé was expected to call every day with a fresh bunch of flowers, and to talk to the girl in the presence of her family. They could go out together publicly only in the company of a male relative. French reformers used to wonder if the German plan of longer engagements with more chance for deep conversations, long walks and the right to correspond might not be better, with "possession purified in advance by love,"[25] but change in French custom came only very slowly.

The arrangement of marriages in France was as much of a parental duty as sending a child to school, and it was admitted even by disapproving foreigners that parental planning could eliminate much of the misunderstanding that comes from financial surprise, though parents were less good at detecting unsuitable temperamental differences. All books of advice, it is true, put "character" above "property" as a guideline, but in actuality what parents were best at was seeking compatibility in property arrangements. They attempted to make life smooth for the children, said Hillebrand, instead of developing their strength of character. Philippe Ariès calls worrying about a child's career and marriage the very pivot of bourgeois consciousness. The tutor in Rousseau's *Emile* had declared that he would have refused the job of educating Emile if he had not at the same time had the right to choose a wife for him, while Michelet, recommending to widows the adoption of an infant, insisted that one must be careful not to take into one's home a child whose birth would keep it from being successfully married off.[26]

The delightful letters of the mother of the poet Alphonse de Lamartine, published by her daughter, show the old French system at its best.[27] There were five sisters in the family besides Alphonse, and they lived on a country estate near Macon with very limited cash income but an abundance of good food and wine, much simple gaiety, hunts for the men, and dances for the young folk where one of the daughters would play for the others. To make ends meet and, especially, to get the girls married happily in spite of the deficiency in dowry money was a constant preoccupation of Mme de Lamartine all during the 1810s and 1820s.

When the time came to marry off Césarine, she was much in love with a neighbor's son. Madame liked the young man and did not want to offend the neighbor, but because of money—"*ce vilain argent*" —she had to say no to the suitor. At the next party, she could not help observing how miserable he looked, and Césarine too looked unhappy, though "of course" she knew nothing and asked her mother what could possibly be the matter with him. It was poignant to watch the couple dance their one dance together, she as lovely as the day in her mother's eyes. A little later Madame urged Césarine's married sister to help persuade her to marry a forty-year-old-man of affluence and status (Césarine was only eighteen). It did not, of course, occur to the girl to go against her parents' wishes. Her mother called her "admirably submissive" but still worried that her daughter was unaware of the sacrifice that would be demanded of her and that it might be more than she had strength to meet. ("And burn these last letters," said Mamma of the paper she was writing on.) When the engagement was announced, the Lamartines found that they had unwittingly offended the family of the first lover. Thinking it over, Madame felt that she had really done the best thing for the girl's happiness but regretted that she had not smoothed over all the bumps. Still, the question nagged at her conscience for years, and by the time poor Césarine died, after having had two babies, her mother had suffered even more than she over the sacrifice of her youthful love.

Another sister, Sophie, had a less tempestuous experience. The family had studied the proposed husband for over a year and finally announced that he would come to call. Sophie wrote to her sister, "I am astonished at being so calm, even though the day of the interview is approaching," and debated whether to wear her pink or her blue dress for the meeting.[28] At the great occasion itself, Sophie looked him over and agreed to accept him, whereupon he asked permission to kiss her. Sophie did not dare give it, but the elder Lamartines pushed her ahead—and so everything went according to plan.

Mme de Lamartine was almost equally active in the marital affairs of her son. His first love affair was with a married woman; his mother prayed at his bedside over this situation, but did not want to know too much about it. She was much happier when he fell in love with a suitable girl, sweet, used to a serious life and to country living, but this alliance foundered on the opposition of the Lamartine uncles, who controlled much of their property. As Madame put it: "I have taken infinite trouble, I have talked, wept, written, done impossible things, and at the moment when I expected to get the fruit of my labor, it was all destroyed. I will have to begin again . . . because one must never get discouraged, nor relax in filling one's duties as a mother.[29]

It was sometimes said that mothers were the most aggressive pursuers of sons-in-law—that it was woman's final passion. Almost any mother, it was said, could give a young man the feeling of "your money or your life," and a mother of three daughters would be capable of anything.[30]

But, said Michelet, we try to assume that the family, at least, is on the girl's side.[31] Well, was this so? Michelet himself knew of several families where girls were married off to rich old men they did not want, and he wondered why mothers stated, "I love my girl so much," and prepared them in neither heart nor mind for marriage. Juliette Adam, who later became a staunch republican journalist, was married in 1852 against her own wishes, and even against her father's, by her old grandmother, whose motive was the hope that she herself could then spend winters in Paris with the young couple. When Juliette appealed to her father to save her, the family scene became so violent that she consented to the marriage just to escape the furor. It turned out disastrously for everyone, even the grandmother, for the man had no intention of letting any relatives share his Paris headquarters.

It was possible for someone other than the actual parents to arrange a marriage. Sometimes an employer of girls, such as a kindly dressmaker, would fix up her apprentices with husbands.[32] And Juliette Adam, forgetting her own youth when middle-aged and famous, and happily married at last *en secondes noces*, did a signal service for Léon Gambetta by arranging a marriage for his sister.[33]

In any case, French happiness in marriage depended very much on other people's management and approval—far more than was true in England, where each couple was told to stand on its own feet, or in Germany (at least those parts touched by the romantic movement), where it was felt that passion should sweep lovers into the union.

Victor Hugo, who finally succeeded in marrying the woman he loved in 1822, had been put off for three and a half years for lack of his parents' consent. Mme Hugo died without having given it, and after that General Hugo waited a long time until he finally gave in. If he had not, the marriage probably would not have taken place.[34]

ᴄᴏ Marriage without parental consent, or proof that the parents and grandparents were dead, was forbidden in France up to the age of sixty.* (According to one authority, it was permitted after that time on the legal

*Since Catholic tradition does not require parental consent (nor does Lutheranism, for that matter), this requirement can only be considered as a return to old Roman law. Interestingly enough, it was also the rule among sixteenth- and seventeenth-century English Puritans (Schücking, 8).

ground that sixty had been the age in feudal periods at which body service of vassals ceased.) If a couple attained a certain age—twenty-five for men, twenty-one for girls—and were determined to marry in spite of their parents' refusal, there existed a procedure by which they could go to court and then officially make three "respectful appeals"* to the parents, naturally a very difficult thing for a young girl to do. Still failing to win consent, they could obtain a court order permitting the marriage to go ahead.[35]

And the rule was occasionally invoked. George Sand's grandmother, who, as we have seen, was unreconciled to her son's marriage, tried for years to get it annulled on the grounds that it had been performed secretly, against her wishes, and without the three respectful appeals. Fortunately, in this case the effort was unsuccessful.[36]

The ideal age to marry was deemed to be thirty for the man, and twenty for the girl.† At thirty a man would have sowed his wild oats—*il faut que la jeunesse se passe*—and would be ready to settle down. Because it was believed that a man's passions were most violent during his twenties, Balzac, among others, stated clearly that no mother would turn her daughter over to a man who was going through this period of fermentation.[37] There was also the point that by thirty a man would have established himself in a career and the family would know what it was getting.[38] From the man's point of view, according to the popular guidebook *Le Livre de la famille*, the girl should be considerably younger than the man because women were supposed to age faster. By the time she was thirty-two, if she had had as many as three pregnancies, she would already be in decline. Her physical condition then would compare to that of a man of fifty.

Social status was viewed as seriously as age and money. Hillebrand noticed that a Frenchman did not care to marry above his station and seldom married beneath it, although Delphine de Girardin satirized those parents who went to the library to consult pedigrees instead of talking to friends about temperaments and habits. It was considered a *mésalliance* for a nobleman to marry a commoner, a nobleman being defined as anybody with a *de* in front of his name, and Hamerton did some rather careful figuring and concluded that the particle was worth at least £10,000 in the marriage market. Even if falsely borne, as often happened, it was assumed to be a guarantee that the young man would not hold liberal opinions.‡

*Reduced to one by a law of 1896.

†See Appendix for detailed analysis of actual marriage age.

‡A book about the Third Republic's army, written around 1877, half patriotic appeal, half gentle satire, pointed out the advantages for a soldier of using his military *livret* when he went wife-hunting. The soldier is imagined, with the girl's assent, approaching her father, *livret* in hand. The mother asks if the good conduct certificate means he has never had a mistress, but the father hastens to say that that is not what it means at all. They study the record, perceive that the soldier's measurements are the same as the father-in-law's (so they could get by with a single evening suit for both of them). And the *livret* obviates the

For every marriageable girl, said Eugène Pelletan in an 1865 book about the family, there was a female neighbor to pass along the news about her dowry. When the two families got together, a figure was mentioned and the assets of the other side toted up—so much now, so much "in expectation." If the girl's family had a farm, would this balance the man's degree as a notary?*

Since the providing of dowries had become a major duty of parent-hood, and since the laws required that each child be given equal treatment in regard to the family property, a French father had to produce as many fortunes as he had children, all within the space of eighteen to thirty years. To some it meant that they must live almost like beggars, econo-mizing and practicing "systematic sterility" (in the reproachful term of their neighbors across the Channel), to enable their children to have an easy life.†

The lower the interest rate fell, the more difficult it became to assemble the needed sum. In 1897 Edmond Demolins wrote a book for French consumption praising the superiority of the Anglo-Saxon way of life. The continued drop in the French birth rate was held up for compari-son. The interest rate had recently fallen to 3 percent, he explained, and this had led to a faster decline in the number of children per French family.[39]

Many are the examples of the sacrifices families were willing to make, from simply weeding their own gardens and sewing their own clothes—an amount of housework shocking to the English of comparable social status—to a bibliophile's selling his library. Hippolyte Taine's

---

need to make personal inquiry of a concierge, who might fear the loss of a bachelor client should the marriage go through and thus be tempted to blacken his character (Huart, 96).

*Marie Bashkirtseff's diary may be enlightening. In 1879, at nineteen, she called France an infamous country for young girls and said that it would be impossible to exhibit more cold cynicism than was seen at most weddings. Yet four years later when she began to imagine marriage for herself in practical terms, she faced the fact that she was not rich enough to marry someone who would leave her free to follow her own desires, and she could not really imagine falling in love (Bashkirtseff, 455, 700).

†The relationship between the French inheritance laws and the falling birth rate had been the subject of much economic and sociological speculation. The idea that the family was disintegrating because of the equal division of estates is associated with Frédéric Le Play, a French sociologist who tried to get Napoleon III to restore the old type of undivided homestead. He painted a sad picture of the sister losing her right to a place at the family hearth while the brother has to marry money in order to recoup the loss of his sister's share. Although the latest modern studies conclude that there probably was little connection between the inheritance law and population decline (Camp, 121), almost everybody in the latter half of the nineteenth century believed that there was. An English clergyman explained as a well-known fact that French marriage contracts often specified how many children were to be reared, thus circumventing the law of the land by violating the law of God (Baring-Gould, 1: 121). Apparently people had begun to comment on the small size of French families back in the eighteenth century, and the two-child family became very common quite early. Until about 1850 nobody worried much; in fact they were rather proud of their "civilized" mode of arranging things.

mother, a widow, had to forego giving him a notary's training because it would have taken her entire fortune to buy him a practice and he had two sisters. By this sacrifice he was preserved for literature.

Up to 1790, the national budget included a considerable sum to dower provincial girls, either for marriage or for entering a cloister. During the Revolution, women petitioned the National Assembly to force men to marry women who had no dowry, but this effort failed.

There was at this early period, however, quite a spirit of self-sufficiency among girls, which did not persist long into the nineteenth century. The first Mme Guizot (Pauline de Meulan), when orphaned, had donated her dowry to her two sisters and declared that she would never marry a man who would not accept her without any *dot*. Meanwhile she supported herself by working on the staff of a small newspaper where young Guizot also worked. When she fell ill, he offered to help her, and at first she was so independent that she refused. Eventually, though the acquaintance ripened into marriage, in 1812.[40] A few years later it would be hard to match this story, although again toward the end of the century girls were beginning to work outside their homes in greater numbers, often in the hope of creating a dowry for themselves. Miss Betham tells of a governess in a Russian family who earned a thousand pounds by long service, the required dowry for the wife of a French officer, whereupon she came home and married one.* As the custom of accepting paid work spread into the middle class, girls came to prefer it, and their fathers began to see the need to train their daughters to earn a living. "I am anti-feminist regarding my wife, but feminist regarding my daughter," one man is quoted as saying.

Often, however, the woman's contribution was expected to take place after the marriage, though this might be discounted, so to speak, at the time the marriage contract was signed. The *Gazette des Femmes* in the 1840s, perhaps as part of the feminist desire to emphasize woman's capabilities, told of a girl who saved her husband 3,000 francs in the first year of marriage by good management, probably in both home and shop. It was noted that to equal this sum in interest, one would need a capital of 60,000 francs.[41] In the same vein, Miss Betham told of a restaurant owner who chose, with his parents' approval, a propertyless girl of character and intelligence over some richer candidates whose brains were not so promising. French life offered many opportunities for the wife to work closely with her husband in small shops or craft industries.

Here as elsewhere Hamerton is enlightening. In the middle classes

---

*Dowries were terribly important even in the working class. In some French towns there were lotteries where poor working girls taxed themselves by the hundreds in order to make up a dowry for the winner. Even prostitutes worked and saved in order to get the sum to make a respectable marriage, thus showing the French feeling that sex and money are not so separate as they seem in other parts of the world. As late as 1935 the municipality of Paris provided eight dowries for working girls in order to encourage marriage (Spengler, 22F).

that he knew best, he insisted, Frenchmen did not try to make a profit out of a marriage settlement, but simply attempted to avoid bearing the entire burden alone. The dowry should pay for the added expense of taking on a wife. Thousands of young Frenchmen, he believed, were willing to marry for 20,000 francs, which would yield a rather modest 1,000 francs a year. In fact it was a matter of self-respect and honor not to seek a big dowry. His inquiries produced the information that a girl with an income of £200, admittedly larger than ordinary, could expect to marry into a household expending £800, indicating that a quarter of the expenses might be met by the wife's income. Such a settlement could not be called gold-digging. A more usual case would be one where a man would acquire £500 capital along with his wife and together they would buy a shop, or he could move up to become a master craftsman, or if he owned a small establishment already they could move into a bigger one.

In a home economics text for schoolgirls published just before 1914, the main character on whom the lessons were pinned, Marie, brought only a thousand francs, earned by herself, to a marriage to which Pierre, her husband, brought five thousand; this gives an idea of what expectations for the upwardly mobile working class might be.[42]

At the other end of the scale were fortune hunters, men who simply set out to marry 300,000 francs. In these circles the woman was valued according to the size of her hoard. The Countess Sophie de Ségur, a Russian heiress, came with a big dowry, to which was added a large estate in Normandy where she and her husband were to live. But the Russian money was lost during the twenties, and Sophie noticed that her popularity within the family dropped markedly. Only the old grandfather insisted gallantly that although they had lost the fortune, they had "retained the treasure."[43]

Like Hamerton, Elizabeth Gaskell, the novelist, found much sense in the dowry system. She believed that girls in England had to hunt for rich husbands because they expected to be penniless themselves, while in France every family started a marriage portion as soon as a girl was born.[44] At the same time, being English, she inquired rather anxiously whether French parents would force the issue in a case where they had made the arrangements and the girl objected. She was much relieved to be told that a match would be quickly given up if either party said clearly that he did not like it.

In addition to these general customs, there were certain particular requirements for dowries. A soldier, for instance, was forbidden to marry unless his fiancée had a certain sum in cash; he was not allowed to marry one who might support herself by working.[45] Even if he seduced a girl and she became pregnant he could not repair the fault and legitimize his child unless she could come up with the needed sum. For officers the amounts were higher, and there were draconian laws prohibiting officers from running into debt.[46]

DISCARDED

LIBRARY
FORSYTH TECHNICAL COMMUNITY COLLEGE
2100 SILAS CREEK PARKWAY
WINSTON SALEM, N.C. 27103

∽ Although she needed consent to get married, a French girl had the legal right to refuse, the trouble being, of course, that she hardly ever had the chance to fiind out if she wanted to. Writing during a period of active feminism in the 1830s, Edouard Alletz wondered why girls did not refuse more often, and why mothers, scarred by their own experience, did not stop their daughters instead of pushing them into the same thing. A truly prudent mother, according to the advice of Ernest Legouvé, who was regarded as an authority on women's problems, would break off her daughter's engagement whenever her child felt repugnance, no matter how irrational; one bride he knew of said she felt horrible when her fiancé advanced to kiss her on the day of her betrothal, and Legouvé commended the mother for breaking the affair off then and there. Lady Morgan, like Mrs. Gaskell, satisfied herself as an interested Englishwoman that repugnance was never forced, but certain French evidence gives the lie to such a sweeping generalization. Although it is fictional, the following conversation must have been repeated in substance many times in life. Edmond About, writing in the fifties, had a young girl disputing with her aunt. The girl says she will not marry any of a series of young men who have been proposing to her.

> "And why not, niece?"
> "Because I don't love them, aunt."
> "Imagine saying a thing like that. I didn't ask you if you were in love with these young gentlemen."
> "I wish to love my husband first."
> "That is not good form."[47]

And here is a non-fictional letter from a girl, Stéphanie Jullien, to her father, dated August 17, 1836. "I would have liked to be able to know, appreciate, and attach myself before tying myself for life, and this is impossible; I am disgusted with this obligation to unite myself with a man in order to have a lot and a position in the world; what appeals to all other girls only disturbs me and makes me sad."[48]

Mrs. Farrar knew of one case of successful resistance to a forced marriage, but this was a French girl who had English relatives. Her brother helped her to escape across the Channel. There she eloped with a man she really loved, and lived happily.

The right to refuse a marriage was one thing. The claim to choose one's own husband was a far bigger step, and one which apparently threatened each older generation in turn. In a book about women written in 1803, revised and enlarged in 1838, the Count of Ségur complained that girls were beginning to want to make this choice. He regarded it as a scandal.[49] Philippe Ariès sets 1860 as the date when *men* might successfully make their wishes prevail over those of their parents,[50] but it was surely much later when women reached the same stage.

For a young woman to assert her freedom by having an affair frequently meant a complete break with her family. Madeleine Pelletier, one of the first women doctors practicing in Paris in the early twentieth century, had a friend, a woman of thirty living with her mother, who decided to take a lover. Although he had promised to prevent conception, she found herself pregnant, and the mother put her straight out of the house. She walked the streets of Paris all night long until Dr.Pelletier rescued her. The next communication from the mother was a little bit of money, it is true, but it was accompanied by a lethal dose of laudanum as the best way out.[51]

Things were just beginning to change before the First World War, and that catastrophe, of course, speeded up the process for women's independence. Fathers were beginning to see that an education might be as good as a dowry, and it was among the women students that camaraderie and even spontaneous matchmaking first began to have their effect. It is significant that about at this time the Sorbonne itself was nicknamed *"l'allée des Demoiselles."**[52]

---

*A word about the marriage bureaus, which were set up to help those whose family system could not meet the strain of matchmaking. They existed all through our period (one observer noticed that it seemed in the 1830s that *all* girls who advertised claimed to be orphans of soldiers killed at Waterloo), but proliferated at the end of the century, when the family arrangements were weakening. They invariably mentioned property and what might be sacrificed for it (Burnand, 1830, 58). Thus in 1900 an engineer, "possessing property," wished for a wife between twenty-six and thirty-two who was well provided for. Presumably if she was still unmarried at that age there must be a reason, so he included the information that he would "tolerate a small fault." In 1910, "a very serious brown-haired young man" who described himself as tall and elegant and the possessor of 3,000 francs, sought marriage and a position within the family of a nice young girl who might happen to be the daughter of the owner of a farm or of commercial property (About, 18; Grépon, 114–16, and passim).

According to a German commentator, these public advertisements were used and accepted by all classes in France (Meisel-Hess, 312), though in Teutonic countries they were limited to those of lower status.

∾ 4.

The Destined Maid

People think women who do not want to marry unfeminine: people think women who do want to marry immodest: people combine both opinions by regarding it as unfeminine for women not to look forward longingly to wifehood as the hope and purpose of their lives, and ridiculing or contemning any individual women of their acquaintance whom they may suspect of entertaining such a longing. This is hard upon marriageable women. Their time is short, in many cases their opportunities are few, and meanwhile they are hampered with difficulties more numerous and more contradictory than were the old man's with the ass when he tried to take everybody's advice. They must wish and not wish; they must by no means give, they must certainly not withhold encouragement, they must not let a gentleman who is paying attention think them waiting for his offer, they must not let him think they would admit the careless homages of a flirtation and are not waiting for his offer; they must not be frank, they must not be coy; they must not laugh and talk indifferently with all comers, they must not show preferences—so it goes on, each precept cancelling another, and most of them negative. How are the girls to get themselves married and escape censure in the process? And if, whether by fault or only worse luck than her neighbours, a mistaken damsel brings herself under a ban of more than momentary censure, gets "talked about," as the phrase is, henceforth there is small hope of her ever accomplishing her destiny at all.

Augusta Webster, 1879

Things were quite different in England.

Tocqueville, in viewing individuality as "the basis of English character,"[1] was voicing one of the ideas which had come to him in America. He believed that in most Protestant countries girls were much more in control of their own behavior than in Catholic ones, and further that in self-governing countries, like England, they enjoyed even greater independence. They could do this, he thought, because their characters were formed soundly, not because their minds had been artificially kept uncontaminated.*[2]

*Tocqueville went on to say that the English formed associations to get things done that no one person could do alone, but that even in these circumstances individualism kept cropping up: "I suppose that if the French could become more enlightened than they are, they would take to clubbing together more naturally. . . ."

A few examples will show what he meant. During Mrs. Trollope's year in Paris, she was much amused by the tale of a young Frenchman concerning his invitation to an English country house for a month of hunting.[3] He was enraptured, especially when he got there and found that the household contained three charming daughters, but his rapture changed to alarm the next morning when the father, being busy, asked his guest to accompany one of the young ladies into the woods where she could show him the pheasants. In fact, he was so embarrassed that he took the next train back to London. Mrs. Trollope laughed heartily at this point in the story until a French lady reproached her for being unable to understand the man's predicament. So Mrs. Trollope tried to explain English mores. The girl, she said, would have been astonished and embarrassed in her turn if the man had attempted to make love to her. Her French listeners could hardly believe she was in earnest, but she went on to explain that the father would only issue such an invitation to a young man whom he trusted. "What sublime confidence!" the French murmured; they could only have supposed the incident was a way of luring the young man into marriage.

Taine too, though he mastered his surprise better, was astonished at being asked while in England to escort a young girl to a house a mile away, and recounted wonderingly the story of two Frenchmen in Manchester who were asked to accompany two girls home from an evening party.[4] The foursome took a cab, chatted freely, and experienced no awkwardness. As was stated in a French play of 1835, "In England young girls count for something; they talk, act, please, and choose; they are elegant, coquette."[5] By these experiences, young girls were acquiring the maturity to make their own choices.[6]

Even in London, Taine commented, a girl was free to go out by herself, or at least with her sister, while in France *jeunes filles* were kept under close and continuous watch. In a book explaining English customs to foreign visitors at the time of the Crystal Palace exposition (1851), it was said that while an English girl might refuse to dance with you at a ball, if she did accept your invitation, you might call on her the next day, and that even very young women might receive such visits without asking parental consent.[7] Mary Somerville, later a distinguished mathematician, recalled the freedom she and her girl friends had to walk through the streets of Edinburgh, where they could talk to yesterday's dancing partners if they met them, and that they could introduce at supper parties men who were previously unknown to their parents.

But it was in the country that girls were freest of all, being accustomed to long walks and rides. (Stendhal said that an English girl covered more ground in a week than a Roman girl in a year.) Acquaintance ripened on such walks and often turned into courtship, as in the case of William and Mary Howitt. When this young Quaker came to her village, it was the first time Mary had ever had male companionship, but she found that William had a very independent mind and she quickly became interested in it.

Max O'Rell (who in spite of his pseudonym was a Frenchman, Paul Blouët) noted that no English mother or governess would think of opening a letter addressed to her daughter or pupil, but that the young people, in turn, would not conduct correspondence on the sly. Apparently the confidence of parents was rarely misplaced. Although Catherine Winkworth wondered whether Miss Brontë could ever have been in love—"surely she could never herself have made love to anyone, as all her heroines . . . do"[8]—Miss Brontë had, as most readers now know, indeed fallen in love, and had refused to carry on a clandestine correspondence with the Brussels schoolmaster who was the object of her desire.

Kisses between unengaged couples were rare; in fact, a single kiss often meant that troth was plighted even without words. When Thomas Hughes, author of *Tom Brown's Schooldays*, underwent a period of forced separation from his fiancée, he used the occasion to flirt with his cousin, and even kissed her once, but when her mother found out she wrote him a scorching letter that made him feel smaller than he had ever felt in his life.[9]

Lord Amberley as a youth used to go on walking tours in parties which included young ladies, and it appears that his mountain climbing with Annie Stoddard included a picnic and "some affectionate passages." They read poetry together, and at the professor's house where they were staying they joined a club, "founded on love and whose principle is kissing." Another professor with his wife came to visit, and they "did not scruple to carry on the rites of the club in [their] presence." But when he met Annie a year later she was engaged, and so forbidden to kiss, and the club "subsided into a mere eating institution."[10]

None of what has been said should be taken to imply that actual chaperonage did not exist to a degree that would seem galling a hundred years later, while the inner restraints were even more powerful. The grip of convention, in spite of everything, was terribly strong. Thoughtful critics like Florence Nightingale used to point out that despite social access to men, girls were not really allowed to know them very well. A man would not risk "trifling with her feelings"[11] by getting involved in deep subjects, and Miss Nightingale's hope was that if they could meet for some common purpose rather than purely socially, they might develop more realistic ties. From the woman's side, the dreadful fear of seeming unladylike would inhibit many initiatives, and families obviously differed in the degree to which they would welcome strange young men as callers.

When the young women who were later to form Girton College were living at Hitchin for a few years (from 1869 to 1872) before daring to move into the university town itself, they received two visits from brothers. Although everybody behaved with the utmost propriety, the chaperones felt thankful that the brothers did not live close by and imagined fearfully what might happen if the college were settled right in Cambridge with two thousand pleasure-loving undergraduates who had not been properly introduced to the girls. Fears like these led Bessie

Parkes, Hilaire Belloc's mother, to insist that *much* freer intercourse between people would be needed before girls could choose that "noble matrimony" which was supposed to be a special British accomplishment. Even the careful Mrs. Ellis felt that it might be better if manners loosened up a little bit, though she wanted her readers to understand that with things as they were, one could not be too exact about the proprieties.[12]

໑ The English believed that love should precede marriage, that love was the only proper reason for getting married, and that "Love wakes man, once a lifetime each." It was hoped that when each man

> . . . meets by heavenly chance express
> The destined maid; some hidden hand
> Unveils to him that loveliness
> Which others cannot understand.[13]

The above quotation is from *The Angel in the House.** The poet, Coventry Patmore, goes on to describe the slow awakening of a girl's heart, like a caged bird not daring at first to fly, but responsive to her lover's hand.

Most people played the game as nearly according to this ideal as they could. Taine was struck by the Englishman's romantic view of marriage, especially in comparison with the cynicism he was so familiar with in France, and felt that the result of prolonged chastity was much silent agony. Emphasis on "higher feelings" concentrated English passions to the point that there was a real trauma if love promises were broken. *Punch*, he noticed, made fun of legitimate, not illicit, love; in its cartoons men were always respectful, there were no high-blown skirts, and the jokes lay in the little wiles of young men and girls maneuvering each other into marriage. In France he had never seen such drawings because there was no such subject.

Of course, the old-fashioned way had been for a suitor to ask a girl's parents for permission to court her, and in the very earliest part of the nineteenth century this was still the most proper thing to do, though the custom died quite quickly and completely. The change was related to growing disapproval of marriage for money or position, a trend which continued steadily. Thus Patricia Thomson, in her study *The Victorian Heroine*, has found that English novels of the twenties and thirties still accepted the marriage of convenience, but by the fifties and sixties it was being condemned.[14] By the seventies Herbert Spencer, in *Principles of Sociology*, forecast the logical conclusion: disapprobation would extend to marriages where love has died, making divorce acceptable.[15]

Yet even under the old, formal conditions, the man at least had felt the stirring of passion. We have already met Hannah More's Coelebs in Chapter I, an idealized and somewhat disembodied young man who woos his chosen Lucilla in perfect style by tackling her father first. Coventry

*A title "which might be bestowed on a meritorious cook," as an old copy of *Punch* (Graves, II, 237) remarked.

Patmore also had his ideal courtship, in *The Angel in the House*, prefaced by the hero's approach to the Dean, the girl's father. Here, the good dean immediately opened up to explain that she would have "only £3,000" for now, but more would come later, during which discussion his daughter remained in lighthearted ignorance of the matters they talked about, almost like a French girl.

Jane Austen's marriages are probably more verisimilar. In her novels the engagements are not arranged by the parents but are made by free, and often secret, choice of the two principals. They could not be announced, however, until an appropriate moment had been chosen and parental approval won, though there was always the possibility of an elopement in the background.[16]

Elizabeth Grant, the "Highland Lady," recalled that her aunt, in 1806, carried on a courtship in London unknown to either family. There was general admiration and amazement when it became public. Years later, Elizabeth's sister got engaged secretly by mail, creating similar surprise, though in this case the father wrote immediately to the young man to ask about his money and prospects. In 1809 Catherine Potter (who was Beatrice Webb's great-aunt) engaged herself entirely on her own, and since she was an orphan she did the requisite checking on her fiancé's character by herself.[17]

The psychologically insecure young Gladstone tried out proposals to several girls through their parents, but the one he finally married, Catherine Glynne, he approached in person. (His wooing technique was to tell each woman how earnestly he wanted to Christianize politics, leading Catherine to confess that she had already admired his writing enough to copy extracts for herself.[18])

By mid-century, at the latest, the typical engagement was arranged after a direct proposal by a man who had had considerable chance to talk with and observe the girl, and who found himself conscious of more intimate desires. Perhaps they were taking a long walk, perhaps they were sitting together in front of a fire alone—for both situations were well within the bounds of propriety. Perhaps he began by asking permission to call her by her first name; if she assented, he was emboldened to push ahead.They sealed the engagement with a kiss, likely to be the first one she had ever received.

Thus when Richard Burton, back from explorations of Mecca and the East, proposed to Isabel Arundell, he stole an arm around her waist, and begged her to take time to decide. Since she was more than prepared, her immediate answer was yes, *yes*, YES, and they kissed. She wrote later, "All that has been written or said on the subject of the first kiss is trash compared to the reality. Men might as well undertake to describe Eternity."[19]

When this system worked, it worked well, as thousands of happy, stable Victorian marriages testified, but obviously there were all too many chances for slip-ups, occasionally comic, often tragic.

For comedy, take the case of Angela Burdett-Coutts, the richest girl in all England, who lived with a chaperone for propriety. She was so accustomed to receiving proposals that the companion regularly left the room when she saw one coming, and Angela used a certain cough to tell Mrs. Browne when to come back.[20] Miss Burdett-Coutts did not actually marry until she was forty-seven.

When the composer Ethel Smyth's elder sister was proposed to in the late 1860s, smelling salts had to be applied. But being a hardy feminist and self-reliant musician, Ethel needed no such props when her turn came.

For sheer sentimentality, consider E. W. Benson, who later became Archbishop of Canterbury. At twenty-three he fell in love with a little girl of eleven; he took her on his knee and asked if she would marry him when she grew up. She cried. But they became engaged, read Tennyson's *Princess* together, and eventually did marry, in 1859.[*21]

Sometimes considerations of propriety could force the issue, even without love, as when Charles Lear (a relative of the limerick writer) contracted malaria while serving as a medical missionary in West Africa. He was so ill that the captain refused to take him aboard ship without a nurse. A native black African had been attending him, but in order to facilitate her continued service in the cramped quarters of the ship, Charles had to marry her. When they got to England, the family paid to send her to school, and she eventually returned to missionary service in her own land.[22]

More tragically, Frank Besant proposed to Annie Wood after following her to a holiday spot. She was taken by surprise and did not say either yes or no, but he was expecting her to be shy and thought she implied consent. So "out of sheer weakness and fear of inflicting pain, I drifted into an engagement with a man I did not pretend to love"[23]—and Annie Besant's long career of suffering for the cause of women and humanity was born.

There was one thing that English girls of good form could never do, and that was to give the faintest sign of interest or eagerness before they had received a clear signal from the man. Mrs. Cecil Frances Alexander, a versifier, called this feeling "the true instinct that woman 'should not unsought be won,' "[24] an instinct that Walter De la Mare says kept more women straight than religion, morality, and calculation together. This quality was not unnoticed by Taine, who found that while lower-class girls sometimes became bold enough to call on young men in their apartments, upper-class girls would rather remain unwed than make a sign. It was all too well known to Charlotte Brontë, whose Shirley said

*Idealizing innocence as they did, a number of Victorian men were drawn to pre-adolescent girls, including Ruskin, who proposed marriage, and Lewis Carroll, who did not.

that a hurt girl had to learn never to complain when a man ignored her, since if she was weak she would only lose his esteem, though it took a strong woman to absorb the lesson.

When "Miss Weeton" (Nelly Stock) worked as a governess in order to support her brother throughout his education, she expected to find a home with him for the rest of her life, and so refused an offer of marriage. As it turned out, the brother rudely cast her adrift, and delicacy strictly forbade that she should tell her admirer that she was at liberty. "For the world, I would not a make a single advance."[25]

This convention too, of course, broke down in the late years of the nineteenth century. The Webbs' engagement was signalized when Beatrice Potter suddenly put her arm around Sidney in a cab. It could not be made public even then, however, because Beatrice's father would not hear of her marrying a lower-class socialist. For a while Lord Haldane acted as a cover for the couple, letting them meet at his house while he went off for long walks. Later on, busy with social studies, Beatrice was able to take a hotel room, letting Sidney act as her secretary, hoping that the hotel clerks would not suspect the intervals of "human nature" which took place. They postponed their marriage until Mr. Potter had been dead six months.[26]

↺ In English law, the consent of the father (or a widowed mother) was formally needed for the marriage of any person under twenty-one. After that age young people could expect a good deal of subtle pressure to make them live up to family standards of money and social class, but this pressure was negative, telling them whom not to marry, rather than positive in the French way. And while advice, good and bad, continued to flow, actual control by parents had dissolved by the end of the century into little more than a formality.

One way in which parental suggestions were given is shown in *A Book With Seven Seals*, the story of the growing up of two little girls. Here they are about to attend a children's ball in 1873:

> As they lumbered along towards the Park through the fog, Mrs. Danvers spoke a few words in season to her little daughters, who sat facing her on the back seat.
>
> "You both look very nice, dears," she remarked as her eyes scanned an outline of round white faces and well-crimped hair. "I expect you to behave nicely as well. Good behaviour and appearance are of great importance in life. It is your duty to make friends, which you can only do by being agreeable. But it is not necessary to know everyone; you must learn to discern between the right and the wrong people. Tonight you will only meet your equals, and you may not have as many opportunities of doing so as I should wish. We cannot entertain, and your Papa does not approve of dancing and parties. But I consider that going into good society is a necessary part of your education, and I think you are old enough to understand what I mean."

"Yes," laughed Hetty. "We are to make friends with the sheep and avoid the goats, Molly."

"Harriet, you are vulgar and profane," said her Mamma. "I wish to impress upon you the importance of making a good marriage when you grow up, for no lady can earn her own living. Therefore you must marry, and I should like you to make a good impression to-night on Mr. and Mrs. Prince and their family."

"We are to improve the shining hour with the sheep because we shall not meet any goats; but I like them quite as much as the sheep," laughed Hetty.

Mary Anne listened to all that was being said, and turned it over in her small mind as they rumbled along. Going to a dance now assumed a different aspect.[27]

Later we shall see what happened to Harriet and her "goat."

Florence Nightingale noticed that heroines of romance almost never had a mother to interfere with their independence, and she attributed much of the charm of reading novels to this fact. In real life, of course, some mothers, including her own, were busybodies, some were prudes, and some were deeply sympathetic with their daughters' needs. Lady Stanley of Alderley wrote of how much thought she gave to approval of an engagement for her daughter Emmeline because of its importance for her character and constitution, but she dared not talk with a young man about a girl's need for affection for fear it would be seen only "in a gross light."[28] Even her own son Henry was a problem because he asserted that a father, mother, and grandfather had no right to check a young man's inclinations in regard to marriage.

Fathers usually operated on a more practical scale, worrying about money, merits, and prospects, and, when carefully done, this concern often won the children's gratitude.* The night before he died, the Scottish Dr. Welsh had a long talk with his daughter Jane (who was to marry Thomas Carlyle), explaining the gravity of choosing a partner, with the happy result that she thereupon decided to take a serious view of life.[29]

Sometimes parents entirely refused permission, often for reasons that seem quite unfair. Ann Taylor laid down the general dictum in 1825 that while elders must not force a marriage, they could quite properly prevent an undesirable connection.[30] This was all too often done, usually by appealing to the loyalty or higher instincts of the young people. Consider the case of Elizabeth Grant. When she was eighteen, in Edinburgh, a friend of her brother moved in their social circle for months. No one ever told her to stop seeing him, as they went on picnics and to dances, until she was peremptorily forbidden to marry him because her father had had a falling out with his father in their university days. She

---

*My own mother-in-law told me how much she owed to her father for warning her in the 1890s, when she was nineteen, not to get serious about a certain young man. His reasoning: "I think you are ambitious, and though Mr. X is a good enough young man, he is not likely to achieve the level of distinction that would make you happy." She appreciated getting this hint before she had had time to become emotionally involved.

never learned the grounds of the ancient quarrel. After the young couple had pledged eternal faith to each other, his mother came to call on Elizabeth and explained how much pain it would cause the two families if the young folk persisted. The argument succeeded, at least superficially. Elizabeth agreed to receive him coldly, as a mere acquaintance and to return his letters unopened; but the experience was a wound that she never got over.[31]

Sometimes other pieties were invoked, as in the case of the elder Augustus Hare, who felt obliged to fulfill an aunt's dying wish that he break off his brother Julius's engagement. Julius made the bitter sacrifice, and Augustus felt noble rather than intrusive.[32]

And now we get back to Harriet Danvers, whose training for marriage we observed a few pages back, from *A Book With Seven Seals*. A gifted singer, she wins a scholarship to the Conservatory, which her father will not let her accept because "no lady can earn her own living."[33] Cut back to singing in parish concerts and attending neighborhood skating parties, she falls in love with a Jewish baritone. But Mr. Danvers will hear none of it, and reproaches the two with having met behind his back, as he puts it. Harriet insists. Her father retorts that a marriage is out of the question. Jews have no nationality. Jews are outcasts. So her family packs her off on a long visit to the country, and she comes back engaged to a forty-year-old cousin. The night before her wedding, she burns a heart-rending appeal from her former lover to elope with him and let her voice be trained. Such a leap is too much for her, even though she murmurs to her sister, "They won't let me marry the right man, *or* be an opera singer, *or* be a hospital nurse."[34]

Once in a while it was the man who could not break the family pattern, like Edward Bond, Octavia Hill's fiancé (Octavia was a pioneer in housing for the poor). The engagement had been contracted after a long friendship, stimulated, like so many others, by walking tours, but when Bond's mother forbade it, he caved in. Octavia was disgusted at his weakness of will and never saw him again.[35]

Short of actually forbidding an engagement, parents often prescribed a period of separation; in fact, it was almost standard practice. Part of the pattern was set out in *Coelebs*, whose hero, as soon as he had declared his love for Lucilla, was ordered to leave for three months on grounds of propriety. In this case the father had no objection to the suitor personally, but in most cases the separation was a kind of test that the parents hoped might cause the love to die. Thomas Hughes met Frances Ford in 1842. Mr. Ford called them silly young people (Tom was twenty), and decreed that they must not see each other or communicate in any way for four years. They faced the separation with romantic courage, and Tom kept a journal for her future reading. "Why should they keep us apart," he asked, "we shall not be such fools as to marry without their consent, and separating us can answer no other end but the prevention of such a step."[36] In spite of Tom's promise not to write, Mr. and Mrs. Ford opened and read Frances' mail during this period, but they did relent and lifted the ban a few months early, in May of 1845.

J. A. Froude had never done very well at college until one summer he fell in love, and immediately his whole character changed for the better. He enjoyed two months of bliss with the girl, taking long walks and scrambles, but his father, who was unusually dictatorial even for that age, wrote to the girl's father that Froude was not trustworthy and had run up great debts. The girl was then ordered to write Froude a letter of renunciation, promising never to see him again until after she was safely married.[37]

When the family of Charles Kingsley's fiancée seemed reluctant to accept him, Charles himself proposed a year without communication, as a kind of purification rite. He had met her in 1839; they were married in 1844. Marriage is so paradisiac, he wrote later, that it needs to be entered through purifying fires, and he felt that they two could wait, endure, and, if need be, find their happiness beyond the grave.[38] Meanwhile, during their separation, he wanted them, at a pre-set time every Thursday night, to imagine themselves in each other's arms (and every Friday he scourged himself for purification).

ᘓ Even when approved of, engagements were often long, mostly because the couple was waiting for money, and this was what the French were particularly critical of, wasting the best years when a small dowry could help out. For instance, we read: "Jane Damer is engaged to be married to Colonel Dunn, but there is not enough money as yet. Two old Aunts of somewhere about eighty-four years of age must die in order to make them comfortable. But I do not know how it is, these old creatures live a long time, particularly when their kind relations think they would be better in Heaven."[39] Lady Jane died unmarried.

Sometimes instead of waiting for an inheritance a couple had to wait simply for the man to establish himself. Tennyson became engaged to Emily Sellwood in 1838 but was not able to marry until 1850, an extreme victim of Victorian rules of behavior. After a couple of years of correspondence, Tennyson lost his independent income. Some people blamed Mr. Sellwood for refusing to let his daughter marry under such circumstances; some say that the poet himself felt it unfair to commit a woman to his fallen fortune. His mother offered to share her jointure with him in order to enable him to marry, but he nobly refused this offer as unfair to his brothers and sisters.[40] The lovers had one last meeting, over an entire summer's night, then separated and decided that they should forego all communication—a principle that they carried out so determinedly that when they met by chance at a social gathering and one of their relatives offered to give up his carriage so they could drive back together, they refused the opportunity. Eventually Tennyson's affairs took a turn for the better, and after receiving advice from Charles

Kingsley, Emily finally accepted Alfred's proposal. The marriage was apparently exceptionally happy.

And we hear from Taine of a twenty-eight year-old inventor who started a factory and had been engaged for three or four years at the time he was interviewed. The young woman waited patiently for her lover's calls each Saturday night, and sometimes they took little trips together, perfectly honorably. Taine contrasted what would have happened in France, where the girl would have helped in the work of the shop but the little trips would never have been permitted.

Even the prudish Dr. William Acton, in his book on prostitution, calls long engagements unnatural, with "two young loves wearing out their best years with hearts sickened and with hope long deferred."[41] It is all summed up in a painting called "The Long Engagement" by Arthur Hughes, portraying a couple holding hands, the man's face full of suffering, the woman's with a kind of puzzled effort at consolation. She cannot quite understand what hurts him so much.[42]

What, then was permitted to engaged couples? The books of advice often told girls that it was their duty to check the ardor of their suitors. But they were free to kiss, and not only in the presence of their families like the French. In 1864 Lord Amberley's mother asked him not to get involved with Kate Stanley, the girl he eventually married. His response was that he felt oppressed by "the great monster 'conventionality,'"* and within three weeks he had asked to see Kate alone. "We met & had one fervent embrace; one long, loving kiss which was worth hours of conversation."[43] Although, as we have seen, Lord Amberley had played kissing games before, many young men would not dare to claim a kiss until they were ready to propose marriage, and the kiss itself was supposed to seal the fact of an engagement.

For Mary Vivian Hughes, her engagement kiss was the first one she had ever received except from her brothers, and her whole life story as she gratefully recounts it makes credible how much joy could be had in spite of the strict following of Victorian convention. Her engagement lasted ten full years (from 1887 to 1897), during which time she and Arthur† made several trips to visit his parents in Wales, and spent as much time together as their two jobs allowed, but always with perfect obedience to the rules of convention.

---

*Even Church of England divines did not always obey the conventions. The Reverend Hugo Reginald Haweis was always a flirt (before and after marriage), and his future wife fell in love with him when he prepared her for confirmation. She continued to help with his Sunday schools from 1864 on. Sometimes, on church business, the two had to ride to London together on the train. One day he put his arm around her. "He had not got me squeezed up *tight* with his arm *far* round—only now and then a little press which felt queer and I was half tickled, half nervous, and I stopped laughing every time I felt his hand" (Bea Howe, 78, and passim). Later he used to drop a sixpence and then use the ruse of hunting for it to pinch her ankle. But for three years he never proposed. When he did, in 1867, Mary Eliza went shrieking to her mother, "He's done it, Ma, done it at last!"

†Not Arthur Hughes the painter, but a solicitor of the same name.

Might an engaged man go beyond the kiss? Mrs. Sewell, writing in 1869, fudged. Woman, she purred, was the most lovely of all created beings with her molded limbs and her rich, full, rounded bust, sacred to him alone who will win her heart. But may he *look* at all these witcheries?[44] She gives no answer.

The mystique of the kiss made broken engagements traumatic. Max O'Rell was fascinated to tell his French readers that English law forbade withdrawing from an engagement (by imposing a financial penalty), on the grounds that, with all the freedom that was theirs, girls would have worn off some of their bloom. They might even have been kissed, and this would detract from their value, for which damages might be claimed. Trollope, in *Can You Forgive Her?*, voiced the sentiment that a girl sinned against her whole sex by breaking a sacred promise and throwing off the aroma of precious delicacy. In another novel, *Robert Elsmere*, Mrs. Humphry Ward shows Rose, a girl who is kissed and proposed to one evening by a man who discovers the next morning that he had not really meant it. Rose is completely overcome and becomes afraid to love or think about marrying anybody else for fear that her own heart would seem shallow. This is quite a lot of mileage for a storyteller to get out of one kiss.

A natural corollary was that many engagements were fulfilled out of honor after the original passion had died. An early example was Richard Edgeworth. Once having proposed to Anna Maria Elers, he met some more glittering ladies at Bath, but since he had obtained the affections of Miss Elers, he married her in 1763, resolving, as he explained, to meet disagreeability with fortitude.[45] Shortly afterward he met Honora Sneyd, who at least equaled his imaginary picture of perfection, but he nobly resisted any approach to the lady until his first wife had died.

The Duke of Wellington's impeccable, though disastrous, behavior could be said to have set an example for noble Englishmen thereafter, for when he returned from India in 1806, after nine years of service overseas, he was informed by a female friend that Catherine Packenham still cherished remembrance of his proposal of many years before. The fact that they had not corresponded at all during his absence did not deter him from making a gentleman's amends, and with a stiff upper lip he led her to the altar. The couple was never happy.

A slightly different case was that of the painter J. M. W. Turner, who promised to write to a girl he was in love with. But her stepmother intercepted the letters, so, feeling abandoned, she gave her hand to another. Turner returned a week before the wedding, but the lady felt bound to honor her promise, and Turner declared that he would never marry.[46] And he never did.

In spite of the older generation's assumption that it had certain rights of control, English young people took matters into their own hands far more frequently than the French. Ann Taylor advised parents whose children married against their will to make the best of it and not interfere further. The temptation for clandestine marriages was strong and the opportunity fairly open because Scottish law differed from the English in that it never required the consent of parents for the marriage of minors. So a couple could cross the border and marry without much ceremony in Gretna Green.*[47] From Carlisle, the last English post stage station, young lovers could always somehow get a fast horse to take them across the border, while the pursuers could never seem to find a beast that was not lame or lazy. As late as 1851 William Farr, in his introduction to the British census of that year, told how certain English parents were afraid to send their sons to the University of Edinburgh for fear of these possibilities.[48]

Once of age, a couple did not need to flee out of England, and there were many elopements, of which the most famous was that of the Brownings and the next perhaps that of the Richard Burtons. Isabel Arundell had fallen in love with Burton in 1850, but her mother told her that Burton was the only man she could never consent to her marrying, saying that she would rather see her in her coffin. Finally in 1861 Isabel ran off from home in a cab, married, and did not tell her mother for several weeks, until the mother heard gossip that Isabel had been seen walking into bachelor quarters![49]

cᴑ Although there was no system of dowries in England, everyone was as much interested in finances here as elsewhere, and a "good match" always meant money in the background.† "In good society," claimed Edward Bulwer-Lytton, "the heart is remarkably prudent, and seldom falls violently in love without a sufficient settlement."[50] What worried the French about the English way was that girls were brought up in affluence, and yet when a suitable young man came along, the father of the young woman was rarely willing to put money down. There might be "expectations," but inherited money might often come too late, and in any case, an English father was not constrained, as a French one was, to leave his money in equal shares. If he favored his eldest son, as was common practice, the girls might get a very short end of the stick.

Testamentary freedom in England allowed writers of wills any degree of eccentricity and became an effective means of control. For

---

*Richard Lovell Edgeworth had been married at Gretna Green.

†It was also a question of having the "right kind" of money. In *Middlemarch* the litmus test of each character is his eagerness or reluctance to touch certain kinds of money. It was hard to earn an honest living, though Fred Vincy does so. Lydgate loses his character and earns dishonest money. Ladislaw does not earn enough but makes do with the honest fraction of Dorothea's fortune. It was better to inherit money than to make it, though it should come from honest sources even then; thus Ladislaw repudiates a fortune that came from stolen goods.

example, Mrs. Menzies (whose autobiography is entitled *Memories Discreet and Indiscreet*) made an indiscreet confession that she had been named after a rich old aunt, in hopes, but that when the aunt heard the child referred to by a nickname, she announced that she would leave her money to a maid.[51] Another confidence from the same lady revealed that her grandfather had informed his son that if there were more than four children in his family, there would be no fortunes for any of them—so four children there were, and no more.*

Frances Power Cobbe explained in 1862 that if a professional man did not have at least a thousand pounds a year he would oppress his wife with household cares and not be able to develop his own career in the best way. Therefore, he should not marry, and no "true woman" would wish to impede him.[52]

In case money was totally lacking, marriage was impossible for a prudent middle-class couple, a precept drilled into them by such people as Miss Cobbe and Charles Darwin. Darwin says, in *The Descent of Man*:

> Man scans with scrupulous care the character and pedigree of his horses, cattle, and dogs, before he matches them; but when he comes to his own marriage he rarely, or never, takes any such care. He is impelled by nearly the same motives as are the lower animals when left to their own free choice, though he is in so far superior to them that he highly values mental charms and virtues. On the other hand, he is strongly attracted by mere wealth or rank. . . .
>
> The advancement of the welfare of mankind is a most intricate problem: all ought to refrain from marriage who cannot avoid abject poverty for their children; for poverty is not only a great evil, but tends to its own increase by leading to recklessness in marriage.[53]

It was felt by the French that English parents spent all their money on the famous *confort anglais*—that they would save for a new piano or a new carpet rather than for their daughter's happiness. Taine was probably showing a touch of malice when he told the story of a wealthy Englishman who was disturbed that his daughter was already twenty-four and unmarried, and "beginning to read weighty books."[54] The father was advised by a French friend to let word get around that she would be given £5,000 at marriage, and a wedding soon took place. (But Taine was fair enough to admire her practical sense in starting to study at a point when she had no hope of such a dowry.)

The French probably were not aware of how much English parents were willing to spend getting their daughters off to a good social start rather than saving for the married ménage. If the girls had to attract their own suitors, at least their parents showed them off to good advantage and spent money on this part of the process. Thus the Arundells husbanded

---

*This may be considered as a minor refutation of Le Play's thesis that while French inheritance laws decreed small families, the freer English system would create the large "stock" families that Le Play considered so much healthier.

their resources for several years by staying away from London in order to make a a big splash when Isabel and her sisters made their debuts. One hoped to get engaged in the first season because having to go through a second "lowered the starting price." It was not Mrs. Arundell's fault that she was to be disappointed by Isabel's unmercenary passion for Richard Burton.[55]

Occasionally people wondered whether this system was not framed to force girls "to make a trade of the warmest feelings of their nature" in order to meet the social expectations of their parents. The sisters Maria Grey and Emily Shirreff, writing in 1851, actually asked whether the foreign system of arranged marriages might not be preferable to leaving such a crucial job up to the girl.[56] Of course, it also became a favorite subject for satire. The Mayhew brothers, in *Whom to Marry*, imagined ten offers of marriage that came to a girl, starting with love but no money from her drawing master at school, and ending with money but no love in the last. Both ends of the spectrum were painted as equally dismal.

Nor, of course, was it unknown for parents to push for money from their child's in-laws. When he was twenty-three, William Harcourt decided to enter politics, but his father warned against it unless he could state that he had been accepted by a girl with at least £20,000,[57] while Lady Stanley of Alderley was determined not to let her daughters marry younger sons, "although they are apt to be much more interesting than their older brothers."[58] (We have noted part of her success: Kate Stanley married Lord Amberley, heir to Lord John Russell; another daughter married the eldest son of the Earl of Carlisle.)

A German adventurer, Prince Pückler-Muskau, who came to Britain heiress-hunting in the 1820s, found that he was wrong in his belief that the English ideal of love was sheer hypocrisy. He had figured out that the best answer to his difficulties back home, where his enormous landed properties were in financial straits, would be a rich marriage, even though he had to divorce his German wife in order to be free. But he could never win the hand of any girl, partly, to be sure, because nobody wanted a divorced man, divorce being much worse thought of in England than in Germany, but partly also because English girls held out for "love," a sentiment quite incomprehensible to the Prince.[59]

In contrasting the French and English experiences of finding a husband, it seems as if French girls were put on a track from which it was very difficult for them to deviate, while English girls seemed to be given their head, only to find themselves frequently checked in mid-course by parents or by unpromising circumstances. The possibility of a girl's choosing her own husband was very intimately tied up with the idea of marriage for love. If money or status were at issue, the parents might do a better job, but only the woman herself knew if she was in love. The change from Regency libertinism to Victorian sentiment came early. The idea that love was the only moral basis for marriage, plus the feeling that it was not right to marry without being able to support a large family, obviously put many young people into a bind, especially because women were dependent on men for both love and money.

But Englishwomen's school of character trained them in self-control and self-sufficiency. We shall watch them freeing themselves by insisting on jobs and alternative ways of life.

French girls followed the same path, but much later, because economic shifts in French society came slower and later than in England, forcing women into a new role. But by 1914 the educated women of France insisted that the most important advantage of education and the careers that it opened up was that they would no longer have to accept the husbands foisted on them, but could meet men on an equal basis and make free choice according to their personal wishes.

∽5.

"German Love"

Wer die Schönheit angeschaut mit Augen,
Ist dem Tode schon anheimgegeben. . . .

Ewig währt für ihn der Schmerz der Liebe,
Denn ein Tor nur kann auf Erden hoffen,
Zu genügen einem solchen Triebe. . . .
                          August Graf von Platen, 1825

(Who has gazed on beauty with his eyes is
reconciled to death. . . . For him the pain
of love will last forever, for only a fool
can hope to gratify on earth such force of
desire. . . .)

Otto von Corvin once compared the different effects of law on character in Germany and England. To his surprise he concluded that England, with the freest laws of any European country, had the most rigid social conventions. All the men on the streets of London looked depressingly uniform, and he found this uniformity extending to social behavior and to character itself. In Germany, on the other hand, under the tightest set of legal regulations of private life, eccentricity of character and behavior flourished. Germany was noted for its oddities, individuals who exhibited their inner feelings to a point uncommon elsewhere. He put his finger on a contradiction within the German character that has often been noticed: the harsh, authoritarian love of rules versus the sentimental, music-loving side with a capacity to go to extremes. It is very likely that the emotional extravagance of private life represented a form of release, or even of protest, against the constrictions of public law.

The contradiction is matched by great divisions within the people as a whole, and this fact makes it impossible to describe German marriages with as much confidence or consistency as French or English ones. Germany, for most of this period, was divided by religion, politics, legal traditions, and what was at the time unabashedly called "race"—by which was meant the fixed belief that the ancient Germanic tribes (Bavarians, Württembergians, Saxons, Prussians) had endowed their descendants with persistent and very diverse traits of character. Religiously, Germany was half Protestant and half Catholic (especially if one includes Austria); politically, there were thirty-odd separate, self-governing states, many of them quite tiny, where patriarchal forms of government were perpetuated.

As for the regional differences, Bavaria was known for its *Gemütlichkeit*. North Germans were more aloof, serious, and male-dominated. The Prussians, who came from the east, were even more patriarchal. It was observed that on family outings the Prussian father walked ahead of his wife rather than by her side. And the Rhineland was supposed to be the most cultured and the most influenced by French ideas. Here houses were more open, architecturally, than the dour *Schlösser* of East Prussia, and the people were given to fun and gaiety, but with less horseplay than the Müncheners.*

It was no wonder that France and England, each with a long history of a single government and, by and large, a unified religious tradition and a coherent legal code, should have a sense of limits on government regulation which was lacking in Germany.

These statements hold true especially for the period from 1815 to 1871. After the Napoleonic Wars, most German states were quick to reinstitute as reactionary a form of government as was possible, and to restore the traditional powers as rigidly. When the Empire was created in 1871, federating all the German states except Austria, there was, to be sure, a swift push towards modernity in economic and political forms, but even then it was thirty years before a new uniform Civil Code, comparable to the French Napoleonic Code of 1804, could enforce the same law for marriage and the family all across Germany.

Although the laws might vary from state to state and region to region, it was a distinguishing feature of German marital arrangements that the governments frequently claimed the right to make minute regulations about who could marry whom, how much money was necessary, and how the marriage was to be performed. This tradition derived from Luther, who declared that marriage was not one of the seven sacraments of the Church, but a civil contract.

At the very end of the eighteenth century, Theodor von Hippel had voiced the opinion that a state needed to be concerned with sound marriages because it had a duty to encourage population growth and to raise men out of poverty so that they would be integrated into full citizenship.[1] But most of the regulations were so limiting that the English clergyman Sabine Baring-Gould was led to ask, eighty years after Hippel, whether the government was not actually infected with "Malthusian ideas" and acting precisely to *slow down* population expansion.[2] The code of 1754, for example, forbade marriages between aristocrats and other classes, but this was rescinded in 1848 as a result of revolutionary upheaval, only to be replaced by laws limiting marriages for various other reasons, including eugenic ones, such as the prohibition in Eisenach forbidding the union of imbeciles.

*Another division separated those parts where the legal system followed ancient Roman law from the ones where the old Germanic tribal law still obtained.

Most of the rules concerned money. In the Saxony of the 1860s, no man could marry until he was twenty-four and could prove to the town council that he had a steady job or property sufficient to support a wife; and if he was a resident of Eisenach and wished to marry a country girl, he had to buy her the freedom of the city for thirty thalers. In Bavaria, likewise, it was necessary to prove self-support, land, or a profession that made it unlikely that a man would become a charge on the parish, and thus many poor couples were denied the right to marry. Some municipalities attempted to limit the sums that could be spent on presents, and some specified a minimum sum that *must* be spent on a wedding.

In Hesse-Darmstadt an 1852 law set the age of marriage at twenty-five, but in 1868 this was lowered to twenty-one, with parental consent. No runaway matches were permitted. Most such petty limitations were abolished when the creation of the Empire provided a greater uniformity, and a sharp upturn in the overall marriage rate followed.

In Prussia there was a longstanding fight to push civil marriage through the legislature, but it was continually rejected by the upper house, and only in 1875 was the imperial government able to decree that marriage in a registry office should be the only legal form. The government hoped that the churches would thenceforth confine themselves to blessing an already wedded couple. While in England the requirement of civil registration barely affected the way in which marriages were performed, in Germany the measure led to a wholesale desertion of the churches, so that in Berlin, after this decree, only 27 percent of marriages were solemnized in church.[3] Henry Mayhew blamed primarily the churches' laxity, but was also indignant that the government "*must* and *will* meddle with matters in which they have no moral nor social right to interfere."[4]

The new imperial law permitted men to marry at twenty and women at sixteen with parental consent, and at twenty-five and twenty-four respectively without it. Non-commissioned officers could be married only with special permission, granted to about 5 out of every 250 petitions, and common soldiers were simply forbidden to marry at all, which led, according to Mayhew, to a ghastly state of morals in garrison cities.[5] As was true in England, the need to accumulate money made the actual age of marriage rather late. Lily Braun, a later German feminist, says that the average age for a middle-class woman in her day was twenty-eight.[6] In the 1880s the average age for Prussian officials was thirty-three.

An important extra provision was that soldiers and government officials were under special regulation. It had always been hard even for commissioned Prussian officers to marry.[7] A lieutenant and his bride must show between them a certain fixed sum (which changed with conditions but might amount to between 6,000 and 15,000 thalers); but a captain's salary was considered sufficient in itself. Though it took a long time for a poor lieutenant to work up to captain's rank, it was comparatively easy to find a lawyer who would forge papers to show that a couple had funds.[8] (But if in fact they lacked the cash, the struggle to keep up appearances after they were married made the hardship as great as that of a laborer's family with much less income.)*

∞ A complicating or mitigating factor, depending on how one looks at it, was that the betrothal was taken as seriously as a marriage ceremony. Breach of promise became as serious as divorce. The custom was based on one of the differences between ancient Germanic and old Roman law; the former stressed the betrothal, the latter the marriage. Luther had regarded the two as practically equivalent and tossed off the remark that it would be best if betrothal, marriage, and consummation could all take place on the same night. While an Englishman who broke an engagement would be considered to have violated his spoken word, a German might be regarded as if he had committed adultery.†[9]

With marriage so difficult and engagements so sacred and often of years' duration, acceptance of pre-marital intercourse spread upward from the peasantry, where it had always been endemic, to higher classes of society than would have tolerated it in other countries.[10] In 1843 the English economist Robert Vaughan judged that Prussia was lower in female chastity than any other Protestant community of Europe.[11] Even in the middle classes, he continued, one out of every seventy-five child-bearing women would have an illegitimate child, a figure unheard of in England or Scotland. Eleven years later, Samuel Laing, who traveled on a fact-finding mission, repeated that if female chastity was the index-virtue for any society, the one that most clearly marked its general condition, Prussia might be regarded as the least civilized nation in Europe.[12] Just before the outbreak of the First World War, a serious German student of public affairs could claim that only in the highest classes was virginity at marriage still greatly valued.[13]

∞ In the midst of all the bureaucratic control, romantic love flourished in Germany in a more soul-drenching manner than elsewhere. If Corvin is right, it was almost the only way to protest against, or make up for, the state's petty infringements of personal freedom. Germans had no place to retreat save into themselves, and a transcendental and absorbing love could make up for many a bureaucratic entanglement.

The romantic style had its origin in literature and provides one of those cases where life imitates art. It went back to Goethe's early romance, *The Sorrows of Young Werther* (1774), and was still going strong

---

*In addition, "caution money" had to be deposited in government funds; it could not be spent, but was kept as a sort of insurance for the widow to live on in case her husband was killed in action.

†The German Civil Code of 1896 eliminated the penalty for a broken engagement and forbade alienation of affection suits. Earlier laws had made an engagement binding, but when they were formulated marriage was more a matter of property arrangements, while by 1896 marriage was felt to have changed into a question of inner feeling for which stiff enforcement was inappropriate.

ninety years later in Wagner's *Tristan and Isolde*. It was preached that love was so much the supreme experience that having once undergone it, one should then prefer death to any paling of the glow (this at a time when French plays were mostly prescribing how to behave "reasonably" in a case of adultery).[14] Young Germans accepted the idea with characteristic literalness. A wave of suicides who died with *Young Werther* in their pockets testified to this influence.

One case aroused widespread public admiration. The poet Heinrich von Kleist tried to get his fiancée to live in a cabin in the Swiss wilderness with him. His letters to her during the years 1800 and 1801 expressed both adoration and the strong wish to mold her character into a pattern sympathetic to himself, but she finally refused to make the desired move. In 1811 he made a suicide pact with another woman, Henriette Vogel. He took her to a country inn for supper and ordered coffee to be brought out to the woods afterward. When the waiters got there, they found two corpses.[15]

Almost as romantic as suicide for love was its renunciation for the sake of some higher principle, even if only obedience to a social code. A memoir entitled *German Love* (1858) explained this notion for English readers. Although published anonymously, it is supposed to embody the recollections of Max Müller, a German-born orientalist who had a great reputation as a professor of linguistics at Oxford. Translated into English by a star-struck girl named Susanna Winkworth, it tells of a student who returns for a vacation to his home at the court of a minor German prince, where his father is an official. As a child the writer used to play with the princess, and upon his return he receives a note from her, in English, inviting him to call. (She explains that she has to write in English in order to avoid the German difficulty with "you" and "thou.") Perhaps the princess's mortal illness makes them realize that they are in love, a discovery that takes them through a long philosophical discussion, at the end of which he kisses her hand and she sends him away. By chance—or destiny—they later find themselves at the same spa, but since the prince, her father, has forbidden meetings they enjoy another renunciation scene. This time he kisses her on the lips. "May God forgive us for this happiness," she murmurs,[16] and soon dies. However much Professor Müller dressed up his story, this was the way he chose to remember "German love."

Obviously this sort of thing was not exportable, as F. D. Maurice tried to explain to Miss Winkworth before she began her translation. "We cannot throw ourselves into that elective habit of mind which characterizes the German,* which was worked into the organization of their empire,† which comes out in their theology,‡ and which, as Mr.

*"Elective" in this context refers to the concept of the one-and-only, which Goethe delineated in his novel *Elective Affinities*.

†The Holy Roman Empire was a monarchy supposedly based on the spontaneous choice of the princes.

‡Luther's doctrine of election.

Scott once observed to me, is just as apparent in their novels, where the affection of the lady so generally precedes that of the man."[17] German love, according to Maurice, was so great an emotion that even women could express it first, and this, as we have seen, was quite contrary to English notions of propriety.

The code and the conventions are brought out quite clearly in an Austrian novel of 1920, *Das Haus Erath*, by Otto Stoessel. Among its meandering characters, spread over three generations, is a young woman who is kissed by an officer carelessly, without preliminaries, in the 1890s. At first she is outraged, but he manages to convince her that they are meant for each other, that they are "elective affinities." Then it turns out that her family cannot command the "caution money" requisite for an officer's wife, and so they have a renunciation scene. Although in actuality the fiancé could hardly care less about her, she is bound to his memory, and when another good man wants to marry her, she feels that she "has loved," and though she accepts the new suitor, she always believes that she has withheld something precious. When he is killed in the First World War, she blames herself for not having been able to give him everything that he deserved.

In *Helmut Harringa*, by Hermann Popert, a best-selling novel of 1910, the old romantic ideas show their continued vitality, but they are also infected with a new quality. The hero meets the girl on a walking tour on a northern Frisian island. Before they have even spoken a word, they realize that they are meant for each other, and they know it because of their "North German blood." She has been hiking in the company of a retired English army colonel who, as an Anglo-Saxon, is felt to be racially akin. When his old war wounds begin to bother him, the young couple walk out alone. Their two hands meet. They do not need to kiss: the author explains that North German souls have no need for coquetry.[18] Here "German love" is no longer just a destiny for individuals, but a call for racial chauvinism.

It could be expected that only a few chosen souls could live up to the highest demands of the romantic spirit. To those who were unsympathetic, including most French people, it seemed to add up to "a nature where conscience had little place."[19] They pointed out that a German girl could have many "loves" before marriage, and yet retain an ingénue quality that seemed hypocritical. French girls, they said, would lead a more regulated existence, but when they met experience, they would respond more realistically.

∽ German girls, like those of other northern countries, had considerable freedom to make friends with men. I have mentioned that theorists of the time assumed a definite racial difference between the Teutonic and the Latin peoples. English, German, and other northern couples were able to converse, and even to kiss and hug each other, without necessarily being driven on to ultimate embraces, though French critics found this most surprising. When Taine read Goethe's account of the way in which young people of his day could exchange tokens of affection, walk out together, and address each other familiarly, his comment was, "They must have had nerves of ice." And both Balzac, a Frenchman, and Karl Hillebrand, a German, explained that German marriages were less unhappy than French because the German girls had privileges which would seem shocking to a Latin. Hillebrand, writing in the seventies, had in mind such things as walks around the public gardens and the many interest groups for music or theatricals. A good example from upper-class life was the Kaffeter Club, conceived as a literary forum by Bettina von Arnim's daughter, Maxe, and some of her girl friends. It was not long before one member proposed admitting young men, and the coeducational staff got out a literary newspaper, which incidentally was the freest in pre-1848 Berlin. They also enjoyed dances and picnics, charades which often became extremely elaborate, wanderings in the Alps, singing in the moonlight, much free mingling of the sexes, many platonic friendships, and a few proposals. Maxe herself, who married rather late (in her thirties), once compared the various men with whom she had been in love. She had loved first Prince Adalbert with a romantic longing; realized the force of carnal desire when Prince Lichnowsky kissed her; felt friendly love for Georg Graeben, to whom she was engaged for a period; and described her feeling for another royal prince, Waldemar, as heavenly and holy. Finally, with her husband, Count Oriola, she thought she had found that true love which comes from deep respect and unconditional trust in a strong and honorable personality.

Though Maxe's opportunities were undoubtedly wider than most, nearly all the German women who wrote memoirs mentioned with keen pleasure the balls of their youth and their encounters with men, especially if they happened to live in university towns or at army posts.

It is true that the books of advice were very cautionary (as they always seem to be, in any culture), particularly warning girls never to betray the slightest interest in any young man of a different social class. Karoline Rudolphi (who died in 1811), carrying the ideas of Rousseau and Pestalozzi to Germany in a handbook of education that was a sort of *Emile* for girls, counseled that young men should never be allowed to meet girls except in the presence of their families, but then she ran into a common difficulty for writers in this vein. If the strictest rules of propriety were observed, it was extremely difficult to imagine how love could ever be declared at all, and so the advice givers usually dodged and created a fictional emergency. Frau Rudolphi makes her exemplary young couple, Bruno and Clara, undertake a journey to Geneva to visit an ill parent. They are accompanied and chaperoned by the family maid and a little sister. But the maid, who is Swiss, stops off for a few hours to see her family, leaving the young couple alone with the child. When little Seraphina says brightly, "Bruno and Clara kiss!" they do so. Apparently it would never have occurred to them by themselves, but under her dispensation they become engaged.

The story strains the imagination, and a much later handbook, *Backfischens Leiden und Freuden* by Clementine Helm, does not do much better. Recounting for its numerous teen-age readers the adventures of a country girl who is sent to Berlin to be "finished" by her more sophisticated aunt, it stresses the moral and social dangers that abound. At a party the *Backfisch** notices a lonely man, and out of impulsive (but unsophisticated) kindness she starts up a conversation. Since no girl has ever done such a thing before, his only conclusion is that she must be in love with him, and out of kindly humor he proposes. It is most improper, for he has the title of baron, while she is middle class, so she is instructed by her know-it-all aunt to refuse his offer. She is not quite cured, however, because on another occasion she begins talking to a man whom she had previously met at her father's house, but though this too is contrary to etiquette, this man turns out to belong to the right class and she is allowed to marry him. Meanwhile the author involves her slightly more noble friend, Eugenie, in a serious accident in order to bring the baron to the rescue, and eventually Eugenie lands him by providing prominent parts for him to perform in the theatricals she organizes for charity. Perhaps, after all, more girls than would admit as much followed Bismarck's advice to a seventeen-year-old: *Kriegt en Mann*"[20]—a vulgar way to say "catch your man."

While in Saxony William Howitt noticed that whereas the girls at the balls would waltz with any young man who asked them, they would not take the arm of the same young man on a Sunday stroll with their parents. To walk arm-in-arm signified engagement, and Howitt himself was regarded with confusion when he, an old married man, offered his arm to a young lady. In the same vein, Edward Wilberforce noticed in Munich that though one could dance with any girl who took one's fancy, conversing with her between dances meant serious interest, and so the awkward custom obtained of the man's dropping his partner the moment the music stopped, allowing the poor girl to find her way to a chair all by herself.

Once engaged, the fiancé could visit like one of the girl's own family, and the couple could walk out arm-in-arm as much as they pleased. Howitt said that they would stand together, sit together, talk together, and go out walking, but mostly in the presence of the entire family, and a surprising feature of the German landscape was the hugging and kissing that went on for all to see. In fact, according to Thomas Hood, the "she-cronies" of the bride went along on walks and scored kisses like runs at cricket. In certain provincial circles the place for a courting couple in winter was in front of the porcelain stove, even though this meant that all other members of the family had to disappear into cold chambers.

*Bachfisch means "flapper."

Yet when Amy Fay from Cambridge, Massachusetts, was studying music in Berlin in the early 1870s, she felt that the sexes were really prevented from getting to know one another in any frank way. She found that the girls had "rubbish" in their heads, and as for the men, she had no idea what they thought because she never got a chance to speak to any of them. It is possible that as a foreigner she had limited opportunity to judge; most reports indicate that once admitted to the social circle of a German family, a visitor was much more informally treated than in France or England.

One place where freedom definitely expanded was at the spas, and many matches were made under their more relaxed vacation rules. Thus, Hedwig Heyl (she to whom Bismarck gave the free advice quoted above) met her future husband on a walk at one of these bathing establishments. Since their first talk proved interesting, she allowed him to escort her to her lodging, a procedure which slightly shocked her mother, who was only pacified when the guest proved able to fix their piano and to accompany Hedwig as she sang. They were married in 1869.

Friedrich Paulsen also met his wife, Emilie, on vacation walks. On the second day they confessed their feelings, which words could not describe. An old suitor turned up and caused a few doubts, but when Paulsen fell ill, Emilie sent him something every day at the hospital and later visited him in his quarters as he convalesced. He served her tea, and doubt was dispelled.

All of these situations allow considerable room for spontaneity, and such opportunities continued to grow especially with the development of sports. Marie von Bunsen described her girlhood in the 1880s as a round of swimming, rowing, hiking, and skating. She adds that when cycling came in, in the nineties, it completed the revolution because mothers could no longer even pretend to keep up with their daughters. Although she described singing and games around the campfire and strolling by couples through the woods afterward, she tells us that up until the age of twenty-two she had never been kissed by any man except upon her gloved hand.

Amid all the outings and skiing expeditions to the mountains without chaperones, formal balls apparently lost much of their charm. It was at this period that Thomas Mann recalled middle-class ballrooms as "excited and puerile, erotic, stiff, formal, obscene, and stupid."[21]

∽ German parents did not keep their hands off like the British, though they did not arrange marriages like the French; and they often showed awareness of the importance of romance.*

*The pre-romantic point of view was expressed in a rather curious piece of advice from Theodor von Hippel. Though Hippel was a warm advocate of women's education and political rights, he felt that members of the sex, as he knew them in the late eighteenth century, had so little wish to be specially chosen that a man might very well pick his wife by

Thus Karoline Rudolphi made a plea to mothers everywhere not to begrudge their daughters the experience of first love, especially if they themselves had been kept from it by *their* mothers' seeking a "good match." Her own cast of characters all end up on the arms of their first loves, but all have suitably asked permission of their elders first, and it is set out with care that the good country pastor would sooner see his daughter dead than betrothed to men of higher status without the approval of the man's parents.

It might be expected that Dr. Riehl would have assigned his patriarchal father the duty of arranging marriages, but instead he adhered to the Lutheran view and observed that among the middle classes of his day, a lover who asked the father's permission to begin courting would be laughed at.*

Letters from mothers repeatedly provide touching examples of concern that their daughters should truly experience love. So Karoline von Humboldt (Wilhelm's wife) wrote of the satisfaction she felt when two of her girls had "found love" and were settled, and of her worry about the third, who was " too womanly" to succeed in life without a man. (In the end, however, this girl rejected two offers of marriage because she did not wish to leave her mother.)

The journal of Frau Karoline von Pichler, of Vienna, a successful dramatist as well as a diarist, provided a running commentary of her daughter's affairs of the heart. She was flattered at first when a distinguished scholar with a European reputation asked for her daughter's hand. The parents would have been glad to comply, but as the girl did not love him they were afraid to push her, lest since she had never loved, this sentiment might arise awkwardly in future. A second suitor, a military man, would never set a date for the wedding, and when his conduct became increasingly strange, the girl plucked up courage to free herself. Another officer cooled off when he discovered the size of the dowry. After so many painful disillusionments, the mother wondered if her daughter's heart would ever trust itself again, but at last along came a man who proved his spiritual depth by opening his conversation with a discussion of the dramatist Grillparzer, and in the spring this marriage was successfully brought off.

There is clearly a marked difference from the attitude of French mothers, who were peculiarly anxious that their girls have not the smallest chance to fall in love before marriage. Far from giving them a broader

---

lot. In the selection of men friends, on the other hand, he should consider individuality and emotional attractiveness. But marriage was meant to bring a person into accord with "nature,"more or less the same for everyone, and was, therefore, a good thing, though by no means an intellectual or cultural companionship.

*In this he was following Luther, who had insisted that a mother must permit a son to marry a wife of his own choosing. Luther wrote to Frau Schneidwin that if she would not assent to her son's marriage, he would perform it anyway, and further, that he would help the young couple out if they were left in financial need (Keyserling, *Book of Marriage*, 174).

perspective on life, such opportunities were felt to prevent a single-minded attention to their husbands. As for English mothers, they were more inclined to treat their daughters' love affairs as none of their business and, as I have shown, they did not feel particularly obligated to sacrifice their own welfare for their children's.

In Germany, parental self-denial was far from uncommon. Mayhew felt that many families in Saxony in the 1860s made ends meet by living like kitchen wenches and eating little better than English cattle in order to show their daughters off to good advantage at the balls. Later, I. A. R. Wylie, an Englishwoman living in Germany just before the First World War, knew several families who had denied themselves necessities in order that their girls might start life fittingly in their new homes. She knew one mother who spent her last penny on her daughter and had to go out to work as a companion.

Sometimes, however, there was parental interference, usually but not always related to money. (We can leave aside as exceptional the case of a mother who mutilated the governess who was attracting the love of her son. The young woman was fortunate enough to have her face fixed up by Dr. Lange, who tells the tale.) A typical example was related by Gustav Freytag, whose cousin was in love with the village schoolmaster; since her father was a property owner, she had to marry property and was not allowed the man of her choice. In *Buddenbrooks*, the husband whom Tony's money-loving parents select turns out to be insolvent; when she makes a second marriage of her own volition, however, it ends up no better than the first.

When Wilhelm von Kügelgen fell in love with his cousin, who was a Catholic, and within the prohibited degree of kinship, he long remembered a sympathetic talk with his father, who told him simply to flee before dawn the next morning. It was arranged for him to live with a country pastor who kept him so busy with social work and gardening that he eventually forgot his infatuation, and was correspondingly grateful.

Otto von Corvin, a live hero of romance, with a career of military engagements, lost causes, prison escapes, and early love affairs, was more fortunate. As a young officer he was quartered in Frankfurt in the home of an Italian merchant named Cardini. The daughter of the house, Helena, seventeen years old, "had not yet loved" and had therefore refused several offers of marriage, but her parents had agreed that she was to marry one of her father's clerks. Helena had not been consulted, but it was expected by both families that the betrothal would soon take place. They had reckoned however, without the German lieutenant, who, after less than a week in this house where "Italian freedom of manners" obtained, found that he and Helena were in love. Helena fled the scene when the expected suitor turned up for the betrothal, but had to confess her love for Otto. Eventually Cardini tried to get Corvin's commanding officer to make him stop seeing Helena, and for insurance sent her off to Paris, where Otto followed. Meanwhile he was trying in every way he could to persuade his colonel to permit him to marry this bourgeois girl, but he was told that since army pay would not support a wife, he would have to resign and start in a new profession. (He did so in 1835. The marriage seems to have been markedly successful. Helena helped him with the literary career he embarked on and stuck by him in the political difficulties of 1848.)

As in France, if parents absolutely refused permission for a marriage, it was theoretically possible to obtain release through the courts. The most famous couple to take advantage of this was Robert Schumann and Clara Wieck, but Clara was such a remarkable woman that I mean to defer her complete story to a later chapter.

Did German girls have unusual opportunities for taking the initiative in love affairs? Were they especially forward, as F. D. Maurice claimed?*

The use of the *poste restante* to carry on love affairs was so common that there was at one time a special staff to hand out missives entrusted to it, until finally the postal service had to deny the privilege to girls under sixteen.[22]

A few examples of female initiative may make the point clearer. Marie d'Agoult tells of her mother, the daughter of a Frankfurt banker, denied permission to marry a French prisoner of war until she visited his prison cell and remained long enough to endanger her reputation. Then her family had to give in.[23]

Emma Herwegh found in Georg Herwegh's poetry the answer to her soul's wishes and declared that she would give ten years of her life to meet him. The technique she chose was to hang around a museum where she heard he would appear. Even more forthright was the girl for whom Ferdinand Lassalle met his death in a duel in 1864. She had begged him to take her to Egypt with him, but although he was willing to do everything in his power to marry her legally, he refused to carry her off. A Jew, he offered to convert to any kind of Christianity that would please her family, but nothing suited them, and he died at the hands of her official fiancé.[24]

When the initial glow of romanticism had worn off, by the 1860s and 1870s, many young people of both sexes began to feel that middle-class life was full of horrors. The materialism, the regimentation, and what Lily Braun called the positive hatred of free and happy things fell like a pall on all too many homes.

*Of course, for Catholic Germany the carnival gave opportunity for a great loosening of convention, making Otto von Corvin feel that the Mainz girls at this time of year had a perfect legion of devils in them. Once six masked girls burst into his room just to watch him comb his hair, but he insisted to his readers that they must not draw the conclusion that these were in any sense bad girls—just carnival crazy.

Lily Braun's own life is an interesting example, complete with a final emancipation that necessitated changing her social class. She called her autobiography *Memoiren einer Sozialistin.** As the daughter of a Prussian army officer, she was brought up in the strictest circles of conventionality and ideals of "Prussian honor," and her first revelation of how tight these could bind came when one of the young men in her father's regiment took her out into the woods and kissed her. She was completely overwhelmed, but her father was furious. That was not the worst of it, because the young blade boasted of his achievement and announced to all the world that he was going to marry her. She felt trapped and was not helped by her mother's simple comment, "You don't kiss if you don't intend to marry."[25] The other officers all took the part of their fellow, and she got out of the situation only at some cost to her reputation, and with a sense of how easy it was for her sex to be wronged.

Her next emotional shock was love for a man so far above her in social rank that marriage was impossible. She does not name him, but he must have been one of the small sovereign princes of Germany or perhaps one of those who lost their sovereignty but not their social rank after the Napoleonic settlements. Even though she gave this man up, her father suffered a military demotion partly on account of her recklessness. A sudden light fell on her when a "good match" was found for her, and she received advice from an uncle: "No one of us has been able to follow his heart."[26] This new suitor made her flesh crawl, but it was only when he commanded her to shut up, as she was uttering her views on a workman's strike, that she found courage to dismiss him. He had spoken to her with the authority of one who had her parents' permission to command her, and she declared that no one had such rights.

Later she met a professor at the University of Berlin, luckily of exemplary family so that his rather radical ideas could be overlooked; but it was hard to overlook the fact that he was paralyzed from the waist down, leading Lily's father to warn her that her blood would scream for physical love of a kind that the stricken professor could not give. But at that stage of her life, Lily was more intellectually than physically hungry, and the professor gave her a philosophy to live by. He told her that if she ever wanted a normal marriage, he would release her, but she waited until he died. Then, fully emancipated, she married an official of the Social Democratic party, had a son, and enjoyed an active professional career.

∽ What was the role of money in German marriages? What became of romance when money spoke?

The most colorful (and probably colored) description of the marriage business was from the pen of August Bebel, whose *Woman and Socialism* took off from the Marxian adumbrations in the *Communist*

Memoirs of a Socialist.

Manifesto.[27] Bebel saw nothing but "the market," with its trade-offs between money and status, the frantic ads in personal columns of those who wanted wealth or security far more than love. There is much evidence that in certain circles this picture was true.

Marianne Weber assures us that while dowries were important in the Rhineland society where she had been born in 1870, the girls were not supposed to know this as they whirled around the dance floor. The Rhineland had a long imbibed French customs, and before 1848, at least, its bourgeois families felt obliged to finance their grown sons to give them a good start in life. The start would include securing a wife with a good portion. The Hanseatic merchants described in *Buddenbrooks* also paid great attention to arranging marriages between persons of approximately equal inheritance, and the woman's dowry went into, or came out of, the family firm, not their private fortunes. Jewish families seemed to carry their concern even further. In the circle of international bankers from which he sprang, according to Stefan Zweig, whenever a girl from the poorer branch of the family reached marriageable age, the rich ones collected a considerable sum just to keep her from marrying beneath them.

In the small provincial cities studied by the Mayhews and the Howitts, the dowry of every girl was known to the last penny, and one German man told Mayhew, "No use in their dancing unless we fancy we can hear the thalers jingle in their pockets as they go."[28] The Mayhews believed that in all their three years in Eisenach, they had never heard of a single love match, and they quoted one bald gentleman who candidly informed them that he considered himself worth 7,000 thalers, and would not walk with any girl with a groschen less.[29]

Then there were interesting patterns of marriage for money arising from a higher aim. William Howitt noticed that German patriots tended to marry women with money just so that they could be independent of the government in the years when patriotism seemed to require hostility to their small principalities for the grander ideal of German unification. Among men who did this he mentions Georg Herwegh, the poet who caused such infatuation in the breast of the wealthy banker's daughter, Emma. It seems to have become common before the First World War for students at Munich to advertise for women who would put them through school, even ones with a "regrettable incident" in their background, but the message usually added that subsequent marriage would be "a point of honor."

In addition to the dowry, it was customary for the German bride to furnish the new household with everything, from plate and linen to furniture, as well as clothes and jewels for herself. The husband was expected to contribute nothing.

In a society with such a set of expectations, there were naturally cases where marriages could not take place because of lack of funds. I. A. R. Wylie knew of a lieutenant who consulted the parents of a girl he loved to see if they could afford him as a son-in-law. They named a yearly allowance that was insufficient, so he went away without ever speaking to the girl at all, and she never married.[30] Miss Wylie also knew a girl whose parents were willing to make every possible sacrifice to give her the husband she wanted, but she refused to buy happiness at such a price, and she too never married. The conclusion was that while Germans could not marry without money, they usually would not marry just *for* money. *"Das Herz müss auch mitsprechen,"*[*][31] and a loveless marriage was the despised exception.[†]

*"The heart must also speak."

†If the first wish of families was financial security, social status and especially racial and religious congruence were nearly as important. Maxe von Arnim describes her horror when one of her cousins engaged herself to a Jew, and Maxe was astonished that her liberal mother, Bettina, actually approved of the union with "an enemy of Prussia." Maxe begged her cousin to think how awful it would be to have little Jewish babies.

∞6.

I Promessi Sposi

Man can never renounce love. But because he does not establish it upon equality, by maintaining the inferiority of the woman, he humiliates himself. He does not wish to raise her to his level? Then Love will compel its wished-for equality in a different manner. Once he is thus humiliated, the woman will dominate by a natural reaction, as it always was and ever will be.

Malvina Frank, 1872

Italy, like Germany, did not attain national unity until 1870. After the sudden and brief influx of French revolutionary ideas, which came to an end in 1815, there was a determined effort by the Church and the victorious powers, especially Austria, to put the clock back and restore the many small reactionary political sovereignties of the old regime. From 1815 to 1870 patriots fought desperately against these influences, at first by individual or conspiratorial resistance, later gathering strength through armies and diplomacy. Although all of Italy was nominally Catholic, the struggle of the Risorgimento was really between the liberals, who wanted national unification with secular government, and the unholy combination of Austrian domination and Papal temporal power.

The patriots won after half a century. From 1870 until 1914 the new Kingdom of Italy, ruled by the House of Savoy, endeavored to unify the nation economically, educationally, and culturally. Regional differences were vast between the highly cultivated, economically forward-looking north and the illiterate, backward south.

There were class differences too, and one group deserves special attention: the liberal-minded upper-class patriots, who were much influenced by English constitutionalism and were imitative of English family habits. Though mainly of the noble class, this elite society was open to artists and intellectuals. From this group emerged a high proportion of the outstanding women and the writers about women's affairs who are discussed in this chapter (and later). There was nothing quite like it in the other countries under consideration. There, bourgeois elements usually took the lead, and mingled with certain parts of the aristocracy. In Italy the sharp separation lasted longer. "I do not know the bourgeoisie at all,"[1] announced Costanza d'Azeglio, a member of a noble and public-spirited family, and when confronted by them in the 1848 upheaval, she did not like what she saw. To be sure, they entered political life increasingly during the next fifty years, but for a long time the girls of the liberal aristocracy led very different lives from those in the classes beneath them.

Every country thinks its own kind of love is special, and Italy was no exception. There is no exact word for "woman" in the language, only "*donna*," which has more the connotation of "lady," and this gives the whole sex a certain elevation.[2] When Mme de Staël visited Italy in 1805, she was so impressed with the status of its women that she put the heroine of her novel about a woman of genius, *Corinne*, in that country. Corinne tells her English lover that in Italy everyone thinks about love all the time, but love there is so quick and so public that if one were to write a novel about it, one would "begin and finish on the same page."[*3] Italians prided themselves, in fact, on the "hot blood" of both sexes,[4] and for that reason made certain efforts to control the emotion in their young girls, though they showed unusual tolerance for more mature passion.

∞ On the whole, love within marriage, whether originating before the promise to marry as in England, or awaited after the wedding vows as in France, was less expected in Italy than in any of the other countries. (This is not to say that it did not ever happen or was not valued at all.)

It was often said, in fact, that the major passion in any Italian man's life was for his mother, and this adoration was often carried beyond the point considered normal elsewhere. A cycle can be imagined of Italian daughters, somewhat left out of things while they were growing up, dreaming of a perfect romance, failing to find it in their mother-centered husbands, and going on to take comfort from their own sons. By romanticizing the image of mature and understanding women as seen in their own mothers, Italian men often developed a respect for women's understanding quite different from that of men of other countries who derived their inspiration from virginal innocence.

A son's feeling for his mother is described in a little book, *La mia mamma* (1876), in which the distinguished physiologist (and sexologist) Paolo Mantegazza eulogized his mother, Laura,† who, he noted, had been married too young to a husband picked out for her. Mantegazza had every reason to be proud of her, for she was famous all over Italy for her work in setting up infant schools. Still, few men from England or Germany would have described their love for their mothers as the devotion of a son, a brother, a friend, and a disciple. The heart of his mother, as

---

*"There was never such a book,—such a compound of genius and bad taste. . . ."—Hannah More on *Corinne* (Yonge, 169).

†When Gabriella Parca made a sort of Kinsey study of Italian males in the 1960s, she found that most of her respondents still separated sex and sentiment, as she expected in a society where the male's main attachment was to his mother (Parca, 3).

Mantegazza depicts it, was profound in its mysteries, high in its aspiration, delicate in its demands, touchy in jealousy, impetuous in sacrifice, dazzling, and many-splendored.

In the diary of Grazia Mancini—a record which covers the adolescent years (1856–1865) of one of the most attractive Italian girls of the period—a recurrent theme is the pain suffered by her father during his enforced exile in Turin because of the separation from his mother in Naples. Grazia was brought up to venerate the old lady, who is scarcely ever mentioned without the adjective *adorata*. She had devoted her life to the education of her only son, studying herself to keep up with his progress, and when she was apart from him she composed a little book of good counsel about marriage.* (Among her pieces of advice was that men should value and appreciate women in general.)

The emotional intensity of this relationship was increased by the fact that in many families the sons and even the daughters lived on with the parents after they were married and had children of their own. In 1886 Augustus Hare described an evening he spent in Florence with "the most perfect type of a grand old Italian household, consisting of between eighty and ninety persons."[5] Of the four sons, each with his wife had an apartment of his own under the maternal roof. Frances Power Cobbe experienced the same sort of arrangement when she visited a family of three brothers and two sisters who jointly owned a town house and a country villa.[6] An English family would have sold and divided the property, but the Italians chose to live together in one house or the other, and were apparently perfectly happy. Count Keyserling believed that a hundred Italians living together in the same house would actually be less in each other's way than a German and his neighbor across the street.[7] An Englishwoman living on the east coast of Italy knew seven brothers, all married, and all under one roof. They explained that in such a household, one brother, not always the eldest, was called the *vergaro* (literally "the flogger"), while one of the wives, not necessarily his own, was the *vergara*, and that these two took charge.[8] Lady Duff-Gordon concluded that there was, in general, far more long-term sympathy between blood-kin in Italy than between spouses.[9]

Massimo d'Azeglio once declared that love between the sexes was a purely literary concept, that a couple who had never read a book would never come to believe that only one person in the whole world was worthy to be loved.[10] Perhaps it *was* from the books they read, perhaps it was part of their conviction of their own hot-bloodedness, but Italians were taught to believe that nothing would make up to a woman for a disappointment in love, not children, not a career of good works, not even a new love affair. (This statement was made, significantly, at an 1889 conference on women's rights and women's achievements.) The author of these remarks

---

*Published by her granddaughter under the title *Il Manoscritto della Nonna* in 1879.

believed that unrequited passion was a common cause of tuberculosis, and could frequently cause death.[11] When a young girl succumbed unexpectedly, it was usually rumored that she had died for love and she was regarded as a martyr, like the young marchesa Vittoria Savorelli, whose corpse was laid out in white satin with jewels and borne through the streets of Rome. Another young woman, who was supposed to have caught cold at a secret rendezvous, was kissed in her coffin by droves of worshiping girls.

Taine believed that in Rome, at least, and perhaps in other cities, young girls commonly had half a dozen "passions" before marriage.[12] (Obviously this was quite contrary to what he was used to in his native France.) He felt that these were naive and dreamy affairs because he saw young lovers at soirées looking across the room at each other but hardly conversing. Italian girls often "took the air" by sitting at an open window, and a common way for a young man to show his interest was to walk down the street. If a corner of the curtain was raised a bit, he knew that his *innamorata* was aware of his efforts.*

In 1860 a doctor advised Grazia Mancini to fall in love. Most girls do, he told her; it is something like measles.[13] Grazia, however, was a girl with a different ideal, belonging to the favored class I have mentioned, more serious and better educated than most. Her father was a professor of law at Turin, the capital of Piedmont, where manners were unusually free. The Mancini household was a haven for political exiles from more repressive regimes in the turbulent Italy of 1859, many of them young men on the way to war, and Grazia seemed perfectly at liberty to walk with them or to correspond, noting in her journal that she had received a chess set from one, a book of English poems from another, without sentimentality. On a visit to her grandmother in Naples, she was interested to note how much less freedom girls had there than she was used to in the north.

౿ A Frenchman writing in the 1860s, commenting on the more typical condition of girls belonging to conservative families, thought that the Italian girls he saw at that time were very like French ones of the *ancien régime*, mostly educated in convents and let out only in time to marry. An old marchesa told an Englishwoman how her marriage had been announced to her. One Easter day her father, mother, two aunts, and a married sister came to spend the day at her convent school. She was so taken up with looking at their Easter finery that she hardly noticed a little dried-up old man talking with her father. The family left, having crammed her with sweetmeats. Two days later her mother called again. Though she had never had a chance to get to know her parents at all, she dropped a deep curtsy as her mother said, "I suppose you would like to

---

*An advertisement in the personal column, ca. 1905: "Beautiful Florentine, I thought I understood the signal of your fan. If it is so, be at the window, same hour." Another: "A thousand kisses, *bacini, baci, e bacioni*" (Bazin, 59, 60).

come out into the world a little." The girl, in awe, faltered, "*Sì, signora,*" but already her imagination was at work thinking of the fancier clothes that her married sister had worn. Her mother went on to explain how hard she had worked to find a husband whose age would "counterbalance" the girl's extreme youth, while the daughter was thinking of theaters, jewels, and carriages. So she clapped her hands and cried. "*Mamma mia.*" Eight days later she was led to the altar without a tear. The only men she had ever previously met were her father, the priest, and the convent gardener.[14]

Laura Mantegazza too, and many other women who became famous for their independence during the Risorgimento, remembered being married ignorantly and too young, accepting the husbands picked out for them. When her parents came to tell Giuditta Sidoli, at seventeen, that she was to marry Giovanni Sidoli, she was terrified and begged to be allowed to remain at school for a while longer, but they insisted, and her fiancé exerted so much charm that she changed her mind.[15] (This marriage turned out happily.)*

A last anecdote in this connection is of a father who created a sensation by announcing that he would not marry off his daughter without her consent. The daughter's view was, "Now, isn't that good of Papa? Perhaps it is because Mamma, *poveretta*, had never seen him till her wedding day, and at first she didn't like him at all."†[16]

In general the right and duty to marry off one's female relatives had belonged to the male head of a family, no matter what his age or degree of wisdom. The poet Giacomo Leopardi had several bad examples in his ancestry. His father was left at age eighteen to dispose of a sister's hand (in 1794) and picked a Roman noble who took her to live among nine in-laws, providing "ample exercise for her many virtues."[17] The elder Leopardi went on to contract a marriage of his own choosing, though against the wishes of his mother. When the match turned out badly he felt that he was being punished for ignoring her advice. Notwithstanding this run of bad luck, Leopardi himself took on at an early age the task of finding a husband for his rather unattractive sister.‡

Although mothers lacked the legal authority, their sentimental influence was often smothering, and sometimes their jealousy prevented marriages from taking place. Some women pushed their sons into the priesthood in order not to have to give them up to another woman. It is quite obvious from her letters that Costanza d'Azeglio really did not want her only son, Emmanuel, to marry. She proved it by breaking up all his

---

*After Sidoli's premature death, Giuditta had her great love affair with Mazzini.

†A friend of mine who attended the Collegio Reale delle Fanciulle in Milan from 1924 to 1926 assures me that most of her classmates followed the same pattern as their mothers and grandmothers: boarding school until age eighteen, perhaps a short social season, then marriage, and with it, the beginning of relative freedom.

‡When the Italian Civil Code was adopted in 1866, it copied the French, giving men of twenty-five and girls of twenty-one the right to marry without parental consent.

chances.[18] When he was stationed in Holland in the diplomatic service, he fell in love with a rich Dutch Protestant. Costanza declared that Catholic principles were worth more than money, and that even if the girl converted, large fortunes often made heiresses presumptuous. Subsequently she wrote of how grateful she was to have an obedient and respectful son. Later someone proposed a rich and pretty girl who seemed suitable until Costanza found out that she had spent some time during the revolutionary upheavals of 1848 in military camps. Though she had supported this patriotic war as holy, Costanza could not favor going quite so far in the direction of fraternity.

The most widely admired mother of the whole Risorgimento period was Adelaide Cairoli, four of whose five sons died in the struggles for Italian freedom and unity.[19] Her devotion to them all was intense and full of daily concern, and considering the military hazards this is surely understandable, but it is also significant that during her lifetime only one of these young men dared to become engaged, though all but the youngest were fully adult and the eldest practically middle-aged; the only one to marry, the survivor, did so only after his mother's death.[20] A biographer comments without disapproval that their family devotion was so close there was no room for another woman to move in.

It is noteworthy that devotion to the mother became generalized into patriotic love of the country, so that, for instance, Carlo Cattaneo talks of Italy "like a mother, of which a man ought never to speak as he does of another woman."[21]

∽ If a girl happened to come home from the convent before a suitable party was found for her, she could be subjected to the strictest discipline. She could be locked in her room at night, and her reading so censored that she might not be allowed *I Promessi Sposi*,* the most famous Italian novel of the century.† The mother's ideal, as Mariotti explained it, should be, that "the girl must feel that she is never left alone, not because she is mistrusted, but because her mother loves her too well to spare her company." To the mother he added, "keep sharp eyes out, and trust no person whatsoever where your daughter is concerned."[22] The prescription seems to have worked on Olimpia Savio's daughter, for one; her personality is said to have simply "disappeared" while her mother was living, though she and her brothers did not so much love as "adore" their mother.

In some country places a girl could never leave the house except with her father, since neither mother nor brother was considered escort enough. In the cities girls were often sent out with servants, but even

**The Betrothed Lovers.*

†The only novels Cristina Belgiojoso was allowed to read before her marriage were those of Maria Edgeworth (Gattey, 3).

there, brothers were considered unreliable. Fanny Kemble tells how one woman was recognized to be English by the fact that she let her two young nieces follow rather than precede her on the streets.[23]

When Mrs. Gretton, another Englishwoman, was young, she had visited her uncle in the diplomatic service in Italy. The girls she met used to ask if it would not look suspicious, back in England, that she had been gone so long. "Who will vouch for your having really been under the care of your uncle?"[24] She explained, or attempted to explain, that in England marriage was based on mutual trust. Later on, as a married woman herself, Mrs. Gretton had to bring up two adolescent daughters in Italy. She did not try to overhear their chatter with young male houseguests but let them talk freely, and this too was a new and surprising idea to her Italian friends. She could only reiterate that she had confidence that young Englishmen would not say, nor her daughters listen to, a single word incompatible with the strictest propriety.

Lady Duff-Gordon, another English resident, explained how shocked her servants were when an engaged couple were left alone in the living room with orders that no one was to disturb them. The servants' comment: "Englishmen must have cold blood."[25]

Though Italian suitors might try to take advantage of the girls they courted, they by no means wanted their brides to be free and easy. Another of Mrs. Gretton's stories is of a young man who was attracted to one of the new breed of village schoolmistresses called into service by the young Kingdom of Italy after 1870.[26] For six months he made conventional calls at her home, at the end of which time she agreed to take a walk with him without her chaperone. In line with the expectations of both of them, he attempted to kiss her, but when she actually returned his kiss, he was so shocked that he dissolved the engagement.

What could happen when a girl really broke the traces was observed by Lady Duff-Gordon, calling on a family whose daughter had run off. She found them all huddled in one bedroom, sitting for hours with drawn blinds. The father wailed that he had never let her out of his sight, had protected her like the *Bambin Gesu*, but now he swore that she should never lift the latch of his house again.*[27]

cᴏ In planning Italian marriages, money was often the first consideration. Even today in Sicily a marriage is preceded by secret dealings and close bargaining down to the value of the mattress the bride will bring along. In the nineteenth century such planning was more widespread, and it was dignified by political theory. Lecturing at the University of Paris, the Roman Count Pellegrino Rossi told his students that lightly con-

---

*Taine heard of a girl in Rome who was sentenced to prison for life for having had an intrigue. When he asked if there was no way to get her out, he was told that there was only if someone was willing to marry her. "What a price!" was the Frenchman's comment (Taine, *Italie*, 1:322).

tracted marriages injured the state by creating poverty, so it was in the govenment's best interest to insist on parental planning.[28]

Primogeniture, which had been going out of fashion since the days of French occupation under Napoleon, was legally limited, in some states at least, by a law requiring a man to divide half his property equally among his sons and daughters. In practice, this was often done with the entire amount. This meant that younger sons were less pressed to enter the Church and could afford to get married,[29] especially as many civil and military positions opened up when administration became professionalized. At the same time, girls could be more easily married off. According to the Countessa Pepoli, writing in 1838, parents no longer had any motive to place girls in convents,[30] although, as may become evident, she was generalizing from the vantage point of her own liberal class.

The way in which the condition of the family fortune could still affect the life of a young woman was vividly described by Margaret Galletti, who lived in a villa on the Adriatic coast. A young neighbor wanted a wife. Since his family was in great need of money, the head of it explained that the young man's bride could come and live in their *palazzo*, and if this led to overcrowding, the family could *then* marry off a sister; but no money could go out for a dowry until some had come in with the first bride. This family even composed a circular discreetly advertising for a woman with 100,000 francs, and then felt betrayed because the best candidate was snatched out from under their noses by an "enemy" who lived across the street.*[31]

Occasionally, to be sure, girls won the right to marry the man of their choice. Grazia Mancini knew one, in love with a soldier, who survived three brothers, each of whom had in turn forbidden her marriage, and who in middle age bestowed her hand upon her aging suitor.[32]

Adelaide Cairoli, whose role as a mother was just described, fell in love at seventeen (in 1824) with a professor of medicine, a widower much older than herself who already had two teen-age children. Adelaide had unusual fortitude and wrote to her fiancé directly that she would confide not in her mother, but in him, "my sweetest friend and future husband."[33] At a five-hour family council, in which everything was discussed from money to the likelihood of her falling for some handsome seducer in the future, her fiancé explained that it was her gifts of mind that interested him and would interest him always, and finally she received her mother's consent "to make two people happy."

Difficult cases could sometimes be taken to a king for decision. The grandfather of an Italian-born friend of mine was a penniless young socialist journalist, in love with a marchesa. In order to get permission for such a union, the suitor had to kneel before King Ferdinand of Naples

---

*With money so all-important, poor girls in need of dowries became a natural object of charity, and no country in the world had so many institutions set up to provide them. In Rome these took the form of public workshops where girls could find employment while being protected from seduction and prostitution and thus build up a sum of money to be given them on their departure (Daubié, 416; Story, 37).

while the young lady's uncle pleaded their case. The King, always something of a boor, declared, "So she wants to marry this fool scribbler of foolish ideas? Well, let them get on with it, and the devil take the hindmost." And with a Bourbon kick on the posterior of the young socialist for a blessing, the audience ended.[34]

One of the most important writers to argue that the whole system of training Italy's young women should be changed (thereby incidentally revealing a good deal about how things were) was Malvina Frank, a Venetian who composed a polemic to stir up engaged girls in 1869 and completed her thoughts on husbands and wives three years later.*

It was important, she advised, for young women to take time after their betrothal and before their wedding to study their future duties. Of her four proposals, two are familiar: that engaged girls should take up home economics (with field trips to butcher shop and laundry) and child study (with a side excursion on hereditary, that is, venereal, disease). But, in addition, Malvina offered two unique prescriptions. As soon as girls came home from the convent, parents should put them through a course of "intellectual gymnastics," including a series of exercises that forced them to make choices and in which they would not be allowed to fall back on other people's opinions, successively training independence in thought, judgment, and will. This, she hoped, would do away with the mush of concession which had been their too frequent response to life. Lastly, let them think hard about their rights as women, study the existing laws on the subject, and then address themselves to what justice would demand.

She had one other major concern—professions for women. A dowry, she thought, gave a woman importance in her family because, under Italian law, she could add it to her husband's store or withhold it, and in any case she could feel that she was a giver. But a profession, carefully trained for, would have this advantage and more, in that it would offer her an alternative to marriage with a man she did not love. She imagined three sorts of marriage: one from necessity (a girl pushed out to relieve the burden on her parents), one from vanity, and—the only kind she recommended—one for love.[35] Let us suppose, she said of the last sort, a young girl whose parents noticed her musical ability and trained her so that she could teach music, who then fell in love with a young man who had the courage to resist his parents' plans (financial and marital), and decided to fulfill his own wishes and become a teacher.[36] Together the two could make an emotionally and economically happy home.

After the country was united, and the cause they had fought for so long was won, new opportunities for women did begin to open up, slowly. For upwardly mobile girls from the lower classes, positions as teachers in

*The latter volume was presented first as a series of public lectures in Milan.

the towns and villages became available. For girls of higher station, not only better education but also sports gave them more chances to meet men and to become independent. The vogue for walking and cycling spread here, as all across Europe. Still, those concerned with women's rights, in the 1880s and later, continued to ask why some parents would hunt up any old husband for their daughters. For a long time to come the very idea of a girl's employment terrified many upper-class mothers and fathers.[37]

∽ In each of the four countries we have talked about, marriages were made with some sort of balance between inclination and material considerations. The French were the most realistic: they felt that affection would grow between a couple for whom all other matters of concern were well attended to. The English gave the young people the largest individual choice, hoping that marriage would be based on love alone, though they hesitated to marry without financial security. The Germans at their most romantic seemed to rely not on individual choice so much as on fate to bring two chosen souls together, but when they were not so bemused they jingled money as openly as the French. Italy was considered the place where love apart from marriage thrived most easily.

In all these broad generalizations I do not wish to deny that there existed in every country many loyal and devoted couples, many examples of quite cynical selling of brides for cash or status, and, of course, everything in between.

There were, however, certain clear differences between the dowry and the non-dowry countries. In the dowry countries (France and Italy), extramarital love was tolerated and often smiled upon. It became an effort of the feminist movement to make marriages for love both possible and popular, and in these countries the leading argument in favor of education and professions for women was that they could endow themselves, so to speak, and make their own marital choices.

In the non-dowry countries (England and Germany), extramarital love was not openly favored. And here, when the question of jobs and professions for women opened up, the theme of making a better choice of husband was hardly mentioned. Girls from these northern nations already had a say in their marital choice. If they wanted to support themselves, it was either because they could not find a husband, or because they needed something interesting to do.

ɔɔ 7.

"If Ignorance Is Bliss . . ."

Marriage is the only contract ever heard of, of which a necessary condition in the contracting parties was, that one should be entirely ignorant of the nature and terms of the contract. For owing to the voting of chastity as the greatest virtue of women, the fact that a woman knew what she undertook would be considered just grounds for preventing her undertaking it.

Helen Taylor

It sometimes seems as if the people of western Europe spent the nineteenth century in a gigantic conspiracy to keep children from knowing that there was such a phenomenon as sex, and even grown women from knowing much about it. A completely false front was erected to cover wide areas of life, and nearly everyone joined in the confidence game. Women themselves unconsciously furthered the illusion on which their precarious innocence rested. The conspiracy affected family life, changed the nature of art and literature, education, and even politics,* and, of course, women in particular, who were thus imprisoned in forced immaturity.

Today, obviously, the tables have turned. From being a hidden reality, sex has become so prominent that it dazzles away many values that the last century celebrated. Though their technique was insolently false, the middle-class Victorians and their counterparts on the continent really tried to combat prostitution and drunkenness, faithlessness and neglect of children, and the disorderliness that emerged from the total self-expression of the romantic movement.[1]

To make sure that young girls did not learn about the processes of reproduction, conversations were carefully monitored, reading was censored, newspapers were kept from view—everyone joined in what was felt to be a benign effort to keep childhood, and especially girlhood, pure. The process was made possible for the first time in history by affluence sufficient to provide privacy in middle-class dwellings, by the removal of many households from farm processes, and by the consciousness that they were all carrying civilization upward by concentrating on higher intellectual and emotional values. In the social classes where one or more

*Her Majesty's ministers felt that they could not lay certain sorts of bills before Queen Victoria; hence such bills could not be passed (Lytton Strachey, 194).

93

of these factors was missing, girls were unprotected and often sexually abused, but these are not the ones I am writing about.

As so often when questions about childhood come up, Rousseau proved an effective spokesman. Emile, the hero—or victim—of Jean Jacques's great educational romance of 1762, was brought up to live according to "nature," and part of the process was to live out a childhood untouched by any of the things, such as sex, that properly belonged to adulthood. Rousseau himself, it will be remembered, had early and extensive sexual experience; perhaps that is why he deprived Emile of it. For although Emile was to learn the principles of physics, gardening, and private property by direct observation and discovery, Rousseau believed that his curiosity would never direct itself toward where babies came from or why people marry. Since the discourse was meant as a textbook for parents, Rousseau, in an aside, advised any parent who was not positive that he could keep the forbidden knowledge from his offspring until late adolescence to make sure that the essential facts were delivered before the age of ten, and in such a way as not to pique curiosity. (To tell them that women *piss* out babies would, he thought, be a clever gambit.) But since Emile himself is being given an ideal education, no such early explanations are necessary, and he is represented as never giving the matter a thought until he is eighteen. At this age, Rousseau admitted, certain inner pressures would begin to build up, but in order to hold off sexual interest still longer, he advocated teaching Emile to hunt. This new skill would excite him, keep him physically active, and tire him to the point that he would sleep soundly. Then, at twenty, Emile is introduced to Sophie, who, needless to say, is equally unaware of the facts of life. They fall in love naively. Only after they have promised themselves to each other (for Sophie was given by her father the unusual privilege of deciding for herself) is Emile trusted to go on a tour of the big cities of the world, during which trip he is given a real, planned sex lecture, sufficiently gruesome about disease and prostitution and sufficiently idealistic about chastity to make him cry. The thought of Sophie's love keeps him pure, naturally, while he has a safe chance to inspect the evils of civilization. His tutor explains to him that his engagement would subsequently seem the happiest period of his life, being the "purest."*

Throughout the nineteenth century, lip service was paid to the ideal of keeping boys as chaste as girls, but here the actual difficulties proved insurmountable. Boys almost always found out about sex at school, if not earlier. In fact, during the perennial debate over whether girls should go to school or be educated at home, one of the hardest obstacles for those who were trying to advance women's education proved to be the parental fear that girls would learn the same sort of bad things at school as their brothers.

---

*Oddly enough, he does not award to Emile and Sophie a faithful married life but one troubled with infidelity on both sides, although this episode is rather a postscript, and not a part that parents seeking pedagogic insights would turn to.

Boys would be men, it seemed, and women would remain girls. Wives and mothers were not to talk about their experiences. The consequence was that they had no vocabulary, either technical or homely, in which to discuss these matters, so that even when it seemed really necessary to say something, they lacked the words to do it. This reminds one of Wittgenstein's theory that deliberately unclear language disintegrates the sense of reality and diminishes the moral life.*

So we have the memory of one little English girl who was cold in bed and looked for a place to warm her hands, and was completely mystified by the injunction "Don't touch yourself."[2] The same command could come in a more sinister fashion, as in Lily Braun's case, where her mother came to her bed at night, red in the face, saying in a threatening voice, "Keep yourself free from the secret sin,"[3] and even though the child had no idea what her mother meant, she felt guilty anyway.

Preparation of girls for sex in marriage was usually even more incoherent. Probably many mothers would have been relieved to leave their daughers totally ignorant right down to the day of their wedding, but occasionally there are stories of what some of them attempted to say, of conversations that nearly always broke down in the middle. French accounts of this experience are more interesting than English ones because, although they never explain very much, at least they record the bafflement of the girls, while the English tend to deny even this.

The French countess who wrote light novels under the name of Gyp, described in *Marriage No Mystery*† the marital history of a heroine named Paulette, who, although she is cynical and exploitative, is not very much more knowledgeable about the said mysteries than most of the girls who might read about her. When she considers engagement to a man selected by her parents, she inquires what the duties of marriage are, suggesting that this information might help her in making a decision. Paulette's father tells her that her mother will explain; her mother says that her future husband ought to do it—all of which leaves Paulette with a shrewd suspicion that she would rather have a tooth out. On the night before the wedding, her mother starts to explain that she must, of course, obey her husband in everything, and asks if she knows what "everything" means. Paulette only remarks that when you get married, all words seem to acquire a double meaning. Her mother fumbles on. After the civil and religious ceremonies, she murmurs, the last word will not be spoken until her husband has taken her into his arms . . . and . . . and . . . the mother hopes it won't be too painful. Paulette, more uncomfortable than her mother with the course of the conversation, tries to cut it short with the statement, "I know all that quite as well as you do." The mother gasps . . .

*Also of Robert Louis Stevenson's comment that the rift between the sexes was astonishingly widened by the teaching of one set of catchwords to the girls, another to the boys (Stevenson, 37).

†*Autour du mariage.*

how on earth? In a manner of speaking, Paulette mumbles, but after all we *are* living in an era of progress. The next day, talking with the bridesmaids who are helping her dress, she reveals her true ignorance. They ask if she knows what will happen, at which point a young married woman leaves the room abruptly. They comment: "Like everyone else she respects the professional secret." Paulette admits that she doesn't know any more than the rest of them, though they all agree that "something very strange must occur, for on a wedding night the relatives have such queer looks."[4]

It turns out that Paulette has at least read an enormously popular book, *Monsieur, madame et bébé*, by Gustave Droz. Her husband, thinking to use it to enlighten her, is astonished to find that she has read it already. "So your parents allowed you to read this book. How surprising!" "No," she responds, "it was strictly forbidden." In fact, the copy had been chained to the library table and the library had been locked, but Paulette got up in the middle of the night and stole downstairs to read it anyway. "Didn't *you* ever eat forbidden fruit?" she asks her husband. "Oh, that is different," he says.

We shall come to Droz's full account of a wedding night in due course, but here as a preliminary let us review the conversation which he devises between mother and daughter on the duties of marriage. The mother pulls the girl from the wedding reception and takes her up to the nuptial chamber, but when she sits down and begins to talk, the bride goes off in a daydream about what her husband will look like in his nightcap. She does not really want to listen, although she has the general feeling that she would give ten years of her life to have the next two hours over with. She is roused when her mother stands up and says, in effect, don't worry, darling, perhaps I have painted too dark a picture, but my experience makes it my sacred duty to tell you. . . . Your husband is a man of delicacy, but your title of wife will expose you to these things from now on. The surprise will be painful at first but will leave delicious memories. Yet, as her mother helps her out of her veil, the girl realizes that she has not understood one word of what it was her mother's sacred duty to tell.

Even when the need for knowledge became crucial to a woman's health, the effort could still fail. In the German novel *Helmut Harringa* (1910), written when frankness was becoming less unthinkable and a novel could expose various sexual dangers, there is a subplot concerning a society girl who becomes engaged to a man whom the hero knows to be syphilitic. The intended husband is a university corps comrade of the hero's brother, and, shocked beyond words, the two Harringas try to think how they can get the engagement broken. The girl's father, they agree, will not intervene because of the fiancé's social prominence, and perhaps his wealth; neither the girl nor her mother would have heard of venereal disease and could not be made to understand the problem; and if they confront the fraternity brother directly, he will only challenge his accuser to a duel and undoubtedly kill him. In the course of the discussion it becomes clear that nice girls are brought up to ignore their healthy instincts. This particular girl has a moment of revulsion at the engagement party, but her resistance is killed by a few shots of champagne. (The novel was written as part of a temperance campaign.) So she is married, has a miscarriage and then a defective child, and eventually goes mad.

A similar theme was handled in a more gingerly way by Sarah Grand in *The Heavenly Twins* (1893), in which two young Englishwomen marry syphilitic officers. One of them hears the news right after the wedding, and therefore refuses to live with her husband, but she suffers a nervous breakdown from sexual frustration. The other bride, totally innocent and ignorant, even though the first tries to warn her, is infected by her husband, has a sickly baby, and dies in agony.*

In 1849 August Debay, in *Philosophie du mariage*, asked rhetorically whether women who complained of ignorance at the time of their own marriage did anything to enlighten their daughters. "*Eh, mon Dieu, non,*" was his answer.[5] This was true on both sides of the Channel, but there does seem to have been a difference in tone between the two sorts of silence. English mothers seemed to be implying, "Let's keep the girls from knowing this unpleasant truth as long as possible, because if they knew the real facts they might be unwilling to marry," while the nuance in France shaded more often into: "We must keep the girls in ignorance because if they suspected such a delightful possibility they might want to try it out, and it is important for their husbands to be the ones to arouse them." This contrast is naturally oversimplified, but again and again one runs into remarks that tend in these divergent ways.

Mrs. Jane Ellen Panton, of England, remarks that at the very best, "a woman's life is a complete martyrdom,"[6] and that some women, at least, would have "kept out of it . . . had we been told in the least what it

---

*Mrs. Grand was one of those feminists who veered off into a distinctly anti-male direction satirized by the *Westminster Review* shortly after the publication of this novel:

Tell me, Mrs. Sarah Grand,
(What I ill can understand),
Why your men are all so horrid,
All with a "retreating forehead"?

Why your women all are decked
With every gift of intellect,
And yet — invariably wed
These knights of the retreating head?

She, as bright as a geranium;
He, a simian type of cranium —
Why, with decent chaps all round her
Choose an atavistic Bounder?

We are apes — well, let that pass;
Need she, therefore, be an ass?
Tell me, tell me, Sarah Grand,
For I do not understand!

[Quoted in *Boston Daily Advertiser*, October 10, 1884]

meant," leaving the strong ones to undergo what no man would be willing to bear. Mrs. Juliana Ewing, the writer of delightful children's stories and in most respects a more cheerful individual than Mrs. Panton, commented, "One could do anything for a home *but* marry."[7]

Even English men seemed to believe that sex would be unpleasant for women, as will become clearer. For example, William Cobbett felt that no proper man liked to think of a widow's remarriage, when "the person has a second time undergone that surrender, to which nothing but the most ardent affection could ever reconcile a chaste and delicate woman."[8]

And if a woman actually did seem to enjoy sex, that fact could be horrifying. When Madeleine Smith was tried for the murder of her lover, her love letters were made available to the judge, whose shocked comment was: "It is the letter of a girl rejoicing in what had passed, and alluding to it, in one passage in particular, in terms which I will not read, for perhaps they were never previously committed to paper as having passed between a man and a woman . . . and she talks of the act as *as much hers as his*" (emphasis added).[9]

In France, on the contrary, the undercurrent was an expectation of ultimate pleasure. Rousseau specifically stated that the knowledge of such things would only be a temptation to try them out prematurely, while the parting shot of the mother in *Monsieur, madame et bébé* was, "My darling, we have to pay for *happiness*" (emphasis added). This sentiment was a factor in the argument for the age difference (see Appendix) considered desirable between man and wife, so that the son-in-law could "know the world" and as an experienced lover could initiate his wife into marital pleasure. As Chantepie explained, on her wedding night a bride awaits from her husband, as he penetrates the bed curtains, her ultimate perfection and the revelation of her nature, the opening up of her body and mind. It should be an honor and privilege to initiate her into the harmony of the senses.[10]

Later in the century a few voices were raised in favor of treating girls more honestly. Even an occasional Englishman, such as the Reverend Edward Lyttelton, an Eton schoolmaster, in the 1880s, who had advocated a certain amount of sexual instruction for boys, said that he had heard (at second hand) that girls might have complex difficulties of their own. Without venturing to lay down a hard and fast rule, he raised the question of whether it might not be appropriate to explain to them that the father was allowed to give his seed to the woman with whom he had fallen in love.[11] He gave no indication of believing, however, that the girl was anything but passively interested.

As might be expected in the more erotic climate of France, certain writers were willing to go much farther than Lyttelton. As early as 1822 Stendhal (shocked at hearing a mother telling two little girls that "love" and "lover" were meaningless words) advocated that girls should be taught about love, marriage—and the lack of masculine integrity.[12]

Debay, in *Philosophie du mariage*, told his readers that when one has their confidence, married women will tell one that ignorance caused many tears which might have been prevented, and he concluded that it was not safe to trust to nature alone to tell women what was hidden so scrupulously from them.[13] In Janet's 1857 lectures on the family, there was a carefully reasoned outline of what he thought it proper to tell future wives.[14] Although innocence was the chief virtue of young girls, it need not be *ignorance*. Curiosity was natural in a girl, and her questions should be answered step by step. This was especially worth doing to keep her from trying to find answers by other, "restless," means. His ideal was neither the slightly dumb simplicity of the convent-bred, nor the restless affectation of girls brought up too much in the world, but rather a sweet tranquility that knew a little and did not wish to know more until life and the heart insensibly rendered up their secrets. He thought this could be achieved by a motherly conversation about human affection, its fragility, and the tests it must meet, and he quoted Mme de Rémusat, who had declared that she could not imagine why a girl who had been told what the obligations of marriage were offered her husband less chance of happiness than another.

Michelet also believed that a mother's most sacred duty was to tell her daughters exactly what they would consent to and submit to in marriage. "Nothing is easier than the revelation of sex to a child who is prepared [he means by birds and animals]. . . . What are we to think of the imprudence of those parents who leave this revelation to chance?"[15] Unfortunately, we have seen what could happen to the idea of "sacred duty." Revelation of sex has never been as easy as sex educators want to make it seem.

By the end of the century, the popular *Livre de la famille* was a conservative voice. It was intended as a sort of encyclopedia of etiquette and social advice for the average family. Its comments were limited to saying that girls must be prepared bit by bit for the part they were to play. Shouldn't they know why nature made them so beautiful? Meanwhile, chaperone them carefully and *never* let them waltz; the chaperone who let young girls (or young wives!) perform that dance had lost either her memory or her mind.[16]

Nevertheless, schools, sports, easier transportation, and a new freedom of manners made it increasingly difficult to guard girls in the old way, so that such advisers as the Vicomtesse Adhémar felt that some sex education was a positive necessity. She considered the illusion that girls had no spontaneous sensual feelings dangerous, insisting that they did, and that the best protection was intellectual training.[17] The French have always trusted reason as an antidote to passion.*

In 1907 Frédéric Passy wrote a little book, entitled *Entre mère et fille*, intended as a text for home economics classes in public schools. Here we find a child asking whether it is just a coincidence that mothers are always in bed when babies come. The mother is pleased with the child's intelligence and explains birth with pleasant references to snakes, chickens, and the Bible. The child is in ecstasy.[18]

In Germany too sex education became an issue. The saddest commentary and the most passionate plea for enlightenment was Frank Wedekind's famous tragedy *Frühlingserwachen*.† In one early scene, Wendla, the fourteen-year-old heroine, simply begs her mother to tell her how babies are made. She no longer believes in the stork, and promises not to flinch at anything her mother says. Giving in, as well as she knows how, the mother says that a wife must love her husband as a girl Wendla's age is incapable of doing. That's *all*, she insisted; now you know what trials lie before you. Then, of course, in a later scene Wendla turns up pregnant, having dissociated sex from anything she knows as love, and protesting that she has never loved anybody but her brother. She bitterly reproaches her mother for her lack of clarity. "How could I tell such things to a fourteen-year-old girl? It'd have been the end of the world."[19] So an abortion is arranged and the girl dies.

An instructive story comes from an old Virginia lady I knew, a perfect exemplar of Victorian womanhood. When she became engaged, in the mid-nineties, her married sister, Alice, came to her and said, "Now, Ella, there is one thing you ought to know before you get married. It is that men, *nice* men, have certain desires repeatedly, perhaps as often as once or twice a week!" Alice had become mixed up from reading about bees before she was married, and had gotten the notion that sex involved a single consummation which lasted for life. Ella was not in the least fazed at her sister's words. "Oh, I know all about that," was her cheerful response. "*I've read my Bible!*" To my natural inquiry whether Alice had not had just as much chance to read the Bible, Ella answered that she supposed so, but somehow "that part" had gone over her head. When Ella's wedding night came, she told me, "We had a very funny time. My husband had been told to expect I would know absolutely nothing, whereas I knew everything, from the Bible."‡ Throughout the married

---

*Even the Church got into the debate when the Archbishop of Avignon endorsed sex education for girls. He apparently recommended that this be imparted in convent schools, but the commentator Turgéon, who was writing a not-altogether-favorable book on women's emancipation, felt that the mother was the only one who could identify the *moment juste* (Turgéon I, 357).

†*Spring's Awakening*, published in 1891, first performed in 1906.

‡Mme Roland in the eighteenth century had also used scripture as a source of sex instruction. She reported that sex did not sound attractive in those old frank translations, but at least she learned enough to be able to laugh at the stories of children found in cabbage leaves.

lives of these two sisters, it is quite clear that they always responded differently. Ella enjoyed physical love, but she never felt that Alice had come to terms with the sexual aspect of an otherwise happy partnership.

These seem to be the two basic ways in which well brought up girls could react to the conspiracy of silence. Most parents were not going to say a word. Some girls would have the curiosity and healthy confidence in life to scrape together what information they could and count on nature to reveal the rest, while others were content not to know very much, often resisting what was available; and these were likely to be the ones who experienced sexual shock.

Emmeline Pethick-Lawrence, born in 1867, later an ardent suffragette, told how at her Quaker boarding school she was chastised for asking a question about birth, and hence corrupting the mind of a younger child: "the result was that for many years I tried to put the whole subject of sex completely out of my mind," which resulted later in "the tangle of emotion which I and many others of my generation have had with much difficulty to unwind."[20]

In addition to reading as a source of information, girls might hear talk from servants or from other girls, or they might get ideas from spontaneous uprisings of bodily sensations. Unfortunately, none of these sources transmittted much accurate information.

Of course, the trouble with all sex education, even the most complete and honest, is that facts alone have little importance compared with all the unconscious influences, such as good mothering and a certain amount of give-and-take with the peer group, which have been shown to be so necessary to healthy sexual performance in all primates.* It seems as if in the nineteenth century the French had more good mothering, which might develop interest and trust in their children, while the English may have had more of the aggressiveness that came from camaraderie with their age mates. Remembering this, let us consider some of the sources of sexual enlightenment that were open to middle-class girls.

Books of advice were constantly warning against allowing servants to become intimate with children, largely because of the fear of contamination by lower-class morality, but at the same time, supervision of servants in real life was so distant and so careless that a good deal of information (from stories or from physical contact) passed over to the children anyway. The literature is full of such episodes; Lily Braun, for instance, remembered that the first personal maid she ever had, at the age of thirteen or fourteen, was the daughter of a brothel keeper, who instructed her with such graphic detail that she was both horrified and nauseated.[21]

Girls' schools were also considered to be dangerous establishments. Dr. Albert Moll (in a 1913 book called *The Sexual Life of the Child*)

---

*As demonstrated in Harry Harlow's experiments, and others.

described the thoroughly obscene writings that often passed from hand to hand among schoolgirls of twelve to fourteen.[22] One earlier report noticed that these girls would blush and giggle if "stockings" were mentioned, thus revealing to an attentive viewer that their minds had already been corrupted by forbidden knowledge.[23]

The spontaneous awakening of sexual feelings in girls was not often described in the nineteenth century. Occasionally some of its women recalled reading the dramatic eighteenth-century recollections of Mme Roland, written from her French revolutionary prison. She told how her girlhood nights had been disturbed by sensations which roused her from sleep and which she felt to be so wicked that she did all she could (standing on cold stone floors) to stop them.[24] (One who had read this account in her girlhood, Lady Stanley, remarked that the reading had not tarnished her, and yet I have not found any similar confession from the nineteenth century.)[25]

On the other hand, the repression or sublimation was certainly not entirely successful, and most adults had no idea at all of what was going on in the heads of their children. At a Pomeranian houseparty, Maxe von Arnim remembered being thrown in with a group of young girls who started asking each other at what age they felt the first erotic stirrings. Their parents would have supposed that this might occur at seventeen or eighteen, but one named Ida said it had happened to her at twelve, Lenka remembered blushing when she met a friend of her brother at ten, Armgart was disturbed by a kiss at eight, while Maxe herself recalled the deep emotion she felt when she was very little and her cousin carried her on his back in the rain. Only Valeska complained that she could not fall in love and never had.[26]

There was the fear, in addition, that girls would arouse each other, in spite of Dr. Auguste Forel's dictum that women liked to kiss each other and normal girls liked to sleep together but that such caresses did not awaken the same kind of sexual appetite that they would in men.[27] I have found little trace of such activity from the pens of women, though men sometimes either knew that it happened or imagined that it did. (Frank Harris says that he made systematic inquiries among young country girls in the South of France, and that most of them said they learned about sex by older girls' rubbing them.[28] A fictional example from a woman's pen was Pulchérie, the sexually giving-and-receiving foil of the frigid heroine in George Sand's novel *Lélia*.)

Dr. Robert Carter's *On the Pathology and Treatment of Hysteria*, published in London in 1853, remarked that prurient desires could often be increased by Indian hemp, and then could be partly gratified by medical manipulation with the vaginal speculum. Hysterical girls, in his opinion, would hear about the pleasures of pelvic examinations, would enjoy the speculum more each time, and would crowd the doctors' offices with trumped-up excuses to have it again. That this could happen was, he thought, a disgrace to the medical profession, since it reduced the girls to the condition of prostitutes.[29] (And it seems to reduce the doctors to a condition of hysteria at least as disturbing as that of their patients.)

What could girls learn from reading? Scripture and the church marriage service were an inalienable heritage of an earlier era of frankness, but they were not aways the help they might have been. While the devout allowed themselves to skim over the sexy parts of Holy Writ, the rare freethinkers used them as a club with which to beat the superstitious. Thus in the 1830s Flora Tristan, on her English travels, was struck with the incongruity of forcing young girls to read the Bible when they were not allowed to use such words as "chemise" or to refer to the breast of a chicken.[30] More strikingly, Annie Besant, who had rejected the doctrines of the Church of England and therefore separated from her clergyman husband, was convicted in court of not allowing her little daughter, whose custody she had kept, to read scripture. Thoroughgoing radical in every sphere but sex, Annie obviously felt that she was standing up for a higher level of civilization by insisting that the Bible was "too coarse."[31]

For Roman Catholics, who were discouraged from reading the Bible, the questions of a priest at confession could introduce sexual matters that a girl had never thought about. Michelet, who was strongly anti-clerical, stated that a French girl of fifteen would have been forced by the confessional into a maturity in sexual matters equal to that of an English girl three years older.[32]

Flora Tristan was avoiding this when she decided not to subject her daughter to this "impure questioning."[33] And in Bavaria, Lena Christ first learned about sex when her confessor asked if she had touched an unclean part of her body or allowed other children to do so. Later, when Lena was a novice in a convent, the rules were that the sisters could never touch each other, and that they could never touch their own skin except for face and hands. They could not undress even in the bath.[34]

On the other hand, F. W. Newman, writing in 1869, believed that the high degree of chastity among Irish Catholic women could be attributed to the faithful warnings they received from their priests. He urged that this fact (statistically borne out by the low rate of illegitimacy in Ireland) be recognized to balance "our Protestant horror of the Confessional."[35]

Even the marriage service itself seemed questionable. George Holyoake—another freethinker—declared that the Prayer Book contained "things no bride could hear without a blush *if she understood them*."[36] (The italics are his.) Long before this, Miss Burney had lamented, "A public wedding! . . . Oh, what a gauntlet for any woman of delicacy to run!"[37] Coventry Patmore sentimentalized the same idea:

Pure as a bride's blush, when she says
"I will" unto she knows not what.[38]

Madame d'Agoult fretted that the indecent gaze, the jokes, the raillery a girl must endure on her wedding day would be unbelievable in a society supposedly civilized, while the ceremony itself was even more difficult to bear in Protestant countries because the text read in the vernacular, not Latin, unmistakably concerned "avoiding fornication."[39]

The liturgical passages offensive to critics were those thrusting "into prominence that which constitutes the 'sequel' " to all the "love,"[40] the part of the text which called marriage an "expedient," a little bit lower than virginity. Sometimes the text was actually altered, as it was for Princess Alice, married by the Archbishop of York in a service from which "the worst coarsenesses had been purified."[41] At Italian weddings no bridesmaids were allowed because it was not felt to be in good taste for unmarried girls to be present.

If the Bible was of such dubious help, what about other reading? "A mother ought to be answerable to her daughter's husband for the books her daughter had read, as well as for the company she had kept"[42] was Maria Edgeworth's dictum, and she informs us approvingly that her stepmother, Honora Edgeworth, read every book available to her large family and marked out unsuitable passages with black ink. Similarly, Erasmus Darwin, who wrote a treatise on girls' education, felt that while they should never even see a copy of *Tom Jones*, or *Gil Blas*, in the case of less improper novels, a governess could mark with disapproval such passages as young ladies would recognize as bad.[43] Surprisingly, this technique must frequently have worked, since even so lively a girl as Kate Stanley (later Lady Amberley) obeyed docilely when she was told that she might read the *first* parts of *The Mill on the Floss* but must break off at a certain point. She supposed her parents must know best.[44]

The proper tone for girls' reading had been made plain by Fénelon, back in 1687, in a famous treatise that set the stage for Frenchwomen's education for two centuries. Let them never read anything with a love interest, he instructed, even if it was delicately handled; in fact, the more glossed over, the more dangerous. Interestingly enough, when Philip Hamerton found a French girl with a novel, it was usually an English one, which calls to mind the shock felt by Mrs. Trollope that a Paris educator, Mme de Genlis, had insisted that her daughter, at eighteen, read *Pamela* and *Clarissa* as examples of "pure" literature,[45] though Mrs. Trollope felt that they were full of "revolting coarseness."[46] The English apparently were more afraid of physiological detail, and the French of emotional arousal.

Mrs. Gaskell would not allow her novel *Ruth*, whose heroine lapses from virtue, to be read in her household. It was not for young people, she explained, unless read with someone else.[47] At this time her elder daughters were aged sixteen and nineteen. When Otto von Corvin's racy autobiography was translated into English, he winced at each cut made by the English publisher, but his consolation was that his book, "in its trimmed state, is fit for every drawing-room table, and may be read even in the nursery without injury to the feelings of the most immaculate governess."[48] A comparison of the English and German versions is quite illuminating about the standards of the two countries.*

Thomas Hughes, author of *Tom Brown's School Days*, wrote to his fiancée that he planned to read Sterne's *A Sentimental Journey* with her on their honeymoon, since it was a book he was sorry to say no lady could read by herself.[49] Parenthetically, he was shocked that Nassau Senior's daughter was allowed to read *Vestiges of Creation*, the new geology, for he would have expected any girl to put it down in disgust.[50] A similar point is made in Massimo d'Azeglio's boast that his mother had kept her reading to such a level of purity that she was unfamiliar with the story of Mirra, Alfieri's great tragedy of incest.[51] A German bookseller reported to the poet Heinrich von Kleist that unmarried people simply did not dare to make purchases from him of any sort, for fear of what people would think.[52]

Naturally newspaper reading was censored. Eleanor Farjeon noticed at the time of Oscar Wilde's trial that the daily papers mysteriously disappeared from the family table, and at the same time that her parent's conversations were apt to be broken off whenever she came into the room.[53]

Nor was it any use, for a curious girl, to go to the books of advice specifically written for married women or those about to be married—at least until the early years of the twentieth century. In *The Wives of England*, the prolific Mrs. Ellis made suggestions on how to be a successful wife, what to do if your husband was habitually late to dinner, how to divide the responsibility of running a home—indeed, how to handle every exigency except those arising in bed. But a young girl could read the book through and never imagine that her relationship with her husband would involve anything more than an intensification of the affection she felt for her brother. The closest the book gets to sex is the earnest advice to girls not to indulge in fantasies, since the duties of marriage were such that no woman could render them without the most complete devotion.[54]

There were, of course, some under-the-counter tracts, such as those advocating birth control, with methods described, but they do not seem to have reached young girls. In England the strong feeling that they were immoral kept them even from middle-class wives. Here too attitudes became freer with time. In 1905 Dr. Forel, a Swiss, wrote a complete treatise on the physiological and psychological aspects of sexual adjustment, and because of his professorial prestige and his scientific

---

*As William Bell Scot described Englishwomen: "They shut their eyes to every form of the Social Evil and take it as an impertinence in any man, poet especially, who draws their attention to these matters; and I have never known the woman yet, however 'strong-minded', who will allow any poem to lie on her table or within sight that has any allusion to Cyprians or bastards. 'Serve them right' is the verdict of the sweetest and gentlest of creatures" (quoted in Thomson, 122).

approach, his book met with wide acceptance.* In the second edition, he quotes a letter in which a young girl had written to him of her gratitude for explanations of natural facts that had been so hard to understand. She said that her mind had been in chaos, that she had never felt like asking her mother, and that although her first reaction to his book was disgust with the human condition, this passed away. She still believed however, that girls would be little attracted by the sexual side of marriage.[55]

It was an important part of the great conspiracy that the girls themselves were so often prevented, by fear, disgust, or the simple wish to be nice, from going too far in the pursuit of knowledge. An occasional few scoured the Bible or rose at midnight to read forbidden literature, but many more were content to follow Charlotte Yonge's advice to abstain deliberately from reading anything improper.

Byron was credited by girls all across Europe with upsetting their emotions, one dramatic sufferer being Fanny Kemble, the actress, child of a distinguished and liberal theatrical family, who listened to her teacher read some Byron aloud in school. Its impression was so overwhelming that she begged to be allowed to take the book with her overnight, but when she got to her dormitory, the schoolmate in the next bed was so shocked that Fanny actually took the volume back the next day, unread.[56] Later, at eighteen, she renounced Byron entirely, a process she described as "a severe struggle" to break the thralldom of that powerful spell, because she had found after indulging in this passion that she was unable to work.[57] The withdrawal process took two years, but as she looked back from middle age she was ashamed of having liked Byron—and Shelley too, for that matter—at a time when Wordsworth and Scott were writing. Byron, she insisted, added poison to the fermentation of youthful brains in the climate of the twenties, although later on, in the fifties, young people were less effervescent and the effect was not so great. It was not only the accounts of profligacy in *Don Juan* that she disapproved of, but the defiant, questioning, bitter, proud sentiments of *Manfred* and *Childe Harold*.†

Another woman, Frau von Pichler, in Vienna, recollected how overpowering Byron had seemed in her youth. His poetry struck deep inside her and monopolized her fantasies, till she felt horror at the secret crimes, forbidden desires, and restless passions that he aroused in her.[58]

---

*Dr. Henry Arthur Allbutt, who published in 1886 *The Wife's Handbook* (Subtitle: *How a Woman Should Order Herself During Pregnancy, in the Lying-in Room, and After Delivery, with Hints on the Management of the Baby, and on Other Matters of Importance, Necessary to Be Known by Married Women*) and sold it for sixpence, was stricken from the register of English medical men, apparently largely because the work was so *cheap*. The result, however, was that in twenty editions it sold 180,000 copies.

†"Byronism was not, of course, in reality so much a pessimism about civilised things as an optimism about savage things" (Chesterton, *Robert Browning*, 19). Which is precisely why the Victorian ladies were afraid of it. The phenomenon was not limited to women, of course. The young Dr. Arnold refused to soil himself by reading *Don Juan* at the age of twenty-four.

A number of writers capitulated to the great conspiracy, either because they really believed that it represented a step forward for civilization or because they hoped for a large audience. Some of the very best, as might be expected, felt their restrictions keenly, beginning with Goethe, who wanted girls to be left in convents and not taken to the theater where their presence could only emasculate plays.[59] "They give us a little box of toys," complained Robert Louis Stevenson, "and say to us. 'You mustn't play with anything but these!' "[60] And he wondered what Dickens and Thackeray might have produced if only they had had the same freedom as Flaubert—but Flaubert's freedom, it will be remembered, led to criminal prosecution for *Madame Bovary*. Henry James's comment on Zola was "Half of life is a sealed book to young unmarried ladies, and how can any novel be worth anything that deals with only half of life?"[61]

Quoting this statement with disapproval, Eliza Chapman, an ardent feminist, explained that in her opinion the refining of literary standards was a measure of the progress of civilization, while Frances Power Cobbe congratulated her century on having produced two such authors as Tennyson and Browning, men of beautiful personal lives who had never written a word that would have to be blotted out by any recording angel.[62] As for Tennyson's ideas, he said once that if a woman had character or will, she was the more likely to be impure, or to invite impurity. Thus, he felt—as had Sir Walter Scott—that the nice ones had to be insipid.[63] When Charles Reade once imprudently suggested that it might actually be a fine idea for girls to sow a few wild oats, he was barred from several fashionable homes, though the homes had no difficulty in accepting young men who had actually sown them.[64]

A family magazine in Germany directed its writers not to introduce political or religious material, and never to mention divorce or suicide;[65] descriptions of passion must be suitable for younger family members, and all stories must end happily. The editor of the most popular woman's magazine in Germany, *Die Gartenlaube*, which flourished after 1870, complained that he had not only had to cut out a story about Josephine Bonaparte's amours, but that he could not even go into detail about a new elastic corset, invented by Dr. Eulenburg, which was supposed to have great health benefits.[66] In the same vein Marcelle Tinayre saddles a woman journalist in one of her novels with the problem of writing a story about a home for unwed mothers without including any detail that might arouse the faintest suspicion in young girls.[67]

Not very many girls were frank about how all this affected them, but there are occasional clues. Mary Vivian Hughes, who was devoted to her family, was grateful all her life that she had been kept from a knowledge of the evils of this world by the common conspiracy of her parents and four brothers,[68] whereas Ethel Smyth, who was to have a notable musical career, contrasted the surface of life in and around 1870 with the "orgiastic whirlpool below," and was amazed at how completely the women of her generation were taken in by the pleasant illusion.*[69]

French girls were even more carefully shielded than English ones, if that was possible, and Philip Hamerton assured his English readers that they simply would not believe stories which he knew to be true about girls in Picardy, but which he could not "with propriety" recount.[70]

Naturally, guilt was aroused very easily in these tenderly nurtured young women, and they felt it when they overstepped the line in fantasy, by accident, or on purpose. Not all could have been quite so meek as Eugénie de Guérin, who was brought up to walk out with her mother and never to look up unless the mother pressed her arm lightly. If she happened to look up secretly to see something else, she always felt a pang of remorse, and when her mother said, "*Ceci n'est pas convenable,*"†[71] she never questioned the judgment. Such feelings of guilt and fear must have driven many girls into the convent to escape from the dangers of daily life. Later on Eugénie's *Journal*, covering the years 1834 to 1842, became a manual of quietism from which a generation of girls tried to learn lessons of resignation.

Fifty years later styles had changed, and another young girl, Marie Bashkirtseff, determined to give to the world for the first time the absolutely honest record of everything a young woman experienced or thought. She began to do this at the age of twelve, and kept it up until she died of tuberculosis at twenty-four in 1884. In the hundreds of pages of this document, there is almost nothing directly about sex, though she does talk about her infatuations with various young men and the efforts of others to flirt with her. In 1880 she was reading Dumas and came to the conclusion that what he called "love" must mean "sex," which she considered a natural complement of love "at least . . . as far as people who are at all decent."[72] A bit later on she says of sex, "I know nothing of it," and yet she imagines that it would be repulsive with someone she found disagreeable. "What would disgust me most, would be to kiss the lips of a man to whom I was indifferent."[73] She was rather a cold fish, at best, and utterly wrapped up in herself, but she admitted that she dreamed of love, of a kind pure, tender, and beautiful; once, when much younger, she had asked herself if she had ever had "delicious moments" of feeling with a man, and concluded that perhaps she did once, in Italy, but that it might have been mostly imagination.[74]

It seems possible that Italian girls had more freedom to be passionate, perhaps partly because, as Stendhal suggests, their mothers were

---

*An example of how well the suppression worked: during the Second Empire an unmarried Frenchwoman wrote a book in which she remarked that many babies had no fathers, drawing the conclusion that they must have been engendered by their mothers alone. This drew the disgusted judgment of M. Maillard (who considered her a bad example of emancipated womanhood) that while she could not be expected to know how babies are made, she should at least be prevented from writing about them until she was no longer a virgin (Maillard; 239).

†"That's not suitable."

freer in discussing their own affairs in front of their adolescent daughters. There may have been more to it than that. With an upbringing far removed from such low talk, Grazia Mancini was led to think about her mother, who married, when poor, for love. "I think, I think! of what nights of love I was born, I was born to feel strongly."[75]

∽ The effect on women of all this concealment and the occasional taste of forbidden fruit was that growing into adulthood was an almost impossible task. The worst of it was that girls began to stagnate just at the time when the boys they would marry were testing both intellectual and sexual freedom, and the rift between the sexes was astonishingly widened by the teaching of one set of words to the girls and another to the boys. Englishwomen could not even mention trousers, though they were permitted to watch cricketers with their jersey drawers sweat-soaked and clinging, an anomaly which struck certain French observers as funny.[76]

It was not funny, however, for the parents of marriageable daughters. A mature personality might turn out to be a great disadvantage for a young woman, and if she was to grow one at all, her husband was its proper instigator. In the end, of course, such limitations could only make relations between men and women harder.

Let us return to the description of a French wedding as presented in the invaluable *Monsieur, madame et bébé*. This book was propaganda, conscious or unconscious, for the kind of ideal family life needed by the Third Republic for the recovery of national strength. The author, Gustave Droz, was so obviously pleased with his performance in the role of husband and father that he wanted to show other men how to share in the delights of domesticity. Though lightly fictionalized, and surely embellished, it is quite clearly the record of the author's own experiences.* Enormously popular, it was sometimes used for sex instruction, as we have seen, and it attempts to tell about the bridal events, first through the husband's eyes, and then through the wife's.

Included is a sermon by the officiating priest, which is interesting in that it urges the husband to be patient, even though his ultimate aim should be to reach a delicious intimacy. The woman is told to forget most of her education, which will soon come to seem like one of those cheap pieces of furniture that crack up in six months. It takes sixteen years to create a wife, the priest goes on: ten years of preparation by the mother and six more of "study" with the husband, and since those sixteen years are mostly lost to happiness, people should try to make up for them and not treat their emotions as Chinese people treat their feet. Be seductive, he urges; use perfume, tease your husband a bit, so that when he finally asks you, "You love me a little, then?" you *say* no, but you offer a kiss that means yes—by such tricks is love maintained throughout marriage.

_____
*This is confirmed by the fact that he wrote another book, not intended to be fiction, in which many of the same situations are described with identical details.

The account of the wedding itself begins in the Mayor's office, depressing with its pictures of Napoleon III, the signs on the walls, the forms to be filled in. According to the law, the Mayor has to read appropriate sections of the Code to the couple; the bride's reaction is a wish to point out to him that what he is reading lacks common sense, as, for instance, in the section that informs her that gendarmes will come if she disobeys her husband. She keeps her mouth shut, however. The job is done and the party goes to a pastry shop and then home. The bride sleeps in her own bed that night, but notices that the servants now address her as "Madame." The next day is the religious ceremony, which the girl finds more elevated in tone, though her husband merely remarks that the civil service did not cost anything.

Now come the groom's recollections of what happens next. Because the affair is held in the country, the reception breaks up early, and as his friends depart they press his hand as if offering condolences, or else with a meaningful cordiality that borders on the indiscreet. He has been able to talk to everyone at the party except his dear little wife, but when he looks across the room at her, she blushes, and he wonders if she is feeling more ardor or more fear. To encourage himself he remembers the kiss she gave him at the end of the church service, but just then his commanding officer comes up and burts into laughter as he remarks that now has come the moment to prove that "he belongs to the regiment." The bride has disappeared, and presently her mother emerges from the chamber, grabs her son-in-law's hand, and breaks into tears. A little nuptial apartment has been prepared in the family chateau, and as the groom hesitates outside the door, he rehearses his role. "Be passionate, be restrained," he tells himself; "be calm, but show warmth. Be sweet and tender, but show a nature of iron." Pondering these alternatives, he begins to disrobe in the dressing room, then gives three small taps on the bedroom door. No answer. He realizes that if he speaks at that moment he will not be master of his voice. Then he hears a dry little cough, which seems to him like the heavens opening. He enters, and approaches the bed, from which emerges a vague sense of warmth and perfume. Two candles are burning, Louise's head is lost in the pillow, she pretends to be asleep, and he is frightfully embarrassed. Should he take off his underwear and climb in? This might savor of brutality. He has to figure out how to eat the peach without breaking the skin; he must make her cry without hating him; and he most certainly must not let her make him feel ridiculous. She trembles when he touches her shoulder, so he asks if he could kiss just her fingertips, whereupon she smiles and he dares to take off all his underclothes and insert a leg into the bed; but at this she screams in fright, curls up against the wall, and sobs. He is getting very cold, but he leans over and whispers, "*Je t'aime, ma petite femme*," and in a very small voice she responds, "*Mon ami je vous aime*, but let me sleep." A slap in the face could not have humiliated him more, but as he backs away he begins to realize that he is judging her, poor little soul, by rough masculine standards. Sleep, angel, he says as he sits down in the armchair, wishing he had brought his warm robe. He begins to think about the ridicule tomorrow if he spends the night in the armchair, and he wraps her silk dress around himself as he tries to light the fire. He sneezes. Then the girl in the bed laughs, and in a tiny, flutelike voice asks, "Did you hurt yourself?" And after a silence, "Georges . . . ?" He says, "I'm pretty funny, aren't I?" and she says, "You aren't funny but you'll catch cold. It would be cruel of me to let you become ill." So she moves over to make room in the bed. She asks if he would like to say goodnight, and she lifts her cheek to be kissed; but the candle goes out at that point, and he misses the cheek but finds her lips. She apologizes for being frightened, and he says, "I want to embrace you." "Go ahead and embrace me, Monsieur *mon mari*," whereupon he climbs into bed and immediately forgets his good resolutions. Their lips meet, a long kiss, and he feels her heart beating against his chest. "You love me a little, then, darling?" he asks. An almost inaudible "*oui.*" "I don't scare you, then?" "*Non.*" "You want to be my wife then, you want me to teach you how to love me as I love you?" "I love you," she says, so sweetly and simply that she seems to be dreaming . . . . How often they laughed about those moments afterward.

When it comes to the woman's impression of the same event, the bride remembers that at about midnight, at the reception, her mother made a sign and led her through the hallway where the servants, backed against the wall, gazed on her with curiosity. Her own feelings are neither for laughing nor for crying, but she feels confused, triumphant, and humiliated, all at the same time. A collection of female relatives gathers in the bedchamber, and as she wishes to be left alone, she retires to the dressing room, where she can hear the four old women cackling. When she does get into bed, she perceives at once that it is not her familiar hard, narrow bed. The women finally go away, mother and all, and she is left waiting. She spends the time practicing kisses on her own shoulder, and prays, "Dear God, protect me," but cannot resist adding, "but don't protect me too much,"* while feeling a soldier's sharp pleasure in not retreating before danger. Then she hears the knock at the door, but cannot find voice to answer. He knocks again and she coughs, but dares not look up, although she sees his shadow and is pleased that he does not wear the nightcap she had wondered about during her mother's earlier lecture. She wants to be taught, but not too fast, and she is ashamed of her ignorance before a man whom she loves—but loves still "with precaution." It helps when he calls her "darling," still more when he presses her hand, but when he comes closer she prays to God to protect her " all the way" this time. Not until hours later does she "understand the intentions of Providence." When her husband says he is thirsty for a kiss from "*toi,*"

---

*"Don't protect me too much" became a proverb and was quoted by Kipling in his souvenirs of France as one everyone would recognize.

the use of the intimate form seems sinister, somehow, but this too moves things along. At this point she feels herself slipping into a big river, and as she lets go of the last hold on the bank, she says to herself, *"Oui, je t'aime*, Yes I want to follow you, *je suis a toi, toi, toi."* As she repeats *"toi"* to herself, she feels him approach, and he says, "Do you want to embrace your husband?" Her *"si"* is so low she hopes he will not hear, but he does hear, and she feels herself die before the force of the embrace which follows.

The author alleges that he discovered this account in an old blue notebook in the drawer of a second-hand bureau. The manuscript was said to conclude with the sentiment that the best way to learn to swim was to be thrown into the water. Marriage was like a storm, something unheard of and horribly violent, when what was forbidden before became permitted overnight, and (once again we hear this) words changed their meaning.

All this sentiment, though mild enough, seems to have been just what French readers wanted. The enormous success of the book—the copy I read was the 131st reprint, dated 1886—shows that the French were not afraid to think about marital sex and its pleasures; yet the book horrified most foreigners, including Karl Hillebrand, a distinguished German commentator on French life. It offered, in his verdict, a curious view of the delicacy of the French bourgeoisie. "A German would rather have courtesans introduced than see the veil thus drawn aside from the mysteries of marriage."[77]

It is impossible to review the implications of *Monsieur, madame et bébé* without realizing that whether or not being thrown into the river was the best way to learn how to swim, at least Frenchmen *hoped* that it was, and the idea certainly offered an excellent rationalization for not carrying out sex education. What advice there was on the subject was given more to men than to women, and it usually urged restraint and tenderness. How hard it must be, mused Michelet, for a young wife to find an imperious master. Although your bride loves you and feels no real fear, her poor little heart is beating wildly. Let her sleep if she is not ready and she will wake beside you in confidence, and on all accounts do not let sex become a matter for your own impatient vanity. Next morning she will be ashamed for having suffered and try to smile. *You* are already happy, she is not, yet, though she will become so; and a good way to cheer her up on the first morning is to pick that moment to show her her new house, her chests and drawers, her fireplace and garden.[78]

In a similar spirit, Dumas, who was a confidant of many women, urged husbands not to expect to find immediate sexual response in their brides—in fact, if they did, it would be cause for alarm![79] Women who talked to him remembered with sadness their bridal moment; and once he was told by a high prelate of the Church that of a hundred girls he prepared for marriage, eighty would come back in a month regretting the step.[80] Alfred de Musset was also sympathetic to women, but angrier at society: we hide our young girls, was his view, and they get pale and weak, then suddenly we "whisper an obscene word at them and throw them into bed with an unknown who violates them"[81]—and we call this marriage.

When women talked about it they were still more angry. It was one subject on which the great French women writers were unanimous. George Sand stated that the experiences of the first night could lead to a lifetime of illness and painful childbirth later on;* Flora Tristan compared a bride in her white dress to an ancient victim of sacrifice;[82] and Hortense Allart, a feminist of the 1830s, declared that most girls decided that the universe was drunk.[83] Fifty years later Colette described the experience in this way: "The rough and graceless husband proceeds to the assualt. Overgrown appetites shine in his face, he stinks of cigars and chartreuse, and to achieve his due he has the gallantry of a sailor on leave. Older men have assured him that love is only good if it is brutal."[84] She added, however, that a girl's pride will keep her brave and self-contained even in the moments when she will utter "the inevitable and sincere great cry of awakening and fear."[85] A woman confided to Armand Lanoux that when she saw her naked husband advancing on her, having no idea of the male sex, she fled, cried, climbed up on the furniture, that he pulled her down, threw her on the bed, violated her several times—and that the next day she tried to kill herself.[86]

Withholding information about sexual matters surely contributed not only to suicide but also to husband-murder. The famous poisoner Marie Lafarge, married to a husband she barely knew, was taken by her aunts into a small salon after the wedding and the wedding breakfast. They wanted to impart the secrets of married life, but she was so horrified that she ran out screaming. Later that evening she refused her husband access to her chamber. No one is certain whether the marriage was ever consummated, but it ended after a few months when Monsieur Lafarge died of arsenic-flavored cakes sent with a tender message from Marie.[87]

A twentieth-century historian of love attributed the disillusionment of these women in part to the fact that they had been raised in mysticism and prepared by the Church for a marriage with Jesus Christ, and then they were expected to accept a *petit bourgeois* in their bed until the end of their days[88]—this for a girl who, before marriage, had never been permitted so much as to walk across the street with a friend of her brother. No wonder that for some the cloister seemed a welcome escape.

There was less frankness in England on the part of both men and women, but we do have the record of the outspoken Annie Besant, who had married at twenty in the customary state of ignorance. "Many an

---

*Sand to her brother: "Take care that your son-in-law does not brutalize your daughter the first night, for much illness and painful childbirths come from this cause. Men are not sufficiently aware that this amusement is a martyrdom for us. Tell him to limit his pleasures " (Decaux, 8:248).

unhappy marriage," she wrote, "dates from its very beginning, from the terrible shock to a young girl's sensitive modesty and pride, her helpless bewilderment and fear."[89] Or take the confessions of a more obscure lady, Mrs. Menzies:

> I was shot out into the realities of life after the manner of those days, in a condition of absolute black ignorance of practically every fact of life that would be almost unbelievable to girls of that age today—happily for them. The fact that I had not the faintest idea of what I was doing was a matter of legitimate self-congratulation to my parents as a proof of the success of the upbringing they had bestowed on their child. It seems a little incongruous that a man who, say, for instance, murdered an aged aunt, should be regarded as such a naughty fellow, and probably hanged, while the people who launched their daughters into life before they knew what they were about should be adjudged quite praiseworthy. The gentleman who murdered his aunt had only shortened an old life while the others had done their best to ruin a young one.[90]

Similar stories come from Germany, such as Lily Braun's about her mother. Like all well brought up girls, says Lily, her mother had no suspicion of what was involved in marriage, and her husband, also a virgin, had such enormous pent-up desire that she thought he must be mad.[91] She often wanted to run home, but was too ashamed, and of course, it was not long before she came to understand that her husband was not unusual. One of Stefan Zweig's aunts actually did run to her parent's house at one o'clock on her wedding night, screaming that her husband was a madman who was trying to undress her and that she had only escaped with the greatest difficulty.[92]

∽ The two sexes were balanced off against each other, and each was divided within itself.

For men, sexual affairs tended to be split from the rest of their lives, their public concerns, their intellectual interests. Whether they had their sexual experience at home or abroad, it was commonly consciously separated from their other life. If cold baths and self-discipline were used to discourage sexual expression, men employed them with full awareness of the power of the drive.

Meanwhile, women were told that the most precious part of themselves was their femininity, which could be destroyed by contact with such male public concerns as voting or scholarship. This femininity was never clearly explained, and its implications were often suppressed into the unconscious portion of their minds. The resulting inability of either sex to understand a great part of the other's lives led to considerable fumbling on the part of all those, including the members of the burgeoning women's movement, who wanted a more rational relationship.*

*Malvina Frank's interesting suggestion that people should pass an examination to prove their capacity for marriage was, of course, not taken seriously then, nor has it been since (Frank, *Mogli*, 410).

It should be clear, however, that the sexual patterns of the middle classes here described were able to exist only because there was a huge submerged world of prostitution and vice, just as the economic pattern of their affluence depended on the existence of a huge, hard-working, ill-paid working class.

Throughout history there have been periods when women were valued for their erotic potentialities, alternating with times when they were regarded chiefly as mothers. The eighteenth century might be considered broadly as one of the former, while it is clear that during the nineteenth, erotic values were subdued and motherly ones received unusually high acclaim. Probably Britain was the most cursed with the "absolute non-recognition of sexual needs,"[93] and enlightenment came slowly there. Edward Carpenter (1844–1929), sexologist and sociologist though he was, pitied his unmarried sisters because they had to wear themselves out while their primal needs were unspoken. On the continent too, it was stated by Grete Meisel-Hess that sex caused more misery than poverty, with the added burden that it could not be talked about. Meisel-Hess was grateful that in her day Sigmund Freud began to describe the consequences of enforced sexual abstinence as it worked itself out in anxiety neuroses.[94]

The prohibition against discussing sexual affairs ate into women's physical and mental health; Bebel noticed that doctors dared not even protest against the corsets of the day.[95] In a way, the clothing they had to wear was part of their unspoken sex education. Women themselves often reported that they felt a sense of security from being all laced up and tightly covered, and any looseness of fit or relaxation of squeezing in their garments came to seem a dangerous divestment, not only of modesty, but of personal integrity. This accounts for the hostility to dress reform (often proposed by people with dangerous socialist leanings) and the complete horror of trousers ("dual garmenture") for women, even underdrawers, although doctors tried to persuade them that these would prevent much unhealthy chilling.

Luise Otto, in a most interesting discussion of how the modes of dress she had observed in her long lifetime changed to accord with changes in public affairs, complained that an argument used against women's emancipation was that they could not even dress themselves without help.[96] In the 1840s, for example, the style was for buttons to fasten down the back, and only very old women and female servants were allowed dresses which opened in front.)

If women could not talk about sexual matters, which men discussed so constantly, and could not think about all the inplications, it is little wonder that men accused them of having childish minds, incapable of abstraction, unable to cope with higher education, political decision, or careers in the higher professions.

The underlying anxiety, of course, was only rarely understood and still more rarely voiced. One man who let it out was George Jessel, Annie Besant's judge, whom she heartily disliked; he stated that *fear* was the only bridle that could restrain women's sexual impulses.[97] If this fear was indeed at the back of the great conspiracy, a still more deeply buried fear lurked in many minds: how could women in such circumstances remain physically and mentally healthy?

But women were fighting cobwebs in the dark. They did not know how much they did not know, and the consequence was that much of their effort to attain equality was, at first, misdirected. Not understanding what they were up against, they wasted much effort in the wrong place. Only when women became erotically free could they take their place beside men as equals.

8.

Self-Reverence, Self-Knowledge, Self-Control

The passions are always foes, but it is only when they have been encouraged that they are able to become masters. . . . They resemble wild beasts. . . . What miseries they cause, how many intellects they paralyze, how many families they ruin, how many innocent hearts they break. . . .

Winwood Reade, 1872

In this chapter I want first to discuss the ways in which the ideal of sexual continence was applied to men, and then to compare the materials available to them for sex education with those listed for girls in the last chapter. The difference in both aspects of their preparation is important for understanding the difficulties of communication between the sexes.

Chastity in men has never been a widely practiced virtue, except perhaps among special sacred categories set apart from the world. In the nineteenth century, however, there was considerable propaganda to the effect that men ought to take the Christian marriage promises as seriously as women, and in one way or another this ideal was probably adhered to more strictly then than before or since. Every country seemed to have some rationale for continence, though the different ways in which boy babies were treated and the different expectations of the masculine role provided each with disparate reasons.

Men are more sexually irrepressible than women in the sense that sexual feelings and orgasm are inevitable for them, while for women these things have to be learned (even though the female response may ultimately be stronger than the male). In the absence of such learning experiences, women may actually lack sexual drive, an explanation offered by some modern anthropologists that contradicts the common assumption that such drives are merely repressed. Furthermore, men are more likely than women to want intercourse for its own sake, independent of any particular partner or relationship. Thus the emotional, intellectual, and sexual rhythms of men can diverge so sharply from women's that empathy is hard to achieve. There have been many periods in history when men have wondered why can't a woman be more like a man. But there have been relatively few when women tried to change men to fit a female pattern of chastity, fidelity, and tenderness. Perhaps the medieval Courts of Love were one such episode, and the nineteenth century another.*

At the start of that period we have seen women encouraged to become the angels in the house. Thus was prepared a seedbed for cultivating feminine values in the rising generation, and it is easy to imagine that boys in these households could acquire two sorts of guilt— personal guilt when they broke the sexual taboos, and a kind of social guilt about the fairness of the system, which later on became one of the forces aiding the women's movement.

༤ Honors must go to the English for being the most literal about a single standard. Matthew Arnold laid down down the dictum that the two great virtues of a Christian society were charity and chastity, the former meaning kindliness to others, and the latter mastery over oneself. The Victorians thus equated chastity with the progress of civilization, a victory over the barbarous past of the race—and possibly over the subcurrents of their own suppressed working classes.

"Blameless" or "stainless" were the highest accolades a man's character could receive, and once accused of failing in this quality, like Charles Stewart Parnell, the leader of the Irish Home Rule party, could be quickly ruined. By attributing France's loss of the war of 1870 to the "lubricity" of the French character, it was suggested that such ruin could overtake a whole nation.

Still, the people who propagated this ideal genuinely wanted to erect a single standard for both sexes. When in Meredith's *Diana of the Crossways*, a maid tells Diana that her follower is "quite like a female," Diana longs to tell him that he has received the highest of eulogies. At the same time, while boys should be brought up to be pure, girls should learn to be brave. In the reformers' view the female character was not to be clinging or incompetent.

Continental observers, admitting that the English gave more than lip service to continence, puzzled over the reasons. Taine finally came up with nine explanations:[1] that Teutonic senses awakened later than Latin ones;† that the English tended to be shy; that they indulged in a great

---

*Here I am following Eleanor E. Maccoby and Carol N. Jacklin, whose *Psychology of Sex Differences* surveys the entire literature of sex differences and conclude that the males' greater aggression has a biological component, that they are more irrepressible than women, that this difference is observed in other primates and in crosscultural studies among humans. Furthermore, they conclude that society does not reinforce aggressiveness more strongly in boys than in girls.

†Max O'Rell noticed that in English parks couples could embrace for hours without becoming overly excited, while at the same time Englishwomen would let their skirts drag in the mud rather than lift them up as in Paris, where the young men loved to follow a trim pair of ankles (Blouët, *Womankind*, 2). More scientifically, Salvador de Madariaga believed

amount of physical exercise; that London was simply a less seductive city than Paris; that public opinion was less tolerant of breaches; that Englishmen often maintained their religious beliefs into maturity; that they adhered to an ideal of marriage and deglamorized easy sex; that the sort of women available for pick-ups were unattractive streetwalkers, not at all like the Paris grisettes; and that married women were almost all faithful.* Taine was aware, however, that English customs were not easy to live up to, and he observed many cases of "silent agony."

Whereas in France morality was often an object of curiosity, in England it was for practical use,[2] and many exhortations were provided to sharpen the tool. Englishmen were told that "a man's body is given him to be trained and brought into subjection, and then used for the protection of the weak, and the advancement of all righteousness and the subduing of the earth. . . ."[3] They were told that

> The happy husband is . . .
> He who, scanning his unwedded life,
> Thanks Heaven, with a conscience free
> 'Twas faithful to his future wife.[4]

They were told, "I dislike as much as you do the assumption that men cannot be chaste, for I believe they can & ought to be,"[5] and they were told that in a mature adult sex united with the wish to be a father and so became spiritualized.[6] Yet when Francis Wey, a Frenchman, inquired how the Englishmen controlled their feelings, he was told that while an elevated soul could master itself, "We all have our scars, which we guard in silence."[7]

The moral justification was strengthened by a biological one, so they believed, to the effect that the reproductive organs contained something not to be carelessly poured out, because, reabsorbed, the semen became a source of strength for both brain and body. Even Dr. Knowlton, whose book on methods of birth control was radical enough to be prosecuted, wanted young married women to realize that the male system was exhausted by gratification, and that the loss of one ounce of semen was equivalent to the loss of forty ounces of blood.†[8]

It should not be supposed that all young men lived up to their highest ideals, but adolescence, when the hormones ripen, was also for many English boys a time of religious or romantic idealism. By no means all university men used the freedom of these years to sow wild oats.

An American Yale graduate, Charles Bristed, who spent five years at Cambridge University during the 1840s, was confounded at the open

---

that race, climate, and athletic education retarded for many years the onset of British sexuality.

*J. B. Priestley, for one, considers still more important the habits of thrift in all affairs of life inculcated by Britain's commercial mores (Priestley, 30).

†The equation between sperm and blood had been worked out in the eighteenth century by Tissot, and was a commonplace (Newman, 2).

immorality he found there, quite different from anything he knew at New Haven. (Yet musing on the relativity of moral standards, he added that Cambridge men would never cheat on an examination, a lapse that he remembered vividly having witnessed at Yale.)[9] But he also found a large number who kept chaste through frigidity, religious scruple, or physical training, and he was puzzled that the two sorts of students at Cambridge, the reading and the "rowing" (rhymes with "allowing") men, were equally likely to have irregular connections, or to remain pure.

When the idealistic were falsely accused, they reacted as to an affront to their honor; if they had really fallen, their guilt could be overpowering. When Earl Russell, Bertrand's elder brother, was accused of immorality, he chose to leave the university, defiantly wearing in his buttonhole "the white flower of a blameless life."[10] He later said of himself at the time that he was "entirely possessed by that white virginal flame of innocence which I think is even stronger in adolescent boys than in girls."[11] But the unfortunate Charles Kingsley, led to an encounter with a prostitute by his undergraduate companions, felt when he became engaged that he was not worthy to consummate his marriage.*

While men were often said to "rise" toward feminine values, women were not to be allowed to fall into masculine habits; but Winwood Reade explained that women were not to be pitied for this: "it is they who alone are free; for by that discipline they are preserved from the tyranny of vice."[12]

Publicly there was a good deal of self-congratulation concerning the heights to which this mixture of civilization and liberation was carrying the European peoples. Westermarck, in his monumental *History of Human Marriage* (first edition 1891), traced the increase of affection in sexual relationships and related it to a general growth in altruism. Love had now become "the refined feeling it is in the heart of a highly civilized European." At the same time Sir Patrick Geddes had just completed studies of sex that bore out the theory that evolution's grand design was to make romantic passion the highest product of natural selection.[13] It was also hoped that as a single sexual standard became the norm for all classes, it would create a moral bond between the rich and the poor.[14]

Darwin felt that immorality was always "outmoded behavior," once appropriate but soon to die out, and in the seventies and eighties, when this ideal reached its apogee, Englishmen were able to look incredulously at their grandfathers' morals, "when a man might indulge in pleasures which seem to us coarse and degrading, and yet retain all the pride and all the bearing of a gentleman."[15]

Beatrice Webb too placed her hopes in evolution, though she thought its main work concerning sex morality was still in the future.[16] As for the time in which she was living, she expatiated on the dangers and

---

*"You, my unspotted, bring a virgin body to my arms. I alas do not to yours. Before our lips had met I had sinned and fallen. Oh, how low!" And he talked of getting French monks to scourge him (Chitty, 57).

ugliness of sex "in our present rather gross state of body and mind,"[17] but she concluded with the hope that physical desire would be subordinate to intellect (ignoring the difficulty that natural selection could hardly work that way). Such a possibility, she stressed, was her only hope, and without it she could not struggle on.*

By 1909 Ellen Key was proclaiming that chastity would become a positive instead of a negative virtue,[18] while Edward Carpenter could boast concerning his gentle homosexuality that it represented a higher, because more feminine, nature. He shared the common belief that for most women sex was a real, though willing, sacrifice.[19] Women in the meantime had begun to raise their consciousness of this form of victimization. Mrs. Anna Jameson had noticed at mid-century "a sort of mysterious horror of the immorality of men"[20] among women of the world; fifty years later this horror had grown into the angry blaming of most of the world's troubles on masculine sexuality, so that "votes for women, chastity for men" became the slogan of one segment of the English women's movement.[21]

Evolution, however, did not perform according to the hopes expressed above. Today's views of mental health and those of a hundred years ago are nearly 180 degrees apart, as is nowhere better exemplified than in the case of Augustus Hare, expounded in F. D. Huntington's introduction to Hare's memorial to his mother. Huntington avers that the one trait that dominated Hare's life was what "we should call moral healthiness."[22] This because he never married and very likely never had any relations with women at all. Hare was brought up by a widow, his adopted mother, whose first duty as she saw it was to "break his will," and to effect this she had him brutally beaten by his uncle, Archbishop Julius Hare, whose visits were described by the same editor as "errands of delight and cheer." (Julius was the author of a book called *The Mission of the Comforter!*) Far from exhibiting moral healthiness in modern terms, Augustus's story could be used in a casebook of child psychiatry.

Nor was Hare's case the most disturbing. The roster of Victorian males with sexual problems includes many men of the highest distinction: Dickens suppressed "certain criminal tendencies,"[23] Kingsley and Gladstone whipped themselves to atone for their sexual fantasies, Swinburne was a masochist, Ruskin and Carlyle impotent, Samuel Butler a repressed homosexual, and Oscar Wilde an active one.

It is easy, and rather fashionable, to use cases like these to indict the Victorian sexual system as particularly cruel and ineffective. Yet many people living today have known products of repressive Victorian childhoods who turned out to be affectionate, public-spirited, and humorous adults, interested in ideas, art, travel, and sports. If their background gave them a certain hauteur about physical pleasures, and if their level of

---

*At the wedding of one of her former students, Miss Beale, the head of the North London Collegiate School, was heard to murmur, "The lower life, my dear, the lower life" (Fremantle, 70).

sexual activity was almost certainly low compared to that considered normal in other times and other places, they had a great deal of other kinds of pleasure in life, as well as a notable integrity of character that prevented certain kinds of pain.*

 ∽ Germans traced their idealization of chastity back to the time of Tacitus, who had described ancient Germanic youth as coming late to the pleasures of love, so that they passed puberty unexhausted. When both sexes were fully mature, they contracted marriages that produced notably healthy offspring.

The early nineteenth-century student movement made of chastity a cardinal virtue, especially for those caught up in the patriotic organization called the *Burschenschaft*. Members swore to remain chaste while they devoted themselves to the redemption of the German fatherland, and those who violated that provision were expelled. One can speculate about how far such an ideal was lived up to, but as late as the 1860s it created enough of an appearance of virtue to lead Julie Daubié, a French feminist who was trying to improve the morals of French students, to state flatly that German university men were "all chaste."[24] And indeed in World War I a group of medical students and professors founded a Union for Sexual Ethics, pledging themselves to total celibacy until the age of twenty-four in order to concentrate on winning the war and saving German culture.†[25]

The ideal North German, as pictured in the novel *Helmut Harringa*, was brought up not to let sex bother him until the time came when it could "lead to a future." Helmut's brother, weaker than he, kills himself when he discovers that a night's drinking with his corps brothers has ended in venereal infection; as for Helmut himself, if his sexual feelings disturbed him before the appearance of the North German girl described in a previous chapter, he would start to think about sailing or

---

*As Ethel Smyth described her eldest sister: "Just a very pleasant-looking typically Victorian woman, full of interest in life, and conspicuously kind and thoughtful for others. But behind a taking little manner . . . was a fund of quiet heroism, and a liberality of outlook that never ceased to astonish me (St. John, 65).

†A perfect example of propaganda for sexual purity is *The Wanderer between Two Worlds* by Flex, a novel of an ideal young German officer in the early days of the 1914 war. The hero, Ernst, is a graduate of the youth movement, which had always stressed chastity, along with friendliness to people of all classes, love of nature, and folksinging. The young man enjoys from his trench in France the sight of wild geese flying north, and later, on the Eastern front, the soldier's life is represented as consisting of sunbathing, swimming in the cold rivers, reading Goethe and Nietzsche, and sending money home so that his young siblings can "wander" through the countryside. There is no hint of sex. He is represented as an officer who provides his men with inspirational sympathy, so that each one can be built up both as a man and as a soldier. After he is finally killed in a quick ecstatic burst of fire, his mother's chief concern is whether he had experienced the joy of combat before he died. So different from most modern war stories.

rowing instead. Of possible significance is the fact that his best friend is English.*

Although those Germans who followed the ideal of sexual restraint greatly admired the English, the sentiment was tied to several elements that were not so apparent among the Anglo-Saxons—namely, patriotism, a special racial pride, and the romantic feeling that unconsummated love was the most deeply felt. Both German and English commentators have noticed that the stress on continence represented an effort of the rising middle class to set itself off from a corrupt nobility.[26]

∽ In France it would seem that most of the factors that led to male continence in the northern countries were absent. Most cosmopolitan, middle-class Frenchmen did not take religion so seriously, they were painfully indifferent to physical health, and they lacked mystical racial sentiments. Among a few literati, however, intellectualism worked to downgrade sensuality. Sex not being a rational activity, some of these men came to think of it as silly, certainly not so important as excitement in the brain. They talked about it constantly; in fact, when Turgenev came to Paris, a barbarian from Russia, he was surprised that there was so much to talk about, because in his native country people made love so simply that there was nothing to discuss.[27] Yet the Goncourt brothers mentioned in their *Journal* on September 22, 1864, that the two of them had probably had only eleven nights of love all told in their lives. Stendhal complained about penis failure, while even Englishmen noted Renan's sexual repression.

An interesting conversation is reported in the *Goncourt Journal* for January 18, 1864. In a long discussion about sex, Flaubert is supposed to have declared that copulation was not needed for health, while Taine remarked that copulation every two or three weeks freed him for work. Flaubert then complained of the difficulty of getting a nervous thrill in a brothel, to which the Goncourts added that most people did not get these nervous thrills anyway, either because they had old mistresses, or wives, and that at best a man could hardly expect to have such a nervous thrill three times in a lifetime. Cynical as these old roués were, they reflected the general belief in France that sex was something to talk about without shame or idealization.

The one French savant† who glorified chastity instead of muttering

---

*This idealization of chastity, endemic throughout the nineteenth century, reached a mad climax in the work of Otto Weininger, whose *Sex and Character*, weird but popular, appeared in 1906. It suggested that the solution to all moral problems in the world was to give up sexual intercourse entirely. (Only the most masculine men masturbated, he said.) Women must cease to demand sex from men. If German males worried that the race would die out, it only proved that they had no faith in immortality. Weininger committed suicide at twenty-three.

†Proudhon believed that giving in to love would lead to promiscuity, uni-sex (*l'uni-sexualité*), sodomy, pederasty, hysteria, and nymphomania (Adam, Idées, 26).

about it was Comte, who, as we have seen earlier, felt that he had been purified of his animal desires by the woman he loved. He preached "altruism" and considered sex "coarsely personal" and women, with their less intense sexual demands perfect teachers to discipline the male sex.[28]

⌦ It is notable that in these various mythological or ideological patterns of masculine continence only rarely does the love of a sexual partner emerge as a motive. Self-mastery, service to the state, even idealization of women, are not elements likely to improve sexual contacts with flesh-and-blood partners. What was missing was any sense of mutuality. Equality is measured by the responsibilities that are assumed by both partners, and—at the start of our period at least—men were making the sexual decisions. They were accustomed to doing this heedlessly, just as in politics they claimed that women were "virtually" represented though only males voted. As Georg Simmel put it in 1911: "If we express the historic relation between the sexes crudely in terms of master and slave, it is part of the master's privileges not to have to think continuously of the fact that he is the master, while the position of the slave carries with it the constant reminder of his being a slave. This fact is evident in the extremely frequent phenomenon that certain judgments, institutions, aims or interests which we men, naively, so to speak, consider purely objective, are felt by women to be thoroughly and characteristically masculine."[29]

Even when they tried to be kind, they were patronizing; thus Michelet's book on women, for instance, tells much more about how he imagined they must feel than about how they really did feel. With women of their own class, but even more poignantly with those of the lower classes, with casual contacts or long-term mistresses, it was the man's decision when to start and when to stop—and they did either seemingly without compunction.

It was a common view, though not one held by the admirers of self-control of course, that for a man to overstep the sexual line was really something secretly admirable or at least easily condoned. The majority report to the Royal Commission on Contagious Diseases Act of 1871 told the British Parliament, and the world, "There is no comparison to be drawn between prostitutes and the men who consort with them. With one sex the offence is committed as a matter of gain, with the other it is an irregular indulgence of a *natural* [emphasis added] impulse."[30] It was odd, said Legouvé, that in a country like France, where a girl's honor was equated with her chastity, the aim of most young men was precisely to take it away, and still odder that men should be acclaimed for wrecking girls' lives.[31] When Josephine Butler was a young faculty wife at Oxford, a particularly painful seduction case was hushed up; Josephine was furious, but received only a negative answer when she asked whether the man could be brought to any sense of shame.[32] In fact, the Yale graduate at Cambridge mentioned earlier concluded that there was more brutality toward women of the lower classes by men (of all classes) in England than in any other country, except perhaps Russia.[33]

Among German men of the aristocratic and officer classes, there was a tradition of sexual excess and contempt for women. Demonstrative examples ranged from the ball in *Naturkostum*[34] given during the days of Otto von Corvin's lieutenancy to the famous trial for homosexuality of Count Philipp zu Eulenburg, scandalous enough to threaten the Wilhelmine monarchy.*[35] There was also a prestigious club for officers limited to those who had contracted a venereal disease.

When German men wanted philosophical backing for their indifference to moral standards, they could always rely on Schopenhauer, whose book on women carelessly pictured all men living polygamously part of the time, and most men all the time; this was considered to be excellent because in Schopenhauer's opinion it would bring women back to their proper sphere.

✍ English mothers of the middle and upper classes took little physical care of their children, turing over such tasks as bathing and feeding to a special nurse who came to be called the nanny. Children were taken, often quite formally, to spend an hour or two a day with their parents, or they might come in to dessert after dinner; later in life many of them expressed gratitude for the spiritual ideals which their mothers and older sisters had implanted, but for direct physical contact a little boy was more likely to climb into his nanny's lap. Such a separation of roles in the first two women he was close to might well account for the fact that an Englishman made a clear distinction between the women to be idealized and those to be exploited.

In any case, at about the age of eight an upper-class boy would be withdrawn from almost all feminine contact when he was sent off to school, where the older boys were full of suggestions about masturbation and homosexuality, and the male teachers were quite regularly celibate. Mrs. Ellis, who so often urges on her readers the ideal of womanly submission, comes close to losing patience with the male sex when she discusses public schools, which only encouraged their "precocious selfishness" and where "the influence, the character, and the very name of woman was a by-word for contempt."[36] There was little women could do to combat the masculine belief that school was a place for toughening up young males and the less women knew about what actually went on there,

---

*Eulenburg, a brilliant figure at court, was accused by a journalist, Maximilian Harden, of homosexuality. By swearing that he was innocent, he got Harden sent to jail, but on release, the journalist proved that Eulenberg had been in a homosexual ring at Capri, where a Krupp committed suicide because of all the publicity. It is interesting that among Italians homosexuality is known as the "German vice."

the better. Josephine Butler, the great crusader against prostitution, felt that the notion that boys *had* to experiment sexually was specifically the result of their being "driven away at an early age from the society of women, and thrown upon the society of each other only—in schools, colleges, barracks, etc.; and thus [they] concoct and cherish a wholly different standard of moral purity from that obtaining among women."*[37]

There was no lack of discussion of ways to keep boys on the track, of course. The Eton schoolmaster, Edward Lyttelton, felt "spiritualization" was the best way.[38] It was natural for British parents to be shy, he thought—perhaps the fathers remembered their own youth too well—but if mothers could impart the spiritual quality, while fathers threw in "science," the problem should be met much better than by silence.

Doubtless many parents added religion to their sanctions, as George Meredith wished he could do in writing to his doubting son Arthur. The father told him that if he lacked religion to float him "through the perilous sensual period when the animal appetites most need control and transmutation," the boy would just have to summon something out of his own resources. Otherwise he would be doing "only half [his] work."[39]

Obviously even some women actively disagreed with Matthew Arnold's hierarchy of values with chastity at the top but they were classed as rebels against society. Eliza Chapman, a champion of women's rights, argued (in *The New Godiva*) that purity was simply not in the same class of universal virtues as honesty and kindness,[40] while Dr. Drysdale, a pioneer in sex liberalization and an early advocate of contraception, was vehemently against abstinence.[41] He noted the large number of spirited young men who wore themselves out in the struggle for chastity; and even when they won, he felt that it sometimes cost them the ability to have erections when they married. In fact his catalogue of horrors is a mirror image of his opponents' fears about masturbation: the penis shrank from non-use, the intellect became turbid, and woman-shunning became a bad social habit. Far better to marry young and indulge sex for health's sake, as many French doctors were advocating. Meanwhile Herbert Spencer was noticing with surprise that several of the promiscuous young engineers he had worked among turned into exemplary husbands and citizens.[42] But plain common sense on either side of the debate was hard to find.

co The young Frenchman would grow up in a climate where sex was more freely discussed, where both within and outside the family it was

*As might be expected, H. G. Wells has provided us with one of the most outspoken accounts of an Englishman's early sexual life. At his first little grammar school, he learned about sex "with guffaws." To his generation, masturbation was "a horrifying, astounding, perplexing individual discovery . . . black with shame," but he says he had relatively little experience with homosexuality, though at some schools it was certainly rampant. When his shame at his virginity became unbearable, he visited a prostitute (Wells, *Experiment*, 57–58, and passim).

regarded as a natural phenomenon. Furthermore, at least according to Karl Hillebrand, the intense emotions generated by the family itself would tend to defuse the emotional charge related to falling in love. Women were less idealized, but also less disregarded. Love was more matter-of-fact, more integrated into family life, and perhaps there was less "silent agony" for the French adolescent.

In contrast with the Englishman, the young Frenchman would have had more motherly attention in infancy, he would be more likely to have lived at home during his school years, and when at their end he seemed to have a sudden burst of freedom, he could often turn back to his mother for guidance. Many informants tell us that when, with passions rising, a man was first let loose into the seductions of city life, he would find that his mother was flattered rather than scandalized to be made a confidante. The English simply had no notion, declared Taine, of "those long, long conversations, those complete outpourings of the heart, in which the difference in age neutralises the differences in sex, and in the course of which a son, who is beginning in the world, finds in his mother, who is withdrawing from it, his cleverest, subtlest guide and his most perfect friend."[43] O'Rell said the same thing: "In France, our mother is the recipient of our tenderest caresses, our nearest and dearest friend. We tell her our secrets . . . even our escapades."[44] In his study of the family, Pelletan explains that man "perfects himself" by having poured into him the feminine hearts of his mother, sister, wife, and daughter, and only so could his soul become strong and beautiful.[45] (Query: how did woman perfect herself? Apparently only through her son.)

When young men reached adolescence, we often hear of their seduction. In the days of thick clothing, any glimpse of the female figure uncovered had a powerful erotic effect. In his bachelor days, the hero of *Monsieur, madame et bébé*, billed as a typical young Frenchman, begins by looking through a window at a careless woman undressing and then has a much more traumatic experience when a female cousin invites him to come to a bathing establishment with her. While he himself is hidden by a high-necked costume buttoned at collar and sleeves, her arms are bare, and when her suit is wet it reveals all the lines of her body. Warned about sensual desires at the religious school from which he has just graduated, he prays that the monster will not awaken, but when his companion wants to learn how to float and actually asks him to hold her up, he faints.[46]

The women with whom young men embarked on sexual experimentation could be older married women, the grisette type of lower-class mistress, or, of course, prostitutes. In order to keep their sons safe at home, some mothers encouraged liaisons with chambermaids, and they would sometimes hire pretty ones on purpose.[47] As Julie Daubié complained, the same woman who would not let her son steal a toy would be happy if he stole a chambermaid's honor.[48] In any case, all these women acted as "substitutes" for the *jeunes filles* looking forward to marriage. (The comparison was with the *remplaçants* who could be hired to do a young man's military duty for him.) While preserving the dowried girls from amorous attentions, the substitutes had the bad effect of training young men through their weaknesses, not through their strengths, so that French reformers complained that their compatriots grew up lacking the strength of character that it was assumed Englishmen possessed.*[49]

Hamerton's comment was that it was doubtful that any age or country ever worked the brain with such complete disregard of the body as France between 1830 and 1870. While Englishmen tried to subdue the body, Frenchmen attempted to ignore the rules of health.

This ignoring of the body, the preference for the training of the mind over the sort of character building chosen by the British, was reflected in Julien Benda's sexual odyssey.[50] Benda, who was born in 1867, believed that as a Jew he was perhaps even more committed to abstract cerebral processes than the average Frenchman. He remembered sitting on his father's knee when he was ten, and inquiring where babies came from. The reply, "You will find out later," he accepted without surprise, and then he stopped thinking about the subject. As he looked back, he regarded this not only as a sign of perfect confidence in his parents, but also as showing his lack of interest in experiment, adding that he was similarly uninterested in learning how an automobile worked. When he was eleven, a slightly older girl who had come over to play proposed that they "verify their sex," and to this end she exposed herself. He found the game bizarre and rather ugly, but she persisted in explaining how to make love. He was still bored. At fourteen he remembered looking through a keyhole at a young aunt in her tub (his interest in experiment rising, apparently), and the same year a big boy explained to him what you do with a wife. It was only when he had finished his education and was out "in the world" that Benda came to understand how many sensual pleasures were available for enjoyment. In his own family and throughout his school life, intellect had been preeminent. Dimly he had been made to feel that sexuality was secondary.

Similarly the Abbé Ernest Dimnet denied that he had ever had a moral crisis in all his education for the priesthood. His teachers felt so safe in ignoring the subject of sex that it was first discussed with his class the night before they were to be ordained, when the head of the seminary gave a little talk about the danger of "causing the Church to weep."[51] They should have been given a bit more preparation than this, Dimnet felt, before they went out the next day licensed to hear confessions in total ignorance of applied psychology.†

*Rhoda Métraux and Margaret Mead found the pattern still common in the France of the post–World War I era: young men learned sexual technique from older women, and then passed it along to their own wives. Because the older women were often of the same generation as the men's mothers, the mothers were able to keep in touch with the sons' sexual development (Métraux and Mead, 42).

†The discipline of the Church could be very hard on its priests, of course. Proudhon felt, on the basis of discussion with some of them, that it amounted to torture. One priest,

∞ Early nineteenth century German opinion about women's sexuality fitted in with the general European idea that women were to retreat to their homes. A Dr. Pockels of Hanover made a survey of female characteristics in 1799 and concluded that nature had kept women pure by giving them a low sex drive, that their highest and most lasting joys came from their children, and that they disliked purely animal responses from their husbands.[52]

A strong attack on this mode of thought was mounted by Dr. Roderich Hellmann in 1875 when he tried to import the liberal ideas of Dr. Drysdale into Germany. Hellmann felt his countrymen suffered from crippling limitations on sexual behavior, which he did his best to relieve. Apologizing for his use of taboo words and for voicing opinions so different from those people were used to, he yet hoped his readers would be repaid by new insights. As he watched boys and girls in whispered searching for the sexual instruction that was withheld, he looked forward to a day when universal perfected contraception would permit these unmarried youngsters to experiment more freely with healthier bodies and minds and the prospect of happier marriages.[53] The society of the future would, he felt, enjoy general nakedness without embarrassment, making public urinals unnecessary and certainly obviating the need for separate women's toilets, while free speech would let children understand sexual matters without dismay.[54] But with all this, Hellmann was not in favor of political and social equality for women, just erotic liberation. He was certain that enfranchised women would vote against progress.[55] Such political views failed to sweeten Hellmann's recommendations in sexual areas, and like his English mentor he had little success in loosening the grip of conventional teaching and repressive practice.

German *gymnasia* were hothouses of hard work, and in the more intellectually stimulating ones the students were so interested in ideas and idealism that they resented the efforts of adults to joke about sex with them.[56] In other schools nightmare conditions, like the ones set forth in *Frühlingserwachen*, combined overwork, excessive competition, and schoolmaster brutality with sexual ignorance to create the wave of student suicides that began in the 1890s.

When Fritz Berolzheimer wrote a guide to twentieth-century morality in 1914 he told his readers that steeling the will would remain the only way to get through puberty—the will, not the brain, for he found the intellect helpless before these matters.[57] (*Pace* the French on this subject.) Deliberate sex education was no use, since he had found that enlightened people indulged in unwholesome sexual practices (by which he apparently meant masturbation) as often as did the unenlightened.

---

aged sixty-five, told him that he would rather be shot than relive his twenties (Proudhon, 3:323), and reformers of the 1870s, like Angelo Mazzoleni, spoke strongly of the useless and heartbreaking struggles of young priests and nuns to keep their vows (Mazzoleni, 177).

Nor did he endorse the then-fashionable interest in British team sports. For Germans it would be better to go back to the traditional emphasis on *turning* (gymnastics), fencing, hiking, and wandering.

Havelock Ellis reports a survey among German and Russian physicians who nearly all gave the opinion that continence was harmless. This is what they presumably would have told their patients, but Ellis also tells us that when eighty-six doctors of the same nationalities were asked about their personal lives, only one had been sexually abstinent before his marriage.[58]

This attitude of hypocrisy and self-indulgence was anathema to the German women's movement. They declared that nature itself "speaks as with tones of thunder against promiscuity."[59] "Celibacy is the aristocracy of the future," cried Gabrielle Reuter; she and her fellows believed that the sex education that German youths were receiving was painfully inadequate to counteract the crudeness and ignorance around them.[60] In 1897 the German women's *Bund* sent a letter urging sexual purity to every student matriculating at any German university. By 1914 the women were still angry because the directors of the war effort devoted more time to training women in home economics than solders in sexual responsibility.[61]

∞ The duel of the sexes, dissipation for the men, horror at such behavior in women, was fought in Italy as elsewhere. The artist and statesman Massimo d'Azeglio has left a record of his growth into sexual maturity, beginning with his years of life in Rome as an artist which he described as a round of cafés, theaters, and girls in abundance. He had so little regard for them as people, in those days, that he used not to scruple to lie to them, until one day he had a conversion, and decided from that moment to study, paint, and exercise regularly.[62] He disappeared from the lives of his previous companions, and although he nearly burst, he managed four years and eight months of chastity. He could never describe the violence of the storms he went through, but he felt that they were a tonic, and recommended the practice for "the exhausted Latin race."[63] Along with sexual self-denial in his case came a devotion to truth-telling, and he laid down the rule for himself that he must speak truth and keep promises to everyone, "even women." This period of his life ended when he fell in love with indescribable violence and had an affair that lasted many years.

Possibly no one but Massimo himself would have complained in the 1820s if he had continued his dissipated life, but fifty years later the women's movement began to attack the easy assumptions of conventional Latin males. So when they set up an institute for the study of women's affairs in 1874, it was significantly called the Society for Science, Letters, and Ethics. Its first president, the poet Erminia Fusinato, expressed the gratitude of all Italian mothers to Luigi Chierici for a handbook for youth entitled *Wine, Tobacco and Sex* (*Bacco, Tobacco e Venere*), pointing out the evils of all three.[64]

Though one ought not to project the findings of the early 1960s back a hundred years, when Gabriela Parca made a survey of the sex habits of Italian men, she noticed a shocking ignorance about sex on the part of boys, whose mothers instructed them by fanciful tales while their fathers usually would not talk at all. And most of her informants remembered playing sexual games as children, with little sense of guilt. These games were initiated equally by boys and girls.[65] These stories and these diversions could hardly have been invented in the twentieth century.

She also found a significant difference between the north and the south. As that was one of the most frequently noted facts about Italy in the Risorgimento period, the modern findings strengthen one's belief that women in the north were far more likely to be considered as persons in their own right. It is not rare there even today, as it is in the south, for both partners to be virgins at marriage, and when this happens it is a source of lifelong pride. In the south, we hear even now of the custom we have met elsewhere of hiring a maid to give the adolescent sons experience.

∽ "The passions are always foes."

Perhaps the passions might instead serve to unite the sexes, if they were understood. In 1912 a Frenchman, Camille Mauclair, told his countrymen that the whole false theory of "sin" was based on a separation of body and spirit—an ancient religious heresy—and that this separation created the whole system of prostitution as well as the system of lies that it supported. Many men, he said, would rather suffer the pangs of jealousy than face the hazard of a free woman; for while men could understand the lies easily, they could not comprehend a free will like their own in women. The idea that one could own property in a woman's body, he warned, was the height of masculine egoism, and the demand for fidelity in love a silly and impossible one.[66]

Mauclair drew hope from the new discoveries in the physical sciences of his day. Just as an earlier generation of Englishmen had attempted to justify their sexual morality by appealing to evolution, which they supposed led to constantly higher levels of purity and self-mastery, so Mauclair tied the new morality he championed to recent discoveries in physics. Such phenomena as polarization, molecular dissymmetry, radioactive elements, and cathode rays were doing away with the line between matter and energy. Applying this concept daringly to morals, he said that the dualism of mind and body was also dissolving. Only outworn theology could support the morality of dualism. The subconscious mind, he said, was worked upon by both physical and mental forces, and when men absorbed this lesson, then the passions might indeed become friends.[67]

⌘9.

"A Woman's Profession": Housekeeping

Infallible man, like a little Prometheus, brings woman fire—in the shape of the cook stove. And the punishment? Not he, but she, is put in irons; the vulture devours not his, but *her*, liver.

Hedwig Dohm, 1876

If the interior of the house was to be regarded in a new way—as a refuge from the press of business and the corruption of politics—and if women were to preside there busily, protected from that press and corruption, what was it that they actually *did*? Was housekeeping a sacred, priestess-like duty, both fulfilling and necessary, or was it a trap of monotony and triviality? Just how interesting, and how responsible, was it?

With his usual irony Byron concluded:

Man's very sympathy with their estate
Has much of selfishness, and more suspicion,
Their love, their virtue, beauty, education,
But form good housekeepers—to breed a nation.[1]

But sometimes this male sense of irony degenerated into panic, and in 1870 we find W. Landfels remarking in all seriousness that no man *could* perform a woman's domestic duties, that so long as the world should last, women would be required to do them.[2] The meaning is clear: women must be kept at it, while men continued to flaunt, often rather proudly, their own incompetence.

A preconception of the masculine sex was that they were totally dependent on women for physical care, food, cleanliness, comfort, and consolation. These came as their right, and they did not have to pay for them with any particular consideration. Whatever else they did, women of high station and low, in England and on the continent, always provided these services.

Many people felt with Landfels that this was a crushing argument against women's emancipation. Even Ruskin, who wanted men to carve stone for churches instead of jewels for adornment, and who felt that personal service was humiliating for men, agreed that it was so pleasant to

132

be cared for by women that he was willing to allow maidservants in Utopia.*[3]

A well-run house *is* decidedly a satisfaction, and Mrs. Hugo Reid gave a spirited defense of the challenge to intellect and self-discipline called forth by its proper management.[4] Most masculine jobs, she felt, were routine and consisted in following orders, a fate which only men at the very top of their professions escaped, while even ordinary women had daily opportunity to make important decisions and choices. (Her opinion of men's jobs is buttressed by Herbert Spencer's rationale for not marrying: *he* did not want to become an office drudge.)[5] Gina Lombroso points out that after the French Revolution former *grandes dames* found interest and unexpected pleasure in running their smaller ménages; she felt that only later on, after feminism questioned the old division of labor, did women begin to suppose themselves bored with housework.[6] To do so was one way to assert equality with men.

How women managed their duties or responsibilities varied greatly from country to country. In general, English ladies did not actually get their hands dirty. They presided over their households like managers, limited to giving orders. The French, while still executives, were thoroughly conversant with the practical details—able either to oversee or to lend a hand. Housekeeping for them was a chosen art. For German ladies it was not so much an art as an imposed duty. German wives had the most drudgery and the least freedom of choice.

∾ Let us start with Englishwomen. Until about the time of Victoria's accession, the master of the English house had taken most of the responsibility for its ordering and even its appearance.[7] Flora Tristan was struck by this facet of English life during the 1830s, but in the following decade a reversal of roles began to be noticed, and women became the ones to select furniture, curtains, and carpets. By 1850 it was considered effeminate for men to pay attention to such things, and the housewife came into firm control of her domestic staff.

---

*An attitude nicely sentimentalized by Arthur Hugh Clough in his poem about some university students on a reading and walking tour in Scotland (ca. 1848). The lassies who serve them draw their admiration, performing their "household work, which someone, after all, must do":

> How the old knightly religion, the chivalry semi-quixotic
> Stirs in the veins of a man at seeing some delicate woman
> Serving him, toiling—for him, and the world; some tenderest girl, now
> Over-weighted, expectant, of him, is it? who shall if only
> Duly her burden be lightened, not wholly removed from her, mind you
>
> . . . .
> She will rise like an urn-bearing statue of Hellas; —
> Eve from the hand of her maker advancing, an helpmeet for him
> [Arthur Hugh Clough, 124]

"The usual method of London housekeeping, even in the ranks of the middle classes, is for the mistress to give her orders in the kitchen in the morning, leaving the cook to pass them on to the tradespeople when they called," reported a grumpy article in the *Saturday Review* on the sliding standards of housekeeping in 1868.[8] The editorial point was that women were selfish enough to be bored with this work, even though "men bear with the tedium of office work." (The *Saturday Review* was known for its anti-feminism.) Yet women themselves often claimed that those who spent more than an hour or two in the morning on such tasks, including doing up the accounts once a week, were simply inefficient. It was absurd to talk about household affairs with a degree of pompous mystery that would be laughable in Secretary of State, according to the sisters Maria Grey and Emily Shirreff.[9] (If things got too complicated, they added, a housekeeper would be engaged to take over, though one could ask what was she but another woman doing woman's work?) Miss Emily Davies reiterated that an hour a day was enough. Her opinion was that running a household took judgment, tact, organization, decision, and an inner sense of the beauty of order, such as could be acquired in a liberal college like the one she devoted her life to starting—but it did not take much *time.*[*10]

They did, of course, all have servants; we are considering only women of the middle class or higher, and one definition of that middle class was that the household should employ at least one maid.† Today, servants, if one can find them, may or may not save more time than various household appliances, but in the nineteenth century, when water had to be heated and carried up to bedrooms, coal hauled upstairs, ashes and slops down again, when quantities of white linen must needs be washed and ironed by hand, household service was a necessity to anyone who wanted to live a life of comfort or intellectuality. Management of a household of servants of both sexes was, of course, an executive job.

*The Duchess of Rutland found that it took almost as much effort to direct the household concerns of a large party in a country house as in guiding a hunter across a stony country in a mist (Shelley, 131)

†Patricia Branca, in *Silent Sisterhood*, deals brilliantly with a different "middle class" from mine. She limits her discussion to families with incomes under £300, usually with just one servant. The budget of my typical family ranges upward from £500, an income that Mrs. Haweis believes a young couple might just get started with. Branca might call my characters upper class; yet surely professional men are middle class and quite clearly separated from the aristocracy of wealthy landowners, peers, and industrial millionaires. Froude wrote at the time of his marriage that his wife would have an income of £300 a year, which with his own £60 would involve serious sacrifices of comfort unless he could add £120 or so by writing. (Dunn, 186) William R. Greg, in 1874, felt that £400 or £500 was inadequate for "cultivated refinement" in England, though quite adequate on the continent, where the cost of living was about the same but the style of living quite different (Freg, 293). The census of 1851 calculated that one family in about eight or nine kept servants. Branca deals with the lower segment of these; I mostly with the middle.

Here is what Mrs. Gaskell, the novelist, had accomplished before ten-thirty one morning in 1857:

> decided how long to boil the beef;
> told the gardener what perennials would survive the Manchester smoke;
> decided on the length of skirt for a gown undoubtedly being made up in the house;
> decided on the salary for a nursery governess;
> read up on the Indian Army and returned some letters on that subject with a polite note;
> answered twenty questions of dress for her girls;
> saw a lady about a manuscript;
> arranged to sell two poor cows for one good one, talking to the purchasers and discussing cattle keep and price.[11]

A versatile lady, indeed, for whom, we are assured, household cares were a positive delight, who trained a succession of first-rate cooks, and who was prouder of her pigs than of her literary triumphs.[12] She wrote to her publisher, who questioned some of these skills, that if he came to dinner, she would prepare him a lobster sauce with Brobdingnagian pieces.[13]

Only rarely did the Victorians contemplate the possibility of doing without domestic service. To be sure, William Cobbett, who represented the back-to-nature movement of his day, the 1820s, had advised that a young couple should start without servants. But though his newspaper column was rather a fad among the higher classes, he was directing his counsel to those artisans and small farmers for whom having a servant might be a way of impressing the neighbors. He told young wives that to cook, clean, wash, and mend for two people would preserve their health and beauty and keep up their spirits besides. He found servants expensive, interruptive of privacy, stimulative of laziness in the mistress, creative of pretentiousness, and in general destructive to conjugal felicity. With her food, fire, and space, a maid could use up thirty to fifty pounds a year.[14]

Few women in a class that could afford servants took Cobbett's advice seriously, though it is on record that in her early married days on a Scottish farm, Jane Carlyle used Cobbett's manual to learn how to bake bread and manage the stable.[15] (As Jane baked, brewed, sewed, and washed, Thomas explained that these activities were delivering her from the slavery of frivolity and the imbecility of her sex.)[16]

After Cobbett's time the standard of living, among the classes we are considering, rose, and with it the number of servants and the insistence on comfort and privacy. When the Kingsleys married in 1844, Charles's parents suggested that his ménage, that of a young clergyman, would require a man as groom, gardener, and table waiter; a cook who would have some housemaidly duties; and a lady's maid to take care of the bedroom and help wait on table.[17]

Harriet Beecher Stowe attributed Englishwomen's fine complexions and good figures to the fact that they did not have to lie awake nights "ruminating the awful [American] question who shall do the washing next week," nor were they obliged to choose between washing their own dishes and leaving the best cut glass to the mercies of coarse immigrant help.[18] (And Mrs. Trollope thought it a pity that an American senator's wife should need to spend her day cooking, or even sewing for a missionary society.)

With the enormous number of servants (there were 1,038,791 domestics in England in 1851) came an increasing separation of the mistress, not only from active housework, but also from the personalities of the help. The relationship was quite different from that obtaining on the continent. Factors may have been not only English affluence, which could afford such separation, but also the English attitude toward individuals and their private lives. They did not want their servants to become intimate with the family, nor were they eager to intrude upon the servants' privacy. Reinforcing the idea of separation between upstairs and downstairs, Arthur Hugh Clough in 1846 proposed engaging daily servants, who living outside the home would not oblige the mistress to control their dress and conduct.[19] The admirable Mrs. Isabella Beeton, in her famous book of household management, thinks only in terms of directing servants, and the more the better. She talks of "duties clearly assigned" to different categories of maid and man, and explains the mental function of the housewife in economics and organization.[20]

Mill wrote to Harriet Taylor in 1832 that no woman who could possibly afford help should do the housework herself, but that the main thing was to establish such a good system that constant supervision would not be necessary. (Even with children in the house, mothers' time would not be required, he felt, just their love.)*[21] From Germany, Hedwig Dohm explained to her feminist readers that the reason English homes were the most comfortable was that English cooks would not stand for "interference" from their mistresses.[22]

---

*Mill, to be sure, changed his mind about women's role, perhaps under Harriet's influence. Freud, who translated an essay of Mill's on discrimination against women, had this to say in a letter dated November 5, 1883 (translated by Ernest Jones):

> I recollect that in the essay I translated a prominent argument was that a married woman could earn as much as her husband. We surely agree that the management of a house, the care and bringing up of children, demands the whole of a human being and almost excludes any earning, even if a simplified household relieve her of dusting, cleaning, cooking, etc. He had simply forgotten all that, like everything else concerning the relationship between the sexes. That is altogether a point with Mill where one simply cannot find him human. His autobiography is so prudish or so ethereal that one could never gather from it that human beings consist of men and women and that this distinction is the most significant one that exists. In his whole presentation it never emerges that women are different beings. . . . He finds the suppression of women an analogy to that of negroes. Any girl, even without a suffrage or legal competence, whose hand a man kisses and for whose love he is prepared to dare all, could have set him right. [Ernest Jones, 176]

Various stories from below stairs indicate that the servants were sometimes amused at the helplessness of their employers; and from above stairs Josephine Butler used to wonder if just telling servants what to do gave adequate exercise to ladies' need for activity. But the rationale was clear, and it was as much a matter of class as of sex. No upper-class man would do physical labor. (Ideally he should not even be in manufacturing, since being a poor landowner or in a genteel occupation was viewed more favorably than being filthy rich "in trade.") This is one reason why physical housework was seen as degrading. Beatrice Webb, when running her mother's house as a young girl, "had neither need nor ability to cook or mend or do household chores."[23] (Mrs. Beeton suggested that if one must be personally useful, one could visit the poor, and in this way subtly spread information about the well-run house.)*

The nature of the supervision required if the house was to run smoothly is outlined in Mrs. Haweis' *Art of Housekeeping*, written for her daughter in 1889, in a way that makes it sound far from simple. Her first piece of advice was: understand your *drains*. The second recommended a thorough knowledge of accounting, for it behooved the young housekeeper to keep track of every penny. In regard to lighting, for example, lamps were preferred as the most economical and pleasantest illumination. The light of the future would surely be the just-introduced electric, but at the time she wrote, that system would cost £50 the first year, and £25 annually thereafter, while gas (which she disliked for its dirtiness) would come to £10, and old-fashioned lamps only to £7. All household supplies were to be locked up. It was cheaper to buy in quantity, a month's supply at a time, but the goods should be handed out daily to the cook and maids. Everything was to be recycled, with many hints on how to use up the outside leaves of greens (soup pot), uneaten bread from the plates (pudding), tea leaves (to sweep the floor), newspaper (it could be recycled, as could old tin cans). The mistress should check on every room every day, moving furniture to hunt for dust, being sure that the grease in the kitchen was covered tightly, and that the servants had no chance at the perquisites that they often appropriated in carelessly run homes. *Write out* the orders for servants, the author commanded, including the schedule for each day, the hours for rising, the rules concerning followers, the quarterly days off. But she, like other English mistresses, advised that servants simply detested personal intrusion into their private affairs. Most housewives, surely, failed to live up to these counsels of perfection, and indeed Augusta Webster laughed heartily at most such books of advice, on the ground that they were utterly impractical because English servants would never put up with what they felt to be such unwarranted bossiness.

*To show that there was no universal pattern, Lady Morgan wrote in 1830 of how she worked "like a galley slave" at cleaning a house with 3,000 books, cleaning and varnishing her thirty pictures, washing up her old china, all this time talking with the charwoman and trying to instill better ideas of cooking and nutrition, such as using beef instead of salt bacon (Morgan, *Memoirs*, 3:66).

A consequence of this English policy of not intruding on their servants' privacy was not, as one writer has put it, "unthinking blindness" to what was going on in in their own households, but rather a whole philosophy of independence. Prince Pückler-Muskau said he found that it was considered an insult to inquire of a footman how he felt in the morning, as this was his personal business.* With their employers, of course, servants were not to cultivate intimacy, not to speak first, not to hand things directly but to put them on a tray, thus physically emphasizing their psychological distance.[24] A servant was hired to do a particular job. He should be left alone to do it; he was not expected to do the job another servant was engaged to do. This excessive formality could lead to abuses, which were particularly horrifying in the case of incompetent nurses entrusted with the care of children; countless instances of brutality, stupidity, and carelessness never came to the attention of the parents at all, or did so too late. Even if they were forced to notice, the parents would often assume that nurse *must* know best and support her position.†

Few wives could expect any help in practical chores from their husbands, who could always escape to their clubs, luxurious in service and comfort. Bulwer-Lytton estimated that a club would enable a relatively poor man to command the standard of living of one ten times as rich,[25] while Mrs. Beeton held it over her women readers' heads that their homes had better measure up to the competition. Lady Morgan felt that club life was so much the perfection of comfort that it could provide a sufficient reason for a man's not marrying,[26] while Bulwer-Lytton hoped that at the very least it might offer an alternative to "imprudent" marriages.‡

⅓ An anecdote will illustrate the difference between English and German ways of housekeeping. About 1900 an English friend of Mrs.

---

*"*If you meet some of your servants in the streets . . . you would not know their faces,*" said Thackeray in *The Newcomes* (149). "You know no more of that race which inhabits the basement floor than of the men and brethren of Timbuctoo. . . ."

†Sometimes girls of good family were sent to learn housekeeping when they became engaged. Mrs. Panton felt that they should be taught to market as soon as they got out of school—all except university graduates. (*They* should never marry!) Mrs. Panton was remembering that in her own girlhood she had never laid eyes on anything uncooked. (Panton, 130). But Isabel Arundell spent a summer on a farm learning to cook, clean, milk, and care for chickens, before marrying Richard Burton, and in 1902 Kathleen Isherwood took a class in housewifery. These girls did not, however, learn such skills in their homes.

‡A recent study of helpless British husbands, as reported in the *Courier-Journal* for October 10, 1976, shows that men in bureaucratic jobs learn not to take the initiative and typically never lift a finger at home. Their wives are likely to espouse women's rights. Men in more independent work, whether self-employed or craftsmen or with management responsibilities, are more likely to cook the spaghetti for dinner and ask themselves why the wives should bear the whole burden of the house.

Sidgwick engaged a German governess who was an accomplished musician and linguist. But the mother complained:

"The other day I actually caught her teaching Patricia to *dust*."
"If you don't watch her," I said, "she'll probably teach Patricia to cook."
My friend looked anxious first, and then relieved.
"I don't see how she could do that," she said. "The cook would never have them in the kitchen for five minutes. But now you mention it, I believe she can cook. When things go wrong she seems to know what has been done or not done."
"That might be useful," I suggested.
"I don't see it. I expect my cook to know her work, and to do it, and not to rely on me. I've other fish to fry."[*27]

Here we see the determined ignorance of the English mistress contrasted with the German woman's ability to perform "servant's work" without any shame attached, no matter how many fish she had to fry.

In general, where an Englishwoman would delegate all her work to her two or three servants, the German family of comparable status would commonly get by with a single maid-of-all-work.[†] It was their policy to keep breathing down the maid's neck—check her every quarter-hour, advised Hedwig Dohm satirically, and keep all the supplies locked up—thus betraying a lack of trust.[28] On the other hand, it was assumed that a German servant who never saw her mistress in the kitchen would despise her as a poor housekeeper and would probably start thieving.

When her children were little, a German mother spent more time with them than an English mother might; when the daughters were grown, the German mother often became utterly subservient to them, scrubbing the sitting rooms and cleaning saucepans while the young ladies were getting dressed.[29] The Germans would even answer the front door themselves if their maid was busy washing. (The reason an English couple needed at least two servants was so that one would always be free to answer the door. A German friend asked the Sidgwicks why they could not open the door themselves. Mrs. Sidgwick thought it over and could only reply that it would seem "odd.")

Compared with English households, there was a general picture of hard housework and lack of creature comforts. The Leipzig of 1854, with an opera and a university and two or three theaters, was yet without piped water in the houses, a situation that led the British traveler Samuel Laing

---

*This was the same Mrs. Sidgwick who once shut up an argument with some foreigners about bad English food: "We have a great contempt for people who pay too much attention to food" (Sidgwick, 235).

†In Luise Otto's childhood home in the 1820s, for example, there were nine people to care for: the parents, four daughters, an aunt, two of her father's law clerks, and only one maid. Her father was a judge and director of law courts. The household was frequently expanded by long visits from nieces or the sudden incursions of wandering students on holiday, for whom they kept a separate room always ready (Otto-Peters, 4).

to say that the civilization of an English village was a more *real* civilization.[30] (One can imagine the German retort.) The newest houses in Berlin began having piped water and gas about 1870, but the general level of comfort in German houses seemed low, with primitive sanitary arrangements, stiff chairs, no closets, and not enough fire.

It was all part of a scheme of economy that offended English sensibilities. The German diet contained far less meat than did the English. Most of the Germans whom Mayhew knew got by with small pieces of meat two or three times a week; in poor families, meat was eaten only on Sundays. In studying the budgets that some Saxon families showed him, he found that a third to a half of the money was spent on beer. In order to show, as he thought, how outlandish the food could be, he provided his readers with some recipes and a whole week's menu, including marinated herring, beer soup, buttermilk soup, and potatoes cooked with plums.

English visitors to Germany were often critical of the way the natives ate breakfast. No tablecloth, an earthen coffee pot, ill-matched china, no butter, people shuffling in and out in loose dressing gowns and caps—not at all the way the homesick travelers remembered England, with the girls in pretty print dresses, a fresh tablecloth, and a steaming silver pot.*[31] On the other hand English visitors sometimes expressed surprise at the pleasantness of German kitchens, where there were no black pans, no grease in the sink, and no cloths with holes,[32] perhaps because of the housewives' physical presence.

Linen was hoarded, a relic of the old days when washing was done only once or twice a year, so that it became a habit for Eisenach matrons to count stockings by the hundred and shirts by the score.[33] Old women, Mayhew noticed, still knitted all the time, though young girls were beginning not to. (This was in 1865.) Mrs. Howitt, during her sojourn in the Rhineland in 1843, found knitting a constant female activity. She also knew of one man who had so many shirts that it would take six years for him to wear each of them once. On the other hand some families practiced economy by using dickeys instead of real shirts, so that Mayhew, with his passion for making lists, studied a civil servant's laundry as it was spread out to dry and concluded that he had not a single shirt to his name.

The economy the English found hardest to understand was the amount of work German middle-class women were willing to perform themselves: "How often have I not seen, with a sadness I dared not show, the indefatigable *Hauptmannin* von Z.——baking, boiling, stewing, pounding, sifting, weighing, peeling, with an energy that positively para-

---

*To Englishwomen's disgust, German ladies defended their dress as required by their life in the kitchen: "[They] are not nearly so much like *ladies* as our own *cooks*, who have scrubbed, and hearthstoned, and blackleaded, and sent up an elaborate breakfast, and yet are ready at ten o'clock to take orders for dinner in clean cotton gowns, tidy aprons, and trim caps" (Bothmer, *German Home Life*, 138).

lyzed me at my post of observation?"[34] Later we see the *Hauptmannin* (an officer's wife) chaffering with the egg lady as well as scolding the servant.

Compare with Mrs. Gaskell's morning a day in the life of Helene Weber, Max Weber's mother, about 1875.[35] The German lady got up at six and fed the baby. At seven she had breakfast and got Max ready for school, then she made sandwiches for the other children, trimmed the lamps, and issued supplies until about nine. Then she bathed the baby, served breakfast to her husband, taking a cup of coffee with him, and had a chance to scan the newspaper and exchange a bit of gossip. After that she returned to jobs in the kitchen or around the house; at noon she fed the baby again, then gave snacks to the boys, and served dinner at three or four for the children; but since her husband, Max Senior, came home later, she fixed him a separate meal. At seven she gave the children supper, put young Max to bed, and prepared supper for the grown-ups. By now it was nine o'clock, and she wondered just what she had accomplished.

Anna Mary Howitt, one of the first English girls to go by herself to study art in Munich (in 1854), felt that the sight of a *Frau Geheimräthin*— the wife of a man fairly high in the administration—hanging out clothes in the garden was "truly German." The previous evening Anna Mary had danced with the lady's son at a grand ball at the royal palace.[36]

Few, if any, German men were willing to help with the housework. I. A. R. Wylie declared that she knew gently nurtured German women who endured hardships that would disgust an English housemaid, and even sacrificed a whole life's happiness just so that the honored male in the family could live as became his rank and profession.[37] He would never be expected to spend days and nights without sleep watching over an invalid's slightest movement, as nearly all the women of the day were prepared to do; it was sympathetically assumed that even a deeply affectionate man would not be able to do it.*[38]

The German housewife's obsession with details—which Robert Lowie considers the feminine form of the German man's devotion to hard work—may have made it harder for these women to cultivate intellectual interests than for those of other countries. An incident of 1834 recounted by Anna Jameson, an Englishwoman much admiring of most things German, shows what could happen. An expedition to a picture gallery was planned, but the wife of a minister of state, described as one of the most accomplished ladies Mrs. Jameson had met, excused herself because it happened to be her day for counting up the household linen—an all-day job, presumably.[39] Likewise Marianne Weber, Max's wife, clearly felt that her mother-in-law had separated herself from her husband's interests by her determination to wash so many diapers herself.[40] It took

---

*I have not been able to find a copy of a book recommended by Bebel as giving a picture of the misery in which most housewives lived: *Randglossen zum Buche des Lebens* by Gerhard von Amyntor.

an ardent feminist like Hedwig Dohm to remark rather pointedly that a mother who spent too much time in the kitchen would become cross with the children when they interrupted her—more so, she felt, than would be true of a mother who was writing or painting.[41] Henriette Feuerbach, a determined if much put-upon intellectual, found that the only way she could manage was to divide her time, so that if she did up the laundry one week, she could read and write the next.[42]

Mary Howitt, a resident English writer, thought the solution would be for German women to train their servants to take more responsibility, like English ones,[43] and Marianne Weber seems to have actually done this, acknowledging that she owed the possibility of her intellectual career to the women who helped her in her home, about whom she wrote several touching reminiscences.[44]

Another way out would be to turn housekeeping itself into a fine art, worthy of being a true vocation, as it was for the French. Luise Büchner wanted women to realize that a liberal education was needed for this,[45] though she explained that cooking could do for girls' brains very much what training in logic did for boys. At the urging of Crown Princess Viktoria, Hedwig Heyl opened a cooking school for middle-class girls and wrote a textbook, *The ABC of Cooking*, to go with it. The book was an enormous success, going into thirteen big printings very quickly. At a chef's exhibition held in the 1890s (with sections covering good nutrition for the common people, cooking for soldiers, bourgeois and luxury cooking, and foreign foods), exhibits from women were accepted for the first time because of Frau Heyl's work.[46] In 1905 Käthe Schirmacher began research into the economic and social values created by housewives, so often underrated in government statistics as well as in popular values.

No woman thought harder about the problem than Marianne Weber. As a young girl she had come to Berlin in pursuit of better and more professional education than was available in her Rhineland village. She lived with the Webers, who were related to her and sympathetic to her endeavor; yet as soon as she became engaged to Max, everyone in the family agreed that "now" she would have to learn to cook. The young couple were advanced in their views and determined to have a free and equal marriage. In hunting for some area of expertise for Marianne that would counterbalance his assumed superiority in "thinking," Max hoped that superb mastery of housewifery would qualify.[47] He feared that she could never be on a par with him in the former area because of women's disqualification from university study, but cooking was to exercise her reason in much the way laid out by Luise Büchner. In reality Marianne's happiness proved to come from intellectual rather than practical activity, with Max's full approval, and even before they married she began to help him with his research. Later on, working in the women's movement, she studied the problem of women's work and considered housework as an art form, but she clearly stated that no one, not even servants, should have to devote a lifetime to it. (A childless woman herself, she did not consider whether a mother would be justified in spending her life at home.) But when Max had a nervous breakdown that lasted for years, Marianne regretted that he had no handskills. If only she could let him cook, she lamented.[48]

ᑲᑯ Count Keyserling commented that the French regarded women's work, even in his post-war day, as essentially equal to men's in value, and because of this high regard France was the land where women found the greatest satisfaction in their assigned role. It was scarcely an exaggeration of the common attitude when Mme Thérèse Blanc told her home economics students in 1899 that their vocation was "sublime" because women prepared the destinies of societies.[49] Their work, she hoped, would give them pleasure, both in the attention to small things and in the sense of the vast design.*

On June 30, 1848, the streets of Paris were filled with fighting in the "June Days" of the Second Republic. Delphine de Girardin and her husband Emile, editor of *La Presse*, discussed what to do if the insurgents should attempt to storm their house. Emile went to his office while Delphine gave orders to her servants—but what orders!—to collect water and store it in the cellar, then to wet down the roof. Delphine decided to go to the office to be with her husband, but she told the servants that if the insurgents should attempt to enter their house, to open all the doors and tell the crowd that M. and Mme Girardin made them a present of everything in it. They wanted to do this to save their fellow citizens from the charge of pillage.

Looking back, after nothing had happened to the house, Delphine drew the contrast with the sort of orders she gave every day: to put the flowers so; to carry the piano to a room where they would make music in the evening; to plan for her sister to come to dinner and to make bonbons for her children.[50]

Our friend Janet, whose views on women's place have been quoted already, believed that household management was ideally suited to women's capabilities: they thrived on details instead of abstraction, and their work could be a school for economy, order, and taste.[51] The philosopher of marriage Debay wrote that the occupations and duties of family life were so serious that they pulled a mother away from frivolity and dissipation, the only other role he could imagine for women.[52] Delphine de Girardin, in a newspaper column, told her readers that the right feeling about her work could make a plain woman pretty, and she suggested such exercises as giving courage to an old man, patience to a

*After World War I, Margaret Mead and Rhoda Métraux found that a French wife still enjoyed much more power inside her home than an American one. It is interesting how the patterns hang on (Métraux and Mead, 41).

young husband, inspiration to a bored poet, or amusement to a sick child.[53]

The characteristic of good French housekeeping was economy, the careful counting of every penny, not only for food, but the cost of the fuel to cook it, and the saving of each valuable juice afterwards.* The French also used many more vegetables than the British, and more bread per person(400 pounds per year, compared to 330 in London). An English admirer, Frederic Marshall, calculated that small economies and lack of waste saved about a third of what a comparable English family would spend.[54] A German critic of this English writer pointed out that though his observation was exact, he failed to see the underlying philosophy, which was that such tiny economies, endlessly repeated, represented "organized rationalism."[55]

The French books of advice depended on such rationalism. The *Manuel complet de la maîtresse de maison* (1834) urged the housewife not only to budget and spend carefully, but also to schedule everybody's time. "In agreement with her husband," the mistress must set hours of sleep for everybody, have them wakened by alarm clocks in every room, remembering that women need more sleep than men, and children still more. The concern went at least back to the seventeenth century, when Fénelon's celebrated essay on women's education was mainly motivated by the desire to teach them how to run households effectively.

As for how much work French ladies did themselves, it was certainly more than the English and less than the Germans. Mrs. Gaskell's observed that a French girl would come to breakfast in negligée (not "the finished toilette of an English young lady"), but two hours later she would appear in a clean print gown, her hair brushed and plaited, and she would have helped Julie, the maid, to make her own bed, and would certainly have dusted her own room, while her mother went to market.[56]

In addition to their roles as mothers and household managers, Mmes de Ségur and Octave Feuillet also performed the duties of general overseer on their country estates, spending part of the day walking on the farm itself, talking to the workers, and checking the details to make sure everything was running smoothly.[57] Mme de Lamartine, whose adventures in marrying off her daughters have already been described, gives an enchanting picture of this sort of life in her *Confidences*. Like Mme de Ségur and Mme Feuillet, she performed varied jobs in the domestic and business aspects of the home, but on top of that, she managed to find time

---

*Blackwood's Magazine in 1874 stated that the average Parisian consumed 130 pounds of meat a year, while a Londoner would eat 211. These figures are not explained and seem extraordinary if the whole population is considered, but they may bear some relationship to what the upper classes ate and the relative proportions of the two nationalities' consumption. Mrs. Haweis's household in 1889 used meat at the rate of three pounds a day for four adults, and she figured that with what was lost in cooking, it would amount to a half-pound a day per person.

for offices like running a bureau for public welfare that helped fifteen thousand people in a single year.[58]

It seems that at many levels of society, exclusive probably of the highest nobility, women took an active part in making their homes attractive. Even women of great personal distinction and involvement with careers were interested in their houses too. Thus George Sand explained that housework could be a soothing occupation, and she felt that most women, including herself, found sewing a pleasant one.[59] As a bride Marie Curie studied housekeeping in order to be able to get it done well and quickly, so that the rest of her day would be free for long sessions in her laboratory. She used to go to market herself in those early days.[60]

The literature of housekeeping tended to keep it high in public esteem, as a true profession. Janet argued that it was what women made of it; they could regard it as a low occupation, a humiliating necessity, or a pleasurable duty to which they could devote passion, interest, and taste.[61]

Extensive sale of a work called *Maison rustique des dames* did much to create a class of women who were used to consulting scientific authority in their work.[62] The Librairie Agricole had long passed out household hints from the pen of a Mme Millet-Robinet, but when they decided to issue a complete manual in the 1870s, they enlisted the collaboration of a medical specialist, so as to give their readers both the delicacy of a woman and the science of a doctor. The collaborative work covered all aspects of household care: the duties of the mistress, the treatment of servants, the organization of time, attention to beauty in dress, the care of furniture, cleaning, lighting, laundry, preserving, cooking, and menu planning, with a list of foods suitable to different seasons. In a second volume were medical suggestions, including advice on how to tell if a doctor was needed, care of children, gymnastics and swimming, the garden, the farm, and management of farm animals and poultry. The preface urged the need for women's education in household arts as well as men's in improved agricultural methods. By the time she got around to the eighth edition, Mme Millet-Robinet commented on how many changes had been needed since the seventh (which was sold out rapidly), indicating that she always wished her readers to be at the forefront of progress. Mrs. Philip Hamerton found the book indispensable, even when her husband took her to live in a remote part of Scotland.[63] It is interesting to compare the French and English manuals—Millet-Robinet with Mrs. Beeton. The former seems to be both more comprehensive and more exact about the findings of science, while the latter relies more on the exposition of the tried and true. When universal compulsory schooling was established in France in the 1880s, the curriculum for girls of all ages included home economics, sewing, cooking, the care of the house, hygiene, child care, and laundry.[64]

Although as far as comfort was concerned, the British surpassed every other country, in elegance the laurels went to France. A French boudoir done up in pale blue satin might be the acme of taste and charm, but in England water would be piped up to the second story or even the third. In 1860 only one out of every hundred Paris homes had piped water.

Actually the whole basis of architecture was different. Some contemporary observers derived a theory of national character from the fact that the English preferred to divide up their houses vertically—one family, one house—while on the continent it was quite usual to divide families horizontally, so that in one *hôtel* (as they called it), families would rent accommodations in layers, with common use of stairways and halls, and the servants were all relegated to the common attic space.[65] (The English particularly disliked this feature of French life, and when they at last came around to accepting "flats" in London,[66] they made a point of keeping the servants of each family separate, fearful no doubt of gossip, and perhaps wishing to give their servants some of the privacy they so valued in their own lives.)[67]

Small flats had long been considered suitable in Paris, where families were smaller and there was less of a fetish for bathing.[68] In 1871 the Royal Institute of Architects in London heard a disquisition on French flats that explained their lesser need for water on the grounds that the French would wash with the corner of a wet towel, and concluded with the estimate that a French family could live in a quarter of the space used by the average English household.

When Frenchwomen looked for help from their men, the picture was less discouraging, if only slightly, than in other countries. Some of France's greatest men, like Dumas and Brillat-Savarin, were not ashamed to cook meals for their friends, proving that cooking at least was considered an art of which males need not be ashamed.[69] Books like *Monsieur, madame et bébé* also tended to make men feel that an interest in small children was not beneath their dignity. As servants became scarcer toward the end of the century, and as married women of the employing classes went out to find careers, they were faced with the same double responsibility that met the women of other countries. Even husbands who encouraged their wives to find careers usually proved unwilling to help with the work at home. After two world wars, however, we find that even though ladies have to scrub floors, their husbands will at least push baby carriages in public.[70]

∽ Italian women were not regularly commended for their expertise as mistresses of their households like the French, or exploited and pitied like the Germans, or even harangued about efficiency like the English. I suspect, though I cannot prove it, that their relationship to their cookstoves was neither so close as the German woman's nor so formal as the English. Their minds seemed to be on other things. But it is clear from Malvina Frank's essay for young women about to be married that there existed very little training for marriage and house management, and the lack led Cecilia de Luna, a feminist, to cry out that before women's powers could be freed, a complete change in housekeeping routines would have to be instituted.*

English tourists regularly railed at the lack of system in Italian households. A possible, partial, explanation may be embodied in Samuel Laing's hint that because fuel was not needed to keep houses warm, it was cheaper to eat out and not waste it at home just for cooking.[71] Since men went to restaurants freely, while women were left at home to pick up snacks, a gross separation of the sexes ensued, deplored by the indefatigable Lady Morgan.[72] Frances Power Cobbe described the average middle-class Italian matron as spending her days "half-helping, half-scolding, half-gossiping with her maids," with hours spent gazing out of the window and exchanging comments with the maid next door.[73] What she may not have fully understood was that these maids were often brought into a family as children of ten or twelve, grew up and lived in intimacy with their mistresses, and expected to serve all their lives in the same place. In middle-class Roman houses, the husband commonly dealt with the servants and arranged for the delivery of supplies, while in richer homes they often hired an *abbé* who would combine the duties of *major domo* with those of tutor to the children.[74]

At the Women's Exposition held at Florence in 1889 the speaker on the family described the old-fashioned housewife, obedient to her spouse, dedicated to the care of her children, a busy maker of jelly and sausage, but with a limited mind; she did not read, could not follow her husband's conversation with his friends, and in fact was proud of that fact. At the same time, intellectual Italian women did not wish to be reproached for neglect of their household duties, and their ideal was to balance brain work with good household management,[75] as was done by Erminia Fusinato, a poet and a director of a higher school for girls. We are told that in Florence in 1876 she attended a conference on social hygiene and heard Luigi Chierici lecture on "Woman and Her Pretended Emancipation." A few days later he went to call on her, and as she started looking through her desk to find a particular piece of paper, something fluttered to the floor. It turned out to be her laundry list. "Ah, there," cried Chierici, "was a woman usefully and wisely emancipated."[76]

∽ The possibility that a time would come when people would refuse to enter domestic service seemed like a cloud no bigger than a man's hand at mid-century, but in 1849 the *Westminster Review* published an article foretelling just such a dire future. Ladies would have to meet the crisis, it

---

*In 1909 Lady Duff-Gordon compared Mrs. Beeton with the Italian manual of her day by Signor Pellegrino Artusi. The chief difference she noticed was that the Italian book recommended all fresh ingredients, while the English writer devoted considerable space to using leftovers (Duff-Gordon, 70).

said, either by greater self-dependence or by the use of mechanical appliances.[77]

As for self-dependence, Augusta Webster mused about what it would be like if housewives did all their own work. It would clearly bring about a revolution in social life, with much less time spent on dressing and paying calls, less table service, and earlier mealtimes. She feared that the unhappy consequence would be to separate ladies even more from their husbands' companionship and to curtail their time for study, art, or music.*[78]

The question would not go away, however, especially as during the latter part of the century certain groups began to question the morality of employing domestic help. Luise Otto, the founder of the German women's movement, asserted in 1876 that living without servants was the only basis for true emancipation and a very worthwhile goal.[79] In England the Fabian socialists came up against the problem early in their debates when one of their members, Marjorie Davidson, asked whether it was right for her to employ a maid. Sidney Olivier hastened to assure her that so long as she worked full time as a teacher, she simply could not do her own housework and cooking. He proposed using an unmarried and presumably unpaid relative, if one could be found, or else a proletarian worker, but in order to prove that socialists honored physical labor, the servant should eat at the family table.[80] (Reports from visitors in a few households where this was tried indicated that it caused visible social strain on both sides.)†

Perhaps Frenchwomen, who have been shown to be the most adept housewives, managed servantless houses the best. Wally Zepler told German socialists in 1909 that there was quite a dearth of maids in Paris at that time, but that professional women, such as journalists, loved to boast of how well they kept up their houses, partly by simplifying the work and eliminating heavy draperies and hard-to-clean furniture coverings. Even before 1900 Frenchwomen were also thinking about appliances—the other part of the *Westminster Review*'s prescription. One housewife is quoted as saying, "But with electricity it is all done so quickly. Crack, a button."[81]

In 1876 Luise Otto took a long look at the changes in household routines during her lifetime, most of them due to industrial processes carried on outside the home: factories that knit stockings on machines, commercial laundries, gas lighting on the streets and for houses.[82] She

---

*Men who urge girls to learn how to cook, explained Miss Emily Davies, do not realize "that if mistresses are to do the cooking, masters must dine alone. Dinners cannot be cooked an hour beforehand, and left to serve themselves" (Emily Davies, 46).

†In 1902 Edith Nesbit, a Fabian herself, wrote an entertainment called *The Red House* about a young couple—he a writer, she an illustrator—who inherit a large house and who find much more fun in the dishwashing, paperhanging, and gardening than in their professional work. It is "play," they explain, because "it is not what one ought to be doing," but it comes to be their full-time occupation. One might add that only in England could it be what women, at least, were not supposed to be doing.

remembered the enormous amounts of time spent cleaning the old-fashioned lamps, and that before the days of matches it sometimes took a maid half an hour to get one lighted. It seemed only reasonable to expect the continuation of such progress. In 1889 Mrs. Haweis was recommending "one of the easy and economical washing machines."[83] Feminists, naturally, all approved these hopes, even though certain men felt endangered. Fritz Berolzheimer, about 1914, worried that vacuum cleaners and like helps would merely free women's hands for an "American" type of extravagance and enable them to take up sports, and that then they would disparage their marriages.*[84]

By far the most radical proposals for lifting the burden of housework from women's shoulders were the many plans for communal living, part of the agenda of most socialist groups and of a few individual women who wished to get on with their careers. The German feminist Hedwig Dohm, writing in 1873, foresaw a future of communal kitchens where those who really loved to cook could do it for everybody; where communal laundries could make it easy to keep linen clean; where children would be cared for in kindergartens. Then other women could concentrate on other sorts of work.[85] Even the individualistic Augusta Webster examined thoughtfully the possibilities of cooperative housekeeping to save money and trouble, although she concluded that the English liking for complete separation of each family's life from the rest of the world would militate against such a solution in her country.[86]

Housework was one of the many things whose effect on women's progress could be either positive or negative. If managing a household well is an executive and responsible job, then it is reasonable to believe that the training women received here carried over to the professional jobs they moved into. The same process is visible today when middle-aged women entering the job market are urged to consider their unpaid work for family and community as an asset to be vaunted. Caring for a home could be a valuable experience, but its demands and its limitations often bound women to the past, and from this past neither mechanical appliances nor socialist regrouping provided a completely satisfactory escape.

*Winwood Reade in 1872 projected three inventions, expected to be forthcoming soon, that he declared would make women truly the companions of men: a less cumbrous motor to take the place of steam, the conquest of flight, and the creation in laboratories of unlimited quantities of synthetic foods (Reade, 513–14). At the time, the book was felt to be wild and hysterical, but when it was reissued in 1909, the editor pointed out that electric and gasoline motors had come into use, the conquest of the air had just been achieved, and science had greatly improved the yield of most grain foods, even if not in the laboratory. Still more hopeful, he felt, would be the direct use of solar energy, and he directed his readers' attention to an article in the *Anthenaeum* for July 31, 1909, in which the projects that had already been devised to use it were described. Unfortunately this article does not consider ways to use sun power for household tasks.

∾10.

To Have and To Hold

Women have served all these
centuries as looking-glasses
possessing the magic and delicious
power of reflecting the figure of
the man at twice its natural size.
                    Virginia Woolf, 1929

Some states of Europe, before or during the nineteenth century, abolished laws for general male stewardship over all women, but all of them retained some form of the peculiar power of husbands over their wives. It was pointed out that this power was the only form of guardianship that was not based on the incapability of the ward and that did not have the purpose of protecting his welfare. A man could be brought to justice for neglecting his children's health, property, or education, but there was no such check on a husband's prerogatives over his wife.[1]

It is, nevertheless, a truism that the law does not usually reflect the actual behavior of people: it merely defines certain limits. Modern sociologists believe that the distribution of power between two spouses reflects directly the comparative resources that each one brings from the outside world.[2] Such assets as inherited money, status, and education all count, and so, of course, does employment with its double bonus of income and status. What is rather surprising in the sociological findings is that membership in organizations weighs as heavily as outside employment. Almost any sort of organization has this effect—church groups, charitable service, political or cultural organizations, or even sports clubs. Furthermore, the more deeply women become involved in such activities, the greater, as a rule, is their satisfaction with marriage.

If the most important consequence of the Industrial Revolution for family life was the separation of the man's workplace from his home, it can be seen that this affected his marital power in two opposite ways. While it lessened his ability to impose discipline on the spot, at the same time his involvement outside the home increased his authority. Women, who were left at home, could not fully take advantage of their husbands' absence to take charge of things because they lacked this outside reinforcement. Or, as Horkheimer pointed out some years ago, the impulse of submission comes more from the structure of the family than from whether the husband employs coercion or kindness.[3] In a word, the confinement in their homes could be a cause as well as a result of their marital submissiveness, even while it offered some wives a first taste of autonomy.

This analysis demonstrates the importance of a woman's having a dowry or a job, and the change in status that accrues to her from working outside her home, or joining a church or the women's movement, or undertaking charitable work. This fact was perceived by various nineteenth-century observers, though without the panoply of science. Thus Louis Larcher in 1860 believed that Frenchwomen's near equality with their husbands stemmed from their frequent involvement in business, whereas Englishwomen, who did not work in this way, were in his view enslaved.[4] In 1896 Bulling, a German lawyer, observed that just because women's "natural calling" was one entirely lacking in outside contacts, men must compensate by insisting that their wives share in all the husband's privileges and pleasures.[5]

There is considerable evidence that husbands' power weakened significantly during the nineteenth century, and this was very largely thanks to a change in manners and in people's minds. The new laws that were passed to protect women's rights were both a sign of this change and a victory for militant women,

By mid-century Herbert Spencer was telling his readers that "the desire to command is essentially a barbarous desire,"[6] and he discussed at length the change that he believed civilization was working in men's sentiments. He described how a man of refined feeling would strive to put his poorer neighbors at their ease, encouraging them to be less submissive and more self-respecting. (Such a man even says "please" and "thank you" to domestics!) With his friends he shuns the appearance of anything in the form of supremacy. Thus there would be nothing utopian in supposing that this delicacy, which had come into existence between men, could now carry over into married life. For himself, he declared that if he were to marry he would forget, if he could not destroy, the legal bond. For some men courtesy may have been only skin-deep, but others truly renounced the supremacy that the law gave them because they no longer felt comfortable in that position.

In 1912 the question of whether submission should be held as the *only* duty of a wife to a husband was debated within the church of England.[7] It was proposed that the marriage service be revised so as to leave out the word "obey," and perhaps that the final exhortation copied from Saint Paul, outlining a wife's obligations, be changed. The Dean of Winchester explained that civilization had moved ahead since the Book of Common Prayer had been composed, and that other passages of scripture could be drawn on to emphasize the new, higher ideal, but since the Dean of Canterbury felt that to challenge the apostle was a "somewhat alarming and distressing principle," the changes were not in fact approved.

Thus though the law and the church held back the emancipation of women, other factors moved it along. It is time to look at the way marital power was exercised in countries with varying traditions.

ᑎᔭ "When a Frenchwoman gets married, her good time begins; when an Englishwoman gets married her good time is over."[8] So declared a French observer in 1884. He was commenting on something many others had noticed: the striking contrast between English and French wives. English girls seemed to go from freedom to dependence, while the French bride won a thousand liberties by the mere fact of being married.*

Several factors entered into this set of conditions. I intend to take up some general aspects first, and then go into the way in which decisions about money and the household were actually made within the families of the different countries.

First of all, there was an interesting and subtle difference in the legal status of women. Although the man was greatly favored in the laws of both France and England, in the latter a married couple was treated as one person, a concept that, taken literally, meant that the wife could not own *anything* (not even her clothes) until the first Married Women's Property Act of 1870, and certainly she could not sue at law or sign a valid contract. As expressed in Blackstone: "By marriage the husband and wife are one person in law; that is, the very being or legal existence of the woman is suspended during marriage, or at least is incorporated into that of the husband. . . ."†[9]

The Napoleonic Code, by contrast, never lost sight of the legal personality of the woman. True, she owed "obedience" to her husband, while he only owed "protection" to her, but though she was, so to speak, a minority stockholder, she still had a voice; and though her husband could administer her estate, he could not sell her dower property without her consent.

Even more important than what the law said abstractly was the practical effect of the French dowry system. Economic weight adds a mysterious reinforcement to personality, and contemporaries were very clear about what a bit of money could do for a woman.[10] Frenchmen lived in the belief that a dowry was "the best defense of feminine equality"[11] and that it would increase the likelihood of love between a couple, since property is a more permanent interest than romantic love.

We have noted that by law the property of a French family had to be

---

*Tocqueville had said that American women lost their independence forever in the bonds of matrimony, indicating that they followed the Anglo-Saxon pattern.

†Compare Alexander Herzen's letter to his fiancée, Natalie: "In my embrace your separate existence will disappear, in my love all your needs, all your thoughts will be drowned. . . . You are *I*; Alexander and Natalie do not form a *WE*, but only my own *I*. My *I* is full, for you have been completely swallowed up; and *you* no longer exist" (Carr, 21). Herzen was a Europeanized Russian.

distributed equally among the children, girls as well as boys, and this practice gave the girls, as they grew up, an equal interest in the family fortune. English girls had no such expectation. Their marriages, based upon "idealized sex," were not supposed to be sullied by financial cares, and girls were to remain above such things even while their fiancés struggled to make money to marry on. Frenchmen regularly blamed the secondary position of the English wife on her lack of a portion, and sometimes even wondered if Englishmen might be so eager to be complete masters in their homes that they actually *preferred* not to receive a dowry, in view of the independence it would confer upon the woman.

Bringing property (by dower or inheritance) into a marriage did not mean, of course, that the woman retained the right to manage, but Mona Caird—admittedly something of a man-hater—noticed that one seldom heard of bad treatment toward a woman who had private means, and that when a wife came into money you could see a sudden difference as her husband gave unconscious recognition to her new importance.[12] This was true even though the husband could control both the capital and the income of his wife's estate. In England, two Married Women's Property acts of 1870 and 1882 put certain limits on that control. Before that time the wife's parents might try to protect her by setting up a fund with trustees to manage for her, but to do this only increased the separation of interests between the spouses, which was the direct opposite of the effect the French attributed to their dowry system.*

A third difference underlying the marriage systems of the two countries is embodied in Salvador de Madariaga's remark that the English trusted individuals, while the French did not.[13] The English seemed to care more about the happiness or autonomy of particular people, and even inside the family preferred to let decisions be made by one person, without consultation, whether it was a young person choosing a husband or wife, or the father of a family ruling the budget for everybody. Within the French family far more of a group process was at work, and their joint efforts were commonly devoted to furthering the welfare of the family and its fortunes through generations.

It is obvious that while a woman's personality could be submerged under either system, under the French she had much more chance to take part in a family democracy and to give her counsel in matters that would affect the whole group. In contrast, in England one who wanted to express herself often had to break away completely and assert her indi-

*In France there were three ways to make up a marriage contract. In the South, under old Roman law, the traditional form was the "dotal" regime, which put the woman's estate in the hands of trustees (Gide, 490). Even there, in the middle part of the nineteenth century, lawyers worked to make the contract more like one for a joint partnership. Social philosophers, however, much preferred the system of "community property," the usual pattern in the north of France, stemming from the old common law. It created a fusion of interests that was especially suitable to the more active bourgeois classes who wanted to give women an equal share in family life. The third system, which became increasingly popular, was one of complete separation of goods.

viduality by making decisions for herself alone, and this individualism turned out to be a stepping stone to wider liberation when women had the courage to assert themselves.

It is perhaps worth noting that the Victorians' notion of what constituted psychological maturity was distinctly different from ours. For them it was a matter of taking responsibility for other people, for reciprocal duties and obligations nobly borne. For us it is more likely independence and self-sufficiency. For them the lieutenant could die for his men, or the slave demonstrate the highest qualities of Christian manhood by sacrificing himself for his master: equal moral credit was given to both of these acts. Today it is hard to praise *noblesse oblige* without seeming elitist, while "Uncle Tomism" is a term of reproach. For the Victorians, marriage was one of these mutualities, with reciprocal rather than parallel duties and performances. It took them a long time to give up the idea that woman's role was different, even while they strove to have it accepted as equal in value. This was assuredly a slippery slope to climb.

∽ "An English father is absolute master in his own house; something of the father of antiquity,"[14] said Max O'Rell. As was noticed in the preceding chapter, when Flora Tristan came to England in the 1830s she was astonished to find that ordinary Englishwomen were not the mistresses in their own homes as Frenchwomen were, but that the husbands held both the purse and the keys.[15] The master budgeted, he dismissed servants, he ordered the meals and issued invitations. And he alone decided the fate of the children. The persistence of this pattern is shown in Elizabeth Haldane's family. Growing up in the seventies, Elizabeth was made to feel grateful to her father for his kindness in providing, while her mother was to be regarded on a more spiritual level. Although Mrs. Haldane had money of her own, she never received any of it except through her husband, and though she no doubt ordered dinner, it was the master of the house who examined the books and paid the bills and the servants' wages. Maurice Baring recalls his father's summoning the cook each morning after breakfast to order the dinner—this in the eighties.*[16]

In the thirties Cobbett, who loved to share his experience of life with his many readers, made a list of things he thought the man should decide, and another for the woman. To the husband went the responsibility for choosing what calling he should follow, what house they should live in, what scale of expense and style of living was right, what was to be done with the property, how and where to educate the children, what *their* callings were to be, who was to be employed in the household (he was thinking in terms of a tradesman's or artisan's household, where perhaps there would be apprentices as well as domestic servants), what principles should be adopted by the family on public affairs, and whom to

*Even so late as 1927 a study of English character demonstrated that the mistress of the ménage was less likely than in France to be the one who really ran the house.

have for friends. The wife's assignments were limited to what to have for dinner, how to furnish the house, and how to manage the day-to-day work of the domestic servants.[17]

Cobbett was not the only Englishman who liked to make lists. When Charles Kingsley was going to be married, he wrote to his fiancée outlining the rule of life they should live by; he prepared a schedule of duties including family prayers, a regular time for casting up accounts (which should never be mentioned at other times), time for work, time for study, and the evening assignment—"we will draw, and feed the intellect and the fancy."[18] Similarly, when J. A. Froude was engaged, he busily asked advice on household and kitchen because "Charlotte knows nothing."[19]

Obviously such a pattern of masculine management could become oppressive. Lord Berners describes the position of his insane grandfather. The old man would sit in a dark room all day, groaning and cursing, but at mealtimes he always sat at the head of the table, even when they had visitors, and he was taken to church every Sunday even though once he cursed so loud that the service had to be terminated.[20] The patriarchal idea was so inflexible that he was treated as head of the house as long as he could stand on two legs. Even John Bright, a good Quaker, felt that his sisters had no right to hang on to money inherited from their father if it could be used to help the brothers in business.

Among the more famous male-mastered households was that of Thomas Carlyle, who kept his brilliant wife "like a caged mockingbird,"[21] unaware that this seemingly natural arrangement crippled talents that might have been as great as his own. In sum, many homes must have resembled the one George Crabbe pictured in 1812 in Jonas Kindred's household, and its "peace":

> Yet not that peace some favoured mortals find
> In equal views and harmony of mind;
> Not the soft peace that blesses those who love,
> Where all with one consent in union move;
> But it was that which one superior will
> Commands, by making all inferiors still;
> Who bids all murmurs, all objections cease,
> And with imperious voice announces—Peace![22]

Even as late as 1889, Professor Alfred Marshall, in a dinner conversation at the house of Beatrice Webb's father, held that if women were not subordinate, body and soul, there would be no reason for a man to sacrifice his freedom and marry. He thought that contrast was the essential element in marriage and, evidently, that the only worthwhile contrast was between a master and his submissive helpmate.[23]

On the other hand, not every example of womanly "submission" was a response to masculine "tyranny." The subtleties of relationship cannot be defined so simply. Robert Browning's poem "A Woman's Last Word" (1855) describes a situation that some commentators have taken as an example of capitulation at its worst. A couple who have had a dispute are in bed together. The woman is frightened. The question is: does she feel dominated, or is she rather hurt at having a precious relationship torn?

> Let's contend no more, Love,
>   Strive nor weep—
> All be as before, Love,
>   —Only sleep!
>
> . . . .
>
> Teach me, only teach, Love!
>   As I ought
> I will speak thy speech, Love,
>   Think thy thought—
>
> Meet, if thou require it,
>   Both demands,
> Laying flesh and spirit
>   In thy hands!

Maurice Cramer, who has analyzed the poem in detail, urges a closer look. The woman is after all, he points out, managing the affair, making the decisive choice as to how the situation will end. And at the end of the poem she will set her own time for doing it. Far from being a cowed mush of concession, she is an adroit peacemaker. Cramer reminds his readers that Browning may have been expressing his own gratitude to Elizabeth Barrett here: there had been a time in their courtship when he "acted with such incredible stupidity that only Elizabeth's heart . . . saved them from catastrophe."[24]

The main secret of man's domination of the household was his control of money. As we have seen, the husband had the legal power to do anything he wished with his wife's money, her landed property alone excepted—and the nineteenth century was the period in which landed property declined in importance relative to other forms of wealth, a change that had not been envisioned when the arrangements were first drawn up in the Middle Ages. But as late as the eighteenth century, women had apparently been freer to earn or spend money on their own.

Even though Lady Sydney Morgan had earned and handled her own money for years before her marriage, and even though her marriage contract stipulated that the £5,000 that she had saved was to be under her control,[25] when she wanted a greenhouse behind the stairs of her house in 1831, and offered to pay for it, her husband vowed that she should never have it. The ultimate disposition of the affair is not clear. Her comment was, "Upon this occasion I am a bore, and he is—a bear."[26]

One rationalization was that women had no training in the use of money, thus providing the menfolk with an excuse not to entrust them with any. Mrs. Ellis even apologized for including in her treatise for young women advice on pecuniary honesty, imagining that her readers would protest that they had so *very* little to spend, so very little to do with money.[27] At the time of her marriage Annie Besant had never so much as bought herself a pair of gloves.[28]

Certainly many husbands thought that managing finances was a friendly as well as a suitable service. William Gaskell, for example, took charge of all the money his wife earned from her popular novels as part of his natural duties as husband.[29] The couple had a deep mutual affection; he encouraged her to write and left her free to do so; yet she told her publisher that she had never made out a check for herself. She was without funds at one time when he went off to Ireland, for he had left the checkbook locked up, and even when he was at home she could not subscribe to a desired journal but had to read discarded library copies. When the Married Women's Property Bill was being agitated in 1856, she gladly signed the petition in its favor.

In the case of a less well known woman writer, Mrs. Margaret Gatty, the checks for her popular children's books went straight into the household budget, and she never handled the money again.[30] But the day her daughter, Juliana, later Mrs. Ewing, earned *her* first check, about 1857, and her father's hand went out for it, everyone marveled at her temerity when she stated that she had decided to keep it.

Some husbands gave their wives housekeeping allowances, but even among the very rich many of those sums were notable for their inadequacy. In 1849, when her husband was taking in £3,800 a year, Lady Eddisbury begged for a bigger allowance than the £100 alloted her. "I never bought a pretty thing in my life,"[31] she cried, and yet she was in debt because it cost her £140 to live. She traced *all* the troubles of her married life to want of money.

One of the difficulties in the Duke of Wellington's unhappy marriage was that his wife would not spend the housekeeping money he gave her the way he thought she should, and she refused to follow his orders about the servants. He accused her of "misappropriating" his funds by lending money to her brother, and when she asked for a raise, from £500 to £670 per annum, he flatly refused. He told her that the amount she was getting was generous, that only princesses had more.[32]

Similar tales come from Miss Weeton, a governess, whose rich employer was himself "master, mistress, housekeeper"[33] while his wife was penniless; and from Leslie Stephen's daughter Vanessa, who kept house for him in his old age (he died in 1904) and who had to enter into collusion with the cook to falsify the accounts because he accused her of overspending.[34] Jane Carlyle, with her usual wit, once presented her husband with a "Budget of a Femme Incomprise," explaining the inflation in food prices and suggesting that though she could cut her dress expenditures, she would still lack money for wages and candles.[35]

One of the books that depressed Florence Nightingale in her years of seeking a vocation was called *Anna: or Passages in the Life of a*

Daughter at Home. In it she read that women sometimes wondered why they were not allowed to diminish the luxury of their own dress, or impose upon themselves a simple privation, in order to use the money for a charitable cause.[36] They were to be assured that Father Knows Best. Or as Lord Fraser put it in the House of Lords debate on the Second Married Women's Property Bill in 1881, "The protection which has been thrown around a married woman already is sufficient, and why she should be allowed to have money in her pocket to deal with as she sees fit I cannot understand."[37]

By this time, to be sure, such ideas had begun to seem old-fashioned, and the bill was passed in spite of him. On the other hand, there is much evidence that for the first part of the century at least, women not only acquiesced in the system but often embraced it. Richard Burton's wife, Isabel, whose elopement has been mentioned, wrote a set of "Rules for My Guidance as a Wife" that deserves to be placed opposite the list already mentioned from Kingsley as a husband. Among her rules were such reminders as: never refuse Richard anything he asks, and never let anyone speak disrespectfully of him.[38] Lady Dufferin, we are told, was an active and independent lady when by herself, but she rose when her husband entered the room, never called him by his Christian name, and would cease speaking the moment he appeared.[39] Another active and intelligent woman, anything but immature in her perceptions of life during her career as a teacher before she was married, and as mother afterward, described how she felt at her wedding: "On the arm of an ideal brother I was walking to an ideal husband."[40] She had insisted that the word "obey" be in her vows, and tells us that she was full of pleasure at the idea that she no longer had to order other people's lives, but would "be ordered" herself. She agreed warmly with the proposition that one of the pleasantest things about married life is *not* having money of one's own, but having to go to one's husband for every sixpence.*[41]

One small point should be made clear: upper-middle-class women

---

*It may be worth quoting Mrs. Ellis's advice, even more sanctimonious than usual:

> It is here, the privilege of a married woman to be able to show, by the most delicate attentions, how much she feels her husband's superiority to herself, not by mere personal services officiously rendered, as if for the purpose of display, but by a respectful reference to his opinion, a willingly imposed silence when he speaks, and, if he be an enlightened man, by a judicious turn sometimes given to the conversation, so that his information and intelligence may be drawn forth for the benefit of others. [Sarah Ellis, *Wives*, 33–34]

Mrs. Ellis wrote confidently for her female audience in 1843. Thirty years later the drive toward feminine equality spearheaded by John Stuart Mill had assumed such menacing proportions that Leslie Stephen addressed a predominantly male readership with the heavy guns of philosophy. In a dispute between husband and wife, he announced, "the wife ought to give way. She ought to obey her husband, and carry out the view at which he deliberately arrives, just as, when the captain gives the word to cut away the masts, the lieutenant carries out his orders at once, though he may be a better seaman and may disapprove of them" (Leslie Stephen, 197).

were made to feel that earning money of their own was distinctly vulgar.* This was probably partly to set themselves apart from lower-class women, who sometimes did help their husbands in a shop or craft, and, of course, from millions of working-class wives who labored in factories. In fact, the *Edinburgh Review* for April 1859 expressed astonishment at the amount of female industry disclosed at the hearings of the recently established divorce court, where it seemed that the majority of aggrieved wives could prove that they had actually supported their husbands.[42] But this was not the way of the ideal upper-middle-class household.

The notion that women should be trusted to spend money grew with the passing years, however, as Englishwomen came more into command of their own households. Mrs. Haweis described the process rather charmingly to her daughter: "Penny by penny your father built up his income, to give his children that 'good education', which is said to be, but is not always, a sufficient panoply for the battle of life. Penny by penny I have guarded the store, with self-denial laying out what his self-denial laid by. When you were a wee child, penny by penny you asked for little pleasures, which it was a pleasure to give you. . . ."[43] (This description of the Haweis family is touching but not accurate, for the Reverend Haweis kept them all in debt, while Mrs. Haweis created a new profession for women, that of interior decorating, and earned money for the support of all the family.)

It seems, then, that after a long period of separation from the management of both their money and their homes, Englishwomen gradually obtained more control. An important step for improvement in English marriage would be having money entirely of their own; the first legislative changes, ardently campaigned for, were the two acts of Parliament (1870, 1882) allowing married women more control over their inherited or earned money. One of the first women to profit by the new law was Elizabeth Garrett Anderson, England's first woman doctor, who stipulated at the time of her marriage in 1871 that her earnings should be her own.[44]

∞ If visitors were taken aback by the inferior position of English wives, foreign reaction to French home life regularly stressed the superiority of the woman's position compared with that of other countries, often by using similes derived from monarchical privilege. As early as 1830, an Italian named Mothe-Langon who used the *nom de plume* Lanfranchi, stated that women were "sovereign" everywhere, in the noble *faubourg*, in the banker's house, and at the merchant's counter.[45] The French husband was alleged not to be allowed to have anything to do with linen, silver, furniture, even his own clothes. He was kept ignorant,

---

*While the proceeds of her children's books went into the charge of her husband, Mrs. Gatty kept the money she earned from her hobby, a scientific study of seaweeds, for charity. In no way would she keep money to enrich herself (Maxwell, 100).

according to this Italian, of the price of groceries, did not know what he would have for dinner until the plates appeared before him, did not know the names of his guests until they were presented. Possibly this was an exaggeration, but in almost equally strong terms Frederic Marshall, forty years later, called the woman's "reign" absolute in the drawing room, in the direction of the family, and in the management of the children, though he noted that this rule seldom extended to opinions on public questions.[46] Forty years later still, in 1910, Miss Betham explained that the reason Frenchwomen could reign unchallenged in the household was that they did not fritter away their mental and physical energies, as Englishwomen did, on social and political committees, sports, or church work.[47] One last testimony to the "almost total royalty" exercised by the French wife came from Julien Benda, in whose own Jewish home a different pattern obtained, so that it was only when he began to move in larger circles that he was struck with the importance generally attached to women's responsibilities in France.[48]

Women's maiden names survived more often after marriage, so that many French couples hyphenated the wife's surname into the husband's, and the linen and silver would be marked with both initials.[49] Even when the wife's name was not doubled with the man's, she would be referred to as "Madame de B., *née* de C."

Taine may have put his finger on it when he attributed this quality of French life to their feeling about equality in general. Equality, he stated, was "almost complete" between parents and children, husband and wife, the oldest and the youngest, noble and commoner, rich and poor.[50] This did not mean, of course, that everyone had identical responsibilities, but merely that in face-to-face intercourse Frenchmen were more willing to listen to all parties without the sense of ritualized hierarchy that might interfere with free discussion in England or Germany. In France, hard decisions were made with the consent of all concerned parties, said Emile Boutmy, and the French wife, with her clear head and judgment, was a wise counselor. He had to admit, however, that the English system, where the father took command, did get things done faster.[51]

Of course, when it came to total disagreement the wife would have to give in. It was explained that this was just like the husband's having to give in to his superior at the office, but the whole French nation lived by the principle of administration and by an instinct for harmony that Mme Thérèse Blanc explained as being diametrically opposed to the development of individuality.[52] (The American Albert Rhodes buttressed this opinion when he declared that "angular, strong-minded" women did not exist in France.)[53] In the distribution of roles, the father had the duty to administer and augment the patrimony of his ancestors and his wife's dowry, while she had undisputed care of the interior of the house and the education of her daughters.[54] These roles were considered so non-interfering that the spectators at a wedding would regularly show by their smiles that they understood the irony of bride's having to promise obedience.*[55]

Michelet believed that more than those of any other nation, Frenchwomen were ready to second their men and to become not only *compagnes* but *compagnons*† of their husbands, and that such relationships led to prosperity in the commercial classes and to broad mutual discussion of ideas in official ones.[56]

The very fact that she had not won her husband through erotic attraction meant, in Henry Bulwer-Lytton's opinion, that the French bride was able to enter at once into his pecuniary and intellectual interests.[57] In spite of her sheltered girlhood, we are told that within a month after her marriage any young Frenchwoman could entertain a cabinet minister, or, if in a more humble sphere, manage the shop; and this ability to take part in business was one of the clearest differences between her and her English counterpart. Laing, another Englishman, felt that "females" in France occupied "a higher and more rational social position certainly than with us," and that they often took over "the thinking and managing department in family affairs."[58] Michelet felt that it was a young husband's job to initiate his wife into full appreciation of his business, and the women could be capable of great effort. He gave as an example Mme Pouchet, who helped her physiologist husband discover the human egg.[59] He also described the wife of a shopkeeper in the Rue des Lombards who passed her life at a desk, giving orders to twenty younger men while her husband ran around all day on business. When he came home at night, they would go upstairs together. No union was stronger, said Michelet: did he love her? No, but he adored her.[60] Such employment in shops and offices was almost universal.‡ Julie Daubié reported in 1866 that fewer than three million French wives (out of about seven million married women) lived solely on the income of their husbands' work; the others contributed by their dowries, and also by their own labor.[61]

This ability of the sexes to work together to increase the property was not evident in English and German families, at least in the opinion of

---

*Métraux and Mead noticed just after World War I that Frenchwomen's earnings were seen as replacing a dowry, not as trespassing on the male sphere of major earner. They felt that French women detested asking for money and enjoyed earning the money for their own purchases rather than having to ask for it (Métraux and Mead, 38).

†Not only consorts but companions of their husbands.

‡In 1840 there were 1.4 million little shops in France, mostly run by a couple, and a few of them made it big. Mme Marguerite Boucicaut, with her husband Aristide, began with a very small boutique of novelties and by 1869 had an empire—*Au Bon Marché*—employing thousands of young girls as clerks, a new role for women (Decaux, 9: 100–101). When Pasteur needed funds to set up a research institute, he called on Mme Boucicaut. She went to her desk and handed him a folded check, which he took, and he bowed and went out. Only later did he see that it was for a million gold francs. He returned to thank her and burst into tears, and so did she (Burnand, 1870, 176).

Karl Hillebrand, and the difference often showed up after the husband's death, when Frenchwomen were able to keep on with the business, as the many signs over shop doors saying *"Veuve une Telle"* indicated.[62] Englishwomen left in reduced circumstances had to become companions or governesses.*

Naturally there were vehement French feminists who held out for keeping the woman's property completely separate and for training girls in jobs outside the family enterprise. Some of them felt that the girls were coming to hate their dowries and the ties that these created. Chantepie wrote a treatise against the dowry in 1861, asserting that the most important social reform he could think of would be to suppress the woman's privilege of making a life on its basis instead of by working.[63] But this radical idea found few converts at the time, and several strong opponents. Jürgen Meyer considered France the country offering the least inducement for the emancipation of women, and it was apparently true that family-style democracy gave them enough sense of responsibility and participation in a common life to keep them relatively happy, and to endow the nation with considerable social cohesion.

∽ As for Germans, let Heine speak first: "German marriage is no true marriage. The husband has no wife, but a serving-maid, and he still goes on living his intellectually isolated life even in the midst of his family."[64] This relationship was codified in the laws of many of the small states, such as the provision of the Saxon Code that allowed the husband to require a wife to perform her housekeeping duties. One assumes that such provisions did not often need enforcement by the police power of the state, but at the same time the husband was empowered to make household decisions. Even the modernized imperial Civil Code of 1900 gave the man of the house the right to fire the maid.[65]

Foreign women visitors usually got the impression that German housewives lived like upper-class servants, and as a proof of this inferior position they adduced the practice of giving butter only to the master of the house and guests, none to the wife and children.[66] Mayhew believed that German men spent far too much money—sometimes half their incomes—outside the house, on beer, tobacco, and gambling, and he contrasted their houses with English ones, where the money was spent on household comforts. German ladies told Mayhew that while English married couples strolled arm-in-arm, they themselves were used to staying behind with the children while the husband walked on ahead.[67]

Early in the twentieth century, Irma von Troll-Borostyáni was

---

*Herbert Spencer: ". . . among shopkeepers in England [the housewife] is not required to take so large a share in the business as she is among shopkeepers in France. . . ." Spencer considered this an advantage for England, where women could be kept clean of mercenary affairs; he could only believe that the French were forcing women into them (Spencer, *Principles*, 1: 741).

visiting in an Austrian country house and watched while the fourteen-year-old son ordered his sister to pull off his boots. When she refused, he demanded that she be deprived of supper. He explained that the servants were either busy or clumsy, and that naturally he could not get his own hands dirty—but that he would certainly know how to train his wife.[68] She then quoted Goethe's story of a man who met a coquette at a social gathering and remarked, "I would like to marry her, so I could beat her."[69]

Old German law generally permitted corporal chastisement by the husband of a wife, a parent of a child, a teacher of a pupil, and the head of a house of the servants. The rule in Hamburg was that the man could decide how much was proper.[70] The practice was certainly more usual in the lower than the upper classes, although Mayhew declared that wife beating was "as common in Saxony" as it was "exceptional in England,"[71] and he went on to reveal that until the 1860s, a husband could take his wife to the police station to be beaten, and that a pair of linen drawers was kept on hand there for this purpose.* To its credit the imperial Civil Code abolished the right of wife beating.

For the ordinary middle-class woman, even if she was not beaten, life was a ceaseless round of drudgery. "For the wife the baking and brewing, for the husband the cakes and ale; for her the toiling and spinning, for him the beer and skittles; for her the sheep-walk of precedent and the stocking of virtue, for him the paradings and prancings; for her the nippings and screwings, for him the pipings and dancings; for her the dripping-jar and the meal-tub, for him the stars and garters, and general gallooning, glitter and sublimity."†[72]

Max Weber's mother, Helene, had inherited enough money in 1885 to make her income twice that of her husband, but she had to watch helplessly as it went for things her husband wanted, unable to claim any of it for her favorite charity. As Max wrote later, "the demand that he should give his wife independent means contradicted all firm tradition."[73] Bringing up a large family, Helene had neither a set allowance nor any

---

*It may not have been as rare there as Mayhew thought. The Criminal Law Procedure Act to prevent it was passed in 1853, with a statement in the introduction that "no one could read the public journals without being constantly struck with horror and amazement at the numerous reports of cases of cruel and brutal assaults perpetrated upon the weaker sex by men one blushed to think were Englishmen" (Burn, 155). The act raised the permissible fine to £20 or six months in prison, but this had little deterrent effect, judging from the hideous revelations that came forth at the opening of a divorce court a few years later. On the other hand, Lucy Aiken, answering a query from Channing in Boston, declared in 1838 that she had never heard of one single instance in her limited, upper-class circle (Channing and Aiken, April 18, 1838).

†It is interesting that even in 1961, when the German Home Economics Institute took a poll, 90 percent of the women called their lives a slave existence, although 90 percent of the husbands called their homes happy (reported in *Louisville Courier-Journal*, February 17, 1961). The German Public Health Association attributed the problem to the German male's refusal to allow his wife to be free of the traditional ties to children, church, and kitchen.

special sum for her personal needs, but she had to bring every item to her husband for approval.* The historian Theodor Mommsen was considered unusual in letting his wife manage the family finances, even to the point of asking her for pocket money, though he liked going to market and was remarkable for his ability to help in practical crises such as a flooded cellar.[74]

In 1908 Professor Paulsen of the University of Berlin, an educational reformer, at least for boys, wrote an essay on women's rights in which he expressed the common view that women were less able to handle money, and he gave three reasons: their fatal tendency to keep up with the Joneses, the bad habit of spoiling their families with luxuries, and a general inability to keep accounts. He admitted that he could not convince "modern" women, but he felt that ordinary wives would not feel degraded by the husband's being the head of the house. On the other hand, he felt it *would* be degrading to have to beg for money, and recommended that a fixed allowance or a fixed percentage of the family income be allotted to the wife.

Paulsen imagined a conversation between a married couple. The wife wants a more expensive house. The husband explains why they cannot afford it. Her counterargument is that the Müllers have one. He still does not see how they could manage. Whereupon she cries that she is sorry she ever got married and bursts into tears. Paulsen's recommendation in such circumstances was that the husband simply go ahead in silence and rent the house he could afford.[75]

Taine, who had noticed the Frenchwoman's ability to control fifty clerks, or face bankruptcy proceedings, or argue with an official about taxes, said simply that any German woman would be out of her depth in such circumstances.[76] Taine was, to be sure, chauvinistic, but he may have made a correct generalization.†

There were, indeed, German wives who managed very well. Some of them lived in the early part of the nineteenth century, when Enlightenment ideas still worked to free intellectual women there as elsewhere. For instance, when Karoline Herder married a head-in-the-clouds philosopher, Johann Gottfried Herder, toward the end of the eighteenth century, *he* at first did the cooking, and she managed the money, even to the point of borrowing secretly to handle his debts.[77] By such means she hoped to keep him free to write, though she also worked on his manu-

---

*In 1913 a Braunschweig court ruled that a wife had the right to receive her housekeeping money in advance (Zahn-Harnack, *Frauenbewegung*, 64).

†One's attention is drawn to how often the wives of radicals even of the northern countries took over with full competence when their husbands were jailed for political activity. Bebel's wife kept their business going for two and a half years under such circumstances (Bebel, *Life*, 106), while in England, Cobbett's wife took a lodging near Newgate (where he was sent for protesting against the flogging of English soldiers) to keep in touch with him and their work (Cobbett, 163). Similarly Richard Carlile's wife and sister ran his print shop when he was imprisoned for his birth control manual (E. P. Thompson, *English Working Class*, 725–30).

scripts and educated herself in order to be qualified to edit them. Those few women in later periods who matched her success were either highly talented themselves or belonged to families with strong liberal ideas.

Talent is what freed Clara Schumann. Though Robert Schumann made part of his musical reputation with a song sequence about the life of a woman devoted to love, home, and children, his own wife far transcended such limitations. Clara, a distinguished pianist, for years earned all the money that was needed to educate their eight children, and eventually to pay for her husband's care in a mental institution. She was a woman in a million, both in strength of character and in earning power.*

A woman from a liberal family who made a success of her husband's business was Hedwig Heyl. Born in 1850 and married at eighteen, she immediately began helping her husband run his paint factory, where she became interested in the condition of the workers;[78] to help them she installed a bathing facility and later started a cooking school, writing the first scientific cookbook. She kept on managing the factory after her husband's death and was particularly proud of her decision to introduce electric power.[79] Eventually she turned more to public service, organizing the four-week-long 1912 exposition of women's work that involved ten thousand participants and a half-million visitors. Its catalogue was three hundred pages long. When the war came, she was asked to head up the soup kitchens.

In thinking about ordinary German women and their reaction to the circumstances of their lives, we might go back to Dr. Riehl. His theory, quite simply, was that women had no individuality and were not supposed to have any. Only ugly, sour, and bitter women would go so far as to practice *art*, he pontificated, utterly ignoring all the qualities of Clara Schumann, who was giving concerts as he wrote. Even keeping diaries would be too individual and "French" in Riehl's opinion, since the true German way was to keep family Bible records[80] (as was done in *Buddenbrooks*).

As seemed to be the case elsewhere, women often liked what their particular tradition dictated. Thus Karoline von Humboldt wrote to her husband, Wilhelm, "I am not much at commanding and find it much nicer to be commanded. But you take care of me so well that I don't get upset, and you make me believe that I am commanding you."[81] Henriette Feuerbach complained of lacking a master because her husband was morally weak. Ethel Smyth, an English feminist and composer who studied music in Germany, said that she got tired of hearing so frequently on the lips of German women, always with complete assent, "mein Mann sagt. . . ."†[82]

*See Chapter 26.

†Even today elementary textbooks used in German schools present women as lacking individual identity, stuck in what the reporting sociologists term "primary group affiliations." They found that the man was shown as dominant in thirty-nine examples as compared to three for the women (Sibermann and Krüger, 26). Of course, this situation is by no means unique to Germany but is true of many western European textbooks.

Michelet summed up the situation, as perceived by the period, in saying that the French woman was an admirable partner, the English woman a reliable wife, while the German woman was humble and obedient.[83]

∽ When Giacomo Oddo gave a series of lectures on the Italian woman as wife, mother, and daughter, roughly comparable to Mrs. Ellis's disquisitions on Englishwomen, he wanted them to be trained to *help men*, and not for their own advantage. He wanted them to take his assignment seriously, explaining that they were not married just for their husbands' pleasure, but to meet economic responsibilities in a way that would require much more stringent training than was commonly available.[84]

For an Italian bride, the patriarchal system created generational as well as marital control, so that she might well have as much trouble adjusting to her mother-in-law as to her husband. Mrs. Gretton, who lived in Italy for ten years, knew of a married woman who dared not sit down in the presence of her mother-in-law unless invited, a situation in which her husband felt it would be impossible to intervene.[85] Another young nobleman, after ten years of marriage, was unable to invite any friends of his own to dinner without his father's permission. With a disposable family income of £4,000, the young husband was given £4 a month and his wife £3; but all their bills, even theater tickets, were paid for them.*

Yet once again, the description of what seemed to be average situations does injustice to the large number of individual women who did much to hold family and household together in the period of intense nationalistic struggle.

The story of the poet Leopardi's mother was well known throughout Italy for the way in which she single-mindedly set herself to restoring the family fortune after it had been gambled away by the male heads of the house. With a cold heart and a will of steel, by starving her sons emotionally and physically, she achieved her goal.

There were more genial cases. Many of the leading patriotic families belonged to the genteel poor—titled families whose land was encumbered or failed to produce needed revenues—and their ability to contribute to the national cause was often due to women's wit and skill.

∽ The question arises: Did the European pattern of family life add up to masculine tyranny?

*A 1960 scientific sampling of Italians reports that 41 percent said that they grew up in a patriarchal system, compared to 28 percent of French people, 20 percent of Germans, and 12 percent of English people questioned (Lupri, 99). (Note that a patriarchal system is not the exact equivalent of a "father-headed" family.) Other recent interviewers have found

inly, sometimes. Whenever a husband wanted to dominate
law in every country gave him all the support he needed, as
s in this book will show.

'y most of the dominating husbands believed that they
sponsibly—in fact, "naturally." People's behavior is
ower relationships of their culture, and at the start of our
dividuality in women was both less expected and less
'. Men were told that it was a duty, not a privilege, to
uecisions for their families, and women that it was their
uion and relief to give in.

There were three possible ways for women to react. Most submitted, with good or bad grace (sometimes even "decking the altar with flowers");[86] some did what people in inferior positions have always done—manipulated behind the scenes;* and a few rebelled outright.

At the same time, it is important to remember that founding a family meant a sudden loss in freedom and decision-making ability for men as well as for women, a narrowing of their choices both human and financial. This was especially true if the number of children was left totally to chance, as an 1872 article in the *Fortnightly Review* explained to its readers. Though both parents would be under severe constraint, that on the wife might be so heavy as to destroy all chance for personal growth. The magazine suggested that a lower birth rate (in obedience to natural laws, which "all may discover and verify if they will")[87] would solve most of the educational, personal, and economic problems of the age. The article was ahead of its time, but it pointed the way toward the single most important area of choice within a marriage.

On the continent, as well as in England, there was a steadily growing revulsion against the use of marital force, beginning with very moderate statements like Janet's, that for women to try to dominate was revolting and ridiculous, but for men to use force was base and cruel.[88] In the happiest homes, said Turgéon, the husband commanded without seeming to, and the wife obeyed without realizing it,[89] and such was surely Dr. Riehl's vision of the natural ordering of a family. Riehl made a great point of family happiness and cheerfulness; he would not have considered a grumpy, rebellious household right, though any complaint from a female was taken as evidence of something bizarre in her individual make-up.

---

persisting fear that the new type of woman being developed by industrialism and urbanization will no longer accept the role of obedient wife (Parca, 101).

*Marie Corelli:

The clever woman sits at home—and like a meadow spider spreads a pretty web of rose and gold, spangled with diamond dew. Flies (or men)—tumble in by scores—and she holds them all prisoners at her pleasure. . . . One never sees any pretty women among those who clamor for their rights. And why? Because every pretty woman knows she has every "right" she can possibly want—the right to govern man completely and draw him everywhere after her like a steel filing drawn by a magnet. [quoted in Blease, 220–221]

Such sentiments, undoubtedly usually genuine, could also be easy paths to hypocrisy, as when Max Weber declared of his father that he *thought* authoritatively even after he had lost faith in authority.[90] Another rebellious son, Edward Kellett, ruminated, "It is a mark of tyranny that it has the power of concealing itself from the man who exercises it; the tyrant tends to think of himself merely as the president of a republic, or even a private citizen who, by his personal virtues, has attained authority."[91]

This leads to the question whether there was a connection between the different kinds of family relationships and the kinds of government in each country. Hippel, writing about 1800, remarked that in a monarchical state the husband will act like a king, and in a democratic state he will act democratically,[92] and I would like to follow out his suggestion in a spirit of speculation without in any way insisting on a cause-and-effect relationship.

In the mid-nineteenth century, the French were the only people here considered who had had political experience of universal male suffrage and an ideal of equality that seemed to have penetrated part of their social structure even in periods when their government took a turn toward authoritarianism. Hillebrand compared the bond of reason in French marriages to the bond of reason between the people and their state, and explained that in neither case was their devotion to any liege lord.[93] In 1848 Legouvé, as he studied the problems of women, presented the idea that unity in the modern democratic state came not from the imposition of one will but from the fusion of many, and that ever since 1789 authority had derived its legitimacy not from power but from the benefits that power conferred.[94] It is very much in this spirit that I see the French family as actually functioning. In 1902, whatever the law said, in a magazine survey of female readers only 963 respondents out of 6,512 (less than 15 percent) said that they had included the promise to obey in their wedding vows.[95]

English political life at the time could be considered a masked despotism of the upper classes, smug in their conviction that they knew best how to govern. The English paterfamilias undertook his duties in a similar spirit of *noblesse oblige*.

It might be noted that democracy within the family did not mean that Frenchwomen would be the first to get political suffrage. This aspect of democracy was more likely to be sought in a country of overt individualism.

In Germany, the historian Heinrich von Treitschke argued, "Already in the family we find the *political* principle of subordination. The father is the supreme head, he administers justice"[96] (emphasis added). At the same time, German rulers often presented themselves as the fathers of their people, and in a country where many jurisdictions were tiny, and where many lacked constitutions, this fiction was easier to maintain.

Ralf Dahrendorf, a modern student of German democratic institutions, has a different theoretical explanation, one that, in a way, is consonant with Riehl's of a hundred years earlier. According to Dahrendorf, German family life has been so self-contained that it fails to reach out to influence public affairs. Inside the family private virtues come to flower, while in Anglo-Saxon countries public virtues are inculcated because the school, rather than the home, is the prime character-building agency.[97] The school forms the life of an English young person, with emphasis on team sports, school spirit, and participation. Dahrendorf suggests that when the family outranks the school, authoritarian political institutions such as have repeatedly appeared in Germany cannot be checked, while in countries where the school outranks the home, liberal democracy can flourish with the participation of millions of prepared citizens.* If this theoretical framework is valid, it would follow that the even greater weakness of girls' schools compared to boys' would make it particularly hard for German women to enter political life.

*Montesquieu had said just the opposite; that the more liberty in the state, the more need for authority in the family (Turgéon, I:370).

$\backsim$ 11.

To Love, Honor, and Obey: England

I flung closer to his breast,
As sword that, after battle, flings to sheath;
And, in that hurtle of united souls,
The mystic motions which in common moods
Are shut beyond our sense, broke in on us. . . .
　　　Elizabeth Barrett Browning, *Aurora Leigh*, 1857

You do not think for instance that *marriage*
as it exists on all sides of us, is a better,
happier, holier condition *far so* than a single
life. You do not deny it to be an *abomination*. . . .
　　　Elizabeth Barrett Browning, 1845

　　　We have discussed the use of money and the distribution of authority between the sexes, especially in marriage, but what of love? What was the nature of the emotional relationship that held two people together?

　　　Clearly, the sexual tie was one determinant. But though sex is nearly always one motive for marriage, it is mixed with other concerns. Romantic excitement may sink into domestic habit, comfortable though not intimate, or it may change into warm affection, or grow into intellectual companionship. For each of these benign mutations there is a malignant counterpart: sexual excitement may turn to distaste; if home seems a refuge to some people, it becomes a prison for others; and intellectually one partner may quite outgrow the other.

　　　What was relatively new in this period was the idea that home ought to be a place of refuge, and then, gradually, the idea that personal and especially intellectual compatibility might be a goal within the reach of most couples. What made it different from life in the twentieth century was that the pattern was harder to escape, for women at least. The doors were not absolutely shut for a person whom marriage did not suit, but it took exceptional vigor, ability, and usually luck, to be able to push one's way out.

　　　Marriage was not only socially desirable but religiously sanctioned—Charles Kingsley believed that Christ taught the Teutonic races something about wedlock that he had not bothered to teach the Jews. The special gospel to the northern peoples was the idea of love matches, that love could be a total physical and spiritual union. Of himself he stated: "I am so well and really married on earth, that I should be exceedingly sorry to be married again in heaven. All I can say is, if I do not love my wife, body and soul, as well there as I do here, then there is neither resurrection of my body or of my soul . . . and I shall not be I."[1]

Though Levin Schücking's study of the Puritan character concludes that English marriage was differentiated from the continental by a religious change, he moves the change ahead to the seventeenth century, with Puritanism as the motivating factor. He demonstrates how the Puritans spiritualized the relationship of marriage, telling husbands and wives to study and attend to each other's characters, and how this directive became a key part of the growth toward more personal attitudes about women.[2]

Those emerging feelings were well described by Dr. Thomas Arnold when he declared: "The most certain softeners of a man's blood, are, I am sure, domestic intercourse in a happy marriage, and intercourse with the poor"[3]—an interesting pairing. "My dearest M——," he wrote to his wife on their tenth anniversary (August 11, 1830), "How much of happiness and of cause for thankfulness is contained in the recollection of this day: for in the ten years that have elapsed since our marriage there have been condensed, I suppose, as great a portion of happiness, with as little alloy, as ever marked any ten years of human existence."[4]

When Mary Vivian Hughes's husband, Arthur, was fatally injured in a traffic accident after twenty years of marriage, he spent the last half-hour of his life, while the blood flowed from him, pouring out expressions of how "glorious" it had all been, a feeling he had rarely put into words before.[5]

Such expressions are not unusual, and they do not seem to be perfunctory. Mary Howitt writes to her sister that a ten-day absence of her husband makes her feel as if she has lost her right hand or an eye.[6] William Gladstone, who wrote once or twice to his wife every day they were separated, said on his forty-seventh wedding anniversary, "My own own, we are away from each other, but not in spirit. My mind travels back to the 47 years of blessed memory. . . . Thank you for all you have done, for all you are, and for the lovely example you have been to me in sorrow, or in joy. . . . Darling old thing, I long to give you such a kiss."[7]

William Cobbett explained that his wife was so disinterested, generous, and devoted that she helped him accomplish everything he wanted to do.[8] There is a charming story that Cobbett was once held at a meeting past eleven o'clock, but still insisted on riding the twenty-three miles home that night. His guest was sure that Mrs. Cobbett would not be up when they got there, but she was, with a nice fire going, and she remarked, "He never disappointed me in his life." Told that in France most husbands went to the café each evening, Cobbett retorted that a husband should show by his actions that he prefers his wife's company to all others', and that he should make a point of telling her about daily occurrences.*[9]

Though it was certainly usual for the husband to be the one coming home and the wife to be the one who waited, the Victorian ideal of marriage was broad enough to allow for occasional reversals. When a woman was outstanding, her husband very often supported her efforts without any loss of dignity. The best example is probably Josephine Butler, who undertook one of the most difficult assignments of any Victorian woman, since she ran the crusade against legalized prostitution. In this work she was upheld by "a perfect marriage,"[10] and although she believed that all the great work of the world should be done by both sexes together, in her case, she actually did the bulk of the work while George Butler offered support and domestic tranquility.[11] Another famous woman was Mary Somerville, the mathematician, whose home was the happiest that Frances Power Cobbe had ever seen.[12] Mrs. Somerville herself described her wedded life as "a marriage of sympathy, affection, and confidence,"[13] but she was certainly the acknowledged intellectual superior.

So also the first English woman doctor, Elizabeth Garrett Anderson, wrote of her husband, "The only possible basis for us is warm personal love and utter truth and outspokenness,"[14] and she lived with him on this principle for thirty-six years, always receiving complete support. Nor is there any indication that Lord Amberley offered anything but encouragement to his wife, Kate, in her public talks on women's rights—even though some of the newspapers waxed satiric that he should have been "permitting" his wife to do such a thing.[15]

Sarah Ann Sewell, a lesser figure, expressed touching gratitude to the husband "from whom I have received for more than twenty years, the tender joys of married life," saying that his love had rendered it one long sunny day.[16] Among other services, he had nursed her through illness. In something of the same vein, Beatrice Webb remembered her father, Richard Potter: "His own comfort, his own inclinations were unconsidered before the happiness of his wife, the welfare of his children. With him the domestic instinct was a passion to which all else was subordinated."[17]

Even in the absence of outstanding personal devotion, there were many factors that drew Englishmen to their homes in a routine of enjoyable domesticity. It is, and was, often remarked that "home" is a word for which the French language lacks an equivalent. Every Englishman wanted his own little detached house, and was encouraged by the climate to stay within it. Schücking believed that this kind of family life was developed by the bourgeoisie and that it involved the creation of a role

---

*Once when Disraeli came home at three in the morning after a vote on the Second Reform Bill, his wife had waiting for him a pie from Fortnum and Mason's and a bottle of champagne. His comment: "My dear, you are more like a mistress than a wife!" (Magnus, 187).

for the wife and mother as the center of radiating warmth.[18] What Tocqueville said about American family life held true for English too: since most men worked outside the home and had limited incomes, women had a greater need than previously to stay home and watch the domestic economy.[19] Or as John Stuart Mill put the same point, men were increasingly thrown on their home and family for personal and social pleasures, and as women's education and preparation for the new role improved, satisfactions should increase.[20]

There is a wonderful picture of Dr. Arnold's family life. "From about a quarter before nine until ten o'clock every evening, I am at liberty, and enjoy my wife's company fully; during this time I read out to her (I am now reading Herodotus, translating it as I go on), or write my sermons, when it is my fortnight to preach; or write letters, as I am doing at this moment. And though the space of time that I can thus enjoy be short, yet perhaps I relish it more keenly. . . . I ought to think how very many situations in life might have separated me from my wife's society, not for hours only, but for months or even years; whereas now I have not slept from home once since I have been married."[21] Another pleasant vignette is that of the Gladstones waltzing around in front of the fire, or singing at the top of their voices, "A ragamuffin husband and a rantipolling wife."[22]

Though no one should downgrade the genuine happiness shared by a multitude of Victorian couples, there were many for whom things did not run so smoothly, for whom, as for Leslie Stephen, it proved hard to make the shift from the ideal of devotion into daily understanding and sympathy.[23] There was much temptation to pretend that one was happier than one actually was. When Augustus Hare was bitterly criticized by the family for suggesting in his biography *Two Noble Lives* that the married life of Lord and Lady Canning was not cloudless, Hare's excuse was that, after all, "what made Lady Canning's so perfectly 'noble' a life was that, however much she suffered, she allowed her mother and sister to live and *die* under the impression that she was the happiest of wives."[24]

From across the North Sea, Karl Immermann proposed that the English were often not really aware of the meaning of conflict within a family.[25] Boz, he said, saw no irony in letting his characters retreat to their homes. The author (who, of course, was Charles Dickens) seemed unable to imagine that strife might arise there when the home was meant to absorb the whole person.

If the possible conflicts were masked, either from the partners themselves or from their closest relatives, there was a reason, or at least a mechanism, that made this possible—namely, the general coolness of relations, the Englishman's hesitations about intimacy, his formal respect for the female sex in general, his suppression of such weaknesses within himself as self-pity or vanity, his substitution of courtesy for sympathy. Schücking feels that the phenomenon that strikes the modern continental observer more than any other is the English way of regarding emotion, and the "astonishingly small" vocabulary used for the ordinary purposes of life, a verbal reserve that, he notes, is supported by the cool expressions of face and body.[26] French visitors too agreed that every Englishman held some part of himself back, that their intimacies were incomplete (symbolized by the lack of the delicacy of *tutoyment* in their language).[27]

Indeed, the more we find out about marriages that would have been called happy, the easier it is to find flaws in them. Thus the Kingsleys, as we noted, had what was called an ideal union, and yet even by reading the letters published soon after Charles's death, it becomes clear that he was always the one who went off on fishing trips, alone, or visited the West Indies as the guest of the Governor, accompanied by his daughter. By a closer reading of the original correspondence, his latest biographer has shown that his wife simply refused to go along to America. We can only wonder about the deeper reasons.[28]

"The cross of matrimony lies heavy on many a woman who never takes the world into her confidence, and who bears in absolute silence what she has not the power to cast from her."[29] So declared Mrs. Lynn Linton, explaining why some widows were so uncommonly cheerful. Barbara Leigh Smith was also made aware of a dark side to Victorian marriage when she carried around her petition for a divorce law and heard horror stories from the various women she solicited for signature.[30] Her own marriage was to a Frenchman whose ideas were of greater equality and who left her so free that her friends marveled.

Brutality did not have to be physical, and lack of sympathy would only be natural for men who had never had to think in terms of women's predicament. Edmund Gosse told how his father repressed his second wife, with constant, cheerful, and quiet pressure; never unkind or abrupt, he went on "adding avoirdupois" until her will gave way.[31] John Duguid Milne thought middle-class women were hurt simply by being left alone all day, comparing them with the upper class, where the sexes could mingle, or the lower, where women were more likely to share the lot of their men whatever it was.[32] Mrs. Ellis listed the hardships of married life as men's bad tempers, their dislike of housecleaning, their unpunctuality, and their occasional infidelity—all of which the wife had to bear with Christian sweetness.[33]

No wonder that by the last third of the century, writers commonly reacted against the assumption of domestic bliss. Yet Edith Nesbit took issue with H. G. Wells's picture of the total disintegration of the institution, as she insisted, "Love is . . . much oftener than you admit, . . . 'nice straight cricket.' . . ."[34]

დ So much for the ties of domesticity. What of the sexual lives within this domestic interior?

To the twentieth-century consciousness, the power to give or withhold sexual intimacy is a privilege of maturity. The nineteenth century did not so regard it. At least for the women of that day, sex was rather an obligation than a privilege, a more or less agreeable burden, but it could only be withheld at the cost of giving up a whole complex of other things, such as home, status, and security.

Of course, men were bound by the system too, but with weaker chains. The glorified family was meant to limit male roaming, and as women gained in power and self-consciousness, though not in sensual freedom, they made some interesting attempts to restrict the total quantity of expended semen by urging men too to be chaste, within and outside of marriage.

It is hard to get at the facts, however. Balzac pointed out one difficulty—namely, that the English marriage chamber was so sacred that no outsider entered it;* sometimes it was even closed off from the servants, and the housewife made up the bed, a notion that won Balzac's approval.[35] Louis Larcher reinforced the idea that it was a much more mysterious place than a French bedroom, and hinted darkly that it was where female alcoholics retreated to drink.[36] On the other hand, another Frenchman, Max O'Rell (who must somehow have penetrated the sacred enclosure), reported that it was the least attractive room in the house. In fact, it resembled a servant's room, with no cozy armchairs, only straight-backed ones, and an iron or brass bed, the inevitable washstand with sponge bath, and "it" actually on the floor beneath, in plain sight. He was shocked that there was not even a screen to undress behind—"Is John no longer a man in your eyes?"[37]

To many continentals the English habit of using a double bed was incomprehensible. Dr. Paulsen of the University of Berlin, who toured England in 1904, used to try to get a second bed set up in his hotel room for his wife, but this was not always possible and he simply could not imagine how English couples managed.[38]

Of course, there is no way of knowing what proportion of these embedded couples enjoyed sex, though the double bed was widely given as the reason for their great fecundity. It is sometimes possible to guess about an individual couple, even though they lacked today's need to discuss the matter. Often those who expressed a sense of oneness with Nature, or God's purpose, were revealing their sexual satisfaction. Those who disliked sex were more likely to be indirect in explaining that "many women" felt shocked or betrayed. Naturally those who were indifferent were the least articulate.†

*Charles Kingsley called the bedroom their chapel, their study, their heaven of earth. Although he allowed the maid to clean it up, no one else must ever be permitted to enter.

†Anne Fremantle tells a delightful story of her mother's bridal night. When she woke up in the morning, her maid brought her bath while the young husband was still asleep. After some hesitation she slipped out of her nightgown and stepped into her bath, at which moment her husband awoke. Long afterward she asked him if he had been shocked. "No," he responded. "All I could feel was wonder that there was anything so lovely in the world" (Fremantle, 143).

The most over-quoted medical opinion of the time about female sexuality was that of the remarkable Dr. Acton, who declared, in the well-worn phrase, that he had *compared abundant evidence* and concluded that "the majority of women, happily for society, are not very much troubled with sexual feelings of any kind." The average woman, he was certain, "submits to her husband's embraces, but principally to gratify him; and were it not for the desire of maternity, would far rather be relieved from his attentions."[39] He was writing for other doctors, but seemed to suspect that his book might "accidentally" fall into the hands of laymen, for whom, he realized, the subject would be novel and painful.

Acton is often made fun of, though he was obviously a serious man and told the truth as he saw it. His analysis may be questioned, however, especially for his lack of curiosity about what social attitudes might prevent women from expecting sexual arousal. He himself may have added to the pressures of restraint, perhaps unconsciously, as when he wrote of a female patient that she was "the perfect ideal of an English wife and mother," whose marriage was nevertheless unconsummated (how then was she to become a mother?) because she was "so pure-hearted as to be utterly ignorant of and averse to any sensual indulgence."

Medical opinion was by no means unanimously on Dr. Acton's side, however. Because he provided a convenient quotation for those who like to expose the backwardness of Victorian life, he has been cited far beyond his contemporaries who held the opposite view. In obstetrical lectures at the North London School of Medicine in 1839, for example, Dr. Michael Ryan vigorously supported the view that sexual gratification should be mutual, and that consummation of marriage should be done gently and carefully. He believed that women's enjoyment, evidenced by erect nipples and a tremor in all parts of their bodies, was much more intense than men's.[40] In the same vein, Dr. Alexander Walker, in *Woman Physiologically Considered* (1840), upheld the opinion that natural desires were felt equally, and that while regular exercise of the reproductive organs in marriage was beneficial to general health in both sexes, it was something that women needed even more than men.*[41]

---

*Besides these respectable voices of professional opinion, there were a number of radical propagandists who directed their pamphlets toward the working classes in a vigorous defense of sexual pleasure, but these barely touched the middle-class women who are the subject of this book. The main reason was that they all advocated some form of birth control device (usually a sponge on a ribbon), which, of course, offered the only means by which the poor classes could be free to enjoy sex without fear of conception, but which was considered filthy by the higher orders. Even Dr. Ryan had attacked the spreaders of Malthusianism as grossly immoral (he named Bentham, James Mill, and Miss Martineau, among others), and their doctrine as contrary to nature and religion. A self-respecting middle-class woman would have hesitated to enter one of the working-class bookstores where these little volumes circulated quietly. One such book was attacked for immorality in 1876, when Charles Bradlaugh and Annie Besant were prosecuted for trying to sell it. The books here alluded to include: *The Fruits of Philosophy* (published anonymously in 1832 but supposed to be by an American doctor, Charles Knowlton; this is the book for which Bradlaugh and

Even though such a view of sexual pleasure was available to them, it seems at least reasonable to guess that English women, and perhaps men too, had a comparatively low level of sexual enjoyment. Dr. Drysdale, the birth control advocate, who warmly wished that the English had "a more vigorous relish for sensual pleasure," said that he could hardly imagine a society where there was less of it, even among the rich, though it was worse for the poor, with their ignorance, ill-health, and unrelenting fear of pregnancy.[42] Havelock Ellis too said that he was constantly astonished at the rarity of "erotic personality" and the general ignorance of the art of love among both sexes in Britain. Few people realized, he added, how much women lose when they miss out on sexual climax.[43]

Legally, until 1884, a woman could be imprisoned for denying her husband his conjugal rights. There might be extenuating circumstances for such refusal, and these were listed by Dr. Ryan in his obstetrical lectures, in which he specifically said that it was wrong to abstain for reasons of poverty or because the couple had too many children already.*[44]

Consider the case of Mr. and Mrs. Cochrane, who were married in 1833 and had two children. In 1836 Mr. Cochrane sued for restitution of his conjugal rights in the Court of Common Pleas, she having refused to obey a previous order of the Ecclesiastical Court that she must "perform the contract she has entered into." Her response was to abduct her one living child to Paris, where she stayed for four years with her mother, enjoying such dubious pleasures as "masked balls." Mr. Cochrane got her back to London by an admitted stratagem, and then locked her up in their apartment. In the court's opinion, "the husband hath by law power and domination over his wife, and may keep her by force, within the bounds of duty, and may beat her, but not in a violent or cruel manner."[45] And the judge added that the husband could force cohabitation in the interest of the happiness and honor of both parties.

Armed with such marital authority, many men "regarded the marriage ceremony as a rite which absolved them from the laws of health and temperance"[46] (according to Bernard Shaw), and from any consideration of their *wives'* health. As bad an example as any is that of Catherine Gladstone's sister, Mary Lyttelton, whose doctor pronounced at her ninth delivery that another pregnancy would kill her. Nevertheless, she became pregnant for the tenth time at forty-two, and did indeed die. It is

---

Besant were prosecuted); *Every Woman's Book* (1826) by Richard Carlile, who, though not a doctor, quoted a gynecologist who attributed five out of six deaths from consumption to lack of sexual intercourse; and *The Elements of Social Science*, by Dr. Drysdale.

*Dr. Ryan thought refusal was justified if there was doubt about the validity of the marriage, if the woman's life was endangered (deformity or too-frequent miscarriages), if she was solicited in drunkenness or madness, in a public place, in an unnatural manner, or during menstruation, or if either party asked too frequently (without defining this point) or suffered from a loathsome disease. He was violently against birth control (Ryan, 128, 14).

not clear whom the doctor told—Mary or her mother or her sister—but *nobody* had had the courage to mention the little fact to George Lyttleton, with whose masculine prerogatives it would have interfered.[47] Mona Caird bitingly quoted from an essay of Kingsley's in which he described a pleasant, peaceful home, full of swarms of beautiful children whom the young wife and mother watched from a sofa, having become a confirmed invalid.[48] The irony of her sacrifice was pointed up by the belief that her husband was saved thereby from licentiousness; the price was obviously, in male eyes, cheap. All too many Victorian wives paid it. Men's personal testimony often indicates that marriage was their only means of preventing (as Francis Place said) "moral ruin"; or, as Lady Morgan's fiancé put it, without woman's love "there is a void in existence that deprives me of all control of myself, and leads me to headlong dissipation. . . ."[49] The abstemious Shaw declared that if he had followed the marital sex patterns of the average businessman, "a startling deterioration would have appeared in my writing before the end of a fortnight, and frightened me back to what they would have considered an impossible asceticism."[50]

Many of her subjects would have endorsed Queen Victoria's *cri de coeur* in a letter to her daughter: "The animal side of our nature is to me—too dreadful"; and she went on to write that "our poor degraded sex" was intended for man's pleasure and amusement. "Papa is not even quite exempt, though he would not admit it."[51] George Egerton, the pseudonym of a female fiction writer concerned with women's problems, declared (using the the unfortunate racial stereotypes of her day) that many women felt something like physical disgust for men, akin to the racial disgust of white for black.[52]

An interesting and well-documented case is that of Mrs. Mark Pattison, who maintained an uneasy relationship with her husband, a distinguished university don, before she became free to marry Sir Charles Dilke, with whom she had been in love for many years. In spite of that, she tried to make a go of her marriage, and once wrote to her husband that she wanted to come back to him (from a trip away for her "health") and was willing to share all aspects of his life but one, "and that is so distasteful to me that the fear of its renewal has often preoccupied me to the exclusion of all other considerations. It is a physical aversion wh.[ich] has always existed, though I strove hard to overcome it. . . ."[53] She explained that she had "feigned pleasure"[54] in his embraces. Apparently she did not feel the same way about Dilke, for that marriage seems to have been congenial. George Eliot is supposed to have modeled Dorothea Casaubon on Mrs. Pattison.

Claiming ill-health was one of the easiest means of escape for Englishwomen, especially when the need to flee the climate of their country sent them off to sunnier places. Mrs. Pattison wrote from the south of France, but German spas, or even the warmer parts of England, could provide suitably inviting excuses for living separately.

Modern psychologists would expect that there was a price for so much dissatisfaction and repression, but in pre-Freudian days few called attention to it.* Richard Burton was one who did, remarking that Englishwomen when insane or delirious often broke out into language that would shame the slums, thus relieving their pent-up feelings by mental prostitution.[55] Burton did his best to share with Englishmen some of the Indian arts of love that he had studied during his years as an explorer.

Dr. Acton's approach to sex was exactly the opposite, as might be expected. His advice was that married couples should have intercourse very rarely: every ten days, he suggested, though he thought that by doing it twice in one night a man might be able to hold out for a fortnight.[56] The liberal position was expressed by Dr. Drysdale, who felt that twice a week was a good average for sex among city-dwelling couples.[57] (Even Dr. Acton's position became more flexible with time. In his 1857 edition he had written that intellectual qualities are usually in inverse ratio to the sexual appetite, but later he noticed many exceptions to this rule, and in his 1894 edition he admitted that when celibate university fellows married, their health often improved.)[58]

When an intellectual woman told Acton that she thought the wife should sometimes be the one to decide when to have sex,[59] his response was that she could hurt the health of her husband by doing so, though it was not quite clear whether he expected her to ask for too much or too little. In any case, he felt that restraint was needed for the sake of the wife too. Women could get epilepsy, in his opinion, from long-continued sexual shocks, as well as uterine infections that would make them look haggard, pinched, and feverish.[60] Ellen Key claimed to know of cases where insanity ensued.[61]

One response of women to their unsatisfactory erotic experience was to try to persuade men that this was a low, animal activity. By the 1870s, according to C. W. Cunnington, a new sense of personal rights began to surface in women's magazines, which for the first time were willing to print such outpourings as "I have borne for twenty-two years all the insults of a coarse nature. I have been a devoted slave to the man I swore to love and obey."[62] Dr. Acton noted sourly, in a late edition of his tome, that the women's movement had caused many wives to resist normal sexual demands, and he named John Stuart Mill as the chief perpetrator of the disastrous encouragement of "women who regard themselves as martyrs when called upon to fulfill the duties of wives."†[63]

*Another effect was pointed out by Count Keyserling, who found that nowhere in the world were there so many *mariages blancs* as in England. A number come to mind at once: the Ruskins, the Carlyles, the George Bernard Shaws, and probably the Jamesons (Clara Thomas, 196). Effie Ruskin explained after many years of unconsummated marriage that she "had never been told the duties of married persons to each other and knew little or nothing about their relations in the closest union on earth." John explained to her that he did not like children, that he wanted to preserve her beauty, but actually, Effie believed, "he had imagined women were quite different from what he saw I was, and that the reason he did not make me his wife was because he was disgusted with my person the first evening" (Evans, *Ruskin*, 135, 200).

†When Geoffrey Gorer made his survey of English character in 1951, he came to the conclusion that general interest in sex was low, and he found that Englishwomen of his day

∽ We turn now from the consideration of sex to the question of the intellectual relationship between husbands and wives. If a man's home was his refuge from the office, many a husband neither expected nor desired to find his wife an intellectual and spiritual companion. He might very well prefer to relax there and enjoy the respite from the discussion among equals in his world of work, and from the need to compromise. At home he could be undisputed boss and have everything arranged for his ease.[64] Some people have blamed the Hanoverian dynasty, and especially Queen Victoria, for importing German ideas about the inferiority of women. Her widely praised purification of the royal family life also provided a model for less independently thinking female subjects.

But it was well established even in the time when Mme de Staël wrote *Corinne* that an Englishman simply would not tolerate a wife's independent career. Corinne's dilemma was that she could flourish as a woman of genius only in Italy, and if she married her English lover, she would have to give up the expression of any of her talents.

In the two-volume collection of the life and letters of Dr. Samuel Butler, who was headmaster of Shrewsbury School from 1798 to 1836,* Dr. Butler's only reference to his wife, except for her health, was to note that she had kept three houses with fifty boys each and thus had helped with the budget. He never mentioned his daughters, except at their weddings, though he wrote several letters to his son.[65] Yet his correspondence to a wide variety of other men showed sympathetic understanding of the boys in his care, real attention to the problems of educating them, a lively concern with public (mostly church) affairs, and a sense of fun that shows up in Greek puns and accounts of fishing trips. His wife simply had no part in any of these interests.†

Many of the men most noted for intellectual achievement indicated that they did not look for this quality in their wives. Thackeray wrote to his mother in 1840, "I like this milk-&-water in women—perhaps too much. . . ."[66] Even Charles Kingsley told his fiancée (in 1844) to "think little and read less," and always to have some sewing in her hand,[67] presumably to keep her mind out of trouble.

---

regarded physical love as less important to them than it was to men, and the older his sample, the lower was the regard for sex. None of Gorer's informants, obviously, could have begun an active sex life in the nineteenth century, but the attitudes he found suggest a moraine left behind by a retreating glacier of earlier sexual indifference and distaste (Gorer, 114).

*Edited by his grandson of the same name, who though he showed his dislike for his father in the novel *The Way of All Flesh*, nevertheless apparently admired this more distant ancestor.

†Dr. Butler's feeling that women were unsatisfactory mental food was doubtless intensified by the sort of women who occasionally wrote to him: "Now I want to fidget out of you a wee bit more on this interesting subject; and if you are sitting very prettily in your easy chair by the library fire, who knows but that you may take compassion on the little lady in Wiltshire, who lives in the world through the medium of Bath vellum. . . ." (Samuel Butler, *Life and Letters*, 2: 36).

In his extraordinary poem *The Bothie of Tober-na-Vuolich* (1848), Arthur Hugh Clough repeats the lesson. He makes an Oxford student fall in love with a Highland lassie, and when the time comes for him to return to the university, she asks him to leave her something to read. "Not a volume," replies her lover. We men are weary of our books, he explains, and come to women to find again the freshness of nature. Women should not want books, "as if they didn't know it all beforehand."[68] She retorts, however, that she will read as she chooses.

An 1869 essay explained the position of an ordinary office worker: he did not want to be reminded of his bookkeeper when he got home, so he hoped his women would not be educated into a state of "energetic acuteness."[69] Husbands could be absolutely devoted to women who did not profess to understand their ideas. Sometimes they started out with the idea of instructing them and found the process more boring than they expected. Shaw, of course, was being deliberately outrageous when he found at the end of the century that a "man as intimate with his own wife as . . . a Prime Minister with the leader of the Opposition, is a man in a thousand,"[70] but he had the point.

∽ A new idea, however, came slowly into prominence during the period we are concerned with. Critics of the social scene came to feel that the estrangement between the sexes was a very serious matter, that diversity of pursuit, incongruity of taste, clash of sentiment, and lack of common reasoning powers detracted from the satisfaction of both sexes. This was one of the main arguments in favor of educating women, and Emily Davies, founder of Girton College, declared herself motivated by "the enormous loss to general culture entailed by the solitude of the male intellect,"[71] as well as by the fact that children brought up in a home where ideas were freely discussed would gain an enormous advantage.

One of the techniques for making the male intellect less solitary, as well as for educating children, was the widespread custom of reading aloud in the family,* and the credit for this habit goes back to Ann Taylor, wife of Isaac Taylor of Ongar, in the first years of the nineteenth century.

Early in her married life, a friend had told her: "Your husband has got a housekeeper and a nurse for his children, but I am sure he has no companion: it will be well if in due time he does not grow tired of you. The

---

*Harriet Mill, John Stuart's sister, explained how her mother and father lived under the same roof but as far apart as the North and South poles. "How was a woman with a growing family and very small means . . . to be anything but a German Hausfrau? How could she 'intellectually' become a companion for such a mind as my father?" (Packe, 33).

In his own marriage John Stuart Mill rather curiously lived out the abstract hopes of his father, James Mill, who had said that a stress on intellectuality might draw men and women closer together in a higher bond so that they would not need to think about sex all the time. It remained for John Stuart Mill to live by this precept in his relationship with Harriet Taylor, whom he loved for years and with whom he worked in close collaboration before they were able to marry, being too proud to have a sexual liaison.

affections of a man of taste cannot fix permanently on a mere plod, and you are certainly nothing better!"[72] The friend managed by keeping two servants, but Mrs. Taylor, while admitting the truth of the friend's remarks, could not at first decide how to remedy her own case, until a brilliant idea struck her. She decided to read aloud to her husband during breakfast and tea so that "I may at once revive my dormant taste, cultivate a mind now rapidly degenerating to its former state of ignorance, direct my mind from these harassing cares which beset me on every side; and thus subjects may be brought before us on which we can converse with mutual advantage." The plan was well received, she tells us, and "instantly adopted."

By passing along the idea in her popular manuals of advice, Mrs. Taylor started a widely adopted custom, and we can see the idea of intellectual fellowship between men and women growing among different groups and classes. It often began with reading together, later progressed to joint walking tours, which were fashionable among university men, sometimes extended to attendance at scientific congresses together, and occasionally ended up in actual joint production of works of scholarship or papers on public affairs.*

By 1870 Angelo Mazzoleni was able to advise Italian women that they should imitate the English home, where, he told them, books, maps, and equipment were available so that every member of the household could think, read, study, and work.[73]

A married couple who exhibited the new style were Mary and William Howitt, both prolific writers throughout a long marriage, during which, they said, "never once did we cease in the pursuit of knowledge."[74] But they also became famous for their long walking tours in Scotland.

A still more famous equal marriage was that of William and Catherine Booth, founders of the Salvation Army. When they became engaged, Catherine had a set-to with her fiancé about the social and mental equality of women, declaring that she would never marry anyone who would not endorse this proposition[75] and telling him that the examples of inferior women whom he had observed were created by training from infancy which cramped and paralyzed them. The couple were married in 1855. The rules for the marriage were that they were to have no secrets relating to the family (although confidences from their converts could be kept) and that they would reason out any differences of opinion but never argue in the presence of the children.

When the Reverend Arthur Rees attacked the right of women to preach, Mrs. Booth wrote her first pamphlet to defend it, and soon she herself began preaching even when to do so she had to leave William at home minding the children. In 1870 when he became ill, Mrs. Booth took over the entire executive function of their mission for three months, besides carrying on her household duties and continuing to preach and write. Within her own large family, she ground into her sons that their

---

*"Why, being married to you is like chumming with a chap!" (Bright, 25).

sisters were just as intelligent and capable as themselves, and the Salvation Army had a policy of appointing women to stations as important as any given to men. Mrs. Booth lived to receive the gratitude of "tens of thousands of women whose lips she had unsealed, whose timidity she had overcome, whose rights she had defended."[76]

Many politicians' wives contributed to their husbands' careers behind the scenes. Gossip in the 1820s had it that George Canning's wife had written many of his speeches.[77] Somewhat later, Lord John Russell's wife defined another sort of contribution: most of us, she declared, have had "the blessed experience of seeing woman the companion of man in his highest thoughts and leading and helping him as much as he does her in general."[78] Her son and daughter-in-law, Lord and Lady Amberley, who during their brief career together sought to have a hand in every good work going on in England, were (said their son) "devoted to each other spiritually, mentally and physically, and acted and reacted on each other with the happiest results."[79]

Early in his career William Gladstone gave his wife, Catherine, the choice of knowing all his political secrets, with a pledge of secrecy, or of knowing none. She chose to know all of them, and during their marriage he credited her with making only one little mistake.*[80]

Of course, the marriage of well-known intellectuals of approximately equal stature created the highest interest. In the middle part of the century, the most famous such couple were the Brownings; at the end, probably the Webbs. Both these couples are too well known to need much description here, but it may be worthwhile to comment on a few others. Isabella and Sam Beeton—she of the famous book on household management—traveled together, played together, picnicked together, and sometimes she made up the magazine he edited, while he followed with interest her manifold experiments with cooking and assisted in the preparation of her magnum opus, all before her death at twenty-nine.[81]

Mrs. Humphry Ward tells how, in 1881, her husband had to review a long book for the *Times*; he had so short a deadline that could only be met by her taking half the book to read and he the other.[82] She herself often wrote independently for the *Times*, contributing articles on fiction and on religious questions.

Unfortunately women who were capable of this kind of intellectual work were likely to be so strongly individualistic that if things worked out less well, they became unhappy with the institution of marriage. Schücking's close study of the British family led him to notice the number of loveless households represented in late nineteenth-century fiction, when

---

*Although Schücking believed that this spirit of cooperation grew out of bourgeois family life, the working classes were also touched. William Lovett, a labor leader, wrote: "We seek to make the mothers of our children fit instructors to promote our social and political advancement, by reading to and conversing with them on all subjects we may be acquainted with; and thus, by kindness and affection, to make them our equal companions in knowledge and happiness, and not, as at present, the mere domestic drudges, and ignorant slaves of our passions" (Lovett, 134).

unfeeling independence got the better of mutual confidence. He wondered whether the modern idea of family life had got stuck halfway, or whether Britain was moving toward a new sort of impoverishment of feeling.[83]

If there was substance to the "impoverishment of feeling" theory, it may go back to the sexual question and the desire of upper-class Englishwomen to avoid sexual experiences classified by them as "coarse" and hence uncivilized. It seems as if they might have made their demand for more satisfactory (rather than for less) sex, but because of their ignorance, and the tradition of hushing the subject up, this course was not widely pursued. In countries where erotic techniques were more advanced, like France and Italy, there is no indication that continence was included in women's demands for a larger say in affairs. But in England, as I have tried to show, men often accepted the argument, with the result that sexual activity was presumably lowered.

Several possible benefits can be discerned: a higher evaluation of women's non-sexual functions, a turning toward intellectual and joint social activities, and a reevaluation of spinsters as not, in fact, having missed the essential ingredient in life. On the other hand, the relative neglect of physical sex may very well have held Englishmen and Englishwomen back, in all too many instances, from the complete fulfillment of their emotional needs.

12.

To Love, Honor, and Obey: France

If a man wants a soul that responds to his with the light of reason as much as with love, who cheers his heart by a charming vivacity, gaiety, sallies of courage, a woman's words, or songs of birds, he needs a Frenchwoman.

Jules Michelet, 1858

In France, as elsewhere, the celebration of domestic pleasures was a relatively new thing for the nineteenth century. Back in the seventeenth (according to David Hunt),* men actually felt threatened by the role of husband and father.[1]

By the late eighteenth century (here we follow Léon Séché), domestic love flourished only among certain old *"parlement"* families;[2] it was a Jansenist flower, much as the English love of the time was a Puritan one. In certain landed, conservative households like the Barantes and the Rémusats, it lasted right through the Revolution and on into the Restoration period of the 1820s. In 1805 Mme de Rémusat's mother asked her what she would do if M de Rémusat was unfaithful to her while he was away in Milan. Her answer was that she would not even think about an impossible situation. Her image would always remain between him and seduction, and she thanked her stars for such luck and happiness.[3] But such households as these were in contrast to the general moral climate of the *ancien régime* in noble and courtly circles, where custom almost dictated that a young countess have a lover after six months of marriage and that after the birth of her first child her husband should practically disappear from her life.[4] In the bourgeois classes life was far more strait-laced, as we can tell by the rigid standards of Mme Roland's girlhood.

The effect of the Revolution was to dissolve both aristocratic conventionality and middle-class puritanism, and for a while Frenchwomen had a great deal of freedom. Mme de Staël, who was the greatest exponent of the feminine point of view before 1820, felt that the new

*He suggests that Erik Erikson's "intimacy" phase of human development may be a relatively recent phenomenon (David Hunt, 55).

freedom gave men a chance to detach themselves, leaving Frenchwomen "the least happy at heart" of any nation.[5] She joined her voice to those who preached that love ought to be the prime value in marriage, and she reproached those philosophers of the Enlightenment who had come to regard married love as secondary to parental.[6] In practice, obviously, she was far from these ideals, and her husband complained that she had deprived him of "the only happiness a rational being and a sensible heart can desire—the happiness that can be found only in a tender and intimate marriage."[7]

For whatever reasons in the early 1800s—the return to religion, the *embourgeoisement* of society, the small homes for single families that sprang up as the result of the subdivision of property, the sober thoughts induced by the Revolution itself, and the retreat to the home as public life became dangerous—almost all commentators noticed that married and domestic affection suddenly sent out deeper roots. Lady Morgan felt that it was no longer bad form for a lady to be accompanied by her husband, and she thought that even after intimate ties had ceased, French couples often remained close friends.[8] As an example we might present the case of Chateaubriand, who never "loved" his wife but who acquired a warm friendship for her when he found out how clever and devoted she was.[9] His official mistress (he had others) was Mme Récamier, and he often used to write letters to both ladies on the same day.

By the 1840s and 1850s the process of domestication had gone much farther in the middle classes. It was here that the arranged marriages discussed in Chapter 3 flourished, and they usually turned out well by all accounts. If erotic love failed, at least friendships nearly always developed and infidelity became rare. In an 1838 book about the new democracy and the manners of the middle class, Edouard Alletz pointed out that with life so precarious, man demanded a loving, close, cheerful family, and he thought it was a sublime task for a bride to set up a sacred asylum where honesty and consolation could thrive.[10] ("Sublime" and "sacred" are two favorite French adjectives.) Mrs. Trollope commented in 1835 that if she looked around her instead of reading books about French life, she would conclude that its most remarkable feature was conjugal and family affection. "It is rare to see either a man or a woman, of an age to be wedded and a parent, without being accompanied by their partner and offspring."[11] Whatever pleasures existed were shared equally. Likewise Frederic Marshall, in 1874, observed that the careful attention paid by parents to the selection of mates produced enviable results. It was not easy to discover really unhappy marriages, he thought.[12]

Taine, with his usual eagerness to give explanations, made a list of the assets a French couple brought to marriage: they were protected by prudent financial planning; most French homes were models of gentleness and kindness; the skills brought to marriage were of a high order (sexual, does he mean, or domestic?); the children, though fewer than in some other countries, were warmly cherished. Particularly in the lower middle class, he found the intensity of partnership unparalleled.

Noticeable was the relaxation of the old patriarchal discipline. Although some people, then as now, blamed permissiveness for all the evils of the day, Janet, discussing the family from a sociological point of view in 1857, found touching intimacy, confidence, and freedom.[13] He felt sure that the benefits of increased affection outweighed the loss of hierarchical principles.

Michelet, as might be expected, joined the chorus of praise for the new sentiment. Woman, he sang, who used to be only a thing, had now become a person and a soul.[14] Marriage as the union of two persons had just begun to be possible, and since religion was decaying, love had become the only valid cement or source of moral authority.[15] Likewise Hillebrand, that German student of French customs, reported in the seventies the unusual social ease within the family, and that except in the highest social class, men usually stayed home and shared social life with their wives.[16]

In 1919 Charles Lefèbvre was asked to deliver a series of lectures on the subject of French family life to American soldiers still stationed in France. They are a paean to this old French idea of domesticity, and he explained how the laws against bastardy and against the rights of women and minors were designed to preserve the family as an ongoing entity through generations. Praising Paul Janet for his exposition of the best French tradition, he warned his American audience not to take the French theater too literally. The highest ideal of many newlyweds was to create a home where both partners could work together to bring up their children in a continual concert of care and effort.[17]

A few examples from life and fiction may illustrate the point. Women themselves began to express the intimate affection they felt for their husbands without shame or coyness. A French wife of Spanish descent, a poet by profession, wrote to her husband: "You are at once my friend, my lover, my husband, my brother, my father and my child. . . . Forgive me if I have omitted any tenderness." Her bed, she said, felt hard when he was not in it. "I don't exist without you."[18]

The case of the Girardins was somewhat unusual. Emile was the most sensational journalist of the Orléans period and Delphine already a renowned poet when they married. Childless herself, she had brought up one of Emile's natural children, but there were never any scenes of public jealousy.* In the June Days of 1848, when Paris was in a bloody rebellion, Emile wrote to tell her he was under arrest, and asked to have a warm coat and linen sent to the prison. "In all circumstances you have proved that you are my equal in courage—don't disprove it now. *Je t'embrasse.*"[19]

*The first duty of any woman, declared Mme de Girardin, was to be *pretty*. Not everybody could have beauty, which was given from above, but prettiness could be achieved by a simple desire to *please*, and to please everyone: an old aunt, a young relative, or an important deputy. She offers a suggestive list of ideas: to don a pretty bonnet with a pink ribbon, or to put a bouquet of perfumed violets on the table, to serve a glass of true Spanish sherry, or to have a well brought up child. The most important thing of all, however, was to be an angel in the house for one's husband, who would be oppressed by cares at his office (D. Girardin, 350).

Glorifying the happy new ideal, Gustave Droz (in *Monsieur, madame et bébé)* pictured his bride and groom (whose wedding we watched in Chapter 7) a few days after their marriage. When for the first time she discovers her husband shaving, she playfully dabs his nose. Delicious moments, these, the writer exclaims, and then moves on a few months to depict Christmas Eve. They sit together discussing Christmases in their childhoods, and then she produces a surprise supper of cold chicken and other things, which they devour in front of the fire. He is charmed. She sits near him and sews his gift—a pair of braces.

The feminist movement and the other changes in housing and in opportunities appearing during the last quarter of the nineteenth century began to turn French family life around again. Marcelle Tinayre, a prophet of femininity rather than feminism, regretted the disappearance of the old-time "queen of the home," who enjoyed more privileges than rights, although she felt that a new kind of happiness would be possible in the twentieth century.[20]

In 1946 Marguerite Grépon described the results of these long-term trends. Out of date by that time were jealousy, adultery, and vanity. Equal education had at last led to a happy, balanced home, and the new interest in sports had replaced the exclusively indoor interests of the married couple.[21] Such happiness, she felt, was shared by thousands of couples in post-war France, and was surely a logical offspring of old-time domesticity coupled with newfound human rights.

∽ The French regard for sexual experience has been well celebrated. In fact, they believed that Latin women's strong sexuality raised them above the Anglo-Saxons and contributed to equality between the sexes.[22] Their advice on the subject was accordingly franker. Marriage, cried Debay, whose *Hygiène et physiologie du mariage* was in its forty-seventh printing by 1853, is a great regulator of health and promoter of long life for both sexes, although he felt that extremes of either continence or indulgence were equally damaging. He was insistent that the first requirement for a happy sexual life was gentleness and mutual understanding, and in case this was lacking, he recommended an earlier volume of his, *Philosophie du mariage.*[23] The clitoris was the organ of pleasure for women, he told his readers; but unfortunately many more women than men remained unsatisfied, and he spent considerable time in telling them how to overcome this condition. In any case, a woman should show signs of pleasure even if she had to pretend because a refusal would drive her husband away. On the other hand, the man must consider her pleasure because to insist in a despotic manner would send her to the arms of a lover. Camille Mauclair, writing much later, believed that gentleness on the first night was quite uncommon, that men, in fact, got a sadistic pleasure from rupturing the hymen, so that when the woman had her first orgasm, often years later, it would come as a thundering surprise.

Women with this experience could be said to lose their virginity twice, but it was only the second, the sensation of true sexual delight, that made them into full women.[24]

A more psychological counselor was Michelet, who as a historian pointed out that the expectation of complete and absolute possession in love was an invention of the nineteenth century, and that the only way to get it was to consult the partner's needs.[25] Among women's rights he placed high that of never being impregnated without their own consent, and he recommended a sort of rhythm method to help control fertility; meanwhile, he instructed husbands never to accept pleasure without being sure the wife shared it. In preparing for his study on women during the 1840s Michelet explained he had become the confidant of many who spoke frankly with him as soon as they found out that he was an impartial investigator. They came to appreciate the fact that he saw into their souls. Modestly, he attributes the closing of some brothels to the beneficial effects of his marital counseling.[26] In his book *L'Amour*, he imagines an ideal couple, aged eighteen and twenty-eight, and follows them through all the stages of their marriage, through the initiation and the young husband's "creation" of the wife's personality and happiness, to the birth of their child, the subsequent languishing of sexual love, and the need to reaffirm it in middle age.

What women want—according to Michelet's findings—is to be the center of desire. To be loved is not the heart of the problem; nor do they seek physical pleasure principally, though they enjoy it; nor is their central wish to be mistress of the house, though they like that as the best means to attain their desire. Love in men is impatient and easily satisfied, coming once every three or four days, but in women it crests only monthly, and is less exigent; in fact, it is a time of sadness. Men love after a good dinner, especially in the harvest season, but women who feel the sweet pricking are likely to feel it on spring mornings. Because of such differences in timing and mood, it is essential to study women's feelings at all times, study their background, study their taste.

Although the French middle-class bedroom was usually furnished with two very small beds, set very close together,[27] what Michelet recommended was an old-fashioned, oversized bed, which might take up half the chamber, and it was to be low, almost at floor level. This promoted easy conversation, so that things would get said that would never be shouted to a separate bed.* Intimacy was not easily achieved in the presence of a maid, so let the husband assist his wife with her clothing.[28] He hoped his couple would not be rich, but let them arrange to have plenty of free time and to live in the country, where the wife could work a little, sweat a little (but very little at first), bathe in water that had been exposed to the sun and was nearly cold, and sun-bathe alone in her garden to turn her skin brown.

*Louis Philippe used to show with pride the big bed where he slept with the Queen (Burnand, *1830*, 62).

Since he noted that there was a frequent let-down in mid-marriage, Michelet devoted considerable attention to the need for new communication with a wife after a period of childbearing had seemed to bring about a separation. An experienced physician told him that women of thirty-five often had an increased need for love, even though their desires might be more fitful as their blood circulated less regularly. This was no time for the husband to seek laughing beauties elsewhere.*

Among the marriage counselors of France must be admitted Balzac, even though the title of his *Physiology of Marriage* is misleading. It is not a description of how the human body works, but an analysis of how to keep a marriage going. He uses the word "physiology" with the same sense of metaphor that Robert Burton employs in the *Anatomy of Melancholy.*

Balzac described his book as meant for the husbands of those million women who cultivated the privilege of inspiring passions that a gallant man admitted with shame or hid with pleasure.[29] To him a French married woman was like a conquered queen, free and a prisoner at the same time, and he wished that somehow girls had a chance to get some of their flirtatiousness out of the way before they were married. He would prefer that they had no dowries but could be picked by character and talent alone. But with things as they were, Balzac advised men to cope with the dangers by a combination of the carrot and the stick. In the first place, he advised, never begin a marriage with a rape. As for the question of double or twin beds, or separate rooms, he believed that the double bed would enable the man to know how his wife was feeling, even though to sleep this way was an example of the sacrifices he must make. From then on the husband must spend nearly all his time paying attention to what his wife was up to, to give her enough real satisfaction to keep her from straying, and also to enable him to notice the start of any misstep. In order to reduce her vitality, he advised allowing her to eat very little meat and keeping her indoors, where she would not get fresh air. If the thin diet failed to quiet her, keep her busy, he advised; get her something to do; remember that after all she is your property, something you have acquired by contract. If she has a baby, make her suckle it; to persuade her to do this, read *Emile* aloud and appeal to her sense of morality; but be careful not to let her read anything on her own; make fun of her if she betrays a taste for books; tell her it will make her eyes dull. The danger, of course, is that books may give her an imaginary world in which she can learn to do without you. If she insists, let her have access only to dull reading matter. Add to this bag of Stephen Potter tricks an attention to such physical arrangements as will thwart a lover: have no cupboards, corners, or wardrobes where he can hide, and be sure to train your wife in habits of neatness so that you will detect at once an extra book or disorder

*By 1898 Michelet's ideas were the subject of a satiric blast from Jules Lemaitre, who laughed at his orphic style clothing commonplace ideas. Particular fun was made of Michelet's idea that yielding to a husband's desires signified that the wife was willing to die for him (Lemaitre, 743).

on the bed. The last part of Balzackian advice dealt with truly desperate measures to keep an unruly woman under control: traps, reading her mail, setting the servants to spy, and careful management of money. You should make a practice of handing over two-thirds of your income to your wife with a show of absolute confidence, but be sure to withhold the other third secretly for your own defense. No husband should allow himself to feel bored with all this; it was part of the art of keeping a wife.

Turning away from Michelet's dreams and Balzac's cynicism, let us try to deduce from more ordinary examples how average French people felt about women's sexuality. One of the many French theorists of love, Camille Mauclair, thought he observed that women easily became accustomed to having sexual relations with a particular man, even in cases where they wished it could be with someone else.[30] Other writers believed sexual feelings were dormant, waiting to be roused by a husband's attentions, but they acknowledged the possibility that lack of tact or something else could turn them off for good.

Hillebrand, whose Teutonic sense of contrast is so useful, believed that sex among the French was an area of cool wit, less slippery than sentiment, less seductive than passion.[31] He felt that this relative coolness in marital relations could be accounted for by the overheating of French family life in childhood, so that a person's passions might well be exhausted early. This is not how the French thought of themselves, of course.

The French did admit the existence of "those curious misunderstandings of the flesh which freeze the most ardent."[32] Sometimes this was inexplicable, although at other times it might be caused by clumsy handling on the part of the husband. George Sand said that when she was married she had no knowledge of what marriage required, but she felt that her later refusal to sleep with M Dudevant was based more on a total lack of sympathy and love than on purely physical repugnance. She believed that a sense of marital duty could overcome physical repulsion but that when all love was gone, the sexual connection became ignoble.[33] On the other hand, her husband's response addressed her as "You who repel my embraces, you whose senses seem to me proof against anything. . . ."[34]

And so she wrote *Lélia*, the great novel of feminine frigidity that she hoped would speak to millions of women in post-Napoleonic Europe. Successive biographers have tried to fit the theme into her own life and to speculate about which, if any, of her many lovers may have given her the physical fulfillment she desired. Whatever its relationship to herself, there is no doubt that the book was a sensation across Europe, partly because of its romantic theme and partly because of its explicit descriptions of sexual activity, even though these were not pornographically expressed.

Lélia is beautiful, rich, and intelligent, and she has nothing to do in life except contemplate her own problem and console herself with the idea that suffering somehow ennobles. In her case suffering has been endured in the long months she has lain beside a man and pretended to achieve orgasm while actually striving in vain. At times she retreats to the forest, living under a vow of silence in an abandoned monastery; at other times she casts a world-weary eye upon revelers at a masked ball. She then decides to have one last fling with a young man who adores her and who describes in detail the techniques he will use to overcome her frigidity. When even this does not work, she deceives the lover into spending the night with her sister (and exact opposite), Pulchérie. Pulchérie and Lélia enjoy a long discussion, the cheerful Pulchérie explaining the importance of using one's gifts and taking life as it comes. Pulchérie is a high-class courtesan, but she is not ungenerous or indifferent to pain. Sleeping with her, however, brings the young man only disillusion, and in revenge he enters on a life of total debauchery, ending in suicide. Lélia falls on his corpse muttering that she has at least been true to him and to herself by not repeating her pretenses in his bed. While moaning, she is conveniently strangled by a mad Irish monk.

Frigidity may have been a dramatic problem, but perhaps more common was a general lack of vitality. For women, youth was brief.[35] Debay believed that after thirty-five their trumpets of desire faded out,[36] while Balzac set forty as the time when nature, "with a summons sufficiently brutal, bids the passions cease."[37] This was known as the *coup de lapin*, the rabbit's blow (an expression not heard in the drawing room). Thus a pencil sketch observed by an American visitor showed a mature woman in evening dress with a rabbit sitting on its haunches on the back of her chair, ears pricked, one paw raised, about to tap her shoulder.[38] She could not hope to recover from the blow.

As for men, vitality was sometimes considered a question of class more than of age. We have noted a certain lack of passion among male literati. It was perhaps an illusion that the working classes kept hold of simple vitality, but Zola depicts the mine owner in *Germinal*, facing his starving, striking miners, willing to exchange "his education, his comfort, his luxury, his power as manager if he could be for one day the least of the wretches who obeyed him, free of his flesh, enough of a blackguard to beat his wife and to take his pleasure with his neighbors' wives. . . . And those fools complained of life when they could take their fill of this supreme happiness of love."[39] Happily would he starve as they did if he could begin life again with their facility in coupling.*

It will be noted that one of the pleasures Zola's employer felt he had missed was beating his wife. And although it is hard to think of the French as a nation of wife-beaters, certainly one of the charges brought by the feminists when they began to organize in the eighties and nineties was brutality. A woman doctor in 1911 made a passionate plea on the subject, describing women who were kicked and dragged around by their hair when they tried to resist their husbands' demands because they were ill or

*In Germany Treitschke voiced the same idea: the lower classes had lots of simple sex to console them for their lack of culture.

had just given birth.[40] Doctors, she said, often had to artificially prolong the time a new mother stayed in a maternity hospital, knowing that the minute she got home she would be subject to the assertion of marital rights. (After all, Proudhon had said sharply, "If your wife resists you to your face, you must beat her at any cost.")[41]

Frenchmen were also well aware of flagellation as an erotic technique and as a cure for frigidity.* Debay has a whole chapter on this. He told his readers that while in the Middle Ages whips were used for penitence, nowadays their only purpose was to stir desire.[42] In Russia, he believed, many people needed a good whipping in order to be able to make love at all, and though this was not true for France, he gave specific advice on how to practice it if desired. On the other hand, Michelet told his followers that no matter what was true in Russia, Frenchwomen were uniformly too nervous to stand being beaten. Even if you caught your wife in the act with a lover, Michelet's advice was to spare her corporal chastisement unless, out of great remorse, she begged for it and offered herself. Then you might whip her lightly, so as to heal her soul by inflicting pain on her body.[43]

In regard to birth control, the French were widely believed to use it more than any other nation of that time.[44] The practice was widespread enough that a French bishop told the Pope in 1842 that he was simply powerless to halt it, and that to try to do so would only drive people away from the Church.[45] The techniques were passed from woman to woman without being widely discussed in print; amateur efforts in this direction were not always harmless, leading to many inflamations and minor feminine complaints.†[46]

In general, though, the French were probably more adept at sex than their neighbors. Maupassant told Frank Harris that it took brains to give a woman the greatest possible amount of pleasure[47] (not for him the belief that intellectuals were unsatisfactory lovers), and Frenchmen were trained to believe that such effort was worthwhile. Emily Boutmy explained that while in England sex was enjoyed without preliminaries, the French were wont to delay their own satisfaction in a mood of chivalry to their partners, in order to blend sex with affection.[48]

∽ A striking aspect of the French attitude toward marriage was the change it was expected to produce in the wife. Sometimes the change

---

*Adèle Esquiros, writing on love (*L'Amour*) in 1860, included material on the necessity and the art of whipping women. She described the husband as physician, confessor, and, when love has cooled, flagellator. So did Claude Anet (Jean Schopfer) in 1908.

†Paul Bureau, in 1919, summed up his glum statistics. According to him, 51 percent of French families contained one or two children; 23 percent, three or four; 16 percent were childless; and 8 percent had five or six. He calculated that 2.7 were born to an average family, of whom 2.2 grew up. Such figures are probably more valuable as representing the perceived situation than as literal fact, as he gives no full explanation of how they were gathered (Bureau, 163).

happened almost overnight, from "the dreamy monotony of *Mademoiselle*" to "the vivid charm of *Madame*." Mrs. Trollope compared the change to the awakening of a sleepwalker, and numerous other observers mentioned the alteration in girls' voices, their handwriting, and even their facial characteristics. Mrs. Trollope knew an Englishman who had been received into the bosom of a French family. He felt close to the adults, though the only daughter seemed plain and unresponsive. Some months later, visiting the Louvre upon his return to Paris, he was greeted by a strikingly beautiful woman who inquired about him in the kindest way and invited him to dinner. It was the same girl, now married and utterly transformed.[49]

Though the change was partly due to the new freedom and sense of power that the title of *Madame* conferred, most French people felt that it was the husband's duty to help his wife grow into just the sort of companion he wanted. This was why she must not have read or experienced too much beforehand, even though this meant that the couple started out with a great disparity of knowledge. But, says Michelet to the new husband, most people have a passion for creating growing things. What joy for your bride, with her Byzantine education, to find that you know all about science and modern ideas. Nothing is sweeter than to teach a woman, since her intellect is equal and in some respects superior to men's, and she will feel grateful to you for freeing her from her mother.[50] Such counsel was often repeated; for instance, Janet said that there were many things a young girl was not allowed to know, but once married, you may read anything to her, every evening, and show her even pictures like those of Correggio.[51] In 1869 Charlotte Yonge heard of a French girl, convent-bred, who when married, had never read a single book straight through.[52] Her intellectual husband made her undergo a three-year course of study to enable her to fit into his family. But it is important to stress that the theory had a second part, and in Michelet's view again if you deliver your wife, as Perseus delivered Andromeda from her chains, she will return the favor. In later life she will deliver you from baseness and from sorrow, and she will offer you the priceless gift of a balanced judgment against the overspecialized view that most masculine vocations entail.[53]

The result of this process was that Frenchwomen were commonly assumed to have immense influence. Hillebrand considered them morally and intellectually far ahead of men, with a decisive voice in the family, the salon, the house of business, and even the ministerial office.[54] It was noted that whereas in a salon all the men betrayed their social origin by what is now termed "body language," the women were indistinguishable by reason of their elegance and charm, so that it was impossible to tell the daughter of a notary from the daughter of a courtier.[55]

It was only to be expected that there would be a certain number of exploitative wives. In *Marriage No Mystery* Gyp's young heroine looks forward to theater and opera, dining out in restaurants, and acquiring lots of new Paris clothes, including a riding habit like the Empress Elizabeth's.*[56] Her husband meanwhile is planning to teach her only what he believes to be right and intends for her to go out only in family gatherings. Simple-mindedly he congratulates himself that she has not been brought up in the English fashion to do as she pleases, but he is obviously unprepared for the metamorphosis of the French bride. He is specifically against tight riding habits. As they discuss her allowance, on their honeymoon, he finds himself promising more than he intended, and is ultimately helpless when she decides to go to Deauville and bathe there in mixed company in a short and skin-tight bathing costume.

∽ Whether men joked or agonized about women's role in marriage, underneath there was the feeling that the essential basis was not physical, nor yet domestic habit, but a union of sensibility and of intellectual interest. When this ideal foundered, the most common cause of disagreement was religion. Convent schools were giving young girls ideas so adverse to what their future husbands were probably thinking that there would be small chance that they could ever agree, according to Michelet. Hamerton observed the separation of the sexes that was common in Picardy at social gatherings, noted the domination of the ladies by their priests, and concluded that only in Paris was the wider intellect cultivated.[57]

Michelet, who had a particular animus against the Church, partly because a priest had kept him from going to the bedside of his dying mistress, wrote in 1845 an influential book about the marital relationship of a husband, his wife, and her confessor; the last he considered more potentially disruptive than a physical lover and said he was an invisible man who sat between the head of a family and its womenfolk. Michelet was writing about the grave trouble created inside a family when the confidant of all the wife's secrets, including those concerning her intimate relationship with her husband, set the standards for her life. This effectively prevented the husband from talking freely about serious matters that ought to be decided strictly within the home.[58] The Catholic church had recently taken up the psychological explanations for sin, according to Michelet, and this made the modern act of confession more damaging than the straightforward medieval confessions.[59] Priests were enemies of the modern intellectual spirit, and because many of them felt keenly their own lack of family warmth, they would console themselves by directing other families. When one considered that two hundred thousand boys, six hundred thousand girls, and millions of women accepted spiritual direction from this source, one could see what a profound effect it had upon the state itself, as well as on the happiness and integrity of numberless families.[60] Michelet's book was a ringing cry to French husbands to

*Her comment about sex: "I believed it was more terrible, but I also thought it was more amusing" (Martel de Janville, *Marriage*, 76).

reassert themselves and make their relationships with their wives into "true marriages" once again; and in order to facilitate the process, he called for the abolition of clerical celibacy.*

Michelet's indictment became more searching. Young priests used to undergo explanations of every sexual detail, as part of their training, in texts that had to be copied out by hand because no printer would dare to set such words. When ordained, the confessors were required to pry into the imaginations of young girls with suggestions that to Michelet were monstrous.

His message concluded that a married man would often find that while he owned the body of his wife, the priest would own her soul. The tug of war could become disastrous. Imagine meeting in the street a man who knew all your secret weaknesses and might be laughing at you. The priest could also create frigidity in the wife; he could declare so many days for feast and fast that the husband had little chance to assert his marital rights. When a confessor became a spiritual director, he could call at home at any time, and was then told more things than would come out in confession. The marriage sacrament ought to give a man a unique moment to win his wife away from psychological dependence on the priest, but too few men used the moment to good advantage.

What evidence is there that Michelet's diatribe was in any sense correct? In another place, Michelet himself recommended French wives above all others, partly on the grounds that they had been instructed precociously by the confessional. But Dumas felt that women who gave their bodies often hoarded their minds, so that a chaste priest after six months of confessing women would know more about them than any Don Juan,[61] and this posed a dilemma for a man who seriously wanted a complete relationship as a husband. Dumas did not want couples to be united against God in free thought; nor did he want the other form of the triangle, the priestly God-woman alliance against man.[62]

More interesting are women's reactions. We might start with the highly emotional remarks of Eugénie de Guérin, showing what a confessor could mean to an unmarried and deeply religious woman. "The world does not know what a confessor is to one: the man who is the friend of the soul, its most intimate confidant, its physician, its master, its light. . . . When I am at his feet, I see in him only Jesus listening to the Magdalen, and forgiving her much because she has loved much. Confession is but the expansion of repentance into love."[63]

On the other side, Flora Tristan said that the reason she did not go to church, or take her daughter, was the fear of subjugating her dignity as a woman to the impure questions of a priest. She considered the assi-

---

*In an interesting aside, Michelet apologized for a mistake that he had made when writing his history of France in 1833. In that book he declared that no married man could have raised such a sublime monument as the Strasbourg cathedral. Subsequently he found out that it was the work of a married architect who had, moreover, had his daughter associated with him in his work (Michelet, *Pêtre*, 180, n. 2).

duities of women at confession a violation of natural right.[64] George Sand had to dismiss one confessor whom she accused of confusing the curiosity of a man with the function of a priest, and in a novel (*Mlle la Quintinie*) she portrayed the dangers that could follow the intrusion of the clergy into the life of a family.[65]

Much later, at the end of the century, the Vicomtesse d'Adhémar, a devoted Catholic, showed how old-fashioned ideas could damage the Church's influence in a story of a woman whose confessor forced her to resume marital relations with her husband while she was still nursing her baby, with the result that a new conception took place, her milk supply dwindled, and her baby died. The writer felt that it was only natural for a mother under such circumstances to turn against the Church.[66]

The obvious cure for this alleged disruptive factor in marriage was better education for women, much favored by secular thinkers who assumed that this would be the way to make women as anti-clerical as men, but also by Catholics who hoped to retain women's loyalty if only certain reforms could be instituted. Notably the influential Bishop of Orléans, Monsignor Dupanloup, rebutted the traditional argument of Joseph de Maistre that it was best to leave women totally ignorant. He issued a series of pamphlets in the 1870s urging serious education for young girls. The Bishop's declared purpose was to help the wife, not just the husband, apparently hoping that women would accept the will of God more easily if they had greater inner resources. By the end of the century, the enlightened view had become dominant; people now expected women to continue to interest their husbands by keeping up with them in history, science, hygiene, and philosophy.[67]

In view of the tragedy that was assumed to befall women after the menopause, the idea of intellectual potential became unusually important. The physical crisis in itself might occasion a sort of demi-divorce, but it might also be the time when a wife could reach out to help her husband with his work and become truly his associate;[68] in any case, when the charms of youth disappeared, this was the only way for a woman to hold on to her husband. "She must make him love her inner being"* was stated as an ideal whose "grandeur" all civilized men would recognize.[69] Instead of following the English custom of reading aloud to her husband, the French wife was more likely to sharpen her wits by lively discussion of political and literary affairs.[70] It came to be a commonplace that if a man was a writer, his wife should be his first critic; if in politics, she should sharpen his judgment; and if a mere citizen, she should be able to help him decide how to vote.†[71]

*"*Elle doit lui faire aimer son intérieur.*"

†Many nineteenth-century Frenchwomen remarked on having read the eighteenth-century memoirs of Mme Roland, who may have set the style. Intellectually, she tells us, she learned about happy domestic life from reading Rousseau, but she never saw how the care of the house could occupy much time for an intelligent and orderly woman (Roland, 302). Although she did all the necessary household jobs, she also worked side by side with her

The history of French science records an unusual number of men whose wives helped in their research and got credit only for being good wives, not for being good scientists. The marriage of J. L. Gay-Lussac lasted from 1804 until 1850 and was considered one of the great love stories of the century.[72] He first noticed his future wife reading chemistry at the counter where she was a shopgirl, and impressed at the sight, he presented her with a pile of books out of his modest salary, so that she could read while he went away for a year and a half on a research expedition with Alexander von Humboldt. The list included certain classics of literature and also works of modern science and geography. After the couple were married, they worked so closely together that their handwriting came to seem identical, and scholars now cannot tell who wrote the manuscripts.*[73] Mme Pasteur, likewise, was an intelligent collaborator with her famous husband and was especially helpful in his work on the silkworm disease, setting herself to learn how to raise the worms.[74]

The most famous scientific couple of course, were Pierre and Marie Curie. Although Mme Curie's enormous personal reputation is owing partly to her husband's early death, while Pierre was alive no couple could have been more devoted, and their work was completely shared. Their daughter, Eve, remarks that they would have made very poor material for a modern novel because there was complete family loyalty and no treachery; parents and children loved and respected each other, and their characters were uniformly candid and generous.[75]

Other intellectuals of lesser renown that the Curies often married each other, too. We have the word of Mme Edwards-Pilliet, one of the first women doctors in France, that most female physicians of her generation had married their colleagues, and that the marriages had turned out extremely well.[76]

The difference from England is interesting, for in England women gifted in science, like Mary Somerville and even Mrs. Gatty, did their work in their own names, without intellectual input from their husbands.

Collaboration was often seen also in French literary families. Guizot picked both his wives for their literary ability, and they helped him in his own historical labors. They were both of a Catholic and conservative family (the second was the niece of the first), while he was Protestant and liberal, but as the first one put it, his rationality carried harmony into her soul. "Oh, how few people know what happiness is," she exulted, to which he replied, "With you, Pauline, I can't regret

---

husband at his literary work every, day, declining all credit for this even when he was a minister in the government and she was drafting some of his decrees. Another much admired woman from that period was Mme Lavoisier, who educated herself in order to be able to help her husband.

*Mme Gay-Lussac was the daughter of a music teacher who lost his job, and so his daughters' dowries, when the Revolution repressed the convent schools where he was employed. In order to build up dowries for her two younger sisters, Mme Gay-Lussac, at seventeen, went off to earn her living in a lingerie shop (Blanc and Delhoume, 76).

anything, nor desire anything. Everything is good, all complete."[77] As a historian, in fact, he was much more interested in private lives than most of his contemporaries, and he wrote a whole book on married love in history.[78] Mme Michelet is said to have been another creative co-worker.[79]

A rare couple for whom we have testimony from both partners were Charles and Elisa Lemmonier. Protestant in religion, and Saint-Simonian in politics, they were married at Bordeaux in 1841. They had already organized a conference on the future of women, the first of their many joint efforts to improve the world. In a letter to a woman friend in the first years of the marriage, Elisa wrote about the happiness that marriage had given her. The sweetness of companionship and of sharing things made up for any cooling of passion or monotony.[80]

Charles, however, renounced his teaching chair rather than profess Catholicism, and the young couple, finding themselves at odds with the majority of people in their city and isolated by their intellectual interests, moved to Paris in 1845. Here Elisa devoted herself to starting trade schools for girls. After Elisa's death, Charles wrote her a memorial letter, summing up what their life together had meant to him:

> My dear wife,
>
> For thirty-four years I have shared your life, for thirty-four years we have had in common our work, our sorrows, our hopes, and our joys. We gave ourselves to each other out of choice; out of choice we remained united, and our union has never impaired our liberty; we have each worked according to our strength, following our vocation.
>
> I saw come to birth in you the idea of the work to which your memory will be justly attached; without other resource than the passionate energy of an indefatigable courage, frail of body but strong of heart and will, I have seen you for fourteen years gather little by little your friends, communicate your enthusiasm. . . .[81]

Such a couple were clearly exceptional in their social views and in the freedom that belonging to a minority culture gave them.

⚭ A favorite pastime of the French and English during this period was weighing their two marriage systems against each other and trying to deduce which was the happier, naturally without conclusive results.

It is worth suggesting that the reason the Vicomtesse d'Adhémar was so eager to smooth out the disruptive forces, even those caused by her own church, was that she believed feminism was born out of unhappy marriages.[82] Insofar as this explanation is plausible—it is certainly not sufficient in itself—the relative weakness of the feminist movement of France could sensibly be related to a greater totality of successful marriages in that country.

∾13.

To Love, Honor, and Obey: Germany

In Germany a young woman does not arrive at her own gender till she marries and becomes somebody's *Frau*. Woman in general, girl, and miss are neuter; and the fried-fish girl is masculine.

Cecily Sidgwick, 1908

For German Protestants, at least, the style of marriage was set by Luther, who, though no defender of women's intellect, wanted marriage to be based on the warmest possible affection and mutual respect. By denying its sacramental character, he paradoxically created a more viable human institution.[1]

Luther's idea of love, to be sure, was not exactly that "divine emanation" which was discussed in an earlier chapter, and which Stendhal thought he perceived as an active principle in the Germany of 1822.[2] German patriots heartily endorsed the myth that theirs was the only land where marriage was holy, but even Immermann, one of the most ardent protesters about the depth of German commitment in the good old days, which for him were the days of his childhood and the War of Liberation, saw trouble ahead in 1839. Formerly, he explained, lovers were content merely to desire one another, but now, he complained, they added to this the wish to be "understood."[3] This new, individualistic desire went with a demand for talent and the wish of women to be equal to men, all of which he considered but a disguise for their underlying desire, to be cherished more warmly by their husbands. This analysis, while it was both sentimental and incorrect, indicates how threatened the patronizing, authoritarian males in German families were by any talk of women's rights.

It is possible to be extremely fond of a little woman confined to *Kinder, Küche, und Kirche,* and yet be startled when the same woman asks for a larger share of your life. As Fanny Lewald explained about her father, "His wife was subordinate to him, the marriage happy through lack of insight into what a happy marriage in the higher sense would be."[4]

Stories of comfortable friendliness are anything but rare, and William and Mary Howitt (who spent several years in Germany because they found better and cheaper schools there for their sons than were available in England) reported, in 1842, that there were not in the world more attached and affectionate couples than the Germans, even though intellectual companionship was not usually part of the picture.[5]

Perhaps Theodor Billroth provides as good an example as any. He was a German-born surgeon who taught at the University of Vienna. Soon after he was married, he wrote that his wife was "a cheerful, wide-awake, always lively creature, and with it all very sensible. Being married is just too nice."[6] Twelve years later when he volunteered to serve on the battlefield in the war of 1870, he wrote that the bandages she had rolled were much the best, and that he read each of her letters three or four times. As their children came along, he bought her a little suburban home, which she adored, even though it cost him many an extra night's work to pay for it. And then when he got home, dead tired after twelve hours with his sick patients, he found a wife who, having spent the day with the young, was ready for some adult conversation and a share in his life. Theodor felt, wearily, that she had a perfect right to expect this, since he was her reliance and her support.*[7]

One of the most charming customs of intellectual German families was the composition of little verses on all sorts of occasions. This art, of course, was not unknown in England; perhaps, if there is a difference, the German verses were more sentimental, the British more witty.[8] Pastor Wiedig sent out from his political imprisonment in 1836 two birthday poems for his children, one of whom had been born during his incarceration, along with a note to "the dear wife of my heart."[9] When Professor Hermann Kurz, the librarian at the University of Tübingen, died, his wife recalled in verse how much she used to enjoy carrying his lunch to his desk so that he would not have to leave his books.[10] Theodor Mommsen, the great historian of Rome, was constantly inspired to address his family in rhyme, sometimes with little jokes, sometimes seriously, as in the following:

> My darling, since our earliest kiss
> Our lives have been as one,
> We've faced together storm and mist
> And shared the shining sun.†[11]

On the other hand, since German women's companionship depended so heavily on the willingness of their husbands to give it, many of them were seriously neglected. English visitors were inclined to pity German married women, according to Mayhew, because they had to

---

Stütze.

†Mein Lieb, seit unseren ersten Kuss
  Lebten wir insgemein;
  Wir teilten wie den Regenguss
  So auch den Sonneschein.

My translation lacks the original's charm and elegance but may provide some idea of the sense and rhythm.

sleep in single beds and often, indeed, separate rooms.[12] (This pity, to be sure, was reciprocated, as was pointed out in Chapter 11.) Moreover, German men were unlikely to spend their evenings at home (we have seen that it was a sacrifice for Dr. Billroth), and in fact it was part of the duty of a good middle-class wife to send her husband to the tavern, where he could pick up business acquaintances.[13] Women might hold *Kaffee Klatsches* to discuss things interesting only to their own sex, leaving the social life of the country seriously split in two. For wives left so alone, physically and spiritually, for women when the light had gone out, there remained, in Henriette Feuerbach's words, "only the little candle of duty."[14]

The Kurzes' daughter, Isolde, lived in a university town where she saw the best of German home life. In the 1870s she took a short trip to France and compared German views of marriage with those of young people there. The French considered the German way of freedom for engaged couples and marriage for love impractical, she found. Generalizing from her observations, she concluded that while many unions in both countries were boring, a few German ones reached heights of devotion untouched by any in France.[15]

ᴄᴏ Talking openly about sexual experiences was frowned upon in Germany to the point where even such mild revelations as the French absorbed happily in *Monsieur, madame et bébé* were felt to be offensively frank. Evidences of public and private censorship extend through the whole nineteenth century. At the beginning, Johann Gottlieb Fichte, the Berlin professor who inflamed his students to fight idealistically for a restored and united Germany, also told them that the woman who acknowledged her sexual needs forfeited her self-respect.[16] In mid-century a Prussian judge, von Kirchmann, was dismissed from his post on grounds of immorality because he lectured in favor of birth control.[17] Later, the first German woman to talk frankly about prostitution and try to stop it, Frau Guillaume-Schack, was subjected to a police trial and eventually had to leave the country. And in the 1920s, when such censorship had come to seem absurd, Helene Lange looked back over her long life as a pioneer in the women's movement and remarked how nearly impossible it had been to start any discussion of sex in the 1890s.[18]

A sort of running debate can be traced among doctors and philosophers on the question of women's sexual nature, with the radical views almost always so startling as to be generally discounted by the public. The man who might be said to have begun the discussion was Friedrich von Schlegel, whose novel *Lucinde* (1799) was prime underground reading for many years. It told its readers that women "know everything" because they are at the womb of nature, and so provided a rationale for free experimentation in the field. In opposition to this view, a Dr. Karl

Friedrich Pockels decided that nature's method for keeping women pure was to give them a diminished sex drive.[19]

It has already been mentioned that the man who tried to bring the most radical British ideas on birth control and eroticism to Germany was Dr. Roderich Hellmann, who observed that in most civilized countries sexual pleasure was attained only with difficulty. After describing five techniques of birth control (rhythm, withdrawal, the sheath, the sponge, and the douche), he goes on to list the positions of sexual intercourse (in two pages of Latin, alas, since even he could not bring himself to write about the subject in the vernacular). His conclusion was that orgasm should be mutual and simultaneous, and accompanied by a vivid pleasure in the partner's feelings.[20] He was countered by a Dr. Windschied, who believed that sexual appetite is acquired, not born, in women; for it to awaken spontaneously would be an abnormality, and therefore old maids did not miss sex.[21] After him, Dr. Alfred Hegar, a gynecologist at Freiburg, wrote a treatise on the sex drive in 1894, delivering the opinion that the natural inclination for sex in women was rather low, and that they often experienced nausea even in the arms of a man they loved. He felt that most of his profession would agree with this opinion and quoted some English doctors—though not Acton—to support it.[22] Most women, he found, would like to give up sex for good after they had borne two or three children.

The man whose views on sex Hegar was most anxious to neutralize was August Bebel, who by virtue of being at the head of the Social Democratic party commanded a large audience, much to Dr. Hegar's distress. Bebel's argument that the nervousness and anemia of most women was "nature's revenge" for lack of sexual fulfillment led up to a demand that every organ be exercised.[23] So his volume on woman and socialism was widely interpreted, by those already terrified, as advocating unbridled sensualism.[24] Though not the most important tenet of socialism, or one accurately described by its enemies, free love was often used as a means of decrying the entire philosophy.

Meanwhile, a truly distinguished student of sexual pathology, Richard von Krafft-Ebing, after gathering material from all over the world, concluded that frigidity was abnormal in most cultures. Another serious and dispassionate student, Auguste Forel, a professor in Switzerland, disagreed; he did not think that frigidity was abnormal, though he had found that most women could be aroused and develop a desire for coitus after repeated sexual experiences.[25] Forel's book, whose German edition came out in 1905, was accessible to a great many more people than any of the earlier books, either the popular or the scholarly treatises. With his help, the new century was bringing a new point of view about sex world wide.

It is much harder to find out what women were feeling than it is to know what men were thinking about them. Goethe had an anecdote

about his sister that shows sympathy and a rather interesting foreshadow-
ing of the concept of psychosomatic disease. He noted that the idea of
resigning herself to a man was repulsive to her, and supposed that such a
"peculiarity," where it existed, must make for many unpleasant hours.
Even though she was married to one of the best of men, she was still
unhappy and nervous to the point of getting skin eruptions at every
dance.[26]

The few hints that come through here and there mostly concern
women who were very unhappy, and they should not be considered a fair
sample. Lily Braun tells us that her mother came home from the honeymoon a pale wreck, having left in blooming health.[27] Frieda von Richthofen's wedding night with her first husband, Fred Weekley (her second
was D. H. Lawrence), was "hideous." Marianne Weber, in spite of being
in love with her husband, Max, offered herself as a "sacrifice" and in
some way must have contributed to his impotence.[28]

A poignant account of a truly painful marriage was Lena Christ's,
though it reflected a lower social class than most of the families here
discussed. Lena was the natural daughter of a bigoted Catholic. At the
age of seventeen she was not physically ready for marriage, having begun
to menstruate only a few weeks earlier, but she was married anyway and
gritted her teeth for the sake of having a baby. After her first child, her
husband had to force her every time he wanted intercourse—once when
she was in labor, and several times the day after she had given birth. By
great good luck a man in whose house she worked as a maid discovered
that she had literary talent, and he helped her to get her poems published
and eventually, in 1912, to get a divorce. She had a physically satisfying
love affair after that, but eventually committed suicide.[29]

⁓ Before considering intellectual relations between German men and
women, it is enlightening to quote Goethe's dictum to the effect that "the
things we love in a young lady are something very different from understanding." They included beauty, youth, playfulness, character, and
caprices. Still, he admitted that "understanding could fix affections once
aroused by these other qualities."[30]

Goethe pronounced this verdict when he was seventy-five years old
(in 1824), and if he had looked back to the marriages of the friends of his
youth, he would have noticed a change in the interval. The Age of
Reason everywhere had been a period of considerable intellectual equality and social freedom. A representative union of that time was that of
Wilhelm and Karoline von Humboldt, who represented the Enlightenment at its best. (Wilhelm, the brother of Alexander von Humboldt,
founded the university that, in the eastern zone of Berlin, still bears his
name.)[31] At the end of his life, in 1835, Wilhelm declared, "I do not
believe that there were ever two people on earth in whom married love

was so deep and so mutual as in us. There never was so perfect and womanly a person as Karoline, in the highest as well as in the simplest sense of the word.''[32] During their engagement he kept encouraging her to read and to create a high sense of herself as a person, and one of the first things they did after their marriage was read Homer together. When Wilhelm's career took them to Paris, she opened a salon for artists; later, in Rome, they shared domestic chores, and when she took one child to Germany in quest of better medical treatment, Wilhelm took personal charge of the two small daughters. During the War of Liberation in Germany, Karoline spent her time collecting money and linen; during this period, when they were much separated, she hoped that their girls would learn from their example to enjoy every happiness they could snatch with their husbands, to understand every feeling, to honor every tear. The daughters remembered the times of family reunion as full of laughter, but Karoline was also able to give her husband serious advice about his career, urging him to separate himself from the Prussian chancellor, Hardenberg, who she thought was taking advantage of him.

The Humboldts' story is on the whole a happy tale, as if intellectuals born under the Enlightenment expected to be happy, but as the sunlight of the eighteenth century dimmed into the romantic moonlight of the early nineteenth, the sense of equality declined. Many young Germans took their cue from the letters of Heinrich von Kleist to the fiancée he never married, written in 1799 but published after his suicide (see Chapter 5). These came to be regarded as the very model of what an earnest young man would say to his beloved. He wants to explore her heart. He declares that he will share every thought with her, will work for her development.*[33] He even consults her about what career he should settle on, though he does not promise to follow her wishes. Law is too rational for a romantic like him; as for diplomacy, he does not imagine a love like theirs could blossom at a foreign court; finance might be an alternative. He will take her views very seriously. Meanwhile, which of them would lose more by the death of the other? Man, he instructs her, is both a husband and a citizen, while woman is only a wife, so she has more to give and less to lose. And he wants her to learn his instructions by heart:

> Yes, Wilhelmine, if you could give me the joy of keeping up progress in your education of mind and heart, if you could give success in forming out of you a wife such as I wish for myself, a mother such as I wish for my children, enlightened, free of prejudice, always obeying Reason, gladly following the heart—yes, then you could reward me. . . . [34]

He imagines their household after five years of marriage comprising two children and one more to come, so she is to cherish the idea that she "was born to be a mother.''[35] To sharpen her mind for this enterprise, he

Bildung.

sets her problems, such as: Who is lovable? What is uplifting? What is frightful, disturbing? Such exercises, he believes, will fit her for her task.

In spite of the egoism of Kleist's attitude—which might be partly explained by the very limited facilities for girls' education in those days—there is visible here a genuine expectation that marriage could have an intellectual component, and that husbands and wives could converse about serious subjects all their lives.

During the succeeding period, when the cult of domesticity flourished, the opposite was often believed: that intellectual freedom for women went with loose morals. By 1839 Karl Immermann was able to congratulate his period that morals were growing purer—but alas, he went on, he could not account for the fact that nobody seemed to be as happy as before![36] To William and Mary Howitt, shortly after Immermann's time, there seemed to be a serious denigration of women's brains; in their view even intellectual men picked cooks and housewives for marriage partners, and then treated them like peasants.[37] They felt that German men had to be great everywhere, both outside and inside the home, and "to be the sole burning and shining light here, they put out that secondary and moon-like light, the mind of their wives."[38]

The great difference in the education offered to girls and boys made this treatment easy. Although Germany led all other countries in compulsory primary schooling, after its completion the boys could go on to publicly supported *gymnasia* and universities, while for girls there were only poor, scarce, and expensive private schools.[39] Back in Karoline von Humboldt's day, when the cultural leaders of the country had been aristocrats, girls like her often benefited from private tutors,* but when higher education spread widely into the middle class, girls were left to stagnate just when their future husbands were tasting intellectual freedom. The middle class became infected with the positive belief that girls ought not to develop interesting personalities or become familiar with scientific ideas.† One of the things the Howitts missed in Germany was the sort of popular literature on science and history that was so freely

---

*Karoline had been educated by an extraordinary tutor, who had taught her to observe nature, study her own feelings, and also notice the nuances of situations involving other persons. He was almost certainly in love with the girl, but the conventions of the day would have made marriage between them impossible.

†The problem was taken up in a novel by Berthold Auerbach called *Die Frau Professorin* (1846). It tells of a painter who falls in love with a village innkeeper's daughter while on a walking tour. She is a nice, innocent, well-motivated, far-from-stupid girl, but she cannot keep up in the city and court circles where he finds his career. Partly it is his fault, since he has decided to keep her as "a child of nature." At first she meets everything on a plane of spontaneity and good sense, and even charms the Prince with her earthy heartiness. But since her husband feels that he cannot discuss his philosophical ideas in *dialect*, and he always speaks to her in the language of her native village, he stops telling her about his life at all. She finds it sad that a city wife is unable to help her husband in his work and finally retreats to her village, where she lives thereafter in an uncomfortable position as neither maid, wife, nor widow.

available in England. They also commented on the lack of good women writers, ones who might compare with Mrs. Howitt herself, or Mrs. Somerville, Mrs. Norton, or Miss Martineau.[40]

Gustav Freytag, it is true, stated that most of his friends had wives who were confidantes and companions, but in his own memoirs he makes no mention of his own marriage whatsoever, save to record that it took place.[41] One gets the impression that during this time there was far more domestic warmth than intellectual magnetism among the wives of men who were themselves intellectual

In fact, declared Dr. Riehl flatly, the higher the calling of the man, the less help a woman could be. Theodor Fontane remembered how his father always took a light tone in conversing with women,[42] perhaps following rules for etiquette stipulating that in mixed company discussion of scholarly, religious, political topics and "dry" talk in general should be eliminated.*[43]

Hedwig Dohm, a feminist, observed that the happiest marriages in her acquaintance were among the merchant classes, where the education of both sexes was the most alike, and the unhappiest in the high official circles, and among artists, writers, and professional men. The few supremely happy couples she knew lived with complete freedom and equality—no one over, no one under—but she had the unhappy feeling that many German men actually preferred stupid wives.[44] Certainly English visitors noticed how German men left women out of their conversations and out of the taverns where they gathered at night.[45] Particularly when the husband was promoted and entered a world of more exciting meetings, travel, and theater, the wives were left behind and frequently lacked any interest in keeping up with newspapers or books.[46] In 1850, at a Peace Conference at Frankfurt, where the English and American delegates brought their wives, the German men (as well as the French) seemed glad to get away without theirs.

One of the famous Berlin salon keepers, Fanny Lewald, blamed the men for being too caught up in business to enjoy the society of cultivated women even when such women were at hand. Fanny herself was a thoroughgoing intellectual, and she made an exception of her own husband and a few other humanists.[47] But a certain separation of the sexes, and a separation that left women far behind, was surely apparent from about 1840 through the 1870s.

Occasionally a woman novelist would draw attention to the ironies of the period. It was a favorite theme of E. Marlitt to show a man whose love for his wife developed as he came to appreciate her learning and cultivation, even though he had at first scorned these accomplishments. The Grand Duchess Amalie of Saxony, who wrote plays, allows one of her characters, a doctor who thinks he does not like women at all, finally

---

*This set of rules was printed in a 1910 etiquette book, *Der Mann von Welt*, but it seems to represent an old tradition. Etiquette manuals are often guides to fossilized manners.

to fall for one who knows Latin and can play the harp—but is also capable at applying a bandage.*[48]

Better educational facilities for girls and the sense of personal identity that women had achieved by the end of the century promoted intellectual and social intercourse between the sexes, but this by itself did not guarantee happier marriages. It might have the opposite effect as two strong personalities clashed.

There are many records of university circles in the 1880s, 1890s, and 1900s that show that faculty wives at that time were expected to join clubs for intellectual discussion with their husbands, while their joint recreation often took the form of elaborate charades or skits with authentically fancy costumes. Stories from the Billroths in Vienna, the Friedrich Meineckes in Strassburg, and others report on academic high spirits that involved both sexes equally.

The best example of an intellectual couple, each with his own work to do, yet bound in close cooperation, is Max and Marianne Weber. Max was determined that his wife should be not only equal to himself but also independently creative. He found that she needed training and freedom to develop, so he encouraged her to attend university lectures at Freiburg. When a philosophy professor, Dr. Rickert, praised her first seminar paper, Max was as thrilled as she was.[49] Later, when he moved to Heidelberg, they joined a university club for young couples for discussion of natural science and philosophy. Even during Max's breakdown, he urged her to work for the new women's movement, to write books, and to develop her own career.

Adele Gerhard explains in her memoirs that her husband, Stephan, whom she married in 1889, wanted them to share experiences such as visiting the poor so that they could ponder together how to relieve poverty. Systematically they examined all current philosophies, including socialism, which, however, they judged too materialistic.[50]

A different kind of marital cooperation was Hedwig Heyl's, mentioned in Chapter 10; though her head for business enabled her to revolutionize the methods used in the little factory her husband had inherited, she was careful to let her readers know that such concerns did not keep their love from being poetic, their friendship fast, and their mutual confidence endless.[51]

But, as I said, intellectual growth in women did not ensure marital harmony. Even Marianne Weber, who early in her thinking about women's lives felt sure that every woman should have her own career, lost this conviction with the passing years and came to believe that the most important mission for a woman was to protect her husband from his self-dissatisfaction, as he moved to accomplish his ideals.[52]

---

*A possibly exceptional example shows how the tables could be turned: Dr. Billroth wrote to a friend's wife, Frau Professorin Seegan, that he owed to her his introduction to Turgenev, and he remarked gallantly that he was willing to be pulled up to a higher cultural level by a woman (Billroth, 163).

The life of Lily Braun, coming almost exactly a hundred years after that of the Humboldts, shows some of the changes that the century had brought and illustrates some of the difficulties attending an equal marriage.[53] She was much more frank about herself than Marianne Weber, even though she wrote her autobiography with fictionalized names. After her first husband died, she fell in love with an official of the Social Democratic party, Dr. Heinrich Braun. He was unhappily married at the time she met him, but his pregnant wife was away, and for a while they enjoyed their love chastely, spending the days with his two little boys.

Not all socialists would have insisted on a legal marriage, but Braun was one who did, so he got a divorce even though Lily declared that she might actually have preferred a free union, which was then popular among freethinkers. In any case, they were married, and for a wedding trip took a walking tour. In a little mountain hut with golden stars in the heavens and student voices singing in the distance, Lily recalled, "I became his wife."

Lily wished to carry on with her own writing—she was at work on a book about women—and found it difficult to do so while being as good a housewife as Braun required. Eventually she came to the conclusion that both she and her husband were too modern to give each other what each one secretly desired: he a housewife, and she a protector. (She noticed, however, that when her father died it took ten years off her mother's age, proving to her that women needed a kind of freedom for self-development that her mother had never been able to enjoy inside marriage.) Pondering the question of love versus work within marriage, she soon realized that duty to the party was keeping her from taking a holiday with her husband. Finally, when their son developed a high fever, their relationship reached a crisis, particularly as she chose to stay home with him even though her husband's career was at stake at an important party congress. He became furious, and she found that she was now estranged from both her husband and her son. As she nursed the boy back to health, she remembered how little attention she had really paid to him and felt all the more keenly that her life had become shattered among claims of husband, son, party, and herself, all complicated by a need for money.

So at a women's congress held in Berlin in 1902, Lily found herself rising to tell the delegates that the old maids were wrong when they stated that the most important thing in marriage was intellectual companionship. She told them with conviction that it was not brain power but sexual love that made marriage a success. If love remained, all else could go. And though her liberated audience blushed and squirmed, she had the feeling that she was not speaking for herself alone. Her husband had sneaked into the hall during the last part of her speech, and afterward he asked her if her talk had been a confession. She nodded. Out of this experience came a reconciliation and a softening of her militancy.

A few years later, in 1906, Lily noticed a new public awareness in discussions of marriage. Just as predicted, sexual questions had come to the foreground. She felt that real intimacy between the sexes was only then becoming possible, when Dr. Riehl's extended family had disappeared, and women could be companions to their husbands and real mothers to their children, but perhaps not fully independent professionals at the same time.

∽14.

To Love, Honor, and Obey: Italy

An English lady asked of an Italian,
What were the actual and official duties
Of the strange thing some women set value on,
Which hovers oft about some married beauties,
Called "Cavalier Servente?"—a Pygmalion
Whose statues warm (fear, alas! too true't is)
Beneath his art:—the dame, pressed to disclose them
Said—"Lady, I beseech you *to suppose them.*"
Byron, *Don Juan*, 1818

Italian women were more directly affected by national politics than the other women discussed in this volume. After 1815, the Kingdom of Piedmont was the only state with a native Italian ruling house, and here, and in some of the semi-independent duchies, a great movement of patriotic revival enlisted the aid of large numbers of mostly upper-class, highly cultivated, patriotic, and independent women. But because this movement set state against church, other women, including the majority of middle-class ones, were held back by loyalty to the Roman Catholic church. By the Treaty of Vienna the rich provinces of Lombardy and Venetia were awarded to the Hapsburg monarchy, which worked in close collaboration with the Papal States, at that time covering a large chunk of central Italy. Both regimes were hostile to modern science, "progress," and, of course, to the ideas of democracy and citizen participation in government.

It is thus necessary to describe two quite contrary sorts of women: in rough generalization, those loyal to the state and those loyal to the church. Both organizations cut deeply into family life, and it seems likely that the two sorts of women knew each other only very distantly. There is an oft-quoted remark of Costanza d'Azeglio—one of the patriots—that she would like to enlist some middle-class women in the struggle for nationhood, but that she had never known any.[1] It is certainly not right to assume that the division by social class exactly coincided with the political division, but these two tendencies were reinforced by the education available to the two classes. There were more convent-bred women in the reactionary states and among the less wealthy classes, while girls in upper-class homes and under the more liberal governments had access to a wider range of modern thought. The first great Italian feminist, Anna Maria Mozzoni, described the situation as she saw it in 1866: side by side with "the new nineteenth-century woman," who had been educated in the new schools, there existed the "asiatic or medieval woman," convent-bred, who was particularly common in Sicily and Calabria.[2]

When Mrs. Humphry Ward went to Italy in 1889, the difference between the two classes of women was still so obvious that she referred to them as the "liberal" and the "devout," or "black." She enjoyed the former sort, with whom she found a mysterious kinship, and she thought English and Italian minds at that level were more compatible than, say, the English and French, in such matters as managing servants, bringing up children, and feelings about marriage and politics.[3]

౿ Italian women had a long history of certain unusual freedoms— sexual freedom to have *cavalieri serventi*; intellectual freedom even to the point of holding university chairs; and certain civil rights that had been given during the enlightened Austrian administrations of Maria Theresa and Leopold II. As noted before, the fever of revolutionary enthusiasm that was brought to Italy by Napoleon's armies in 1796, though it lifted many age-old tyrannies from men, caused some of women's special privileges to disappear. The new ideas of the day embraced efficiency, rationality, and closer, healthier home ties paralleling the cult of domesticity that was sweeping the western world. There was, as in France, a regeneration of family life, but in the course of this women had to give up their civil rights, their university posts, and their *cavalieri serventi* or *cicisbei*.

Cicisbeism was an old Italian custom. Stendhal explained its history in his notes on Rome. He thought that it had been imported from Spain about 1540, when it became fashionable for every rich woman to have a man who could give her his arm in public when the husband was busy.[4] Soon middle-class women took it up, flaunting their escorts at mass or the theater. A noble husband could repay such a favor by advancing the young man's career, but as this was beyond the power of the middle class, they took to escorting each others' wives instead.*

Taine filled out the picture by writing how in the eighteenth century it came to seem a public disgrace for a woman not to have a man attending

---

*Another theory of the origin of this peculiar institution is that it came from the France of the seventeenth century, demoralized by Louis XIV, who did everything to maintain his absolute power. Inflexible absolute rulers of Italy had the same motive for encouraging frivolity among their courtier class.

her; and if the man accompanying her was her husband, they would only be laughed at.[5] It was true that the woman was not supposed to appear with her *cicisbeo* until after the birth of her first child, but once through that ordeal she was free to pick a lover (often with the help of her husband, sometimes even with express stipulation in her marriage contract), and to this chosen man she was supposed to be faithful for many years.[6] If the lover was of slightly lower social status, he could be employed as a tutor or estate manager. When Byron became the *cavaliere servente* of Contessa Guiccioli, she was criticized not for accepting him, but for her timing, because she had only been married for a few weeks to the rich, elderly widower who had been presented to her at her convent school.[7] Even young nuns occasionally had their *cavalieri serventi*. Lady Morgan, in 1821, added the piquant detail that husbands might return to their wives as a penance during Lent, and she records the shock to her British sensibilities at seeing a Florentine lady entering an assembly between her *cavaliere servente* and her marriageable daughter.[8]

Italian defenders of the hearth and home were never completely lacking, but their arguments seem usually to be of the "things are much better now than formerly" kind. Ginevra Canonici reacted violently to Lady Morgan's accusations, and it is indeed possible that the Irishwoman's harsh judgments were based on incomplete understanding and the wish to titillate her readers. Still, there is much evidence to support her statement that love was not felt to be sinful in Italy, and to refute Canonici's insistence that because Italy was a great nation, therefore the families of Italy necessarily presented the image of that greatness. For what it is worth, however, Canonici averred that the *cicisbei* were all gone by 1824 and that it was absurd to think that a father would provide one for his daughter.

Let us consider an actual case.[9] In the 1820s Massimo d'Azeglio went to Rome, where he wanted to take up the slightly *déclassé* occupation of a professional artist. He was extremely poor because his family had cut down his allowance in disapproval, and he was doubtless pleased to be invited to dinners every other day with a lady ten years older than himself. It turned out that she was only using him to fill a gap in her love life, until her regular *cavaliere servente* came back. Massimo described the type thus: "one who is about the house from morning to night, on whom the husband relies, who takes the children to school, and who even boxes their ears. Despite all this, he does not accompany the lady when she goes to a party but arrives a quarter of an hour before, or a quarter of an hour later, so as not to 'strike the eye'—a technical phrase."[10]

D'Azeglio went on to expound what he called the laws of cicisbeism: that the relationship should not be based on pecuniary advantage, that a roué was excoriated, that the honesty and morality of the affair could be endlessly discussed, and that it was very bad form for the husband to express disapprobation. Once he happened to witness a scene where a young officer reproached his wife on this subject, with the result that everybody turned against the husband.[11]

The custom disappeared at different times in different parts of the country and was not completely gone until the 1870s. The first blow against it, according to the received opinion, had been struck by the conquering Napoleon, who with charactertistic forthrightness decreed that all cards of invitation bear the names of both husband and wife—a complete innovation in Italy at that time.[12] As part of the same process, the French invasion ushered in a period when men could be active in their profession, military or civilian, so that they had less time to relapse into vice.

Stendhal in 1824 believed that only in those places where the bracing Napoleonic influence had not been felt was cicisbeism still functioning.[13] There ensued a short period of relapse as the reactionary governments set up by the Treaty of Vienna condemned the upper class to idleness once more, giving them no role in public affairs. Gradually, though, an underground movement was formed to work for national independence; during this time active patriots sometimes wore the *cicisbeo* mask in order to avoid the ubiquitous secret police of Rome or Vienna. As the resistance grew stronger and engaged the energies of both men and women, a sharp decline in the old futile pleasures was evident. D'Azeglio estimated that by the 1860s the people he knew spent only a third as much time making love as the same sort had in the 1820s.[14] By the 1860s no one could any longer afford to play the full-time "gentleman-in-waiting," except in certain centers of despotism, like Rome. From there Taine, in 1864, was still regaling his readers with the depiction of the lover as one constantly on call to pick up packages or carry flowers—or even accompany the lady to confession. Like D'Azeglio, he attributed the enormous leisure required for this way of life to the fact that Italian men, and in his day particularly Roman men, were not allowed to take part in politics, nor did they have the habit of serious reading or the study of science.[15]

At the time Taine was writing, Paul Desmarie, another Frenchman, says that he searched actively to find Italian women who were attached to their husbands and to their duties in the home, and he found very few.[16] In France, he said, one could count the women who strayed from their husbands, but in Italy, those who lacked a *cicisbeo* were the exceptions. A frequent caller might not find the husband at home for months on end; Desmarie's conclusion was that the custom had survived the general *embourgeoisement* of manners of which he also took account. This, however, was not a universal view. There were many signs of decline.

In 1864 Frances Power Cobbe believed that rumors of Italian mistresses were much exaggerated, except again in Rome, even though she realized that fidelity did not have the same value in Italy that it did in England.[17] One change in manners that signaled something new was mentioned by Mrs. Gretton about the same time—namely, that the husband was by then the one to escort his wife to the theater, even though he would leave her in her box while he waited upon other ladies and she received other gentlemen. But he would come back to take her home.[18]

By 1869 Jessie White Mario, who lived in a circle of the most active freedom fighters, repeated in the New York *Nation* that Italian women had by then completely given up their *cavalieri serventi*.[19]

෬ Among the Piedmontese nobility there was a different tradition, one of marriage based on intellectual companionship and a common patriotic purpose. A good example of the type is Cesare d'Azeglio, who took up his wife's education in a serious way right after they were married in 1788, and for several years spent four hours a day in this task.[20] Together they read all the great literary classics, in several languages, which she was required to learn well enough to translate freely. The love based on this experience lasted forty-two years, boasted their son Massimo, who enjoyed recounting the story of his father's loyalty to the King at the time of his abdication. When Cesare found himself obliged to accompany his master into exile, he embraced his wife, who was ill at the time, telling her he would have to stay away as long as duty called, and that perhaps she would never see him again. She had the strength to reply, "Go! Stay there! If it must be so, die! I should be too unworthy of you to speak otherwise!"[21]

The persistence of such a pattern of *noblesse oblige* is demonstrated by Ubaldino and Emilia Peruzzi, who married for love in 1850 and who soon adopted the custom of studying together for several hours after breakfast. Their example was an inspiration to the niece who lived with them. Her aunt and uncle proved to her that integrity and affection were possible and taught her to laugh off any cynical whispers deriding the ideas of family and marriage.*

Massimo d'Azeglio, though he had an eye for women, valued them for more than prettiness. In general he considered them worth far more than men. "If I have had to suffer much on their account," he declared, "I did once find the compensation of an affection which never failed and persisted through all possible vicissitudes. Those who can say likewise should be satisfied. Not many can."[22]

He does not say who this woman was. His relationship with his second wife, Luisa Blondel (his first had been Manzoni's daughter), was rather stormy, but even so, the intellectual respect continued after her jealousy had brought an end to their physical relationship. Luisa was rich, beautiful, cultivated, a charming talker, and the match had been made for love, but women were irresistible to Massimo, and he could seduce

*The Peruzzis maintained a salon where such guests as Longfellow, Renan, Samuel Smiles, and Karl Hillebrand loved the fine talk, and Emilia knew how to learn from all her guests.

and be seduced by them with ease. Even when he was over seventy he declared that he needed female intimacy to keep himself feeling alive. Luisa's response to such affairs was to make scenes, which only drove Massimo away for longer and longer intervals. One day, when they happened to be driving together along the Roman Corso, a trasteverine flower girl threw a bouquet at their carriage, and Massimo responded with what Luisa thought, rightly or wrongly, betokened undue intimacy. She gave him a smart smack right in the public street. Massimo did not speak. He got out, closed the carriage door, lifted his hat as though to a stranger, and left her forever, demonstrating the dramatic sexual code of Italians. He continued to write to her, however, both about their daughter and about his ideas. These letters embrace all his intellectual, artistic, and social interests. He was very active in the work of creating a new social consciousness for his country and asked Luisa to help him by collecting reminiscences of their friends in a sort of oral history. And when she finally visited him at his deathbed, he told her he was glad to see her.[23]

At the feminist congress of 1889 at Florence, it was reiterated by many speakers that equality of intellectual level was the condition for the happy marriages of the future;[24] yet a few years after that Luigi Villari found that the possibility existed *only* among aristocratic ladies with literary, linguistic, patriotic, and charitable credentials. In the middle class the fairly well educated wife who could be a companion to her husband simply did not exist.[25] The class difference and the two types were a persistent phenomenon.

∽ Turning away from the "liberal" women to the "black" ones whose training Villari deplored, it is well to recall the ways in which the Catholic church attempted to regulate marriage among the faithful. Italian priests referred to a manual, *De Matrimonio*, which had been composed by Saint Alphonso Liguori in the seventeenth century.

The saint referred to the sex act by the good old medieval phrase "paying the marriage debt," and he discussed all sorts of situations that might cause a woman to ask her confessor's advice. She must follow the husband wherever he wanted to live, but she must not journey alone, even on pilgrimages, without his consent. Although women's natural modesty would make it unnecessary for her to seek actively the debt in ordinary cases, if the husband was in danger of incontinence, she would have an affirmative duty to solicit its payment. To deny the debt to one seeking earnestly or urgently was a mortal sin, except when it meant serious danger of defilement (disease?). Beatings did not justify a wife's leaving her husband. Unjust beatings, frequent violent harangues, and similar dangers would be of serious concern only to noblewomen, but they would not constitute a sufficient cause for a woman in a humbler condition to refuse payment. It seems that the Church believed that women did not have strong sex drives, but must accommodate their husbands "for charity," and that conditions of what was "unbearable" varied very much with one's social class.

In *The Ring and the Book*, Browning depicts an Italian woman's conflict between her spontaneous feelings and the commands of the church. Pompilia is represented as being only twelve when she is married off, and not yet at puberty. Right after her first menstruation her husband orders her to his bedroom. The experience is unendurable, and she flies to the Archbishop, begging to be allowed to go into a convent. Her husband, she explains, married her for her money and does not love her, which is why she cannot bear to have physical relations with him. The churchman sternly points out that sexual submission is in the covenant of her marriage, whether she likes it or not, and bids her, "Swallow the burning coal he proffers you!"[26] Although this poem grafts English romanticism onto Italian Catholic doctrine, it shows poignantly what the letter of the law prescribed to devout wives, and what was reinforced by their convent educations.

It is possibly unfair to begin a description of these women by quoting the impressions of a number of English visitors, who surely carried the prejudices of their island with them, and yet the picture they present is remarkably consistent, and one that supports Villari and other Italian critics of the same social problem.

In 1833 Lady Shelley wrote that she found Italian women so bigoted by their religious training that they could be cruel to any Protestants with whom they came in contact.[27] The discrepancy between these women and their husbands was often so great that the men preferred to dine at a hotel rather than create social obligations that it would be beyond the capability of their wives to handle.[28] (Such a contrast to the universal admiration that French wives of all classes won for their social ease!) In the sixties Mrs. Gretton attributed the vulgarity and illiteracy she found to the low standard of girls' education in Italy.[29] Even wives of scientific men knew no better than to scream at their husbands, to gossip with their neighbors, and to avoid all serious subjects. One of her friends regarded Protestants as no better than atheists, but, of course, she had little understanding of true Catholicism, and Dante would be way beyond her comprehension.[30]

Frances Power Cobbe knew of a daughter in a noble Roman family who had been educated according to what the family considered "new" principles. In order to enable her to carry on discussion at evening parties where foreigners were present, she was supposed to have read *one* interesting current book. *Uncle Tom's Cabin* was chosen, but as it contained heretical chapters, her confessor made a sixty-page abstract. Then she could ask people ingenuously if they had read that *charming* book, *Lo Zio Tom*—giving away by her choice of adjective both the sense in which the cutting had been done and her total lack of understanding of its serious theme.[31]

Lady Duff-Gordon, who had a villa on the Adriatic, declared that her neighbors lived in *houses*, not *homes*, defining a home as a place where a wife was ready to take some share in her husband's intellectual interests. It was impossible, she went on, to exaggerate the position of the Italian *madre*, but her extraordinary influence was exercised without sharing the concerns of her husband or sons; she nevertheless received the sort of deference that would lead her husband to give up a good promotion in order to gratify her whim to live in her native town.[32]

In 1838 the Contessa Pepoli decided to vindicate the women of Italy from the false accusations of foreigners[33] and composed a treatise on their excellent performances as housekeepers, as instructors of their children, and as social beings, only to have the book put on the Index, thus giving color to the very accusations.[34] The Italian critic Mazzoleni lamented in 1870 that while Italian brides all knew the catechism by heart, they had no ideas about the world, life, men, and themselves.[*35] Even those Italian feminists at the 1889 conference who wished for equal marriage were forced by a self-survey to the conclusion that the old-fashioned housewife was obedient and a good cook, but that she did not read, could not follow her husband's conversations with his male friends, and was even proud of that fact.

The discrepancy between the two types of Italian families paralleled the great political difference between the state and the church, and was felt by patriots to be a huge stumbling block to national regeneration. The battle lines were described in a novel by Giovanni Ruffini, himself a member of a famous liberal family, who hoped to show his fellow countrymen the dangers of religious control over women's minds. Ruffini's mother, Eleanora, could be considered an outstanding example of an enlightened woman. While bearing thirteen children, she endeavored to keep on with her self-education, and her powers grew to the point where her husband, a judge, relied on her to draft legal documents.[36] Several of her sons died for Mazzini's cause, but Giovanni survived to write *Vincenzo: or, Sunken Rocks* (1863). Its story is worth retelling.

Vincenzo, an orphan, is brought up in the household of his father's old employer. Destined for the priesthood, he enjoys a childhood intimacy with the daughter of the house, Rose; while he is at the seminary, she is sent to a convent school, where she is imbued with all the most clerical and reactionary ideas. She is totally without sympathy for the new political ideas that are thrilling so many hearts, but her rather liberal

---

*As a "diverting," though not "guaranteed," picture of Italian married life, Mazzoleni offered some figures on the Italian marriage of his day (Mazzoleni, 120 n.). Out of 872,564 marriages in all, he supposed the following:

> 1,360 wives who have given their husbands the slip in order to keep lovers behind their backs;
> 2,361 husbands who have fled so as not to have to live with their wives any more;
> 4,102 spouses who have separated voluntarily;
> 191,025 spouses who are at war while living in the same house;
> 162,320 spouses who detest each other cordially but maintain a mask of politeness;
> 510,132 spouses who live in mutual indifference;
> 1,102 spouses who are comparatively happy though with unhappy episodes;
> 9 spouses truly happy.

father only shrugs. "What does it matter, she is only a girl" is his sentiment, which, as the author points out, only proves that he is not really "a man of his century." Vincenzo finds that he lacks a religious vocation and so decides to study for the bar, still spending his vacations with Rose and her father. Because her mother is dead, she has more freedom than is customary and she personally rejects the proposal of a young nobleman, thus angering her father, who demonstrates once again that he lacks any high concept of women's rights. By this time Vincenzo is working up to a promising career in the new politics of liberal Italy, and he hopes that he can bring Rose along if only he can be married to her.

The "sunken rocks" of the title become apparent on their wedding trip. Such trips were a new fashion in Italy, but Vincenzo takes his bride to see cities where she has never been, and only then begins to notice her total lack of appreciation for architecture, music, or politics, and, at the same time, the absence of all passion in her make-up. At this point she tells him that she married him to save his soul. The suitor whom she rejected, meanwhile, has married an energetic liberal wife, one who turned her father's house into a hospital during the insurrectionary days of 1848, and who loaded muskets for her father and brothers when they defended Brescia in 1849. The unhappy Vincenzo feels torn apart by fate; he turns down a flattering offer from the Piedmontese Prime Minister Cavour to enter political life in order to live at home with his wife and infant daughter, trying to bring up the little Rose so that she will not become a clog in another husband's life. At the end of the book, we see him living at his wife's *palazzo*, unable to be happy or to make her so. At thirty-two he looks forty-five. Would to God, exclaims the author at this point, that such cases were rare, but instead you find them in all corners of Italy, and throughout Europe. The best that Vincenzo can hope for, at the end, is that his friend's patriotic wife—strictly platonically—can revive his interest in politics and good conversation. The best that the author could hope for was that his novel might spread the word to families like Vincenzo's that they were not alone, and so perhaps bring them together.

By the 1880s feminist ferment and industrial development wrought changes in Italy as elsewhere and raised hopes among Italian girls that their marriages would be better than their parents'. Yet when Anna Maria Mozzoni, the leader of the feminist cause, wrote a message to girls preparing for professions in the new secular schools, all she could find to tell them was that to live peacefully they would have to give up their dreams of accomplishment, of freedom, of love. All that marriage offered them was hard continuous work, with no rights, pay, independence, rest, or dignity.[37]

∽15.

Extramarital Affairs

To take a woman without taking
marriage is like eating a piece
of meat raw that ought to be
cooked.
                    Louis Veuillot, 1886

Although it will be forever impossible to obtain even approximate statistics on the number of marital infidelities in the century before Dr. Kinsey, we can test some common views: for example, that French marriages were more vulnerable than English ones, that the French and the Italians took a relatively benign view of adultery, while the Germans, like the English, seemed inclined to the view that renunciation was noble.

Karl Hillebrand explained that Frenchmen were not restricted by a belief in the purity of women (as presumably English and German men were) and that in France success with women brought rather admiration and respect.[1] We have indeed seen that *sex* was regarded by Frenchmen as a natural phenomenon, but we have Balzac's word for it that their view of *marriage* "in no way owes its origins to Nature" and that although as a young man he had been struck with horror and shame at the word "adultery," later he came to realize that it not uncommonly mitigated the severity of the marriage law and helped ease the condition of that large majority of marriages that he judged to be unhappy.[2]

The widespread tolerance of adultery was attributed in part to the custom of leaving sexual love out of the original choice of marriage partners. Girls, said Legouvé, were made to expect rather a paternal affection from their husbands,[3] and this, combined with the general observation that a woman's passions rose in intensity between the ages of eighteen and twenty-eight, made taking a lover only a natural outlet. At this time she had a *nouvelle pousse*, she was ripened; her family was complete with the birth of two children and who could blame her for doing at thirty what her husband did at eighteen?[4]

The reading of romantic fiction could easily stimulate such desires. According to Louis Maigron, literature began to have this effect on life rather suddenly when George Sand's first novels were sweeping the country about 1832,[5] and the tradition was continued through Dumas and other writers. According to their gospel, repressing love was as great a mistake as it came to seem to some Freudians a century later.

Maigron explains his point by telling a true story from 1837 concerning a young engineer in the French provinces who devoted himself to the machinery of his trade and found in it a source of doting pride and constant satisfaction. The machines provided a sizable income, enough to dress his wife in the prettiest clothes in town and house her, their two children, and a maid in a fine home. The wife became as idle as the engineer was busy, and she fell to reading, though her literary tastes were regrettably uncensored. (Her mother had chosen to bolster the daughter's dowry by working in the family boutique instead of directing the daughter's intellectual upbringing.) And when the indulgent husband brought copies of George Sand's novels home from his business trips to Paris, these became the young woman's bedside reading. The husband, a pragmatic industrialist, thought her tastes infantile but not insidious. Meanwhile, his assistant at the factory, a man whose inclinations were distinctly more human than mechanical, gained access to the house and inflamed the wife's imagination with the news that he had actually met George Sand in Paris. The two began passing notes and finally made an assignation. Alas, the maid, whose job it was to babysit with the five-year-old son, at the crucial moment imitated her mistress and chose that hour to meet her own lover. In her absence the child drowned. The unmechanical assistant was subsequently maimed by a machine at the factory and died of tetanus, but not before he could give back the incriminating letters, save one that he asked in his will to have buried with him. Thus the pair expiated their sin, and the woman devoted the rest of her life to refuting the doctrines of George Sand. M Maigron explains that Flaubert must have had access to hundreds of such tales before he wrote *Madame Bovary*.[6]

Stendhal duly delivered the opinion that for a woman to remain faithful to a loveless marriage was so contrary to nature that to resist a new love was "the most amazing thing that can exist on earth."[7] Women married, he thought, to escape the slavery of their mother's house. Only if they had more liberty in their girlhood and the possibility of divorce later on could they be expected to be faithful in marriage.[8]

In 1913 Camille Mauclair delivered one of the most extensive panegyrics on the love that knew no fidelity or law because the partners made law for themselves. Society, meanwhile, he explained, kept trying to pull them back under its discipline, because society wanted marriages to produce "combatants and the mothers of combatants."[9] And so the Code allowed the adulterous woman only the right to be killed—and for something that no one in real life dared compare to a crime!

A different interpretation of French extramarital affairs, hardly congruent with the romantic view, dwelt on their long-lasting character, which was often based not on physical pleasure alone but on friendship and companionship. Hamerton, while explaining that he could not fully discuss the matter "in an English book," told his countrymen that they should not assume that extramarital cohabitation necessarily lacked durable commitment;[10] or, as Alletz explained, men often took mistresses because they needed a friend.[11] In Bulwer's view, while many Frenchwomen had lovers, they generally lacked *passion*.[12] (Italians had passion, in his opinion, while English and German women had mere sentimentalism.) Often, said Hillebrand, a relationship endured for years, not too warm, not at all romantic, but nevertheless one of the most beautiful ingredients of French life just because the women were so cool and disinterested.*[13]

Both Chateaubriand and Victor Hugo had such famous long-lasting affairs, plus many minor ones.† Chateaubriand's was with Mme Récamier, to whom he wrote daily for twenty-five years, besides calling in person every evening.

Juliette Drouet, Hugo's mistress, was of a different class and character. Hugo's wife, Adèle, whom he had married in 1822 when he was a virgin, was seduced by Sainte-Beuve.[14] Though her husband forgave her, he felt he could no longer love her, and in 1833 he met Juliette, a model. Their initial passion was such a memorable experience for both of them that they celebrated the anniversary for fifty years, even though Hugo was not always very nice to her in the meantime. At first he kept her living alone and forbade her to talk to other men or to receive mail. She stayed in her hole for twelve years, mending his socks, copying his manuscripts, revolting, unsuccessfully, only once. In 1851 someone cruelly sent her a packet of Hugo's letters to another woman, and Juliette nearly went mad. Eventually she was able to forgive him, and he, impressed by her generosity, took her back. At the end of his life she became the publicly recognized mistress of his household in Paris and was widely honored. The newspaper notices at her death were most respectful, referring to her as Hugo's "muse."‡[15]

Once a love affair developed, there were certain ways of handling it intended to minimize pain and lessen the possibilities of disruption of ordinary life. Of course, the rigidly correct official etiquette paid lip service to morality. However unhappy a woman might be, Madame Staffe informed her readers, she must never seek forbidden consolations, but cling to her dignity and to her children.[16] But when concealment

*Apparently it was this coolness in the French character that misled Fanny Burney in her observations of Mme de Staël, who came to England with a group containing her lover of the moment. Fanny was sure their relations were innocent, deceived by their uncoquettish rationality, and so she defended what she could never have justified if she had had the clue (Herold, 151).

†Chateaubriand's relations with Hortense Allart are described in Chapter 20. At sixty-four he told another lady that if she would meet him in Switzerland, he would give her more in a day than others had in long years. She did not test this offer. (Greg, 235).

‡In a different segment of society, there was often a casualness about sex that struck the English eye. Both Thackeray and Hamerton told stories of their Paris boarding houses, where they each watched a lady who posed as the wife of one of the boarders suddenly appear with a new husband. In one case the first husband saluted the lady by her new name; in the other she was said to be so well-spoken and so accomplished that one would never have suspected anything amiss though she changed hands several times (Hamerton, *Autobiography*, 173; Thackeray, *Paris Sketch Book*, 17).

became necessary, it was handled less nervously than in England, as when Mme de Staël remarked when asked about self-revelation: "I only portray myself from the neck up."*[17] According to Lady Morgan, the general gallantry of French society, where even old women were politely flattered, camouflaged what liaisons existed, so that vice (as she put it) was never rendered dangerous by visible example.[18]

Men's advice to other men ranged from Debay's sensible suggestion that it was puerile to try to force a confession of previous amours,[19] to Paul Bourget's hints on how to get your wife to take a lover and give up her bourgeois prejudices.[20] Michelet felt that an erring wife should confess and then be pardoned.†[21] Scribe, the playwright, shows (in *La Deuxième Année*) a husband emerging as the hero by talking his wife out of having an affair.[22]

It is likely withal that liaisons among the married were far less common than was supposed by readers of scandalous literature. A Pole, Charles de Forster, living in Paris in the 1830s, praised highly the women he met, calling them mostly good housekeepers who were not easily seduced and who rarely forgot the duties of wives and mothers.[23] By the 1870s, Hillebrand's opinion was that all the public coquetry rarely led to actual unfaithfulness, and he judged that English people, under their weight of repressed passion, misunderstood French grace and their flirting-to-please within recognized limits.[24] Frederic Marshall, apparently one Englishman who was aware of this, wrote in *Blackwood's* that infidelity in French marriages was so rare that one could look around a large circle and not find a single example.[25] If they wanted to point a finger, the French looked upon the English divorce court, set up in 1857, as far more disquieting. Hillebrand explained that French family affection was so close and warm ("overheated" was the way some people put it) that children who grew up in this kind of home had no extravagant need for extravagant emotion later on. As he saw it, parental love acted as a vaccine against later passion.[26]

Just having the children in the home instead of out with a nurse had improved the moral standard, at least among the upper classes, where Tocqueville said that people had become more natural and serious and had less time for adulterous pleasure. Balzac felt that it was mostly among parvenus that "novelistic" situations occurred.

One must, of course, separate the premarital affairs of young men from the liaisons of married persons. A good part of the French reputation for gallantry depends upon the first category. It was Bulwer's view that though there was more early libertinage in France than in any other civilized country, it led to less later depravity. (This even though he called the hospitals set up for foundlings monuments to "a human sacrifice to

*"*Je ne m'en peinte qu'en buste.*"

†Lemaitre, in his comments on Michelet dated 1898, remarks that Michelet never raised the question of perversions, and wondered what would happen if the wife had any of these activities to confess (Lemaitre, 137).

sensual indulgence.")[27] In discussing the philosophy of marriage, Debay stated, "There are very few men who, during their bachelor days, or even their married ones, have not paid homage to the wives of other men,"[28] but "statistical studies" (not described) told him that the number of adulteries by bachelors was a hundred times that of married men.

The women who took these men as partners, whether on an amateur or professional basis, actually ran "a prep school for marriage" while at the same time protecting the girls who had dowries from undesirable attentions. Certain disadvantages of this system were sometimes discussed, such as that the young men arrived at marriage "exhausted," and that the mistresses had trained their characters through their weaknesses instead of their strength. But law and custom urged young men to keep their liberty, and to laugh if anyone inquired about their chastity.

When moral sentiment overtook the French, it was not so much a personal ideal of self-control such as motivated the British, but the awakening perception that, after all, the French way was extremely unfair to women. Even men who loved their mistresses for a while and learned much about psychology as well as physiology would leave them abruptly to marry the girls picked by their families. Michelet especially rebuked men who congratulated themselves on getting out of an affair easily, regardless of what happened to the woman, while Legouvé advised mothers to be far more severe with their sons for seducing poor girls during their expected ten years of sowing wild oats. As the feminist movement began to gain strength, young men took over the ideal of earlier marriage—more for love, less for money—and the reform was easier to carry out in France than in other places because of the clear need for change and the much greater frankness on the subject of sex.

പ It is easy to observe the differences in the English scene. The English by and large did not consider sex a natural function in the way the French did. They were uncomfortable with it as somehow disruptive of what *they* considered to be "natural"—namely, monogamous marriage.* Taine took some pains to try to get Englishmen to open up with him about their illicit affairs, and found he was not getting very far. "An Englishman in a state of adultery is miserable: even at the supreme moment his conscience torments him" was his conclusion, and it followed that, of course, there were fewer such moments, though he heard of mistresses on

*In his study of English marriage in the early 1950s, Geoffrey Gorer pointed out that even then most English people regarded marriage as more important than love, and that faithfulness was its most important attribute. He found that half of his respondents had never had a real love affair outside of marriage and that 40 percent had, but he did not discriminate between premarital and extramarital affairs. He doubted that any other urban population could produce comparable figures of chastity and fidelity, and was obviously proud of the situation (Gorer, 86, 155). If these figures are valid for 1951, then it is reasonable to suppose that a hundred years before, when pressures and dangers were even greater, the chastity and fidelity rate would have been substantially higher, but there is no way of proving this.

the outskirts of London who were visited on Sundays.[29] As for English wives, Taine felt that most of them would lack the dexterity to handle an intrigue, even if their consciences would allow it.*[30]

Another obstacle was the large size of many families. A mother of ten children would certainly have less opportunity for adultery than the mother of two. And there were the brutal social punishments meted out to breakers of the code. Neither rank nor wealth could protect a man whose scandalous life became known, so what liaisons existed were kept secret.[31] Many of them have been discovered by twentieth-century scholars after they had been successfully kept from public knowledge at the time.

An Englishwoman might condone a husbandly lapse. Though (in contrast to Michelet's tolerant attitude) "no man . . . in whom remains any sense of honor, could receive back to his embraces the violator of his marital confidence, . . . there are few cases in which an injured wife might not gracefully pardon an erring husband."[32] Mrs. Sewell's judgment was almost universally accepted: "an unfaithful married woman is the only irrevocably lost human being, and richly does she deserve her doom."[33] Cobbett explained that a wretch who could even think of putting himself between the sheets with his unfaithful wife was beneath contempt.

A series of French visitors commented on the English scene. Admiration for the Englishwoman's virtue was expressed as far back as the eighteenth century, but let us turn to Taine's discussion of the subject, dating from his trip to England in the 1860s. He opined that he could remain in England for a year and a half without encountering a single exception, and even in the very highest class he heard only one affair discussed.[34] He attributed this virtue to the fact that decent women were untouched by temptation.[35] The women (and he said that this was particularly true among the dissenting sects) "always lived in a moral enclosure and never dreamt of leaving it."[36] Thinking it over, he came up with six explanations.[37] Having been used to freedom, these women were used to controlling their own behavior; since they were brought up in the company of young men, they succumbed less easily to romantic fallacies; their serious education and their contact with the parish poor endowed them with basic common sense; they lived much in the country, out of the way of a city's temptations; their many children took up their time; and they had so many intellectual and social interests (making their scientific collections, running their little schools) that their minds were occupied.

The two other factors were often noted: first, a bored husband in England would seek refuge in drink or hard physical exercise rather than with a mistress; and second, the social costs of having an affair could include the loss of a man's position. In France there was a graduated

*Shaw in the preface to *Getting Married*: "men who are bolder free thinkers than Shelley himself can no more bring themselves to commit adultery than to commit any common theft, whilst women who loathe sex slavery more fierce than Mary Wollstonecraft are unable to face the insecurity and discredit of the vagabondage which is the masterless woman's only alternative to celibacy."

ladder between respectability and debauchery, but in England the separation was a gulf.[38]

Max O'Rell pointed out that the husband of an unfaithful wife in England was the object not of good-natured ridicule, as in France, but of contempt.[39] And any piece of fiction that attempted to show the faintest sympathy for an adulteress—from Kotzebue's early *The Stranger*, to Froude's *Nemesis of Faith*, to *Adam Bede*, and *Tess of the D'Urbervilles*—was roundly denounced. Holman Hunt made vivid in a series of pictures called *Past and Present* the tragic effects of a wife's infidelity. Christina Rossetti poeticized about a woman's sin and long repentance. Meredith's poem sequence, *Modern Love*, concerns a husband who cannot take back his wife, even though he feels physical desire for her, because it would violate his integrity to do so. As Shaw remarked, sex can be enjoyed between strangers who differ in taste and social class; it is not the most intimate and personal relationship, but if people believe it so to be, then violations become a matter of "honor."[40]

Though sexual pressures exploded from time to time, even in Britain, a more characteristic and specially British feature of social life was resistance to them. The large number of women to whom sexual experience was "coarse," and the men whose sense of honor caused them to flee from unlawful affairs, sometimes managed to achieve very interesting and productive partnerships with the opposite sex. At other times, of course, the renunciation left permanent scars.

Back in 1791 Mary Wollstonecraft set a pattern by calling sex a villain that distorted relationships between men and women that she thought would otherwise be friendly and intellectual.[41] This recurrent theme was encapsulated by Meredith in a conversation in *Diana of the Crossways* in which Diana considers what to do when her new suitor calls her by ner nickname, Tony, and wants to hug her, though she is still technically married:

> "You see, Tony, my dearest, I am flesh and blood after all."
> "You drive me to be ice and door-bolts!"
> "The only woman I could marry, I can't have."
> "You have her in soul."
> "Body and soul, it must be! I believe you are made without fire."
> "Perhaps. The element is omitted with some of us, happily, some think. Now we can converse. There seems to be a measurement of distance required before men and women have a chance with their brains."[42]

Here we have quite plainly both the suspicion of frigidity and the demand that one's "soul" should be respected and attended to. It was all too often true that men who possessed the body were inclined to settle for that alone, a situation that created a good deal of the poignancy of Victorian women's demands for something better.*

---

*It is instructive to compare Diana's stiffness vis-à-vis a man with her free expression of affection and intimacy when confiding in her friend, Emma. Intuitive understanding here is linked up with physical comforting and cosseting, kissing, and at one point an effort by

Madariaga called frequent friendships between men and women a peculiarly English phenomenon.[43] He judged that they were often really without sexual element, though he realized that sometimes the sexual feelings were only disguised. Still, England had the greatest number of men and women without strong sex drives, he thought, and because such men and women often were deeply interested in public causes, they had opportunities to work together that were not so available on the continent.*

The most famous such collaboration was that between Florence Nightingale and Sidney Herbert. Nowhere but in England could two such people spend hours in each others' company and never even be suspected of passion. Similarly, Annie Besant maintained a decades-long professional relationship with Charles Bradlaugh, with whom indeed she may have been in love. She felt free enough to allow him to work for hours at her house, and apparently they never overstepped the line of legality, even though in her writing she favored the idea of free unions and urged her friends to give support to young couples attempting to live in this style.†[44]

In the case of John Stuart Mill and Harriet Taylor, the couple agreed to forego sexual intimacy so long as her husband was alive, and having done this, to allow themselves every other freedom of social and intellectual closeness.[45] Mill spent weekends at her country house, while he worked with her on essays and books that he called as much hers as his.

Thackeray's intimacy with Mrs. Brookfield started off in somewhat the same way, since her marriage was unhappy and she defended her right to have friends of her own. For a while the two lovers looked forward to a lifelong, though unconsummated, relationship, but after

---

Emma to warm up a chilled and disconsolate Diana by getting into bed with her. Though some critics are quick to call this behavior homosexual, it was not so intended by the author, and it reflected rather the natural expression of womanly feeling at a moment when it did not have to adopt the defenses considered necessary with men. There was wide tolerance for such expression, and in fact a fashion that exaggerated feminine endearments.

*The general feeling of trust in the honor of the other sex is demonstrated in the large number of women who accepted men not their relatives as escorts for extended travel. Splendid examples turn up on nearly every page of Middleton's delightful *Victorian Lady Travellers*, with its tales of intrepid women who went unselfconsciously to Colorado mining camps or central African jungles. Besides these, there were more ordinary trips to Europe. Augustus Hare arranged several tours abroad, once with the Misses Holland and again with Miss Sophia Wright. His 1872 trip to Spain was planned for a party of five, but the others fell away and Hare found himself touring with Miss Wright and her lady's maid, who used to have to make their tea in a saucepan (A. J. C. Hare, *Solitary Life*, 181, and passim). When Mrs. Farrar, in Massachusetts, announced at Sunday dinner that she would like to visit her mother in England, a friend spoke up to say that he would accompany her, and they booked passage for the following Wednesday (Farrer, 263).

†Annie Besant wrote of Auguste Comte's friendship with Mme Clotilde de Vaux: "Those who are too base to believe in a true and noble friendship between a man and a woman will alone try to cast any slur on the frank and noble love . . . " (quoted in Nethercot, 104). Her biographer points out that this was probably more relevant to herself than to Comte.

three years or so Mr. Brookfield took his wife back to his home and ordered Thackeray never to have anything more to do with her. Unforgivable words passed, and the relationship ceased when the novelist returned a letter from her, unopened.*

The friendship between Coventry Patmore and Alice Meynell began with a purely literary admiration, she calling him the greatest intellect she had ever known—right next to Shakespeare as a poet—while he stated that she was a woman whose qualities demanded an enlargement of the ideas of what a woman could be. Later, it is true, Patmore went further and fell in love with her in such a way that she had to draw back. After all, she was a busy wife and the mother of a large family. In an anonymous poem in the *Pall Mall Gazette* in 1895, she wrote, ". . . above / All price is my refusal, Love. / My sacred Nay / Was never cheapened."†[46]

In discussing this kind of friendship, John, Viscount Morley was of the opinion that it was almost always the growth of later years, being too hard to carry off in youth.[47] He also felt that the kind of woman who would be ripe for it would be "masculine in a womanly way." But once established, this was the most delightful form of friendship, and one that, in Morley's view, should not in any way interfere with a man's fervor in loving his wife.

In writing about her life as the wife of a young Oxford don, Mrs. Humphry Ward mentioned a large number of men friends who had a personal relationship with her, not just with her husband or with them both as a couple. Her social group was one of personal, albeit not sexual, intimacy: these men helped her in the development of her ideas and in her writing.[48]

On the other hand, a few years later Beatrice Webb pondered how hard it was to keep relationships with the opposite sex purely friendly. Fiercely she wanted to have a chance with her brain, but "do what one will, sentiment creeps in, in return for sympathy. Perhaps as one loses one's attractiveness this will wear off—*certainly* it will!" And than she adds a word that shows how impenetrable the barriers of class still were: "At present it is only with working men one feels free to sympathize without fear of unpleasant consequences. . . ."[49]

Men too shied away from breaking the sexual code. Dr. William Acton told them that there was nothing for a husband to do while waiting for divorce but remain continent,[50] while Frederick Harrison told his son, who had asked what a man should do if he fell in love and could not

---

*Shaw's open flirtations with his friends' wives can hardly be put in the same class as the cases above, even though he said that if the wife had an intellectual-romantic relationship, it would improve the marriage. He called his services being a "Sunday husband" (Muggeridge and Adam, 137).

†Alice Meynell first fell in love with the priest who received her into the Catholic church. As soon as his superiors found out about it, they ordered him to leave and never meet her again. In a poem about this incident, she expressed a hope that perhaps their angels could meet and kiss in heaven, sentimentalizing the renunciation (Dallyn, 47).

marry, "Do! Do what every gentleman does in such circumstances. . . . A loose man is a foul man. He is anti-social. He is a beast."[51]

Tom Brown at Oxford was a work of fiction but undoubtedly one where Thomas Hughes was giving a very literal picture. He makes a big point of Tom's struggle to resist seducing a barmaid, describing the long walk during which he attempts to deal with the wild beast within him; but Tom has his final reward when he acts as best man at the wedding of the still-pure girl to one of Tom's old village companions. Hughes makes it clear that just as there is a moral struggle at Rugby, where Tom learns both to be honest and to become a governor of other boys, so the struggle in the university years is for self-control. The reason college life is not organized in such a communal way as public school life is that every man must handle this struggle for himself.

In spite of what seem like impassable physical, mental, moral, and social obstacles, adulteries were committed in Britain, and their frequency, so far as it can be gauged, followed the now familiar pattern of greater laxity at both ends of the century with a period of sterner conformity in the middle. Elizabeth Grant, the "Highland Lady," remembered how easily natural children were accepted and provided for in the Scottish countryside where she grew up soon after the nineteenth century began, and while tolerance was probably less in the more sophisticated areas, it could hardly be said that Shelley and Byron concealed their affairs as Dickens had to in mid-century. This phase of the romantic movement ended in England when Jane Digby, Lady Ellenborough, left the country to follow an Austrian diplomat to Paris, subsequently fascinated King Ludwig of Bavaria, married one of his barons, exchanged him for a Greek diplomat, and ended up with an Arab sheik. As her biographer says, she took the romantic age with her. But even in 1840 Dr. Alexander Walker, a physician, stated that there were few men, and fewer women than was commonly imagined, who had not indulged in irregular passions.[52] And however well the majority of them were kept secret, certain ones inevitably came to the shocked attention of ordinary English society. It seems as if the English exaggerated their faithfulness in love and marriage just as the French loved to imagine themselves more dashing in these matters than they actually were.

At the top of the scale, Victoria, of course, gave both precept and example of good domestic fidelity, but her predecessor's infatuation with the Countess of Jersey was famous, as were the relations of her successor, Edward VII, with his "fallen angels."[53]

In high political circles Lord Melbourne, widely suspected, was acquitted in a court of law in 1836 of having had carnal knowledge of Mrs. Norton. The judgment exonerated him, and he went on to become Prime Minister. Fifty years later just the suspicion of bad conduct was enough to ruin a man. This conclusion was ruefully drawn by Sir Charles Dilke after he was accused of having a liaison with a Mrs. Crawford, never proved and probably groundless (though he may have had other minor affairs). He had to leave public life because, as he himself put it, by the 1880s the middle classes felt that adultery was as bad as murder,[54] whereas in the first part of the century aristocratic society had enjoyed scandal. It is pleasant to recollect that when the scandal broke, Dilke's courageous fiancée, Mrs. Mark Pattison, took the occasion to announce her engagement in the *Times*, and shortly thereafter married him.

Parnell's case is a little different. There is no doubt that he had been carrying on an affair with Mrs. O'Shea during most of the 1880s, and that this was condoned by her husband. The news surfaced just when Parnell's Irish policy was meeting unexpected success, and it seems possible, though his gleeful enemies took advantage of it, that he unconsciously brought much of his doom upon himself.

Turning from politicians to intellectuals, here too occasional lapses would stun the community, as when George Grote, the historian of Greece, stepped out with a young sculptress after thirty years of subservience to the extremely bossy Mrs. Harriet Grote. Then there were those who practiced what Froude seemed to preach in the *Nemesis of Faith*—a free love believed to be so entirely pure that the lovers made no effort to hide it, like that of the Unitarian preacher W. J. Fox and his mistress, Eliza Flowers. Such a couple were slightly different from those who simply did not care enough about the world's opinion either to flaunt or to conceal their liaison, a practitioner of this style being Mrs. Hodgson Burnett, who lived for many years after her divorce with a man she eventually married, meanwhile calling him her "secretary." Much more typical was Dickens's long relationship with Ellen Ternan, unknown to the world. It would have been impossible in his society to get away with anything like Victor Hugo's public acknowledgment of Juliette Drouet.

Far and away the most famous case among writers, and in a way the exeption that proves the rule, was the relationship of George Eliot and G. H. Lewes. They were prevented from marrying by a divorce law that denied him a full divorce from his first wife (after she had borne two children to another man) because he had forgiven her and condoned the adultery. According to law, the fact that a husband could condone such behavior proved that he did not deserve what pure outrage would have entitled him to. So when he fell in love with Marian Evans, all he could do was ask her to live with him in a union that both of them would consider as sacred as a marriage, no matter what the world's opinion. On July 19, 1854, they eloped to Europe, where they were warmly welcomed. When they came back to England they found that very few of her old friends would accept their action at first, though as the fame of "George Eliot" grew, her salon began to attract first men and then eventually ladies. (On one trip to England, Charles Eliot Norton exclaimed that no one could forgive her breach of convention and that the only women who called on her were either emancipated or *declassées*, but on a subsequent visit Norton actually took his wife to meet her.) Or witness Mrs. Gaskell's dilemma, as she put it in 1859:"I have *tried* to be moral, & dislike her & dislike her books—but it won't do. There is not a wrong word, or a wrong thought in them."[55] So her decision was to shut her eyes to the awkward blight on the author's life. By 1866 George Eliot's station had improved to the point where the Queen's Lady-in-Waiting, Mary Ponsonby, accompanied by two princesses, stopped in. But the novelist still could not be received at Girton College, in spite of having donated money to it.

If she had lived twenty-five years later, her fate might have been quite different, for there came at that time a new burst of interest in free unions among the literati, particularly among the people connected with the Fabian Society. That society, it must be remarked, was a curious mixture of sexual experimenters like H. G. Wells and Hubert Bland, and sexual puritans, among whom should probably be considered Bernard Shaw, the Webbs, and at least Mrs. Bertrand Russell, if not her husband. The division followed a familiar radical pattern: there are some for whom the idea of freedom embodies freedom in all areas of life, while others feel that the Revolution is too important to get mixed up in sex, a distraction to the initiated and a stumbling block to the populace they hope to convert.

Wells at least balanced practice with theory. While still married to his first wife, he ran off with the student who was to become his second, and though the second marriage was long and understanding, he never restrained himself from carrying on outside affairs whenever he felt like it.

Edith Nesbit married Hubert Bland at a time when she was already pregnant by him, and she soon found that another woman was in the same condition. Through Bland's various illnesses, and through business losses, other affairs, and his other babies, she worked to support the lot of them, living a life of great courage and generosity. All the while, Bland, contrarily enough, took the side of severity in the Fabian debates on sexual freedom.

Among socialists who were afraid of sex, Shaw might be named first, with his well-known unconsummated marriage and his expressed alarm that all too many people used a marriage license as a permit to wreck their health with sexual indulgence.

Beatrice Webb's opinion was that if she were a man, "this creature would be free, though not dissolute in his morals, a lover of women," but since she was a woman, "these feelings, unless fulfilled by marriage, must remain unsatisfied," except, she thought, in religious exaltation.[56] The Webbs were horrified at Wells's seduction of a girl of good family who became the Ann Veronica of his novel, and Beatrice would have liked to take the girl in hand but was baffled by her preference to remain in the little cottage where Wells had set her up.

For unliberated souls, it was a matter of greatest urgency to maintain a front of domestic devotion. The hypocrisy was so sanctimonious that it often succeeded in deceiving both its own age and ours. We are so used to having marital spats aired, and value sincerity so far over fidelity, that it is hard for us to credit that the Reverend Hugo Reginald Haweis, after having cheated, lied, fornicated, and run up debts, and after his mistress with his child had demanded blackmail from Mrs. Haweis, would still state when his wife died that he had given thirty years of his life of toil and labor only for her, while she could dedicate her last book to the husband to whom it owed "everything."

∽ In Germany, the men of the aristocracy had long been used to having a free run among the peasant women on their estates. Otto von Corvin describes this life as enjoyed by his own father, who had "the faults of his time and rank"[57] and gave great offense to his wife (who subsequently got a divorce and was able to marry a *gymnasium* teacher for love).*

When the Prussian Junkers moved to the city, they brought their morals with them, so that Berlin became notorious, even in Germany, as a place with a hypocritical double standard, a haven for rich men's mistresses, for bordellos, for the sale of obscene pictures, for cabarets featuring naked dancers. Count Paul Vasili (pseudonym of Ekaterina Radziwill) said in 1884 that the city still had the customs of an earlier age.[58] She did not call it dishonest so much as simply uncivilized. Adultery flourished there like a plant in ideal soil; most married women had, or dreamed of, a lover. (Love with a married woman, said Stefan Zweig of the nineties, was the literary dream, but few were so lucky in life; others had to settle for shopgirls.)

Marie von Bunsen, who was born in 1860 and lived unmarried in court circles all her life, mentions that she only gradually became aware of liaisons among her acquaintances in the highest society. Her judgment, after receiving confidences from women who were happy with their lovers, was that adultery by no means always entailed an upheaval in married life, but might be a safety valve to keep a marriage together. Many of her confidantes convinced her that their lives were richer and fuller for the experience.[59]

Only occasionally were aristocrats brought to account for any sexual sins, though Prince Kaunitz was finally sent off to prison after an outraged father (one of many) complained to the Emperor himself.[60] Lily Braun reports that her own father lost his officer's commission because he loved the wife of another[61] (though in his case there were the other factors of his insubordination and personal dislike on the part of the young Kaiser Wilhelm II).

Among intellectuals and middle-class civil servants, convention was much more strictly observed. In Karl Immermann's view, German

*Many of the peasant women were of a minority Slavic race. Bebel noticed that in France, where there was no such minority to practice upon, people obliterated the results of sexual contact by resorting to infanticide (Bebel, *Die Frau*, 105).

family life rested on personal respect for all members, and he explained that while it was very common for husbands to have innocent platonic friendships with women, and for women to have male friends, this did not disrupt the marriage bond.[62]

Farther down in the class structure there was apparently greater laxity than among comparable classes in France and England. Certainly English travelers were shocked, and they liked to shock their readers with accounts of more illegitimate births than occurred in any other country of Protestant Europe.* As Samuel Laing reported:

> It is no uncommon event in the family of a respectable tradesman in Berlin to find upon his breakfast table a little baby, of which, whoever may be the father, he has no doubt at all about the maternal grandfather. Such accidents are so common in the class in which they are least common with us—the middle-class, removed from ignorance or indigence—that they are regarded as but accidents, as youthful indiscretions, not as disgraces affecting, as with us, the respectability and happiness of all the kith and kin for a generation.†[63]

Certain radicals found charm in this attribute of German life; in 1826 Richard Carlile, the birth control advocate, was favorably impressed that Prussian society did not ostracize women who chanced to have an early affair, and that this relationship did not prevent their marrying well later.[64]

In the last quarter of the nineteenth century there arose several schools that preached free love in a far more wholehearted way even than the Fabians in England. Certain socialists took up this cause after Marx and Engels had instructed them that marriage was only a bourgeois custom. Lily Braun was greatly impressed at party meetings to meet a certain Wanda Orbin, whom she held to be the type of the woman of the future, earning her own money and living in a free union with a Russian socialist by whom she had a child.[65] Rosa Luxemburg, the only socialist woman to reach really top rank in both the theoretical and the leadership aspects of socialist party life, refused, it is true, to marry Leo Jogiches, whom she loved for many years, though she was said to adopt a middle-class deference toward him, especially in matters of household finance. But once she found him unfaithful, she broke off with him instantly and completely,[66] a typically middle-class piece of behavior.

A non-socialist reaction against the authoritarian family of the German Empire period was started in the immediate prewar years by Otto Gross, a disciple of Freud, in Schwabing, the artists' quarter of Munich.[67] Gross and his women friends had read the new anthropology of

---

*"Illegitimate fertility in Germany has been high by European standards"—higher than Scandinavia, lower only than Austria, Hungary, and Portugal (Knodel, *Decline*, 75).

†When Horace Mann came to study the German educational system, he disputed the truth of Laing's observations, though he added that even if chastity was low in Prussia, the government schools that he admired so much should not be expected to cure a deep-seated vice in a single generation. For Mann, sensuality began at the *top* of German society.

their day, especially Bachofen on the matriarchal origins of society, and became enamoured of the idea of relinquishing the puritanical standards of culture for the gratification of primal instincts by orgies, the use of narcotic drugs, and the systematic breakdown of conscience. The group was somewhat cautiously analyzed by Max Weber, several of whose friends were involved and who was himself drawn into its fringes. As a student of the sociology of religion, he was struck with how sexuality offered some of the same psychological compensations as religion. At that time he considered both a flight from rationality.*

Marianne and Max Weber may be compared in some ways with the Webbs. Both were highly intellectual couples, believing in hard work, mutual succor, and personal independence, and both feared that sex might lead them into frivolity or too much time away from work. Marianne tells us that Max studied, intellectually, the effect on personality of relaxing all restrictions, and he concluded that monogamy might not be the single answer; nevertheless, she was grateful that her own devotion to him spared her the desire for sexual irregularity, and Max was careful never to let her know about the deviations that he undertook later in life.[68] But with Else von Richthofen, one of his early woman students, Max eventually found sexual release that stimulated a new creativity.[69]

It is hard to imagine more of a contrast in ways of feminine emancipation that between Marianne Weber and, say, Franziska zu Reventlow, one of the women at the center of the Schwabing movement. A girl from an aristocratic family, her first interest in both sex and modern ideas came from membership in a literary association, called the Ibsen Club, formed by her student friends in high school. Unfortunately her mother opened her locked desk, retrieved a bundle of love letters, and was so shocked that she packed Franziska off to one of those good Protestant pastor's homes that were supposed to settle the characters of so many German girls. Legally free on her twenty-first birthday, Franziska fled to Munich, where a lover taught her to paint. With lovers, a child, art, alternate periods of riches and poverty, and her social *savoir-faire*, she became a natural center for the Schwabing experimenters.[70]

Meanwhile women like Marianne and the leaders of the official women's movement believed that for women to be free, they must be purposeful and autonomous, actively pursuing thoughtfully chosen goals into which sex was felt to be something of an intrusion. The espousers of eroticism believed that to be free meant precisely to be liberated from such thoughtful choices, free to indulge in the spontaneous joys of primal instincts.

*Among the people involved was Else von Richthofen. She was a sister of Frieda Lawrence; the marital tangles of this group of friends remind one of the Schlegels and Schleiermachers a hundred years previously (see Chapter 25). Otto Gross married Frieda Schloffer, but later fathered a child on Else, and later still became the lover of Else's sister, who was married to an English professor named Weekley before she married D. H. Lawrence (Martin Green, 35–55).

The Italian women we shall now consider seemed not to suffer from this particular contradiction.

∽ L. Mariotti had explained in 1840 that Italians had never been subjected to the wave of "bourgeois" morality that held sway farther north. He attributed this to the smallness of the industrial and commercial classes in his country, the upwardly mobile, anti-sensual classes that had made "sex" into a dirty word in England and Germany.[71] Lady Morgan in 1820 had told her English readers that love was no sin in Italy, while Karl Immermann insisted to his German ones that it was the *wife* who there enjoyed her pleasures outside the marriage bed. (In France, he thought, it was the husband's pre-marital experience that took the charm out of marriage. Immermann, of course, believed that Germany was exempt from both hazards.)

Of all the nationalities here being considered, the Italians had the highest tolerance for irregular relationships, and though looked at askance by northern visitors, they were inclined to give themselves high marks for the moral superiority inherent in the long-lasting quality of their sexual partnerships and the rarity of passing intrigues. Byron notices that a woman was called virtuous in Italy if she had only one lover; it took two or three to make her seem a little wild.

Often separated husbands and wives continued to live under the same roof—though in separate apartments if they could manage it.[72] There the wife's long-term male companion would call on her daily. Heine in 1828 saw an old woman who was still visited daily by two lovers, perhaps, he mused, out of habit, perhaps out of respect for their earlier feeling, perhaps out of feeling itself, now independent of the present state of its former object.[73]

The great patriotic hostesses, the ladies who maintained salons for the discussion of politics and the arts, usually had a set of habitués, among whom one might be a specially favored friend. Laura Mantegazza's son, writing her biography after her death in 1873, never stated clearly that she was not living with her husband for most of her life, but referred delicately to her male friends, among whom were an *abate* (a cleric who was her "companion in thinking" for forty years) and a distinguished secular literary Brescian, Pietro Zambelli.

More striking, because so clear, is the case of the Contessa Chiara Maffei, who separated amicably from her husband in 1846 with a letter—"*Addio, Andrea Mio*"—explaining that they parted with affection and mutual esteem.[74] The legal separation of the Maffeis, asked for by her and willingly agreed to by him, was covered by a decorous formula blaming her health. On the day of the decree, she wrote a farewell letter "with a pained heart but a secure conscience,"[75] regretting, among other losses, their dead baby. The couple met again eighteeen years after their separation. During the interval the count, a poet, had ceremoniously sent her a copy of each of his volumes as they were published. One Sunday she chanced to meet him at a friend's reception; she bowed slightly to him, and he asked his hostess who the lady was. The others present were alarmed at the social awkwardness until they heard the couple addressing each other as "*tu*."[76] But they made no effort to come together again until Andrea fell seriously ill in Florence, whereupon the countess closed her salon in Milan and spent three months nursing him like a sister.

Her permanent male friend, who called on her daily, spent long vacations at her country house, and helped her run her salon as a forum for Italian patriots, was named Carlo Tenca. He lived in bachelor quarters with an old servant, showing his love over the years in sympathy and concern for his mistress's welfare.

Through all their affairs, Italians imagined that they were capable of greater passion than the rational French or the "cold" members of the Teutonic races. For many of them, love was an almost exclusive subject of conversation, as Desmarie found in Rome. It was so much an expected part of girls' futures that mothers would talk about their affairs in the presence of young girls, and would even boast, "My daughter does not sleep or eat. She is in love."[77] Even priests played the same game; Desmarie had seen them dancing with young girls while making remarks that would cause a grenadier to blush, though the girls just laughed and took it in good part. They would carry physical virginity with them into marriage, but not "virginity of the heart," he feared; and perhaps some received the same advice as Nievo's character in *The Castle of Fratta*, who told her confessor that she would like to marry the man she loved, and was ordered by him to yield to her parents' choice instead. The priest told her that God would extend to her the grace to fulfill the duties of her new condition, but that parents did not rule her heart, which would "*think for itself later.*"[78]

Stendhal too found that passion was so accepted that women talked about it everywhere, both in public and private, and that moreover it was not considered to be absurd. Byron added the observation that Italian women kissed better than any others, which he attributed, perhaps tongue in cheek, to their practice of osculation of saints' images. When Hortense Allart chose Italy as the birthplace of her illegitimate baby, fathered by a man she adored, she felt Italians understood the beauty of her feeling. Marie d'Agoult, arriving in Italy with Liszt, noticed that free liaisons failed to scandalize and that no woman hesitated to refer openly to her lover.*

Whereas a Frenchwoman would dream of winning a man by coquetry for a short term, the Roman woman cared only for a man she was sure of. Stendhal knew of men who had been discredited for feigning a passion they did not really feel, though here he felt that French influence was weakening good old-fashioned Italian constancy. Frenchmen would

---

*She may have taken too much for granted. The Countess Maffei recorded her disgust at the intimate signs of affection exchanged between Liszt and his lady love (Barbiera, 64).

be bored by such steady openness, since they liked to be led a chase, but even the appearance of coldness would be sufficient to repel an Italian, and the slightest hint of preference for another would kill all love and often lead to violence.[79]

Violence was of several sorts. Lower-class girls sometimes carried poignards. Massimo d'Azeglio believed that a woman who had shown him affection had been poisoned by one whose advances he had rejected. Then there was the subtler revenge of suicide. A young noblewoman, Anna Guistiniani, fell madly in love with Cavour and threw herself out of a high window, hoping to be reunited with him or dramatizing her hopelessness. Her tolerant husband said that she must be crazy and sent her off to the country. Suspecting correctly that Cavour was eager to repudiate her, she joined a patriotic society in hopes of winning him back, a tactic only moderately successful. Cavour gave her three days of love, and they parted with an exchange of lockets. Her parents made her swear to give him up, but she broke out of her confinement anyway. Cavour had had quite enough of her by then, and after several attempts she did succeed in killing herself.[80]

Another kind of violence was that of an outraged husband. Thus when Giovanni Prati, at eighteen, fell in love with a married lady, her husband, having threatened much worse things, began to carry a whip and set upon young Prati whenever he met him in the street. Since the youth felt himself guilty, he accepted the punishment meekly. The wife, meanwhile, was locked up tightly until her hair turned gray from misery. She too attempted suicide, but was fated to live a long time in despair.[81]

ᴄᴑ Generalizations that attempt to differentiate among nationalities in regard to marital infidelity are sure to be rough and subject to exception. After all, Europe as a whole had a common Christian tradition, based on monogamous marriage, that was strengthened (in varying degrees) during the nineteenth century by an ethic embraced by the middle classes because they could not afford the extravagance of the aristocracy.

It seems safe to say, however, that tolerance for extramarital affairs was greater in those countries where parents customarily arranged marriages for their young people[82]—France and Italy—which also happened to be countries with a Roman Catholic view of the indissolubility of marriage. In countries where marriage was ostensibly for love, it was conventionally assumed that young people who had chosen each other would live happily ever after. This expectation was probably lived up to most consistently in England. (Browning was insulted when Frank Harris asked him if he had learned all the passion revealed in *James Lee's Wife* from one woman.)[83] And in England, and Germany too, there was no accepted way to handle an affair. One did not acknowledge one's mistress or one's lover.

Nor is there any doubt that women's expectations in love climbed throughout the hundred years. They demanded "to be understood," and this changed the nature of commitment both in and out of marriage. George Eliot's choosing to live with Lewes represented the pattern of the future, it seems to me, a step beyond the stylized intrigues in early France or Italy.

APPENDIX: COMMENTS ON PROSTITUTION

Although prostitution was extensive and visible across Europe, travelers felt that among all the big cities Berlin most resembled a gigantic brothel.* Carl Scheffler's autobiographical character Johann arrives as a young man from Hamburg and is solicited six times during his first night in town.[84]

There had been strict police restrictions since 1790, with a prison sentence to anyone, male or female, who transmitted a venereal disease. Anyone suspected of being a prostitute, however innocent, could be hauled in by the police and subjected to a pelvic examination with instruments that were considered particularly brutal.[85]

In 1905 the novelist Margarete Böhme got hold of what she alleged was the diary of a successful prostitute. She explained that her first idea had been to use the material as the basis for a novel, but her publishers recommended simply printing the text, with names altered and certain unsuitable portions cut out. The book was a sensation, appearing under the title of *Tagebuch einer Verlorene* (The Diary of One Lost). The editor hoped that printing it would enable respectable women to sympathize with, or at least understand, a girl who was originally perfectly nice but who had succumbed to ordinary social pressures of the day.

I put the story in an appendix because of doubts about its authenticity, but at the very least it presents a picture that seemed credible to readers at the turn of the century and makes vivid such problems as the sexual ignorance of girls, the carelessness of men, the total lack of understanding of what the girl needed, the blind faith that the way back to respectability was to spend a year in a pastor's house, the social downfall after a single (and repented) slip, the nature of police surveillance, and the difficulty of getting respectable work.

According to the story, the girl, called Thymian, was the daughter of an apothecary in a small village. When her tubercular mother was removed to a sanatorium, the child was left with a sixteen-year-old maid, while her father lived it up with wine and song. Thymian could not understand why the maid had to leave in a hurry—nor why, after this episode, she herself should be sent away, ostensibly for education, to a pastor's house, where, in fact, the three boarders had to do all the housework for his family of five children. Things were not much better

---

*In 1880 Baring-Gould estimated that Berlin had 1 prostitute for every 62 inhabitants. London at the same time, 1 in 91, and Paris only 1 in 247, perhaps because of the custom there of taking more or less permanent mistresses. He did not explain how he got such figures (Baring-Gould, 1: 167).

when her aunts and uncles sent her to a regular boarding school, because she was soon dismissed for having stayed out too late on an outing with some boys from a neighboring school. (The wagon in which they were riding broke down.)

Home again, she still could not figure out why a second housekeeper had to be dismissed, but she made friends with a third one, Elisabeth, and welcomed her warmly to her room one night when Elisabeth had to flee from Thymian's father. Unfortunately, Elisabeth became pregnant and drowned herself in the river; this was a horrible shock to Thymian.

Her father's assistant in the shop was quick to offer the explanation she was seeking—namely, that men "need" women—and he kissed and stroked her to show her in what way. Soon, her unsympathetic stepmother dropped her right into the assistant's arms. By watching the laundry the stepmother discovered when Thymian became pregnant, but the girl rejected the possibility of marriage to her seducer, and in a family council it was decided to send her off to a midwife at Hamburg. Longing for love, but understandably not much attracted by the idea of marriage, Thymian nevertheless protested vigorously when her child was snatched forcibly from her arms and carried off for adoption. Meanwhile, her own reformation was supposed to be furthered by that most German of methods, another stay at a clergyman's house. Here she was given no freedom, no money, and not even the privilege of meeting the "nice" girls who came to the house, even though the pastor himself maintained a peasant mistress. Thoroughly outdone with the church and its hypocrisies, she stole enough money to pay her way to Hamburg, where she hoped to find her baby, but when she arrived, being under eighteen, she was allowed no legal claim to the child. After this she drifted into a high-class brothel, where the personnel combined to break her in very gently, bribing her with silk stockings and luxurious meals since she was still naive enough not to want to give herself for money.

At the point where she stepped over this financial boundary, the point of no return, the editor notes that several pages were torn out of the diary.

In 1893 the friendly madam warned her to flee a police raid and gave her the name of a contact in Berlin. Until now she had played the role of ingénue at the house, and one man had actually proposed marriage; but he turned white when she confessed her true condition, leaving her more desperate than ever for understanding and forgiveness.

In Berlin she pretended to give lessons in foreign languages and in this way hoped to evade police control. (The give-away in the advertisement she placed was describing herself as "Fraülein Thymian," without a surname.) Here, at least she found the neighbors all eager to rally round and protect her when the police came on their searches.

A doctor whose wife was "too ill to be a wife" set her up in an apartment in a new neighborhood, where she had a chance to start a new life renting out rooms. And by luck (here one suspects the *romancier*) she ran into an old and titled schoolfriend, the one she was out late with in the broken wagon. By marrying him she acquired the title of baroness, and no one suspected her past life. Alas, the husband turned out to be totally debauched, his wild affairs drove her honest tenants away, the good doctor abandoned her in disgust. A rich count eventually set her up in a cottage, in luxury but very lonely, and so she decided to try to get useful work, only to be told that, at twenty-six, she was much too old to learn new skills.

Receiving an inheritance from her father's estate in 1899, she generously gave half of it back to her stepbrothers and donated the rest to a home for unmarried mothers. Such largesse attracted the attention of society ladies who asked her to join their charitable committees, but she found these ladies far more malicious than the women in the brothels; and this phase came to an abrupt end when she was recognized by one of their brothers.

An old friend from the brothel had by now risen in life and married; she offered to share some interesting secrets of her trade as a marriage broker. Meanwhile, Thymian made a new friend, the lady in the zoo to whom she entrusted her precious journal. The editor reports that on Christmas, 1902, which was to be her last on earth, Thymian had a happy day as she and her rich protector entertained eleven poor children from the streets with a tree and presents.

Prostitution, however invisible to respectable women, still had a chilling effect on their lives. It caused men to divide women into two classes, gave them a double vision of the female sex, and in that way intensified the double standard of morality, all the while keeping their relationships with respectable women sincere enough to make such women naively certain that society was on its way to a single standard.

Germany may have had the highest rate of prostitution, but many Frenchmen felt that England was where unrespectable women were treated the worst, where seduction and complete abandonment were most frequent. "It seemed as if I were watching a march past of dead women," exclaimed Taine after he had prowled around London's red light district.[86] French society, he felt, had a graduated ladder of respectability, and Frenchwomen, even of the lowest class, had an ingenuity and feminine skill that would enable them to better themselves.

∽16.

Dissolving the Marriage Bond

Divorce is the sacrament of adultery.
                J.-F. Guichard

Today unhappy marriage always raises the possibility of divorce. In the nineteenth century the social, economic, and psychological costs of divorce varied widely among different countries. In France and England, it took long, hard legislative fights to win eventually the option of complete legal separation. In Germany, on the other hand, where divorce had always been freest, the Civil Code of 1900 actually tightened up the rules.

∽ Law, tradition, and public attitude made divorce easier, more common, and more accepted in Germany than in most other places.[1] The tradition goes back at least to Luther, who favored easy breaking of the marriage bond just as he thought monastic vows should not be considered binding.[2] Thus thanks to this religious permissiveness, Prussian law, before the creation of the Empire, allowed divorce for uncontrollable aversion or by mutual agreement.[3] Even after several separations, the woman as well as the man could retain an unimpeachable reputation. Prussia was the most latitudinarian, but the Protestant states usually granted divorce for adultery, desertion, cruelty, or imprisonment of a spouse, and even the Catholic states often allowed for divorce in principle. The property settlements giving married women control over their own money, which could not be seized by the husband's creditors, facilitated the process.[4]

In her famous treatise of 1819 on Germany, at the height of the romantic period, Mme de Staël found that the marriage vow was freely broken by both sexes—equality with a vengeance she considered it—and she did not approve of the ease of divorce, even though she recognized that little bitterness attached to the process. She said that for German women love was a religion, and they changed husbands as casually as if they were staging a play.[5] A telling example of the German forgive-and-forget attitude toward divorce, reported sarcastically by the author of

German Home Life, concerned a man who played whist nightly with his three ex-wives.[6]

As might be expected, Dr. Riehl claimed that Mme de Staël's picture was unrecognizable.[7] Being in favor of a patriarchal family, he stated that even an unhappy marriage could be a blessing through the discipline it demanded. The two writers were talking about different groups: she about the intellectuals she met, he about his partly imaginary old-fashioned, ordinary citizens.

Consider Clemens Brentano, Bettina von Arnim's brother. While a student at Jena, he fell in love with a professor's wife. After struggling for three years to overcome their mutual passion, she got a divorce, but died within two years of her marriage to Brentano, who then fell in love with a banker's high-keyed daughter.[8] (She happened to be the sister of the future Marie d'Agoult, of whom more later.) This marriage lasted barely three months, since she is said to have driven him wild by drumming her feet on the foot of the bed and scratching on the sheets with her nails.[9] Her family finally provided her with another husband in Paris. Meanwhile Brentano converted to Catholicism, and his series of marriages came to an end.

An even more piquant case was that of Prince Pückler-Muskau.*[10] This owner of a large landed estate married Lucie, Countess Pappenheim, a daughter of Hardenberg, the Prussian chancellor. After some wavering over his choice, he apparently became rather fond of the lady, but when their property ran into financial difficulties, the way to solve the problem seemed to be for him to divorce Lucie (with King Frederick William's help) and hunt a rich English heiress. In 1826 he landed in England with this stated purpose. As a matter of fact, he had previously been engaged to an English lady who had provided him with £2,400 to set up a house for them before she backed down. He then refused to return the money, stating that the costs of his courtship had totaled over £4,000. Now, in 1826, this same lady, Countess Landsdowne, welcomed the prince back to London, assuring him at the same time that English society would not recognize his divorce, or approve of his intention to marry for money, since English ladies married for love. He found out how right she was after trying to persuade an heiress or two that German husbands allowed their wives "reasonable liberty"; but the young ladies in question were not persuaded. (The prince never did marry again; instead he traveled in the Near East, acquired a harem, and even returned to Germany with two Abyssinian slaves.)

Other examples of the casualness of divorce in Germany abound. When Otto von Corvin was five or six, his mother had had enough of her horsy, sporting husband, and finding plenty of legal grounds, she won a divorce and an annuity.[11] Later she married, for love, a young high school teacher who became a noted Greek scholar, an editor of Aristophanes.

---

*Whom Lady Morgan's butler used to announce as "Prince Pickling Mustard."

When Johanna Mathieux fell in love with Gottfried Kinkel, a prominent art historian subsequently imprisoned for his part in the 1848 uprisings, she was unable to get a divorce in the French-law Rhineland where she lived, so she escaped to Berlin, where she was harbored for six months by Bettina von Arnim, and obtained her freedom there.*[12]

Yet in spite of the fact that it was such an accepted feature of German life, the actual number of divorces was not great by modern standards. John Russell, a Scotsman traveling in Prussia soon after the Napoleonic Wars, was shocked that there were three thousand divorces in 1817, out of a population of ten million.

Divorce was made even easier by the fact that it cost so little—about ten thalers in 1865 if both parties consented, and only about six times that if it was contested.† Germany was the only country in which divorce was freely available to the poor.[13]

A great change occurred in 1896, when the draft of the new Civil Code for the Empire was unveiled, and people perceived that it would reverse previous policy and make divorce as difficult as possible. (The Code went into effect in 1900.) The new rules required that the grounds be specific rather than general; dislike and apathy were no longer sufficient reason, and the procedure itself was lengthened.[14] Apparently the drafters of the new legislation were stung by the common perception that laxity in divorce made Germany "less civilized" than her European neighbors, ironically just at the time when those neighbors were loosening their own laws. The German Empire was set up to control people, not to meet their needs, and divorce was seen as a behavior that would weaken the social fabric. Bitter protest from the women's movement did nothing to change the new rules.

ᴄᴐ Under the strictly Catholic *ancien régime*, France had not permitted absolute divorce, though limited separation might be obtained. The Revolution of 1789 did away with the restrictions, and set up several grounds for divorce, including mutual consent, incompatibility, cruelty, insanity, and criminal conviction. At the same time it made mere separation unlawful.

Under the 1804 Napoleonic Code, legal separation again became possible, on grounds limited to adultery, cruelty, criminal conviction, and mutual consent. In 1816 the restored monarchy again proscribed divorce, which remained impossible until the Naquet law of 1884. Separations rose steadily in the interim, but as soon as divorce was legal the separation rate fell off sharply and the number of divorces began its steep ascent—from 1,640 cases in 1885 to 7,496 in 1890.

Popular pressure to reintroduce divorce after 1816 varied. In the

*Later on Johanna supported herself and her children in London by giving piano lessons until Karl Schurz managed to help Kinkel escape from his prison.

†A thaler was valued at about three English shillings.

early thirties there were no fewer than five motions to sanction it—a suitable reward, the sponsors thought, for the successful revolution of 1830, which put Louis Philippe on the throne—but though they passed the Chamber, often overwhelmingly, they failed each time in the House of Peers. Under the short-lived Second Republic, a divorce measure again failed to pass, and hope died under the Second Empire, which tried to copy the first in all such details.

A measure was drafted in 1851 to make the process of separation cheaper, and this helped women especially, since women brought nearly 90 percent of the separation suits under the Second Empire.

But even when they won a separation decree, women might still have to take a second case to court for a monetary settlement, and they could easily be left without resources. George Sand, who went through the process with the aid of an able lawyer, a distinguished reputation, and even a willing husband, found the procedure inexpressibly ugly. It required one party to wound the other, and the husband had the power, if he won the suit, to put his wife in prison, to condemn her to return to his embraces, or to make her life one of public reproach.

During all this time stories circulated showing the misery and the often desperate remedies of those for whom an unhappy marriage offered no prospect of release.*

A certain woman who was forced to live in the same house with her husband's mistress stood it until the latter put in a demand for the keys to the wine cellar and the office—the most precious badge of domestic sovereignty. The wife then ordered the mistress to get out, whereupon the husband threatened to send their child to the colonies where his mother could never see him again. The mother went on her knees to beg the mistress to remain.[15]

In 1847 a twenty-one-year-old woman named Mesnager came to the police court, stating that her well-paid husband would not support her and that often she and the children had nothing to eat while he went to a café every day for lunch and dinner. Finally her husband, saying that he was tired of her complaints and the children's crying, threw them out of doors. She was taken in by their lodger, a man named Sombret, who told her that he loved her and would take care of her children as if they were his own. The court was moved by their story to make the punishment light—a week in jail for Sombret and Mme Mesnager. The neglectful husband got off scot-free.[16]

A favorite subject of gossip, and a favorite argument for easier dissolution of marriage, concerned those women who got their "divorce" by murder. The most notorious was a Mme Lafarge, who was convicted of killing her husband in 1840 and given a penalty of life imprisonment

*Though Jenny d'Héricourt said that one could hardly believe the number of married couples who reformed their treatment of each other in 1848, when they were fearful of the restoration of divorce (Héricourt, 280).

because of extenuating circumstances. She was released in 1853, after her case had become a romantic cause. As a girl Marie Lafarge, who was born in 1816, had been an avid reader of romantic literature, including the novels of George Sand, Victor Hugo, and Dumas, but her marriage was arranged through a matrimonial agency that falsified the facts about her husband-to-be.[17] He was an ironmonger who needed capital to expand his plant, and she had a comfortable dowry. She herself was not consulted about the marriage, but was allowed to meet the suitor as if by chance at a concert, and three days later the banns were published without asking her consent. She never had a moment alone with him, but was fed stories of a fine country house with a ruined convent picturesquely nearby. She was stunned to find the property ugly, run-down, and out-of-date, the new husband a widower rather than a first-time bridegroom, and the family provincial and uncongenial. Thoroughly unhappy, she felt that the only way out of her dilemma was to buy arsenic "for rat poison" and bake it into cakes, which she served him with affectionate words. Although many more separations were caused by financial problems, murder made far better copy for the French press and for the proponents of reform.

Under the Third Republic hope sprang up that a free and secular government would establish a liberal divorce law once more, and the question began to be agitated with the publication of a number of pamphlets by some of France's most renowned writers. Dumas, *fils*, and Emile de Girardin both had a say in the discussion. Dumas, although declaring excusable the murder of an unfaithful wife, also reported anecdotes of marital trickery that made divorce seem a rational alternative. Girardin had a more radical plan; while agreeing that divorce might bring temporary benefit, he favored a long-range easing of the expectations within a marriage, so that both partners would remain free, and all their children, legitimate or illegitimate, would have equal rights vis-à-vis their mother.[18] An injured wife should be able to leave her husband without a court case and live in dignity with all her children about her. He also proposed setting up a fund for a universal dowry for women.

In 1874 Léon Richer came out with a little book, *Divorce*, trying to prove that the Bible was not against it and that legal separation without the possibility of remarriage led to a situation whereby two-thirds of the separated spouses would take lovers, leaving the children as the chief sufferers.

The Republic was not responsive at first, though a number of grisly murders continued to titillate: in 1880, a story in the *National* of a man who killed his wife because she was planning to return to her parents; from 1882, a tale of a woman who helped her husband murder her lover, under threat that the children would be killed if she failed to cooperate.[19]

The most logical and powerful plea for divorce came from the pen of Alfred Naquet, a man who devoted his life to getting a divorce bill passed and sought a seat in the Chamber for that single purpose. He placated his opposition by stating that the vast majority of marriages were happy, and that divorce would only interest a tiny minority: 1 in 150, he estimated. For that small group, however, it was crucial; having fallen into a condition of hopelessness, they had adapted to their despair by various unsavory means. He compared France with Belgium, where divorce was permitted. France had one separation for 152 marriages, while in Belgium there was one divorce for 452; and even if one added separations the separation plus divorce rate in Belgium was only 1 in 235.[20]

Naquet's first bill, introduced in 1876, would have made divorce as free as in 1792, but finding that public opinion was not ready for such a strong measure, he weakened his provisions until by 1884 his successful bill was more like that of 1804, giving as grounds cruelty, adultery, slander, and criminal conviction, but denying divorce for incompatibility or by mutual consent. In 1900 France had 7,363 divorces; by 1913 the number had a little more than doubled.[21]

∽ As in Germany, the Reformation in England made marriage into a civil contract, but after the Restoration the ecclesiastical courts would not give an absolute divorce and the civil courts were held to have no jurisdiction. The only way to obtain one was by special act of Parliament.[22] Such a bill could be introduced on behalf of an innocent husband against a wife guilty of adultery, but until the law was changed in 1857, it had to be preceded by a successful suit against the paramour for damages (and how the French railed at the thought that an Englishman's honor could be assuaged by cash)[23] and an ecclesiastical court's decree for separation.[24]

Cases brought before that time averaged less than two per year, while only four cases in 150 years were known where a wife was the petitioner to Parliament. For the wife to make such application, adultery had to be aggravated by such crimes as bigamy, incest, or rape. One such case was that of a Miss Turner, in 1827, who was abducted across the Scottish border and fraudulently married when she was only fifteen. She won her case in Parliament, even though she could have gotten a much easier decree in Scotland. The last case before 1857 when a woman obtained an act of divorce was that of Mrs. Battersea, in 1840, who was infected with an infamous disease by a man who later entered into a bigamous marriage and was sentenced to transportation.[25]

In Scotland, where the wife was not legally a chattel, she had exactly the same right to sue for divorce as her husband, and she was allowed to defend herself. Furthermore, the cost there was only about twenty or thirty pounds; yet the total number of divorces there was hardly high: about twenty a year, compared to less than two in England.*[26]

*The difference in the two countries led Mrs. Norton, whose children had been torn from her when she tried to separate from her husband, to reflect in a satiric letter to the Queen "that whilst your Majesty is surrounded with faithful wives and discreet ladies in

Pressure for change rose. Mr. Justice Maule helped sway public opinion with his gravely ironical remarks at the Warwick Assizes when he sentenced a man for bigamy. He pointed out that the petitioner had married a woman after his first wife had deserted him to live in adultery. The proper procedure would have been for him to institute an action for damages against the man who was living with his wife, and then go to the ecclesiastical courts to obtain the equivalent of a judicial separation. Only after successful conclusion of these steps could he arrange to have a bill presented in Parliament for a full divorce. Of course, said the judge, this might cost five or six hundred pounds, but the law was the same for the rich as the poor. Part of the fault lay in the defendant's trying to marry the second woman. The law would not have been nearly so severe had he merely taken her as a concubine.[27]

The first relief came with the Matrimonial Causes Act of 1857, when a secular court was set up to hear divorce cases, with the effect of making them easier and cheaper, though still not cheap enough to help the poor. The grounds were the same as before and still greatly favored the husband. Collusion or condoning created an absolute bar.* From less than two a year when a divorce had to come through Parliament, the number of petitioners rose immediately to about two hundred annually.

Reformers began to collect stories of abuses against women who could not get relief through the new provisions and to keep statistics of the number of aggravated assaults by husbands against wives, finding that they totaled nearly 1,500 reported cases per year, while, of course, many more would remain unknown. It was pointed out that, by law, these battered wives still had to render sexual and household services to their husbands.[28]

Furthermore, the argument that the husbands were providing shelter and support for their wives was broken down by the revelation that most of the aggrieved wives whose cases came before the new divorce court could prove that they had been the financial mainstay of their households.[29] In 1878 Frances Power Cobbe wrote *Wife Torture*, a pamphlet describing conditions among the working classes where divorce was still too expensive to enable the beaten wife to escape.†

Some relief from these conditions was given by an act of 1878 that allowed a magistrate to grant a separation to a wife if the husband committed aggravated assault upon her, and also allowed her to retain custody of children under ten.

As might have been expected, the new courts did not solve all marital difficulties. Ernest Kellett heard from a medical man that prob-

---

London, Windsor, and Osborne, the less cautious portion of the realm in which Balmoral is situated, is plunged in the grossest immorality" (quoted in Kaye, "Outrages," 546).

*"Condoning" was defined as forgiveness followed by cohabitation.

†I have been unable to locate this pamphlet, nor have I succeeded in tracing a volume by Elephine Rose called *European Slavery: Or, Scenes from Married Life* (Edinburgh, ca. 1881).

ably every physician who had practiced in London for twenty years would have good reason to believe that some wives in his practice had poisoned their husbands, or the husbands their wives.[30] Sir John Kaye, historian and man of letters, felt that while having an outlet in law would enable certain betrayed spouses to carry the case to court, and would therefore prevent some murders, the only real way to discourage adultery would be to give women honest employment.[31]

Far louder than these appeals to common sense rose the moralistic cries of the orthodox, from Queen Victoria down. Her Majesty became alarmed at the startling tidbits now printed in the daily newspapers, which seemed to her worse than French novels.[32]

Even very unhappy couples who wished to stay on the good side of public opinion dared not admit to anyone how they really felt. They tried to hide their private miseries from the servants, even from their own families. Far better to live that way than to undergo the torments that Thackeray describes as suffered by Lady Clara Newcome, who fled with a former suitor from a husband who beat her and knocked her down repeatedly. What a rescue, moralized Thackeray. Her savior himself pitied and deplored her conduct, while all the sisterhood of female friendship was immediately cut off. Her new husband was driven from his miserable house to seek rough companions, while even the cottagers whom she would have liked to help scorned her. Worst of all was that people who were just as criminal as she (for the law stated that what she had done was a crime) feared contact with her, lest they too be polluted.

A good part of the opposition to divorce, however thickly covered up in sanctimony, was based on economics. Gladstone felt that only because marriage was indissoluble were the lower classes moved to obey the laws.[33] The economic system forced the poor to live together, and obeying the marriage code would tie factory labor down and prevent farm labor from migrating. When the court in the so-called Clitheroe case ruled in 1891 that a husband, after all, did not have the power to carry his wife off by force or imprison her until she restored his conjugal rights, Mrs. Lynn Linton called this ruling not only a triumph for promiscuity but a blow at the foundations of social order.[34]

Even feminists were not unanimously in favor of an extension of the divorce law because part of their appeal lay in their determination to make people live up to higher standards. In 1888 the *Daily Telegraph* published some hundreds of letters from its readers on the subject of marriage, and it was noticed how many of them came from men (of the sort who would be called male chauvinists today) expressing themselves in favor of looser divorce rules. Elizabeth Chapman, writing in the *Westminster Review* (1888), was shocked at this laxity. As a defender of women's rights, her interest was to tighten the bonds, create secular standards stricter than the old Biblical ones; even if this rigidity caused private misery, people should be willing to bear it for the sake of public decency.[35]

The cumulative effect of these attitudes was to make respectable people shrink from going through the divorce process. Two fictional examples may indicate how such people were affected. Meredith has Diana plan to flee to Europe rather than stand as a witness in her own case. (If she testified, her testimony would be construed as self-defense, and no divorce could ensue in a defended case.) Even as late as 1906, Arnold Bennett, in *Whom God Hath Joined*, presents a daughter who faints in the courtroom rather than testify against her father, and when her mother perceives the strain on the child, she withdraws the suit. The burden of both books, and many others, is that people could not get satisfaction in the courts.

After 1878, the most spectacular proponent of further reform was Earl Russell (Bertrand's older brother). In 1890 he married a woman who had apparently chosen him for his money, and who left him after three months and sued for divorce.[36] (She accused him of homosexuality.) The suit was dismissed as groundless, whereupon the wife turned around and sued for restitution of conjugal rights, which was the last thing he wanted. In 1895 Russell obtained a decree of separation, but she appealed the case and had the judgment reversed. Thoroughly outdone, he fled to America, where he married an American divorcée in 1900. Upon his return to England, he was slapped with a penalty of £1,500 for adultery (the cash payment again) and had to serve three months in jail for bigamy. By bribing his first wife with a handsome settlement to make the accusation that would lead to a divorce, he finally managed to make his second marriage legal.[37]

Predictably eager for reform, Russell introduced a divorce bill in the House of Lords in 1902 that would have made various grounds, including three years' separation, or one year's separation with both parties agreed, sufficient. But his fellow peers attacked him with rage and went to the unusual length of rejecting his bill outright rather than employing their customary polite method of tabling it.

What brought about the next push for change was not a noble lord's eccentricities, but rather the increasing conviction that to enforce a single standard of morality was an obligation of every well-ordered, civilized state. When early twentieth-century reformers looked back on 1857, it seemed a semi-barbarous age; by 1909 the alteration that had taken place in moral standards was proclaimed by a Royal Commission. The different penalties for adultery meted out to wife and husband no longer seemed appropriate,* nor did the exclusion of the poorer classes from the possibility of divorce fit in with the new egalitarianism. A third facet of reform, the one that had interested Queen Victoria, was the curbing of unrestricted newspaper reporting of sex scandals and intimate details of private lives. Over strong minority protest led by the Archbishop of

---

*A reason given in 1857 for treating a wife's adultery as more serious was that she could thereby introduce into her husband's family a child that was not his. At that time no comparable injury seemed to be done by the husband's straying, but the 1912 report pointedly explained that even a small accidental act by the man was by then known to be capable of causing a loathsome disease in the wife, permanently ruining her health.

York, the Commission in 1912 issued a report that recommended that desertion for three years be added to the grounds for divorce.[38] But Parliament did not actually agree; nothing was changed until after World War I.

From 1897 to 1906 six hundred divorces were granted annually in the central divorce courts, with eighty judicial separations, while poor people, unable to afford the costs, obtained eight thousand separation and maintenance orders in the magistrates' courts.

Apparently a large segment of the population had ceased to feel the commitment that led one nineteenth-century lady to say, "Once married, you no more think of changing your husband that you would of changing your parents."[39] Instead, as E. M. Forster remarked, "People today love each other from moment to moment as much as ever their ancestors did, but loyalty of soul . . . is on the decrease."[40]

∞ The reason why there is no section on Italy in this chapter will become clear from the accompanying table, which also codifies information about the other countries.*

Divorces and separations granted per thousand marriages celebrated

	Years	Divorces	Separations
Prussia	1891–1895	18.01*	0.0
France	1884–1894	21.0	8.0
England / Wales	1890–1894	1.6	0.1
Italy	1890–1894	0.0	2.9

*Demands only.

What stands out are the very low numbers for Italy (restrained by the Catholic church) and the very high numbers for France and Prussia. (The table apparently does not include the judicial separations granted by the English magistrates' courts, but only those adjudicated by the central divorce courts. In 1897–1906 the former courts granted 8,000 judicial separations, while the latter granted 600 full divorces and 80 judicial separations.)

The comparison between the number of divorces in England and Germany is somewhat misleading because before 1914 the cost was such that only the middle and upper classes could obtain divorce in England. Thus though Germany still had a far higher rate than England, the difference between the upper classes was not so large as the overall rates suggest.

*I owe this table to Steve Hochstadt, who found it in M. Emile Yvernès, "Essai d'une statistique internationale des divorces et des séparations de corps," in *Bulletin de l'Institut International de Statistique* 2, pt. 1 (1899).

Even though the German Civil Code of 1896–1900 was intended to slow down the divorce rate, it failed to do so; after it came into force, the rate per thousand marriages went up to 38 per year.

∾ To many women divorce seemed the pivotal issue of liberation. So long as marriage could be forced—or foisted—upon them, the right to get out as nearly unscathed as possible was only simple justice, and yet this was extremely hard to do. Even women who did not want divorce for themselves still felt the underlying injustice of the situation of their sisters.

The intensity of these feelings can be partly gauged by the popularity of naturalistic fiction. If a woman felt unjustly entrapped, reading about Mme Bovary could speak to her condition in a way that nothing in real life could do, and so the basic thematic reservoir of a whole school of novels and plays came to be the lack of practical escape from intolerable domestic situations. When *The Doll's House* let Nora out, the drama played all over the world as a universal symbolic scream.

In Germany, the country where divorce was freest, fiction stayed longer in a romantic vein than in France. And when divorce became commonplace everywhere, naturalism ceased making entrapment a central theme.

Socialism too offered a way to obtain some emotional release. There is no way of telling how many people embraced the doctrine because they desperately needed marital liberation, but it certainly promised this kind of freedom along with others. Germany again provides an instructive example: the imperial government put in tighter marital controls just at the time, about 1900, when socialism was becoming a real threat to the burgeoning capitalist order. Today, with easier divorce, socialism has lost this part of its emotional appeal.

ᦔ 17.

An Unclaimed Dividend

We seem only recently to have waked up in England to any distinct
perception of a fact which has now been at work for years in altering,
without any one's premeditation, the position of our women. The
dearth of husbands was known as a statistical discovery, but it was not
recognised as a practical fact with direct bearing on the everyday life of
the everyday world. Men enough to match the women, and a few to
spare, are born into England, but, as each generation ripens into marriageable years, a large proportion of the men and scarcely any of the
women have left the country.

Augusta Webster, 1879

For several reasons, in the middle of the nineteenth century people
began to consider the unmarried part of the female population as a
problem. For one thing there seemed to be more of them, rather suddenly. They were pushed into the public consciousness by the fact that
they were in the way, being no longer so usefully absorbed into families
and less willing to enter a religious community where they could be
honored but also fairly inconspicuous. When people began to question
why this phenomenon had occurred, uncomfortable ideas arose. Were
economic conditions making it more difficult to support a large family?
Or was the sex drive weakening across western Europe (raising the
possibility that Civilization itself might be at fault), and would the nations
face depopulation? It sprang to mind that if unmarried women had to
become self-supporting, they would likely have to be admitted, threat-
eningly, to such all-male strongholds as universities and professions.

In his great study of human marriage, Edward Westermarck told
his contemporaries that in the year 1874 a third of the population of
western Europe lived in voluntary or involuntary celibacy.[1] His figures
are highly suspect, though his voice would add weight to an already
strong sense of alarm. Among contributing factors to the distressing
situation, he believed, was the possibility that the development of mental
powers had reduced the reproductive ones—the zero-sum game again—
although he added that this was not proved. Or else the new higher
demands on marriage might have slowed down the rate at which people
were willing to enter it. A woman who had to develop "character" before

a man would fall in love with her would need time to mature, and this would prevent very young marriages.

∽ The crude figures of the British census of 1851 showed 600,000 more women than men over the age of twenty. This figure was to become part of the conventional wisdom of the day, and was widely, if inaccurately, taken to mean that a quarter of the women of England could never find husbands. The actual rate of never-married women hovered around 12 percent until the end of the century, then rose to about 16 percent just before 1914, but the census-takers did not break this down by class, and it is almost certain that in the upper strata of society the rate of celibacy was indeed higher.* The French commentator Louis Larcher calmly told his readers in 1860 that in London alone there was a surplus of 120,000 women[2] plus 100,000 unmarried men over twenty-five (who by refraining from marriage prevented an additional 100,000 women from attaining that fortunate state), totaling 220,000 unmarriageable females.† French and Italian journalists were already commenting pointedly on the situation within a very few years after the census figures appeared.[3]

In England a spate of articles explaining what the figures meant and what the consequences might be followed one by Harriet Martineau in the *Edinburgh Review* for 1859. Before discussing this article, let us look at the old expected course of life for a maiden aunt. Fanny Kemble's Aunt Dall is a good example. This lady's romance had been wrecked because she was an actress and her lover's father had forbidden him to marry anyone in such a profession. The lover refused at first to give her up, but the father summoned all his servants and tenants, and made a public statement that the boy was illegitimate, disinherited, and disowned, whereupon there was nothing for him to do but enlist in the army and go to India. After that, Aunt Dall made her home with the Kembles. As Fanny explained:

*The proportion of women in England and Wales who were unmarried at the age of 45–55 was 12.2 percent, and it remained between 11.9 percent and 12.4 percent until 1909, when it slowly began to rise, reaching 15.8 percent in 1911. (Steve Hochstadt got these figures from the Census of England and Wales, Vol. 7, House of Commons Sessional Papers, 1912–1913, v. 113, p. 429.) But when in 1911 Lee Holcombe compared the ratio of men to women in three wealthy neighborhoods and three of the working class, it turned out that the former had 19,738 women to 5,758 men, while the latter had only 3,850 women to 5,185 men, thus showing just how different the ratios could be in different classes (Holcombe, 11).

†Steve Hochstadt, who has studied the figures more thoroughly, believes that there was no demographic shortage: the men were there, but perhaps less emotionally pressed by the situation, since the life of a bachelor was not so doleful as that of an old maid. In 1860 *Punch* seems to support this view:"Thanks to the prevalent taste for a profusion of finery, combined with a rising income tax [at that time ten pence in the pound after an exemption of £150] girls are getting too dear, that is to say, too expensive creatures to find husbands . . . " (Graves, 2: 246).

Without any home but my father's house, without any means of subsistence but the small pittance which he was able to give her, in most grateful acknowledgment of her unremitting care of us, without any joys or hopes but those of others, without pleasure in the present or expectation of the future, apparently without memory of the past, she spent her whole life in the service of my parents and their children, and lived and moved and had her being in a serene, unclouded, unvarying atmosphere of cheerful, self-forgetful content that was heroic in its absolute unconsciousness.[4]

Maria Edgeworth was a maiden aunt too, although her reputation made her something more besides. But when Mr. Edgeworth died, her eldest living brother inherited the estate. He begged his mother and sisters to live there with him, and Maria seems always to have played the part of a dutiful sister and daughter, deferring to her brother and to her young stepmother.[5]

Dickens, who had a sister-in-law of this type, speculated on "whether it is, or is not, a pity that she is all she is to me and mine," thus hovering between compassion and admiration. Compare Lady Constance Lytton, a suffragette, who, not allowed by her parents to study music professionally or become a journalist, called herself "one of that numerous gang of upper class, leisured-class spinsters, unemployed, unpropertied, unendowed, uneducated . . . economically dependent entirely upon others. . . . A maiming subserviency is so conditional to their very existence that it becomes an aim in itself, an ideal."[6]

The expected pattern and its religious sanctions were set out in a book called *Anna: or, Passages in the Life of a Daughter at Home* (by Sara Stephen), which followed the life from twenty to eighty of an unmarried woman who had to learn not only to be orderly and loving but not to rebel against her narrow sweep. Her little difficulties of adjustment were helped into resignation by a Christian cousin.

Even so late as the eighties the expectation had not completely changed, for Beatrice Webb explained how she had to fight against the assumption that an unmarried daughter would be endlessly at the service of her family until the moment of taking a husband would miraculously free her.[7]

The condition of those who had neither inheritance nor families to support them was often desperate. With luck some might become governesses or companions, but age would overtake even these, and charity never reached them all. Augustus Hare tried to help the few his means could encompass by setting up a little guest house where "impoverished gentlewomen" could live for a month at a time with their groceries delivered and their transportation paid.[8] The Governesses Benevolent Association tried a more systematic approach and was simply overwhelmed by cases of tragedy that it could not begin to meet.

Although there was an actual shortage of potential husbands, so that in the game of musical chairs some women were bound to be left out, in each individual case it presented itself to the girl as if it must be her fault—that she had been too shy, too forward, too unlucky, or too inept to achieve the chief thing she had been brought up to look forward to.* Only those who tried to help such poor ladies knew the miseries they endured, declared Mrs. Sidgwick.[9] Sometimes it seems from the literature that half the women of England were hiding broken hearts.

The training they received, of course, was never, never, never to show any interest in a man until he had given unmistakable signs first. If the man they loved went away without speaking, they might well spend a lifetime brooding about what might have happened, smiling at grief like patience on a monument. In view of this it is ironic to read in thoughtless modern articles that men were the ones who had to repress their emotions and could not cry when they were hurt, with the implication that women through centuries have had free access to tears. This is simply not true. Men were the ones who had the right to speak out if they loved (providing they fell in love with a suitable woman). Women's mouths were locked.†

Any misstep would be irrevocable. Mrs. Trollope, hearing from Frenchwomen that they simply could not believe that English old maids had never committed any sexual fault, acidly commented, "It is as well known as that a Jew is not qualified to sit in Parliament, that a single lady suspected of indiscretion immediately dies a civil death."[10] Eventually both these taboos would be lifted, but while they lasted they were ironclad. Mary Clarke, a lively English girl living in Paris in the 1820s, was expecting to marry a Frenchman, M Fauriel; but when he suggested accompanying her and her mother to Italy before the ceremony, she explained that no Frenchman could imagine the effect on her English family: such a move would ruin her sister's and her niece's chances to marry even though everybody knew nothing untoward had really happened.[11]

Dr. Robert Carter studied hysteria and in 1853 wrote a book in which he blamed the prevalence of this disease among women on their having to conceal and restrain all sexual passion, which he called "a modern necessity."[12] (He treated the disorder by removing the patient from her family and by talking with her extensively.)

When medical training for women was being discussed, Sir Almroth Wright wrote to the *Times* that doctors were appalled at the terrible physical havoc that a disappointment in love could wreak on a girl. He thought this a reason for disqualifying women from becoming doctors, even though Barbara Bodichon had pointed out that the reason it was so much harder for a girl to get over a broken love affair was that

---

*Writing at the age of twenty in her self-reproachful diary, Anne Jemima Clough accuses herself of laziness, boastfulness, and "wildness" that *must* be controlled. Her "idle, foolish thoughts about marriage" were dashed since nobody danced with her twice at balls.

†" 'But if I feel, may I *never* express?'

'*Never!*' declared Reason." —indicating the terrible revenge for those who break bonds. In 1903, in one of the first scientific efforts to link mental traits and sex, Helen B. Thompson concluded that women had a far greater tendency to inhibit expression of emotion (Viola Klein, 99).

she did not have *work*, which was so healing in the case of men.[13] Fairly happily married herself, she devoted her life and fortune to finding and opening opportunities for other women.

In fortunate cases disappointment in love might strengthen the character. Women could find that "the heart, though broken, can endure," and develop what their age would have meant by "maturity."

In the twentieth century maturity is presented as the ability to release emotion, as self-development and self-assertion, even as the capacity to inflict pain on another. It requires a certain stretch of the imagination to think back to a time when maturity was defined as endurance, renunciation, and the capacity not to inflict pain on others, but to absorb it.

In this process the renunciation itself often became eroticized, a feeling that found expression in nearly all the women poets of the period, who seemed to have a near-fatal tendency to fall in love with men they could not marry—all except Elizabeth Barrett, that is—the Brontës, Christina Rossetti, Alice Maynell, just like Emily Dickinson in America.* While male poets wrote of dead or faithless loves, women sang of the men they loved, who loved them, and whom they could not have.

Christina Rossetti's biographer notes a certain broken betrothal motif in her writing even before her experience could justify it, but she did later fall in love with a married man, thus fulfilling her poetic destiny; in true form she spent her time trying not to show how much she was hurt both by the impossibility of marrying him and later by his unfaithfulness with another woman.[14]

Concern about unmarried women went back at least to Malthus, who was anxious that women be treated justly and who hoped that his efforts to lower the marriage rates would, among other things, have the effect of raising the social prestige of women who never married.[15] Ann Taylor, setting a pattern of child-rearing advice early in the century, told mothers firmly that they must prepare daughters for both wedlock and celibacy and that no girl should be made to feel that marriage was essential.[16] But sporadic expressions of such opinions did not change very much the social perception of woman's vocation as that of wife and mother until about the time of Harriet Martineau's already mentioned article of 1859. Then suddenly the problem was discussed everywhere.

Even nature was occasionally called in to justify the existence of successful single women, as when William Greg (in one of his "social judgments") admitted that there were some natural celibates—perhaps 3 or 4 percent of the female population, he estimated—"to whom Nature never speaks at all, or at least speaks not in her tenderest tones," who were nevertheless diffusively charitable and a few of whom were brilliant

---

*Hope "might blaspheme the place ordained to suffering." And "It might be easier to fail— . . . than to perish of Delight" (Emily Dickinson).

enough to reach "almost" the same heights as a man.[17] Such women were the objects of admiration, but not of tenderness, to men.

Drawn from such celibates and from the women who overcame their disappointments, there arose a whole class of busy, active, and cheerful old maids. Prince Pückler regarded them as a by-product of the national insistence on love or nothing and the failure of confidence that affection might grow after marriage;[18] Mrs. Trollope defended them ringingly, explaining how high-minded they could be and that their freedom from domestic cares gave them unusual power to manage their own time and resources.[19] Taine was astonished at the dangerous journeys they often undertook alone, saying that he could enumerate fifty examples of women who took off for places like Khartoum, or tropical America, or conducted parties of emigrants to central Australia.*[20]

Many of the best-known unmarried women had been engaged, or had had the chance to become engaged, and had resisted the temptation to be crushed by their failure to marry. Hannah More, for one, was left at the altar by her bridegroom. The man later, anonymously, settled an annuity on her, sufficient to keep her free for the rest of her life for the sort of literary and philanthropic work she wanted to do.[21]

Harriet Martineau's is a more famous case. Her fiancé died of a fever in 1826, and she retreated like a well brought up young woman into the bosom of her family. What eventually freed her was a financial crash that forced her to make her own way in London. She found the experience so bracing that thirty years afterward she wrote how glad she was that she had never married. (She was thirty when she moved to London, and felt that she was too old, as well as too busy, for further romance.)[22] Describing herself as the happiest single woman in England, she also wrote of the satisfactions unmarried women could have: "There are substantial, heartfelt interests for women of all ages, and under ordinary circumstances, quite apart from love. . . . " At the age of fifty-two, though, she requested that people address her as "Mrs."†[23]

She took political economy as her subject, did a great deal to popularize the theories of the classical economists, including Malthus, and—for delving delicately into his theories of population control—underwent considerable persecution.‡ She was also the one, in her famous *Edinburgh Review* article,[24] to call attention to the fact that with the rise of the middle classes, women were going to have to work outside

---

*Anyone who wants to pursue this matter should read *Victorian Lady Travellers* by Dorothy Middleton.

†In 1871 and again in 1879, the German women's movement's paper, the *Frauen-Anwalt*, urged its older unmarried readers to take the married title "*Frau*." It explained that a man would not be called "*Herrlein*" just because he was unmarried. But the protest had no effect at the time (Twellmann, 128).

‡In *Bluestocking Revels*, in which Leigh Hunt arranges to have the god Apollo meet the writing women of the day (1837), the encounter with Harriet Martineau refers both to

their homes, just like men. In former days women worked just as hard as men to keep the entire household going, but no one was individually responsible for his own maintenance. The rise of industry forced men to go outside their homes to work, and women were beginning to understand that they would have to follow. Her article was succeeded, in the *North British Review* for 1862, by Dora Greenwell's "Our Single Women." No woman was single from choice, she asserted firmly, but because there were so many of them, they had become "an unclaimed dividend" that society ought to utilize instead of letting it remain idle.

The clearest expression of a woman's determination to choose a career, and of the contradictions that at that time interfered with a married woman's having one, was Florence Nightingale's well-known analysis of the choice between a man and her vocation:

> I have an intellectual nature which requires satisfaction, and that would find it in him. I have a passional nature which requires satisfaction, and that would find it in him. I have a moral, an active nature which requires satisfaction, and that would not find it in his life. . . . To be nailed to a continuation and exaggeration of my present life . . . to put it out of my power ever to be able to seize the chance of forming for myself a true and rich life would seem to me like suicide.[25]

And that she would not, finally, do. This refusal of marriage bewildered Florence's mother. But Florence believed that God had marked out some women to be single as clearly as he had picked others to be wives. For these women, marriage would mean sacrifice of their higher capacities "to the satisfaction of their lower."[26] She had an ideal of marriage where two strong personalities could unite in some purpose for mankind, but since the men who would share this ideal were scarce, she decided that her strong will should control her strong passions, and so she could serve God and man by herself.

Another kind of spinster was Frances Power Cobbe, who declared herself never to have been in love at all. When her father died, he left her £200 a year, with the comfortable expectation that she would live with her brother and use her legacy as pin money. She decided, however, to live alone, and the sum was barely enough, so she supplemented it by writing. Looking back in old age, she wrote of how happy she had been in a life in which exercise, rest, food, work, play, and sleep had all been delightful.[27] She was able to travel unimpeded, pay country visits, and go to Europe

---

the stories she wrote to popularize political economy and to her Malthusian passion for population control:

> Ah! welcome home, Martineau, turning statistics
> To stories, and puzzling your phylogamistics!
> I own I can't see, any more than dame Nature,
> Why love should await dear good Harriet's dictature!
> But great is earth's want of some love-legislature.
> [Leigh Hunt, 183]

when she wished, and finally she was able to build for herself a little house
that she could share with her close women friends—something bachelors
could never do half so well.[28]

⤳ No matter how happy the English old maids may have seemed to
themselves, their number quite regularly horrified the French. Although
their boast (to Mrs. Trollope)—"we pride ourselves on making the
destiny of our women the happiest in the world. We *have* no old
maids"[29]—was not quite accurate, as we shall see,* these women do seem
to have been less conspicuous in France. Of course, a considerable
number of them were concealed behind convent walls, where they did not
count, socially, as "old maids." Mrs. Trollope believed, furthermore,
that a certain number of the secular ones called themselves "widows,"
and that this sort of deception could remain a family secret even from the
nieces and nephews.†

The question that became pressing as the century advanced was,
what were they to do? Dumas described a whole new class of women who
were too well educated to do manual work, too proud for domestic work
or for prostitution, too timid to revolt or seek adventures, and too much
women to enter a convent. Dumas believed that they often simply abandoned hope.[30]

Well beyond the age when her married sister might be enjoying
complete social freedom, the unmarried one would still be bound by the
ridiculous conventions of youth. Her reading would be censored, she
could not dine in a restaurant, and it was not the habit of French parents
to pay an allowance such as English girls customarily received.[31] Miss
Betham told of the astonishment of a French lady at seeing an English girl
of twenty-five cash a check, something never heard of in France.[32] When a
jeune fille finally had enough of this and was willing to turn herself into a
vielle fille, Hamerton said, it could be done by simply walking out one day
without a maid. Tongues would wag at first, but after that the way was
clear.[33]

*In fact, the percentages of women in the whole population remaining unmarried by
age fifty in France were almost the same as for England; between 1850 and 1900, the
percentage hovered between 12 and 13 percent (Etienne van de Walle, "Marriage and
Marital Fertility," *Daedalus* 97 (1968): 472). Part of the illusion that England had the most
old maids came from the later age of marriage. While France had only 58 percent of its
women unmarried at ages twenty through twenty-four, and 30 percent between twenty-five
and twenty-nine, the corresponding figures for England were 73 percent and 42 percent.
The figures for Germany were 71 percent and 34 percent; for Italy, 60 percent and 30
percent, respectively (Hajnal).

†According to Lily Braun's study of 1891, 62.0 percent of Frenchwomen over fifteen
were married, while in England the proportion was only 42.0 percent—a difference that
could partly but not completely be accounted for by the later age of marriage in England.
When she counted women over forty, Lily Braun found 12.7 percent unmarried in France,
14.0 percent in Britain (Braun, *Frauenfrage*, 162). Lily Braun's figures, however, do not
agree with the findings of modern demographers. See the Appendix.

In view of the denial of their existence, it is surprising how many French men and women of distinction had maiden aunts living somewhere in the country; and what beneficent members of the family they often turned out to be. Apparently many provincial families sent their sons to Paris, leaving the daughters at home. Taine, for instance, explained that his father's sisters, elderly maiden ladies, had developed a taste for abstract ideas and were excellent conversationalists, despite their ostensibly restricted lives.[34] As for Juliette Adam, her three aunts in the country, to whom she was happy to be sent from time to time, seemed to her like heroines; they saved the little girl from too much city refinement and an overdose of propriety, since they were natural, healthy, and yet thoroughly literate.[35] Abbé Dimnet also was sent to live with three aunts when he was six. The eldest one had the business head and managed life for the others, while their mother commented firmly, "*Nous ne nous marions pas.*"[36]

Sometimes it was a sister rather than an aunt who played an important role. Eugénie de Guérin lived, breathed, and had her being in her brother, Maurice, who had been entrusted to her care by a dying mother when she was only eleven.[37] Maurice was a poet, and it was for his eyes that she wrote her famous *Journal* of meditative religiosity. She explained (in 1837) that she was left alone in the country while he was off, first at school, then making his career in Paris. Her life at home was one of depression, and she sometimes despaired of doing good to a single soul; she did not even dare to read that new novel, *Notre Dame de Paris*, because certain blots on its pages shocked her woman's eye. When her brother died, in 1839, she was still more in despair. "Maurice and I were internally linked by rose-colored ribbons."[38]

A more useful and practical sister was Ernest Renan's Henriette. When she died in 1862, he wrote her memoir as a sacred duty to one who had had no pleasures in life save the practice of virtue and the heart's affections. A very bright girl, educated in a Breton village by a remarkable teacher, she early attached herself to the little brother who was twelve years younger. When she found that the family needed her earnings she began to teach, and she kept at it after declining a proposal of marriage that, though it was a good one, would have separated her from her family; but she separated herself from them voluntarily when they needed still more money, going to Paris to teach in a school where she received niggardly treatment and had to work sixteen hours a day. In spite of this she managed to pass the public teachers' examinations, and when her brother was fifteen she brought him to Paris to join her. He was being educated as a priest, and received so many scholastic honors that the renowned Monsignor Dupanloup, Bishop of Orléans, gave him a scholarship. This took care of Ernest for a while, and Henriette turned her attention to paying off her deceased father's debts. This she accomplished by going as a governess to Poland for ten years, whence she kept in touch with her brother by letter. Her mind was flexible enough that when she noticed he was losing his faith, she encouraged him to give up the priesthood and enter the Ecole Normale. Her letters advised him on what kind of secular dress to adopt, sending him money to help and locating a boarding house with the help of one of her friends.[39]

Greatly aged by hard work and still more by her indifference to hair style and dress, Henriette came back to Paris in 1850 and rented a small apartment with Ernest, whom she supported by editorial work while he tried to decide what to do with himself. And then, as he put it, "My inexperience of life, and my ignorance, especially, of the profound difference between the male and female heart, led me to ask a sacrifice of her, which would have been beyond the powers of any other woman."[40] Ernest had finally decided to marry! When her response was that in that case she would leave, his heart stood still; and, in fact, he did not carry out his plan to marry until Henriette had relented and agreed to live with the couple, even though her "sacrifices" threw a kind of shadow around the household. He had to admit that she was jealous; only the appearance of a baby reconciled her a little bit—that, and the invitation to accompany her brother on a scientific expedition to the Near East in 1860. He had been sent out by the Emperor and needed her company, he explained, to manage the expenses as well as to give him the personal care and the collaboration in his work that he was used to. Here she began helping him on his most famous work, the heretical *Life of Jesus*. At the same time she begged her brother to take her savings and make a family tomb, so they could all remain together in death. She could never, in her brother's opinion, "have developed a higher degree of perfection than that she had attained" when death took her in 1862.[41]

All this strikes a twentieth-century intelligence as morbid, unhealthy, and rather unattractive, but it is important to keep in mind that in its own day it seemed an example of pure and lovely devotion. Eugénie de Guérin's *Journal* became an inspiration and consolation to thousands of women, while Renan was sure that his tribute to his sister would find nationwide sympathy.

For Catholic women, religious life always offered dignity, and for ambitious ones the possibility of work and accomplishment. Here too the new equal inheritance laws of France made a difference. Under the *ancien régime* a father could put his daughters into a convent in order to make his sons rich, but after the new laws were passed, even nuns received their share of the family fortune.[42] This made them less of a drag on the budget at home and at the same time more desirable acquisitions for the religious orders. On the whole, however, it seemed that most of the girls entering religious life in the latter part of the nineteenth century were of peasant families, and this was especially true after Michelet had spread his strong disapprobation among the literate classes. He wrote a lurid chapter on the evils of a cloistered life, where women turned into pale flowers that would never bloom, prey to jealousy and to passions substituting for the motherhood that would never be theirs but that could never be quite thwarted. He described whippings that, he alleged, went on unregulated in convents long after they had been abolished in French prisons and in the armed services.[43]

To Michelet the power of religious life was a threat to civil society. To many French Catholics, on the contrary, it presented an entirely viable alternative style of life, and the ideal of consecrated virginity was present in their minds in a way that English people found hard to understand.[44] Convents were for a long time the only place where women of ability could be trained for professions of healing or teaching, where they could rise to executive positions and even get the Cross of Honor, which was denied to the most distinguished laywomen.[45] Nuns had, after all, been doing for centuries what Florence Nightingale almost broke her heart trying to be permitted to do; and when she went to study nursing, she found the only training institutions were a Protestant sisterhood in Germany and a French congregation in Paris. She might have made the French order as famous as Kaiserswerth had she not fallen ill herself almost as soon as she got there.

Before the French Revolution the military and naval hospitals had been under the management of the Sisters of Charity, and although the Revolution, with its passion for secularization, closed the orders, the sisters were recalled under the Consulate, and they served all during the Napoleonic Wars.[46] One French nun received battlefield awards from Austria, Russia, and Prussia and was permitted to wear the decorations on her habit. The French government gave her the unusual privilege of pardoning each year two soldiers condemned to death.

The Ursulines had made the decision to educate girls in the seventeenth century and had maintained a long tradition of picking their teachers by ability, not birth.[47] They educated wealthy girls, it is true, but also took care of numberless poor children and had set up "ragged schools" well before the English thought of such a thing. Thus they continued to prove, in an age that often denied it, that women could teach and that women could learn.[48] Miss Betham claimed that in 1900 there were 64,000 French women teachers inside the cloister, compared with 43,000 lay ones.[49]

As secular, middle-class jobs for women increased during the last third of the century, the tally of girls who chose not to marry and not to enter convents also increased. But for a long time their lives were not easy. About 1910 Brieux wrote one of his social comedies, *La Femme seule*, concerning the plight of an affluent bourgeois orphan who loses her fortune and her *dot*. Her guardians retreat to a country house, but she is determined to stay on in Paris and earn her own living. The drama displays the obstacles she meets—from people who will not hire her to men who want her to sleep with them as a condition of giving her work; from landladies who will not rent to single girls to the desperately low pay. When she finally gets a good job as a bookbinder, she organizes a union among the women in the shop, only to have the male workers go on strike and physically attack the women for fear of competition in the workplace.

ᑫᑐ In Germany, no less an oracle than Fichte had declared that marriage was a duty and that an unmarried person was only half a person.[50] Dr. Riehl, the universal mentor of the "true" Germanic family, naturally believed that everyone should be absorbed into a family circle; there ought to be no leftovers in society. His corollary was that an unmarried woman would do better as an aunt than as a club president.[51]

Something of what they meant, in human terms, can be deduced from Fanny Lewald's story of growing up in a family with five sisters who suffered sorely from the realization that there would not be dowry money for them, and that family pride would not permit them to go out and earn money of their own.[52] Their father grew gray trying to support them all, Fanny said, but he would have felt utterly dishonored if he could not do it; and meanwhile the two brothers who would inherit the job of looking out for the girls felt as if they were carrying the Alps on their shoulders, and this inhibited the girls' ability to express affection for them.[53] Later on, when she was famous enough to have published her memoirs, she said that she got a hundred grateful letters in response, mostly from unhappy old maids who had felt superfluous and unfulfilled all their lives, but also from young girls who dreamed of choosing their own way.*[54]

Yet in Germany as elsewhere economic and social pressures on middle-class girls kept rising. According to a very recent careful study of the German women's movement, in 1864 there were over two and a half million unmarried or widowed women over sixteen.[55] According to Lily Braun, an earlier student of the same subject, Berlin had 1,167 marriageable women for every 1,000 single men (compared to a French ratio of 1,069). Bebel claimed from his socialist angle that 20 to 30 percent of upper-class women remained unwed, often because they refused to marry a man beneath their station in life even though there were superfluous sons among the proletariat.[56] Another socialist of the pre-war time blamed the unwillingness of German men to marry. There were six million bachelors in Germany to eight million unmarried women.[57] Of course, many of these would marry later. These figures disagree markedly with other studies, including the ones used in the Appendix to this volume by Steve Hochstadt, who quotes a figure of less than 10 percent overall never marrying. But they represent common perceptions of the period and explain the strong feeling that something would have to be done about middle-class girls.[58]

The strength of the traditional solution, in the footsteps of Fichte and Riehl, was voiced in a learned journal by Dr. Eduard von Hartmann

*". . . *auf ihre Façon selig werden.*"

in 1896. His cure? Get everyone married. Make marriage a civic duty. Tax bachelors so heavily that each will be in effect supporting one woman, and so he will prefer to choose one of his own.[59] To handle the sex ratio problem, Hartmann showed true Germanic faith in governmental regulations: he would simply arrange that males not be allowed to emigrate. It was widely supposed that the reason for the extra number of women was that the men took off overseas.

While waiting for Hartmann's total solution, there were luckily other ways of taking up the slack. For some, there was an institution called the *Stift*, a house of refuge where unmarried and widowed Protestant women could live in comfort and dignity.

Places in the *Stiften* were endowed, sometimes for charity, sometimes by a woman's family. Vows of celibacy were not required, although if a woman from one of them married, she lost her place. Many of them dated from the Middle Ages and had become extremely wealthy. Otto von Corvin, when a young man, visited his cousin at one and found her with a house, garden, and servant to herself, a cow with cowfeed provided, and an annuity. Male cousins were welcome guests, and young Otto stayed there without raising any eyebrows.[60] Her standing in society was high, comparable to that of a married lady of high official position. Though she could leave for extended visits each year, while she was in residence she was expected to wear a special religious garb and to attend certain church offices. A parent could buy a girl a place in a *Stift*, so that at fifty she might have a retreat; or the *Stift* itself might pension an old teacher, or even a cook.[61]

Anne Fremantle's German governess retired to one of these houses, where the family went to see her and found her in her own sitting room, in quarters much superior to anything available to English governesses.[62] Several of the women described in later chapters of this book were offered such residences and rejected them. Malwida von Meysenbug, for one, had to decide between accepting the place that her family had secured with considerable political pull and taking the chance of making her own way as an independent teacher, a risk she decided to take. When Lily Braun's family fell on hard times, someone got the Queen to guarantee Lily a place in a *Stift*, and for a while it seemed to Lily that she would be helping her family if she accepted, though it would be a personal sacrifice. In her case, it was her father who rejected the plan and said that he wanted to keep his daughter with him.*[63]

Of course, there were a few women with money and social prestige who could live enjoyable independent lives of parties and travel. Marie von Bunsen was one of these.[64] She wrote a popular book entitled *Through Germany on a Rowboat* describing some of her adventures. She and her sisters made their debuts, danced, had love affairs, and she

---

*Something similar was available in France. Miss Betham describes a *Maison de Retraite* in Rheims where the ladies got room, board, service, laundry, and a small garden, all for between £16 and £24 a year (Betham-Edwards, 103).

speculated at one point on why neither she nor any of her sisters married. She explained that there were so many of them that each would receive only a small portion; and because they had been brought up in England (she was the daughter of the Prussian ambassador to London), the girls had grown up expecting to marry for love, not for good connections. (In 1930, at the end of her life, she reflected on how many love matches she had observed that turned out wretchedly, while there were many happy marriages of convenience.)[65]

If money was the key to a good life, work was for most women the key to money, which is why there was such an enormous demand on the part of the women's movement for jobs and education. Let us look at the fate of many ordinary girls who could not overcome their families' or their own hostility to remunerative jobs. A novel by Gabriele Reuter, *Aus guter Familie* (*From a Good Family*), tells of a young woman named Agathe whom we see first at her confirmation party, about 1867. The only interesting gift she receives—a copy of Herwegh's revolutionary verse, sent by a boy cousin—is instantly confiscated. A little later she is rudely pulled from her daydreams by the discovery that her brother, though engaged, has seduced a housemaid. Later, when the maid has his baby, Agathe tries to relieve her distress, but the money is stolen, and Agathe begins to ruminate about why it is so fatal to do before marriage what becomes all right afterward.

Her disillusionment is carried further by a month's visit to some artistic cousins. At first they seem to give her a new vision of life, but it turns sour when she finds that the husband has an illegitimate child by an actress. This experience, plus a visit to a former music teacher who makes pitiful efforts to create some social life with other governesses, leads Agathe to feel that she had best settle for any marriage bargain she can get, so she responds warmly to the embraces of a middle-aged suitor. Alas, her father decides that he is not rich enough. How hard it is that she cannot take part in the discussion between the two men by which her fate is settled. Excited by the kisses she has received, she decides that she will in future take absolutely anyone that comes along.

At this time her family fortunes fall off, and like many girls she has no skills for self-support. Her last effort at freedom fails when, on a trip to Switzerland in her late thirties, she runs across the cousin who had sent the Herwegh book so long ago. He is by now a professor at Zurich, and begs her with all his powers of persuasion to come there, where he promises to find her interesting work and independence. By now, however, her spirit is broken; and it is the last straw when her cousin begins making eyes at a waitress. All the men who might have helped her— father, brother, suitor, cousin—turn out to have feet of clay. Sent to the baths, she tries to kill her sister-in-law, and so before she is forty she is institutionalized. Gabriele Reuter was saying that every time in her life Agathe had a chance to express her real feelings, or to make a move toward liberation, she was prevented by well-meaning people. She was therefore driven into a life of fantasy, which the Germans always considered a particular danger. The fantasies, in turn, filled her up with so many false ideas that she was unable to profit from her opportunities.*

∞ Nearly all the unmarried women of Italy went into convents, at least until the formation of the Kingdom of Italy in 1866, when new opportunities arose in secular professions, particularly schoolteaching. Mrs. Gretton says she only met one old maid in all her protracted sojourn in the country before 1863,[66] while Lady Morgan had earlier declared that those not in convents had been banished to the attic.[67]

It should be noted here that during the Risorgimento period numerous orders of sisters had to be created to cope with the increased demands for care of the sick and the education of the young.[68] Many capable women chose this avenue for serving their country. Franciscan sisters set up a hospital in Florence, and in 1857 they were allowed for the first time to take charge of the men's ward.[69] On the battlefields of several wars, Count Arrivabene saw Sisters of Charity tending the wounded of both sides and uttering prayers for the dying enemy and the Italians alike.

On the other hand, religious life had been used as a means of getting rid of one's unmarriageable daughters (unmarriageable perhaps for lack of a good monetary settlement), or for living a fairly luxurious and dignified life without working, or again as an outlet for a few women who felt strongly motivated toward nursing or teaching or administration and could find no way to exercise their talents in secular society. Count Arrivabene explained that every noble family in Sicily had at least one daughter in a convent,[70] that the rank of abbess was almost hereditary in certain families, and that many of the nuns were young, pretty, and very sociable. When he called upon his aunt, who was one of the Noble Virgins of Jesus at Castiglione, he found that she could receive visits and entertain her friends and that her habit of fine black wool was most becoming, being fitted at the bust and caught with a silver belt, and topped by a starched white headdress.†[71]

Pressure to enter a convent could be quite severe and was backed up on occasion by the police power of the state. The idea was often implanted in girls' minds during the week's retreat that was commonly offered before their first communion, when the nuns would use the period of separation from their families to proselytize.[72]

---

*A comparable English novel is George Gissing's *The Odd Women* (1894), which tells of three sisters who were raised by a father who did not want his women to learn about money but who left them destitute. One became a miserable governess, one an alcoholic, and one married for security. They are played up against a group of energetic women who are hunting new occupations, but the three sisters are psychologically incapable of benefiting from their help.

†In 1864 the Italian Parliament found that there were about twenty-five thousand nuns in the country, about two-thirds of whom were professed sisters. The rest were lay sisters recruited from the peasant class, who did the menial work and who wore coarse black gowns and aprons (Mozzoni, *Passo*, 20).

The ceremony of taking the veil became something of a tourist attraction, spectacular and invariably shocking to English and American eyes. Thus Charles Eliot Norton, in 1856, attended a service where the girl, led to the altar in a ball gown ornamented with diamonds, and followed by a matron of honor in full dress and two flower girls with wings of painted feathers, was disrobed behind a grating and had her hair cut—all with what Norton felt was a striking lack of sincerity in both the girl herself and the cardinal who was officiating.[73] Charles Greville noted in his memoirs that the ceremony he watched in Naples in 1830 was neither imposing nor interesting nor even affecting, with the guests dressed as if for a ball and an air of general heartlessness toward the fate of the postulant.[74]

Once inside the convent walls, it was almost impossible to get out, though it could occasionally be done, as it was by Angelica Catalani, who became a famous singer.[75] She was forced into a convent about 1800 by a father overburdened with children. When the beauty of her voice began to attract attention and opened the possibility of a secular career, her father hesitated a long time before letting her study under lay teachers, but she did emerge, and enjoyed a long success.

The outstanding example of unwilling cloisterization and an ultimately successful struggle for liberty was that of Enrichetta Caracciolo, who was born to a noble family in Naples in 1821.[76] Her father was the military governor of a province. In her engagingly frank autobiography, she describes the early signs of her interest in the opposite sex. At fifteen she ogled from her balcony the boy across the street. Her account describes the development of her body, the precocious advancement of her heart, and her troubled sleep. Her capriciously severe mother began to ration her hours for balcony watching, but in the time still allowed Enrichetta managed to attract the attention of several young men, one of whom sent his grandfather to propose marriage. The Caracciolos rejected the offer, on financial grounds, without letting their daughter know. At a masked ball she managed to kiss another candidate, but his father cut off his allowance in retaliation, since he had other plans for his son. Then her father died, leaving the family so poor that the mother could think of nothing to do with Enrichetta but leave her in a convent where two eighty-year-old aunts were abbesses, presumably victims of a similar fate. Enrichetta, who had received promises of eternal devotion from her current love, a certain Domenico, broke into tears at the news and begged on her knees not to be sent away, but her mother assured her that it would only be for a short time, until the mother's pension came through. And she reminded the young girl that the old aunts were rich.

Rich they may have been, and of high birth, but Enrichetta soon discovered that most of the nuns were low in intellect and morals. Cloistered by the selfishness of their parents, they found nothing inside the walls either to enlarge their small stock of ideas or to give them experiences of the heart. In her own case, the "short time" lengthened into twenty years. Her subsequent exposé was translated into many languages and angered most of Europe. Better than anyone else of her day, she described the allurements and the intimidations applied to hapless novices and the deliberate instillation of jealousy and rivalry, which drove some young nuns to suicide. In her own case, her fiancé (if so he may be called), Domenico, became discouraged and married someone else.

The feature that made female monasticism worse than the male variety, in her opinion, was confession. Since only secular priests (who did not understand cloistered life) were allowed as confessors, and since mortal sins could hardly be committed in the convent, nuns spent hours confessing their venial ones as the only channel through which to vent their feelings.[77]

At one point Enrichetta escaped and stayed for a while with her married sister, but her mother enlisted the police to escort her back to her cell. The old aunts used this moment of discouragement to talk her into taking her first vows, and, in the usual bridal regalia, she did so. While her hair was being cut, she heard through the screen an English tourist remonstrating, but, of course, it did no good.

The year of novitiate was hypocritical, she said, because at the end they did not ask you the *real* questions that would have gotten honest answers—such as, would you go out and marry your lover if you were given the chance? If she had insisted on making such a statement anyway, she felt that she would have been turned out into the street in disgrace, something no young girl could easily face.[78]

Being bright and energetic, she chose as her field of work the infirmary, repressing a passion for the doctor who made the rounds. Soon she determined to get out if she possibly could and won the belated support of her family, who now tried to use their political leverage in her favor. But by this time both church and state were allied against her for fear of the unfavorable publicity her release would create. For a period, however, with some relaxation of rules, she was permitted to go out to the Conservatory to study music and to bring a piano into her cell. She also used some of her new-found freedom to work in the foundling hospital, and she began to read about the political struggle of her country at a time when patriotic emotions were engaging the loyalty of a great many women. It seemed as if the 1848 rebellions would give her a chance to break away entirely, and she even started to distribute patriotic literature in secular dress. But again the police caught up with her and reincarcerated her, this time in solitary confinement in a religious prison, where she fell ill. The only way to communicate with her family was to conceal notes in the laundry parcels she sent out. Though her mother sought an interview with Pope Pius IX and won the support of a cardinal, this very success had the effect of mobilizing the local bishop and his faction against her, and she was kept in prison for three years and four months. Finally, in 1854, she did win release, and quickly joined a secret political society. She found a good job teaching in a girls' school, and at the age of thirty-nine, in 1860, she finally took off her veil and married an English-man in an Anglican service. Her story ends this way:

> I am at last happy. By the side of a husband who adores me, and to whom I respond with equal love, I am where the Almighty had placed the woman at the close of Creation's first week. Why may not I, in fulfilling the duties of a good wife, a good mother, a good citizen—why may not even I aspire to the treasures of the Divine mercy?[79]

∽ Out of the seemingly desperate problem presented by the unmar-ried and ill-supported women came a new type of woman, individualistic, self-reliant, eager at once for independence and for the chance to use her powers. A married woman, after all, could find some kind of fulfillment in the old ways, but these became increasingly constraining for the unmarried. In England and in Germany, the new women became the most clamorous; this was probably because marriage was more fulfilling in the Latin countries and because of the recourse to the cloister there.

The new women found the solution to most of their difficulties (but not, of course, their lack of sexual fulfillment) through satisfying work. Freud was the first person to explain the effects of sexual repression, but by no means the first person to have noticed it. The damage to some women's personalities was constantly being thrown up in their faces as a matter of pity or reproach. On the other hand, many of the women mentioned here and later in this book seem to have had such exception-ally satisfying lives as to support the theory that if sex drives are not aroused in women by some sort of "education," they may not emerge spontaneously.

While the role of old maid was a fairly standardized one, recogniz-able in every country, much less attention has been paid to that of bachelor. Extra women were supposed to attach themselves to their own families (unless they were cloistered), but extra men often found well-prepared niches inside other people's households. Their privileges there-in and their restrictions varied from place to place, and certainly no figures are available on their number. Yet thousands of households across Europe must have included this seldom-considered supernumerary figure.

Marie von Bunsen tells about the northern European custom of the "house-friend," a man who was a friend of the family, who spent great amounts of time in their home, and who had a privileged position as friend of both husband and wife. Ibsen shows such characters in several of his plays. The taboo against sexual involvement was so strong that one pair Marie von Bunsen knew of, who married each other when the wife had become a widow, kept the marriage a secret even from the woman's children.

In Italy the *cicisbeo* performed much the same role. Though he certainly might be a lover as well as a friend, his duties in smoothing domestic routines were even more important. Nor was sexual involvement the invariable rule. Many reports emphasize that the *cicisbeo* might live with the mistress of the house like a brother with a sister.

In England there was no name that I know of for this character, but there are traces of his existence. The clubs, to be sure, siphoned off a great many young men into luxurious quarters, thus providing an alternative retreat. But perhaps Augustus Hare might be considered a typical ladies' man. A "ladies' man," in the parlance of the day, was not one who attempted to seduce ladies so much as one who lived in their midst performing small services such as handing them to their carriages, and yet was perfectly friendly with the men too. Hare was a much sought after houseguest because of his good manners, because he was always at the beck and call of the ladies, and because he could beguile an entire company night after night with ghost stories. He won a good part of his literary reputation by writing biographies of Englishwomen (for example, *The Story of Two Noble Lives*) in which his extreme sensitivity to their feelings was admired. He had been their confidant, certainly not their lover.

A case that is harder to fit into a pattern was that of T. J. Sanderson, a long-time houseguest of Lord and Lady Amberley. When Bertrand Russell published his parents' papers in 1937, he included an excerpt from his father's journal in which he comments on Sanderson's relation to Lady Amberley:

> Although, of course, he has never said a word that was not proper: his devotion to her is extraordinary & he calls her his wife & says he could not think of marrying anyone else while he has her: this sounds odd & hardly proper, yet his character is such that I feel there is no harm in it.
> All he says is in a pure spirit. Besides he abstains altogether from any sort of unchaste relations with women, leading a life of perfect continence. . . . I allow him & have allowed him ever since his visit in the winter of 1866 to touch and caress Kate & even to kiss her. . . . Now Kate thinks he ought to leave off & has told him so. He has agreed yet cannot resist. I feel so sorry for his lonely & unhappy condition that I do not want to stop it altogether. A kiss is a little thing to give when one has everything that love can grant.[80]

Bertrand's older brother mentioned the situation in his autobiography, telling of his mother's involvement with women's rights meetings and "incidentally also cheering up Sanderson and preventing him from making love to her."*[81]

*In Bertrand Russell's autobiography, which was drafted in 1931 although not published until he was over ninety, he tells a different story: that Lady Amberley allowed another man—the tutor, Spalding—to sleep with her because Spalding had consumption and it was considered unfair to require him to remain celibate, although he was not supposed to marry. In those days tuberculosis was considered to be more of a hereditary than a contagious disease. Bertrand Russell added that there was no evidence that his mother either enjoyed the experience or was expected to. It is hard to see how Bertrand could have known of this situation, since all the principals died when he was a child, but if it is true it is only slightly more peculiar than many Victorian family secrets.

This leaves France as the single country under consideration here without some established role as family friends for unmarried males. The centripetal force of the French nuclear family is well known, and it allowed little room for extraneous personages. Adeline Daumard, in her study of the French bourgeoisie, says that unmarried women lived so much at the margin of society that they scarcely belonged to the bourgeoisie, while Rhoda Métraux, observing French family life right after the First World War, explained that people who failed to fill the role of father/mother or parent/child were seen as "incomplete; they were believed to lack the techniques of social reciprocity."[*82] When French married women took lovers, they were decidedly not friends of the husband, and the affairs had to be carried on in secrecy. Even Michelet's priest was regarded as an intrusion, a disruptive force that could break up the marriage rather than, as was often the case elsewhere, a solidifying element.†

*An interesting new law in France allows all women over twenty-five to be addressed as *"Madame"* (Hartman and Banner, 81).

†One wonders, of course, about Lesbian relationships among unmarried women, but there was little understanding and correspondingly little public interest in the matter. Certain mannish characters were often described with amusement as eccentric. Fanny Kemble so treats of "the dearest friend I have ever known," who lurks in her memoir behind the initials "H. S." This friend was tall, thin, and active, and she always had her boots made at a man's bootmaker to get them thick, heavy, and cumbrous enough to suit her. She wore no ornaments, but had her "scantyskirts" made of the very best materials (Kemble, *Girlhood*, 91–93). In the *fin de siècle* atmosphere, when all brands of eroticism were considered and tried out, interest rose. Colette, in Paris, for example, was under the spell of a certain "Missy" for a while (Yvonne Mitchell, 81). Camille Mauclair commented that upper-class male homosexuals were often charming people, with stable and interesting relationships; among lower-class men such relationships were only brutal and disgusting, but he believed that this class difference was not true among women, and that, indeed, the Lesbian caress was often the only kind touch that a prostitute ever received (Mauclair, 178).

∽PART 2

Breaking the Pattern

Like Galileo, armed with facts, rebelling against dogmas, you will say:

"No, O priest, it is not true that I am made to be a slave. The need for liberty rages within me,—it is not true that I have sinned,—I am innocent and I do not deserve to have my mind and body imprisoned. It is not true, O legislator, that I am a lesser being than you and the persons of your sex. My ability to reason is the same as yours. I see through your complicity with crooks, with politicians, and with egoists. I understand your words that denigrate human beings and idolize money and power. Your judicial learning, which you use to deprive me, is an adulterous mixture of modern justice with powerful dogmas of another era. It is not true, O moralist, that my mission is to work without recourse in physical service to one individual, no; my capacity exceeds this task, I am part of humanity, I am both means and end for myself.

"I feel that my mind generates ideas and my heart follows, reaching out to all humanity with maternal feelings. Injustice revolts me, dogma arouses rebellion in my heart, the wiles by which women are demoralized and trained to accede to this way of life repel me. The shyness that keeps them from speculation, and that leads them to flatter men's wishes, saddens me; the slave in body and soul whose mind has been trained to erase every thought, and whose body is no longer that of a person nauseates me."

Anna Maria Mozzoni, 1885

∽18.

French Law

We have to understand that in the eyes of the old French bourgeois class, the family satisfies simultaneously the highest religious ideal, the deepest sentimental needs, and the most durable social necessity. It is like the primeval cell from which individuals learn about the domestic virtues along with the great human joys, where society bases its discipline and respect for law, and finally which Christianity has clothed with the high dignity of a sacrament.

Louis Delzons, 1913

Before taking up the question of the dissatisfaction that French-women felt with their condition, it might be well to review the law under which they lived. French law was originally based on old Roman law, which made of woman a perpetual minor and at the same time safe-guarded for her certain inheritance rights. In the Revolutionary period, the Declaration of the Rights of Man and subsequent acts based on its philosophy attempted to reform marriage by making it a civil affair, with the right of divorce; it also suppressed some forms of paternal authority, such as singling out a particular child in a will, since all children, girls as well as boys, younger as well as eldest, were now entitled by law to an equal share in inheritance.[1] Family life was supposed to reflect the new principle that governed the relation of the state to its citizens—pure reason—but, of course, the nature of family traditions and habits and the inability of new laws to make a clean sweep meant in actuality that even though a king could be dethroned, a husband's power proved much harder to topple.[2]

When Napoleon codified all French law, he undid some, but not all, of the reforms of previous decades. He believed strongly that if women emerged from dependence, it would bring disorder throughout society, and he devoted much personal attention to this part of the Civil Code; his work was not consistent, leaving girls, for example with equal rights of inheritance, and yet insisting that the wife owed obedience to her husband.[3] It even prescribed that in the civil marriage service, which was a legal requirement, the officiating mayor should be dressed in an impos-ing costume in order to add to the ceremony "a terrible authority." Jenny d'Héricourt referred to the Code as "that inelegant paraphrase of the Apostle Paul."[4]

The Code is still the basic law of France, though it has been modified in many particulars. According to its original provisions, the wife had to accept the domicile of her husband and have no other. The husband had to provide her with the necessities of life according to his station and income, and in various ways protections were built in; indeed, to many people of the period, women's insulation from the coarse affairs of men seemed like one of the protections.[5] Both wife and children were hedged from desertion, neglect, and even financial speculation on the part of the husband, and the husband was not empowered to punish his wife.[6] (In fact, wives occasionally sought beatings from their husbands because visible evidence of injury was required to get the husbands locked up.)[7]

The Code was, as I have said, inconsistent on the subject of women as legal beings. Apart from marriage they were considered almost equal to men in civil (but not, of course, political) rights. An unmarried woman or widow could do many of the things a man could do, and her inferior powers in marriage were justified on the grounds that a family had to have a single legal head, so that a wife on her marriage assumed the nationality as well as the name of her husband, and she was forbidden to earn or save money for herself, buy or sell, plead in court, or perform any civil act without authorization. On the other hand, the individuality of the wife was never so completely suppressed as it was in England, and Barbara Leigh Smith, who made a thorough—and angry—study of the matter, felt that women were far better off under French law. In any case, in practice, the husband's authority steadily dwindled throughout the period, though more from new economic conditions and increasing urbanization than from actual changes in the law.[8]

A Frenchman, though he came of age for most purposes at twenty-one, was not allowed to defy his parents' wishes about his marriage until twenty-five. A young woman could do so at twenty-one, but under the onerous obligation (described in Chapter 3) of making three respectful appeals to her parents. Once contracted, marriage was indissoluble, for Napoleon abolished the freedom of divorce that the Revolution had briefly established. Naturally the subsequent monarchs, good Catholics all, maintained the same rule. The law was finally relaxed in 1884, well into the Third Republic, thanks to the persistent efforts of a member of the Chamber of Deputies named Alfred Naquet.

Born a Jew, Naquet married a lapsed Catholic without the blessing of clergy, but when two of their children died without religious funerals, his wife revolted, carried off her single surviving child, and sought the consolation of the church. Though it was agonizing for him to have his child brought up in what he conceived to be a false religion, he renounced his legal right to keep the boy with him rather than drive his wife to despair, and instead took his quest for justice to the legislative chamber, where he introduced, in 1876, a bill for divorce. It was an uphill fight, against most of the women of the country and the priests who counseled them. Still, his 1879 speech, an hour and a half in length, was, he said, a revelation to the country of the dark side of marriage. As he toured the provinces with his message, men turned out in droves to hear him, even while priests organized demonstrations of women against him. The law as finally passed in 1884 contained some compromises; for instance, it did not include divorce by mutual consent, or even after a three-year separation, but Naquet felt that his mission was nearly fulfilled and that many suffering couples would be grateful to him.[9]

The Napoleonic Code showed its favoritism toward men most strongly in its penalties for adultery, a crime for which a woman could go to prison for from three months to two years, while the husband would be subject only to a fine, even for aggravated adultery (which meant something like bringing his concubine under the same roof with his wife).[10] Thus the husband of Victor Hugo's mistress was able to set police to catch the couple in the act, and then get her hauled off to prison, while Hugo, a peer of France, remained scot-free.[11] This inequality became a public issue when some women on trial for murdering their husbands were acquitted because (as Dumas explains it) the people realized that the real culprit was the man, unreachable by the existing statutes.[12] In 1884 changes in the Code made both parties in adultery equally responsible.

The husband's right over the property his wife brought by dower or inheritance created another masculine domain, that of administrator or guardian, though he was not supposed to sell it without her consent. Over what was acquired during the marriage he had complete rights. The provisions could be altered at the time of the marriage if the wife's parents had arranged a marital contract to such effect, but in the absence of this, the man had the right to include the wife's dower as part of the property used to establish his right to vote or be elected to the Chamber, both of which capacities required, until 1848, ownership of a certain fixed sum. The property of a widow could be credited to some male relative whom she designated, who could derive the same benefit.[13]

Without a marriage contract to protect her, under the so-called communal regime, an unfortunate woman could see her furniture sold out from under her. Even with a contract, if the husband violated it, the wife would have no funds with which to bring suit, and so redress was extremely difficult. A legally separated wife still needed her husband's signature on business papers.

A married woman could not receive a gift without her husband's consent, nor could she give assistance to a friend in need or to an aged parent. She could not enter into any kind of business on her own, though with her husband's permission she could acquire the power to make contracts that was needed for such a venture. Under the Second Empire a celebrated woman writer signed a contract with her publisher, and then decided the next day that she wanted a more favorable one. The editor refused to change the terms, indignantly saying that he would stick by the first agreement, until she pointed out that her signature had no force at law whatsoever.[14] When Colette wrote the best-selling *Claudine à l'ecole* (in 1900), the copyright went to her husband, Willy, who took the advantage that the law gave him.[15] And yet in a book comparing the status of women in various countries, Dora d'Istria noted the astonishing unanimity with which the French declared that it would be simply impossible to change the law so as to allow women to administer their own property.

The laws were designed with a loving couple in mind, which meant that they offered little protection to a woman whose husband gambled, drank, or cheated. Cases of this sort were so visible and clearcut that they proved to be a place where reforms were started. In 1881 married women were authorized to deposit funds in a savings bank, although they could not withdraw them without the husband's consent. Since many of them used their maiden names, and the banks were forbidden to reveal to the husband or anybody else the existence of the accounts, no doubt some women circumvented the legal restraints. It was estimated that eight million Frenchwomen were living on their own earnings in the 1890s, even though their legal right to do so was ambiguous, but already the Office of Public Assistance was defying the Code by giving money directly to nursing mothers instead of their husbands, while some private employers took to paying wages to their female help in person, knowing that the husbands were alcoholic.[16] In 1907 the Code gave Frenchwomen the right to keep their own earnings, and thus legalized what was by that time common practice, at least in affectionate relationships. At the same time functionaries could make it hard to enforce this provision if there was any challenge, forcing the woman to prove that she had such a right, until World War I put so many women on their own that custom as well as law changed. The law about handling money was not made completely equal for both sexes until 1965.

The Code inexplicably left out any provision for a widow's support. She had no right to an inheritance from her husband's estate.[17] Some French commentators believed that this was an oversight in the drafting, and it was consequently laxly enforced; but others thought that it showed how partial the law was to the ongoing family and how little concerned with individuals.[18] (Children, however, were obligated to support their old parents.)

The laws of the end of the century allowing women more direct control of their property were widely interpreted by conservatives as a deliberate interference by the state in family life,[19] and in fact a direct attack on the family itself. Nevertheless, a relatively new form of marital agreement called the "separation of goods" became increasingly popular. This arrangement provided that each partner could control his own property. In 1900 only 9 percent of marriages were formed under this plan, but by 1914 it was 14 percent, and by 1945, 66 percent.[20]

Since most European countries favored male heirs, the act of the French Revolutionary Assembly in equalizing inheritance among all children was truly innovative. At most a fourth of a father's estate (depending in part on how many children there were) could be left at his own discretion as a testator.[21] All agreed, however, that the freedom of disposing of property was limited as much by custom as by law, and the French seemed to regard property as a family trust rather than an individual possession.[22]

Article 372 of the Code stated: "The child remains under the authority of his father and his mother. The father alone exercises this authority." The mother was not completely incapacitated and could exercise some of the father's rights in his absence, but there were curious limitations. Thus a father could ask a court to confine an unruly son in prison for a month, but the mother could only do so (in the father's absence) with the consent of two male relatives.[23]

When a French father died, the court set up a family council to act as a collective guardian. The mother or grandmother, as a direct ancestress, could serve on this council, but no other woman, not even an aunt or elder sister, was given this right, while the father could name by will any man he chose to serve with her.

Legouvé, writing in the middle of the century, told of a mother of nine children in a well-to-do family whose husband forbade her to see them.[24] Hearing that a daughter was ill, she disguised herself as a servant and went to the child's bedside, where from a window she watched her husband walk in the garden with another woman. The wife's family, of high rank and fortune, helped her to appeal to the courts, but the judgment came down that the father's rights were supreme, and the young mother died broken-hearted.

Another example of the man's undivided authority over his children occurred in May of 1879. A father of five daughters placed them all in a convent against the mother's wishes. He wanted them all to take the veil, and the three oldest did so, while the mother was forbidden to see the other two. Appealing to the courts, she received the verdict that the father alone had the right to decide their future, and all she got was permission to talk to them through the convent grille.*[25]

When it came to the question of illegitimate children, the old French law almost completely exonerated the man and then failed to protect the children that the law allowed to be born.[26] According to the Code, girls became "responsible" at age fifteen for sex crimes, although they did not reach majority for property crimes until twenty-one.[27] (Until quite late in the nineteenth century, English girls became "responsible" at twelve.) Thus a man could only be punished for seducing a girl over fifteen if he used violence. He could not, however, solicit her to become a prostitute at that age.[28]

*Only in 1938 was the law changed to abolish the marital supremacy of the man, and even then it still referred to him as "the head of the family." In 1970 the equal responsibility of both parents to take care of and educate the children was provided, and in 1972 equal rights were accorded legitimate and illegitimate children (Venezia).

The father of an illegitimate child could not be prosecuted or held responsible for its support, though under the *ancien régime* he had been so obligated.[29] It was strictly forbidden for a natural child to try to find his father, although he was allowed to search for his mother, so that a woman who had once borne such a child could never feel secure from detection.[30] It was felt that to allow the hunt for the father would encourage debauchery—which only shows that the male lawgivers wanted to attribute all possible debauchery to the women involved.* An unwed father could voluntarily acknowledge his child and offer it support, though we are told that this happened in only one out of fifty cases.[31] But he was not allowed to leave property in his will to natural children, and young men under the legal age of twenty-five could not be made to marry a girl whom they had seduced. (In most countries of Europe at the time—including England, Spain, Austria-Hungary, and parts of Germany—the hunt for the father was permitted, and if found, he could be made to pay support.)

A mid-century case concerned a man who had lived nineteen years with a working woman who had borne him five children. He acknowledged them and sent them to school, where they used his name. He then decided to marry, abandoned his children and their mother, and refused all further support—and the courts backed his right to do so.[32]

Reformers preached that the French laws doubled the illegitimacy rate, encouraged libertinage, punished children, destroyed public health, and made half the population prey to the other half.† The law increased the danger of seduction in France to the point where it was very hard for parents to allow daughters to accept employment, or to go out to study. The only safe thing was to keep them at home.

In 1846 a twenty-four-year-old servant was caught by five young men and held in a room at night while she fought them off. Finally she agreed to accept one of them, provided they put out the light while she undressed. Making the sign of the cross, she jumped through an open window, breaking her thumb and several teeth, and when the men followed her she fell again. Thoroughly bloodied, she took refuge with a concierge. Four of the youths were acquitted, and the only one punished was the owner of the room, who had to serve two months in prison.[33]

As far as the duties of citizenship were concerned, the Code masked in verbiage innumerable prejudices against women. Women could not witness any civil legal document, although they could be witnesses in criminal cases and even serve on juries. They were barred from publishing a political newspaper or calling a public meeting. They had to take their husband's nationality at marriage. If the husband was a

---

*The law required that the natural child of a married woman be given the name of her husband, but that the natural child of a married man have inscribed on the record, "*Père inconnu*" (Laya, 54).

†Dr. Madeleine Pelletier stated that thanks to the spread of abortion, many situations that would have been serious earlier became relatively easy to deal with by the end of the nineteenth century (Pelletier, 53).

minor, absent, or in prison, the wife could not make a contract without the authorization of a (male) judge.

The lack of legal protection for women and the inconsistency of treatment between them and men was clearly shown when they came to court. An 1874 case concerned Mme de Bauffremont, who separated from her husband, moved to a German state where she had herself naturalized, got a divorce, and remarried.[34] Her French husband brought suit, and the French court ruled that all these acts had been illegal, and that she would be swiftly punished if she set foot in France. When Mme Jules Simon was attacked by a libel in 1880, she could only sue for reparation with her husband's graciously given consent, and in a later case, a certain Mme Kaulla was unable to bring a complaint against her husband for lack of such consent.[35] Frenchwomen could not vote until 1944, being enfranchised by the Second World War just as Englishwomen had been by the First.

With so many restrictions during most of the nineteenth century, it is hard to see just where Barbara Leigh Smith found the greater freedom that she believed French women enjoyed, as compared to English ones. They could make their own wills, take personal responsibility for fraud, and officially acknowledge the birth of children, so that they had a few privileges denied Englishwomen. But the men who favored women's emancipation, like Victor Hugo, justly insisted that the law needed to be changed from the ground up, and that women must be removed from their role as civil minors and moral slaves.

∾ 19.

French Feminism and Utopian Socialism

*Les femmes, je le sais, ne doivent
pas écrire J'écris pourtant.*
   Marceline Desbordes-Valmore, 1860

A legislative assembly entirely composed of
men is as incompetent to make laws to rule a
society composed of men and women as would
be one composed entirely of privileged classes
to discuss the interests of the workers or an
assembly of capitalists to uphold the honor of
the nation.

Jeanne Déroin, 1849

As reformers from the nineteenth century looked back to the eighteenth, they realized that women had once had much actual freedom, which was lost when the ideal of the mother-centered household became prevalent and as the law was codified, often for the first time containing specific provisions limiting women's rights. It was not so much that the earlier period had cherished freer principles as that it overlooked many loopholes through which energetic women were able to slip. By making successes of their own lives, they removed some of the pressure to make general changes. The laws and customs tightened up in the first years after 1800; women who wished to escape from their appointed role had to join together for the first time *as women*, in order that any individual might be really free. They began by reviewing their assets. Much of the writing in the thirties, when the subject became popular, clarified what women had done up until that time in science, art, and letters. When they tried to go farther and organize, however, they lacked so many needed skills and habits that most of their first efforts broke up over unresolved objectives or tactical disagreements.

   The first big split was between those who wanted a new sex life and marriage reform and those who wanted political reforms, the vote, and the right to work. Although these two purposes could be pursued together and be mutually reinforcing, this did not always occur. Later on another division appeared, often with deleterious results for both sides, between those who thought that women had a higher destiny than men and should set out to organize society in a new way, and those who wanted merely to insinuate women into all the places where men already were.

The views of the philosophers of the Age of Reason had hardly been flattering to the female sex. Diderot considered woman a courtesan, Montesquieu considered her an agreeable child, while Rousseau felt that she was created especially to give pleasure to men,[1] although in *Emile* there is a tantalizing hint that in an uncorrupted society there might be more outside jobs and interests for her.[2] Voltaire hardly mentioned the rights of women. In the Revolutionary period Robespierre and Danton were anti-feminist (though from opposite standpoints—Danton as a sensualist, Robespierre as a puritan). As for Napoleon, even though he was not born a Frenchman, he declared that "there is one thing that is not French, that a woman should do as she pleases." The Abbé Siéyès had been a bit more favorable, and Condorcet was the shining exception, feeling that women were entirely fit for public affairs.

Women themselves, in 1789, were more concerned with the general revolution than with any specific redress for their own sex, though some of the *cahiers* of 1789 had petitioned for an equal education for girls and free schools where women could learn to teach their children. There was also an interesting petition to the National Assembly of 1791 requesting the new government to purge French grammar of the differences between the sexes.[3]

The Mary Wollstonecraft of France—Olympe de Gouges—was the natural daughter of a poet and a laundress. She married early (and disastrously) a military cook. The only way out was up, she found, and the only method was by using her sex. During the Revolution she began to write, asking for equal education for girls, demanding National Workshops for women, and finally composing a "Declaration of the Rights of Woman," for which Robespierre sent her straight to the scaffold.[4] The government thereupon closed all women's clubs and forbade more than five women to meet together for any purpose.[5]

Only a woman of great wealth, talent, and sex appeal could challenge the system that developed thereafter, and Mme de Staël, the outstanding woman of the Napoleonic period, commanded all three. The daughter of an enormously rich Swiss banker, Necker, she was born as close to the top of society as Olympe to the bottom. Napoleon, who, at best, did not like *femmes de lettres*, and who felt that the greatest woman in the world was she who had the most children,[6] simply detested Mme de Staël, who reciprocated by defending women and criticizing the sort of society that kept them down. Her early novels depicted the suffering of talented women under social conditions that made both thinking and loving difficult for them. She herself practiced both on a major scale, but although she had many admirers, she had few imitators.

It took some time for society to recover from the Napoleonic Wars. Families had been broken up, the economy was drained, political involvement seemed dangerous. Mme de Rémusat, a representative of the best of the old aristocracy, noticed women's discouragement in the 1820s and tried to tell them that the world was not so bad as they imagined, but that they must train themselves for a new time when, she hoped, there would come an empire of reason. But the Bourbon government was not very favorable and even passed a special law in 1821 forbidding women to be managers of newspapers.[7] Still, there was much seething beneath the surface, which exploded into a real feminist movement as soon as the July Revolution of 1830 had established Louis Philippe as a king with a bourgeois point of view and a new Charter guaranteeing freedom of the press and association.

Albums of pictures of beautiful women soon began to lie on drawing room tables, while books about women's achievements became fashionable. When writers began to investigate the subject, they found many examples of productive women whose careers had previously seemed isolated.[8] There was Mme Arago, wife of the astronomer, who added deep learning to domestic excellence; Elisabeth Celnart, who tried to bring up-to-date medical knowledge into the field of child care and who had married her lawyer husband for love. Mlle Sophie Germain made such solid contributions to mathematics that she was awarded an honorary degree by the University of Göttingen in 1831, but she unfortunately died before she could accept it.*[9] Cornelia Lamarck collaborated with her evolutionist father, publishing his works after he lost his eyesight. Louise d'Aumont was an entomologist of prominence.[10]

While there were a few cases of prominent women in science, it was in the field of letters that women were most prolific. Under the July Monarchy the writing bug seemed to bite women of all classes, from duchesses to working girls.[11] Four times (1839, 1843, 1852, and 1855) the French Academy gave its prize to a woman poet, Louise Colet, who wrote *"Ce qui est dans le coeur des femmes,"* and who at various times of her long life was mistress to Victor Cousin, Musset, and Flaubert (among others).†[12] George Sand came to prominence at this time. In 1836 Alfred de Montferrand collected biographies of all the women writers of the previous thirty years, and explained in his introduction that during this period women had silently changed from slaves of prejudice into independent creatures. While people used to make fun of women who wrote, he continued, now these authors aroused enthusiasm both for the quality of their product and for the modesty and simplicity with which most of

*Sophie Germain conducted part of her education by what were in effect correspondence courses, writing to the greatest mathematicians of her day, Lagrange and Gauss, under a boy's name. Her death certificate was not bold enough to call her a "mathematician" but listed her simply as a *"rentière"* (Robière, 117).

†Her many prizes were probably due more to her manipulative tactics than to inherent excellence. Her interest in her lovers seemed to peak just before the time when prize books would be chosen, and she was a vehement beggar. An anecdote tells of a time when she shut Flaubert and Bouillet in her library and ordered them to compose a prize poem, due the next day. The two friends copied out an old poem of Lamartine's, and Louise sent it in and won another prize (Pange, 225).

them conducted their private lives. Obviously he wanted his women to be admired as women, in the role which the period assigned them, and he pointed out that those who stayed home to write did not gamble away their fortune or dance away their health. Even if they had less time to manage their homes, they were so intelligent that they would oversee everything carefully, and they were so full of sensibility that they could respond quickly to the needs of their children. Their great advantage, as he saw it, was that they were not constantly competing, as male authors were, for academic honors. Art, for women, was more of a religion than a profession.[13] (The implication was that it would be dangerous for them to be "professional.")

Meanwhile studies of women's place in history and law engaged the attention of scholars. Edouard Laboulaye traced their condition from Roman times in a massive volume, *Recherches sur la condition civile et politique des femmes* (1843), and he was only one of several in the field.[14]

Concurrently, as has been hinted, there was a considerable amount of strictly feminist organizing and the whole question of women's rights was ardently discussed by women themselves. Leaving aside for the moment those who were caught up in the various socialist movements, let us turn to some who wanted more limited reforms. Eventually the women's movement would concentrate on getting the vote, but in those early days suffrage seemed a relatively minor matter among all the reforms that were needed. Probably a change in marriage topped the list in the 1830s. The reformers reproached the whole nation as one great house of prostitution where fathers sold their daughters, and therefore insisted that the dowry system must end and marriage for love come to be the norm. Some women devised imaginative ways to demonstrate their protest aginst the existing marriage laws, like Jeanne Déroin, who kept her maiden name. She had to explain to a court that she did not wish to implicate her husband, a civil servant, in her efforts to eliminate servitude for women.[15]

On a slightly different tack, new professions were to be opened up, at first not so much to enable women to earn a living as to meet the needs of women patients and clients who would prefer to discuss their problems with doctors and lawyers of their own sex. But in 1836 the University of Paris rejected the attempt of a midwife to enroll in the Faculty of Medicine, and in the same year, when some women tried to win admission to the stock exchange, the president called their demand "indecent."[16]

At this period, too, there began to appear a profusion of journals edited by and for women, though most of them were evanescent, reflecting either the lack of business experience of the staff or the lack of readership beyond the committed few. Thus the *Femme Libre*, founded by some socialist women, changed within months to the *Femme de l'Avenir*, then to the *Femme Nouvelle*, but still finding opposition to their radical ideas, they changed once more into the *Tribune des Femmes*, which reached for a broader consensus and was specially concerned with girls' schools.[17]

The most durable editor and petitioner for women's rights was Mme Herbinot de Mauchamps, who founded the *Gazette des Femmes* in 1836. This lady's aunt had petitioned for a restoration of divorce back in 1814, and on her deathbed had entrusted the task of continuing the struggle to her niece.[18] The causes embraced by Mme de Mauchamps were not limited to this one, but included most of those that would constitute the foundation of the women's movement of fifty years later. The technique she chose was to petition the Chamber for the changes she deemed necessary. Her first effort was to ask for an alteration of the law forbidding women to be managers of newspapers, although in her own case her husband was so helpful and sympathetic that some people (possibly unwilling to credit executive ability in a female) speculated that Monsieur de Mauchamps was the real power behind the editorial success of the *Gazette*.[19]

She then petitioned the Chamber for a divorce law, pointing out that a mere judicial separation did not allow a woman to be as happy as her ex-husband, who could freely take a mistress.[20] Editorially she recommended that unfairly treated wives take direct action, such as breaking the glass or china if a husband lifted his hand against them, or better, by cutting or burning the piece of linen he planned as a gift for his mistress.[21] Nor was she against using all the powers of seduction and influence that could be mustered to gain a favorable vote in the Chamber. Not winning much support for divorce she went on to urge woman suffrage.* The Charter, she pointed out, gave legal equality to all French citizens, and she petitioned that Frenchwomen who fulfilled the stringent property qualifications applying to men should be allowed to vote on the same terms. She would have liked Louis Philippe to adopt the title *"Roi des Françaises et des Français."*[22] This petition came to the personal attention of the king himself, who responded that while the Charter recognized women's political rights in theory, they were in no condition to exercise them. Let women—and the working class—study, prepare, improve their condition, and then (soon, he hoped) the Chamber would allow these two groups to vote.

Mme de Mauchamps was said to be delighted with this answer and advised parents to start preparing their girls for entrance to the University and the professions of law and medicine. Among her other petitions was one to abolish, as unworthy of French citizens, the requirement of wifely obedience, and this one earned the distinction of a committee report from the Chamber, though they treated it satirically. Another petition begged for equalization of the penalty for adultery for both partners. Adultery, she said firmly, was not a public nuisance when

---

*Actually women had voted for the Estates General, in occasional cases, from the fourteenth century down to 1789 (Chéliga, 272).

committed by two people in private and therefore it should not be the subject of criminal penalties at all.[23]

With so many desires, and so many rebuffs, it was only natural for women to found groups to help each other. Like their press, their clubs were usually ephemeral. In 1834 Adèle Saint-Armand called on women to join a society for mutual help.[24] They would agitate for women's rights, including the right to vote, "like the women of the United States," she insisted, in a burst of undeserved enthusiasm for the New World. The society would also found schools and colleges and gymnasiums where women could obtain the physical exercise that their way of life made so difficult for them.*

As early as 1827 Louise Daurtat had opened a public course of lectures in the history of religion, but the police had closed it.[25] Under the more liberal policies of the new government, she opened a course on the social rights of women, but the attendance proved disappointing.[26] Eugénie Niboyet formed an *Athénée des Femmes*, a sort of club in which, for dues of twenty francs, each member could attend lectures and use the library.[27] The directors hoped that their courses could lead to examinations in science, literature, political science, and ethics. Courses were also projected for public speaking and grammar.

Not all of the failure should be laid to women's own inexperience, of course. There was also formidable opposition from men, whose easiest weapon was satire. The whisper that took most of the wind out of their sails was that pretty women married; only homely ones organized.† Even Henry Bulwer, who was spurred on by his French mistress, Hortense Allart, to attend a feminist meeting, was repelled by the unprepossessing countenances.[28] The theater too took up women's rights as a source of irresistible laughter. A play by Theodore Maret showed a woman who pretends to be enslaved while actually exerting the most insufferable tyranny over her whole family, her worst act being to forbid her daughter to marry the man she loves.[29] The farcical cure, suggested by a lawyer, is to let the mother have her head; it quickly becomes apparent that she lacks even the language to communicate in the law courts or stock exchanges, and she returns repentantly to her husband's protection. The lesson that women needed better education was palpable, but it was not the one drawn upon the stage.

In a different plane from the rebels so far mentioned because of her firm position within the establishment was the longest-lasting woman columnist, Delphine de Girardin. Born Delphine Gay, she had enchanted Paris as a young girl with her poetry and the charm she displayed

---

*I have found no record of how long this society lasted, but it probably disappeared quickly, like most other women's organizations in this too-early spring.

†Although the unhappy marriages of people like George Sand and Flora Tristan gave some color to this assertion, other active feminists, such as Eugénie Niboyet, were conspicuously happily married, while Jeanne Déroin's feeling for her husband was said to be that of a loyal comrade (Thibert, *Féminisme*, 265; Dolléans, 254).

in her mother's salon.[30] By marrying the influential editor of *La Presse*, Emile de Girardin, she acquired a secure base from which to spread her perceptive views of the passing scene from 1836 to 1849. Under the pseudonym of the Vicomte de Launay, she covered everything from fashions and society to letters and philosophy.

Her conclusions about women's role were discouraging. Although a decade or more of agitation had resulted in some slight change in women's lives, creating a style of clothing termed *garçonnière* and a new feminine type, *la lionne*, who pretended to disdain feminine graces,[31] the actual state of the sex was summed up in her article of March 23, 1844. A woman in France is denied all personal dignity, she exclaimed; she can only shine by reflection. Why do men so love *ladies*, while they mistreat *women*? How can we reconcile the politeness of manners with the malevolence of the laws? And why grant women privileges when you deny them rights?

After the enthusiasm of the thirties, the women's movement slackened off in the forties until the Revolution of 1848 stirred it to a last gasp of activity. The difference between this revolution and that of 1789 was that then women had worked very largely for the triumph of the revolution itself, while in 1848 they paid more attention to women's own problems. The Second Republic lasted from 1848 until 1852, but only for the first few months was it in the hands of liberals.

Under the period of the Provisional Government, from February to December, the Minister of Public Instruction, Hippolyte Carnot, announced a plan to equalize the number of government-run schools for the two sexes, but he was cast out of office before he could implement his intention.[32] During the same first period of fine rapture, the Second Republic had called upon Ernest Legouvé to give a course of lectures at the Collège de France to rouse women to their rights and to suggest revisions in the Code. Legouvé was the leading intellectual expert on the subject, and his conclusions might be called middle-of-the-road.[33] His views may be summarized as follows: he deplored the lack of public educational facilities for women, their dependence on a dowry to make a good marriage, their inadequate civil rights even in areas closest to their interest, such as the guardianship of their children.[34] He felt that the socialist solutions of free love would be degrading to the point where he would prefer even the existing degree of subjection to that kind of liberty. He told his listeners that the First Republic had fallen for lack of a feminine contribution, and that the law must now become the protector of women. In advocating changes, he felt warmly supported by the sympathy of his young audience at the Collège de France. Though he could not go so far as to call the sexes equal in marriage—that might throw discord into the state—sometimes, he believed, the woman might be allowed to make the decision instead of the man.

Forty-five numbers of a sheet called the *Voix des Femmes* appeared between the successful February Revolution and the violent June Days, which put an end to other utopian hopes besides those of women. The journal was supported by a liberal banker, Olinde Rodrigues, and edited by Eugénie Niboyet.* In April, 1848, it opened its pages to propose both an organization of women and a political constitution for them.[35] This last document, while having little noticeable influence at the time (in fact it was quite unrealistic), did indicate the concerns of the editors, and, indirectly, of advanced women of the period. It divided women's rights into public and private ones. By public rights they meant equality of the sexes in civic privileges, property, education, and employment, including a provision that certain young girls should be drafted by lot to serve with the armed forces, where they were to provide food, hospital care, and social service. Among the private rights enumerated was the provision that marriage should be obligatory, at twenty-one for women and twenty-six for men, exemption being granted by a court only in exceptional circumstances. A childless widow would be under obligation to remarry within two years. At the same time, all these marriages were to be between equals, and the housework was to be carefully divided so that each partner would have his share of supervising the servants, or the children, or doing household jobs himself, while both partners were expected to have outside employment. For a husband who refused to cooperate around the home, the penalty would be to perform certain public tasks.†

The document stated that divorce must be allowed under certain circumstances—namely, excessive cruelty, condemnation of one partner to a disgraceful punishment, or adultery—but the last was to be severely punished. Women were not to promise obedience, nor were they expected to be silent; in fact, women who condescended to their husbands were to lose their rights. Houses of prostitution were to be closed.

The *Voix des Femmes* also pushed for equal education, In their editorial view, a girl should stay home until she was eight, and then be educated at the same *lycée* as her brother, only at different times of the day. The feminist movement in later years would favor special girls' schools with women teachers, but this could only be hoped for when the professions had opened up to train such capable women. Meanwhile Eugénie Niboyet demanded a reading room for women at the Bibliothèque Nationale and the right to study law and medicine so that women could defend their rights and take better care of their children.

The swarm of young editresses who worked on the *Voix des Femmes* also organized an association of working women, teachers, mid-

---

*For her, feminism was one cause among many. She was the granddaughter of a Protestant clergyman of Geneva, and in 1832 she had founded a feminist paper in Lyons. From 1838 on she had directed a society for Christian morality, advocating education for the blind, reform of prisons, and world peace, all of which, in Eugénie's opinion were closely related to the women's movement. Rather naturally, she had links with the Saint-Simonian movement too (Dolléans, 248; Thibert, *Fémisme*, 202).

†Another provision was that women should strive, unobtrusively and within the bounds of good taste, to eliminate the difference between male and female clothing.

wives, cooks, and modistes, to protect the rights of employed women, to help them find jobs, and incidentally to guarantee their capability and their morality. They wanted the Second Republic to set up public workshops employing women, as it had for men, free day nurseries for their children, a library for improving their minds, and a cooperatively run restaurant and laundry. The effort to organize working women was more or less successful, and five women were chosen as delegates to the Luxembourg Commission, which the Provisional Government had set up to consider problems of labor.

Lastly, the *Voix des Femmes* set up a *Club des Femmes*, where policies concerning their sex could be discussed. The Second Republic was at first a heyday for clubs of all sorts, but the women's club was so heckled by male visitors that it finally voted not to allow any men to be present. The men got their revenge after the suppression of the June rebellion of the working class, when the newly conservative government on July 25, 1848, forbade women either to be members of a club or to be present at any club meeting.

The general middle-class reaction to the idea of women in clubs was, predictably, mocking, even though one man remarked that his sex's weakness for gallantry prevented his penetrating the mysteries of feminism.[36] *L'Illustration*'s reporter at the May 21 meeting commented on the huge flowered hat of Eugénie Niboyet in the chair, and decided that the whole idea was "piquant."

But in the opinion of Marie d'Agoult, writing under her pen name of Daniel Stern, the *people* had no such prejudices. They remembered Joan of Arc and that France had always been saved by its women. Delphine de Girardin's comment at this time was that only women could have the generosity of spirit to mediate between the two groups of men who were tearing the country apart; those who wanted to hang on to everything, and the others who wanted to grab it.

As is often the case, a new interest in workers grew up side by side with the women's movement. The common problems of oppression have often led the groups to mutual consideration. So now in 1848, various working-class and religious journals devoted increasing attention to the problems of women.[37] For example, *L'Atelier*, a Catholic workers' paper, advocated higher wages for men as a necessary step to enable working women to stay at home and give the care to their families that was already part of bourgeois morality and that they wished to imitate.*

When the Second Republic instituted universal male suffrage by abolishing the property qualification, it naturally reawakened the question of votes for women. It was felt to be a particular insult that male servants were now enfranchised while their mistresses were not. Marie-

---

*Likewise the first expression of interest in women's problems among organized German workers was in favor of freeing them to stay at home. Only later did socialists demand equality in the job market, catching up with still newer middle-class concerns.

Antoinette Rolland forced an official at the polls to register her protest against his refusal to let her vote for Pierre Leroux,[38] while Jeanne Déroin went further and was actually allowed to inscribe her name among the candidates for the Constitutional Assembly, only to be told two weeks later that such a candidacy was unconstitutional. She was very roughly treated.[39]

When the nine hundred delegates of the Constitutional Assembly finally met, only Victor Considérant, an old socialist, spoke in favor of women's political rights, not really hoping that they could be adopted then, he explained, but as a matter of record for the future.[40] Later on, in the first Legislative Assembly, Pierre Leroux, another old socialist, offered a women's suffrage amendment, but although he won warm compliments from John Stuart Mill for this action, the response of his fellow delegates was to pass legislation preventing even the right of petition by women.[41]

After the June Days and the closing of the clubs, in the period of general reaction, the leadership of the women's movement passed to Jeanne Déroin. In the spring election of 1849 she mounted a campaign for herself as a delegate. It was hopeless, of course, but she struck some noble notes about how mothers would demand a world free of violence, and how women needed ways to live that did not exploit their health or their morals. After the 1852 *coup d'état* by Louis Napoleon, which put an end even to the pretense of republican government, she was arrested and tried. The new President, soon to become Emperor, had acquired a peculiar animus against the women's movement. In court she appeared thin, pale, and indefatigable, and is said to have disarmed her judges by her mastery of ideas.[42]

In general, with the collapse of the Second Republic came a sudden loss of interest in the more radical aspects of feminism. For a few years Mlle Déroin courageously continued to issue an annual *Almanach des femmes*. The table of contents for the 1854 edition shows how her interests had broadened and become less activist. There was an essay on the Shakers; notes on an association for *Amour Pur*, which meant love freed from sex; a poem to a young man who was guillotined; a story about the factory girls of Lowell, Massachusetts; a discussion of temperance; an essay on women violinists, one of whom had received second prize at the Paris Conservatory; another on day-care centers; another on vegetarianism; and yet another on the protection of animals; and a hint at the possibility of freeing women from the necessity of becoming mothers. The movement was turning away from hopeless political action to various sorts of asceticism and benevolence.

Very little had been accomplished. As Victor Hugo declaimed over the grave of a feminist martyr in 1853: "The eighteenth century proclaimed the rights of man, the nineteenth will proclaim the rights of women, but we have to admit that we haven't been very quick about it."[43]

∽ It is necessary to backtrack a little in order to pick up the story of the really radical women—those who worked with the various groups of utopian socialists.

The Revolution of the eighteenth century had toppled the feudal structure and declared all men politically equal. The hierarchical social ties between man and man were loosened, and the solvent was universal male suffrage. But each man could be master in his own household, and master over women in general, for those organic ties had not been broken.*

During the nineteenth century, true revolutionaries shifted their focus from political to economic change, and, as is often the case with reform movements, this was announced first by some small, extremist sects. In France in the 1830s, such were the utopian socialists. They wanted to equalize not votes so much as the value of each person's economic contribution, and to obliterate the economic dependence of one person on another. For most of them this led to a very radical view of women, the group whose dependency in the past had been most conspicuous. The technique that many of these sects proposed as a start was to set up new communities where production for use could be put into effect.

Of course, women in their own households had been contributing heavily to production for use over centuries, but this had not seemed of economic value because no wages were paid. In the new communes, domestic contribution would take its place beside other forms of productivity, and women's love life for the first time would not be tied to an economic contribution, whether as a dowry or as housework. Until Marx heaped scorn on the simplicity of the idea, this was what most people meant by "socialism."

To those women who wanted a freer life, sexually and economically, marriage had seemed the most confining aspect of their ordinary role; so when they discovered that the socialist sects were willing to give up marriage in its familiar form, a close relationship arose between socialism and a certain segment of feminism. Over the next hundred years, to be sure, the connection would create more problems than it solved; the kind of feminism that eventually would win victories would have to discard socialist ideology and limit itself to gaining for women the same capacities as men in a capitalist society—votes, property rights, and earning power.

The utopians began in great variety. An early French thinker, Charles Fourier, who lived from 1772 to 1837, wanted to found ideal

---

*The ultimate expression of this masculine power and freedom from restraint was the Marquis de Sade's proposal for public brothels to which any women could be brought, by force if necessary, at the request of any man. This, in the opinion of the marquis's past and present admirers, would "free" women from the tyranny of monogamous marriage and nationalize a valuable product (Corey, passim).

communities called phalansteries. He envisaged people living there a simple, unconstricted life in which they could obey their healthy passions. Passions, he thought, were the elements of human progress, and the chief obstacle to their free development was family life, which held people in such a grip that they were mostly miserable. He had some very modern ideas about sex equality; for instance, he noticed how girl children usually had to play second fiddle to boys, so he recommended that the two sexes be dressed alike in infancy to avoid falsification of their natural interests.[44] Once grown up, women were to be freed from the chains of marriage and also of domestic servitude by the provision of central kitchens and nurseries, where those who liked such work could do it for everybody, freeing others of both sexes for different careers.[45] Fourier believed that the reason women seemed intellectually inferior lay in the dullness of the daily chores assigned to them, and in an early effort at affirmative action, he proposed that at least an eighth of the workers in any occupation should be required to belong to the sex that did not customarily perform that work. Some men would thus do housework, while he particularly looked forward to women's becoming doctors and professors. A basic guaranteed income would free each individual from the need to sell herself, whether in prostitution or in marriage.

Fourier must be regarded as the seminal thinker on women's emancipation. Later thinkers on socialism and feminism acknowledged their debt to him, not only the Saint-Simonians who followed on his heels, but also such theorists as Karl Marx and John Stuart Mill.

Another early French socialist who was particularly vehement in defending the rights of women was Etienne Cabet. There was a chapter on the subject in his visionary novel *Voyage en Icarie* (*Voyage to Icaria*) of 1840, and he wrote a special pamphlet on women in 1848. Some of his ideas came from having read Thomas More during a period of exile in England, and he apparently also admired the English way of allowing young men and women to meet and get to know each other. In his imaginary country the education given equally to both sexes would embrace all fields of human knowledge, although he did not definitely decide whether it should be imparted separately or in coeducation. There would be a program of sex education by books, parental guidance, and special religious counselors, with a great deal of freedom for young couples to walk and talk, and possible pre-marital experimentation—at the very least, a six-month engagement period. Divorce would be possible, though occasions for it would be unlikely where there was so much good education and freedom and where all women would understand the "celestial delights" of sex. Icarians adored women, Cabet exclaimed, and sought every opportunity to make them happy. The two partners in marriage would be equal, he contended; however, the husband would be given the preponderant vote in disagreements. This was one major area in which Cabet's reform seemed incomplete. Politically, also, women in his Utopia could only vote in a "consultative" role, and at a separate polling place.*

Of all the utopian sects, the most flamboyant and much the best organized was that which called itself Saint-Simonian. Claude Henri de Saint-Simon himself died in 1825, and a group of young engineers who were gathered at his funeral decided then and there not to allow the ideas with which he had inspired them to perish. The main tenet was the organization on a rational basis of goods for use, not profit, by an organizing committee for all of Europe consisting of the greatest scientific minds. Although Saint-Simon had apparently had no special theory of feminism, he held women's brains in high regard and would have allowed women to vote for his council of Europe. Prosper Enfantin, his chief follower, picked up a much more radical feminist theory largely from Fourier.†[46]

The first group of Saint-Simonians consisted of men only, but they spent a good part of the year 1829 in intellectual discussion over the place of woman, and at the end of the discussion Enfantin, who had been elected one of the two *pères*, proposed admitting to membership Claire Bazard, the wife of the other *père*, and Cécile Fournel.

The two *pères* did not get on very well, and in the end they split bitterly over the question of women, but it was largely a temperamental conflict.[47] Bazard had been chosen to represent "reason," and Enfantin "feeling," even though he was a Polytechnic graduate. Actually Enfantin turned into something of a sexual mystic, arguing that God was of two sexes and that the couple was the natural unit of human society. At the same time he wanted to release the members from the prison of the nuptial bed, and felt that the secret of who was a child's father should be the mother's alone. He envisioned priestesses who could use any power, including sex, to comfort or console the people or hold on to the backslider, and he decided to begin a hunt for a female messiah who would be qualified to become the *mère* at his side.

The public reaction was sensational. Conservative bourgeois circles nicknamed one figure of the quadrille *la Saint-Simonnienne* because in it one changed partners.‡ More seriously, Enfantin soon found himself in court to answer charges of corrupting public morals.[48] True to his principles, he insisted on being defended by two women lawyers, Cécile Fournel and Aglaé Saint-Hilaire, who was the *père*'s faithful companion and

*When a group of enthusiastic Icarians set out for Texas, eventually settling in Illinois in 1848, report had it that the women were not very well treated.

†Saint-Simon was popularly supposed to have suggested a mating between himself and Mme de Staël, the greatest man and the greatest woman of the age—a legend only slightly more credible than the other one, that he mated his wife with a man he believed to be a genius in order to further his experiments in heredity (Thibert, *Féminisme*, 5; Maillard, 27).

‡Another subject for bourgeois outrage was that the Saint-Simonian women sometimes wore trousers beneath short skirts.

obviously hoped to be called to be the female messiah. As lawyers, naturally, the women were quickly thrown out of court, and Enfantin was condemned to a year in prison.[49]

As soon as he was released, he organized a voyage to the East, where he thought the messiah would reveal herself.[50] On March 22, 1833, a dozen people set sail for Constantinople and Egypt in the ship *Clorinda*, whose first mate was none other than the young Giuseppe Garibaldi, who incidentally picked up many radical ideas from the long discussions on board. The party included two physicians, some sculptors, a black whose parents had been slaves, and a few women. They explained that when the female messiah was found, she would do for women what Jesus had done for men; he saved men from slavery, and she would redeem women from prostitution.

The hoped-for savior was, of course, never found, and the group broke up in some disarray. But at least one of the voyagers deserves a special mention. Suzanne Voilquin was one of the lucky few who were able to use the Saint-Simonian movement as a launching pad into a fulfillment a woman could never otherwise have attained. She was from a poor family and called herself *"une fille du peuple."* She had had an unhappy childhood with a very strict and pious mother. (When her nose was broken in play, her mother refused to call a doctor to set it, telling the protesting neighbors that the child would be "pretty enough" if only she were devout.) She learned to read from a brother who had started training for the priesthood and continued her education in a convent until overwork produced symptoms of St. Vitus's dance. At home she suffered intensely from her father's rudeness toward her mother. His motto was "where the she-goat is tethered, there must she graze," but Suzanne began to wonder why she did not have the right to break her chain. Falling in love with a medical student, she ran afoul of his father's refusal to sanction the marriage, stalling the couple until the young man's restraint broke down and he attempted to seduce Suzanne, at first gently, then more violently, until his final success threw her into convulsions. When he abandoned her, she wanted to commit suicide. Meanwhile her father and brother had failed in business, and she and her sister had to go to work in an embroidery factory. Eventually she married a man named Voilquin, but found the wedding day a trauma. Her despair increased when she found that she had a disease that prevented her having a healthy child.

Into her life the news of Saint-Simonianism came like a breath of freedom. When Voilquin sailed for America on the arm of a new love, Suzanne dedicated her life to fighting for the rights of mothers. Soon she was put in charge of a little Saint-Simonian journal, but her true destiny only became manifest during the voyage to the East. Landing in Egypt, she got a job as tutor to a physician's children; in turn, they taught her Arabic. With this tool she was able to study medicine in the hospitals of Cairo. Her ambition was to help women in the harems, and she hoped that by attending to their bodies she could eventually impress their minds with a wider view of freedom. In 1836 she came back to France, where she organized a society of unmarried mothers whose babies she delivered for free.*[51]

If her life could be regarded as a success, this was not true for most of the women connected with Enfantin's cult. He himself turned out to be far more interested in erotic freedom for his female proselytes than in their political power, one of his techniques being to encourage confessions, which he told them would be healing, though they did not always prove to be so. Claire Bazard, for one, from whom he had extracted a confession of adultery, tried to accept his discipline for a while but ended up feeling that he was using his erotic techniques to throw his weight around. "Today a period of suspense exists among the followers of Saint-Simon," she wrote in 1831. "They preach the love of all and the love of each; as for the love of each, they don't know a thing about it, since individual ties are yet to be formed among them. Family morality is still unknown to them; then when they talk about holiness and the delicious charm of the marriages of the future, they are making *tours de force*."[52]

Eugénie Niboyet, too, broke with Enfantin over his ideas of the *femme libre*. She was a happy wife and mother with a wide social life, and for a while she could profess the Saint-Simonian faith while allowing it to overlap other interests. We have seen that she never gave up her work for women's rights, but she turned her concern into more conventional channels.

In November, 1834, George Sand was asked to become a *mère* in the Saint-Simonian family, but she refused, feeling that the movement had little to offer women. Equal women, getting equal treatment, she said, would be able to be chaste.[53] This could be considered rather prim; still, like so many beleaguered Frenchwomen, she felt that if their marriages were not so contrived, they would be able to make better choices and to stick with them without the benefit of socialism.

Jeanne Déroin was another who repudiated the concept of free love as defined by Enfantin. Her hope was for women to prove that they could exercise their rights while still minding the sacred duties of the home, and she came to believe that Saint-Simonian eccentricity held back serious consideration of feminine causes.[54]

Another ardent feminist, Jenny d'Héricourt, described her first moving vision of the Saint-Simonians as a young girl when she was walking with her austerely Protestant mother. The company of men in graceful costume† were going to the Palais de Justice to defend their

---

*But she also says, rather mysteriously, that she practiced medicine successfully for seven years in Russia. It should be kept in mind that her own autobiography is the only source for her tale.

†One of the features of the Saint-Simonians at this time was their distinctive uniform, semi-military in its red trousers and tight jackets, but with most unsoldierly long hair and mustaches.

organization, and she was greatly upset to see them being dispersed by police. Later she studied their doctrines and came to the conclusion that imitating masculine passions was not the way for women to find genuine liberty: "those who make use of the most liberty in love, neither love nor esteem the other sex."[55]

Enfantin's destructive impact on his cult victims is nowhere more clearly shown than in the life of Pauline Roland, the daughter of a postmistress in Normandy. While still a schoolgirl, she developed a crush on a teacher, a Monsieur Desprez, who happened to be the local Saint-Simonian and thus part of the network that spread the doctrine all across France.[56] He had already converted the editor of the local paper, and now went to work on his girl students. Pauline and her sister fell right into step, and before long Pauline was writing to the headquarters in Paris. She was enraptured to receive a response from no less a person than Aglaé Saint-Hilaire, though her joy was short-lived because a scandal developed in the little town when it was discovered that one of the teachers had been preaching socialism, and Pauline's mother quickly forbade her to have anything more to do with the sect or her teacher. When she said goodbye to Desprez, he kissed her hand, the first time he had ever touched her. Pauline had romantic hopes that the Paris leaders might "save two human souls" by letting them come to Paris together, and a job was indeed found for Desprez. At that point, however, he chose to stay with his wife. The correspondence between Pauline and Aglaé, mostly about women and free love, had been heating up, and Pauline made her way to Paris alone, and to the inevitable interview with *Père* Enfantin. The sexual passes he made left her in a state of great excitement, wondering how she could ever be content again with any ordinary soul. Aglaé commented sarcastically that she must think herself the first![57]

In November, 1832, at the age of twenty-seven, Pauline made up her mind to devote her life to the cause. She was still a virgin at that time, but the next year, under the erotic gospel, she was brought to the decision that she must give "all of herself" and that she must not reserve her favors for a single individual. Apparently she thought of herself as a priestly prostitute, although it is not clear how many lovers she actually accepted.[58] She finally had four children while living with a certain Monsieur Aicard and supporting herself by writing for the new *Encyclopedia* of a rival socialist, Pierre Leroux. After Aicard had been unfaithful to her (though, faithful to Saint-Simonian principles, with another member's wife), she withdrew from the sect and went to teach school in a colony run by Leroux.

When the Revolution of 1848 broke out, Pauline tried to organize a teachers' union. Still protesting against marriage and preaching socialism, she was sent to prison in 1850, where she found a new apostolate among the women prisoners, meanwhile supporting her two surviving children by writing in her cell. In observing the 1,400 women prisoners, including many prostitutes, and the forty nuns who were charged with supervising them, she concluded that both groups had been cruelly deceived about the nature of love and sex; the only remedy would be to reform male ethics. After the *coup d'état* of 1852, she was deported to Africa and might have been forgotten if her young son had not won a national Latin prize and through this achievement and the attendant publicity attracted attention to her plight. She won a pardon on the basis of this interest, but was too ill to get home.

Among other women touched by Saint-Simonianism, Elisa Lemmonier should be mentioned, who along with her husband joined the movement in Bordeaux. The young couple sank their small inheritance of 50,000 Francs into the cause, but, unlike others, Elisa had the spunk to oppose Enfantin on the sexual question and even disagreed with her husband, who did not want to break with his friends. Later, in Paris, Elisa carried out some of the economic ideals of the movement by founding schools to train young women for various technical jobs.[59]

Finding jobs was one of the ways in which Saint-Simonianism acted substantively to improve the condition of women in France. If the sensational aspects of free love are discounted, there was a solid core of accomplishment toward equality of work and education stemming from the engineering aspect of the movement. Quite early Saint-Simonian engineers persuaded the first railway in France (from Paris to Saint-Germain) to use women guards at the crossings.*[60] Elsewhere, in later years, there could be found here and there women of clear intellect and reasoning powers who had been educated right alongside their brothers in families touched by Saint-Simonian educational theory.†

Though some later students of the subject, such as Marya Chéliga in 1897 and Léon Abensour in 1913,[61] have agreed with Jeanne Déroin that the eccentricity of the early socialists aroused hostility to the cause of feminism, others, like Marguerite Thibert in 1926, believed that the general stirring up of the woman question had beneficial ramifications far beyond the limited range of the small sects. Even Catholic interest in the position of women would not have advanced as it did without the general discussion primed by the socialists.[62]

---

*". . . to Saint-Simonism, that strange affair, to this humanitarian Utopia in part bizarre, in part grandiose, which has aroused ridicule, touched scandal, had a bone to pick with the law, and which, with all that, has collected a true intellectual and moral elite, which turns out to be the source of nearly all the works of economic and industrial and social progress of our times" (Henri Marion, 250 *L'Education des Jeunes Filles*).

†The chief theoretician for putting women back in the home and restoring the patriarchal system, Frédéric Le Play, worked out his ideas in controversy with the Saint-Simonians. As a student at the Ecole des Mines, Le Play made friends with one Jean Reynaud, a sincere adherent of Saint-Simon and of Saint-Simon's technocratic ideas. The two young men took a walking tour across Germany in 1829, arguing all the way. Neither convinced the other, but Le Play can be considered to have laid the groundwork for the subsequent stand of the Christian Socialist party against the Marxians. The latter, as I have already mentioned, took over many of their ideas about women from the utopians (Herbertson; Clark, 12).

In this time and place—the 1830s in France—began the long and troubled relationship between socialism and feminism. The situation was remarkably similar to that of the 1930s, when the Communist party dominated the lives of a few deeply committed individuals (including some who later became bitterly disillusioned), and a large proportion of all western European artists and intellectuals were touched in some way and were more or less sympathetic. In both periods the general population was scandalized, and socialism became a *bête noire*, the partly imaginary specter that haunted Europe.

Nothing shows so clearly that men felt that their rights over women were property rights as the fact that the only party that clearly declared for sexual freedom was the same one that would abolish all other private property. While the connection was strong in the 1830s, the inevitability of the link has now been broken. Women have, in fact, been largely liberated in many countries that have not notably advanced toward socialism.

The truth was that socialist movements aroused distaste on two fronts. Many women shied away from sexual freedom, wanting to maintain traditional ties to family and children while getting wider vocational and political choices; others found that socialist parties were always male-dominated in spite of their fine phrases. The socialist fathers turned out to be either exploitative, like Enfantin, or patriarchal in their own lives, as Marx was.*

The most logical and precise contemporary rebuttal to all the various masculine theories about women came from the pen of that remarkable woman, Jenny d'Héricourt. Accomplished in several fields, both scientific and literary, she worked on the *Révue Philosophique* alongside Charles Lemonnier, among others. She was also a medical practitioner, having passed her examinations .as a *Maîtresse Sage-Femme*.[63] There is a tantalizing hint (in an Italian book of 1872) that Jenny, unable to rise as high as her abilities warranted in France, went to America, and there, in Chicago, was immediately offered a chair of anatomy in a medical faculty.[64] We are not told the name of the institution, and I have been unable to confirm this story from any French or American source, although another Italian writer referred to her as "Franco-American."

Her book of 1860, *A Woman's Philosophy of Woman: or, Woman Affranchised: An Answer to Michelet, Proudhon, Girardin, Comte, and*

---

*An interesting conversation between Betty Friedan and Simone de Beauvoir, reported in the *Saturday Review* for June 14, 1975, shows how little the terms of the debate have changed. Friedan felt that too great concern over sexual issues would distract the feminist movement from the paramount issue of equal pay, and she wanted to upgrade the value placed on housework. Beauvoir argued for collective living in the best utopian style and against the myth of the family, wanting free sexual choices, especially in decisions about motherhood, and *no* housework to be done by individual women for their men.

other modern innovators, was first printed in Brussels because the French censors swore to seize any copy found in France, giving no reason, but stating that they were following their regular policy. Jenny met this challenge by sending a copy directly to Napoleon III and requesting a chance to defend herself. Shortly thereafter the book was permitted to circulate.

In it she divided French thinkers into those who had been in favor of equality for women, such as the Saint-Simonians, Fourier, and Emile de Girardin; those in between, particularly Legouvé and his "innumerable adherents," whose position was that women should be given, by stages, a chance to become equal; and those who were opposed to any such equality—namely, Comte, Michelet, and Proudhon. The difference between Michelet and Proudhon, she declared, was that the one was as sweet as honey and the other bitter as wormwood, but she said pointedly that neither of them recognized that women had a life of their own to live.

In fact, she had a genius for turning theories of female subjection on their heads. People say that women are not equal to hard labor; surely it will soon all be done by machinery. Military service? With the growth of civilization, this type of service will disappear. As for Proudhon, after having published an article about him in 1856 in the *Révue Philosophique*, Jenny engaged him in correspondence, demolishing his famous "laws" of female inferiority and defending the right of women to feel sexual emotion. Of August Comte, she declared, like many subsequent readers, that not only his prose but also his ideas were murky. She was in an especially good position to expose the weakness of his hopes for parthenogenesis because she was herself a practicing midwife. She was sharp to criticize the way things were; yet she was not hopeful for the future. The Revolutions of 1789 and of 1848 were supported at their starts by great numbers of women hoping to be included in the great liberation, but they were quickly disillusioned. If Jenny d'Héricourt had lived longer, she would have found the pattern repeated in 1871—she was all too good a prophetess.

∽20.

A Gallery of French Feminists

The law of life was passion then,
as it is now scepticism.
George Sand, 1868

Four women who became prominent during the 1830s showed in their success as well as in their sufferings much of what was possible for women at that time. The changes that those years brought can be seen in a figure who rose to fame some twenty years later.

The earlier four were George Sand, or Mme Dudevant, née Aurore Dupin; Daniel Stern, the pen name of the Comtesse d'Agoult, née Marie de Flavigny; Flora Tristan, who resumed her maiden name after separating from a M. Chazal; and Hortense Allart, who late in life, after most of her adventures were over, married a certain Monsieur de Méritens. All four were born between 1801 and 1805. The later figure is Juliette Adam, née Lambert, born in 1836.

Though widely different in class and upbringing, there were interesting common factors in their lives. For one thing, the first four were products of marriages contracted by French citizens who had been flung outside France by the Napoleonic Wars and thereby were touched with some sort of cosmopolitan influence. Monsieur de Flavigny was French officer who married a wealthy Frankfurt banker's daughter, much against her family's wishes. Monsieur Dupin was another French officer, serving in Italy, where he fell in love with a young milliner who was something of a camp follower. Their eventual marriage was contracted only four days before George Sand was born and was opposed violently by the dowager Mme Dupin. Monsieur de Tristan was a Spanish officer who fell in love with and married a Frenchwoman who had fled from the horrors of her own country. Hortense Allart was born in Milan to a Napoleonic official.

The daughters grew up in greatly diverse circumstances. The Flavignys were at the pinnacle of French society and moved easily in court circles, while the Tristans, on their return to France, were classed as enemy aliens and deprived of the income from their Spanish possessions overseas, so that Flora grew up in poverty and had to go to work in a lithography shop at the age of fifteen. The Dupins were somewhere in between, for young Aurore grew up with the freedom and comfort of a country estate but without great wealth. The Allarts were originally wealthy but lost their fortune; Monsieur Allart died a poor man in 1817.

It may or may not be significant that each of the girls lost her father at an early age. And all except Hortense Allart claimed that they were forced by their families into arranged marriages, which is interesting in view of the freedom with which the parents themselves had married. This fact may indicate how thoroughly the more conventional mores had swept the country in thirty years. ("My mother forced me," said Flora; "I told them I would marry anyone they picked," declared Marie.)[1] And not one of the husbands was in any way suitable for these extremely bright and temperamental women.

Each of them proceeded to bear children, Hortense doing so out of wedlock. Only subsequently did the other three discover that they could never be happy with mediocre or unsympathetic husbands. They all made contact with Saint-Simonian ideas, telling us that they gained thereby the courage to break loose and seek their own fortunes. They all became distinguished for their writing and notorious for their love affairs. All of them but Fora found Italy the country of greatest freedom for these affairs, and Flora at the time of her death was planning to take a holiday there with a man. Monsieur d'Agoult behaved like a perfect gentleman when his wife ran away with Franz Liszt, but Flora Tristan and George Sand fought long battles over separation agreements and custody of the children, and both of them had their little daughters kidnapped by the husbands.

All their lives these women were preoccupied with questions of their children's ill-health and wrong-headed education, and (except for Hortense) by the anguish of having to be separated from them so much of the time. Yet one reason they were so free to pursue their careers and their love affairs was precisely that they lived in a period when even devoted mothers could by custom leave the day-to-day or year-by-year care of the children to others. Convents, tutors, and foster parents were available, and though these women suffered from the separation, they enjoyed a kind of freedom that might not have been possible in another country or at a later date.

Nor did any of them face social ostracism. Their love affairs may have been the subject of gossip, but both George Sand and Mme d'Agoult enjoyed long and honored lives, while Flora Tristan, who was the most radical and who died young, was widely respected, had many friends, and was apparently on the way to even greater success.

Each of them wrote the story of her own life. Since they were romancers, their words must be taken at times as symbolically true, rather than literally, but their own perceptions of themselves, and the way they wanted to be perceived, have their importance for our subject.

∽ Far and away the most famous was George Sand, whose novels spread throughout Europe the doctrine of spontaneous love and of dissatisfaction with the sort of society that prevented it. In later years she told Juliette Adam, "I was born to the literary life at the epoch when the Saint-Simonians had preached to young imaginations the law of pleasure. . . . At that time we lived in an enclosed world where only those ideas fermented."[2] By 1868 she could admit that she was disquieted by the consequences of the romantic theory because, as she put it, the law of life had changed from passion to scepticism.[3] But in the 1830s, except for the fact that she was a woman of genius, George Sand was perhaps typical of the kind of young person to whom the then-new ideals of passion and sexual liberty would appeal.

Although her aristocratic grandmother, who was in charge of her education, had been eager to marry the girl off before she herself was dead, a long illness kept the old lady from attending to this, and in those years Aurore, while technically chaperoned by virtue of her grandmother's existence, had a rare chance to be left to her own devices and to meet more kinds of people than did most French girls. She later felt that without that extra period of maturation, she might never have been able to break loose from convention. As it was she wandered through the woods near the estate on which she lived, Nohant, cultivating an intimate love of nature.[4] She used to go on medical calls with her brother's tutor, who had taken it upon himself to attend to the sick in the village, for there was no doctor, and in this way she learned how to set bones and assist at operations. Incidentally, the tutor told her that boys' clothing would give her a good deal more freedom to walk and ride about the countryside, so she adopted it, unaware until years later of how much criticism it had caused.[5]

After her grandmother died, she went to live in Paris with her much less well born mother; thus, although she had inherited Nohant, her marriage prospects were not very bright, and she was thought lucky to have attracted the attentions of M. Dudevant, who, though born illegitimate, had been adopted legally and was entitled to the rank of baron.[6] In her autobiography she does not admit that they were in love, but only that he did not fill her with instinctive disgust, although a French scholar, Ernest de Seillière, has studied the letters from her engagement period and feels that her sentiments were much warmer than she later allowed. He quotes a letter to a school friend containing a disquisition about what an inexhaustible happiness it was to obey the person one loved.[7] The marriage took place in 1822, but whatever affection she may have had at the start was lost by 1828, when she caught her husband in adultery. The two of them could never explain things to one another, she found, and however hard she tried, she could not reach an understanding of either him or herself.[8] Although at first she had been entirely willing to accept the conventional view of the husband's intellectual superiority, she developed a strong wish to forget all the ties of marriage and property and to become "as nearly a free woman as our wretched civilization permits."[9]

Her first effort to earn money was by sewing or painting small objects for sale, but this brought in so little that she tried her hand at writing, and in order to pursue this vocation she needed to go to Paris. Her husband believed that she was suffering from a whim, and since he did not love her, he arranged amicably for her to go there with her daughter, Solange. She was supposed to spend three months out of every six back at Nohant, whose revenues, by French law, were to be enjoyed by M. Dudevant; she also renounced the 1,500 francs a year that her marriage contract had allotted as her personal pin money. She accepted an allowance of 250 francs a month for the time she was in Paris (compared to the 14,000 a year she had spent running the house at Nohant). Her little son was left with his father, in the charge of a tutor she trusted.

Life in Paris was hard but stimulating. The only apartment she could afford was five flights up, and the only service was part-time help from the concierge's wife, whose wages were 15 francs a month. She arranged for Solange to stay with a neighbor's family where they had a private teacher.

Aurore Dudevant found that she could not knock around Paris in fine, thin shoes and long skirts, so she went back to the boys' clothing she had worn at Nohant, encouraged by her mother, who told her that when she had been in love with Aurore's father, dressing like a boy had enabled her to effect great economies. In her new uniform Aurore looked like a young student; her boots, in which it was impossible to trip, proved so delightful she says, that she felt like sleeping with them. Now she could wander around at night with other young writers and artists, could eat at cafés, sit in the top balcony at theaters, and be free like no other woman in all of Paris.*

Despite her newfound independence, she found it very hard to get a start in writing. The first editor she went to see told her, "Don't waste your time making books, Madame, make babies,"[10] to which she retorted, "Keep the rule for yourself, Monsieur." Eventually her first novels, *Indiana* and *Lélia*, came out under the pseudonym "George Sand." Some of her companions speculated that she might be the author, but one of them once turned to her and remarked that the author could not be the Aurore Dudevant he knew, since Lélia, who was born to tragedy, did not resemble "you who are gay, who dance the *bourrée*, who appreciate butterflies, who do not scorn jokes, who sew not too badly, and who make very good confections."[11]

Although she probably did more than anyone else to spread the idea of a new personal freedom for women, unbound by the old sexual or domestic taboos, she resisted joining either the feminist or the socialist

---

*Compare Rosa Bonheur, the painter, who lived from 1822 to 1899. She found that she had to adopt male attire to hang around the parts of Paris where she could sketch the horses that were her favorite subjects (Decaux, 9: 112).

organizations of her day. She refused to become one of the Saint-Simonian *mères*, as we have seen, and in the popular surge in 1848 she declined to run for office or to let anyone vote for her. She was not given to ideological expression, and when she did say something about women's role, it was merely that women had a very high mission, but that they were not fitted by character for public office.

Her whole concern was for personal independence—more for this than for happiness. The liberated female characters she drew are not shown to be happy, not nearly so happy as we can suppose her to have been in her own life, but neither did they obey the usual call of "duty." Early on, George Sand had rejected the preachments of Thomas à Kempis as stupid and cruel, and there more than anywhere her difference from George Eliot—a woman she is often compared to—is apparent.[12] The latter was passionately pro-duty all her life, as she showed in her hymn of praise to the *Imitation of Christ* in *The Mill on the Floss*.*

It was in her own life as much as in her books that George Sand spoke to young women, for she became a legend for her style in lovers (quickly taking them on and casting them away again), her cigarettes, her masculine clothing, and her free manners. Still, she respected the taboos of the day in her autobiography, and after reading it through one can never be sure whether she did take someone as a lover, so proper is her language and so apparently frank her accounts of friendships with a great number of men, all of which somehow sound platonic. Thus she tells how Jules Sandeau locked her up once, but not that he stayed in her apartment; that she nursed Alfred de Musset through a long illness in Venice, where he "happened" to be, not that they had gone off there to spend the winter together. Nor does she mention that she had an affair with Alfred's doctor at the same time. (She explained, to her friends who wondered, that God had wanted her to love again.)

Thinking it over much later, Juliette Adam explained that George Sand's love affairs were based on friendship and pity, and that while she knew how to give this kind of love, the men did not know how to receive it. The novelist herself came to the view that the Saint-Simonians had soiled the question of love and declared that if she had her life to live over again, she would be chaste.[13] She felt that the two great passions of her life had not been erotic at all, but motherhood and friendship. She certainly lost the conviction that all of society had to be overturned for women to be free. In her earlier romantic period she acted out in life, as she wrote in her novels, the principle that to love with one's total being was all that mattered, and that when one affair turned to disillusion, it was right to seek another.[14]

Her works satisfied an enormous unfilled demand. "Why talk of the

*George Eliot on George Sand: "I cannot read six pages of hers without feeling that it is given her to delineate human passion and its results . . . with such truthfulness . . . that one might live a century with nothing but one's own dull faculties and not know so much as those six pages will suggest" (Redinger, 152).

morality of my books?" she asked the judge who upbraided her when she sought a separation decree. "They are everywhere, people acquire them, they read them avidly. If you blame them, blame the century too, or better, blame only the century because it alone is guilty, since readers always create authors."[15] Hardly one child in a thousand was conceived in real love, she felt, though the will of providence was contradicted every time a man and woman kissed without a union of their hearts and intelligence.

Eventually, whether from difficulties with her husband or the sheer hardship of never being able to play with her children, read books of her choice, attend the theater, or see friends because of the pressing need to write for money, she began to wonder why she had surrendered half her revenue. Nohant was hers, but the law made her husband its master. In 1838 one of her lawyer friends filed a suit in which she requested a legal separation, her estate, the custody of her daughter, and the right to be known as Mme Sand. She won her case, but the father still insisted on certain rights over their son, a delicate boy whom he wanted to toughen up by sending him to a hated school. At one point in the controversy, M. Dudevant kidnaped Solange too, dragging her off screaming at a time when George was in Paris attending to her invalid mother. All of these acts were within a father's prerogatives, but after a handsome cash settlement, Casimir Dudevant surrendered his rights. Young Maurice was to be allowed to study art, and George was left with Nohant and a second house, which, though heavily mortgaged, could be used for Solange's dowry after it had been paid off in ten years—this from a mother who had so heartily decried the whole dowry system in her youth.

In the 1848 upheaval she worked for the Provisional Government as a propagandist, but refused to become interested in woman suffrage, and rather looked down on the agitators for such cause: "I have not the honor of knowing a single one of the ladies who form clubs and direct journals";[16] and she shortly retired to Nohant, where she lived for a great many years enjoying the roles of grandmother, hostess, and honored *femme de lettres.*

༄ One of the women who responded strongly to George Sand's early novels, with their cry of women against the tyranny of men, was Marie d'Agoult. She was almost an exact contemporary of the novelist, but had a more protected life, into which had come the troubling effect of this still-mysterious writer at a deeply unhappy period.

Born Marie de Flavigny, she spent her girlhood partly with her rich bourgeois grandmother in Frankfurt and partly in the high society of Paris. She once explained the effects of this mixed heritage. When her German half fell poetically in love with a certain Auguste de Legarde, her French half restrained her from uttering the word that would have made him hers, and he departed not knowing of her sentiments.

This misunderstanding left her so despondent that she told her parents to find a husband for her. Being famous for her beauty and her accomplishments in music and languages, and bringing with her a considerable dowry, she was soon provided with a brilliant match in the person of the Comte d'Agoult. He turned out to be noble, generous, and dignified, but unequal to her quick wit and her aversion to being dominated. She soon began to ask herself "by what unbelievable power of custom" this marriage had taken place. Though she was the mother of two charming children and had the almost total liberty that accrued to a woman of her status and fortune, these did not make up for the complete separation of heart and soul from her husband. She tried to console herself by adopting the Christian resignation advised by her confessor and by educating her children, only to find her own education deficient.[17]

About this time she read *Lélia* and began to meet many people who were sick of the old form of religion and government and had visions of a better-ordered society. Thirty years later, looking back on the 1830s, in words strikingly like those of George Sand, Marie explained that it would be hard to make her readers imagine the difference in climate. Youth in the 1860s, she felt, held itself on guard against excess and was afraid of suffering, but in the romantic heyday of the 1830s young people were tormented by the desire for an ideal life and were willing to try out the extraordinary, the impossible. And in this mood she learned that communities were being founded outside of Christianity, announcing the revolution, the priesthood of art, the search for a female messiah, and a new role for women.[18]

Among these ardent spirits was Franz Liszt, the Hungarian composer. His playing delighted her musical temperament, and there was no social impediment to keep him from coming to her house every day. For a while they met with pleasure and without tension, and he told her of the preachings of the Abbé Lamenais, who wanted a renewed and purified Christianity, of the writings of Lord Byron, or of Saint-Simonian meetings. They even talked of starting a Saint-Simonian center for artists and workers to meet. Intimacy grew, until one day, when she was crying, Liszt told her he loved her, they stretched out their hands, their eyes met, and a moment later they had sworn to love each other without end or limit.[19] The obstacles that the difference in status and education placed in the way only gave them an intensity of passion that more sober periods never know. For weeks they cherished their intimacy in secret; then one of Marie's daughters fell ill and died, and she was plunged into guilt and unhappiness. Liszt had decided to go to Switzerland and came to tell her so. "You are leaving?" she asked. "*We* are leaving," said he. And a week later they arrived in Geneva.[20]

They wanted to be alone together; Liszt needed time to compose, and he urged Marie to study. Later they moved to Italy, where she bore him three children (one of whom became Cosima Wagner). Nevertheless, rifts developed. Liszt loved his lionizing and was eager to return to the concert circuit, where he could earn money to support the children. He told her that the three years with her had made a man out of him, and he urged her to create a new life for herself out of her own resources; but when he told her that he was going to Vienna, she fainted dead away and became seriously ill. Unaware of her own capacity, she felt only the brutality of his advice. Thinking about it years later, rereading the letters for the purpose of writing her memoirs, she noticed how much despair, how many tears, sobs, and griefs there were between them, and asked herself whether this was what it took to grow up.[21] The separation occurred in October, 1839.

Back in Paris, at the age of thirty-four, Marie decided to live by herself. Her husband, it is true, was willing to take her back, but drew the line at all the Liszt children, and she refused to cut herself off from the chance of seeing them. (They lived for the time being with Liszt's mother.) Work saved her. She explained that her thinking processes had languished while passion took over, and now she discovered how ignorant her schooling had left her; she began to study seriously, and to reflect on science, philosophy, and history. She found pleasure in sharing her studies with her children—reading Dante with them, for example—and in five years she found herself to be a new person. She still cherished within herself the image of Liszt, and so, apparently, she never took another lover, though she had several suitors and a wide circle of friends. Among those suitors was Emile de Girardin, whose wife, Delphine, had been a girlhood friend of Marie. Unable to seduce her, Girardin yet took the trouble to get Marie started as a writer, picking out for her the pen name under which she became another famous mystery for Paris—Daniel Stern.[22] Her *Essai sur la liberté* (1847) established her right to be considered one of the most powerful voices for feminism, and she produced the most dispassionate and accurate contemporary account of the 1848 revolution.

Even for one so fortunately placed, there developed trouble over the custody of the children. Liszt's children, of course, were debarred by law from inheriting either her name or her fortune, and after a few years, when Liszt acquired a new and jealous mistress, he cruelly forbade any communication with them. He became furious when the two girls, aged thirteen and fifteen, stole off to visit their mother, removed them from the school they were in, and found a strict governess, giving orders that they were never to see their mother again until they came of age.*[23]

Although Marie says that she fought like a lioness for her children, and protested before God and man and all mothers against the injustice that was done her, she felt that children by themselves could not fill a woman's life.[24] They took up only a limited amount of time, she found, and women's interests and talents were as varied as men's.[25]

Her plea in her essay on liberty was that women's potentialities ought not to be constricted. The essay was not an immediate success; in fact, it did not receive due recognition until the publishers insisted on reprinting it in 1862. The 1847 edition hit France at a time of emotional

*Later, to remove them still further, he sent them to Berlin, where they boarded with the von Bülow, family. Here Cosima fell in love with Hans von Bülow, her first husband.

slump, after the romantic excitement of the 1830s had subsided and before the political events of 1848 swept theory away. But up to that time it was probably the best philosophical statement by a woman on the subject of a politically free state and is therefore well worth examining. The modern conscience, its author said, was displeased and repelled by arbitrary or privileged behavior.*[26]

To one form of arbitrary behavior, tyranny in the home, she devoted a whole section, arguing that such a situation was permitted only because women and children had no part in the life of the state and lived isolated from public affairs. In addition to giving women a share in government, she proposed a set of graded political rights that would initiate children slowly as they grew up. She saw all around her the consequences of this displacement of women: hypocrisy and disloyalty in society, aridity of life, the desolation of marriage, and the impoverishment of the race. The women she saw were bored or boring, incapable of discernment, ignorant of hygiene, incompetent to manage even the simplest household affairs. She envisaged better-educated wives; attractive enough to keep their husbands and loyal enough to stick with them. But divorce must be allowed. In a society that resisted capital punishment and no longer made monastic vows irrevocable, why should marriage be the one indissoluble tie?

By the time of the second edition, there had been such a change in public sentiment that she no longer felt herself a voice crying in the wilderness. So many things had happened that the outlook for women was entirely different. In 1847 no one could imagine a life for them other than one of obedience to husband, the requirement to please socially, and the duty to bear children. The suggestion that women take part in the running of the government was a subject for ribaldry. In the interim, the revolutions of 1848, the influence of the socialist schools and of various writers like John Stuart Mill, Wendell Phillips, Henry Ward Beecher, and, in France, Edouard Laboulaye, and the fact that people had found that sterile discipline led to moral collapse—all these things created a fresh outlook.†

ᶜᵒ⌐ The most ardent and consistent advocate of a wholly different life for women was Flora Tristan.

*Here follows a touching—and prescient—section on the relations of mankind with lower creation. She knew that she was "writing for the future" here, that people were not ready yet to listen to a plea for the protection of plants and the affectionate training of animals into all the vigor and grace of which they were capable. She had a sense of the closeness between humanity and the natural world and made a plea for directing water courses, purifying the atmosphere, and controlling disasters, with the purpose of multiplying the joy of existence for all creatures (Agoult, *Liberté*, 100).

†Another interesting section of the 1862 edition is her discussion of evolution and natural selection according to Darwin. She looked for evolution to change from natural selection to social selection, and she saw this process as culminating in a more perfect creature, a superman (Agoult, *Liberté*, 291).

Her first intimation of the unfairness of life may have been the imputation of illegitimacy, caused by the fact that her Spanish father and French refugee mother had been married in a religious ceremony only, not the civil service that was legally necessary in Napoleonic Spain. The Tristan family held great wealth and power in Peru—in fact, her uncle eventually became the first president when that country declared its independence—but the allowance on which the young couple were to live was precarious because of dangers in war and transit, and when Flora's father died, it ceased completely. Mme Tristan's house in France was confiscated as alien property, and she could not establish rights as a widow for lack of a marriage certificate.

Flora, who was born in 1803, spent her adolescent years in the poorest quarter of Paris, among beggars and prostitutes, and at fifteen she had to go to work. She tells us her first love affair foundered on the question of her birth, and the second failed when the young man took alarm at the intensity of her passion, attributed to her Spanish origin. At seventeen she married her employer, who was named Chazal. Various theories are held about this marriage. She herself tells us that her mother forced her into it, but this may be a later rationalization, for there exist some passionate letters in which she lays out for her fiancé her intentions of being a very good wife. In any case, after three years and two babies, she left him, though pregnant for the third time. Leaving the children with her mother, she earned her living in various obscure ways; at one time she was a clerk, at another she apparently went to England as a ladies' maid, and from those experiences she learned a great deal about what women had to suffer in a society with so many prejudices.*[27]

She declared that her husband liked to gamble and tried to force her into prostitution, while he insisted that she was overly ambitious. Her earliest socialist biographer explained that at this period she had not yet gotten over her inherited aristocratic snobbery against petit bourgeois life.[28] Chazal pursued her, as he had every legal right to do, took their son back to live with him, and then asked for the little girl, Aline, too. (One child had died.) Flora kept fleeing across France, until she found a pension keeper who agreed to hide and take care of Aline while Flora made the long voyage to South America to claim the inheritance that should be waiting for her there. She carried with her Simon de Bolívar's affirmation that her parents, old friends of his, had really been married. After a romantic trip under southern skies she reached Peru, only to find the old grandmother who had promised to leave her a substantial inheritance had just died. The other heirs each got 800,000 francs, but they were unwilling to disgorge a share for her. For some months she remained at their princely villa until revolution swept the country, and she began to discover both the widespread nature of social injustice and her

---

*Her modern biographer, J. L. Puech, suggests that this position humiliated her and that she made a point of destroying the letters that would throw light upon the time she spent in England.

own talents as a political organizer. Her sufferings gave her sympathy for the underdogs, but she was unwilling to take up arms against her own uncle and kin. So, in 1834, she decided to return to France with the promise of a modest allowance from the family.

An anonymous letter informed her husband that she was back in the country, and rich to boot, so he conceived the idea of kidnapping Aline to hold her for ransom. Flora, meanwhile, was writing her first pamphlet, an essay on women traveling alone and on the need for a sort of Travellers Aid Society to help them and devise means for them to get to know women of other countries. In her eagerness to redress the wrongs she had uncovered she naturally examined the socialist theories of the day and turned to Fourier as the most hopeful prophet.[29] She also admired some of the Saint-Simonian views of women but was unsympathetic to Enfantin. To Fourier she wrote, "I can assure you that you will find in me an energy not common in my sex, a need to do good, and a profound gratitude to all who will give me the means of being useful . . . . Give me work, oh, give me work!"[30]

Aline was a day student at school and had never laid eyes on her father (she was born in 1825 after Flora's flight from home), but on October 31, 1835, when she was ten, Chazal lay in wait for her outside the school and grabbed her in spite of her screams. When Flora caught up with them the next day, Aline threw herself into her mother's arms, but Chazal was able to persuade the police that Flora was a thief. After a court hearing, Aline was put in a boarding school where both parents had the right to visit her, though Flora had to pay the fees, using her South American Uncle Pio's allowance. It was not long before the parents quarreled about the visitation rights and the father got an order to put the child in a convent school where she was not to receive any visits whatsoever and was not even allowed to go out for walks with her class for fear that her mother might see her. Aline's reaction was to run away, seeking refuge in her mother's apartment. This time Chazal, having sued the convent for negligence, won the right to have the child live with him and her brother. Flora's indignation turned to horror when she received a smuggled note from Aline stating that she was forced to sleep in the bed with the two males, and the child fled again in such a physical and mental state that she was practically unrecognizable. This time Flora got an order for Chazal's arrest. He deposed that he possessed only one bed, and that, in order to keep warm, Aline had begged to get into it.

About this time Flora published the story of her trip to Peru, under the title *Pérégrinations d'une paria*. It was also a study of social conditions, and although a literary success, it had the double effect of stopping Uncle Pio's pension and making the affairs of the Chazal family public.

Flora now sued for separation from her husband and for custody of her daughter. In the proceedings, Chazal's lawyer* stated that Flora was

*Who happened to be Jules Favre.

living "in the dwelling of the man she preferred to her husband," but this individual, a painter, was never called as a witness, perhaps because, as her biographer suggests, at least one of her lovers was of sufficiently high position to cover up any such testimony.[31] Unable to get justice as he perceived it, Chazal became deranged and bought a pistol, announcing that he was going to kill Flora. He did actually shoot her in the shoulder, though not fatally, on a street corner. After a sensational trial, he was sent up for twenty years, and Flora won the right to resume her maiden name and the complete custody of both her children.

After publishing a tract urging the re-establishment of divorce, Flora went once more to Britain and composed a remarkable social study of all classes and of the English way of life, *Promenades dans Londres* (*Walks Through London*), in 1839. She attended sessions of both houses of Parliament, though women were not admitted to the gallery at that time, and she had to borrow male attire from the Turkish Ambassador. (The English M.P. to whom she first proposed such a ruse was so shocked that he walked out of the room without so much as a word.)*

She also attended a Chartist convention. Here she found reinforcement for what she had come to feel was her own vocation. This was to be the creation of a great union of disadvantaged people, including working-class men and *all* women of whatever class, since all were universally oppressed. Male writers, she said had often begged women to tell the story of their wrongs, but only George Sand had done so and she under an assumed name. Flora thought that her own story would help make vivid the nature of the injustice under which women labored. Political rights did not interest her particularly, but she wanted education and work, the right of divorce, and the elimination of paternal despotism. She had great hopes that women could get about the world more easily, so that city women could learn from country women's sound sense and natural manners, while the country women could profit from the progress and higher education of the former. They should all be freed from being kept at menial chores while their brothers went to school, and freed as well from marriage to unknown young men.[32] A woman who had income from a decent job, she felt, could unite herself honorably to a man, inside or outside of marriage, but a union for the sake of money, whether in marriage or not, would always be prostitution. What really crushed women's hearts, after all, was the system of property, and she reported that many of them were becoming furious over its power to hurt them.[33]

She wanted children to be raised in the spirit of universal brotherhood. She did not think that ideas sprang naturally into any child's head;

*In 1822 Maria Edgeworth had been able to listen to a debate in the House of Commons by mounting into a garret. A single candle in a lantern was all the light she had. By climbing on chairs, she could peer through a hole in the ceiling that permitted a view only of the chandelier below (A. J. C. Hare, *Edgeworth*, 2: 66). In 1840, when plans for a new building were being discussed, a ladies' gallery was suggested and rejected with derision (Woman's Rights and Duties, 1: 347).

they had to be put there, and to get the right ones, mothers needed education. They should know how to check up on their child's physical condition and be sure they had plenty of exercise, pure food, no constraining clothes, or clothes in which it was wrong to get dirty, no corsets at any age, and no degrading punishments. Let the guiding principle for teaching be the child's own *"pourquoi?"*

Her heart went out to the working class, where women were often physically abused.[34] She noticed that women of this class were usually affectionate mothers until their children were three or four, but since they had no techniques for handling growing independence, they tended to brutalize their older children, which did not induce better behavior but only turned them *méchant*. With new education and a sense of equality, women would win their husbands' respect, and to help develop ideas that couples could share, she drew up a list of books suitable for reading aloud.

Flora eventually sacrificed her life in an effort to set up a grand union with these aims. Her thesis was the faith of all the utopians: since individualism was the disease of the age, association would be the cure. What made her ideal different, and what makes some people claim that she anticipated Marx, was its universality. She was not content, like Saint-Simon and Fourier, to start with small communities. If all the seven million workers in France gave two francs apiece a year, there would be enough momey to set up a workers' "palace," a refuge where children could be taught and old people retire in comfort. One such establishment would lead to another, until there were enough for all who needed them: pleasant places, she imagined, with such luxuries as running water. She also wanted to set up an office of the tribune, a sort of ombudsman, to represent the workers in disputes with their employers, and she speculated on what man would be good for the office.[35] She thought of Beaumont, Tocqueville's companion in America and Ireland; Louis Blanc, who had a scheme for combatting unemployment by national workshops; Enfantin, who, she concluded, was too eager to regiment people; and Fourier's successor, Victor Considérant. Although she intended to begin her work in France, the union was to be universal. The term later adopted by Marx, "international," she specifically rejected on the grounds that the word implied the possibility of *national* rivalry or war.[36]

To get her project launched she required, first of all, a thousand francs to finance publication of her little book, *Union Ouvrière* (*Workers' Union*). After pondering how to raise the sum for several sleepless nights, she decided to make the rounds of Paris on foot, knocking on every possible door from Baron Rothschild's on down. She even wrote to the King. One peer of France contributed, as did twenty-six women, including George Sand, and many actors and literary people. The list of subscribers, printed at the front of the book, is headed with Mme Flora Tristan herself, at 100 francs; then Mlle Aline Tristan, modiste, at 5; Jules

Laure, the painter with whom Flora was living, gave 20; Marie Madeleine, her servant, 1.5; and she included her water carrier at half a franc and her laundress at one.

By 1843 she was ready to announce public meetings in Paris at which she would talk and read chapters from the book, believing that the working class needed only to be told about this beautiful project in order to adopt it. Unfortunately this hope proved unfulfilled, and Flora soon began to be impatient with them for their ignorance, their dirty habits, and presumably their unwillingness to listen to one so determined to devote herself to their improvement. When one of her committees actually voted to start organizing, to try to get a representative elected to the Chamber, it nevertheless infuriated her by making changes in her politically tactless wording. Forthwith she dissolved the committee. The members complained that she was too stubborn to listen; she retorted that God had put words into her head and no one had the right to change them. They would soon find out how she could fight, she said. "With such people it is necessary to be made of iron."[37]

It is apparent that she was not easy to get on with. The Abbé Constant, who was supposed to have been one of her lovers,* said that she considered herself the female messiah;[38] later he added that what she wanted was vengeance, not justice or equality.[39] Still, while she antagonized some people, she certainly had the ability to inspire others; her charisma persuaded people to go on to do her work. She forced Arnold Ruge, the German journalist, to exclaim, "What a woman in her holy anger! She will seize the flag and march ahead!"[40] (Constant called this the power to "swallow you smiling.")[41]

Personalities like hers usually ignore opposition. "To make a book for the people is to throw a drop of water into the sea," she wrote. "Once my book is published, I shall have another job—that is, to go myself . . . from town to town, from one end of France to the other to talk with the workers *who do not know how to read*, and to those who have *no time to read*" (emphasis hers).[42] And so she planned her last, fatal journey, following the ancient route of *compagnonnage* that traveling journeymen had used for centuries. She started out in April, 1844, apparently contracted typhoid fever somewhere en route, and died in November in Bordeaux.

Her greatest success came at Lyons, where trouble with the police only increased the workers' confidence in her, and here she attracted a devoted follower, a laundress named Eléonore Blanc whom she called her "Saint John."† Eléonore later wrote a little book in which she described the feeling of new life born in her when she heard Flora speak; she followed her and nursed her during her illness.[43] The police at

*He kept his clerical title though he quit the seminary when he discovered that he was not cut out for celibacy.

†At Lyons, too, Flora was touched that fathers would come to listen to her after they had lost confidence in deputies, priests, and doctors.

Marseilles tried to discredit Flora by sending *agents provocateurs* to seduce her and show her up as a prostitute; at Montpellier the hotel did not accept unaccompanied women; but nothing stopped her except death itself. At Bordeaux she met, and inspired, Charles and Elisa Lemmonier, both Saint-Simonians, who redirected their energy to the lifelong task of carrying on her work of internationalism and women's education.

Flora's history is not quite finished without a word about Aline. Many people rallied round after Flora's death, even George Sand, who had never liked her personally, and Pauline Roland, the socialist. George Sand explained: "Mme Roland took this young girl, who proper name I don't know but who is the daughter of Flora and who seems as gentle and good as her mother was imperious and ill-tempered. This child had the air of an angel; her melancholy, her grief, and her lovely eyes, her isolation, her modest and affectionate air went straight to my heart. Did she love her mother? Why, then, were they so separated? What sort of apostolate can make one forget and send so far away into a millinery shop a being so charming and so adorable? I would much rather that we did something for this girl than to set up a monument to her mother, who was never sympathetic to me in spite of her courage and convictions. There was much vanity there."[44] They put Aline in the same school that Solange Sand had attended, but she did not remain for long. She married a Breton sailor and newspaperman, Clovis Gauguin, and when his liberal politics cost him his job during the 1852 *coup d'état*, she took him to Peru to visit her relatives there. Thus the earliest memories of her child, Paul Gauguin, were formed in tropical luxury.

ᐧᗖ Of all her contemporaries, Hortense Allart may provide the best prototype of feminine independence, although she is much less well known than the individuals just described. First in her life and then in her writings of feminism, she insisted on the right of women to make their own choices. "I have felt that the lot of women was often so unhappy that they would like to see one who followed freely her own heart, and who placed love and liberty above all else in her life,"[45] she wrote in the introduction to her autobiographical novel. George Sand, who called Hortense "one of the glories of her sex,"[46] contrasted her life with that of Marie d'Agoult. Hortense had two illegitimate children, whom she nursed and brought up herself, giving them her name and her time and devoting to them her life; whereas Liszt's mistress abandoned hers, forgot them, and let them be raised in wretched lodgings while she herself lived in luxury. Although this judgment is hardly fair to Marie, Hortense was certainly closer to her sons than any of the other mothers here under discussion.

She was born in 1801 in Milan, where her father was helping the French conquerors to liquidate the old Austrian administration. Through her mother she was related to Delphine de Girardin, née Gay, and the rest of the remarkable tribe of Gay women. Though her birthplace was Italy, she tells us that her personality was created at a country seat near Paris, amid fresh woods, pure air, and transparent water. Her childhood was simple and her religion pious until her free-thinking father caught her at prayer and made her read Voltaire. George Sand wished that there were more details about this period, but in recounting her life story, Hortense moved quickly to her first great emotional experience, a passion for an older woman whom she called Laura, and to whom, she said, she owed her delight in being alive and the courage to write. A bit later she began to feel bewildered by her own sexual agitation at the little dances her father arranged on Sundays. She supposed that he would have found her a very good husband if he had not died when she was only seventeen.*

Lacking parental guidance, she fell deeply in love with a man whom it was impossible to marry. In life he was a married Portuguese who had five children, but her novelistic account changes him into a Jesuit priest, equally inaccessible.[47] The pair tried separation, and then came together more passionately than ever, discussed everything, from politics to morality and their own feelings, until finally they made love and Hortense became pregnant. They decided that the best place to have the baby was Italy, so in November, 1825, she bravely set out alone, bearing no grudge. Later on she wrote that she would advise any girl in her situation to yield to love rather than to combat it, because the girl with a lover is at least alive, while the one who avoids love is like a derailed machine.[48] When Marie d'Agoult was having trouble with Liszt, Hortense told her, "You don't forgive enough. As for me, I am for infinite forgiveness."[49]

She had hoped that Jerome (as she called her lover) would get to Italy in time for the birth, but he callously failed to do so. Nevertheless, she soon collected around her a circle of interesting and learned men. It was typical of her style that an Englishman escorted her (dutch treat) to Pisa and Leghorn while they read Bacon's *Novum Organum* together. She chose to nurse her baby herself and consequently could not do as so many other mothers did and send the child away, but she writes serenely that this period of her life was fine, peaceful, and independent. Later she had a second illegitimate child, and visitors recorded how unselfconsciously she suckled him while carrying on a conversation, and later, how devotedly she taught both boys history, languages, and literature, and "made them into men."[50]

Among literary Frenchmen in Italy at that time, René de Chateaubriand, was prominent as the French ambassador to Rome. Hortense had adored his novel *Atala* and wondered if she dared to call on

---

*She tells us that after she turned eighteen, "those torments already described by other women, came to announce the precious duties of maternity and tenderness to which God has called us" (Allert, *Enchantements*, 30). About this time she witnessed the birth of a child. The thing that moved her—besides the interesting process itself—was the happiness of the mother in nursing the baby.

the great man. Finally she wrote a short note, to which he responded with an invitation. He was charming, she tells us—and charmed—charmed enough to call on her the next day, stick in hand, flower in buttonhole. He was sixty at the time, but apparently insatiable for women, and they enjoyed a liaison for the next twenty years.* He pronounced her a genius after reading her novel about Jerome, thus treating her as a perfect equal. Later, in Paris, the two used to meet regularly at the botanical gardens, dining at a restaurant and then making love in a secluded spot before driving back into the city.

In this and other cases, her philosophy was that you could only really know a great man when you had him for a lover. In the course of her life, she attracted an extraordinary number of interesting men; Béranger, Thiers, Lamennais, Sainte-Beuve, and Henry Bulwer were only among the more distinguished of those who were named as her lovers, and at the end of her life she looked back at them: "O my lovers, my charming lovers—lovers for a day, for ten years, lovers of the imagination, lovers of the heart—how much it all comes back in memory with delight when one lives alone and oppressed."[51]

In comparing some of these men, she decided that Jerome had been the important sentimental influence in her life; he dominated her emotions for years and years. Chateaubriand and later Sainte-Beuve had been the most satisfying intellectually, but Bulwer was the man who awakened her senses.[52] (Even Chateaubriand, praising her tenderness, had complained about her physical frigidity, but until she met Bulwer she had no idea of what he was talking about.)†[53]

Henry Bulwer, a Member of Parliament and brother of Edward Bulwer-Lytton, the author of *The Last Days of Pompeii*, fell violently in love with Hortense when she was on a visit to England. Though he proposed marriage, she felt that it would be unfair to inflict on him her lingering regrets for Jerome and the presence of her four-year-old son, but she agreed to become his mistress. Bulwer set her up in an apartment in London, still willing to marry her, even if secretly (to preserve his inheritance), but Hortense hated England and feared that marriage would be an intolerable yoke. When Henry began to dally with other women, she went back to France, asking herself whether he had found a new mistress with more passion, or perhaps one who did not read books!

For all this time Hortense had been writing. Even mediocre writers could not help writing, she said, and it must be admitted that she was really a mediocre writer herself: "The bee and the ant have no vanity: they go, they go by a higher law. People of letters, good or bad ones, go in

---

*As for Mme Récamier, his official mistress back in Paris, to whom Chateaubriand wrote every day, he explained to Hortense that she was neither a love nor a friendship, but merely a habit.

†"I had known up to this point an intellectual love where the senses—pushed away and combatted—languished without awakening. Now I discovered the sacred Venus, or the sacrament of love out of which priests realized the sacrament of marriage."

the same spirit. They work, they work, they publish, they publish. It's a higher law."[54]

Hortense owned a country house at Herblay, and here she retreated when her son was seven, to start a new life of study and work. Although she was still emotionally pulled back and forth by Bulwer, she managed to get her novels and histories written, and all the while her insatiable mind was absorbing new subjects.

As a girl she had studied Latin and poetry with a tutor, until a doctor, fearing for her health, had ordered all her books to be burned; later, with an uncle, she undertook history and philosophy. In her years at Paris she had read algebra and astronomy under masters. Jerome had read *The Wealth of Nations* with her and discussed it in detail. In Italy she took up history and law (Bentham, Vico, Machiavelli), and in London she dug into parliamentary papers.*

When she was sick and upset, she studied Mme de Staël, who became for a time her model, and one of her first books was a biography of that lady. Her schedule was exact. During her year in Rome she used to work in the mornings in order to save the afternoons for sightseeing, and both parts of the day seemed like fun.

Naturally she wanted to examine the ideas of the Saint-Simonian school in Paris, and so she arranged a few conversations with Enfantin, but was repelled by his sexual advances. It may have been here that she became interested in women's problems. This concern soon went far beyond the boundaries of any particular sect, and she began attending women's rights meetings every night; in 1839 she put the fruits of her pondering into a book, *La Femme et la démocratie de nos temps* (*Woman and the Democracy of Our Times*). Its burden was that while most women will be mothers and nurses, just as most men are workers and artisans, if *all* women were free and well treated, *some* women would arrive at professional success. The first step would be to educate French girls at the expense of the state, and educate them at least as well as the slaves of Constantinople, trained as they were in the arts, languages, music, and history. Then, to help poor girls, why not create a fund out of the dowries of dead girls? And why not marry priests to Sisters of Charity; and why not let religious women be ordained too, so that they might confess young girls? No one wept, she exclaimed, at the injustice done to women; yet it was one of the crying shames of the century. Still, she was not for a general democratic leveling but for the encouragement of special talent. Freedom, she felt, depended on "exceptional laws."

In 1837 she returned to Italy with her son, who was now eleven; here she continued his education, taking him to the theater and explaining about religion. On this trip she met the father of her second child. Several people disapproved of this second child, among them Chateaubriand, who told her that at her age she would die. This only made her

---

*Her writings include histories of the republics of Athens and of Florence, an essay on political history from the barbarian invasions until 1848, and a volume on "interior religion."

laugh because he had often expressed a wish to have a child by her; besides, she believed that freely chosen pregnancy and childbearing should be a plank in the platform for women's emancipation. After women had obtained the freedom of the press, she claimed, it was time to announce the freedom of having babies when they chose. She was elected to the Academy of Arezzo at this time, and for her inaugural speech she read some pages out of her book on women.[55]

It is hard to imagine what led her to the disatrous mistake of her late marriage. M. de Méritens was of noble family, though with little money, and she admits that she was pleased at the idea of entering the French nobility and carrying thither the principles of women's emancipation. The experiment did not last long, but at least it showed her from experience what marital rights could mean legally. Amidst furious scenes her husband demonstrated how horrible the law could be when it ordered the submission of frailty to force. Now she became convinced that women should demand not to be treated like harem slaves; nor should they have to suffer the indignity of exposing their bruises or broken limbs in court.[56] Eventually she fled, throwing her wedding ring into a river as she drove toward Paris. Chateaubriand, highly amused, offered her five hundred francs to start a new life, but she returned the money, insisting that she who had never known a yoke need not succumb now. She returned to Herblay with her two boys and rejoiced in her approaching old age, as she had rejoiced in all other phases of life. In 1854 she wrote to George Sand: "I marvel—do you do the same?—to see how men carry off the evening of life less successfully than women. Men get discouraged and they suffer, for it seems as if youth had taken everything out of them."[57]

ᏻ The changes that Marie d'Agoult noticed between the 1830s and the 1860s were vividly exhibited in the life of Juliette Adam. She was born in 1836, and thus one whole generation later than George Sand and Marie d'Agoult, both of whose mantles she inherited. She was equally concerned with women's rights, but instead of going off to Italy with a lover, she demonstrated her convictions by a second marriage to a husband of her choice, not with an affair, nor yet with celibacy.

George Sand and she used to talk about the difference. The older woman realized that the life of her youth was no longer possible. In the thirties people lived exclusively inside themselves, she said, while artists of all sorts formed an aristocratic caste. The new world of the 1860s was far more democratic, with art produced for the masses, with less hunting for the impossible dream, probably less suffering, and a great increase in the number of women who valued their own intellectual and moral worth. Previously there might have been half a dozen such women; by the time they were talking, there were at least fifty, according to their reckoning.[58]

Juliette was an only child, brought up by her grandmother, whose money had enabled her son-in-law, Juliette's father, to become a doctor.

Dr. Lambert was a typical character of the Age of Reason, so free-thinking and egalitarian that he expressed the wish that his daughter would not have a dowry, and indeed that she might marry a workman.* Juliette herself resisted passionately the need for a dowry, which her grandmother was determined to provide, even selling off a beloved garden for this purpose.[59] But she also resisted the idea of marrying outside her class. Proposals began to be made, for her dowry and her person, when she was still only fourteen years old, and this led to a number of family quarrels. The grandmother finally settled on a M. La Messine, largely because he promised to let the old lady live with them in Paris for half of each year. Dr. Lambert was so opposed to the marriage that he refused to come to the wedding, which occurred in 1852, and in fact it turned out almost immediately that Juliette was one of the worst-matched young wives in all of France. She was too proud to appeal right away, as she realized later she should have done, but instead waited to tell her father until after her baby was born. By this time even the grandmother had turned against M. La Messine, he having coldly informed her that he had no intention of letting her share his house in Paris and had only promised to do so in order to collect the dowry. Juliette believed that remorse over her dreadful mistake led to the grandmother's death by half-willful slow starvation.[60]

Meanwhile Juliette, like most of the other bright young spirits in Paris, ran into the Saint-Simonians, and in fact the aging Enfantin, at sixty-two, considered her, a ravishingly pretty twenty-two, as his last chance at finding a possible female messiah. At this point she proved that she belonged to the new generation. She rejected the honor specifically because she did not believe in free love ("Woman needs a certain dignity"),[61] although she attended a Saint-Simonian banquet in the company of Arlès-Dufour, a pacifist, feminist, and friend of John Stuart Mill, and, soon decided to leave her husband on the advice of her Saint-Simonian friends. Her father said at first that, having married, she ought to stick with it, but his libertarian sentiments soon reawoke, and he welcomed her home, advising her that the only way a woman could win true liberty was by working, writing, and becoming known. He promised to finance her first book.

Her first piece of published writing was no book, however, but simply an anonymous letter in response to a newspaper article by Alphonse Karr in which the author glibly stated that there was no young and pretty woman in all of France with the courage not to wear the crinoline. Juliette wore the full skirts of her day, but never put hoops beneath them. "There *is* a pretty woman of twenty," she wrote, "who

*Later, after Juliette's second marriage, he lived on the left bank of the Seine among scientists, while she lived on the right among politicians. During the Paris Exposition of the later sixties, no member of the general public was admitted on the day that the Emperor was to open the show. Dr. Lambert circumvented this rule by disguising himself as a wagon driver carrying in supplies.

does not wear the crinoline, who has never worn it . . . and that one is I, Juliette."[62] This letter was printed in the *Siècle*, and when the paper reached her provincial home, she burst into tears, overcome at seeing her work in print.

When Proudhon's book, *La Justice*, came out, announcing his violently anti-feminist ideas,* Dr. Lambert advised his daughter to read it, particularly the vicious attack on the women writers of the day, George Sand and Marie d'Agoult, whom Juliette worshipped. Not feeling capable of responding to such an important man herself, Juliette's first idea was to ask Jenny d'Héricourt to do it.† Getting a negative response, and believing passionately that women must be defended *as women*, Juliette decided that she herself must rise to the occasion. Reminding her father of his promise to pay for her first book without telling him what it was, for she knew that generally he admired Proudhon, she extracted a thousand francs and launched *Idées antiproudhoniennes* (1858).

Proudhon's discussion of the female sex contained, she declared, "things which every woman who knows how to hold a pen has the right to regard as personal insults."[63] First of all she attacked Proudhon's coldness, his hostility to love, a force she thought caused even the beasts to sing.[64] Because he saw in woman only the female, he completely failed to comprehend how two beings of different sex might fuse, mingling their intellects, enhancing their personalities. He actually seemed to take satisfaction in his belief that marriage was the graveyard of love, while she felt that marriage was to love as the fruit to the flower—an institution for the sake of children, pleasure, the moral growth of individuals, the perfecting of the race, and, in fact, for infinite progress. It is plain that ideas about marriage had advanced greatly since the thirties.

She next took up Proudhon's effort to prove women's constitutional inferiority. Were they really as physically inferior as he thought? Did not beauty and the power of endurance count as much as muscular strength? She neatly spiked his claim that men were worth far more than women because they produced more by pointing out first that his own socialism denied this sort of valuation when applied to males alone, and secondly that he disregarded the time spent in procreation and the nurturing of the young as economically wasted. She figured that women devoted an average of seven years per child to this task alone.

Work, she declared, was the only path of emancipation for women, and for this they needed education and training in a variety of occupations.[65] Why were they not permitted to become doctors? Why could not each mayor have an equal female official at his side, a mayoress who would see to infant schools, welfare, hospitals? Home life, she

*See Chapter 2.

†She was a natural person to ask because she was so good at pinning Proudhon's philosophical mistakes, but in this case her refusal to go farther was apparently based on the feeling that his personal vehemence against the immorality of Sand and Agoult was justified, while Juliette felt that they had to be defended (Stephens, 52).

believed, was important, but in itself it did not take a as much time as Proudhon imagined, and after her maternal tasks were over—and a woman as young as twenty-seven might be finished with motherhood— she should have a long life opening out for other useful activity.[66]

Shortly after the publication of this book, Marie d'Agoult wrote a congratulatory letter to its author. Juliette had used her own maiden name on the volume, leaving off the last letter and calling herself "Lamber." (She was trying to avoid funneling all the royalties to her husband, but he called it a low trick and took them anyway, as he was entitled to do.) Marie assumed that a man was the author and said, "It is surprising, sir, that you should have assumed a woman's name while we women write under masculine pseudonyms."[67] Juliette answered of course, that she was a woman, and the older writer immediately invited her to her salon.

Marie was so charmed with the little provincial that she made up her mind to turn her into a society lady. Juliette forthwith sent her daughter to live with the grandparents in the country and devoted herself to becoming a full-fledged member of the literary circles of Paris, where she commanded attention for her handsome appearance as well as for her original ideas. In 1864 Mme d'Agoult suggested that Juliette set up her own salon. "Mine will remain the great salon of the winter, and yours shall be the little summer salon," and she gave her direction for its management.[68] Both ladies were republicans, in the midst of the Second Empire, and their houses became the only places where republicans could talk freely.

The most colorful republican politician of this period—and well into the Third Republic—was Léon Gambetta, but he was considered a rough diamond. Emile de Girardin was eager to have Juliette meet him, but feared that Gambetta was not sufficiently refined. Without waiting for the introduction she invited him to her house anyway, where he appeared in a flannel shirt and nondescript coat. Even so Juliette let him take her in to dinner, touching him so deeply that he adopted her as his patroness and permitted her to turn him into a man of the world.

In 1867 Juliette's husband died, and the very next day she announced her engagement to M. Edmond Adam, a republican journalist. She had been having the customary troubles with M. La Messine, he insisted on pocketing her royalties, and she knew that if she or her daughter was to inherit the beautiful house that Dr. Lambert had bought in the south of France, he would be entitled to control that too. One day, on holiday there, she received a letter marked "pressing" from her lawyer, which she put aside for a while, too upset to open it and fearing new demands. Instead it bore the news that M. La Messine had died. At once she woke up her daughter, Alice, and cried, "Your father is dead." The two women embraced. Then they informed Dr. Lambert, whose comment was, "I know someone who will not be angry when I become his father-in-law." Juliette knew whom he meant, and dispatched a telegram stating, "I am a widow." Edmond Adam had loved her for a long time and had even talked of becoming naturalized in Switzerland so that they could marry there. Now they announced their engagement, and their friends sent immediate felicitations, except for Mme d'Agoult, who strongly advised Juliette not to take this step. "I didn't think you capable of such folly. An intelligent woman should remain free and the mistress of her own thoughts." "Alas," was Juliette's reply, "I have greater need for happiness than for liberty." And Mme d'Agoult was so disgusted that she never received Juliette again.[69]

Being dismissed by Mme d'Agoult only gave Juliette a chance to cultivate the acquaintance of George Sand, who had written to her at the time of her first book expressing gratitude for its ideas but explaining that the two could not meet at that moment because Sand had quarreled with Agoult.[70] If Juliette were ever to break with that patroness, George Sand hoped that she would call upon her, and now, in 1867, after nine years, Juliette was free to do so. Thro'bing with emotion, she called at the flat. She found the lady rolling a cigarette. Juliette could not say a word, and burst into tears, whereupon George threw away her cigarette, opened her arms, and Juliette flung herself into them with filial tenderness.[71] This friendship remained close until after the Paris Commune of 1871, at which time Juliette turned into a militarist and anti-communist, while Sand remained pacifist and humanitarian. They both regretted this break, but Juliette could not condone George Sand's permitting herself to be moved by pity for those Germans.[72]

One day in 1867, before the rupture, Mme Sand took her young friend to a restaurant to meet several writers. Dumas, who never liked women writers, told Juliette that the main thing was to love, love, love. Flaubert and the Goncourts endorsed the sentiment. "To learn that lesson, gentlemen, I have not waited for your words of wisdom. I love to love the man that I love, and he whom I love loves to see me write." "The fool!" muttered Dumas.[73]

The lovers' first quarrel came during their engagement. It so happened that each of them owned a house in the south of France, where they used to spend the winters. They were both very fond of their houses, and each wanted the other to move. M. Adam was afraid that if he took up residence at her place, the natives would call him "M. Lambert"; the disagreement lasted a good four days. After she promised to be nothing but "Mme Adam" and he agreed to do some extensive remodeling of her house, he declared himself willing to be the one to move. They were married two days after they returned to Paris, in 1868, happy enough, she said, to make anyone jealous, and all their friends rejoiced with them.[74]

Later that same year came another, happily resolved, disagreement over Adam's politics. In a scandal concerning the surveillance of letters the Imperial Director of Postal Service was accused of promising promotions to those employees who dug out the best secrets from reading private mail. As an opposition journalist, Adam excoriated the practice. This was not government corruption, he said; this was government cynicism; and a government in such shape could not cure itself. Nevertheless, at the time when the crown announced a new "liberal Empire," he was strongly tempted to take an oath of allegiance in the hope of getting into the administration. If he had signed, Juliette would have felt their emotional relationship severely traumatized,[75] but when he resisted the temptation, she was prouder of him than ever. It is hard to imagine either George Sand or Marie d'Agoult having this kind of commitment to another person's political integrity.

The war of 1870 broke out while the Adams were paying a visit to Nohant. They heard the drums beat.* Alice said her heart pounded. Juliette's rose in her throat.[76] Maurice Sand took a drum and cried, "*Vive la France!*" George Sand and Juliette Adam broke into tears.†[77]

Juliette was now able to do her share of public service in the cause of her nationalistic and republican ideals. On September 11, after visiting her daughter in the country, she took the last train back to Paris before the siege by the German army closed it in. (She had made the engineer promise to let her ride in the locomotive, along with her maid, in case the train should be stopped.) Once at home, she stocked up her larder and opened a private hospital. She set up a workroom where women could meet and sew and sympathize with each other instead of sitting alone, and she organized the provision of cheap meals for the poor and even took a wounded soldier into her own flat.

After the Third Republic was finally established, she continued to press for the nationalist cause in her capacities as journalist and salon leader, to the extent that her activities threatened the negotiations between France and Bismarck's Germany. The German ambassador called her "*cette diablesse de femme*," and asked Jules Ferry, then Premier, to silence her. Ferry answered that the only man who could do that, her husband, was now dead.[78] Juliette used the money Adam had left her to found a review in 1879, and she worked daily in its office for twenty years, always against Bismarck and Germany. She lived through World War I, and on to be a hundred.

∽ One thing that stands out in the lives of all these women is how much uncriticized freedom they could seize for themselves compared with what was available to contemporary Englishwomen. The fact that Frenchwomen's marriages had been arranged led to a widespread tolerance for those who broke loose, particularly if they could distinguish

---

*After Emile Ollivier, Marie d'Agoult's son-in-law, who headed the war cabinet of Napoleon III, had pledged the war "with a light heart."

†In a letter to Juliette from her former escort, Arlès-Dufour, he wrote, "What is more distressing than the war is the popularity of the war; how it has been necessary to deprave and brutalize this poor people to lead them to applaud the massacre of their own children, to the destruction of the property which they so painfully built up (Adam, *Sentiments*, 466).

themselves by writing. Each of these women suffered in the first place because of her sex, but each of them transcended this set of conditions and went on to criticize the society that permitted it.

George Sand was the one who spread the gospel of personal freedom most widely. She wanted women to stand in judgment on men, and on the laws that allowed so much personal suffering, but her plea was made through art, not reason.

Marie d'Agoult, less gifted as an artist but more committed to the intellectual task of analyzing women's problems through the study of history and philosophy, pondered the subject of generalized injustice (to workers as well as women) until she could write books about the state and revolution and its consequences that were both solid and fresh.

Flora Tristan adopted a more radical approach. She set out to act, not just to think, and undertook the huge task of organizing a protest group. Impatiently she saw beyond sexual problems to those of all the myriad oppressed, and wished to help them all.

For Hortense Allart human relationships were a mode of self-expression, and she used them to demonstrate the way in which she thought all women should live, unencumbered by conventions.

It became clear that Juliette and Edmond Adam were creating a new sort of marriage. The outstanding women of the earlier period had nothing but unhappy experiences with the only kind of marital relationships they knew or could conceive of. George Sand said that she would sooner spend her life in prison than remarry, and she, like Marie and Flora and Hortense, repudiated the institution as unworthy of a free woman. But M. Adam obviously respected his wife's autonomy. He liked and wanted to help her in her writing. In that way their union was something like that of George Eliot and G. H. Lewes.

Hortense and Juliette demonstrated two patterns for the liberated women of the future: Juliette the partner in a genuinely equal marriage, and Hortense the autonomous individual who undertook alone the tasks of work, love, and motherhood.

ᔆ21.

Les Bachelières

La démocratie a trouvé ses principes,
mais elle cherche encore ses moeurs.
                    Ernest Legouvé, ca. 1867

(Democracy has found its principles
but it is still hunting for its customs.)

It was ironical that the Declaration of the Rights of Man of 1789 should have left Frenchwomen in worse shape than they had been before. About that time many avenues previously open to them were closed. In feudal times, as is well known, women could inherit and manage property. Many abbesses had extensive executive responsibility with authority over both men and women, and until 1694, the French king sent out women as ambassadors. During the eighteenth century educated women could practice medicine and belong to the academies, while civil service jobs were frequently offered to soldiers' widows.[1]

Both Mme Roland, the revolutionary martyr, and Mme de Genlis, who lived from 1746 to 1830 and was a tutor in the royal family, had studied and practiced medicine. But the revolutionary government closed even the schools for midwives, and the last medical diploma awarded to a woman doctor who was not a midwife was given in 1794 by the medical faculty of the University of Montpellier. Its recipient, Mme Castanier, practiced medicine for nearly fifty years in the Department of Ardèche, and died as a result of answering a night call in a remote spot. After her licensing, although midwives were still examined in their specialty, they were not permitted to take the title of health officer, a limitation that prevented their giving medication even in desperate cases; and having delivered a baby, they were not allowed to take care of him. In 1836 a midwife attempted to get her name inscribed under the medical faculties of Paris and Montpellier, and was rejected at both places.[2] In order to tend the sick—or to teach, for that matter—it seemed as if a woman had to take religious vows, even though both professions had once been open on a secular basis.

There was no woman in the French Academy. During the nineteenth century a few were selected from time to time for the provincial academies, but even there the proportion was lower than it had been a hundred years earlier. Likewise, there had been eight women members of the Paris Academy of Painting at the outbreak of the Revolution. When this body was re-established under the Consulate, all former members were given the right to sit—except for the women, among whom was the distinguished Mme Lebrun.[*3]

In the civil service Mme de Calonne, a widow, was named Director of the Archives of the Seine in 1800 and remained in the position for forty-two years, winning a great name for her prodigious memory and ability to locate documents. Women born a few years later could never have found such an opening, and they used to comment that Mme de Calonne had started life in a period of more advanced civilization.[†]

In fact it is possible to trace a distinct narrowing of public jobs for women in each administration from the First to the Second Empire. In 1810 they held many high-level appointments in the post office and other governmental offices, and a majority of the clerkships. The July Monarchy put in several hampering regulations: for example, the spouse of a postal employee could not have an independent industry or trade. Though formally treating both sexes equally, this would in practice be harder on a woman, whose husband would be debarred from earning a separate income. And at this time it was decreed that no woman could be appointed to the most important postmastership in any *arrondissement*.[4] As long as the property qualifications for voting were high (until 1848), the administration apparently wanted to save its political plums for voters, who were, of course, all male. Under the Second Empire, which adopted universal male suffrage, women applicants would be in competition even at the lower levels of clerkships, and so when Julie Daubié was writing her book on women's work, she was told flatly that women could no longer be taken on in the post office at all. She knew personally a woman of great ability who had given a quarter of a century of loyal and efficient service as the director of a post office and who was transferred during the reorganization to a distant locality with diminution of pay. The preference for employing male workers extended into such traditionally female jobs as hospital nurses—even into children's hospitals, where their ignorance was damaging to the little patients. Another person interviewed by Mlle Daubié was the widow of a pharmacist who had worked beside her husband for years and who owned the small business; upon his death she was no longer licensed to practice and had to study for

*Anton Hirsch's 1905 history of women in art, *Die Frau in der bildenden Kunst*, mostly about women subjects, included a section on woman as artist in the eighteenth century, but he did not think the work of nineteenth-century women worth mentioning.

†It is true that the Revolution, while formally closing off opportunities, at the same time nurtured self-reliance in a number of women who had to cope for themselves. For example, Mme Octave Feuillet described a Norman heroine who saved her father from the guillotine by riding a horse halfway across France to obtain pardon, and when she inherited his land, she kept busy all her life with the factory on her estate and with the municipal government, working with the poor and making the mayor and the curé toe her line (Feuillet, 3ff.).

an elementary teacher's certificate in order to get into the only profession still open to women.

When Lamartine's niece, who had kept house for her uncle as long as he lived, decided after his death that she would like a position as inspector of schools, she was told there were at most two or three such spots available to women, and they were all filled.

On the other hand, there was not very much of the sort of prejudice widespread in Britain against married women working inside their homes or beside their husbands in their shops or offices, like our pharmacist's wife. There was far less setting women apart (as in England) or down (as in Germany), but rather a sense of economic cooperation that began with the incorporation of the wife's dowry into the family capital,[5] so that the proportion of women working in France was much higher than that of most European countries. In 1906 it was reported that twice as high a proportion of married women (38.9 percent) were working in France as in Britain at the time.[6] Yet however well the French accepted the married woman working in the family business, independent work was for a long time greatly frowned upon. This prejudice was strong enough to stop Elisa Lemonnier from opening a lingerie shop in Bordeaux, even though she wanted to do it to help her young lawyer husband get along.*[7]

Julie Daubié puts a good deal of the blame on the laxity of French laws against seduction, a state of affairs that made parents hesitate to allow their girls to become shop clerks or office helpers. In the 1860s shops actually began to hire women, and they paid a bonus to those who could speak English. Night schools taught English, but even a father who trusted his daughter to go out in the day would not let her out at night, and besides, he would be unwilling to eat into her dowry money to pay the tuition.

Nevertheless, as the possibility of the wife's working outside increased, the importance of the dowry decreased, as can be seen in the declining rate of marriages preceded by a contract. In the 1860s and 1870s, about 40 percent of marriages involved marital contracts; by 1913, this had gone down to 22 percent.[8] Mary Hartman suggests that the slower rate of economic transformation in France permitted the combination of older and newer roles for the wife, and therefore her greater sense of autonomy at home.[9]

With a pattern of life involving close chaperonage for young girls and heavy responsibilities within the family for married women, Frenchwomen did not follow the Englishwoman's path from philanthropy into professionalism. The average French middle-class housewife had fewer servants, had more to do at home, and was less interested in the public sphere than the comparable Englishwoman.†

---

*The stage was, in fact, the only profession where the sexes were entirely on the same level, and where either could be perfectly independent.

†Mrs. Gaskell stayed with a Protestant lady in Paris who belonged to a *dizaine*, a group of ten who picked a particular charity case—a poor family or someone with similar

Miss Betham remarked that the average Frenchwoman was not cosmopolitan; and compared with Englishwomen and their almost compulsory interest in missionary societies and good works for the poor, the French suffered from a lack of training in this kind of cooperative association.[10] Rich members of the landed class in France, as elsewhere, would indeed take care of the peasants in their villages, while the Paris aristocracy gave charity balls, but what private charity they did they often kept hidden. Maxime DuCamp wrote of how, as an adolescent, he used to follow young and pretty *femmes du monde* who would visit the poor, attend the sick, take care of orphans, but never call attention to their work, and the same evening he would meet them at parties, serene and eager to please, with no mention of their secret.[11]

One major reason there was less general philanthropy in France was that much of what was needed was performed by religious orders: nursing; caring for orphans, the poor, and the old; and managing the prisons for female convicts. When Miss Mulock toured the hospital at Caen, run by sisters, in 1867, she admired its clean, airy, quiet atmosphere and the careful watch kept over serious cases. Many of the nuns were high-born, she noted, and brought their dowries to the order.[12] Feminists like Julie Daubié started to complain, in the sixties, that ordinary women should be allowed to do these things and *get paid* for it. But the religious orders created almost impossible conditions of competition so long as they paid no salaries and had plenty of recruits.

However, the necessity of paid work for young girls, outside the home, became pressing after the 1860s. The girls began to be unwilling to stay at home and wait for the promised husband, while those fathers who found it increasingly difficult to collect a dowry noticed that an income-producing daughter could be quite an asset. The idea of training women in modest circumstances for jobs other than teaching inspired certain far-sighted feminists—among them most notably Elisa Lemonnier, who founded the Society for the Professional Training of Women in 1862, with fifteen students.[13] She began raising money for her project by proselytizing among Parisian ladies, who were each to contribute twenty-five centimes a month. By "professional," however, she did not mean the liberal professions. The first school was a workshop for dressmaking. Then followed institutes for bookbinding, commerce and industrial design; but the Lemonnier plan was always to include some general studies along with the technical training. No sooner had the project gotten started than it became apparent how astonishingly unready for this sort of white-collar employment the students were.

This pattern helps explain why there was less feminist agitation in France than in Germany or England. Lily Braun, from her vantage point

---

need—for which each one did what she could; thus a richer one would give money, a more active one could carry groceries up five flights of stairs, and another could spend time writing appeals to her friends. Advice on almsgiving was provided by Jules Simon (Gaskell, "French Life," 739).

as a German socialist, felt that Frenchwomen were degraded because they had fewer public positions and less representation in the professions than women in other countries in the 1890s, but on reflection it occurred to her that perhaps French women were really happier at home than the German ones she knew. Miss Betham made the same point by observing that Frenchwomen who went out to work might do so out of need for money, or from the pleasure they got from a vocation, but that they never did so out of sheer dislike for home life.

∾ Before the universities were open a woman who wanted to do intellectual work (especially if she were not in literature) had to go through many humiliating steps in order to get any part of her contribution before the world. One such woman was Clémence Royer, who was called the greatest feminine brain of the nineteenth century.[14] Today we would term her a Renaissance woman, concerned as she was with all the natural and social sciences, as well as with religion and philosophy; but when, in 1875, she applied at the Sorbonne for the right to give a course in natural philosophy, she was unanimously turned down by the academic council.

She was born at Nantes in 1830 to a Catholic royalist family. After the July Revolution, her father resigned his commission in the army because of his loyalty to the previous dynasty, losing a good deal of money in the turnover, but in compensation he won considerable freedom to spend time with his brilliant daughter. The family did a great deal of reading at home, so that when Clémence was sent to a convent school she quickly ran off with all the prizes, and she was given her first communion early because of her precocity. As a child she often had mystical fantasies, but secular reading and the republican Revolution of 1848 turned her into more of a rationalist. In 1849 her father died, leaving her as a dowry a tiny sum that she determined to use to create a profession for herself instead of marrying. She then recommenced all her studies. She studied physics at the Conservatory of Arts and Industry and passed examinations that would have qualified a man for a good position, but the best she could find was teaching French and piano at a boarding school in England—where, however, she improved her time by learning English. One summer back in France, serving as governess in Touraine, she discovered a hidden library and devoured the books in it, among which were the works of the great French Encyclopedists. Here she completed her emancipation from religious ideas; renouncing Catholicism in an open debate with a priest, she demanded rational proofs, which he could not provide to her satisfaction.

Because heavy floods hit the Rhone valley at this time, she gave all her little fortune to the victims and retreated to a Swiss farmhouse, where she supported herself by her needle so as to have time to think. Dressing like the peasants around her, she used to walk eleven kilometers to reach the circulating library in Lausanne. She began a serious study of the Bible here, at the same time continuing with her chemistry and physics. By 1858 she had produced a treatise on the eighteenth-century French philosopher Maine de Biran, and the next year she moved into Lausanne to be nearer to the book supply. At this time she offered a course of lectures, open to women only, on logic and the philosophy of nature. (The reasons for shutting men out was that they might be disruptive.) In the month in which *On the Origin of Species* was published in England, she had been expounding the ideas of Lamarck, but soon thereafter she became Darwin's first French translator.

Her next book was an introduction to the "philosophy of women." She had noticed that men and women lived with such different vocabularies that they could hardly communicate, an idea that seems still to be circulating among the sociolinguists of the 1980s. She thought she had identified ten thousand words that most women had never heard pronounced, and she explained how difficult it had been for her to master scientific papers under this handicap. Now she wanted to explain intellectual subjects for women in a language they could understand. "Mesdames," she began her lecture, "I have a double emotion, as a speaker and as a woman in a field where women are not supposed to go."[15] And she told them that she did not wish to copy men like Kant and Fichte, who were capable of talking tremendous nonsense. Women needed to think about the same questions freshly. Science, if left to men alone, she felt, would never get around to the profound problems that confronted human beings in daily life and in society. For instance, she was against the male-created standing army, both as wasteful of tax money and as a corrupter of morals.[16] It is piquant to think that in 1860 she shared a prize with Proudhon.

At the age of thirty, Clémence took as a lover Paul Dupret, an economist. Although she did not marry him, she had very high expectations of companionship between the sexes and wrote, "I do not understand how conjugal happiness is possible for any woman except with a husband whose thoughts she shares and to whom she can tell all hers without fear."[17] The couple went to Italy together, like so many others living in free union, had a child, and lived for a while in Florence in one huge room that they curtained off into areas for dining, working, a salon, a baby's room, and a bedroom.

She kept on in intellectual work, and in 1884 Victor Considérant (the old Fourierist) supported her in a series of public lectures concerning a new theory she had developed in physics, the elastic atom. How insufficient Renan's praise that "she is almost a man of genius,"[18] but at least the Republic awarded her one of the very few ribbons of the Legion of Honor given to women in the nineteenth century![19]

❧ A few years later Frenchwomen no longer had to take such a devious route to fulfill their intellectual potential because higher education opened up rather suddenly in the sixties. It happened with a stroke of the bureaucratic pen, so that Frenchwomen did not need to organize, as Englishwomen did, to set up facilities for women, or as the Germans did, to create a mighty wave of public opinion. What opposition there was in France arose more out of surprise at the novelty of the idea than from determined hostility to women's brains. For a while activity in this direction focused women's attention away from the ideas of sexual, or even literary, freedom that had dominated the previous thirty years. The new opportunities were much more practical, and progress could be measured in the ever-growing numbers of women who took advantage of them.

There had been a *lycée* for women under the *ancien régime*, endorsed by Montesquieu and Condorcet, but the Revolution put an end to it, and by closing the religious orders that had provided the bulk of female education, it had thrown women back into their homes while the proceeds of the confiscation went to the endowment of a purely masculine university.[20] (In France the university includes all publicly supported education from the earliest grades through graduate school.)

After the Restoration women could sit as auditors, though they were ineligible for degrees. Lectures were so popular that Lady Morgan described Paris in 1829 as one great university, where nearly everybody was either a professor or a student.[21] She listed some of the courses available: geometry as applied to the arts, at the Conservatory; French literature; the history of Roman law; Professor Guizot on modern history—an immense class; Professor Cousin on the history of philosophy, talking to enthusiastic listeners. Mary Clarke, an intellectual Englishwoman living in Paris in the twenties, used to attend the opera, copy pictures in museums, and study Italian, German, and Latin; she even took a course in entomology.[22] The Collège de France and the Jardin des Plantes were always hospitable to women auditors, but admission to the Sorbonne was prohibited after they took up so many seats that the enrolled students had to arrive an hour early to find a place in the classrooms of popular professors like Michelet and Quinet.[23] In 1848 a poet's daughter took and passed the examinations for teaching, privately, just for the honor, but this action was protested by the conservative press.[24] Certainly the climate was not favorable for any woman who wanted a serious education followed by examinations that might lead to a profession.

Then, one day in 1861, M. Roulard, Minister of Public Instruction, found on his desk a letter from a woman who demanded authorization to take the *baccalauréat* examination administered to boys at the end of their *lycée* course. Success in it ordinarily admitted the *bacheliers* to a university.* Like a proper bureaucrat, he turned down this novel request,

---

*It is dangerous to try to compare French and American levels of education. *Very* roughly, the *lycée* can be compared to a high school, the *licence* to a master's degree, and the doctorate to Ph.D. The *baccalauréat* examination, the *bachot*, comes at the end of the *lycée* education.

but it received a certain amount of publicity and came to the attention of the Empress Eugénie.[25] The applicant was named Julie Daubié; when she reapplied the following year, M. Roulard followed instructions from the crown and investigated. He found out that she was a teacher, not young, already in her thirties. Dismayed by the general lack of knowledge and methodical thinking among her fellow teachers, she had tried to correct her own deficiencies by studying Latin with her brother, a priest. She had also composed a prize-winning essay for the Academy of Lyons in 1859.

This prize had been offered for a work on the social condition of women. The committee proposing the subject, whose reporter was Arlès-Dufour, explained that for eighteen hundred years all laws, both civil and religious, had promoted inequality between the sexes, and in the 1850s the contradictions were becoming so obvious that they required attention. Mlle Daubié's essay, which was published in 1866 under the title "*La Femme pauvre,*" might almost as well have been called "*La Pauvre femme,*" because she covered not only women's lack of money, but their lack of almost everything else that makes people independent and free. The work can well stand comparison with John Stuart Mill's *Subjection of Women*, which came out three years later. The writer's dedication to the Lyons Academy pays tribute to its insight with the moving apostrophe "Be blessed for it—in the name of all that suffer and all that hope."[26]

After a thorough exploration of the actual condition of women in France, both legal and sociological, Julie Daubié listed the reforms she would like to see. Compared with the utopian proposals of the thirties, hers were far more practical and depended far more on governmental action and political power. She wanted public officials to be held responsible for the consequences of their acts; for instance, in administering the law against research into paternity, they would be accountable for the women and children who were hurt in the process. She asked for universal suffrage, with the unusual twist that parents should be able to cast votes in the name of their minor children, so that even the very young should be represented in state policy. She wanted all children, illegitimate and legitimate, to be equal under the law; freedom to marry for anyone of legal age; testamentary freedom for fathers; the disqualification of husbands who misconducted themselves from administering their wives' property; liability for men as well as women in prostitution cases, and the closing down of government-tolerated houses; and she hoped that equal tax money would be spent for girls' and boys' education and that an equal number of civil service jobs would be open. Higher educational institutions should be open to women; schools and charities should be made more human by decentralization; and lastly, she proposed dismissing the standing army that spread so many insolent and unmarriageable young men about France for their seven-year terms, and substituting a national militia.

Unfortunately Julie Daubié died before seeing most of her reforms adopted, but not before she became the first *bachelière* in France. Her second application to take the examination was favorably received because of the Empress's insistence. Having passed it, she applied for permission to continue her studies at a university, and received in 1871 the first university degree in letters granted to a woman, the *licence-ès-lettres*, from the Sorbonne.

She was not, however, the first woman student because she did not follow up her success immediately, while her victory in passing the *bachot* inspired other women and led to a public demonstration in Paris on behalf of women's admission to the university. The Empress Eugénie used to preside at Ministerial Councils when her husband was away at the wars, and she picked one such occasion, in 1866, to get through a decree stating, "Women are authorized to take the examinations of the *Facultés*."[27] Because France was a highly centralized country, this was all that was needed to ensure that women could not be turned down by reason of their sex at any university in France. M. Victor Duruy, who had become Minister of Public Instruction in 1863, was a great friend of women's education and cooperated actively, while the Empress sent her own two nieces to attend courses.[28]

As soon as the decree was passed, Mlle J. Chenu received special permission to submit herself for examination and received a Master of Arts degree from the Paris Academy of Science in 1868. The first regular students were three foreigners; Elizabeth Garrett, who became the first British medical doctor; an American, Mary Putnam, later Dr. Jacobi (who was advised by one professor to attend medical lectures disguised as a man); and a Russian.

I do not know why it took Mlle Daubié nine years to get her degree in letters. Long before then women had received degrees in science, signed by the Minister himself, at Lyons, Bordeaux, Montpellier, and Algiers. It was hardly a flood yet, though it seemed to Mrs. Somerville that at this time, in the late sixties, the French were the most civilized of all nations in respect to women's education and culture,[29] while Jessie White Mario, writing in the New York *Nation* in 1869, stated that France "with her lady students and *bachelières-ès-lettres* . . . seems far ahead of her northern neighbors."[30]

The first native Frenchwoman to apply to medical school was Mme Madeleine Brès. The daughter of a wheelwright, she started toward her career by helping out the nuns at Nîmes when she was still a child. "What a good little doctor you would make,"[31] the head physician said to her one day as he met her, aged seven, carrying a load of supplies. At fifteen she was married, but was soon widowed with several children to support. When she asked, in 1866, to be admitted to the medical school at Paris, they told her that she would need to complete her *baccalauréat* as a prerequisite, so she spent two years preparing for this examination with the help of a manual that she picked up at a second-hand book stall. "I learned pell-mell all that I could," she said of herself. Meanwhile a neighbor gave her lessons in the obligatory Latin and Greek. At the age of twenty-eight, on the second try, she passed her *bachot*, and then began her medical course. But in 1870, when she presented herself for her diploma, it was unanimously refused by the corps of professors, and only after the personal intervention of M. Duruy did she get it. On the battlefields of 1870 she was appointed an emergency surgeon, but once the war was over, she was refused the same position in a civilian hospital.[32] She kept on working, however, and in 1875 submitted a dissertation on breast-feeding that received the grade "extremely well done" and finally got her a full medical doctorate.[33] She acquired a large practice, and in the course of her career founded a welfare center for infants.

Although Mary Putnam declared, after she was through, that she had suffered no difficulty or embarrassment, no trouble at all, in working beside young men in the hospital or laboratory,[34] the path to medicine was not easy for all women students, who were assigned a special place to sit right under the professor's eye, and who were occasionally jeered at. The real difficulty for most of them came, as for Mme Brès, in obtaining staff positions at hospitals. Even in 1881, when officials should have been used to female applicants, Mlle Blanche Edwards, later Dr. Edwards-Pilliet, was to waste eighteen months before receiving permission to be a "dresser," which would open up the way to becoming an intern. She had to use political pressure to achieve the first step, and then repeat the struggle in 1884 to achieve the second. At her final examination, in 1885, she saw herself burned in effigy outside the hall, and was whistled at with the comment, "*Sortez*, Blanche."[35]

Nevertheless, she and other women got their degrees. By 1882 there were twelve women practicing medicine in France. One early graduate, an opthalmologist, died in Viet Nam, where she was called to operate on the Emperor's mother in Hué. The first women to receive doctorates in science did so in 1888; the first one in letters was awarded in 1914. There were six women professors by 1930.[36]

The first woman law student was Mlle Jeanne Chauvin, who used to arrive early at her class every morning, attended by her mother. In 1892 she received the doctorate in law, with a dissertation on the professions open to women, and applied for admission to the bar.[37] In spite of a touching plea that she had spent ten years of her youth and considerable money to qualify herself for a profession that she loved, she was told that to admit her would be "contrary to the progress of civilization."[38] The feminist Maria Deraismes was extremely sarcastic about this decision: she wondered aloud if judges were afraid of being seduced by women lawyers, or whether they feared that one might give birth in court.[39] It took years of effort (until 1900) and the personal intervention of statesmen like Poincaré and Viviani to have the legal profession declared open to women on the same terms as men. A few weeks after this decree, Mlle Chauvin was admitted to practice. (In 1925 she received the Legion of

Honor.) Still, by 1914 only about twenty-eight women had taken their oath in court as lawyers, and of these only a dozen were practicing.[40]

A delightful but somewhat ambiguous picture of the first group of women lawyers was portrayed in a novel of 1909, *Les Dames du palais*, by Colette Yver (Antoinette Huzard). She shows a group of rather shy but idealistic young women eager to take public service cases and to defend juvenile delinquents. The heroine, Henriette, is young, rich, talented, and totally devoted to the young man, also a lawyer, who wins her hand. They attempt to set up a completely modern marriage, with two independent careers and a baby, but trouble starts when the wife wins a spectacular divorce case in which she obtains for her woman client the unusual privilege of child custody. The publicity surrounding the affair brings her a legion of women clients eager for divorce, so that Henriette forges ahead of her husband in money and prestige—a position assumed by the novelist, as it was by most fiction writers, to be fatal for a wife. The marriage comes apart and can only be put back together when she agrees to act as her husband's secretary, an alternative she has formerly haughtily declined. The moral is reinforced when the celebrated divorcée whose case she handled decides to go back to her husband for the sake of the little boy. A novel like this caters to popular prejudices, but also reflects genuine social problems. It could not have been easy then—nor is it now—to create an equal marriage. But occasionally life outstrips fiction, as the marriage of the Curies demonstrates.

It is well known that Marie Curie was the first woman to hold a university chair in France, though she might not have received such an appointment, even with her brilliant reputation, if her husband had not been killed in an accident, leaving her the natural successor to his place. While he was alive she had at first only a teaching appointment at a girls' normal school. Three years before Pierre's death, she was made head of his laboratory.

She was the daughter of a teacher in Russian Poland, where the curriculum of the girls' *gymnasia* was the same as that offered boys. If she had been raised in the part of Poland annexed to Germany, she would not have had such good luck. At the age of seventeen Marie engaged herself as a governess to help pay for her talented older sister's medical studies in Paris. When that sister, Bronia, began to earn money, she reciprocated by bringing Marie to the Sorbonne to study physics. She married her fellow scientist, Pierre Curie, and went on to have two daughters, to win two Nobel prizes, and to inherit her husband's university appointment. Their marriage provides an extraordinary example of an equal partnership. Eve Curie says that her mother was eager to be a wife, a mother, and a scientist, without cheating any of these roles.*[41]

---

*Marie showed her devotion to her small children by making careful records of their mental and physical progress, and later by teaching in a cooperative faculty school for very young children.

∽ The convention that women should not study nude figures hampered the training of women artists until the mid-seventies. For many years before then, Rosa Bonheur had been exhibiting her paintings of animals, prowling around Paris in men's clothing in order to get her material, but she was rather a George Sand of art, a unique example. Marie Bashkirtseff, determined to win regard as a painter, entered in 1877 the studio run by M. Julien, the only place in Paris for women to study art seriously.[42] Whether it was the same one admired by Albert Rhodes is not clear, but that American visitor was impressed to find (in 1875) men and women seriously studying nude models together, and was told that an excessive modesty in a woman painter was taken as a sign of mediocrity.[43]

Marie reveled in the atmosphere of her studio; all the students were equal there, and each one confronted art for herself, as an individual, without the intrusion of family name or fortune. They felt free, and proud—at least until they wanted to move on. Then where could they go? Not to the Ecole des Beaux Arts.[44] Marie used to cry with rage at this discrimination and imagined that if she ever became rich, she would found a whole art school just for women. There were other encumbrances to cope with; men's lives gave them liberty for experiences that could deepen their art, while she had to get a carriage and a chaperone if she wanted to go to the Louvre.*[45] Part of her trouble, she realized, lay in her aristocratic origin, and one way she used to increase her freedom a little was to dress like a woman of the middle classes.

Even with the small amount of liberty she had wrested for herself, she found in 1882 that people were saying that she had been granted a "compromising independence." She denied this, partly in defense of her own standards, partly in protest against how much these standards did indeed deny. Men were free, she insisted, to come and go, dine at a restaurant, go to the Bois, or to a café. Then she imagined an interlocutor saying to her, "Superior woman that you are, give yourself that liberty!" "It is impossible," she mourned in response, "for the woman who emancipates herself thus—the young and pretty woman, be it understood—almost has the finger pointed at her, she becomes singular, commented on, insulted, and consequently still less free than before she shocked idiotic custom."[46]

∽ In order for women to be admitted in any numbers to higher education, they needed to have access to secondary schools, and for several reasons this seemed harder to get than university admission. To let a few extra students use the facilities of existing higher institutions required hardly any tax money. To set up government-sponsored schools

---

*Taine had believed that there was another reason why women could not become great artists. He told his sisters, "You cannot live the tempestuous, mobile and licentious life without which Imagination languishes and Genius grows faint (Taine, *Life and Letters*).

for half the population would double expenses, and hence taxes. There was a great lack of secular teachers, and the Catholic church, with its near monopoly of girls' education, was bitter in its opposition to secular competition.

Nuns as teachers enjoyed two advantages: they cost less in salaries, and they did not have to meet the same stringent professional requirements as laywomen. From 1820 on an ordinance required certificates of both morality and competency for the head of any girls' school, but if the head was a religious, the certificate was given in return for a mere "letter of obedience."[47] At first the competing schools were private, but when public schools began to be set up nuns taught in them too, and until 1881 they still needed only the letter of obedience for certification. Then the thoroughly secular Third Republic rescinded this provision and, after a battle of increasing heat, in 1904 it prohibited members of any religious order from teaching in France.

For secular teachers the certificates were at first hard to obtain. Before 1848, 119 women had applied for the license as headmistress, and of these only 16 passed.[48] One of the very few civil service jobs open to women before 1850 was that of inspector for these examinations.[49] The board of examiners consisted of three priests, a Protestant pastor, a rabbi, some university professors, and three ladies.

The Guizot law of 1833 had set up government-run schools for boys in every commune of France, but for girls it merely stated that facilities could be set up if there were money and demand. Education for girls was a luxury. Obviously this disparity was one of the greatest causes of feminist dissatisfaction.

The Second Empire was more favorable in theory (at least at the end, under M. Duruy), but slow in action. By the time of the Third Republic, however, the question was no longer whether elementary education should be provided for both sexes, but whether girls should have access to secondary schooling just like their brothers. The law allowing the establishment of girls' *lycées*, but not yet requiring them, was pushed through in 1880 by Camille Sée, with backing by Jules Favre, and in the following year the first normal school was set up at Sèvres, in part of the famous old pottery works, to train teachers for the new schools. This institution subsequently won a very high reputation for scholarship. Mme Jules Favre was its head, and M. Legouvé the inspector of studies. It opened with forty students and turned out its first graduates in 1883.[50]

Meanwhile, to implement the new law about the schools themselves, the first *lycée* was opened at Montpellier in 1882, and another one at Rouen; and Paris got its first one, the *Lycée Fénelon*, named for the seventeenth-century mentor of female education, in 1883. There were still grounds for complaint. However high their level of scholarship, these girls' schools were not permitted to offer the *baccalauréat*, the ticket of admission to the university, which was routine for successful boys. Girls who completed their courses received merely a *diplome*, so that they had to train privately for the *bachot* examination, until 1907, when at last it became legal for the public schools to offer it.[51]

Nor did improvement in the laws necessarily mean immediate improvement in conditions for girl students and their women teachers. In 1900 the Republic spent over seven times as much on boys' secondary schooling,[52] though this was, of course, before the alternative of convent education was eliminated. Women teachers were regularly scheduled for more class hours per week and in a wider variety of subjects, both requiring greater preparation time, than were men.[53]

Naturally the Catholic church felt the pressure, and it made considerable efforts to stiffen its own intellectual training and liberalize certain of its ideas in order to keep the education of young women in its hands and prevent the closing of private schools. One of the most thoughtful Catholic commentators on girls' education was the Vicomtesse d'Adhémar, who was forced to admit by 1900 that public education, especially when it took place under teachers trained at Sèvres, was far superior to that offered by convents. She hoped to follow Leo XIII in his effort to Christianize democracy, and she believed that girls would flock to an education provided by the Church if it were freed of narrow throne-and-altar tendencies. Parents, she felt, were dismayed by the materialism and free thought of the secular universities, however brilliant the presentation.[54] It was clearly one of the aims of the government to make education more scientific and less "superstitious." And the Church needed to offer a more attractive substitute.

One of the early attempts proved disastrous. The church hierarchy engaged a lay professor, M. René Doumic, to give a course of lectures to girls with the avowed purpose of keeping them away from university benches. Alas, he alarmed the chaperoning mothers by references to Machiavelli and Boccaccio. After that, the only thing to do seemed to be to open special Catholic courses at the university level, taught by priests, and these were actually started in 1897. Meanwhile, members of all Catholic teaching orders who would have to treat matters of intellectual controversy from which they had hitherto been sheltered were given upgraded training, though this still excluded the literature of passion. This idea foundered on the tough new anti-clerical education laws of the government.

⤳ Meanwhile social life was definitely changing even for those French girls who had nothing to do with the movement for emancipation. Style is often a more potent changer of life than ideology, and Michelet's invalid went completely out of fashion. Sport became the mode, along with more chances for the sexes to meet informally and a new opportunity to have longer engagements and to marry for love. Corsets went out about 1910, and tailored suits came in.[55]

Margerite Grépon insists that feminism started in the provinces under the Third Republic with a generation of girls who refused to marry for money, took examinations to qualify as teachers, and then spread out across the land.[56] They believed that they could organize a better world than the one their mothers had bequeathed them—mothers who had left home, if at all, only for religious pilgrimages. The graduates of the new normal schools, led by Mme Favre, dared to go out alone, to walk, travel, attend the theater, talk openly with men, and dress elegantly, no matter how much the bourgeoisie was scandalized.[57] Restaurants had to start accepting without comment a man and a woman dining together, and if there was any difficulty in getting the waiters' attention, Dr. Pelletier urged such couples to stage sit-in campaigns until the custom became so well established that there would be no further jibes.[58]

A picture of the new women of 1914 in their own words was offered by a professor of secondary education, Mlle Amélie Gayraud, who conducted a sort of poll among her students and other young women of her acquaintance. Her aim was to show what thirty years of education had accomplished since the law of 1880 had opened public secondary schools for women. Mlle Gayraud believed that at the time the law was passed, all enlightened men were feminists, but that by 1914 many of them had changed their minds.[59] Meanwhile, new power was given to feminism by the young women who read, wrote, talked, and attended lectures.

Her poll was conducted by talking to girls or getting them to write letters. In either case, she says, she was aware of the danger of putting words into their mouths, a danger she conscientiously tried to avoid. She questioned only young girls of the bourgeois class, between the ages of eighteen and twenty-five, and she tried to include ones from a number of different schools and localities. Among her sample were a Sorbonne student, two from the normal school at Sèvres, and several from provincial and Parisian *lycées*. At one point she collected twenty-six together and "held a plebiscite." Out of all this informal questioning comes a picture of quite a different type of young girl from the blank-brained creature of the 1850s or the former generation of *emancipées*. The 1914 girls were emphatic that they did not want to copy the eccentricity of the *Saint-Simoniennes*.

Without exception her informants expressed the wish to marry, but they all agreed that they would prefer to remain celibate than to be united to a husband who did not please them. Most of them were not in love with their professions, or with the idea of a profession, but felt that having one was the best guarantee against an unsatisfactory marriage. Only four of the twenty-six in the "plebiscite" insisted that they would like to continue their careers after marriage, though six more would do so if it did not interfere with their household responsibilities. The conclusion Mlle Gayraud came to was that part-time work might be an "interesting solution" to this problem, but as she pointed out, it would be difficult for a teacher to find, though easier for a lawyer or professor. None of the girls was interested in the time-saving proposal for a huge common kitchen in each apartment house where food would be prepared professionally and each family could order its choice sent up to its apartment. That would be all right for the working class, they thought, but not for young *bourgeoises* like themselves.

Patriotism was decidedly their dominant social emotion. Repeatedly they wrote or said that the only way a woman could serve her country was to bear children. "A patriotic girl will want to found a French family and give her country good soldiers," said one, and they would bring their sons up to be willing to sacrifice their lives if need be.[60] Many of the respondents expressed concern about the low French birth rate, and while none of them wanted a large family, they often hoped that the normal number might be three or four babies instead of the one or two that was then standard. (Their interlocutor betrayed her own bias by her evident delight at this nationalistic ardor, because, as she put it, the Latin race was the "civilizing" race. But one of the *Sévriennes*, though endorsing the general sentiment, did remark that everyone realized that men's wars were often stupid and selfish.)

On the other hand, these young girls were surprisingly indifferent to religion. Of the twenty-six who answered the poll together, eight were strongly against religion, while most of the others claimed to be religious only by habit. This was at a period when young men were flocking back to the Church, and Mlle Gayraud remarked that the girls were still expressing the liberal views of Frenchmen of a previous generation, not those of their own male contemporaries.

The two *Sévriennes* who wrote a joint letter were among the most articulate respondents. They represented a minority, said their pollster, but one that pointed toward the future. They were quite self-consciously members of a new generation that wanted to surpass its mothers. We keep their maternal instinct and love of the *foyer*, they insisted, but we want women to have a new dignity based on intellectual equality and, if possible, reinforced by part-time work. They repudiated free love specifically because they had observed so many feminists sharing happy homes with husbands whom they loved. One of the students was a socialist, a follower of Jaurès, and the other a republican; but both had high ideals for their country: the elimination of anti-semitism and royalism, a campaign against alcoholism, and an increase in the population. They were united in repudiation of all religious dogmas, especially the authoritarian ones of the Roman Catholic church, and they intended to base their faith on reason.

The respondents were also asked about sports, to which most of them seemed enthusiastically addicted. Mlle Gayraud explained to her readers that this had been a development of the preceding ten years, during which period girls' schools rushed to put in gymnasiums and began organizing hikes, tennis matches, and bicycling tours. The girls expressed passionate admiration for a famous aviatrix of the day, Mlle Marvingt—the "fiancée of danger," they called her—and many of them stated that they had begged their parents for permission to take a ride in an airplane. They all explained that sports provided the best way to meet young men in the mood of camaraderie that was now preferred to one of coquetry.

The results of the entire survey were presented to several eminent Frenchmen for comment. The most interesting answer came from Romain Rolland, who said that although he felt that the ideas of the working class would be well in advance of those of these merely liberal girls, he had found the new feminine generation, all over Europe, to be much more lively than the corresponding males.*

*Mlle Gayraud could not resist quoting Anatole France's vision of the twenty-first century (in *Sur la pierre blanche*), in which there would be no social distinction, whether by class or sex. There would be "no Monsieur" and "no Madame." Differences in dress would be eliminated and the women would wear trousers. Everyone would work, but the hours of labor would be very short (Gayraud, 148).

22.

The Women's Movement in the Third Republic

But what should fulfill women's lives? Their endless yearnings, countless glowing and extravagant energies, have burned uselessly for four
thousand years, like an offering, before the twin idols of fleeting Love
and Motherhood; those sublime illusions which are denied thousands of
women and which never engross the others for longer than a few years!
Romain Rolland

There was no doubt that the French women's movement got off to a
slow start, compared to the English and German ones, and even after its
beginning it failed to keep pace with them. Much had been accomplished
by 1914, but, relatively speaking, Frenchwomen were legally as far
behind the rest of the western world then as they had been in 1870.[1]

Two reasons for this lag can be identified. The most obvious was
convent education, which left most Frenchwomen thoroughly willing
to take advice from their priests all their lives. In the words of one
male commentator, the Church had so softened and domesticated
Frenchwomen that they could not lift their heads as proudly as their
Anglo-Saxon sisters. Another reason lay in the fuller involvement of
Frenchwomen in the responsibilities of their homes and, often, in their
husbands' business affairs. With more democracy within the family, they
felt less need to press for democracy in the state. This, anyway, was how
the English suffrage leader Mrs. Pankhurst explained the fact that so few
Frenchwomen thought that the vote would increase their power.[*2]

Yet Marie d'Agoult closed her memoirs in 1877 with a moving
account of how mothers, sisters, daughters, lovers, and wives suffered far
more from "the malady of the century" than men, in a world that seemed
to be losing its faith, its traditions, its manners, its morals—where "nothing stays upright, not even a lie."[3] In a democratic society women did not
know what they could or what they ought to do. There were many ways,

*Even French socialists (not the utopians, but the more sober Marxians) clung to the
concept of the importance of the home. At an international congress in 1866, the French
delegation was the only one to suggest that true liberty for women meant being able to stay
home (Pieroni, 108).

343

she felt, that they could influence public opinion, and she used her own experiences to demonstrate that men were quite willing to listen to a woman though she should have realized that her position as a distinguished writer on political subjects and the hostess of a great salon was far from ordinary.*

On the other hand, there were those who discounted strongly the idea that women could influence political trends behind the scenes, even the best and brightest of them like Juliette Adam, who sat at the center of journalistic power. Although she enjoyed a close personal friendship with Gambetta, he would not vote the way she asked.[4]

As for a woman's taking a public stand on an issue, as Lady Amberley was doing in Britain, the supposition that a wife or daughter of a French minister could make a public address was (according to the *Siècle*) a supposition singularly absurd.[5]

⌒ Feminism as a movement was revived toward the end of the Second Empire, largely by Maria Deraismes, with the devoted assistance of Léon Richer; it was a comparatively sober effort to change the laws and decidedly lacked any utopian flair for radical changes in property and sex roles. Maria Deraismes herself was a young woman of great distinction in dress and bearing who never broke with her prosperous bourgeois family, though she fought without cease for the rights of underprivileged women, the poor, and the oppressed. She was fiercely anti-clerical and republican, but disagreed strongly with one of her co-workers, Louise Michel, who was to become the Red heroine of the Paris Commune in 1871.[6] When Louise was incarcerated for radicalism, the field was left clear for Maria and her more conservative followers.

After defeat in the Franco-Prussian War, France uneasily declared a Third Republic and set about the usual process of debating a constitution. Feminists thought it an opportune time to send in a petition urging that thirty articles of the Napoleonic Code be modified in favor of women.[7] They should not have been surprised that there was no response to this petition, since it seemed to be a habit among legislative and constituent assemblies at this period simply to ignore women's demands. In 1874 the subject of women's rights was officially declared to be subversive and immoral, and the Minister of the Interior forbade it to be discussed at a public meeting. In response to this move, Maria Deraismes, with a number of other able partisans, founded in 1876 the Society for the Amelioration of the Condition of Women. Among her

---

*Interest in the woman question seemed to be quiescent during the Second Empire, compared to its conspicuousness under the preceding two regimes, but the slow, steady growth of its importance was shown by the number of books published about women. Between 1800 and 1830, only 20 such books were issued; during the July Monarchy, about 68; during the few years of the Second Republic, 34; and during the Second Empire, over 300, although the issue most of them discussed at that period was education (Maillard, 235).

collaborators were Clémence Royer and Mme Jules Siegfried (mother of André), and they had strong support for a new set of laws from Victor Hugo and Anatole France.[8] But the apathy of the general public was appalling. After sending out seventeen thousand circulars asking support for equal rights for women workers to vote for labor arbitrators, they received only two responses.[9] Likewise, the first international women's congress, held in 1878, passed almost unnoticed.[10]

The next ten years, however, saw a great change in sentiment. By 1885 the legislature had majorities in both houses in favor of women's rights and began to pass, one by one, laws easing their condition. The organizers of two women's conferences for 1889 timed them to coincide with one of the great Paris expositions, so that they were very successful.[11] The first of these conferences, that on the rights of women, was run by Maria Deraismes and Léon Richer, and it finished its work with a unanimous resolution in favor of revision of the Code and equal pay for women teachers; the other, presided over by Jules Simon, onetime Minister of Public Instruction and a former premier, was devoted to exhibiting the achievements of women, including works of charity and teaching. Both were so successful that a popular women's movement in France could be said to have been fairly launched at this time.

In the next decade the pot was kept boiling as a feminist theater was formed, and a women's daily paper, *La Fronde*, with a circulation of two hundred thousand, was launched by Marguerite Durand.[12] It took up such serious questions as voluntary motherhood and revision of the Code and covered foreign news, but it also had supplements on sports, fashion, and spiritualism. Its purpose was to combat the influence of those ordinary women's magazines that preached that women should stay at home in order to keep their husbands and sons happy. Conferences and significant international gatherings continued to be held right up until war broke out in 1914.

Frenchwomen learned by these contacts to compare themselves with women of other nationalities. They realized that on strictly women's issues they were backward compared to English and especially American women.*[13] On some other issues they distinctly kept themselves apart. For example, they could never reconcile themselves to treating delegates from Alsace-Lorraine as German, but insisted that they were representatives of a separate country, and in line with this feeling, they were unable to adopt the enthusiasm for internationalism and peace that characterized prime points of argument for most of the women's movements.[14]

---

*Their vision of America was always highly laudatory. Mme d'Adhémar wrote in 1900 that in the United States women were "the cement of society," that they opened schools, built colleges, ran prisons, farmed on model farms, built workers' housing and workers' clubs, gave help to abandoned children, opened refuges for strangers, disciplined vagabonds, educated blacks and Indians, ran temperance societies and hospitals especially for alcoholics—all this and their numerous literary and cultural clubs (Adhémar, *Femme catholique*, 258).

෮ Voting was not a high priority for most French feminists during the late nineteenth century. Some were more concerned with getting for women the right to manage their own money, and others to have laws concerning sexual behavior changed in their favor, but one woman, Hubertine Auclert, broke with Maria Deraismes and Léon Richer over the issue of suffrage.[15] She adopted the policy of refusing to pay taxes on the grounds that she had no representation in the legislature, and her property was confiscated as a result.

In France as elsewhere during the Middle Ages, certain unmarried noblewomen and abbesses had the privilege of voting. By 1789 this had been diluted into the right of noblewomen to name proxies, and this right disappeared entirely when all men were declared equal and the noble rank was abolished.[16] The question of reviving votes for women was barely touched on during the 1848 period and lay dormant for most of the Second Empire.

The establishment of the Third Republic gave new hope to partisans of republican ideals, and one of the first men to change his mind about women's voting was Dumas. In 1872 he wrote a book, *L'Homme-femme*, in which he said that "feminists"—and he remarked that the word was new—lacked common sense. Eight years later he was brave enough to come out with a new book, *Les femmes qui tuent et les femmes qui votent (Women Who Kill and Women Who Vote)*, expressing a change in his views. For many years people had laughed at Hubertine Auclert as a silly eccentric, but Dumas assured his readers that in twenty years her points wouldn't seem so funny.[17] The fact that some recent murderesses had been motivated by the impossibility of divorce, and that women had no part in making laws that they had to obey, persuaded Dumas that the situation was indeed irrational. He was also influenced by an *Appel aux femmes*, an 1870 manifesto of a familiar sort, in which women once more stated their need to live by independent work, to have equal parental rights and the right to vote and serve on juries.[18]

A famous counterargument came from the pen of Emile de Girardin, who made a strong plea for women's "equality" but explained that "equality" for a woman meant being left free to raise her children in the home while her husband made sure that the money kept coming in. Liberty to work outside was not true liberty for a woman; her triumph would come in the excellence of her children.[19]

The reaction of most Frenchmen to their first contact with the idea of woman suffrage was the usual deep-set hostility to an unfamiliar idea.* This hostility was related to the fear that such a change would undo the

---

*When Marie Bashkirtseff went, in heavy disguise, to a meeting of the Women's Rights Society, in Hubertine Auclert's small parlor, she disliked everyone she met. She considered the women either furies or withered hags, and the men distasteful types who were either socialists or atheists (Bashkirtseff, 522). Her reaction would probably have been widely shared.

foundations of marriage and politics as they knew them. Miss Betham found that Frenchmen were even more unyielding than men of other nations on the subject of the vote.[20] Guizot, under the July Monarchy, had believed that a "providential law" forbade women's taking part in politics, while his colleague, Odilon Barrot, thought any woman who even wanted to vote must be a moral monster.[21]

The usual arguments of flattering denigration were dragged up. The familiar canard that women were swayed by emotion instead of logic was lightly tossed around by those who did not observe the men in government too closely. It was stated that while they might like to sit in the Chamber of Deputies, they would recoil from admitting their age by service in the Senate, a more venerable body.[22] Another approach attempting flattery was: "It is not that we judge *them* unworthy to sit in Parliament, but *Parliament* unworthy of them." Sex was described as the last aristocracy in a world of egalitarianism. To a woman who asked why, with all her new education, she could not vote, one might bow and say, "Madame, you *do* vote."[23] All that men did was fill out their ballots at home, and this was where she could influence them.

The only two important issues on which men supposed that women's vote might actually change the direction of government were war and anti-clericalism.[24] It was widely assumed, without any evidence, that women would be unwilling to declare a war. Until 1914 this issue was hypothetical, and in that event it turned out that women were rabid for war after all (though it is interesting to toy with the idea of what might have happened to Europe if only women, instead of only men, had been in charge of running the affairs of nations at that time).

The other issue concerning religion in the state, however, had sufficient substance to convince even so committed a feminist as Jenny d'Héricourt that women would only use their privilege to sound a retreat from progress.[25] The argument was that they would vote as their confessors instructed. It seemed to most Frenchmen between 1880 and 1900 that there was something fundamentally hostile to French democracy in the Roman church of that day; and religion as practiced was also felt to attack the integrity of the French family, which was considered the foundation of the state.

After the period of general free thought engendered during the Revolution there had been a religious revival under the Restoration, and it was far stronger among women than among men. The practice of religion for the first time became a largely feminine affair, while the characteristic attitude of most middle-class men was anti-clerical if not definitely free-thinking. The possibility that women, so much more religious and suggestible, might reverse the struggle for the separation of church and state was a real stumbling block to many men who might otherwise have been glad to see the extension of the vote as part of their generally liberal principles. Such was Michelet's position, and he stated flatly that while justice demanded votes for women, at the moment when he spoke (1866), it would only mean eighty thousand more votes for the priests.[26]

Michelet was not the only man who was troubled. Taine imagined a scene of clerical influence as it might be played out in a provincial town, such as Douai. The curé pays a visit while the husband is at work. He asks the wife if she wants the destruction of religion and the ruin of the Holy Father. She protests, but the priest continues, asking her why her husband is going to vote for so-and-so. She replies that the mayor gave them the ballot, but she tells the priest that if the mayor's ballot is a bad ballot, he should take it away and give her the right one, and she promises that her husband will cast it.[27]

Some Frenchmen realized that the reactionary sentiments of women were a kind of revenge for the fact that the Revolution of 1789 had given them so little.[28] Women had originally embraced Christianity out of the wish to be free, the argument went, and after a democracy was founded from which women were excluded, they wore themselves out demanding from religion something that it could not give. Even some troubled Catholics added their voice. Only men have entered democracy, according to Mme d'Adhémar, and public opinion subsequently has kept women's intelligence from even thinking about democratic ideas.[29]

When the Third Republic was formed in 1871, voting became an even more significant activity than it had been under the Empire, though Napoleon III had instituted universal male suffrage. Republican leaders quickly showed a vein of anti-clericalism that roused the Church to use every weapon in its power. Never, said Alexandre Laya, had they intervened so directly in intimate family affairs as they were doing in the 1880s. As he put it, women and children had handed over to the priests the keys to "le Home, le Sweet-Home!" Their "black army," he explained, was almost invisible; yet it was constantly interfering with the authority of the head of the house; it was, indeed, the period's Mephistopheles.[30] Particularly the doctrine of the Immaculate Conception, which issued from the Vatican in 1854 as an article of faith, was repudiated by men with scientific educations, but it had a peculiarly overexciting effect on the women, according to Alexandre Laya—perhaps because they themselves wished to be relieved of sexual guilt.[31]

This whole controversy was naturally of great concern to feminist leaders. Hubertine Auclert, in a preface to Léon Giraud's book of 1882, announced their hope that every church door would be firmly closed on the very day that the doors of the polling places were opened to women.

The first bill for woman suffrage was not introduced until 1901, when an international feminist congress had at last put it on the agenda and directed René Viviani to place their petition before the Chamber. The measure passed the Chamber but failed in the Senate. In 1906, when tens of thousands of Englishwomen were marching and demonstrating, a hundred and fifty Frenchwomen went to the Chamber and demanded votes. Mrs. Pankhurst was delighted that her movement had been answered by even this much of an echo, but it got nowhere. French-women received the franchise in 1944, and even for legal control of their own property, which Englishwomen had won by 1882, Frenchwomen had to wait until after World War I.

∽ One thing that kept the organized women's movement all over Europe from concentrating wholeheartedly on issues like civil rights was their more immediate concern for relief from sexual subordination, "the heaviest, the most intolerable, the most degrading of all."[32] They wanted to marry whom they loved, and to count on as much fidelity in marriage as they were willing to give—in other words, the single standard. This is not a great issue today because it has either been won or been bypassed by a new set of expectations. In fact, the adoption of a single standard of chastity had already brought considerable changes in social expectations among many groups of people (like the young women reported on by Mlle Gayraud in the previous chapter). But in those days what seemed like simple justice for women was felt in other circles to be a real threat to male autonomy. Men who tried to comply would have their traditional masculine behavior sharply restricted. Turgéon, who wrote a middle-of-the-road book on feminism in the early days of the twentieth century, felt that for men to adopt women's standards of faithfulness would be "to betray science, and humanity itself." (Did he mean that a man held down to domestic loyalty could not survey the stars?) But the counterproposal, that women be allowed to work outside the house like men, caused him to imagine that they would then "love like men, intermittently and rapidly."[33] (This is just what women were complaining about.) In some complex, unconscious way, the processes of loving and working were tied together, so that there was a masculine pattern embracing both activities, and a feminine one that was different. Most men were not so formally logical as Turgéon; they simply felt that it would be difficult to conceive a passion for a woman doctor or philosopher.*

To men's dismay, women reacted to this sentiment by turning the tables. A spate of feminist books came out encouraging free love and feminine independence of masculine wishes. (Turgéon suggested that the authors were overexcited by the air of Paris.)[34] They recreated the myth of Lilith, the woman who had first been created as Adam's equal; but Adam was lazy, it turned out, and wanted someone who would do his bidding, so God sent him Eve, a pretty slave.[35] Lilith, though, hung around. In the period we are speaking of she was personified by the sort

*Another of the familiar efforts to cut down the women's movement by ridicule was the savage novel of 1901 by Moreau, *L'Un ou l'autre*. It deals with a woman who decides to set up an institute where women can get scholarships, vocational advice, and help in finding jobs. Unfortunately, she wants not only a career but also marriage, and she first shows her mettle by being present at the interview between her fiancé and her parents. During

of girl who, unlike Mme Emma, would have refused to marry Charles Bovary, preferring to go to work,* and perhaps to love before marriage. After all, another interpretation of the "single standard" meant doubling up without marriage. A conservative Frenchman warned his compatriots in 1919 that this practice was already very common in the United States![36]

To refuse marriage altogether was still unusual, but more and more women were refusing to marry any man who would not share his marital authority.[37] Auguste Forel, who wrote the first really clear treatise on sexuality for laymen, believed that in the marriage of the future, both parties would work outside the home, and the husband would share in the personal education of his children.[38] No domestic work would be considered degrading, and servants (he could not, in 1905, envision a world without servants) would be treated as equals. Turgéon believed that already husbandly despotism was quite out of fashion and had almost died out, at least above the working-class level.[39] Dr. Pelletier, an early medical woman, writing in 1908, went a bit further and informed French young people that communal living, sharing the household and social duties among many persons of both sexes, was being practiced by some Russian students and was worth the consideration of her compatriots.[40] (It was pointed out in the last chapter, however, that young French girls of the period repudiated this suggestion.) She also favored abortion. Many women began to demand what is today called reproductive freedom, first brought to widespread public attention in 1892 when Marie Huot, arguing from the high physical and emotional cost of multiple pregnancies, called a conference on birth control and preached the "*grève des ventres.*"†[41]

The novelist Colette, born in 1873, personified the sexual liberation of the early twentieth century as George Sand had done for her generation. She has been called the most truly liberated woman of this century. Her books shocked the bourgeoisie but started a cult among adolescents. She was the last of the great French women writers to feel the full force of the law of marital power, for her husband, Willy, locked her up, forced her to write, and kept all her royalties; when she finally shook him off she was able to taste the pleasures of love in all its forms and all its sensory appeal, and to write about them so that all the world should understand.[42]

---

pregnancy she refuses to follow her doctor's orders to rest, and when the unfortunate baby is born, she refuses to nurse it, and is so busy at the office that her husband retreats to the home in order to nurture his infant. The child, of course, fails to thrive under masculine care. When it dies the father regains his manly courage; when his wife comes home for the funeral, he meets her at the door with one word: "*Sortez.*"

*Jules Bois's sensational book *L'Eve nouvelle*, which I have not been able to find, is said to have done much to change the climate of opinion about women. In it the author claimed that women invented fire, the wheel, the plow, and the boat (Rebière, 324; Lange and Bäumer, 380). Charles Albert's *L'Amour libre* and Jean Deflon's *Le Sexualisme* are other examples of the trend.

†Literally "strike of the bellies."

If the picture of Frenchwomen here presented is correct, one must conclude that they were ahead of the women of the northern countries in control over their own bodies, in erotic freedom, in the use of birth control, in the high status attached to their position as the queens of their households, and in general competence in helping their husbands at work.

They were behind the British and Germans in places where industrialism had forced a faster change, and in the two things that would pull them from their homes into the world of outside work: professionalism and feminist organization.

What they wanted were the freedom to choose their own husbands and better education so that they could bring up their children more effectively. On the whole these changes required new customs and could not be brought about completely either by feminist organization or by new laws. Frenchwomen eventually fitted into the modern world like women of other countries, but in general, they were not the ones who forced the pace.

23.

A Gallery of German Romantics and Others

You wish a Christian paganism and dare not admit it; you wish to emancipate the flesh, and sin, and yet you are ashamed of sin; you only flirt with the old worn-out virtues, because you are really authoritarians.

Heinrich Laube (on Young Germany), 1834

In the same year that Mary Wollstonecraft published her *Vindication of the Rights of Women*, 1792, the earliest modern German defender of women, Theodor von Hippel, issued a treatise on their civil condition that was startlingly different.[1] While she drew on reserves of pathos and appealed to a passionate sense of justice, he, in cheerfully ironic tones, described how much more interesting and sensible life would be if only women had an equal share in it. Some of his critics wondered if he could be serious when he made such apparently simple remarks as that food tasted better, and actually was digested better, when a woman was present, and so all social gatherings should include both sexes.[2] Yet he stated unambiguously that he wanted to "storm the Bastille" in which the female sex was imprisoned. Why not give them full citizens' rights?[3] Why not give them the chance to earn their own living, since they would make excellent doctors or financiers? If they seemed to lack the power to make decisions, he went on, it was usually because they had been deprived of the right to earn money. Surely the remedy was to let them do so.

And why should they not propose marriage? Women did not need protectors, he insisted. Although under existing laws they were hardly allowed to do more than go to bed and get up without permission, all this could be changed.[4] Look at how widows, having been protected all their lives, were usually helpless and crippled in spirit; on the other hand, orphans managed to get along in the world splendidly and showed that dependency was not at all innate.

One of his pet hopes was that the whole sex would reject its ascribed status—in other words, titles or the concept of class consciousness. Women should all start even and then acquire their status by their own

352

work and powers, rather than by taking that of the men to whom they happened to be attached.[5]

No one followed up on these political recommendations, naturally, and in his own day Hippel was regarded mainly as an educator.[6] His was a spirit of the Enlightenment, and when German life turned toward romanticism, all of his questions about women were forgotten, to remain unstudied for fifty long years. In this way his fate was like that of Mary Wollstonecraft, for her ideas too suffered a long eclipse while a romantic, and in her case a Saint-Simonian, period turned the women's movement in a different direction.

Whereas Hippel wanted women to be self-assertive and autonomous, and perhaps rather cool, the romantics defined human beings in terms of passion, what Rainer Maria Rilke was to call "the relation of one individual person to a second individual."[7] Rilke thought this the most significant revolution of modern times, while Helene Lange, historian of the German women's movement and no romantic herself, considered this change in social relationships more important than any political revolution.[8] She must have meant that its importance lay in the high regard for women's intellect and spirit among the romantics, for their versions of love and marriage were often an embarrassment to the very proper feminists who came along in the 1860s.

It might be well to point out the discrepancy between what the concept of natural rights could do for women and the benefits they might gain from romantic idealism. In general the natural rights advocates, of whom Hippel is an example, were not much interested in personality. Hippel himself declared that it could not matter which woman one chose for a wife because they were all so alike. This impersonal approach to equal rights for everyone was picked up by the organized women's movement starting in the 1860s, while the romantic ideal of spontaneity in erotic and other matters would play a return engagement somewhat later. From start to finish, of course, the real conservatives were taking Dr. Riehl's prescription and living without concern for either political or erotic freedom, and they were much in the majority.

The romantic women we are about to discuss, those who lived in the early nineteenth century, demanded that marriage be based on mutual love between highly individualistic partners. Each was to be a complete human being, and the couple were to be concerned with each other's growth—a dynamic concept quite different, for example, from the static medieval adorations of courtly love. In Germany, in the romantic heyday, it was not free love that was wanted so much as an ideal marriage in which men would be drawn erotically to intellectual and spiritual partners.[9]

They played down the differences between the sexes, feeling that these had been much exaggerated by dramatists like Schiller, whose characters followed obviously feminine or masculine patterns. Some

354 Breaking the Pattern

voiced the fear that the trivia of housework might cramp women's free spirits.[10] Thus Bettina von Arnim once said that if "duty" crossed her path, she would wring its neck.*[11]

Perhaps it was the fact that political and social experiment were easier in France that led the French romantics into utopian socialism. In Germany there were severe limits on discussion and the formation of political organizations, and it seemed much harder there to change intractable reality. In a society strongly repressive in economic and political matters, one way to break through was by proclaiming erotic freedom and a sort of situational ethics. The French were able to imagine drafting a new set of laws, while the Germans could only protest the right of each individual to create his own rule of conduct.

Neither in France nor in Germany was the women's movement of the second half of the nineteenth century tied directly to the outpouring of the romantic interlude, though doubtless there were indirect connections.

∽ The group of early nineteenth-century poets and novelists to be considered here definitely included the two sexes. Schleiermacher, one of their leaders, ordered women "to covet men's culture, art, wisdom and honor," and a host of enthusiastic young women seemed eager to follow his advice. Quoting his remark to the effect that education should be directed toward "eternity," Betty Gleim, about 1800, asked that women be given the same sort of schooling as men—in other words, mainly classical—and not be educated for any specialized role, either sexual or vocational.[12] In her period this advice probably had a liberating effect, but later on, when social changes made political activity seem the most favorable avenue for justice, or even for practical survival, German women seemed to be left behind, trapped, perhaps, in "eternity."

The women of Schleiermacher's circle lived proud and independent lives, studying, writing, falling in love with whomever they chose.[13] For example, both the Schlegel brothers, Wilhelm and Friedrich, married distinguished women who are often believed to have done the major part of the well-known translations—of Shakespeare and medieval romances—for which their husbands got the credit.[14] In 1795 Friedrich von Schlegel had published a famous vindication of women's brains, *Über die Diotima* (*Concerning Diotima*), referring to Socrates' wise woman mentor, and a few years later wrote a scandalous novel, *Lucinde*—scandalous because of its insistence that freedom for women would mean freedom in sex, though he also wanted a program of social reform with political rights. When the novel was attacked, Schleiermacher rushed to the defense of his friend and composed a set of Ten Commandments for

*Which brings to mind that Mme de Staël, who coined the word "romantic," noticed that the German women she met were insulted if asked about their children instead of about literature.

noble-spirited women (reprinted in the appendix to this chapter). Among his points: though you should have one lover only, you can be friends with many men without coquetry; try to see your man as he is, and do not idealize him as either an angel or a hero; do not misuse love or let it degenerate by settling down to being just a mother; do not praise men for their coarse qualities; and do not contract any marriage that is likely to be broken. He also advised men and women to prepare for real marriage by such preliminary experiments as would temper the bedazzlement of love at first sight.[15] These are all points that suggest a high level of mutual concern and understanding.

His penultimate piece of advice was the one most often contradicted. The lives of this group in particular reflected the leniency of German divorce laws. Karoline von Schlegel, who had been widowed, and then had an affair that left her pregnant before she married Wilhelm von Schlegel, eventually divorced him and married his best friend, Friedrich Schelling. Dorothea Veit, Moses Mendelssohn's daughter, divorced her husband in order to live with, and ultimately marry, Friedrich von Schlegel. Schleiermacher himself fell in love with Henriette Herz, one of the great salon leaders of Berlin, and then with a clergyman's wife who later went back to her husband; in the end he married a young girl. All of them—the Schlegels, Schleiermacher, Schelling—believed in the total mating of body and soul, and since such matings are notoriously fragile, their philosophy urged them to continue the quest for perfection no matter how far it took them.

However that may be, the German romantic movement was much less socially revolutionary than the slightly later French one with its stress on utopian social change. When Saint-Simonian and Fourierist doctrines came to Germany, it was largely through the dark glass of George Sand's novels.[16] Although these found eager readers among both emancipated and repressed German women, they resulted in the public picture of a woman with a dagger in her girdle, a cigarette in her mouth, and a whip in her hand. Immermann liked to contrast George Sand, who had fled her husband and sought emancipation, and the more self-sacrificing German, Charlotte Stieglitz, who killed herself in 1834 in the fond hope that a great sorrow would improve the quality of her husband's mediocre poetry.[17] (It is true that Charlotte was called *Weltheilige* by her admirers, like a Saint-Simonian female messiah, but she did not belong to any socialist group and was actually a romantic hangover rather than a pioneer of a better future state.)[18]

By the 1830s a new movement was taking root. Young Germany was less cosmopolitan and more patriotic than the earlier romantic movement.[19] It had political hopes for a united country, but it rather dropped interest in women. Enfantin's ideas on economic reorganization were picked up, but not those on the equality of the sexes. Its literary leaders, Ludwig Börne and Karl Ferdinand Gutzkow,[20] were anti-romantic and anti-feminist, although strongly in favor of the Rights of

Man, while Heine, the most distinguished of the group, called Enfantin "the foremost mind of his age," and searched out the Saint-Simonian meeting place within twenty-four hours of his first arrival in Paris.[21] Yet when he came to marry, his wife was not a free intellectual but a prostitute with no pretension at equality. Heine favored emancipation of the flesh but not of the female mind.

∽ Much of the discussion of romanticism and the new woman had taken place in the salons of Berlin, which were under the guidance of a series of highly intelligent, free-thinking, socially skillful Jewish women, among them Dorothea Veit and Henriette Herz. The most famous was Rahel Levin, who eventually married Varnhagen von Ense. It was in these salons that talk about feminism made a bridge to the renewed political consciousness of the 1860s.

Rahel's father was a banker, and apparently a family tyrant. He decreed, for example, that no birthdays were to be celebrated in any form.[22] Rahel grew up in the shadow of his brutal rages. "A more tortured youth cannot be experienced; no one can be more ill or nearer to madness,"[23] she later said of herself. When Rahel left home she could only afford to live in a garret. After her father's death, in 1798, life became a bit easier, though her brothers still held the purse strings. It was not long, however, before princes were calling at her humble apartment, attracted by her charm and intellect. Rahel hoped that life would strike her like "a storm without an umbrella"—a romantic fancy which irritated Hannah Arendt, who wrote a book about her in 1957—but she learned how to transmute her emotional tempests into a political understanding of women's needs.[24]

Soon after she started to enjoy her independent social life, when she was about twenty-five, Rahel became engaged to Count Karl von Finckenstein. The troth lasted for five years, until 1880, but he was never able to get permission from his relatives to marry a middle-class Jewess. The effect of his departure was devastating. "One is no longer a pure creature of nature," she wrote, "when once, terrified by pain and humiliation, one would . . . have given one's life not to be able to feel pain; when one has seen cruelty in *everything*—all nature."[25] (When she met him again, twelve years later, "cold as a frog," talking of his handsome wife, she reproached herself with feeling "like an animal that had belonged to him.")[26]

Ellen Key, another of her biographers (1913) and a more sympathetic one than Arendt, remarked that few women used up their power of loving in a first experience, and that at thirty, when a woman's senses awoke, she found out how to love with more than just her soul.[27] The love that turned Rahel's being to flame and her soul to ashes (the expressions are Key's) was a Spanish diplomat, Raphael d'Urquijo. It was love at first sight in 1802. Eventually this affair, too, foundered, perhaps on the difference in ways of loving between a man and a woman, perhaps on those between a Spaniard and a German. Urquijo was furiously jealous. Rahel gave up society, moved to the country, and saw no one but him for a year and a half, but nothing satisfied him and she suffered anew for her commitment.

Her next lover was Alexander von Marwitz, whom she met in 1809. He was much younger than she, and her motherly sympathy was said to have saved him from suicide. They had a more companionable affair than she had experienced before, for "we live[d] like two students, one of whom is a woman," as she described it.[28] Marwitz was killed in the wars of 1813. Before his death she had already come to know Varnhagen von Ense, another much younger man, whom she hoped to help as she had Marwitz. He was engaged, but was attracted into Rahel's circle by Schleiermacher. Her personality impressed him when he observed her in attendance at Fichte's lectures at the newly founded University of Berlin. By the summer of 1808, he was coming to call on her every day, visits that he said made him feel as if he had spent the summer "in Athens."[29] Obviously he was falling in love, and though she told him that she could never again feel a passion such as Urquijo had awakened —forcing him, like a typical romantic, to read the love letters of the earlier affair—she agreed to marry him if he went back to see his first fiancée and then decided to make an honorable break. "You must be free," she wrote, though she was beginning to feel that her own poor heart might be able to to love again after all.[30] Varnhagen chose Rahel, but they had to wait six years for him to complete his studies and get a position. They married in 1814, when Rahel was forty-three, even though they disapproved in principle of the marriage bond and had agreed to treat each other as if they were not married. In the long run Rahel was surprised at her own happiness; Varnhagen was so attentive and understanding that she finally conceded that she did feel married after all.[31]

Rahel's importance was chiefly as a consciousness raiser. Her letters, published after her death, revealed a new kind of woman to her contemporaries, much as Marie Bashkirtseff's *Journal* would do for a later period. Above all Rahel wanted women to be honest, especially in love. Lying bored her, but she harped on that theme song of the nineteenth century: women were forced into insincerity by men's coarseness. "It is hard that in Europe men and women should form two different nations: one moral, the other not," she wrote.[32] In her mind reform of slavery, war, and marriage went hand in hand, with hope lying in "the new European love." She abhorred patience in suffering (just the opposite of George Eliot), and she looked with scorn on aesthetic flirtation that failed to move on to carnal involvement. Her favorite women friends were those who left their husbands to follow their hearts, like Pauline Wiesel, who went off with Prince Louis Ferdinand.

In order to have new women, new men would be required, and Rahel called for the sort who could unite her "two nations" in total sympathy, while in the process abolishing slavery and war. She felt, in fact, that women ought to turn toward the state out of their innate love for children. She had married too late for a family of her own, but described herself as "a mother without children."[33] Of her nieces she explained, "I put flesh on them by my care and made their souls grow and their minds arise and bestir themselves."[34] It is characteristic of her interest in her own sex that she thought children should have only mothers, and that they should bear their mothers' names and be subject only to womanly authority. Jesus had only a mother, she pointed out as a clinching example, and she hoped that for each child an ideal father could be appointed by the courts, for if the children's own father was at odds with the mother, it could be torture for them, she explained, doubtless remembering her own early sufferings.[35]

During the cholera epidemic of 1830, she volunteered as a nurse and began to study the condition of the poor. It was this experience that convinced her that women needed to be more than great lovers and must turn their motherliness outward. They were needed, among other places, on the directing boards for public welfare. Her own competence at organizing a hospital proved considerable, leading her to cry like so many others, "If only I had some profession!"[36] For a brief moment only, Saint-Simonianism seemed to her the great instrument to heal the wounds of history, and in one of her letters to Heine she described how moving, how shattering, and yet how full of blessing it seemed to her.

For all her social concern, Rahel's chief fame, and her impact on her generation, was as "the President of Germany's Republic of Letters."[37] Her fellow citizens were the literary men and women who flocked to her salon, where, they felt, she knew how to fructify genius, to tie people and interests together, to nourish thought, to mediate between priests and atheists, poets and artists, lords and writers. She described one of her favorite techniques as "penetrating the masks" that people wore, regarding this as a good deed, but she also liked to direct conversations away from empty forms. Heine felt that no other being understood him so well, even though (with her total lack of a sense of irony) she felt that *he* lacked seriousness.[38] Most of the people mentioned so far in this chapter, as well as many others, met in Rahel's salon: Schleiermacher, the Schlegels, the Tiecks, Fichte, Gentz (secretary to the Congress of Vienna), Prince Louis Ferdinand, Heine, Prince Pückler-Muskau. Here, for almost the first time, intellectuals were free to move as equals in high society, and all were treated according to their merits, ranked according to their culture. The salons usually began about five o'clock and broke up after light refreshments at nine. No one was specially invited, but there were seldom more than two other women present, because, with all her hopes for women's future, the hostess found that most of the ones available tended to disrupt the continuity of thought.

When George Eliot, with G. H. Lewes, went to Berlin in 1854, Rahel herself was dead, though they met Varnhagen. They visited instead another of Berlin's salon leaders, Fanny Lewald, with her husband, Adolf Stahr. Fanny has been called a German George Sand, with the important difference that the Frenchwoman lost her faith, whereas Fanny acquired ever-increasing doses of earnestness throughout her life. (George Eliot's and Lewes's complaint was that there was no scrap of humor in the leaders of intellectual life in Berlin.)

Born in 1811 in Königsberg, of a free-thinking Jewish family, Fanny was given the best education the times afforded, though it was hardly enough to satisfy her. Her father planned a strenuous schedule of five hours of sewing and knitting, with two of piano practice daily; she described herself in early adolescence as wanting to know how things worked from the inside, but all that was available to answer her burning queries were her old schoolbooks.[39] Later she was given a chance to travel, and her earliest writings were about England and Scotland. A cousin had noticed her talent for letters and had helped her get some-things printed; this effort scandalized her father, whose own plan for coping with her support was to settle her into an unworthy marriage. Meanwhile he insisted that she keep secret even from her own sisters the fact that she was making money.[40] When she finally left home, wanting to earn her own living, she took with her the same allowance that her sisters were given for pin money. At one time she figured out what her work had contributed to the family finances: how many stockings knit, how many music lessons given to her sisters; and she was convinced by the large total that women's work was always unrecognized and ill-recompensed.[41]

Like Rahel she had a series of passionate affairs before she settled down. At twenty she inspired love in a Protestant theological student and considered converting to his faith until she found, on the eve of her baptism, that she believed hardly any of the dogmas she was supposed to. Being in love, she signed anyway, assuming that the instructor could hardly have believed these things either, but after this sacrifice her lover retreated.[42] Then she fell in love with her cousin Heinrich Simon, who won her heart by making her believe that the most important things in life were self-understanding and self-development.

Her future husband was to win her by telling her that the most important thing was creating love out of a field prepared by passion. She met Adolf Stahr in 1845. He was a *gymnasium* professor and the father of five children. It was ten years before he could get a divorce and be free to marry her; meanwhile they took short trips, and he rented a room near her apartment so that they could spend part of their days together.[43] Thus it seems that even so late as 1855 much was still permitted to a woman "trying to live her own life."

When they finally married, she called it a bourgeois affair; she boasted, however, that she continued to support herself. Though both partners were conscious of her superiority, he was one of those rare men who seem to be attracted to superior women and to bring out the best in them, while she found that being loved by a man at a ripe age is life's highest fulfillment. As long as he was alive, they would talk out their ideas, but when he died, she began to write down her thoughts on feminism. She had already composed several novels.* Now she railed at women who failed to make rational lives for themselves, lamenting the platitude that the natural calling for any woman was to be a wife and mother when men were not described primarily as husbands and fathers.[44] Men planned things *their* way, she complained, while women stood stupidly around to wait for them. She was disgusted with the women she saw about her, with their sentimentality, their unwillingness to commit themselves to passion, and their devouring of fine people and great purposes like Juggernauts. The men in her circle seemed bigger-hearted about most things than the women, though the way they treated women infuriated her. Even a female genius would be told to sit and *knit*, she fumed.[45]

By this time, 1869, she was thoroughly anti-romantic. What women needed was not free love but equal pay, not association into small groups of believers but self-understanding, and, far from needing socialism, women should be grateful to Bismarck.[46] They should also pay attention to personal care of themselves—she was a warm advocate of daily bathing, which first became practicable during her lifetime.[47] Her concern for her own sex included special regard for poor women and for getting the affluent to help them. She looked forward to workers' education, hostels for retreat in times of sickness or unemployment, clubs for their entertainment, and even communal kitchens for lower and middle-class families.[48] Especially she hoped that rich women would treat their own maids well, paying decent wages, seeing that they had comfortable quarters, protecting their morals, and training them to become good wives and mothers in their turn.[49] One of her most radical ideas for promoting understanding between rich and poor was that children of various classes should attend school together and that even the wealthy should send their children to school instead of having them privately tutored.

The fact that Henriette Herz, Rahel Varnhagen, and Fanny Lewald were Jewish may well have played the same part in making them free-standing women as the unusual, non-French parentage of George Sand, Marie d'Agoult, and Flora Tristan. They had all been subject to an unusual kind of patriarchal despotism, combined with an enlightened intellectual education. This enabled them to stand a bit apart from the culture they lived in, a position that sharpens perceptions; any alienation they felt, any lack of total commitment to one set of norms, added to the courage to protest.

Bettina von Arnim, née Brentano, was the product of an Italo-German marriage. Her father was an Italian banker living in Frankfurt, and her brother Clemens was an early collector of folksongs and folklore.

---

*Her 1844 novel, *Der dritte Stand* (*The Third Estate*), was censored. When the authorities found out that she was "only a woman," they removed the ban, which made her even angrier than the original censorship (Steinhauer, 80).

Bettina was known all her life for her originality and impulsiveness. The correspondence she carried on with Goethe was typical. Although she was at least seventeen (and perhaps as old as twenty-two), she later caused a literary sensation by publishing these letters under the title Goethe's *Briefwechsel mit einem Kinde* (*Goethe's Letters to a Child*). ("Some child!" snorted Dora d'Istria; but Bettina excused herself by murmuring that she was so given to fantasy that she could not tell truth from dream.) The story of her engagement goes that one day, when walking *Unter den Linden*, she went up to her brother's friend, Achim von Arnim, impulsively took his hand, and said, in Latin, "I'll marry you if you like."[50] The marriage produced seven children and was not unhappy, though for long stretches Bettina lived in Berlin to enjoy city life while Achim stayed at their country residence, where in the holidays the children were always overjoyed to rejoin him.

After she was widowed, in 1831, with her children grown and independent, Bettina felt free to express her long-slumbering gifts. She began with the Goethe letters, but very soon became enormously concerned with the condition of the poor. She was never as committed a feminist as the other women just discussed, but she attacked injustice and suffering everywhere.[51] (Nor did she limit herself to words, having been a devoted nurse during the cholera epidemic of 1831.) Her literary description of how the other half lived was entitled *Dies Buch gehört dem König* (*This Book Is for the King*), but it was not well received at court, especially as she supported the Silesian weavers in their famous strike of 1844, and the Polish minority who were being oppressed by the Prussian state. She stood up for the Grimm brothers, ousted from their professorships at the University of Göttingen, and for Gottfried Kinkel, the art historian. When she was hauled into a magistrate's office to account for her subversive writing, her defense was composed in red ink, intended to convey to the official the color of the blushes she hoped would overcome him. She remained irrepressible until her death in 1859.

∽ All of these women were at the top of society, respected as intellectuals and protected by love and admiration. But there were women of equivalent gifts who suffered more because they were less fortunately placed. For instance, Mathilde Franziska Anneke won a custody fight against one husband for her child, and then married Fritz Anneke in 1847 and wrote a tract called "Women in Conflict with Social Conditions."*[52] She rode on horseback beside her husband in the 1848 campaign in Baden, cut off her hair, and tried to found a newspaper for women. After the reaction set in, the couple fled to Wisconsin, where she started a girls' school.

More data are available for Luise Aston, the daughter of a German pastor whose love match to a girl of higher social class had proved

*I have been unable to locate this in America or Europe.

extremely unhappy. Luise's birth date is uncertain, being given as anywhere from 1814 to 1820. Perhaps in reaction to his own bad experience with love, her father pushed her into marriage with a wealthy English industrialist. She was just seventeen, she tells us, and gave in only when her father suffered a stroke,[53] indicating some of the tensions surrounding the procedure. The English husband remained a stranger to her heart, she continues, and she was lonely amid his glittering surroundings until the greatest conflict that can hit a woman struck—that between love and marriage, heart and conscience. (She may very well be moralizing here for the sake of convention.) She goes on to explain that at Karlsbad, while taking a cure (and where, if she is to be believed, she refused Metternich's offer to buy her a team of ponies), she fell in love. Though she insists that she refused to sleep with that particular man, her marriage nevertheless ended with the customary German ease, and in 1846 she made her way to Berlin with a four-year-old daughter. She had saved nothing from the shipwreck except the determination to rule over her own life. For this she needed more education and the chance to earn a living, but in her circle of freethinkers, who were also apparently free livers, she was led into trouble with the police. It was alleged that she had founded a club of emancipated women, and she was given a week to leave the city. (The fact that a minor poet had dedicated to her a poem entitled *"Madonna und Magdalen"* did not help her case.) Her first thought was to petition the King, as Bettina von Arnim had done. She described herself as the daughter of a public official who had given thirty years of faithful service to the throne, and as a woman who had been married for nine years to a factory owner from England, and now had a four-year-old child to support. She pointed out that it would be impossible to go on with her writing career in the small village to which she had been exiled, nor could she there find suitable educational facilities for her daughter. While her friends may have *talked* of founding a women's club, she went on, they had no real intention of doing so—let alone the one imagined by the police as a crazy house (*Bedlamstiftung*). In fact, the only radical action she admitted to was asking a man to dance—and this, she coyly remarked, was a custom sometimes followed at cotillions in the palace.

A petition from her level of society intensified the persecution. Now she was expelled from all Prussian dominions, and so she moved to the free city of Hamburg. During the 1848 war in Schleswig-Holstein, she became a nurse, the only woman serving with the German army. Eventually she moved to Bremen, married a Dr. D. E. Meier, and went to live in Russia.

Her novel, *Aus dem Leben* (*Drawn from Life*), has a *Doll's House* theme. The wife of a rich factory owner enjoys her affluent life, while the employees humbly work their sixteen-hour days six days a week. Finally they strike, however, just when the master has made a husky profit from a shipment from England. Mrs. Oburn, his wife, who has been stimulated like so many others by George Sand's *Indiana*, becomes concerned. She tells her husband that if the workers must have a pay cut, the owners themselves should live more simply, and she dismisses some of her servants. Her husband tells her that she does not understand, but that if she really wants to help, she should use her powers to persuade the prince, who has sought to seduce her, to give them a loan. Horrified at such a suggestion, she slams out of the house, free like Nora.

In her relatively obscure life, known more for its scandals than for its achievements, Luise Aston nevertheless managed to express a good deal of the pain of the female condition in her day, but she was not content with a merely emotional statement. To fortify her position philosophically, she studied Kant and Spinoza. She found her best support in the ideas of these men, thereby demonstrating the turn away from the romantic protest of Schleiermacher, for his situational ethics had included a deliberate repudiation of Kant's categorical imperative. Luise Aston universalized her complaint by concluding that women were being denied a basic human right when they were prevented from becoming independent, particularly in view of the common masculine opinion that the development of individual personality was the highest product of the nineteenth century. A general remedy would be total freedom of speech, and by constantly denying this, German police were infringing on the rights of all. For women especially, she added the need for freedom to feel, instead of assenting to artificial and hypocritical marriages that turned women from personalities into possessions.[54] Her daring shocked the infant women's movement in Germany, especially its first organizer, Luise Otto, who fairly or unfairly dubbed her an overexcited coquette and took pains to separate her party from Aston and her ideas.[55]

ᑲᔆ An entirely different kind of struggle, that of Henriette Feuerbach, shows what could happen to a highly gifted woman who felt constrained by poverty or a sense of inadequacy to stick with a disappointing marriage within a middle-class home. By the time she married K. W. Feuerbach, brother of the philosopher, Ludwig, he was already something of a burnt-out volcano, a widower with two small children; and if her sexual longings were never fully answered (as it seems they were not), at least she became a passionate step-mother to the future painter, Anselm, and his little sister, Emilie. Like many women, she worked out her frustrations in long letters to her brother, commiserating with him about the musical gifts that both had sacrificed. She loathed housekeeping, wished to do something in the world, but was diffident about her powers in art or scholarship.[56] She would have liked to collaborate with her brother on a book but suggested that he be the one to propose it because Professor Feuerbach would resent having a wife with ideas of her own. She described the crowded little house in which the only place for her to write was also the only place where her little girl could play with friends.[57] Meanwhile her husband needed a cure at the baths, while Anselm began to develop an artistic talent that would require expensive training. Lack of money drove her to frenzy. She appealed to her literary friends, the Herweghs, then in Paris, to find translation work for her, but felt incapable of writing original pieces because she lacked any relationship to the affairs of the world, though she had already produced, anonymously, a meek little book on the lovableness of women. Her husband would not let her give piano lessons because he objected to such public acceptance of cash, but luckily the compensation for writing was less conspicuous, and when she eventually managed to earn enough she found it an inexpressible pleasure to send him to Italy (he was an archeologist) and her son to art school.

It took war to propel her out of the house and give scope to her unsuspected executive talents. During the 1848 revolutions she wanted to follow the Herweghs into the field of battle as a nurse, but this desire found fruition only after her husband's death. In 1870 she set up a hospital that cared for fourteen thousand sick and wounded. (Even so, the army did not permit her, as a woman, to run it officially, though she was its chief organizer.)[58]

She lived in Heidelberg after her husband died—from 1852 to 1876—and her modest home became a center for music and conversation. She and Emilie were too poor to provide tea or coffee, but sometimes put apples around for the guests. At the end of her life she was still complaining, worried about the superficiality of her daughter, the fecklessness of Anselm, the small size of their crowded home, and the fear that she would have nothing to show for her life. She saw men, by that time, as either common philanderers or tyrannical husbands, and once she extravagantly wrote to Emma Herwegh that her husband, George, might be the only lover of freedom in all Europe who did not fit into one of these two molds.*

Amelia Sieveking was as deeply steeped in the doctrines of evangelical Christianity as other women were in the tenets of romantic love. Both her practical good sense and her eternal mouthing of pious sentiments about the proper sphere of women won the admiration of an English girl with similar problems, Catherine Winkworth, who translated Amelia's biography from the German.[59]

Amelia was born near Hamburg in 1794, lost her mother when young, and suffered from a lack of love all through her childhood. When her brothers went off to school, her dearest wish was to be sent too, but she never mentioned this to her father, who instead hired a tutor whom she soon grew to hate. (One of her complaints was that he had left her so unsupervised that she could read history books that created doubts about the existence of God.)

She discovered her vocation for teaching when she went, at fifteen,

*She must have been unaware that he fell passionately in love with Natalie Herzen.

to live in a family with a ten-year-old girl. A few years later, when she needed to support herself, teaching seemed the natural way to do so, except that for Amelia it was such an act of love that she hated to accept payment, and she feared that books and scientific knowledge might cause her to lose her "womanliness." After telling herself that training children in love and obedience must be a female duty, and that if the old aunt she lived with ever needed her full-time attention she would give it up, she opend her own little school with eight small girls.

Miss Winkworth gives us Amelia's daily schedule in 1832:

7 a.m. Walk to city [an hour] with basket of books
Visit the poor
Three hours of school [11:30 to 3:00]
Alternate Tuesdays reunion of former scholars
Home by 6:30
Evenings reading aloud to adoptive mother.[60]

She saved time by not preparing hot meals four days of the week, and eventually she became so busy that she no longer sat down to eat but simply munched out of her hand. She had already baffled Miss Winkworth by such small economies as doing her own washing. ("She really carried this apparently rather unpractical notion into execution, and for a whole summer washed all her own clothes in secret.")[61]

She tried to teach love to her pupils by turning the last hour of their school day into a play period so that she could study each character while the children had fun. She pondered such questions as what was the right mode of punishment, and how could one instill such unquestioning faith that the pupils would not demand reasonable answers to Biblical puzzles. When her brother inquired whether certain passages of scripture might not prove stumbling blocks, she retorted that God put them into his Holy Writ just to show that there were riddles not meant to be understood, and that a teacher must be careful not to explain the first thing about them.[62] At the same time, she did not feel that innocent pleasure could be displeasing to him who made his creatures for happiness.

She refused to allow a wealthy woman to adopt her legally, feeling the need for greater freedom, though she sometimes agonized over whether she would have to wait for this dear friend to die before she could fulfill herself, remarking plaintively that no one blamed a bride, or a missionary, for deserting her parents. She was fully as introspective as the most self-centered of the romantics. But like many of them, when called to active duty, she could respond magnificently. In the 1831 cholera epidemic, she entered a hospital as a nurse, and lived in quarantine with the patients from October 14 to December 6. Somewhat unwillingly, she even took over the superintendence of the men's wards. But the very day she got home, she started back with her school class.

By 1840 her reputation had spread and her duties widened. She got into prison reform; she worked to set up some apartments for the poor, with common rooms attached, and a children's hospital that grateful citizens named the *Amelienstift*. She tried to interest other women in her work of visiting the poor, and made the judgment that middle-class women were not nearly so good at this as aristocratic ladies, who had more tact.[63]

When Pastor Fliedner of Kaiserswerth asked her to take change of a new institute, modeled on his, at Berlin, she was too busy with her own projects to accept but recommended one of her former pupils. Gradually, finding suitable applicants for jobs became one of her greatest services; she became impatient with those who tried to keep women from useful work, and found it easy to fill the many requests she received because "so powerfully and so generally is the necessity for such employment now stirring in the hearts of persons of our own sex."[64] She was proud, though, that none of her pupils had turned into "a masculine woman."[65] In 1854 she started her sixth class of children,* grateful to find life as interesting in her sixtieth as in her eighteenth year, and she termed herself at that time "a happy old maid."[66]

A world traveler, Ida Pfeiffer, illustrates a more adventurous pattern than Amelia's duty-ridden life. Frau Pfeiffer acquired a taste for travel as a girl. In the early years of her marriage, she used to accompany her husband, and she never really became reconciled to staying at home except for a period when her two boys had to attend particular schools. Once their education was past this stage, she was free once more, and then she enjoyed the agreeable status of being old enough to travel alone. Making the best of such a chance, she went twice around the world, writing light travel books out of her experiences. Her admiring translator explained that she did not answer to that ugly type, the "emancipated woman," but that she had truly emancipated herself from laziness and fear, and was thus an example to her contemporaries.

∽ If any one woman could be regarded as a bridge between the romantic school and the hard-working realistic school of feminists, it would be Malwida von Meysenbug, who lived from 1816 to 1903.[67] Early in life romantic love failed her, but she used her disillusionment to enter into a wide questioning of other facets of women's life: economic dependence, dogmatic religious training, family pressure, and rigid convention. She dedicated her autobiography to the happier women of the future, who would be able to develop in the freer air of acknowledged rights.[68]

She too, like our French feminists, came of mixed ancestry, in her case a father of Huguenot descent and German mother. The family lived at the minor German court of Kassel, where her father had a position. She belonged to a younger generation than the Schlegels, Humboldts,

---

*In Germany it is customary for one teacher to stay with the same class all through the years it spends at a school.

and Schleiermachers, who were indeed friends of her mother, so that she met some of them in childhood. Her education was conducted by a governess along lines considered suitable for a girl of her station, but later on she was to rue the lack of serious secondary schooling that would have taught her to understand the world, she thought, instead of leaving her with dreams and fantasies. In her early teens unanswered questions burning inside her actually made her sick, so that confirmation brought on a real spiritual crisis, as it did to many intelligent German girls. For her, religious answers proved of no use at all, but she sucked some comfort from books by Rahel Levin and Bettina von Arnim on feminism and social action.

Her love life consisted of a series of disillusionments intensified by the fact that she knew "only the poetic side of marriage" and was attracted to a series of men whom the social conventions of the time forbade her to marry—the conductor of the court orchestra, who was beneath her socially, and a Russian fortune hunter, for whom her dowry was insufficient.[69]

To console herself she turned to the only serious occupation open to her, painting (selling her jewels to buy materials), until her eyes became too bad to continue. Meanwhile, through the friendship of "a young apostle," Theodor Althaus, she had discovered another interest—social service. She started making clothes for the poor and visiting the sick in the village, all the while struggling so hard to keep the relationship with the young man on a spiritual basis that she fell ill. Eventually she admitted that she was deeply in love.

Although there was considerable freedom for young people of opposite sexes to go around together openly in the little German town, they rarely had a chance to be alone. Her new mentor had a fine opportunity, however, to inculcate some of his radical ideas, shocking her family with an article accusing the court of extravagance for maintaining a theater and orchestra while their subjects were hungry. Malwida broke with her father, who felt that women should not entertain political ideas of any hue, while relations with her mother were strained because that lady opened the young couple's private mail.

Her first chance to be alone with Theodor came when she went to his home because he was ill; there, as he was helping her into her coat, they kissed for the first time. A few days later, when he returned the call, they were able to embrace again, her family having gone to the opera. Malwida was by this time so totally overwhelmed by love that her mother began to soften and agreed to try to persuade her husband to permit an engagement; but now Theodor's work took him off to another city, and Malwida's pride prevented her from "limiting his freedom" by a formal tie. She was too certain of their undying love to want to make demands upon it.

About this time her father died. Malwida found that she would receive an unpleasantly small inheritance and that she might have to earn her own living, but, generous as ever, she gave her capital to her mother and prepared to teach.

All her good intentions were dispelled by the discovery that Theodor was unfaithful, a poisoned arrow in her heart, she said. She could not understand how a feeling so deep in her could have died in him; while he acted sheepish and evasive, she demanded only candor. This disappointment led to suicidal impulses and the greatest of her spiritual struggles, but in the end she was able to commit herself to an ideal of individual personal worth and (after reading Fichte) to the regeneration of Germany. Still, she was much too unhappy to remain at home. She had shocked even her doctor by keeping a copy of Julius Froebel's *Social Politics* at her bedside and was conspicuously not invited to a court dinner because of her democratic sympathies. Deciding that these ideas were more important to her than family approval, she pondered going to America, apparently entered into correspondence with Froebel, and through him heard of a sort of college for women, the *Hamburger Hochschule für das weibliche Geschlecht*, just founded at Hamburg by his brother, Karl, and a woman named Emilie Wüstenfeld. Malwida was warmly welcomed there, and even her mother approved.

Hamburg at that time was a free city, with old Hanseatic traditions, cosmopolitan and commercial, where women were permitted to act on their own initiative in business, needing no masculine shield.[70] The school that Malwida entered had been founded by a group of German Catholic women (the German Catholics were a liberal dissenting sect) led by Emilie Wüstenfeld, who had heard of Karl Froebel's proposal for a woman's college to train its students particularly in teaching, but also for other "feminine" professions, such as medicine. Frau Wüstenfeld persuaded Froebel to head up her institution in Hamburg, and it opened its doors in 1850.[71] A hundred women registered, drawn from a wide variety of social classes, for there were scholarships available for the poor. A day-care center for their children and a laboratory kindergarten run on the principles then being developed by Karl's uncle Friedrich Froebel were attached.

The group supporting the school, called the Free Religious Society of Hamburg, had money, prestige, and the courage to undertake the risks attendant on running such a school. It acted in fact very much like many American Unitarian churches today, sponsoring lectures by the city's leading intellectuals at which the audience was encouraged to interrupt and ask questions.* After the religious exercises on Sunday morning came a social hour, much to Malwida's delight, and she longed to join the society even though she realized that leaving the church of her childhood would separate her more completely from her family than any other step she could take. Malwida's moment of decision came when her family

---

*Incidentally, Amelia Sieveking, who, of course, was living in Hamburg at the time, worried dreadfully about the forces let loose when the Free Religious Society opened up courses for women where they could be led scientifically away from revealed religion into a mere "love of humanity." She even got into a public argument with the pastor.

wrote that they had succeeded in obtaining a place for her in a Protestant *Stift*. Here she could live for the rest of her life, inexpensively and with dignity. Malwida decided that she could not take the required religious oath, and besides she was just beginning to appreciate her own abilities, so she wrote the formal letter of resignation that cut all her ties to the church she had grown up in.

As assistant to the principal of the school, the post to which she was soon assigned, she laid down the rule that the students should make their own beds and do their personal laundry; this work, she found, not only increased their seriousness but actually bred a feeling of spiritual community. There were weekly parties with free discussion and poetry reading, and weekly business meetings of the religious fellowship at which women spoke as freely as men; and at one point Malwida was named chairman of a planning committee to found a school for city children of all social classes. She outlined a scheme to have the children pay according to their means, with a common education for both sexes, together at the elementary levels and with the sexes separate at high school. There would be no religious instruction.

Meanwhile, Theodor had been sentenced to three years in prison for his radical writings, and though Malwida was thoroughly disenchanted about his sexual morals (she called him a Don Juan of ideals, preying on susceptible women by his intellect), and was certain she could never love again, she continued to be interested in his career and was instrumental in getting him appointed to a top teaching spot at her school when he got out of prison.

At this point the government intervened. Though Hamburg was a free republic, apparently Prussia exerted diplomatic pressure to have Theodor declared *persona non grata*, and he was refused permission to settle there. In the event it made no difference; he fell mortally ill and was moved to a hospital in Gotha, where Malwida spent her last savings to buy him a comfortable armchair and went to see him as often as she could afford the trip.

As political pressure built up against the Hamburg *Hochschule* for women, its board decided to close down rather than compromise their principles. It was a serious blow to Malwida. When the group broke up, she went to Berlin but was quickly asked to leave by the police, who seized her papers. The only course left seemed to be flight to England, where she found plenty of work to do. She became the governess of Alexander Herzen's children, and was so deeply attached to them that she quarreled over their custody when he remarried. In fact, she who Helene Lange said had made "*Hausfrau*" a dirty word, ended up a rather prim old maid. "Flannel had become her religion."[72]

∽ A conspicuous difference between these intellectual German women and their opposite numbers in France lies in their attitudes toward marriage. French free spirits fled from it, at least until a genuinely equal marriage like Juliette Adam's became possible. The German women, even those who had made distinguished reputations on their own, like Fanny Lewald and Rahel Varnhagen, were never really satisfied until they had achieved matrimony, even if this became possible only late in life and to patently inferior men. Part of this can be accounted for by the difference in the divorce laws. While the French used "divorce" (technically legal separation) as a means of escape from their husbands, the Germans, in a land where divorce was easy, used the courts in order to become free to marry new partners. Another part of the difference is perhaps due to national temperament. Even in the case of those women who did not marry, like Amelia Sieveking and Malwida von Meysenbug, we have the feeling that they would have married if they could. Malwida's life was a series of frustrated love affairs, while from Amelia we have the expressed wish for a male intellect to lean on, even if only a religious confessor's. Compare Hortense Allart, who felt no need for a husband at all, and whose ultimate marriage was an uncharacteristic mistake.

APPENDIX: CATECHISM OF REASON

Schleiermacher's *Catechism of Reason for Noble Women* is obviously the work of someone who dared to break conventions when he felt like it, but to whom, at other times, the traditional masculine way of thinking about education, wisdom, and honor came naturally. For clues about Schleiermacher I am deeply indebted to Professor J. Wayne Miller of Western Kentucky University. The ten commandments for women are almost but not quite, parallel to those in the Bible:

I. You shall have no more than one lover, but you can be a friend [to other men] without the coloration of love, and without coquetry or excessive devotion.

II. You shall make no ideal images, neither of an angel in heaven nor of a hero from a poem or romance, but you shall love a man the way he is. For Nature, your goddess, is a star godhead who visits the wild imaginings of girls upon women unto the third or fourth period of their feelings.

III. You shall not profane even the smallest of the holy things of love, for she will lose her ability to love who violates her inner feeling and who gives herself for gifts, or for the sake of being a mother in peace and quiet.

IV. Remember the Sabbath of your heart, to keep it holy. . . .

V. Honor the individuality and stubbornness of your children so that their life may be longer upon earth.

VI. You shall not intentionally incite the passions [of other men].

VII. You shall not contract a marriage that will have to be broken.

VIII. You shall not desire to be loved where you do not love.

IX. You shall not bear false witness for men by covering up their barbarousness with words or deeds.

X. You shall covet [or acquire] men's education, skill, wisdom, and honor.

The Creed:

I. I believe in eternal humanity as it was before it took upon itself the shapes of man and woman.

II. I believe that I do not live either for obedience or for self-amusement, but to be and to become; and I believe that the power of will and education will bring me closer to the eternal, will release the shackles of bad education, and will make me independent of the limitations of sex.

III. I believe in enthusiasm, and virtue, in the worth of art and the charm of learning, in friendship with men and love for the fatherland, in past greatness and future perfection.

ᴄᴏ 24.

German Women in Politics

He who has feeling [and not dogma in its place], *he* senses the new woman arising from the present chaos. In order to appreciate her new, fresh beauty, new eyes will be needed.

Hedwig Dohm

However colorful the romantic life, it was experienced only on a certain fringe of society. If the lives of ordinary women were going to improve, sober thinking had to come from a different source.

As we have seen, the romantic movement itself gradually dissolved into something called "Young Germany," a new generation of artists and intellectuals tied together by patriotic eagerness for a united fatherland. But it is an odd fact—and was to be strikingly true in Italy also—that when men began arguing about constitutions and government, they left women's interests high and dry. The supposedly liberal Frankfurt Parliament of 1848 did absolutely nothing for women, and what small but interesting pockets of feminist activity there had been were destroyed in the subsequent reaction. When the movement started up again in 1865, however, it quickly became too strong to be demolished, even though the Empire of 1871 did nothing to help the women's cause, and the Civil Code as finally formulated by 1896 was designed to push women back rather than to emancipate them.

The political hedging tended to narrow women's traditional sphere considerably, but even more important was the economic revolution taking place at the same time. Distribution techniques improved, heating and lighting became simpler, fewer apprentices were boarded in the homes of merchants and craftsmen, and aunts, sisters, and extra servants were pushed out to support themselves in a market economy that had never had many jobs for women.[1] Even for those who did remain at home, the environment was less stimulating; their role diminished from what it had been in 1800. Many of the accustomed tasks of the household were no longer needed, such as the storage of great quantities of food and clothing, the pride of German housekeepers for centuries. Thus it came about that Amelia Sieveking, for example, found so many women seeking jobs that it was easy for her to fill the requests she got for teaching, nursing, or administrative personnel. And it was this forcing of women into the outside world, whether to defend their rights or earn their livings, that drove them to organizations of their own.

The changes did not happen without strain. The portraits painted in the forties show women with pinched and anxious faces,[2] while the situation reminded the historian Treitschke of the period of decay in ancient Rome when discontented and nervous women thrust themselves into masculine callings.[3] According to Helene Lange, every decent man would be scared if he realized that it was actual misery that caused women to want to organize (for organize they did), and that male derision might kill a thousand possibilities for happiness.[4] At first a few tentative desires took them outside their homes. Political activity might begin when some of them took their problems to an unwilling burgomaster; and perhaps involvement in the German Catholic movement led others to begin attending the sessions of the Saxon diet and studying its proceedings.*[5]

The real founder of the German women's movement, the one who capitalized on the widespread economic and social discontent, was Luise Otto. An admirer called her "the lark" who woke her fellows up.[6] She first came to public attention in 1844, when Robert Blum's *Vaterlandsblättern*, a Leipzig paper, asked its readers, "Have women a right to share in the interests of the state?" A letter came back, signed simply "A Saxon Girl," advancing the thesis that it was not only the right, but the duty, of women so to do. The writer turned out to be the twenty-five-year-old Luise Otto.[7]

She was the youngest of several daughters in the home of a superior court judge in Meissen. Her family life was regarded as very modern at the time because the parents and children used the familiar "*du*" to each other and the girls were allowed to read newspapers.[8] There was a great deal of reading aloud in the household; the mother read Schiller and epics of the Greek wars while the children peeled vegetables or sewed. (Luise remembered appalling stretches of sewing.)[9] On their own the girls got hold of Schlegel's *Lucinde*—contraband, naturally—and began to be concerned about the lives of the poor. When Luise started to write poetry, a relative helped her find a publisher, but she had to use a male pseudonym, Otto Stern.

Her fingers trembled with delight as she penned her answer to Blum's newspaper query. She wondered if she would dare to send it in,

*The German Catholic movement was started in 1844 by two priests who found themselves in difficulties with Rome. One of them was suspended for living with a woman, whom he subsequently married. The new church favored a married priesthood, the use of the vernacular in church services, only two sacraments, and communion in both kinds. Its social gospel favored the equality of the sexes in marriage and before the law and both partners made the same marriage vows in its services. It spread rapidly and by 1845 had congregations all over Germany, including one in Leipzig, where Robert Blum was a leading spirit. Later it was united with the *Freie Gemeinde*, one communion of which sponsored the Hamburg institution attended by Malwida von Meysenbug (*Kirchenlexikon* [1886]).

and after carrying it to Blum's bookstore, she left her sealed paper silently on the desk and stole away.[10] Blum realized as soon as he opened it that he had made a discovery. He was a bookseller, a publisher, a liberal, and a feminist, and he was in a position to encourage Luise to write.

She was emboldened to undertake social criticism by Bettina von Arnim's example, and went on to write a volume of patriotic poetry and a novel, *Schloss und Fabrik* (*Castle and Factory*), which cut sufficiently close to the bone that the censors confiscated it and finally allowed it to be published only with alterations.[11] Blum suggested that she use her royalties to travel around Germany, and she eagerly took up this idea, giving three reasons: love of scenery, devotion to the fatherland, and the hope of showing the world that a young woman could get around on her own without depending on a brother's escort.[12] It was the first time she had ever traveled by herself, and her family warned her thoroughly of the dangers that might be lurking, but in her tour, which lasted several months, she found nearly everybody kind and helpful; the one exception was a bemedaled court official who tried to hold her hand in the woods. She walked for a good part of her journey, but often hired wagons too. Once when she tried to engage such transportation, the livery station manager asked to speak to "the man," but when she explained that there was no "man," he picked out his most reliable driver as her escort.

Meanwhile, Blum's paper went on to print a complete program for a feminist movement, including sections on girls' education, self-support through jobs for women, and the special problems of poor working women.

The Revolution of 1848 inspired both Blum and Luise Otto to renewed activity. Unfortunately Blum met his death before a firing squad later in that year, but Luise Otto was able to continue for a short while editing a newspaper called *Die Gleichheit* (*Equality*), with the motto "I enlist women as citizens in the empire of Freedom."* Eventually it too fell victim to the reaction, and she found her movements limited by the police.

In the middle of the Revolution, she had fallen in love with one of its heroes, a certain August Peters, who had been through the siege at Rastatt and only escaped execution because of his serious ill-health. When he was expecting to be shot, he poured out his love in a letter of farewell to her, to which she replied that she would marry him whenever he got out of prison.[13] She had to wait seven years, during which time she was allowed to visit him once a year, and in 1858 they were married. He died in 1864.

His death by no means stopped her work. In 1865 she called together a women's conference—the first in Germany—with herself in the chair.[14] She had asked a sympathetic male professor to open the proceedings because no woman had ever presided over a large public

*"*Dem Reich der Freiheit werb' ich Bürgerinnen.*"

meeting before, but he told her that women would be lost before they began unless they could manage their own affairs. At his suggestion, men were admitted only as honorary, non-voting members of the All-German Women's Alliance (*Allgemeine Deutsche Frauenverein*, hereafter referred to as ADF), which was formed out of the deliberations.

Their first organized endeavor was to set up an educational program for women. Because Luise Otto-Peters had a strong sense of the solidarity of the whole sex, their efforts were especially directed toward working women. "Life is struggle" was their motto, and their first aim was to train poor girls for paying jobs. At the same time they hoped to broaden the lives of their disadvantaged sisters, so they set up a cultural program where factory girls and servants could discuss such topics as "Schiller's youth" side by side with "the early intellectual training of children."

Twenty-five years later participants recollected these meetings with nostalgia, the sessions that began with coffee and cake, followed by the reading aloud of Kant and Hegel while the rest of the membership knitted, and they remarked on the extremely good manners that characterized any activity organized by Frau Peters.[15] Deliberately they sought to erase the trouser-wearing, cigar-smoking image present in people's minds ever since the days of George Sand. At the same time they wanted to carry on in new social circumstances what they felt were the true ideas of the older period: freedom of expression, care for human beings, the embodiment of "motherliness in public life."[*] With equal force, insists Helene Lange in her history, the movement consecrated itself to the ideal of individuality, the heightening of the modern feeling of personal identity, albeit one that could best be created by work.[16]

In some ways Luise Otto was ahead, not only of her own contemporaries, but even of many of her successors in the women's movement. She was outraged at the unequal treatment often accorded sons and daughters in the same family. Girls were sacrificed to the home while brothers went off to school, and sometimes those boys spent more for beer and cigars in two or three days than their sisters would receive for pocket money in a month.[17] The girls could lose their chance at marriage if their brothers took too much time or money in setting up in their professions. The first requirement in girls' education, therefore, should be to replace their feelings of inferiority with a sense of courage and independence; after that could come training for earning capacity. Although she did not want women to train for "masculine" jobs, she believed that there were enough feminine ones to go around. All women should have a vocation outside of marriage, just as men did, though marriage itself was a calling for both sexes that should be devoted to mutual growth.[18]

She was also ahead of her time in her concern for workers. Her early novel, *Castle and Factory*, had revealed the brutalization caused by mechanization,[19] and she continued to write poetry about poor working

[*]"*Muttersorge im öffentlichen Leben.*"

girls, especially the lace makers with their low pay and their inevitable blindness. August Bebel was one of the men she had invited to address her first women's conference of 1865, though later both the middle-class women's movement and the Social Democratic party backed away from acknowledging the connection. In the last year of her life, she acquiesced without protest to a resolution by the Confederation of German Women's Associations, or BDF (*Bund Deutscher Frauenvereine*), not to allow any socialist groups as members; but in the opinion of Margrit Twellmann, a leading modern student of the matter, this was neither because Luise Otto had changed her convictions nor because she had become weak with old age, but simply because of an alteration in the system of political parties.[20] Her lifelong motto was: "No one must ever doubt the victory of humanity and progress. Least of all should one doubt himself, his own strength."[21]

At the same time that Luise Otto started her work in Saxony, a somewhat parallel beginning was made in Berlin under the leadership of Dr. Adolf Lette. Because he was a man, the *Letteverein*, as it came to be called, was aimed at doing something for women, without the democratic practice of the women of Leipzig. Its management was perfectly frank in stating that "never in eternity" would they move toward political emancipation, since their only concern was getting means of self-support for women who needed it.[22] Limited though it was in comparison with the ADF, it still represented a step forward in that it gave work and education to thousands of young girls who remained devoted to Dr. Lette's memory. He helped them get entry into nursing, midwifery, lithography, telegraphy, the post office, railroad ticket selling, bookkeeping, lending libraries, bookbinding, and kindergarten teaching.[23] The English-born Crown Princess Viktoria, who always worked to move things forward in her adopted country, accepted the honorary presidency. By 1869 there were sixteen member associations of the *Letteverein*, serving the same purpose as the schools of Elisa Lemmonier in Paris. After this, however, it ceased to grow. The work begun in Luise Otto's fashion proved to have more vitality.

Slowly what had begun as a sort of guerrilla warfare on the part of the women turned into a campaign to organize regular troops and carry out a battle plan. By 1877 the ADF had enlisted between eleven and twelve thousand women, and knew of many more in specialized local groups who were not yet ready to join a movement for total emancipation.*

At first it attracted little attention. In 1870 a resident English-woman stated that she heard no mention at all of any women's move-

---

*Both the ADF and the *Letteverein* published newspapers, the former's called *Neue Bahnen* (*New Highways*) because, explained Luise Otto, "women's studies" had become a special discipline (Otto-Peters, 154 ff.). The *Letteverein* paper was called *Frauen-Anwalt*, or the *Women's Champion*.

ment, and for a while the cause spread without even much opposition.[24] In its second decade various men and conservative women noticed its potential with dismay, particularly when Jenny Hirsch translated John Stuart Mill's *Subjection of Women* and Fanny Lewald's essay, *Für und wider die Frauen* (*For and Against Women*), appeared in a Cologne newspaper.[25]

The chief spokesman for the opposition was Philip von Nathusius, who made a broad appeal to German men, at Halle in 1871, not to give up "the still green oasis, the piece of paradise" that women's presence in the home afforded.[26] Heinrich von Sybel, the once-liberal historian, added his voice.[27] And a few women chimed in, notably Laura Marholm, a well-known novelist, who felt that the only women who would stand for women's rights were those in whom sex lay dormant, whose faces were sallow, whose skins clammy. In Russia, she hinted darkly, this type turned into Nihilists and murdered; in Germany they *started Kindergartens.*[28] It was all the same thing in the end, she said.

⚮ Before going on to describe the growth of the middle-class women's movement, and especially its long, hard struggle with the Social Democrats, let us pause and look at German law, which in some ways was more specifically limiting than that of the other countries here under review. In addition to restrictions that were built into German civil law at the end of the nineteenth century, a time when other nations were relaxing their rules about women, German women had to face a set of prohibitions against political action that were more severe than any elsewhere in western Europe.

The legal struggle, the split with the socialists, and the general growth of the middle-class women's movement were all proceeding simultaneously from 1865 until 1914, but they will necessarily here be dealt with one at a time, beginning with a description of German law as it affected women.

As the German states had separate governments until 1871, and as the Empire when formed put off codifying its civil law until January 1, 1900, when the *Bürgerliches Gesetzbuch*—the Civil Code—was promulgated, it is nearly impossible to generalize about the laws prior to that time. In 1873 Hedwig Dohm listed what she considered "marks of slavery" in women's status: they lived under another's will, could not dispose of their own persons, were subject to corporal punishment, had no rights over their children, and had no right to own or earn money.[29] Laws alone, of course, do not account for social harmony or discontent: all they do is to create limits that cannot lawfully be breached, and sanctions to ensure obedience. Not all women felt constricted. Professor Paulsen of Berlin, who was a moderate defender of improved legal rights for women, remembered the stalwart women he knew as a child in Schleswig-

Holstein, which had one of the most backward of all German legal systems; they would not, he said, have understood feminists' complaints that they were in any way hindered in pursuing their goals.[30]

Like women of other countries, German women looked back to a distant past when they had enjoyed more rights, and it was a common belief that they had lost ground every time the ancient Germanic law gave way to Roman or French codes.[31] They recalled that in the Middle Ages, abbesses as well as abbots had sat in the Reichstag, and that the law had not only allowed divorce by mutual agreement but also protected the wife's right to her own property. Over the years these privileges had been worn away by piecemeal legislation in the petty states, and especially in the Rhineland, which was governed by the Napoleonic Code even after the army of occupation left. In some ways the French law seemed sensible and coherent. For women, however, as we have seen, it was at best a mixed blessing.

The formation of the German Empire in 1871 dashed feminist hopes for any serious consideration of their legal status, especially so long as Bismarck was in control, for nothing interested him less. When a divorced princess attempted to establish a legal claim over her child, Bismarck's son commented, "With us that counts as false law—women count for nothing." The iron chancellor apologized once for even mentioning politics to a group of ladies who came with an offering of flowers, telling them that the German home was a stronger defender of the Fatherland than its fortresses.[32]

When the new imperial Code was drafted in 1896, there were supposed to be four years of discussion before it took effect with the new century. It appeared to be a great opportunity for the women's movement to express its desires, and they came up with sheaves of recommendations that seemed reasonable, modern, and likely to pass. They asked for such rights as management of their own property and guardianship of their children.[33] Mass demonstrations were organized, mammoth petitions signed (twenty-five thousand from Munich alone), leaflets, protest meetings, lecture courses on civil rights[34]—but when the Code took effect German women received a slap in the face. Almost nothing of what they had asked for was included, and they learned that in the German Empire, women's rights were less important than a new railroad or even a new election law for men.

The hardest thing for the women to accept in the new Code was that it kept the man as the head of the family. Paragraph 1354 stated that to the man belonged the decision in all matters of common married life.* The wife was specifically assigned a housekeeping role, and if perchance she earned any money, it was required that she pay for common household expenses out of it.[35] It explained that the woman was not obliged to follow the man if he was misusing his rights, but who was to decide? In

---

*"*Dem Mann steht die Entscheidung in allen das gemeinschaftliche eheliche Leben betreffenden Angelegenheiten zu.*"

accordance with a court decision, a husband had the right to open and read his wife's mail, while for her to do the same with his was punishable.

The law on guardianship had never (in Prussia, and doubtless elsewhere in Germany) allowed a mother to serve as guardian for her children even though her husband might have named her so in his will.[36] She had to have a male trustee to serve with her, even if he functioned only in an honorary capacity. There was, naturally, no such provision for a widower to get the necessary motherly oversight of his offspring. The rule of paternal right covered even trivial things. Hedwig Dohm was shocked when her six-year-old girl came home with a piece of schoolwork that had to be signed for, and she learned that a mother's signature was not good enough.[37] When the new Code was written, the old word "paternal" was replaced by "parental," but in spite of this verbal concession, the father was the one who had the right to decide about a child; if he died, the power went to the grandfather before it was allowed to go to the mother; and such a mother lost her rights upon a second marriage. As one commentator put it, *her* parental power was exactly equal to that of a father who had been hauled into court for alcoholism and given a legal guardian. Defenders of the law explained that if the wife of a drunken husband was allowed to be the guardian of her children, she would still owe "obedience" to that husband, and hence could not be considered fully capable. This explains why she could not remain a guardian if she remarried, because then she would owe obedience to her second husband. Another fine legal point revolved around whether guardianship was a "public office," for women were specifically forbidden to hold such offices.[38] Real equality was not given to German women until 1949.*

Although the Code gave formal support to the "civil equality of women" (with some of the exceptions noted), it did not by any means indicate that suffrage could be any part of civil rights. To this it should be added that the women's movement itself came rather late and slowly to the demand for the right to vote. Its leaders decided to consolidate one position for women before moving toward another, and they began with education and jobs. Not until the end of the century did they begin to realize that without the ballot they could not accomplish the rest of their program.†

*German laws regarding seduction and bastardy were more favorable to the woman than the French, generally speaking. For example, most states not under Napoleonic influence allowed research into paternity and made the father responsible for an illegitimate child, although, in Prussia at least, such a child was not permitted to enter the home of his father, nor of the mother either, if she was noble (Koltsova-Masalskaia, 2: 114).

†As far as the vote was concerned, Germany, like most other European countries, had never completely given up the medieval customs that permitted certain women to vote on certain occasions. In some parts they could vote in local elections, and in a few cities qualified women could seal their votes at home and send them to the polls by a messenger (Zahn-Harnack, *Frauenbewegung*, 327). Austrian women who owned land in their own right could cast ballots for provincial legislative assemblies under a law of 1861, though again they often had to carry out this duty by proxy (Stanton, 187). A new Austrian law of 1888 abolished these privileges and at the same time excluded women from political clubs,

To politically active women the denial of the vote may not have been quite so galling as the restriction on other activities. An 1850 law of Prussia, copied in some other states, decreed that: "Political clubs are forbidden to accept women, schoolchildren, and apprentices. Furthermore, such persons must not take part in assemblies or meetings at which political conditions are discussed." A clarification of 1887 added: "Under 'political conditions' must be understood all affairs that concern the constitution, police power, or law making of the state, the rights of citizens, and international relations."[39]

Obviously strict enforcement of this provision would have prevented the women's movement from ever discussing votes, peace, or legislative reform in any of the areas dear to feminists, especially since the schools and universities they hoped to open up were all agencies of the state. Helene Lange explained that one of the things dividing the middle-class women's movement from the Social Democratic feminists was that the police were eager to use any excuse to suppress socialist activity, while they often winked when middle-class women slipped beyond the boundary of strict legality. Even so, at a big evangelical-social congress held in Berlin in 1901, women who had prepared papers and were eager to listen and speak were summarily barred.

Time, though, marched on, and by 1903 women were officially permitted to attend purely *social* affairs of political clubs, and also lectures and readings; and finally—a great victory—on May 15, 1908, came the long-awaited day when women were allowed to join political parties of their choice. Helene Lange was so happy that she marched to the headquarters of the Liberal party that very morning and became the first woman to inscribe her name.[40]

Not that the parties were uniformly delighted at this access of new members. They did not yet realize what a help female volunteers could be. Helene Lange says that the first change in Germany's creaky political customs came when women members refused to sit in smoke-filled rooms, and so they brought a breath of fresh air both literally and figuratively to the discussion.[41] The Conservative party was least ready to use feminine help, even though they could easily have enlisted a large number of devout Protestant churchwomen. The Catholic Center party was also unprepared to receive them, though their press tried to awaken interest and the Pope gave women permission to discuss everything but theology. The liberal parties talked a better line but did not really act to make use of the new energies at their disposal. As Agnes von Zahn-Harnack put it, their brains told them to use women but their hearts still said no.[42] Even so, this political wing was the one most feminists chose to join, rather than setting up a party of their own. Some of the liberal parties endorsed woman suffrage in 1912. As for the Social Democrats,

---

parties, and meetings. Before the loopholes were closed, some women in German-speaking lands had had the right to sit on local committees for welfare, schools, and housing concerns.

they, of course, had long proclaimed women's equality and had enlisted in every possible way the help of their women friends. The prohibition against political activity had been particularly hard on working women, who were thereby excluded from discussion of their own wages and hours. Nevertheless, the Social Democrats turned up very few women leaders, and, as will become apparent, they spent much of their time in internal bickering.

ᑲᔆ Socialist concern with women went back to the brilliant and controversial Ferdinand Lassalle, whose meteoric career had opened in 1846 with the defense of a countess against an unfaithful husband who had stolen her money and would have deprived her of her children.[43] A young lawyer, Lassalle pitted himself against the world, and by this *cause célèbre* he demonstrated how unjust the laws against women were. But his mind was too volatile to lay down a set of abstract principles, a job that was left up to the Marxists.

August Bebel had been present as a guest at the first feminist meeting, the one at Leipzig in 1865, and soon afterward, at a congress of workingmen's societies, he and his friends won an endorsement of various women's rights, including the establishment of schools for girls and organizations for women workers. This little meeting, led by Bebel and Wilhelm Liebknecht, was the forerunner of the Social Democratic party, which in the future, whenever it faced the woman question (which was not all the time), came out for the repeal of laws that discriminated against women in public or private life.*[44]

In 1891, after Bismarck's anti-socialist laws had been rescinded, the party for the first time approved a resolution calling for universal adult suffrage without regard to sex, and in 1894 they introduced the measure in the Reichstag. Their official paper, *Neue Zeit*, published nearly five hundred articles about women between 1898 and 1912, reviewing books on the subject, discussing conditions of work, prostitution, divorce, education, anthropology, civil rights, organization, and women in foreign countries.[45] In fact, Georg Lichtheim is of the opinion that so much attention to women's problems distracted the party from foreign affairs and military matters just before the outbreak of the 1914 war, and so bears some of the blame for the fatal vote for war credits in that year.

At the same time, inside their own houses, German workers could be as patriarchal as their middle-class fellow men.[46] The sharp-tongued Hedwig Dohm certainly did not spare them when she wrote, in 1876, that one cannot be a "perfect democrat" while holding a whip over half the human race and asked why the party leaders failed to chastise their own chauvinists.[47] When Max Weber attended a Social Democratic convention in 1903, sensitized by the passionate interest of his wife, Marianne,

---

*Only Socialist party activity is discussed here. For a fuller account of Bebel's views on women's role and sexuality, see Chapter 26.

he felt that the comrades did not really want to hear about woman suffrage, even though whenever the subject came up in the Reichstag, they obeyed the party line and were the only large group to vote for it.[48]

Active feminists both within and outside the party frequently complained of the lack of socialist women leaders, in spite of considerable efforts to set up meetings, which were billed as educational in order to avoid the law against political work for women, and in spite of the immense cultural and intellectual hunger that middle-class women observed among the poor girls and women with whom they worked.

The split between middle-class and working-class women widened during the nineties. Middle-class women wanted work and more work, freedom to manage on their own, and civil rights. Working women, on the other hand, wanted less work (shorter working hours), less freedom (in the sense of greater legislative protection), and job mobility.[49]

With the government eager to shut the socialists up, working women became embittered when the middle-class ones pulled their skirts away. The law forbidding the founding of political clubs or women's participation in them was the same for all on the books, but still it turned out that police could interpret a particular problem as "political" in the mouth of a socialist and "non-political" when voiced by some respectable member of a middle-class club.[50] Another cause of dissension was that the feminist movement was fighting, in a way, against men, wanting what men had kept from them, while proletarian women were seeking something *with* their men, for they meant to share in the struggle against the capitalists.[51]

Probably the underlying reason for the mistrust between women of different classes lay in the strong class consciousness of German society. Upper-class ladies occasionally barricaded their doors at the time of the May Day celebrations of the Social Democrats. (One comment quoted Bismarck's saying that Germans feared God and naught else in the world, but added that German women feared war in the east and revolution in the streets, and put their trust in the army.)[52] Even the more pacific middle-class leaders, women like Marianne Weber and Marie Calm, and men like Lorenz von Stein, told their sisters that the high cultural mission of the female sex was precisely to combat socialism and anarchy; and the way to pursue this aim was by being kind to their servants and imparting moral instruction to youth.[53] (Stein believed that kindergartens and sewing schools would also help.)[54] Naturally both the stick and the carrot aroused anger among the socialists.

In 1894 a women's congress was held in Berlin. Its aim was to unite thirty-four German women's organizations into a single federation dedicated to a certain limited number of reforms that would benefit all women.[55] The first blow to unity was the refusal of a large church group to federate with any organization that might contain a freethinker; the second was the decision of the congress itself not to allow any socialist members.[56] (This though Bebel was at that time the chief champion of women in the Reichstag. The year before, Clara Zetkin had warned her fellow socialists never to expect anything from the middle class.)[57] Some members hoped that Luise Otto would stand to protest against this move, which succeeded in alienating both sides, but regrettably she failed to do so.

In 1896, when the next women's congress was held in Berlin (an international one this time, with five hundred delegates from thirteen countries), it received a petition the first day from a group of socialist women protesting against their exclusion.[58] Maria Montessori, one of the delegates from Italy, was sent round to speak to the socialist women, and they broke into applause when she told them that for the women of Italy class differences did not exist, that the rights of *all* women were what mattered.[59] She made a far less favorable impression when she addressed the bourgeois congress, although at her insistence they did pass a resolution favoring equal pay for equal work.

In 1912 the Social Democratic women passed a special resolution reaffirming what seemed to be an unbridgeable split between them and the middle-class movement.[60] Yet only two years later, women of both groups found themselves working side by side in the National Women's Service for the war.

For understanding how these conflicts affected an individual, the effort of Lily Braun to keep a foot in both camps is illuminating. She tried to hold the whole women's movement together and was thanked by neither side in the end. From her early love affairs, described above, we might guess that she was destined to be a rebel. It will be remembered that her father was a Prussian officer, and her first effort to loosen the grip of social conventions was a search for meaningful work rather than love. Her love affairs, after all, had only taught her how rigid and confining the class structure and etiquette of courtship were.

At the time Bismarck began attacking the Social Democrats in the Reichstag, Lily had never heard that party referred to except as traitors to the Empire, that new and glorious empire that her father had sworn to uphold.[61] She was interested, however, to note that Wilhelm Liebknecht had spoken of marriage for love as a socialist tenet, and such a remark appealed to her after the pain and disillusionment of her encounters with the marriage market. At this time she read Disraeli's novel *Sybil* about the "two nations" of the rich and the poor, and also Zola's *Germinal*. Contradictions began to fill her mind, for her grandmother, who was very bright and was personally the most sympathetic and understanding member of her family, filled her with tales of how "democracy" would destroy all the values of their class.

None of her aristocratic acquaintances seemed to be happy, though, as she studied the problems of mismanaged love and marriage within her class. This made it all the more striking when she met, in the

Berlin Tiergarten, the first happy man she had ever known, even though he was a cripple in a wheelchair.[62] As they saw each other from time to time, she learned more about him; she found out that he was a professor at the University of Berlin, a socialist by principle (one of the "socialists of the chair" who kept Germany's reputation for academic freedom intact), and, what won her heart, a strong believer in women's working at professional jobs. It was the first time in her life that she had ever heard the idea of a woman's training at a university mentioned without snickers. The professor's name was Georg von Giżycki. Luckily the "von" in his name made him a not utterly unthinkable husband, and her family reluctantly agreed to the marriage.

Lily and Giżycki heard about the Ethical Culture movement in New York and decided in 1892 to found a branch in Berlin.[63] They set it up with a governing board, regular meetings, and speeches, very much like a modern American non-profit organization. Lily actually became secretary of the board, against the orders of her father, who was distressed by a religion that did not command obedience, but he softened as Lily's success in making speeches won her some renown.[64]

For a while she worked hard for this movement and for women's rights. But now the conflict between the middle-class and socialist programs for women was taking place right in her own mind. Helene Lange considered Lily an attractive prospect for the ADF, even though her still purely intellectual predilection for socialism rather shocked some of its leaders. Indeed, Lily was headed toward a different set of questions from theirs. In her concern for poor garment workers, in her wonder at a society that tolerated prostitution, in her searching questions about why women were denied the vote, she failed to keep within the disciplinary limits of the ADF and went way beyond the sympathies of her middle-class audience. Meanwhile, her professor husband was telling her that the pursuit of individual success, the development of personality, on which the middle-class women's movement laid such stress, was contrary to socialist ideals,[65] because socialists wished for the submersion of the individual in the collective good. By this time Lily had begun to work with Social Democratic women, trying in vain to get them to join with the middle-class movement for certain specific feminist goals, and particularly for the conference of 1894, which wished to federate all feminist organizations into the BDF. The Social Democratic women were feeling insulted by the middle-class attitude and refused to attend, so she went alone to plead the socialist cause, but was forbidden to speak by the timid bourgeois leadership.*

Giżycki died, leaving Lily still undecided whether to go on as a middle-class supporter or to go all out with the socialists. For their part, the socialists were not especially welcoming. She proposed, for instance, labor exchanges for women workers, but the women proved distrustful,

---

*It is fair to state that Helene Lange's account of this incident is quite different from the one given by Lily Braun.

and even Liebknecht discouraged her with some disparaging remarks about the backwardness of the female sex. The issue was forced when the socialists ordered her to remove her name from the sponsorship of the international women's congress that was to be held at Berlin in 1896.[66] She had agreed to serve before the Social Democrats had put their official ban on all cooperation, and now she felt that her freedom of conscience had been violated. As she noticed how dogmatic all socialist discussion had become, it also struck her that the most prominent socialist leaders were content to let their own womenfolk sit at home and knit stockings.

Lily was invited to speak from the platform at the congress, and here she made a direct appeal to the middle-class women, begging them to try to understand why the socialists, why working-class women, felt that the movement, as then set up, was only addressing itself to a small part of the needed reforms. She implored her fellow delegates to regard the plight of millions of working women as just as important as the need for thousands to get higher education. Her speech provoked a near riot. Well-dressed women lost all their manners and screamed unladylike insults. Sadly Lily realized that she had quarreled with both sides.

Her second husband, Dr. Heinrich Braun, was an official of the Social Democratic party, and with his help she tried to combat the orthodoxy within that movement. While numbers of formerly good members were going over from socialism to nationalism in the pre-war build-up of German military strength, she found that within the party blind faith in the doctrines received from Marx had never changed. She noticed a lack of willingness even to listen to such new proposals as giving state support to mothers.

Though she tried for a time to submerge her own personality and accept party discipline, she found the women comrades turning very hostile; they gave her the most boring assignments and finally expelled her from the women's section.[67] At a hearing before the men's tribunal, she was cleared, but she was never able to reconcile her individuality with the movement. Her memoirs, dedicated to her husband and son, were well received by all reviewers except those of the socialist women's newssheet.[68]

⌒ During the in-fighting between the middle-class and socialist women, Lily Braun threw part of the blame for the split on Helene Lange. In Helene's view, however, the working-class women were not truly interested in cooperating with the regular feminists. She was outraged, for example, that after the latter had decided to put suffrage on the back burner, the Social Democrats kept it on their list of immediate demands.

The middle-class women felt that their conscience was clear, recalling the time and labor their members had put into forcing recognition of the terrible conditions under which their poorer sisters lived. Luise Otto had started out in the 1840s with her protests in prose and song on behalf of the weavers and lace makers;[69] Bettina von Arnim had shocked official Berlin with moving revelations of just how poor people lived in that city. Then, as the professions opened up to women, many of the new female doctors, sociologists, and social workers turned specifically toward rendering service to poor women. Surveys were made, factories inspected, and a crusade was led by Marianne Weber to improve standards for domestic servants, who had no state insurance and were often given abominable little sleeping quarters without privacy, and yet were unable easily to change jobs or locate new employers.

The middle-class movement's projects for its own membership, meanwhile, gave them cause for a certain amount of self-congratulation. The sixties had been the time of ground-breaking, they felt, with all the excitement of a new beginning. The seventies were passed under Bismarck's political regime, which cast a chill on the movement as on much of the rest of German life. Attendance at meetings fell off in those years, and acceptance was less general, whereas the eighties saw both a revival and a period of discussion about moral and intellectual principles. The nineties moved toward practical considerations, with efforts to improve factory conditions, obtain equal pay, and argue women's rights for the proposed new Civil Code.

This was the time when women of various countries were reaching out to one another, and at an international conference held in Chicago in 1891, German representatives met some of these other women and were inspired to form the Confederation of German Women's Associations (BDF).[70] It quickly rallied other groups, though not as we have seen, all churchwomen or any socialists. The large federation was to work only on interests held in common by all middle-class women's groups, leaving special concerns, such as coeducation or the regulation of prostitution, to the separate member organizations. Without the radical element of socialism, an uneasy compromise was reached between the conservative style of the old ADF and the new militant drive of something called *Verein Frauenwohl*, which stood for "equality now."

Both wings finally agreed on an agenda for the confederation's first year. It included planks that day nurseries should be attached to every primary school to help working mothers; that the curriculum of all schools should include material on hygiene and against alcohol; that women in factories should be protected by female inspectors; that stores employing girl clerks should have earlier closing hours than were customary at the time; that women should be admitted to medicine and other professions; and that training should be provided for public welfare work.[71] A special committee was set up in 1895 for factory inspection, with one for purity in morals and temperance to be added later. In 1897 they opened the first women's counseling center for legal and vocational advice. Suffrage was to come as the final plank.[72] By 1901 the BDF was composed of 137 associations, embracing over seventy thousand individual members.

It puzzled many observers that German women were so slow to ask for the vote. Luise Otto had declared at the beginning that justice entitled women to the *right* to vote, but that in practice it was too early to think about it. Another early feminist educator, Marie Calm, felt that only by imbuing themselves with sufficient patriotism to sacrifice their men for their country would they show men that they were responsible enough to vote. From the time of their first organization, they regularly put enfranchisement at the end of their list of demands, so that it would be the crown of their achievements after they had won education and earning power— a tactic that someone called pulling apart the artichoke leaf by leaf. When Helmut von Gerlach attended the international congress of 1900 in Paris, he was amazed at how puny the demands were. When he heard Hedwig Heyl get up to speak on the benefits of gardening for women's nerves, he rose to tell the audience that they should instead be storming for equal rights under the law.[73]

Because they felt that regimentation within the movement was the only way they would ever get ahead, the general staff of the women's movement was unsympathetic to opposition and looked askance at their most talented writer, Hedwig Dohm, who was utterly impatient with the artichoke approach. She told her colleagues frankly that if they had the vote first, they could get everything else they wanted easily.[74] Unfortunately for herself, she was much too witty to suit Helene Lange and her likes, who conspicuously put her down. She even looked different from the others; she was strikingly pretty, and prettily gotten up, with curly bangs instead of a tight bun, curls hanging over her lace collar, and a bow at her throat. Her face was thin and alert, and it is easy to imagine, looking at her picture, that as a girl she had a hard time filling her mind with the limited material offered at school and at home. But when she was fifteen, she says, she was turned instantaneously into a woman by seeing the dead eyes of the barricade fighters staring at her from the street after the 1848 rebellion.[75] Passionately she tried to listen to the revolutionary speakers until her mother clamped down, but from that moment she was a democrat. When her school years were over, the family knew no way for a girl to pass the time before marriage except at home, mostly sewing. Out of a year and a half of her life, she remembered nothing except the stitch on stitch toward the great rose bouquet destined for a carpet, and she calculated what quantities of antimacassars, table covers, and cushions must have been produced across Germany by young girls waiting for their "rescuers." ("*Freier*" is the German term for "suitor," but its literal meaning is "one who sets free.") As for Hedwig, sewing, sewing without end, she hoped that every ring at the door might be a letter from an unknown stranger, but nothing ever, ever came but bills and packages.

Finally she got permission to go to a school where she could train to be a teacher, but even there life was a dull routine of rote learning geography, history, botany, and the Bible,[76] until she married Ernest Dohm, the editor of the famous humor magazine *Kladdaradatsch*. This brought her into the most interesting literary circle in Berlin, where she met such people as Lassalle, Humboldt, Fanny Lewald, and Hans von Bülow. She was thirty-eight and the mother of five children when she began her brilliant attack on the opponents of women's rights. Looking back later, she said that it had never occurred to her to do anything *but* push for the freest right of all women to choose lives for themselves. All through the seventies articles and pamphlets issued from her pen, blasting male pretensions and urging women to get angry.

If women were naturally dependent on men, she inquired, how did it happen that there was such a rush after rich heiresses for wives? If women did not look good in the new postal service uniforms (a favorite subject for male satire), let the gentlemen take a look at themselves attired for an evening party! And if men thought women's main interest in entering politics would be to get lovers, let women become eligible to vote at age thirty, by which time no man would care to look at them. She defended her sex's intelligence by insisting that it took more to understand the soul of a small child than to teach in a university. She was furious that there was no association in all Germany that insisted on getting votes for women. She told them that men behaved so ungenerously and compulsively to each other that they could never be trusted to represent women's many interests.[77] Not finding agreement within her own class, at the end of her life she became sympathetic to socialism and a contributor to the socialist press.

But, as we have seen, most other women leaders felt that she was talking out of turn, and the general line of the women's movement continued on the course it had appointed, even though their lopsided priorities had produced many able, fluent, but overqualified women with no slots available in public life, no chance to take public responsibility, and no part to play in public meetings.[78]

By 1890 the feminist movement had been organized with true German thoroughness. An official complained that if he got one woman's petition about a subject, then he could count on getting at least twenty more from different branches. Furthermore, they did keep winning one point after another, first the schools, then the factory inspectors—until the war of 1914 put a stop to progress.

Thousands of women contributed and won a sense of release and accomplishment from their participation in the movement. Their day-to-day work was punctuated by periodic conferences, filling their lives with warmth and friendship as well as the opportunity to exchange ideas.

Two of Queen Victoria's daughters, both married to German princes, were interested in the movement, and their sponsorship did much to lend prestige even though they had no political influence. The Prussian Crown Princess, Viktoria, was in correspondence with

Josephine Butler as early as 1868, and complained how hard it was to rouse German women. She was able to help a little bit with money, which was so difficult for German women to beg from their husbands or to save out of their housekeeping funds. (In 1867 the ADF had an income of only 281 thalers or about $200.) The princesses also invited guests from England and started the cultural exchange that was the beginning of many international friendships.

It was soon decided to call large international conferences every five years. The 1896 one, in which Maria Montessori and Lily Braun participated, was unofficial. The first official one to be held in Germany took place in 1904, also in Berlin.[79] By that time the movement had progressed to such a state of public approval that the city fathers put on a public banquet for the delegates. A few years later there was an exhibition of women's work through which half a million visitors passed in four weeks. Max Weber's mother, Helene, was one of the organizers, and his wife, Marianne, lectured there, discussing the monetary value of women's contribution in the home and the irrationality of its lack of compensation.[80]

Despite all these advances, only a minority of German women, after all, took part. I. A. R. Wylie, the English writer, who spent a year in Germany as a young girl, was fairly sarcastic in her judgment. As she put it, the Empress Frederick* announced her intention of raising and freeing German women, only to have them rise en masse with the indignant protest that they already had all the freedom they needed.[81]

The final irony was that the middle-class feminists, who had refused to go after the vote and had rejected their socialist counterparts, received suffrage in the end from the hands of the Social Democratic party in 1918.

*Queen Victoria's eldest daughter and namesake was known in Germany both as Princess Viktoria and, after her husband's accession, as the Empress Frederick.

ᥫ25.

The Academic Woman

Deutsche Wissenschaft ist Männerwerk.
quoted by Arthur Kirchhoff, 1896

In November, 1895, the historian Heinrich von Treitschke threw some ladies out of his lecture hall at the University of Berlin with language so coarse that he subsequently had to make public apology. The widely reported incident came at a time when women were beating at the doors of German universities, but before any one of them had been admitted for credit toward a degree.

The Treitschke incident inspired a journalist, Arthur Kirchhoff, to find out how other professors felt on the subject, so he sent an open-ended questionnaire to every faculty member in German universities and at various other institutions of higher education, such as engineering and art schools, plus a few teachers in the newly opened secondary schools for girls.[1] The answers he got were classified only by discipline and printed verbatim in a book entitled *Die akademische Frau* (*The Academic Woman*). In his brief conclusion, the editor stated that it seemed to him that the number favoring women's admission had strikingly increased even in the year since Treitschke's blast.

The volume is a gold mine for attitudes toward women and education. No more than Kirchhoff shall I attempt a numerical weighting of the responses, which are shaded in innumerable ways, but I shall point out various recurrent themes: the effects that they imagined women's admission would have upon preparatory education, upon the universities, upon the women themselves, and upon society.

ᥫ One of the most frequent arguments was that because girls lacked preparatory schools comparable to the boys' *gymnasia*, they could not be got ready for university work. An obvious solution to this problem would be to erect schools for them, or to admit them to the boys', but as a University of Berlin philologist pointed out, this would cost the German state huge sums of money, which it was not prepared to spend. A medical professor from Leipzig proposed that an elite group of women might be selected without formal training, much as the officer corps was recruited for the army, but he imagined that this circle would remain very small.[2]

Several of the teachers in the girls' schools, including two who taught under Helene Lange, testified that their students were quite equal to males, that they were enjoying their work, seemed fresh and alert, and did not suffer from intellectual fatigue (though this had been widely predicted). A teacher in Weimar insisted, it is true, that girls needed much more physical education than they were getting and that more than half the upper-class girls he saw were nervous and anemic. The remedy he suggested was giving them the same freedom to hike around the German countryside that their brothers had.[3]

Apparently the quality of boys' preparatory schools was of such great public concern that many of the respondents criticized them instead of answering directly about girls' needs. Present schooling pushed boys to their limits, said Professor Conrad, an economist at Halle, while a chemistry professor at Leipzig described the products of these schools as near-sighted, pigeon-chested, pale-faced, and hollow-eyed.[4] Women were simply lucky not to go through *gymnasia*, argued von Hartmann, a philosopher at Berlin, because in such an atmosphere only the gifted and the lazy retained their own personalities. Boys attended only under compulsion, and it would be disastrous to inflict the experience upon girls, especially just at puberty. Professor Conrad felt, indeed, that girls' education was far behind that of boys, and actually behind that of the rest of the world; but while he favored setting up special, serious schools for women students, he did not think that they could be prepared for university work. Kirchhoff's personal conclusions from this material were sidetracked into discussion of the dire need of the boys' schools to become something better than mere *Drillanstalten*;* he failed to address the problems of female education of the day.

The imagined danger of having men and women in the same classroom, of course, was that sexual excitement would debilitate learning. Earnest professors did not want distractions in their serious lecture halls when their listeners were the age when the sex drive was highest. An alternative danger occurred to an engineering professor at Berlin: young women in his discipline might have to listen to unsuitable language during field work. Much better, he thought, to leave intellectual life to men—

---

*A special appendix in Kirchhoff's book was devoted to the ruminations of Hugo von Münsterberg, who had taught at Harvard during the year 1892 and was asked his impressions of American college girls. He was lyrical about the happy lives of Smith and Wellesley students, living in what he could only describe as "parks," looking so charming in their light dresses which lit up the nooks of the library, boating on their little lakes, singing in their glee clubs, enjoying theatricals, dancing. They emerged happier and healthier than ever, Münsterberg continued, but European readers should not assume that their experience proved that they could stand the rigors of a German university. He estimated that only about five hundred of the women in American colleges and universities could qualify as real students by German standards, and he pointed out that the four "best" universities—Harvard, Yale, Hopkins, and Columbia—were closed to them. He failed to mention the "Harvard annex," not yet a full college, which is ironical inasmuch as he was destined to die, twenty years later, while lecturing in a Radcliffe classroom (Kirchhoft, 349).

raising the question (unintended by him) of whether intellectual life consists in hearing coarse language.

Certainly there was no unanimity among the professors. A philosopher at Berlin was sure that progress required that women should be given free admittance to the learned professions, and he rated the danger of mixing sexes no greater in the lecture room than in the ballroom. He had noticed that young men actually did better work if they were engaged to be married, and so felt that the presence of women would have a bracing effect. Kirchhoff's drew the sensible conclusion for his part of the debate that boys and girls should be brought up together from kindergarten on, and then there would be no sudden, unsettling relaxation of tension in the university.

Many German professors were afraid that admitting women would lower the whole tone of their institutions, even if the question of proper preparation was solved. Thus law professor Gierke of Berlin thought that while the work might not damage the women, women would change the character of the university for the worse. The German people had more important tasks than to advance women's study, and one important feature of the national mission was that the men should remain *men*.[5] A Berlin theologian felt that men and women learned in such different ways that they needed different kinds of teaching. It was his opinion that men studied causes, while women studied results.[6] (It is perhaps just as well that he did not try to elaborate.) A chemist at Leipzig would not object to having women sit in at lectures, but patiently explained that if they had been permitted in laboratories during the previous fifty years, German science could not have made its impressive advances. A historian at Breslau made the most impassioned plea against their admission, seeing nothing in the demand except a revolutionary plot.

Ranged on the other side were a scattering of men in the humanities, and somewhat more from the natural sciences. Several of the latter had had experience with women students, either in Switzerland or in private tutoring, and reported enthusiastically, though their responses were more matter-of-fact and less colorful than those of their opponents.

The question of separate institutions arose from time to time. In line with the pattern of special women's colleges then developing in England and America, some German opinion favored the setting up of such schools in Germany, or even, as advocated by a law professor, the turning over of a small university (such as Giessen) exclusively to women.

Turning from the effect of admission on the institutions to that on the women themselves, a small number of professors wanted to take affirmative action to push them into the universities, being sure that they would reap intellectual benefits and not damage their health, but mixed in with these were voices expressing alarm about health, vocations, or ideas. A Heidelberg doctor opined that women became hysterical when they were forced to study, while a philologist from Göttingen, Wiliamowitz-Moellendorff, believed that the ones who succeeded might exhaust themselves in the effort to beat men, and might even succeed temporarily, but that "Nature would have her revenge."[7] A slightly lesser doom was foreseen by a Berlin psychologist: merely that they would lose their freshness and charm. There was a Strassburg gynecologist who actually proposed compulsory marriage for women (thus automatically ruling out university life); this, he thought, would be no harder than compulsory military training was for men.[8] After all, said a Berlin philologist, we might gain a Goethe by educating women, but we should lose the possibility of creating Goethe's *mother*.*[9] The director of the Industrial Arts Museum of Berlin worried that girls who studied art history would demand "Italian honeymoons," while a Dr. Weber, teaching Sanskrit at Berlin, felt concern about the passages of passion they would have to read if they pursued his language very deeply. He praised the creators of Aryan languages for having set a good example in the separation of roles for the two sexes. (For him, the very existence of large numbers of "superfluous"—that is, unmarried—women indicated racial exhaustion.)

As might be expected, the debate on academic women reopened the ancient question of their natural abilities. An astronomer wondered why they should be let into science now after they had failed to produce a great painter or musician after the forty years or more that art academies and conservatories had been open to them. In fact, declared a Berlin theologian (who could never bring himself to say "Ladies and Gentlemen" to a class), if they were reported to be successful at French and English universities, then it was only because those institutions were not research-oriented. Max Planck, the physicist, wanted to let a few talented women in, but felt they would be the exceptions, believing as he did that the law of life was for women to be mothers.[10] A Kiel historian was particularly explicit in stating that in his eyes they lacked the judgment, as well as the experience and training, to undertake the study of *history*.[11]

Some others—a considerable number—wanted the question left open, which surely seems the more research-oriented way to decide. Probably the most distinguised of these was Wilhelm Wundt, of Leipzig, founder of the science of experimental psychology. He described it as an outright injury to women to deprive them of a chance at full development, and ascribed such deprivation to brutal sexual egoism in men. Wundt's own expectation was that women would qualify in almost every subject, though he thought that they might prove physically unfit for military studies and perhaps psychologically unfit for politics.[12] A few

---

*Goethe himself attributed his need to tell stories to his mother's happy nature, and to his father the part of himself that pursued the serious things in life:

Vom Vater hab' ich die Natur
Des Lebens ernstes Führen,
Vom Mütterchen die Frohnatur,
Die Lust zu fabulieren.
[Jardon, 32]

men went farther. Lujo Brentano, the Munich economist, believed that women's brains were actively needed for certain phases of study,[13] notably for their insight into social problems, and a colleague of his in the arts believed that when they turned their minds to literary studies, they would develop important new insights. Preyer, a Berlin philosopher, also expected women's brains to provide a great new source of energy for the world.

As for their alleged mathematical incapacity, a Göttingen professor declared it a myth. He said that the six women already studying at his institution, all foreigners, were doing just as well as the men, while a Kiel mathematician provided a long list of women who had been productive in the fields of mathematics and astronomy throughout history. In fact, most of the men who had ever taught women found them acceptable, and often brilliant, students.

Especially interesting were the debates in the field of medicine, because while there was felt to be a particular demand for women doctors to treat women patients, at the same time the requirements of the study seemed to present unusual difficulties. Again and again the fact that women patients were dying because of their reluctance to consult male physicians about intimate ailments was cited by those who wanted women to be trained to meet the need; and here, too, there was a body of experience to base a judgment on because women had been studying medicine in Switzerland for years. The evidence showed that they worked harder than the men, who were distracted by fraternity life. A Munich medical professor declared that he had interned with forty women from all over the world, and that all but one of them were in practice as he wrote.[14]

The study of law generated less comment, although a professor of that subject at Berlin looked forward to the new legal concepts women might bring forth. But law, more than other studies, raised in the minds of the fearful the possibility that a woman defending clients in a courtroom would soon be demanding full political rights for herself. Another man believed that they were simply not hard enough to be judges.

Lastly, certain commentators brought up the effect of women's study on the fabric of society. The conservative side was explained by a Königsberg theologian who feared the "atomizing" of human life if women gave up marriage as their "career." Whereas in England the decision whether to educate the girl and risk weakening the future mother devolved on the parents, in Germany the state was felt to have this affirmative duty not to let women become unfit for motherhood. The liberal position was expressed by a Berlin astronomer who said flatly that to call marriage women's career was sheer male egoism; he added that there was no doubt that female brains were fully equal. Social life could only improve when women took an equal part in all phases of it.

A Göttingen economist summed it up: the question was not *whether* women should be admitted, but *how*. Plan to get the money, he advised, and make the innovations needed. And let men not assume that they have the right to decide everything their own way.

∽ When the leaders of the German women's movement decided on a step-by-step approach to their problems, they put education first.[15] This was essential, they felt, both for their ideal of self-development and as preparation for professional work and civic responsibility, which could then be asked for later with greater plausibility. Basically they wanted girls' education to be taken as seriously as boys', with eventual state support.

At that time, of course, the boys' *gymnasia* were government-run, and their graduates had to pass a state-set examination to qualify for the university. Naturally, all their teachers were men, and these men enjoyed a rather high status in German social life, being themselves university graduates and often scholars. The schools for middle- and upper-class girls, meanwhile, were private institutions, without set standards, and there was almost no provision for girls to pursue a course of study after their confirmation, usually at the age of fourteen or fifteen. From their sixteenth year on, the fate of most young women was, in Fanny Lewald's words, to "sit and sit, wait and wait."[16] There are plenty of examples among the women in this book.

There were a very few first-class private schools for girls. One of the most distinguished early principals was Marie Calm, who was inspired by an unusual teacher, Ida Speyer, to become a teacher herself, even though it was most unusual for a girl who did not need the money to take up a vocation. In the 1860s she ran an excellent girls' school in the Rhineland. Not satisfied with that, however, she went on to study for three years in England, and even put in some time in Moscow; finally she settled in Kassel, where she started an evening school for girls of all social classes. She also wrote books for young people and founded a women's club.[17]

Strangely enough, one of the people who did the most to get young women to respect their own capabilities, and to get them out of their houses and into the wider world, was Friedrich Froebel. Froebel is always thought of as the founder of the kindergarten movement, but kindergartens need teachers, and in a series of pedagogical lectures at Dresden during the winter of 1848–1849, Froebel opened up a whole new world for his listeners, among whom was his niece, Henriette Schrader-Breymann. He told them that they must build a center for their lives, reaching beyond the subjective fantasy that poisoned so many young women's effectiveness.[18] He came to feel that every girl should undergo kindergarten training, so that if she married she would be a better mother, and if she failed to marry she would have a means of self-support, thereby using her motherly instincts instead of suppressing them. This is, to be sure, a limited ideal for women, but at the time his game was almost the only one in town, and aspirants poured into the work. Forty-four kindergartens were set up in that first year alone.

Unfortunately the King of Prussia decided that kindergartens were a threat to his political dominance—probably not so much because of the children as because of all those ardent young women—and by 1851 he had closed them down. But though the movement was squelched for a while, the enthusiasm did not die, and many of its partisans happily joined Luise Otto's organization when it started in the 1860s. In fact, there were so many of them that they nearly took over the movement. At the meeting of 1869, Luise Otto in the chair could not even get a discussion going about opening other fields to women because the Kindergarteners were so eager to endorse teaching as their natural vocation.[19] By the 1880s, when a princess sent her grandchildren to a kindergarten, the movement had come to seem almost conservative.

The general problem of secondary education for girls also came to a boil during the sixties. It grew to be an accepted sentiment that girls' schools must be brought up to some common standard, with accreditation for women teachers. In the absence of university admission, the question of getting women teachers who would be accepted as equal to the male *gymnasium* teachers, either by the parents or by the students, was never fully solved, but the women teachers kept working at it. The male teachers were mostly opposed, fearing competition for their jobs and scorning women's intellectual capability for such exacting work as they felt themselves to be doing.

One of the first clashes came in 1872, when a conference of teachers of girls was called at Weimar. Both men and women attended, with the men in the great majority. The manifesto that emerged was intended to be conciliatory but was actually so patronizing that it whipped the women reformers into a fury.[20] Its main tenet was that women should have better educations so that German husbands would not be bored at home.* Furthermore, it stated that the teaching force of the secondary schools should consist of a principal trained in scholarship (that is at a university), similarly trained male teachers, certain men who had been licensed for elementary teaching, and such women as had passed the state licensing examination.

After issuing this document the men at the conference went off to a luncheon of caviar, lampreys, and cutlets, while the women delegates were served bread and butter like schoolgirls. While the men were eating, the women took a solemn resolve never to give up the demand to have

---

*From the Weimar manifesto:

It is intended to offer women an education equal to that of men in generality of interests, so that the German man will not become bored in his home through the intellectual shortsightedness or narrow spirit of his wife and thus be crippled in his own devotion to higher interests, and so that his wife can stand at his side in understanding those interests in warmth and feeling. . . . The secondary schools for girls have to try to reach a harmonious development of intellect, feeling, and will, in a religious-national sense with a realistic-aesthetic basis. [Zahn-Harnack, *Frauenbewegung*, 101]

women teachers and principals in girls' schools. At the plenary session only one man supported the women's position; the rest of the men took a vote not to concern themselves with the questions of women's liberation.

Even though Froebel's view of feminine abilities was narrow, it was also a high one. Women who took up his work felt that they were liberated as individuals, while the Weimar manifesto would have reduced all women to mere satellites of men.

The crusade for women teachers was the life's work of Helene Lange. If Luise Otto was the obvious leader of the first phase of the women's movement, acting almost alone at first, Helene Lange (1848–1930) stood out in the second phase among a crowd of witnesses.

Her childhood illustrates, among other things, how differently women were treated in the various regions of Germany.[21] North German girls were brought up with much more freedom than those in the Rhineland, where French culture had had a heavy influence. Helene was a northerner from Holstein, where, in the early sixties, no one had limited her freedom to talk. She had never noticed any intellectual separation of the sexes; no one had suggested that she should not discuss with anyone who happened to be around such subjects as the materialism of Karl Vogt. When her father died, however, she was sent to be prepared for confirmation in the home of a pastor at Reutlingen, in the south. Here, to her surprise, she found that only men discussed serious subjects like theology. If a woman entered the room, the tone changed. (Later she found that in certain of the small court cities, women could talk about art and literature.) She also noticed that men were always given preference in household comforts. The pastor's wife was clever and well-read, but she would never open her mouth among a group of males, even though in private conversation she showed fine feeling, and once Helene even overheard her talking to the vicar about scientific materialism. At church parties and social gatherings, the two sexes seemed like two separate species. Any man, no woman, could voice opinions on ethics and philosophy. Helene's reaction when she got back to Holstein was to buy right away a copy of Kant's *Critique of Pure Reason*.

But before then, at the point of confirmation, she began discussing materialism privately with the pastor, who told her to keep quiet and be good, and not to distress herself if she could not assent to all the doctrines in the creed. It seems as if almost every bright German girl had a similar crisis over confirmation, and neither the girls nor the pastors had any idea of how to deal with it.

Helene's insistence on speaking her mind caused only smiles among her female friends in Reutlingen, as did her quaint idea that she would like to go to a university. Among men she was not even allowed to voice such a hope. At the same time, she had to admit that the social environment in the pastor's house was self-forgetful and hospitable. It was the home of many German virtues, if not of women's rights.

By 1866 she wanted to take the teachers' examination, but inasmuch as no one in her family had ever done so, she was not permitted to; as second choice, at the age of eighteen, she took an *au pair* position in an Alsatian boarding school. Alsace was still French, and here she studied French and music, meanwhile teaching literature and grammar. In her work she met one fine teacher, Jean Macé, whom she was to meet again when he had become important in French school reform and she had risen high in international circles concerned with women's education.

After the spell in Alsace, she moved to Berlin, where, now that she was of age, there was no one to forbid her to study for the teachers' examination she had been denied before. She was able to attend lectures by university professors at the Viktorialyceum, an institution founded in 1868 to give German women some access to higher learning. Thriving on these, and on her regular studies, Helene was at first almost unconscious of the women's movement that was swirling around her. She kept busy learning Latin and attacking philosophy, working up to a real under-standing of Kant at last, and meeting an interesting group of career women in Berlin. By setting up housekeeping in an apartment with another professional woman, she embarked on a new style of life. After passing her examination she went on to a long and honored career in which she developed high schools for girls, created places for more women teachers, and—her final professional service—set up schools for social work, so-called *Frauenschulen*, where she did her last stint of teaching. She was the author of many books on the women's movement, which became the central interest of her life, providing friendships all across Germany (for she had by now learned to value the regional differences in women, the social conscience and earnestness of the ones from the east, the charm and spirit of the ones from the south), and eventually all over the world. Like Luise Otto, Helene Lange remained forever optimistic. At the end of her life she realized that her own generation was not the one that would "fasten the feminine will" on the rest of the world, but the next one would *surely* see this happen.[22]

One of her main ideas concerned women's natural motherly in-stincts, which, in the absence of biological motherhood, only the teaching profession could assuage. She was sure that not even the best male teacher could understand the sensitive feelings of adolescent girls, could know when to humor and when to become strict.* (She was surprised to discover on a trip to England that feminists there did not believe in these motherly instincts at all, though she was delighted to find out that English girls were under women teachers and principals all the way to the university.)[23]

---

*The 1884 program of the Conservative party of Prussia stated that old maids were not fit to teach girls, this outlet for motherliness so highly praised by Helene Lange was seen as fostering in such women an unconscious competition with biological mothers. In addi-tion, it was said, girls could not learn from spinsters, but only from men whom they loved, so let them learn in marriage (Twellmann, *Quellen*, 313).

In 1887 she sent a long memorandum to the Prussian Ministry of Education, to accompany a petition from some Berlin parents and teachers. In it she stressed the importance of first-class training, at that time largely lacking, for women who wanted to teach.[24] She explained that she did not have university training in mind, because she did not believe that women were fitted for research, but they did need excellent normal schools ("like Newnham and Girton," she added, apparently not comprehending the purpose of those institutions). The "higher daughters' schools" or finishing schools, with their dilettante attitudes, must go,[25] and all girls must be trained to stand on their own feet. It was a sign of the times that among the many comments she received was one from the girls of the *Charlottenschule*, coming out strongly in favor of their male teachers.[26]

Helene pushed ahead nevertheless. In 1889 she opened a modern high school (*Realkurse*) for girls, with science and modern language instruction equivalent to that offered in *Realgymnasia*. The teaching of housewifely skills was not, however, neglected. Helene Lange believed in building on the girls' interest in motherhood. Officialdom told her that what she was doing was illegal—teaching without a license—to which she responded that her students were not subject to the school-age law but were free adult women.[27] When the authorities threatened to close her school, a great burst of public indignation made them decide to let her alone. By 1893 she was able to change the *Realkurse* to the *Gymnasialkurse*, going from a modern language and science course to one based on the more pretigious classical languages.

All the talk about motherliness did not go unanswered. Even Henriette Schrader-Breymann, Froebel's niece, felt that Helene Lange was too one-sided. While endorsing the motherly principle in human life, Henriette and her husband, Karl Schrader, found that men could share the same quality and make very sensitive teachers of girls, and, in fact, would benefit from training in this direction.[28] Karl Schrader wrote an article for the New York *Nation* covering both Helene Lange's and the Froebelian view that women's highest calling is to run a home with technical competence and a sense of spiritual values. To this Fanny Garrison Villard retorted sharply in the same magazine that women did not need housekeeping indoctrination, that each person had an individual calling, and that this went for women just as much as for men.[29]

Within Germany, the opposition to Helene Lange's emphasis on a single vocation for women was spearheaded by a faction of the women's movement called *Frauenverein Reform*. At the time it was considered the radical branch. Hedwig Dohm was on the committee; she was always a thorough sceptic about the value of motherliness and an eager supporter of the thesis that women could do anything that men could, and should be allowed to.[30] Her aim for education was to make women better human beings. She was sarcastic about the girls' school her own fourteen-year-old daughter was attending. (The child had been asked to produce a theme on "the cultural-historic difference between China and North America," which Hedwig called simply silly.)[31] The *Frauenverein Reform* petitioned for girls' *gymnasia* equal to boys', with permission to take the sacred qualifying examination, the *Abiturienexamen*, equal access to universities, and training for careers.

During the eighties a major project of the ADF was collecting funds for scholarships so that talented poor girls could have a chance to attend what schools there were. Being private institutions, these schools were much more expensive than boys' *gymnasia*, and they were often so inadequate that girls had to be sent to Switzerland to get the kind of schooling they needed, especially medical training. A large initial endowment for the cause came in 1885, when a married couple, Ferdinand and Luise Lenz, donated 130,000 marks for women's education.[32] Their first idea was to endow a scholarship for women students at Heidelberg University, but the university rejected the money, so they gave it to the ADF, hoping to establish at least a good *gymnasium* where girls could be prepared inside Germany.

In 1892 the small state of Baden permitted women to take the *Abiturienexamen* administered at the boys' schools, and Berlin followed suit in 1896. Baden, meanwhile, had taken over one of the private girls' schools in Karlsruhe to be run by the state as the first girls' *gymnasium*. The first four graduates emerged in 1899.

But the battle had to be fought repeatedly, city by city, and state by state. In Breslau, for example, the officials forbade the opening of a girls' *gymnasium*, having gotten the word from the Prussian Minister of Instruction that he wanted to put out the fire![33] Only after 1906 were secondary schools for girls thoroughly reformed and women given a chance to specialize for a profession. Helene Lange's and other early *gymnasia* had only prepared the way.

Concurrent with the fight for secondary schools was the long fight for teacher accreditation and training. In the absence of university admission, the need for a normal school became paramount. In 1876 there were in all of Prussia only five of what were called *Lehrerinnenseminare*—teacher-training classes supported by the state—in addition to which ten of the best private girls' schools had obtained the right to carry on advanced classes, after the normal graduation time, for girls who wished to become teachers.[34] (Men had a hundred of the seminars, and, of course, the university was open to them also.) The state of Prussia gave the first state qualifying examinations to women teachers in 1874 (other states did so at other times), and that move at least set standards and gave goals for study. Most of the women mentioned in this chapter were graduates of these teacher seminars, including Helene Lange, Hedwig Dohm, and the future revolutionary Clara Zetkin. But in 1888, when Helene Lange sent in her petition about women teachers, only 10 percent of Prussian teachers were women (compared to 54 percent in France and 69 percent in England at the time).*

Instead of establishing a good normal school, the Ministry dallied around with a few window-dressing courses at the *Viktorialyceum*. And even after women were accepted at the universities, in the twentieth century, the graduates who chose to teach were paid like washerwomen, according to Lily Braun.[35] It was not until World War I, when the state needed women as teachers even in boys' *gymnasia*, that they won the right to continue working after marriage.[36] Before then they lost their jobs and all their other benefits if they took a husband.†

∽ Women eager to press their case for university admission used to recall tales of women in academic life in past centuries. There were far fewer in Germany than in Italy. There was a rumor, disbelieved by Riehl, that Greek was taught by a woman at Heidelberg during the Reformation. There seemed to be more solid ground for believing that a woman had graduated in physics at Halle in 1754, and another one in philosophy at Göttingen in 1787, while Giessen in 1817 awarded a medical degree to Marianne von Heidenreich, the daughter of Charlotte von Siebold, who had worked up from midwifery to a licensed doctorate.[37]

About the middle of the nineteenth century, a number of women began to audit lectures. Thus when Maxe von Arnim was stationed with her husband's army unit at Bonn, in 1853, she attended a series of lectures on literature and made an effort to include university people in her social circle.[38] There was at first no rule against auditing, but as the custom spread, alarmed administrations tried to stop it.[39] In Berlin, a dozen ladies obtained the consent of a professor for their presence at his Shakespeare lectures; they sat without interference for a while, and then one day when they showed up as usual, the janitor came and ejected them.

For the first women who actually tried to matriculate, things quickly became tougher. Lina Berger, a Saxon woman who had passed the teachers' examination with distinction in 1871, and who studied in Switzerland to qualify for university admission, came home and attended the University of Leipzig for two semesters (1877–1878). But when she applied for permission to take her doctoral examination (with a thesis on

*These figures include elementary as well as secondary teachers.

†Although the women's movement was not nearly so much interested in training girls to become primary teachers as in secondary and university education, the government made quite an effort in the seventies to get women teachers into the common schools across Prussia. Luise Büchner gave an idyllic picture of the village schoolmistress as a culture symbol of cleanliness and economy. Nor was her usefulness as a bulwark against socialism unnoticed. This pattern should be compared with the similar movements in France and Italy (Twellmann, *Frauenbewegung*, 101).

Thomas More and Plato), she was turned down, even though many outstanding professors spoke strongly in her favor. Some of these gave her a private doctoral examination, and then the Swiss University of Bern awarded her an official degree, *summa cum laude*, in 1878. Later on she taught at the *Vikotorialyceum*.[40]

The rule at that time, at least at Leipzig, was that women could not matriculate and could not graduate, but that any professor could admit them to his classes at his own pleasure. One Russian woman, it seems, was granted a degree, but two German medical women who had been permitted to complete their studies there were refused the right to take the licensing test that would admit them to practice.

Another pioneer was the astonishing Sonya (or Sophie) Kovalevsky, a Russian mathematician of great brilliance. She was born in 1850, in a remote province of Russia, where her father was an artillery general. Her mother was of German descent.

When the family home was being redecorated, there was not enough wallpaper to go round the children's nursery, so the workers slapped on leaves from her father's old student notebooks, which happened to be about integral and differential calculus. As a tiny child, Sonya would stand in front of these walls for hours and learn the formulae by heart. She also learned to read spontaneously, so that she astonished her first tutor. Her father, never favorable to Sonya's studies violently opposed her going to a university. His attitude is shown by a remark he made to her sister, who had sold a story and received a check: "How can I tell, if you would sell your work, you will not one day sell yourself?")

To escape, Sonya, at eighteen, entered into a *pro forma* marriage agreement with Woldemar Kovalevsky, a student who was going to Germany. Somehow she managed to win admission to study mathematics at Heidelberg, and in 1870 she applied to Berlin, where she needed to work with Professor Karl Theodor Weierstrass. Weierstrass thought he could get rid of her by setting an examination that he supposed would be much too hard, but when she passed brilliantly, he changed his attitude. He was a genuinely magnanimous person who delighted in genius wherever he recognized it, and he took her under his wing for four years.

The University of Göttingen, which had last given a degree to a woman in 1787, now gave one to Sonya Kovalevsky in 1874, without an oral examination, on the basis of three original and remarkable theses.

Meanwhile her husband, with whom she had lived as a sister at Heidelberg, was pursuing studies at Jena and Munich that would make him a distinguished paleontologist. The two finally came together and produced a daughter, but they did not live together on a regular basis, and in 1883 he died. Sonya was left with the child and no means of support until she received an appointment to teach mathematics at the University of Stockholm. In 1888 she received France's highest scientific honor, the Prix Bordin. When asked, however, if she was now contented, she declared that she hoped no other woman would be as unhappy as she. A few years later she died of a fever.

It seemed clear in the 1860s and 1870s that German universities were not going to open up for women as easily as the French and English ones were doing. To fill the gap at least partly, a Miss Georgina Archer appeared, a bright and well-educated Englishwoman who had come to Berlin to instruct the children of the Crown Prince.[41] She was warmly supported by the Crown Princess when she announced a plan to set up an institute that would provide lectures for women and named it for her patroness, the *Viktorialyceum*.*

Circumstances had changed a bit since 1841, when Karl von Savigny, the founder of the discipline of legal sociology, was asked to take part in a series of public lectures and replied that this would be a debasement of learning, particularly if women were admitted.[42] But even if any professor was willing so to debase himself, the Ministry of Culture forbade him to take part in any popularization. Part of the reason was certainly fear of letting women into academic secrets. So when Miss Archer took hold, her approach was gingerly.

The *Viktorialyceum* started in 1868 with four courses, taught by university professors and intended to parallel their lectures to their male students. The subjects were modern history, Greco-Roman cultural history, and German and French literature. On the first day twice as many women as expected turned up, and there was so much enthusiasm that the following year ancient languages, mathematics, and some sciences were added.[43] The women who flocked to these sessions had no vocational goals at first, and were mainly interested in general culture; their level of achievement was barely up to that of thirteen-year-old boys. With no examinations, there was no standard of final achievement either, and Miss Archer realized this; but believing that "charcoal must glow before it can be used for cooking," she bided her time and hoped her institution would be a step toward liberating women's minds.

Things moved in that direction. By 1881 the institute was giving public examinations in Latin, Greek and mathematics in the presence of the Crown Princess and the various professors. However, the Princess herself was not in high favor with the Prussian Government, and the regime knew very well how to prevent the institution from growing into a real educational instrument. In 1888, reluctantly, as we have seen, it allowed the *Viktorialyceum* to start a three-year course of advanced training for teachers in place of the higher normal schools that women like Helene Lange were advocating. The *Viktorialyceum* was fine so far as it went, but it was always an expensive establishment, and what was needed was general state support of schools at all levels for women and

*One of the four important institutes named for the English-born Princess. The others were the *Viktoria-Schwestern*, for nurses; the *Viktoria-Fortbildungschule*, a trade school; and the *Viktoria-Studienhaus*, a home for girl students at Charlottenburg (Zahn-Harnack, *Wandlungen*, 36).

women teachers. It did continue, however, as a higher normal school even after the universities were opened up.

Miss Archer had considerable difficulty in finding faculty members because of the official attitude toward popularization.[44] In the London *Daily Mail*'s feature story on the facility, it was remarked that only professors badly in need of money would lecture there.[45] There may have been another reason too—namely, Miss Archer's own timidity, which came close to infringing on academic freedom. For example, when Friedrich Paulsen was asked to deliver some talks on ethics, in 1878–1879, he made the mistake of referring to a dinner party, recently held in Berlin, where each guest had been waited on by a different footman. In Paulsen's view such extravagance violated Christian and philosophic ethics. Unfortunately, one of his listeners had attended that very banquet. The result was that Miss Archer paid Paulsen off and said, very firmly, *no more lectures on ethics.*[46]

One girl who was caught between the pressures for and against higher education was Adelheid Mommsen, daughter of the well-known historian of ancient Rome. There were six sisters in the family, only one of whom married. Adelheid found nothing at all to do at home after she finished school at seventeen; her mother and sisters ran the house with the help of three maids. Looking back in her old age, she told the girls of the 1930s that it would be impossible for them to imagine the crushing boredom of the 1880s. One day she went to see her father in his study—a daring act, as he was never to be interrupted there—and asked him for permission to be trained as a teacher. She hardly expected him to say yes, because her brothers and their friends were thoroughly opposed to any such idea, but the old professor surprised her and agreed to her wish.[47]

Luckily she managed to get into Helene Lange's seminar, where, under the guidance of that brilliant teacher, "meanings emerged from knowledge." Old Mommsen was so impressed by Helene Lange that he became a thorough convert to careers for women.[48] Adelheid went on to study in Paris, and then in England, and when she came back she attended the *Viktorialyceum*. Eventually she was able to enroll in a university. Her father warned her that she was becoming overtrained and that no one would hire a woman with so much intellectual baggage, and this proved to be true. But she built her own house, adopted two girls, and made a happy life for herself.

The first institutions of higher education to accept women on a coeducational basis had been schools for the arts. In 1866 Luise Otto noted that the Conservatory treated men and women equally and should be a model for all other higher schools.[49] Robert Schumann's daughter Eugenie was sent to study music in Berlin about that time, and shortly afterwards Amy Fay came over from Massachusetts, sending home a delightful series of letters, which were later printed. These girls boarded with private families in a *pension* style and seemed to find no social stigma attached to their thoroughly correct but unusual style of living.

Art academies were more hesitant about women students because of the hazards connected with nude models, but as early as 1851, William Howitt's daughter, Anna Mary, ran into few problems when she studied art in Munich.[50]

The first German-speaking university to open its doors to women was at Zurich, and this experiment was naturally scrutinized eagerly by the German women's movement. In 1870 their journal inquired of one of the professors how the women were doing, and got back a warmly favorable reply. For six years, he said, women had caused no problems at all in the medical faculty, they hoped to open up all branches of study soon, and he foresaw a great store of gifts, perceptions, and energy freed for the world. It worked so well, in fact, that the University of Bern planned to follow suit a couple of years later, as did the Swedish universities.

Shortly after this Theodor von Bischoff, professor of anatomy at Munich, wrote a vicious attack on women in medicine, complaining about their smaller brains and seductive tendencies. This goaded the Zurich faculty into issuing an official manifesto testifying to their satisfaction with their women students' tact, industry, and competence.[51] But this was not enough to quiet the anxieties of German mothers who were afraid of unchaperoned living conditions and the Russian "short-cropped female Nihilists," who formed the biggest national group of women at Zurich.[*52]

Even if it gave opportunity to a few exceptionally motivated girls, Swiss education could be no solution to the problem of equal education in the German homeland. The *Kölnische Zeitung* had opened up a wide discussion of university work for women in 1869,[53] but the battle had to be fought out in each separate state, and it was noticed that although there was resistance everywhere, each state had a different reason for not allowing women to matriculate.[54]

Often foreign women were the first to break through the barrier, aided by letters from their embassies. Although not accepted for degrees, there were forty women listed as auditors at the University of Berlin in 1896, and thirty-one at the other Prussian university at Göttingen. They all had had to get personal permission from each instructor, then from the university authorities, and lastly from the Minister of Public Instruction, and they knew that any one of these might be withdrawn at any moment.[55]

Against all these handicaps the women persisted in applying, and in 1899, Elsa Neumann became the first woman to get her doctorate at

*There was a sensation when the Czarist government ordered its women students home in 1874. In 1873 there had been 114 female students at Zurich, of whom 100 were Russian. The next year there were only 29 in all, 12 of whom were Russians brave enough to defy the Czar's orders.

Berlin, in physics. In the Dean's speech for this occasion, he made the point that even if a woman's first line of duty was as the high priestess of her household—here he was interrupted by thunderous applause—still, he went on, deeper learning was no hindrance. Here the signs of approval were noticeably weak, but at least the dam was breached.

In 1887 Austria admitted women to its universities, and in 1896 Leipzig admitted them to the state examination of the philosophical faculty. In 1900 the small state of Baden became the first member of the German Empire to admit them freely and as a matter of course to its two universities, Heidelberg and Freiburg, giving them full equality in admission and degree taking. The Hessian University of Giessen opened up to them about the same time. By 1908 Prussia and most other states had regularized their acceptance. Even after that, according to Elisabeth Schiemann, who got a degree in botany from Berlin, women still needed to get personal permission from their individual professors, and for some reason this was much easier to get in the sciences than in the humanities.[56]

The first woman professor in a German university was Elisa Richter, who taught philology at Vienna from 1905. She died in a Nazi concentration camp.[57]

Several of the most distinguished liberal professors of the pre-war days, men like Meinecke and Max Weber, have written movingly of their pleasure in their first group of women students. Their unerring tact and fine culture[58] made of them a picked and dedicated group, according to Weber, whose first woman student was Else von Richthofen. She had taught school to earn money for her university course, and after graduation became the first woman inspector of factories.*[59]

∽ At the time this discussion about women's higher education was going on, German universities were considered the best in the world. In physics, music theory, philology, and psychology, their scholars were engaged in the most sophisticated research, and their mathematicians also believed they were making great advances in logic.

When academia was confronted face to face with the question of accepting women, all this dispassionate superiority dissolved in emotion. "German scholarship is work for men," they announced in chorus, with a few notable exceptions—an expression that sounds even more uncompromising in the original German (*"Deutsche Wissenschaft ist Männerwerk"*).[60] This male chauvinism was part of the Bismarckian era and was apparent in economic, political, and cultural affairs. Uncon-

---

*By 1917, Marianne Weber reported, the personality patterns of the women students had changed. The first ones had been militant about their rights; now a second generation was far more romantic and eager for love (Martin Green, 220).

sciously they may have hoped that no one would notice the irrelevance of their failure to meet the issue of feminism, but it was proof of that failure that when women were finally admitted—thirty years after the rest of western Europe—not one of the dire forecasts was realized.

ᕤ26.

Careers, Femininity, and Motherhood

From now on woman will not sigh for the lost paradise as though under a curse; through physiological knowledge she has become again the mistress of her own body and of her own destiny.

Marie Stritt, ca. 1912

Any discussion of women's work in the nineteenth century must consider the change in the nature of their work at home. On the one hand, the simplification of household tasks drove them outside to seek careers, and on the other, their responsibilities at home were still sufficient to keep them from being as free as men to give undivided attention to a profession. This dilemma was nibbled at in every country, but the most thoroughgoing discussion took place in Germany.

Georg Simmel outlined the general problem in 1902 in an article in the *International Monthly*.[1] The division of labor in modern times, he wrote, deprived women of most of the household functions that in the past had kept them both efficient and contented. Of all their traditional tasks, only child-rearing still provided a suitable use of their energies, while household machinery and ready-made articles in shops subtracted interest from all other routines. With the original reasons for their staying at home forgotten, most women still stayed there and felt the burden of a senseless tradition. By 1914, home life seemed so unattractive that Fritz Berolzheimer, trying to imagine how the twentieth century would turn out, predicted that fewer and fewer girls would be willing to marry.

The socialists thought they had an answer, even though hot debate on women's proper role continued within the party right up until the outbreak of war in 1914. Marx and Engels had promised that socialism would bring in a new and freer relationship between the sexes; when Engels attempted to spell this out, he found himself following the anthropologist J. J. Bachofen's theory of matriarchy.* The thesis was that

*Das Mütterrecht, 1861.

women had been more important than men in primitive society, and that under these primitive and happy conditions, women must have enjoyed a higher social status than they have had since. Thinking it over, Engels decided that the first step toward recovering their rights was for women to earn their own money by entrance into industry, the corollary being a complete suppression of the family as an economic unit. The care and education of children would become public obligations, and this would benefit children as well as parents, because to Engels it was obvious that it was better for the little ones to be taken care of by well-trained practitioners than by their ignorant or careless mothers.[2]

The debate was continued when August Bebel weighed in with his massive study on women and socialism in 1883, based partly on Engels but also admitting a heavy debt to the French utopians. His goal was total economic and social equality, and it seemed clear to him that until the whole economic system was altered, nothing that the middle-class women's movement could do would bring about any improvement. Publication of so radical a thesis violated Bismarck's anti-socialist laws, and the book had to be printed secretly and distributed only to an audience of committed socialists. Still, it proved surprisingly popular, quickly running into eight editions, and Bebel took pleasure in imagining that the copies confiscated by the police would be read not only by the officers, but by their wives as well.[3]

The socialist society he envisioned would change housekeeping routines far more drastically than Simmel's mechanical devices and prepared commodities. Bebel foresaw central kitchens, cleaning establishments where washing could be mechanically handled, central heating and lighting, hot and cold running water, and great warehouses of ready-made clothing. He waxed eloquent over plans that he thought were going forward in America to serve an entire quarter of a city by a single heating plant providing both hot water and air cooling. (Around 1910, in fact, Oak Park, Illinois, enjoyed a central heating system supplying about 40 percent of the homes. Called Yaryan, it utilized steam distributed in underground pipes.) Not only would the serving maid disappear, but also the lady.[4]

The Erfurt program of 1892 attempted to formalize the Social Democratic position on women by including a declaration about their economic and social equality and a demand for the repeal of all prejudicial laws affecting their public or private lives.[5] It turned out, however, that many workers were unhappy with this definition, and discussion in the party press continued. There had always been a faction that held that women's employment outside the home was a capitalist imposition.[6] Such had been the view of Lassalle and of a resolution passed at an early workers' convention of 1867, and it continued to be warmly defended by Edmund Fischer during the decade before 1914. Fischer pointed out that most people, including socialists, did not really like communal housekeeping, and wanted their own homes.[7] According to him, the women he surveyed believed earnestly that socialism should allow them to stay home with their children. One woman put it this way: when women began to work outside the home, "capitalism smiled." This wing of the party favored mothers' pensions.[8]

Other women party members disagreed, and several published direct answers to Fischer. They explained that work at home could be lightened in several ways: by electricity, by shorter hours of outside labor for everyone so that the male members of the household could help, and by family limitation with cooperative nursery care for young mothers.[9] Under such circumstances women could manage both their careers and their homes with satisfaction. Birth control was essential, however, with four considered the maximum desirable number of children per family.* One woman said that half an hour a day was sufficient for her personal housecleaning and that under socialism no woman would be expected to spend time in "serving men" or performing the rest of the socially wasteful chores that occupied so much time of the woman under capitalism. Some socialists hoped that part-time work could be arranged for young mothers, but others explained that socialist children would be different, that sentimentality about motherhood would have to be erased, and that children would be sent out to healthy country farms while their mothers would acquire the independence of character and the breadth of interests suitable for socialist woman. Work, said Wally Zepler, would give a woman more peace and freedom than marriage, an institution that she thought would disappear.[10]

Though the hostility to bourgeois family life created a sharp difference between the socialist and middle-class women's movements, many non-socialist or half-socialist women were attracted to the plans for making housework easier and distributing family responsibility in new ways. Even Helene Lange's *Frauenschulen* had as part of their aim to encourage the back-to-the-land trend of the 1890s and to intensify this new style of life by a certain amount of communization.[11] A complete blueprint was worked out by Lily Braun (a half-socialist, as I think she turned out to be) for a housing development of small individual living apartments, a central kitchen to prepare all the food, and a central nursery to care for all the children.[12] Though she knew architects who were eager to build this complex, the project remained unfunded.

∾ Another burning practical question for feminists, besides the management of the house, was whether the preponderance of scientific

*In 1912 Julius Wolf presented evidence that the Social Democrats had actually succeeded in reducing the birth rate in certain sections of Berlin and other cities. He compared the birth rates in districts with a high porportion of Social Democratic votes with their opposites and found a much greater reduction in the former (Wolf, 147).

opinion was right: were female sexual functions, especially motherhood, incompatible with creative work?* A sort of pre-Freudian psychology was sometimes applied, as was expressed by Goethe in 1825:

> The conversation now turned on poetesses in general; Hofrath Rehbein remarked that the poetical talent of ladies seemed to him as a sexual instinct of the intellect. "Hear him," said Goethe, laughing, and looking at me: "sexual instinct, indeed! How the physician explains it."
>
> "I know not," said Rehbein, "whether I express myself right; but it is something of the sort. Usually these beings have not been fortunate in love, and they now seek compensation in intellectual pursuits. Had they been married in time, and borne children, they would never have thought of poetical productions."
>
> "I will not inquire," said Goethe, "how far you are right in this case; but as to the talents of ladies in other departments, I have always found that they ceased on marriage. I have known girls who drew finely; but so soon as they became wives and mothers it was all over. . . ."[13]

In 1901 Adele Gerhard and Helene Simon decided to find out if this theory was true, and to do so they went directly to those women who had made a name for themselves in the arts or intellectual life.

They received four hundred signed answers to their open-ended questionnaire (plus a few more anonymous ones), mostly but not entirely from German respondents. The answers are printed in a book, *Mütterschaft und geistige Arbeit* (*Motherhood and Intellectual Work*), sorted out according to whether the women were artists, writers, professional women, or scholars. In the end the editors drew no hard and fast conclusions, content in the main simply to present their evidence, though it seems to me that their summary pays unnecessary homage to conventional sentiments about motherhood as woman's highest function.

The 112 artists surveyed were the group that seemed to get on best of all. Seventy-five of these musicians, painters, and sculptors had married, and 63 were mothers, 4 without benefit of clergy. Of these, 42 had more than one child, 33 had nursed their own babies, and 18 had suffered the death of a child.

Among the performing artists, Adelaide Ristori, an Italian actress, was most decisive in her affirmation. "I have adored my art; I have adored my children. An artist can well have a heart large enough for these

---

*Fairly dismal statements about this question circulated freely across Europe. Frances Power Cobbe wrote: "There appear to be some occult laws in woman's nature . . . rendering it impossible to pursue the higher branches of art or literature, or any work tasking mental exertion, while home and motherly cares have their claims. . . . No great books have been written or works achieved by women while their children were around them in infancy" (Cobbe, *Pursuits*, 69). And Margaret Fuller Ossoli agreed: "The duties of a mother are low and neutralizing" (Kuhn, 34).

Of course, these views could have been refuted by a look at such working mothers of the period as Mrs. Trollope, Mrs. Gaskell, Dr. Garrett Anderson, and Hortense Allart, not to mention the American Harriet Beecher Stowe.

two sentiments and for still more."[14] Likewise another actress, Virginie Demont-Breton: "I hope the result of your inquiry will be to prove that art is not generally incompatible with family life. I believe for my part that, on the contrary, it brings an extra charm to it." She added that a woman needed the experience of maternity to be able to communicate in art.[15] The most famous German actress of the century, Wilhelmine Schroeder-Devrient, was married for six years, producing four children. (One of them died while Schroeder-Devrient was on stage.) In divorce proceedings the father received custody of the others, but she continued to send money for their education. Ernestine Schumann-Heinck, the contralto, nursed seven children and used to practice her operatic roles among them.[16]

Role conflict seemed to be somewhat more prevalent among the writers. It was recalled that George Sand had abandoned all intellectual activity while pregnant, and had felt that seeing her baby was the most beautiful moment of her life. The Austrian writer, Marie von Ebner-Eschenbach, wrote that she did not understand how a woman could summon the fortitude to write at the bedside of a sick child. Others said that it would be impossible to combine the duties of a vigilant teacher of one's children with those of an independent writer, while a "famous foreign writer"—unnamed—who admitted to having had several children out of wedlock, advised women who wrote to live alone; she reported that her own schedule was to work all night and sleep while the children were at school. Somebody said of Marceline Desbordes-Valmore, the most distinguished nineteenth-century French woman poet, that "she had the air of a soul which had met a body by chance, and who managed with it as well as she could."[17] On the other hand, Clara Viebig,* author of the best-selling *Das tägliche Brot* (*Our Daily Bread*) believed that only in marriage could a woman writer truly develop because it gave her a broader basis for human and social understanding. Mrs. Gaskell's daughter testified that her mother's writing never interfered with her housekeeping and social duties.

Fifty-five questionnaires were returned in the field of scholarship, of which only twenty-eight were from married women, a quarter of whom had married rather late in life.[18] Eighteen had borne children, and nine of these had nursed their babies. Only fifteen of these women had received university training—not surprising in 1901—and fifteen worked as teachers besides being concerned with research. (Among them, an American historian, Elizabeth Wormley Latimer, who had four children, attributed her undiminished intellectual activity at the age of seventy-eight to the twenty-year fallow period from 1856 to 1876.)[19]

Of the forty-seven professional women, including twenty-eight doctors, twenty-five were unmarried, twenty-two had married, and twenty were mothers.[20] Twelve had nursed their infants. But among this group were three who had become ill from overwork. An inspector of

*Pseudonym of Clara Cöhn.

primary schools in Paris wrote to the pollsters about how hard life was for teachers who were also mothers, and how even though they engaged baby sitters, they always had to rush home after work to start cooking and cleaning.[21]

A sharp twist in the argument came from Marianne Hainisch (mother of the future first president of the Austrian Republic, and in 1901 a leading Austrian feminist), when she remarked that non-working mothers were usually not at all good ones, because they did not know how to concentrate on essentials.

The editors' conclusion was that while careers might prove a double burden for a while (admitting that the new science of hygiene and modern insights into child psychology required more time for each baby than their ancestors had been expected to give), still baby sitters could be trained, and most women lived for many years after their children ceased to be dependent upon them. Although Lily Braun was not among those whose views were solicited for this book, we may remember her insistence that new household appliances and the fact that children regularly went off to school gave women more freedom for work outside the home than had ever existed before in history. We may also recall what an English lady told Agnes von Zahn-Harnack: that to combine a career with marriage required an understanding husband; and Zahn's reply: that such a man was hard to find in Germany.[22]

The debate about maternal instinct had a tendency to complicate the question of feminine creativity. The unmarried women who sought to become teachers argued that in their profession they could expend a quota of motherliness that would not be available to a physical mother because she spent it on her own children. They defended this theory all the more warmly because their jobs depended on it. Socialist theory added weight to this side of the debate because, although it posited environment as a stronger force than instinct, its proponents talked as if only when the private burden of rearing children had been lifted could women be expected to be creative. On the other side were those whose spokeswoman was Hedwig Dohm, who wanted no specialization of feminine qualities and who pointed out that men often took more time out for gout than women did for childbirth. She observed that even Bismarck had withdrawn to his country estate for long periods because of his "nerves"; if a woman had done so, it would be attributed to her sex.[23]

Publication of the Gerhard-Simon book made people consider the value of combining motherhood with intellectual labor in a new light. It was perceived that women in the professions or the arts could make excellent mothers and that motherhood might be an enriching experience for a doctor, teacher, or artist. This point of view, according to Agnes von Zahn-Harnack, matured the women's movement and turned it away from its early insistence that careers were only for the celibate.[24]

Population control was widely discussed by scholars as well as feminists in the years just preceding the outbreak of war. The economist

Lujo Brentano speculated that the falling birth rate was due to the fact that contemporary life offered women so many competing pleasures. (And in France, declared German scholars a bit scornfully, the cult of beauty for women bore some of the responsibility.) But pleasure was not the only cause, as Julius Wolf pointed out after a careful scrutiny of the census figures in 1912.[25] Women needed to have a worthy human existence, and it was important for them to preserve their earning capacity: creative women, he found, often satisfied their desire for children by having just one, or perhaps two. In any case, he found that women of his day insisted that they should be the ones to decide when and how often they should become mothers, and he believed that men were becoming more sympathetic to this wish.

The idea of birth control was introduced to the German women's movement by Frieda Duensing, a doctor of law, in 1907,[26] and shortly thereafter the official organ of the *Bund für Mütterschutz* urged the right of women to end a pregnancy at will, now declared to be an ancient Germanic right that had been set aside by canon law.[27] But while they wanted no one to become pregnant against her will, the movement was equally eager to assure the right of motherhood to every healthy woman, which they thought could be achieved by making available remunerative work plus a system of mothers' pensions.[28]

Socialists too believed in freeing sexual choices. Bebel had explained (quoting Krafft-Ebing's *Textbook of Psychiatry* of 1883) that while men could find a substitute for the sex drive in work, this was impossible for women. Control over their own persons would mean for Bebel the right to have babies and to fulfill their motherly drives, not necessarily in marriage, because in his opinion sexual frustration could lead to suicide as well as various illnesses, all, in his view, the result of capitalist exploitation.[29] He seemed to feel that socialism would bring an end not only to prostitution, but also to masturbation, homosexuality, and female hysteria. Only by uniting with the proletariat would women become free in this sense, he told them.*[30]

To a middle-class feminist, "liberation" could thus be a decidedly ambiguous term on which much discussion foundered. It could mean either freedom to cooperate with men equally in economic and intellec-

---

*Bebel's views aroused furious criticism, not only from defenders of the status quo, as might be expected, but also from those liberals who believed that a higher state of culture demanded sexual restraint. Bertrand Russell, of all people, in a study of German Social Democracy, opined that Bebel's ideas were suited to men of few pleasures and little imagination, and a chapter by Mrs. Bertrand Russell added that Bebel should have considered far more deeply the evils of sexual excess (Bertrand Russell, 179). Engels affirmed that women in general would prefer the limited sexuality of marriage to the more abundant opportunities of socialist freedom. In this belief Engels, the lover of a factory worker, differed from Marx, the married man. In actual fact, Bebel had urged moderation in sexual activity, and several of his followers, including Bernstein and Kautsky, influenced by English philosophy, were opposed to unlimited indulgence, even in marriage. An interesting article by R. P. Neuman explains that these socialists were men of bourgeois extraction, influenced by the scientific views of their day, and were far from carrying genuine socialist principles to their logical conclusions.

tual, and hence sexual, matters—freedom *for* sex, so to speak—or it could mean freedom from male domination, or freedom *from* sex. At a 1908 women's congress a resolution was put forward that "the woman must, as a free person, be the mistress of her own body." A voice vote was inconclusive, and Helene Lange, in the chair, was too skittish to want her precious organization to go on record in this delicate matter, so she declared that there was "no majority."[31] Though the parliamentary maneuver kept the minutes clean, it typified the confrontation between the older, career-oriented founders of the BDF and the younger members who were stirred by the *fin de siècle* interest in sexual freedom. But on the whole the women's movement found that it could get a broad united front of religious and conservative groups by rallying around the ideal of the monogamous marriage. In 1910 the BDF rejected a well-organized effort by the radical minority that would have given help and support to unmarried mothers.[32]

ᨵ A major obstacle to the first girls who longed for a career, and one only slowly overcome, was the ancient sentiment that work was unworthy of a free man. This prejudice, which was also widespread in England, though overcome there somewhat sooner, was very possibly related to the absence of a dowry in these northern countries. Young French and Italian women, who thought of themselves as invested with a certain amount of capital, did not face exactly the same distaste when they started to earn money. (They met obstacles, but not in that particular form.) In the northern countries there was a long tradition that only slaves "worked,"* and long after middle-class sons had submitted to the necessity of earning a living, people still clung to the hope that a free man's daughter need not soil her hands.[33] For anyone with a pretense to aristocracy, the taboo was even more rigid. Thus when Lily Braun's officer father became *persona non grata* to the new young Kaiser, Wilhelm II, and resigned his commission, Lily discussed the possibility of her earning some money, but even under these conditions her father became furious at the idea. Her mother saw no openings except as a lady-in-waiting at court or a governess. Only Lily's grandmother, a holdover from a generation when respectability was not so tightly defined, told Lily that she must certainly stand on her own feet and offered two examples of self-supporting women, one a writer, the other a painter of china.

Helene Lange was a daughter of the middle classes, but she too ran into a wall, reminding the readers of her autobiography that in 1870 no

*My good friend Dr. Justus Bier gave me an example of how the taboo against physical labor applied to male intellectuals even after World War I. When he first came to America in the 1930s, he was invited to sit with the governing board of a local museum, which consisted of the most prominent and wealthy citizens of the city. He was astonished to see the chairman of the board actually straighten a picture with his own hand. Back in Germany, where Dr. Bier had been a museum director, he would have summoned a menial to perform this task.

girl of good family had ever worked for money except in terrible misfortune. Likewise in Marianne Weber's home village, the boys usually went off while the girls stayed home. Marianne rebelled, until her grandfather agreed to send her to Berlin for a career too, but the question remained: if Karl Weber's granddaughter earned money, what would "they" think?

The plot of E. Marlitt's* *The Second Wife* shows how the unrespectability of earning even a little bit of money could be used as plausible motivation in fiction. The leading character, Liana, is an impoverished countess who, before her marriage, helps her brother by illustrating his treatises on botany. It is not really *comme il faut* for a man of his station to make money even from scientific books, and his sister helps him anonymously. She also paints for her own pleasure, but when her first picture is hung in a gallery, she suffers a nervous collapse. Her life after marriage is rather lonely, and she is eager to continue to help her brother. But when this is discovered by her in-laws, the old grandfather starts as if he has been shot. "In other words, before your marriage you *earned bread* by the work of your hands?" Her answering argument that the masses would lose respect for an aristocracy that relied only upon hoarded money falls on deaf ears.

It was only natural, given this general belief, that literary production by a woman was not considered in good taste. In England this prejudice began to disappear after the 1830s, but English visitors to Germany often commented on how long it hung on there, and one of them described a literary tea at which a German husband, without consulting his wife, gave some of her verses to a famous editor to read aloud. The effort was greeted by total silence on the part of all the guests.[34] Even an intellectual woman like Henriette Feuerbach felt that a woman writer should publish anonymously (as did she) and gave warm praise to a literary bride whose unsuspecting husband presented her with a volume of her own writings on her wedding day.[35] Very few women were able to refer to a sympathetic husband as did Frau Pichler, who talked of "my good Pichler's pleasure in my dramatic works."[36]

Many are the stories of families putting pressure on their girls not to write. Annette von Droste was probably the best woman poet writing in German in the nineteenth century, but at the age of forty-one, when her first book of poems was to be published (in 1838), she had to get her mother's approval, which was only obtained with the stipulation that Annette's name should not be emblazoned on the cover.[37]

When Marie Ebner von Eschenbach took a few of her poems to her grandmother, who lived on a different floor of the same building, the old lady treated it not as a mistake but as a positive sin, and sent her "home" with a servant and no explanation.†[38]

*Pseudonym of Eugenie John, 1825–1887.

†Fanny Lewald told the tale of a girl of good family who was still accepted in Berlin society after she had fallen into straitened circumstances and accepted a position as

As Hedwig Dohm saw it, women could cook, but not become chefs; they could sew, but not run a dressmaking establishment;[39] and the only reason Florence Nightingale succeeded was that she was willing to work for nothing. So if the pay for nursing were suddenly raised to ten gold pieces a day, it would be discovered that women were not fit to do it; it would damage their nerves.[40]

Frau Dohm said of herself, "I had a calling, God's voice commanded me, but I was not able to follow it because I was a woman." The fact that millions of women were unable to find jobs she attributed largely to men's unwillingness to face the competition, noting that every man whatever his profession, felt that women were particularly unsuited to that one.[41]

ᑒ Even though frowned upon, writing was still a relatively easy and inconspicuous way for women to earn money, and because many women needed money, a sort of women's literature was gradually built up. Baring-Gould told his English readers that while science and art were forbidden subjects, German women might write nursery tales, or even translate from the English;[42] and many women found a source of income in writing for magazines like *Die Gartenlaube* (literally the Summer House), which from 1853 on brought information, fashions, housekeeping hints, and light fiction into many a German home. Frau Marlitt was one of these. Her family was in bankruptcy when she was growing up, and although a sympathetic countess paid for her musical education, deafness blighted this career, so she turned to writing fiction. Her first story appeared in *Die Gartenlaube* in 1865; six years later she was able to build her own house from her earnings, and take her father, her brother, and his family to live with her.

For a long time the only respected professions that took women into public view were the performing arts. This is not to say that an ordinary bougeois father would be eager to have his daughter tread the boards, but merely that women who were there, mostly from acting families, were not looked down on. In the eighteenth century a certain Frau Neuber had re-established respect for the acting profession and had often taken unmarried actresses to live with her like adopted daughters.[43] The most famous and beloved actress in the nineteenth century was Wilhelmine Schroeder-Devrient, who had been educated for the stage by a theatrical mother, and whose lovely voice and genial personality had won devotion from crowds all over Germany. Nor was she unique; Karl Kautsky tells us that his mother, bright, energetic, and ambitious, found acting the only profession open to her.[44] She was the daughter of a rather

---

companion to a great lady. But when she was bored with this job and opened up a little business of her own (a laundry), she was cut by all her previous acquaintances.

dreamy scene-painter, and married a man in the same profession. Even after she had three children and had become tubercular, she had to return to the stage in order to support the family, while Karl and the other children lived with their father and a maid.

Music, too, offered careers to outstandingly talented women, like the Swedish Jenny Lind, who had adorers all over the world, but who retired when she married.

Clara Schumann was probably the most remarkable of the women who supported their families unaided, and she is worth a closer look. The daughter of two music teachers who divorced when she was small, Clara spent her childhood with her father, Friedrich Wieck, who early discovered her extraordinary talent and who ordered a grand piano for her when she was only eight. At twelve she earned her first money—thirty thalers for a concert at Leipzig, of which she gave twenty to her father. Three years later, in 1834, after she was confirmed, her father declared that he expected her to be independent from then on, though he wished to continue as "an advising and helping friend."[45] Part of his advice was not to marry one of his students, Robert Schumann, his ostensible reason being that the couple would not have enough money to live on. Clara was sent to Dresden to get away from Robert, though while she was there friends managed to arrange secret meetings between the two. When Wieck found that he had failed to break up the romance, he ordered her not to write to Robert, to send back unopened any letters she received from him, and to refuse to allow him to dedicate his compositions to her. The moment she was legally old enough, in 1840, Clara fled to her mother's house and married Robert Schumann after applying for a court order permitting the marriage in defiance of her father. Her father was so angry that he refused to send the grand piano on to the couple's new home.[46]

As Clara's reputation was far greater than Robert's, she believed that it was her wifely duty to renounce her public performances in order that Robert might shine. She could not even practice because he could not bear the sound while he was composing, so she cut beans in the kitchen and shed a few silent tears, waiting for the evenings when they would read together, and Robert would play Bach. The first of their eight children appeared in 1841.

When Robert showed signs of mental illness, Clara had to undertake the management of the whole family and provide support by going back to the concert stage. She sent Robert to a hospital and tried to give her boys the advantages of a male presence by putting them in boarding schools under men teachers, while she taught her girls herself when she could find time. She used to limit her concert season to nine months in order to spend the long summer with the children; all her life, she continued to be a closely interested and supportive mother while enjoying wide friendships of her own. Her closest woman friend was Schroeder-Devrient. Even at seventy she enjoyed her girlhood friends and liked to walk in the woods with them, laughing and climbing gates.[47] Few people seem to have noticed how different she was from the dependent and idealized female made famous in Robert Schumann's 1840 series of songs on woman's life, *Frauenliebe und leben* (*Woman's Life and Love* set to verses by Chamisso).

Musical talent of the quality of Clara Schumann's is so rare that its exploitation cannot be considered a resource for average girls. Even after conservatories opened up, such as the academy at Berlin where Clara sent her daughter in 1869, most parents were unwilling to let their girls take up serious music study. The musical fraternity itself hesitated about letting a girl student conduct an orchestra. Writing home to Massachusetts in 1871, Amy Fay says that the men in the audience were disgusted to see a young woman directing, and added her own opinion that to hold a baton in the hand is not a becoming posture for a lady.*[48]

There was always the possibility of giving music lessons. Such a career was made for herself by Johanna Kinkel, born in 1810 in Bonn, the daughter of a *gymnasium* teacher. After a divorce, she married Gottfried Kinkel, an art professor.[49] Their life together started out delightfully, replete with such pleasures as the singing club that they founded. After the 1848 revolutions, Johanna had to flee to London with her four young children, where she supported them by giving lessons and kept them happy by composing songs for them to sing in parts, though it was hard for her, accomplished as she was, to have to teach beginners in an unmusical city. Yet once again the general disapproval of the self-supporting woman surfaced. When Kinkel spoke in London to the German emigrés, praising women who could earn their own living, the ladies in his audience sat stolidly beside their husbands. They were not moved to sympathy even by such examples of need and courage.[50]

ꝏ In every country, it seems, there was a legend of one woman physician who had somehow conquered the handicap of her sex and been allowed to practice medicine in the early years of the nineteenth century. In Germany the woman was Charlotte von Siebold, who had become licensed as a doctor and practiced in Darmstadt. It was fifty years before the next woman followed her path. Franziska Tiburtius canvassed the medical faculties of her fatherland in 1870, only to find that she had no hope of acceptance by any of them, so she decided to go to Switzerland. The hospitality she received there and the work she was able to undertake filled her with lifelong gratitude.[51] When she and a woman colleague got back to Berlin, however, with their diplomas in hand, officials told them that they would not be permitted to practice. On the advice of friends, they hung out their shingles anyway, and soon found that the demand for

*I have come across tantalizing references to all-women orchestras—one in Sweden, which was considered a rarity, however, and one that won a prize in 1866 when competing against forty male ensembles in Orbech (Otto-Peters, 170; Mozzoni, *Passo*, 44).

their services was enormous.[52] She lived with her brother and his wife, Henriette Hirschfeld, who was Germany's first woman dentist and who had been trained in Philadelphia.

Although Helene Lange asserted that the training of women physicians had become a necessity, owing to the phenomenal increase of female maladies in the 1880s, officialdom was slow to respond. A woman who had studied at Edinburgh in the 1870s, Anna Dahms, was refused the right to take the state licensing examination in Hamburg and had to return to Scotland to practice.[53] In 1891 the Reichstag, in spite of a huge petition for female admission to German medical schools, rejected the proposal.[54] Only in 1901 were the first women allowed to matriculate at Prussian medical and dental faculties.

Nursing was another matter. Here Germany could be said to lead the world. Even without formal training, German women who had obtained distinction in other fields showed extraordinary willingness to take up nursing in times of national emergency—women like Rahel in the war of 1813; Bettina, who nursed day and night during the cholera epidemic of 1831 and again in the war of 1866, when she set up a private hospital in her home; Amelia Sieveking, who supervised the nursing in a cholera hospital; and Henriette Feuerbach, who set up an army hospital in 1870.[55]

For formal training of laywomen, the initiative came from the Protestant pastor at Kaiserswerth on the Rhine, Theodor Fliedner. He had already worked for prison reform, and in 1836 set up an order of deaconesses to nurse the sick poor.*[56] The deaconesses did not take final vows and were free to return to the world at any time. When he asked Amelia Sieveking to recommend a woman to head his project, she suggested that he use his own wife, who had borne twelve children in her fourteen years of married life, five of whom survived. The poor woman undertook this double job, and died of a miscarriage after she had had to leave her sick husband and two mortally ill children to attend to a

---

*Fliedner started his projects in 1822, when he was only twenty-two years old. Many of his parishioners were put out of work by the bankruptcy of a local manufacturer. Unable to cope with the misery by himself, the young pastor conceived the idea of going to raise funds in Holland and England; in the latter country he met Mrs. Elizabeth Fry, whose work in prisons is famous. Once home in Germany, his first institution was a model prison. In 1833 he started what might be called a work release program for women prisoners, who were given over to his custody. By 1836 he had added an infant school where four hundred teachers were trained in 1851, and in the same year he began the hospital that Florence Nightingale made famous. He began with one patient, one nurse, and one cook, but in the first year they treated sixty patients and graduated seven nurses. While complaining of the bad food, Miss Nightingale had only praise for the "high tone" of the place and the dedication of the workers. Fliedner devoted much of his time to individual counseling. Ninety-four of his nurses had been blessed as deaconesses and twenty-two were still on probation in Miss Nightingale's year. They could look forward to very low pay but some social security for their old age in the form of a mother house to which they could retire. He was eager, however, to have this new profession respected so he designed a uniform that would confer the prestige of middle-class matrons.

neglected hospital ward. Pastor Fliedner turned again to Amelia Sieveking to find a successor for both roles, wife and supervisor. The devoted lady who was chosen bore seven children while presiding over the growth of the order of nursing deaconesses from 50 to 650.[57] Eventually official, state-sponsored schools of nursing were set up, one by the Grand Duchess of Baden, another under the aegis of the Empress Frederick in Prussia. In Vienna, Professor of Surgery Theodor Billroth worked hard againt many prejudices to get a non-denominational *Rudolfinerhaus* started for nurses' training.[58]

But once women became involved in anything as professional as hospital management, no matter how well they did it, the German military and civilian officials tried to take it away from them.[59] Such was the steady complaint of the *Neue Bahnen*, the organ of the feminist movement, which ran a column called "From the Battlefield" during the 1870 war.*

In one field of science non-specialized amateurs could still uncover new information in the nineteenth century, people who would today be called naturalists, who catalogued the species in the still largely unclassified domains of botany and zoology. In this area the story of Amelie Dietrich is instructive.[60] She was the daughter of a pursemaker in Saxony, a distinctly lower middle-class girl but so bright at school that the teacher used to threaten the upper-class girls that if they did not look out, Amelie might move up ahead of them. (German schoolchildren were supposed to be seated in the classroom according to their academic rank; and Amelie thought it a great injustice that she was never allowed to sit at the top of the class.)

Born in 1821 after her parents had lost several boys, she was required to learn her father's trade in order to take their place. Even though her mother was proud of her brains and remarked that if Amelie were "only a boy," she would get her trained as a schoolteacher, her father informed her that he would soon knock all the nonsense about reading out of her head; but fate defeated him. While out picking mushrooms one day, Amelie fell in with a gentleman gathering specimens for his collection. He noticed how bright she was and began to visit her family, somewhat to their consternation. Finally he pressed a love note into Amelie's hand. The parents were hesitant about allowing her to marry a man who, though above them in station, was yet quite poor and who offered the girl only the chance to share in the hardships of his profession. The marriage did take place, under rather unfavorable cir-

---

*There was also something of a female country tradition of herb collecting. When Helene Adelmann was growing up, a wise old woman was able, with an herbal bath and a cold shower, to cure her of a malady that the trained doctors could not affect. This old woman sold medicinals to an apothecary shop. The incident inspired Helene to wish to become a doctor, but she had to settle for schoolteaching instead, since she lived thirty years too early (Adelman, 106).

cumstances. Among them was the parents' moving in with the young couple, with consequent conflict over the use of cupboards, which the old woman thought were meant for linen and which Herr Dietrich consecrated to his insect collection.

When her mother died, however, things grew worse, and Amelie, who had never mastered the techniques of housekeeping, could not get the lunch on time and did not know how to wash and iron. The climax of unhappiness came when her little girl, while playing, found a letter that turned out to reveal Dietrich's infidelity. Meanwhile, Amelie was doing most of the hard work of the collections, and most of the brain work too. Carefully she trained herself to mount and catalogue specimens of plants and animals, and her skill was so obvious that a professor at Marburg asked her to lead a field trip to show the students how such studies should be undertaken. Though she was too shy to accept this offer, she began to be recognized in intellectual circles.

It flustered Herr Dietrich considerably to find that his wife was developing independent ideas, and partly to keep her down and partly to save himself the trouble, he sent her on long trips around Germany to replenish their supplies. One summer she obediently went along the whole coast from Bremen to Rotterdam with a dog cart. Luckily it was not long before the professional botanists of Germany realized what a treasure she was and rescued her from such routine tasks, eventually financing her expeditions around the world in search of new species and new classifications. In 1867 she was made a fellow of the Entomological Society of Stettin, while her husband dropped into obscurity.

The acceptance of women researchers was a come-and-go thing in those years. In 1878, for instance, the Congress of German Scientists* allowed a woman doctor to present an exhibit. Even though the exhibit was praised, she made a very bad personal impression—she was rather weirdly dressed, she had a vile accent (she was English)—and so the following year they formally forbade all female participation. In future, they hoped, women would get visitors' cards only and listen silently.[61] And yet in that same year, in Saint Petersburg, a woman presided over the ornithology section of a large scientific meeting. When Helene Simon prepared a paper on night work for women for a social science convention in 1901, she had to sit in an anteroom and listen to the paper being read for her, but this incident proved to be a turning point because everyone realized how silly the situation was.[62]

⤳ For women who lacked either the need or the drive to get directly into serious paid work, an easy stepping stone was philanthropy, although volunteer activity was far less developed in Germany than in England. Already in 1880 Lorenz von Stein was pointing out that the government had taken over so much responsibility for welfare—Ger-

*Versammlung Deutscher Naturforscher und Aïtzte.

many was the first country in the world to put in social insurance—that it left little for private agencies to do.[63] Moreover, German women had to perform so much service at home that they had less time to go outside;[64]— at least this was the explanation offered by several Englishwomen. Among others, I. A. R. Wylie, observed in 1912 that German women did not do nearly as much for their churches, not even small things like taking care of the decorations.[65] A consequence of this lack of habituation to working in organized groups was that when war came, German women proved less capable of pitching in for victory at a time when 85 percent of the war materiel manufactured in England was produced by women workers.[66]

The fact that there was less philanthropy does not mean that there was none. Lily Braun had some experience of it, not good, in her girlhood. When quite small she would have liked to help her grandmother run the nursery school in their estate's village, but there was so much bad language, drink, and illegitimacy around that it was not considered suitable. Later on she ran into another kind of trouble in Augsburg, where she was visiting her aunt. The young girl was so upset at the child labor in the very factory where her aunt owned stock that the family forbade her to continue visits to the workers' homes lest she develop radical ideas.[67] This sort of thing did not seem to bother the English, whether because the village poor were actually more respectable, or because the English were less sensitive to the injustice of a system that seemed to be working rather well for them.

Under the Empire it came to be part of the proper role of a rich woman to have a favorite charity,[68] and she could take her choice among hospitals and summer camps, nutritious meals and enriched education for poor children—work with "the poor, the sick and the wicked," as Mrs. Sidgwick described it.[69] Alice Solomon developed a sort of Junior League to train idle girls from the upper classes to do humble tasks in the social work field.[70] (She had spent four hours a day knitting in her youth, and was "rescued" by a single advertisement calling for social work volunteers.) Royal patronage was always a help, and the two daughters of Queen Victoria on German thrones did much to import English ideals of service to their adopted country. They were always ready to lend their names to good works of this sort.

As the girls who had been educated through the schools and scholarships set up by the women's movement came to maturity, they tended to prefer professional positions in welfare agencies to private charitable efforts of their own.[71] To these were added a few of the women who had worked so hard for charity that they had become practically professional and even the government acknowledged their capacity. In 1904 Helene Weber was given an official appointment in the public agency for welfare, the first woman in Prussia to be so recognized.[72]

One of the notable movements led in good part by women was the temperance crusade. This campaign had many advantages for the women's movement as a whole because sometimes even conservative churchwomen could be initiated into the skills and rewards of organizational activity and could be led from anti-alcoholism to consideration of those political rights that seemed the only way to make a dent in men's bad habits. The temperance movement actually succeeded in getting anti-alcohol instruction introduced into the public schools, and they set up a chain of hotels where women travelers could feel safe, in which, by 1914, ten thousand guests were received nightly.

The anti-prostitution campaign had far less success. Josephine Butler's most important German follower was Frau Gertrud Guillaume-Schack, who in 1880 sent a petition to the Reichstag against legalized prostitution. Her lecture hall was closed in 1882, and she was arrested and tried for, of all things, "immorality." (The court preacher explained it this way: the end of prostitution would mean the equality of the sexes, and such an aim must be at once rejected.) Although acquitted by the jury, Frau Guillaume-Schack took refuge in England, and German work on that front ceased.*[73]

∽ One of the comparisons bandied about between 1860 and 1914 was that while working-class women needed to work because they needed money, middle-class women worked for the sake of their personalities. The latter salved their consciences by using their personality-enhancing careers for the benefit of their poorer sisters, but nevertheless the difference in incentive widened the serious split between the two halves of the women's movement.†

Much heat was produced by the debate over whether professions for women would masculinize the women or feminize the professions. Those who were sure that motherliness was the dominant instinct in all women continued to be defensive about the loss of femininity, insisting that there were certain things that only women could do, and others that they could do better than men, in such fields as social welfare, temperance, peace, and training others for these professions. They believed that the female personality would flower when these opportunities became available.

Georg Simmel urged them not to theorize but to experiment. He advocated allowing women absolutely free play, with equal pay for equal work, so that the world would find out what in fact they could do. His own

---

*Frau Guillaume-Schack founded a bank and set up an insurance society for working girls, as well as publishing a newspaper, *Die Staatsbürgerin* (the *Woman Citizen*). There is some doubt as to whether she turned socialist in the end, but if she did so, she would be another of the many who found the middle-class women's movement inadequate (Twellmann, *Frauenbewegung*, 167).

†The 1895 German census showed 57.5 percent of women between twenty and thirty working to support themselves. Although 77 percent of those between thirty and forty were cared for by husbands, a quarter of the married women also worked for money, and half of those over fifty were again working for their living. This set of figures gives no indication of the percentages among the class mostly under discussion (Meisel-Hess, 205).

expectation was that women would not feel fulfilled simply by competing with men for unoriginal jobs, and their highest praise ought not to be "no one can tell that this piece of work was not done by a man." He offered the far more radical suggestion that all professions be restructured so as to eliminate their male-oriented patterns.[74]

$\backsim$27.

Italian Women and the Kingdom of Italy

Consider woman therefore as the partner and companion, not merely of your joys and sorrows, but of your thoughts, your aspirations, your studies, and your endeavors after social amelioration. Consider her your equal, in your civil and political life. Be ye the two human wings that lift the soul toward the Ideal we are destined to attain.

Giuseppe Mazzini, 1862

Whatever special advantages Italian women may have had under the law were owed to the Roman Catholic church, or to Austrian rule. In a thoughtful article in the New York *Nation* in 1869,[1] Jessie White Mario explained that the Church supported women's property rights, if only because it hoped for donations, whereas in Protestant countries the governments had no reason for "bribing" women and therefore made no effort to break up old patriarchal ways. If the Roman church made marriage indissoluble, it nevertheless repaid women with certain freedoms in other areas, so that in holding property the Italian married woman was more like the *feme sole* of English law, or like an English wife who had a separate marriage settlement.

Parts of Italy, too, had benefited from the liberal regimes of Maria Theresa and her son Leopold II, who, as the grand duke of Tuscany from 1765 till 1790, had given civil capacity to women as well as to Jews. In his domain, a woman (or a Jew) with landed property could even become a magistrate, so that, for example, a certain Signora Ricci was made treasurer of her commune.[2] When the French armies destroyed this regime, they brought with them the egalitarian ideals of the Revolution, but, as we have seen, this liberation of the rights of the common man had within it a tendency to push women back into civil incapacity, a pattern that was to be repeated in the drafting of the Constitution after 1866. It is impossible, however, to make a clear statement about the actual laws in a country under so many jurisdictions as Italy before the enactment of the uniform Civil Code of 1866.

After the Austrians came back as the dominant power in 1815, actually annexing Lombardy and Venetia and exercising influence throughout most of the rest of the peninsula, the reaction was particularly painful because of the relative feeling of freedom that had been attained under the French. The only way to combat the secret police and the military garrisons was by underground organizations of patriots, and these quickly formed, determined to free Italy from the foreign yoke and to give it back the liberty that it had repeatedly tasted throughout millennia, with the hope of making the nation strong through unification.

It was in this context that Italian women passed through the romantic age. At the time when emancipated women in France were announcing sexual autonomy and dreaming of socialist Utopias, and German women found themselves edged out of men's hearts and minds as their men became concerned with a unified and liberal fatherland, Italian women were summoned to more concrete and dangerous tasks. From 1815 until the completion of the Kingdom of Italy in 1870, women were nearly as involved as the men on the battlefields, in hospitals, as conspirators, or as confidantes and consolers. As Leopardi cried out:

> *Donne, da voi non poco*
> *La patria aspetta . . . .*[*3]

There were major battlefield engagements in 1848, 1859, and 1866, in all of which women took part. Over a hundred women had been confined and tortured in Austrian prisons before 1849,[4] and their lives quickly became legends, inspiring hundreds of other women to volunteer for conspiratorial or military service, to write nationalistic poetry, and to imbue their children with patriotic sentiment.

Erminia Fusinato-Fuà wrote thus to her unborn child:

> Angel, as yet unknown and yet already so much loved, whom I feel moving in my bosom, tell me, do you too feel the torment that the fate of our country causes in me? Oh, how many times have I suppressed my tears for your sake, fearing to upset you; yet these tears fall back like a slow fire into the depths of my heart.[5]

And on another baby's tombstone appeared the inscription:

> I am Enrichetto, of the exile Silvestro Castiglione and Enrichetta Bossoli, a most holy pattern to the mothers and wives of Italy. This woman, because she was guilty of loving her country and her husband, enemy of tyranny, died in the German prison in Venice.[6]

In the 1820s the underground men were called the *Carbonari*, and their female auxiliary the *Giardiniere*, or "gardeners." Its members, mostly from the upper classes, were organized into cells of nine, and as a symbol of their membership they were supposed to wear a dagger in their garter.[7]

A famous activist was Bianca Milesi (Mojon), who went through a

---

*An extremely rough and prosaic translation of these impassioned lines might come out as: "Women, it is nothing less than your lives that your country demands."

series of liberated roles, only to end up in a domestic one. She had been born under the old regime and was sent off to a convent as soon as she was weaned.[8] With the declaration of the Napoleonic Italian republic of 1796, she was able to come out of the convent and began to travel around Europe in the company of someone described as "a virile woman." She also cut her hair. Such violations of the norm of femininity troubled her biographer, though he was happy to point out that independent women like her were needed after the abortive revolution of 1821.[9] At this time Bianca joined the gardeners, where her great contribution was the invention of a secret code based on the popular craze of cutting out elaborate designs from paper. Her system involved writing on a piece of paper, then cutting it up in such a way that the message could only be read by the person with the other half. Shortly after this period, however, she grew her hair long, began to wear earrings, abandoned her hearty laughs, married a Swiss doctor, had children, and devoted herself to pedagogy. (She wrote reading books for beginners and studied the English Lancastrian system, which was just then the rage in popular schooling.) Her early fervor was carried on by her sons, whom she sent to the battlefields of 1848.

The most famous of the gardeners, and one who actually transcended that role, was the Principessa Cristina Belgiojoso, whom a recent biographer calls the most intriguing and original Italian woman since the Middle Ages.[10] Her husband, who had been the lover of Byron's Countess Guiccioli, gave up that lady's favors in order to enjoy Cristina's dowry of 400,000 Austrian lire.[11] They separated almost immediately— some say after the first night—and Cristina compensated for her disappointing marriage by joining the gardeners and taking instruction from Bianca Milesi. To rouse the poor against Austria, she dressed in a boy's rags, but was followed by Austrian spies in spite of her disguise. In Milan she met Saint-Simon's secretary and adopted son, Augustin Thierry, and became interested in socialism. To pursue this study she moved to Paris in 1831, living there in a garret and preparing her meals with her own hands, while her husband still clung to her dowry. She attended debates in the French Chamber, listened to lectures on Saint-Simonianism, and began to write on Italian politics. In 1844 she was able to return to her properties near Milan and became famous for starting welfare projects for her tenants, turning her large drawing room into a recreation center, opening a soup kitchen, a workroom for women's employment, and a children's school. Not content with reforming her own operations, she wrote to all the landlords of Lombardy suggesting that they do likewise and begin sharing their profits with their peasants.

For a few brief moments during the revolution of 1848, it seemed as if everything the most ardent patriots had hoped for might be within their grasp, and the opportunity called out extremes of devotion. Italian women—then and later in the campaigns of 1859 and 1866—had more actual battlefield experience than those of any other country. Stories abounded of girls who joined various armies in men's clothing, like

Erminia Manelli, who donned her wounded brother's uniform and took his place at the front without ever having her sex discovered. Or again, Cleobolina Cotenna, who had written poetry as a child prodigy, dressed as a soldier and went to fight beside her son.[12]

Cristina Belgiojoso's signal service at this time was to organize military hospitals in Rome, under siege by French armies trying to restore the exiled Pope. Four years before Florence Nightingale set out for Scutari, Cristina had opened twelve hospitals. She was aided in this work by the American Margaret Fuller and the Swiss Julia Modena. They appealed to Italian women everywhere to form a voluntary corps of military nurses, and even called on the street women of Rome to redeem themselves by self-sacrifice and the cheerful undertaking of unpleasant duties. After Rome fell, Cristina went off to Turkey, where she bought a large estate and began a new series of reforms, improving the agriculture as well as serving the peasants with medical and other help. Later she put herself at the disposal of Cavour in the work of Italian unification, both traveling around as his emissary and publishing a patriotic newspaper. Her latent interest in feminism rose to a peak at this period as she foresaw a generous new Italy, which, she imagined, would give women a fine education and a new sort of honor within the family.

ᖶ If women supposed they had a great deal to hope for from a united Italy, it was largely because so long as the armed struggle continued, they were constantly flattered by the ideological leaders of the Risorgimento, of whom Giuseppe Mazzini was the most verbal.

As is well known, Mazzini began his career under the influence of the *Carbonari*, but soon became disgusted with their lack of practicality or clearcut philosophy. For a few years he was able to direct the movement toward his more humane program of Young Italy, an organization he had founded on the highest ideals of patriotism and humanity.

He had always urged his male followers to consider women their complete equals, in civil and political life as well as in studies and social endeavors. The women of Italy never disappointed him, he said, and he was deeply cognizant of their contribution to the national effort. In 1855, while the fighting was still hot and there was no sure victory in sight, Mazzini wrote to his "Italian sisters":

> To us [males], death, exile, proscription, anathema. To you, sisters, humiliation, mockery, prison, the rods! . . . Italian women! Those of us who will fight on the field of battle will have a crown. Those of you who remain steadfast, working, faithful in the day of disaster will have two! The redeemed nation will consecrate a monument as much to one as to the other. It was a woman who proposed that divine prophetic motto which Venice inscribes on its coins: *God will award the prize to constancy*.[13]

Nevertheless, Mazzini had long believed that only a republic would emancipate women. He was right, but the republic was long in coming.

Unfortunately Mazzini himself turned out to be nearly as impractical as the scorned *Carbonari*, and he was not able to achieve much against secret police and well-trained troops. Eventually Italy became free and united by a combination of shady diplomacy and war; there is no denying, however, the enormous influence of Mazzinian sentiment on the large number of women, both English and Italian, who were caught up in his cause. Their personal feelings for him were sisterly. His own great love affair, with Giudetta Sidoli, foundered not only on her desire to be close to her children (who were in Italy at a time when she and Mazzini were in exile) but also on his inability to climb down from his cloud of abstraction.

Giuditta had been happily married until her husband's death in 1828. She had followed him to political exile in Switzerland, where she studied and painted and enjoyed music, and bore the last three of her four children. When her husband died, she sent her children to their grandparents in Italy and removed to Marseilles, where her good looks, intelligence, generosity, and funding from home helped create a center for the colony of exiles that soon included Mazzini. For him, to love Giuditta was a passion second only to his devotion to his country, but he concluded, probably correctly, that he could never make a woman happy. So when she, languishing apart from her children, determined to return to Italy to be near them—even though they would still be separated by a political frontier and a hostile administration—Mazzini let her go, while he went off to England whence his letters to her were duly opened and copied by the Austrian police. They have been preserved in these official copies. "Lost soul that I am," he once wrote, "When I love, I love forever." And he described his dreams of their living together. When he returned to Italy to take part in the 1848 revolution, he stopped first at Florence, where Giuditta was living, and spent a fortnight with her.

The revolution failed and Mazzini had to flee again. Years later, when he was able to return once more, Giuditta had a salon in Turin. Perhaps ten times in twelve years the salon was closed when Mazzini came over the hill for dinner with his old love. His last expression of devotion came on her deathbed, in the form of a letter in which he told her once more of his concern and his unfailing admiration for her.

The other great mid-century leader was, of course, Giuseppe Garibaldi, who, because he was a battlefield hero, was able to involve women more directly in physical service. The first of these women was Anita, his wife, whom he had carried off from the arms of another man while in exile in South America. When 1848 brought his chance to return to Italy, Anita helped him round up a herd of cattle to pay for the chartered vessel he took home. She was a true heroine, feeding her brood of children on strict military rations, joining her husband at the siege of the Roman Republic in 1849 even though she was pregnant at the time, leading charges against the enemy as effectively as he did, so it was said. Shortly after the flight from Rome, however, she died of malaria.[14] This romantic story no doubt contributed to Garibaldi's charisma, and in subsequent campaigns great numbers of young women threw themselves at his feet, eager to kiss him, to fight under his eye, and perhaps to die while he was watching.

His own ideas about women were thoroughly republican but sentimentally old-fashioned. Nursing seemed to him the activity most suitable for women volunteers, and many of them were channeled into it. Several won distinction, of whom Maria Martini della Torre, was probably the most conspicuous. Early in her life her family had decided that she must be crazy and they would have locked her up except that she escaped to England. There, in 1854, she met the exiled Garibaldi, with the usual result that she found her cause in his. To prepare for service she went to the Crimea with Florence Nightingale, and afterward she joined Garibaldi in the Sicilian campaign of 1859, where she organized a hospital in spite of the hostility of Italian army doctors. Sometimes, indeed, in a hat with plumes, in trousers and boots, and the famous red shirt, she rode with the troops, smoking cigarettes, but at others she would be found comforting the soldiers undergoing amputation in the field hospital while the wounded sang the Garibaldi hymn.[15]

There seemed to be no limit to the kinds of women who would join up. Once some nuns discovered two of the red-shirted officers wandering around their convent garden and were persuaded to volunteer as nurses rather than remain with their order.[16] A prostitute received the medal of honor for grabbing a cannon and firing right into the enemy ranks.[17]

In a special category were the foreign women who were attracted by an opportunity for activity and self-sacrifice such as their own countries did not at the moment afford. Many of them, like Margaret Fuller and Jessie White,* married Italians. The former, a New Englander, married the Marchese Ossoli and became one of Cristina Belgiojoso's most efficient helpers in the siege of Rome in 1849. Jessie White, an Englishwoman, had been an early woman applicant to medical school in London, but she had been firmly refused,[18] so she assuaged her feelings by following Garibaldi. After marrying Alberto Mario in 1857, she joined the Sicilian expedition, where she too set up hospitals.

If foreign women were much attracted by Italian men, and the men in turn often pleased by the sort of intellectual companionship those women offered, many natives found in patriotism a therapeutic outlet for their unhappy private lives. Of course, countless Italian wives proved their utter devotion to their husbands under great pressure, but there were others who used the occasion to go off with men they thought could better serve their country. Such a one was the Countess Maria dal Varme, married at fifteen, straight out of the convent, who had accepted with her husband's consent a *cavaliere servente*.[19] Later on she fell in love with a more patriotic nobleman, Gaspare Rosales, and she lived with him, fighting at his side right through the campaign of 1859.

Because of the idealization of Italian mothers, many of the most

---

*"Miss Witt Jessy Mario," as Mozzoni referred to her (Mozzoni, *Passo*, 61).

honored heroines were those who had offered their sons to the conflict. Arrivabene tells of a mother who, having lost a son in the campaign of 1859, presented his brother to Garibaldi the next year, along with 30,000 francs.[20]

The most famous mother, a woman whose name became a household word, was Adelaide Cairoli, a "modern Niobe," as she was called.[21] After independence was won, her name was impressed on all schoolchildren. Of her five sons, four were killed in the wars. They all went off talking of *her* sacrifice, not their own; the survivor became one of Italy's prime ministers.*[22] None of them ever professed anything but total gratitude, and for the remainder of her life she clung to the sustaining force of their memory. Garibaldi was deeply touched and said that a country that could bring forth women like Adelaide Cairoli was sacred soil. No nation could fail while it produced such women. "Mother love can never be comprehended by a man. They do not reproach me with their loss but send more sons . . . ."[23]

Women who had less to offer gave what they could, encouraging volunteers by poetry, or by shame—a hesitant youth was presented with a doll in 1859[24]—by opening their homes to the refugees, the wounded, the patriots who needed a chance to talk.[25] It was believed that Victor Emmanuel himself, the Crown Prince of the Kingdom of Piedmont, had received his charge, his realization of a mission to become the first King of Italy, from a poem dedicated to him in 1842, at the time of his marriage, by a young poetess, Giulia Molino Colombini. Her works also developed faith in the new monarchy among his subjects.[26] Adelaide Ristori, the actress, used her talents to build patriotism among her audiences.[27]

Even women who stayed at home could serve the cause. The most famous salon in all Italy, held almost continuously from 1834 to 1886 by the Contessa Chiara Maffei, reached a height of political influence between 1849 and 1859.[28] Here patriotic intellectuals could meet and talk relatively free from police interference, and most of the great men of Italian life passed through it at one time or another.

Housewives also rendered hospitality to political exiles, especially the ones who had to flee from the Kingdom of Naples, the most reactionary of the Italian states. By opening their homes to these refugees, the women of Turin were able to communicate a sense of their common nationality to these citizens of different jurisdictions.

War service not only brought women together from different parts of Italy and from abroad, but it also offered the first opportunity to break down the barriers between classes.[29] When help from all parties was needed, committees of noblewomen began inviting members of the middle class to join in alleviating distress among the wounded or the stranded or those impoverished by economic upheaval. The upper-class women

---

*In a parliamentary election in 1877, Benedetto Cairoli came out strongly in favor of giving the local administrative franchise to women on the same basis as men, but without success.

who had been distinguished for centuries now found allies among those of inferior status.

შ Women who had been told by Mazzini that their services to their country had earned them a double crown, and by Garibaldi that their sacrifices had made Italian soil holy, might have expected an earthly reward when the battle was over and political questions came to the fore. But the age of Mazzini and Garibaldi was fading, and the world was turning from poetry to prose, explained Malvina Frank.[30] A new breed of men was called to write the legal documents on which the Kingdom of Italy would be based.

In the detailed record of conversations which were held over the years at Signora Maffei's political salon, conversations which rambled over economics, law, statistics, art and industry there is never a mention of women's rights. It was men who talked here, while the hostess listened and quietly directed the conversation to what seemed important. The ladies of her circle prided themselves on being patriotic, but not *political*, and her biographer called the transformation of one sentiment into another "degeneration," like wine turned to vinegar.[31]

But other Italian women were enraged at this neglect, and out of their disappointment with the Constitution and the Civil Code, they formed a women's movement to demand for themselves the rights politicians had kept from them.

The Civil Code for all Italy was drawn up at the time when final unification was within sight. In 1863 the government of Piedmont, under whose flag the rest of Italy was rallying, called together a group of the best jurisconsults they could find to unify the laws of the various states. Their work received the royal assent in 1865.

The code of the Papal states had been the worst of all for women, and that of the Austrian-ruled provinces the freest. The code of Piedmont, in-between as far as women's rights were concerned, basically copied the Napoleonic Code, or, as one wit remarked, what the Code had *meant* to say.[32] In any case, Grazia Mancini wrote in her diary, there was no hope in it for any real equality for her sex.[33]

Under its provisions the woman recognized the man as the head of the family, the man accepted her as his companion, and the community of conjugal affairs was managed in the French way. The age of marriage without parental consent was still set at twenty-five, as in France, even though Italians pointed out that in their country the age of puberty varied so much between the south and north that it was silly to impose one uniform marriage age. Hunting for the father of an illegitimate child was forbidden. Dowries were under the control of the husband. Among the few innovations:[34] widowed mothers obtained more rights than were granted under the French Code to be guardians of their children and to hold on to their earnings, although not at first to administer capital. Completely dashed were hopes that women would be allowed to vote in municipal elections (in spite of a forceful petition from Venetian women for the preservation of this ancient right), or that stiff penalties would be placed on seducers.[35]

The foremost champion of women's rights at the time was Salvatore Morelli.[36] Born in 1825, he had spent twelve years in a Neapolitan prison for political offenses arising from his newspaper career. While behind bars he wrote *Woman and Science* (*La Donna e la scienza*), published in 1859.[37] In correspondence with John Stuart Mill, he encouraged the latter to push ahead with his *Subjection of Women* and subsequently became its translator.*

In 1867 Morelli was elected to the Italian Parliament, where he immediately received a woman suffrage petition signed only by women. It was a hopeless cause, of course, even though Morelli was complimented by Garibaldi for his attack against the prejudice of centuries. The old soldier called the emancipation of women "the fulcrum of the social question."[38] Morelli pushed for a complete set of women's rights, but had very little success. His crusades in favor of divorce and against officially regulated prostitution were laughed out of court, and his single successful reform was a law allowing women to testify as witnesses to legal documents. This may seem a small step, but it gave great satisfaction to women like Emilia Mariani, a feminist leader, who was able to act as a witness in her small village in a matter concerning water rights; she was also pleased that to the peasants it seemed perfectly natural for her to act in this capacity.[39]

Three women writers offered strong criticism of the Code—Dora d'Istria, Malvina Frank, and Anna Maria Mozzoni. The first named was an adventurer who traveled into remote eastern civilizations to pry out the secrets of the harem, read obscure classical authors to learn about the status of women in the ancient Mediterranean world, and wrote a comparative study of the condition of women in all countries of Europe and the New World. Through all her works ran an implicit challenge to women everywhere to live up to their highest powers. To her Italian readers she offered a basis of comparison between their Code and others.

Malvina Frank went further: she challenged women to turn the whole country around. Marital power was an anomaly in a constitutional state, she told her readers, if women were subject to laws they had no part in making and were often unaware of and she urged that they study the actual law carefully in order to take advantage of any little loophole, while still seeking to change the whole system.†[40] Writing in 1869, in the

---

*Mill's work came out in two translations in Italy in the nineteenth century, one by Morelli and the other by Anna Maria Mozzoni. For comparison, there were two translations into French, four into Russian, and four into German.

†Malvina drew hope from the condition of blacks in America. It had been proved there, she wrote, that blacks were just as intelligent as whites, and to support her argument

last troublesome years before the final unification, she explained that the values by which Italians had lived for the previous fifty years, values appropriate to a period of conspiracy and universal distrust, would prove harmful in the coming time of peace and national development.[41] Men had been badly prepared for the new era, she exclaimed, and only women could educate a generation fit for the civilization of the future. While the male architects of the Italian Constitution had turned their backs on women, at least this one woman had a vision for her sex that outdistanced contemporary feminist opinion in other countries.*

The person who played in Italy the part that Luise Otto played in Germany—that is, the woman who was totally identified with feminism as a cause and who organized the movement—was Anna Maria Mozzoni. The difference between her and Otto was that while Otto began by cooperating with socialists and then shied away, Mozzoni became more and more radical as she grew older and at the end of her life believed that only through socialism could women gain their rights.

The movement in Italy never became as well organized as that in Germany. When Helene Lange thought about the reasons, she decided first that the long struggle for nationhood had made Italians put off the question of feminism longer than other countries had, and secondly that Italians were too individualistic.[42] The extraordinary effectiveness and discipline of the German women's movement enabled them to move forward on their own—or so they felt—while in Italy Mozzoni, in order to get any strong group backing, had to turn to the well-organized socialists.

Anna Mozzoni was born in Milan in 1837, the daughter of an architect. Such an occupational background placed her far more securely in the middle class than many of the women so far alluded to, but her family had been wealthy in the eighteenth century and were able to place her in a school set up to serve impoverished girls of noble birth.[43] She was there from the age of five until she was fourteen, and long before the end of her term she was made miserable by the bigoted Austrophilia in the classrooms. Her mother, interestingly enough, had always equated Austrian with male domination, so when she got home, the child was given a program of liberal studies to follow including the novels of George Sand, while her father read Fourier with her. Though she owed much to her mother, she felt that her father had trained her in the calming power of reason over passion, and she early learned to distrust all Mazzinian flights

---

she referred to the black Senator of those Reconstruction days. She said it was as if a London workman sat in the House of Lords (*Mogli*, 514). She also informed her readers that at St. Lawrence University in New York, where political economy and mathematics were taught, the chair of English language and literature was held by a black woman (*Fidenzate*, 42n).

*The third architect of Italian unity, Cavour, who died in 1861, would have liked to see complete equality for women, but not at the cost of endangering any of his other programs for a the new Italy. Somehow women always found themselves at the bottom of any list of reforms.

of fancy. (As for Mazzini's reciprocal views, he admitted that she was well-informed, but called her "rather dry," He preferred women with more sentiment.)[44]

In 1864 she published her first feminist tract, on the relation between women and the social problems of the day, including the issue of the reactionary Roman church. Sympathetically she understood that for individual women "bigotry" might represent a protest against husbandly authority even while she deplored the sinister effect of the Roman church on the development of a truly liberal state. The next year, when the new Code was under discussion, she analyzed in detail what it had to say about women. She soon joined a feminist committee presided over by the Caracciolo sisters,* translated Mill's *Subjection of Women*, and opened a correspondence with Josephine Butler on prostitution. The war of 1870 aroused her horror of militarism. Soldiers, she decided, were "the plague of society, its pariahs, parasites, slaves, tyrants, victims, and slaughterers all at once,"[45] besides being the economic ruin of every European state. As soon as the Agnesi High School for girls was founded, she accepted an appointment to teach moral philosophy there, and thence she branched out as a public lecturer on women's education, stressing particularly the need for a rational (that is, anti-Catholic) curriculum.

She bore an illegitimate daughter, whom she brought up proudly under her own name and who subsequently became a suffragist lawyer. In 1886 she herself married, very late in life, like so many other feminists.

Anna Mozzoni's attack on the projected Civil Code began while it was still being debated in the Italian Senate. She realized that she would have to speak out after studying successive provisions that would worsen the position of women. Women, she decided, must examine every man-made law, especially in view of the fact that their laws and "systems" left even the masculine sex unhappy.[46] She attributed the restrictive provisions about women to pressure from the Papacy, but while it was logical for an authoritarian church to speak authoritaritively, she said, it was completely out of consonance with modern life and with a constitutional monarchy.

There was, to be sure, an empty statement in the Code that women were "equal," but a minister of the crown explained that equality did not include admission to public office, and even such an intimate matter as guardianship of children was deemed a "public office." Women were treated as sufficiently strong to support a mountain of burdens, such as the obligations to support the family and pay taxes, and yet too weak to govern themselves. Among the rights Mozzoni argued for, fruitlessly, were guardianship, inquiry into paternity, public money for girls' educa-

---

*I have failed to confirm my hopeful suspicion that one of the Caracciolo sisters may have been Enrichetta, the escaped nun. The introduction to the 1964 edition of *Le memorie di una monaca napoletana* (*The Memoirs of a Neapolitan Nun*), as her story has been retitled, states that in her long life after her marriage she devoted herself to feminist causes, and we know that she had several sisters. Then again, the name is very common in Naples.

tion, and civil rights for single women, which she advocated as the first step toward universal suffrage.[47] She conceived the idea that if women could vote they could do something to abolish war.

Elections in the mid-seventies returned a liberal majority to the Italian Parliament, including a number of deputies outspokenly in favor of at least the municipal suffrage for women. Such a measure seemed likely to pass, and Anna Mozzoni worked tirelessly to get petitions signed by women in its favor. It failed, however, because of fear that through clerical influence the liberal majority would be lost if women had votes.

Unfortunately, in Italy even more than in France, the special "nemesis" (as Frances Power Cobbe called it) of women's progress was the Church.[48] Even anti-clerical men sometimes felt safer if their women had faith. And for certain women, religious zeal offered an unconscious escape from the patriarchal family and from masculine prejudice.[49] Under the guidance of a confessor, a woman had a respectable way to differ from her husband, even in sexual matters, besides having the undoubted consolation that religion can offer those who have lost their independence of action. There are often advantages in serving two masters, with the possibility of playing one off against the other.

This psychological fact was a source of despair to devoted feminists, who soon realized that their cause would be hopeless if women could not learn to abandon superstition and become independent of the convent education that most of them had received. Liberal men, likewise, lost confidence in women's judgment as they found out that the Church, by withholding absolution from the *wife*, was using women to get their husbands to vote against their consciences. The Church was also able to break up women's liberal organizations; so, for example, Caterina Ferrucci was stopped from directing a women's institute by *Civiltà Cattolica*,[50] and later the federation of women's associations (comparable to the BDF in Germany) was dissolved in the 1890s under direct pressure from the Vatican.[51]

∽ The government did present an unusual honor to Signorina Mozzoni: she was appointed the official representative of the Kingdom of Italy to the convention for the Rights of Women at Paris in 1878. As the only officially appointed delegate from any country, she was allowed to open the Congress. She continued to press for suffrage, and in 1881, at Rome, convinced a session of the Universal Suffrage Convention, a group working for universal male suffrage, that voting was a *human* right, needed by every segment of society for self-protection.[52]

Disillusionment, the slowness of progress, and the unlikelihood of success turned her inexorably toward socialism. She had long been concerned with the lives of poor working women, and as early as 1867 she had disappointed Mazzini, who liked to play down the class struggle, by aligning her personal adherents beside a group of workers.[53] She wrote to

Josephine Butler that it was important to get women out of the home and into jobs where they could be producers instead of just consumers, and to fight for equal pay for equal work. This concern deepened during the 1880s, although she never became a dogmatic Marxist and always insisted that some of women's problems were caused by something other than the economic system. She became impatient with men who called themselves socialists and yet liked subordination in their own families, and doubted that they would do much better than the bourgeoisie of 1790, the men of the German Enlightenment, the *Carbonari*, the French Left of 1848, or the Italian fighters of 1859, each group in turn having requisitioned patriotic services from women and later denied them the right to vote.[54]

It is a pleasure to think that Mozzoni lived long enough to attend in 1919 the session of the Chamber at which women's suffrage was debated. It was not granted, however, until 1945.

A feminist press warmly supported Mozzoni and followed her party line. There had been a short-lived women's newspaper in Mazzini's Roman Republic in 1848–1849, with a board of women editors assisted by a group of male collaborators, including a doctor and two professors. Its main concern was driving the Austrians clear out of the country—the grand idea that preoccupied every Italian patriot,* male or female—but there were also articles about outstanding Italian women, a good deal about their need for better education (though with an emphasis on motherhood rather than individuality), pleas for sensible clothing (of a kind not to interfere with military action), and an article or two about the nature of family life.

Only after the Kingdom of Italy had been formed did women's journalism have a chance of permanence. The most famous paper was *La Donna*, edited from 1868 until 1888 by Gualberta Beccari.[55] "Good, brave, and unfortunate,"[56] Malvina Frank termed her, for she was confined to her bed from an early age and did her editorial work from there. It was the only paper that consistently demanded full rights for women and steadfastly backed Anna Maria Mozzoni's campaigns.[57] It also kept in touch with the movement in other countries, especially America, where the newly enfranchised women of Wyoming quickly became à legend.[58]

When Signora Beccari had to give up the journal, it was taken over by Emilia Mariani.[59] Disillusioned, like Mozzoni, by the lack of parliamentary interest in women's problems, she turned its editorial policy in a distinctly socialist direction.[60] The result was to be expected: when desperate women turn to socialist parties as the only ones with sympathy for the cause of feminism, they lose influence with their conservative sisters.[61] For instance, Matilde Serao, the most influential woman jour-

---

*Verdi's operas *Hernani* and *I Lombardi* were so anti-Austrian in sentiment that they brought the composer into conflict with the authorities. They were, however, unable to suppress the tunes, which were sung and whistled all over Italy, and which were felt to be rallying cries for patriots.

nalist in Italy at the time, excoriated *La Donna* for its lack of support for the popular war in Ethiopia (1887–1889).[62]

Even the long-planned exposition of women's work organized at Florence by Conte Angelo de Gubernatis in 1889 attracted little popular attention, though it presented an inspiring and impressive display of feminine activities and a distinguished series of lectures covering every aspect of women's lives and assessing both their condition at the moment and their hopes for the future.[63]

ᴄᴏ28.

The New Women of Italy

The new woman, like the butterfly come forth from the chrysalis, shall be liberated from all those attributes which once made her desirable to man only as the source of the material blessings of existence. She shall be, like man, an individual, a free human being, a social being, a social worker; and, like man, she shall seek blessing and repose within the [home], the [home] which has been reformed and communized.

Maria Montessori

Women were teaching in Italian universities from the Renaissance until well into the nineteenth century. Dora d'Istria traced this unusual possibility to the influence of Platonism, a philosophy that encouraged Italians to regard women as worthy of participation in the highest callings.[1] During the Renaissance, women were listed as professors of philosophy, theology, mathematics, languages, and music—and one Italian woman was said to have lectured at a German university.*[2]

The tradition remained strong in the eighteenth century, when women taught physics, anatomy, Greek, medicine, and mathematics.[3] The most famous was Gaetana Agnesi, who lectured on mathematics at Bologna.[4] When Maria Theresa sent her a present of jewels, Gaetana sold them for the poor; she died in 1799, having taken religious vows. Laura Bassi, on the other hand, was the affectionate wife of Dr. Giuseppe Varati and a mother of twelve, but this did not prevent her from conducting courses in physics that she made notable by performing experiments in front of the class instead of merely lecturing.[5] Maria Dalle Donne earned her medical degree in 1799 and thereafter practiced both medicine and surgery until her death in 1842. She also headed a school for midwives. This work and her regular teaching made her one of the scientific glories of her university.[6]

Eloquent testimony to the impact of these women was offered by Pellegrino Rossi, exiled from Italy and lecturing in political science at the University of Paris in the 1830s. During a discussion of the political duties of women, he recalled his student days and said:

> Heaven preserve me from wishing here to call into question the intellectual powers of woman. . . . I have had the pleasure to know and admire women

*One of these women was so beautiful, according to tradition, that she lectured from behind a screen so as not to distract her students.

440

endowed with the finest talent and even the most brilliant genius. Furthermore I have sat as a student on university benches with women who were studying law and medicine; and I was awarded the degree of Doctor of Law in the same year as a very beautiful lady, whose teaching was not only very good, but ornamented with plenty of wit and grace; I believe she was still alive when I was appointed professor at the same university and that I thus had the honor to be her colleague.[7]

The tradition lasted longer at Bologna, Rossi's university, than anywhere else, and Lady Morgan was able to comment in 1820 on the recent death of Clotilda Ramborini, who had taught Greek until she lost her chair, in 1795, because she was unwilling to falsify her political opinions. Lady Morgan added that certain chairs were still filled by women at the time of her visit, and she admitted, in an unusual access of modesty, that these truly learned ladies made her feel ignorant by comparison.[8]

Women also entered into the Italian academies. Hortense Allart was elected to one while she was living in Italy, and when Charles Eliot Norton visited another, he noted that the only interesting paper was by a woman, Teresa Gnoli, who wrote on "Beatrice and Laura."[9] Even groups like the Philological Society of Milan, which would not have women as members, still invited exceptional ones to lecture—women like Anna Maria Mozzoni, Malvina Frank, Clémence Royer.

This background explains why Mme de Staël had used Italy as the locale for her novel about a woman of genius, *Corinne*. She had been impressed by the intellectual women she met on her famous trip to Italy in 1804–1805, particularly Diodata Saluzzo, who was both a poet and a member of the Turin Academy of Science,[10] and she made Corinne similarly versatile:we observe this heroine writing poetry, singing, painting, dancing, and lecturing. Even though feminine academic activity fell by mid-century to the level common in other countries, nevertheless the image of Corinne kept the heritage alive in the minds of such women as George Eliot, George Sand, Margaret Fuller Ossoli, Elizabeth Barrett Browning, and Harriet Beecher Stowe, all of whom expressed their fascination with this quality in Italian life.[11]

In 1875 Oscar Greco published a biographical dictionary of 427 Italian women who had distinguished themselves by creative work during the nineteenth century.* Most of them were writers of one sort or another, poets, fiction writers, or philosophers, but there was a scattering of artists and at least one composer, Carlotta Ferrari. A rough assessment of their relative importance, at least in the editor's eyes, may be gleaned

*Fifty years before Greco, Ginevra Canonici had prepared a dictionary of Italian women in history. They were arranged according to the century in which they flourished, ending with sections on those who had died during the 1800s and those who were still alive when she wrote in 1825. Her work is too careless to be of much use as a source. According to her, one of her characters would have received a full medical degree from the University of Bologna at the age of 15, while another would have lived to be 138 years old, having published a volume of poems at the age of 126.

from the amount of space he allotted to each. Most of the women were listed only by name and the titles of their works, but a few were given a paragraph or two of biographical data, and certain ones whom he regarded as outstanding had several pages apiece. Not counting Dora d'Istria, who as a foreigner had a special section of the preface devoted to her work,* Greco's favorite was Giannina Milli (thirty-two pages). Next came Malvina Frank (twenty-four pages), and Erminia Fusinato-Fuà (nineteen pages).

Milli, the popular idol of her day, was described as "a miracle of a woman" ("*questo miracolo di donna*").[12] She was a practitioner of a peculiarly Italian art form (the one practiced by Corinne)—the improvisation of poetry.† After her audience suggested a subject, she would retreat into a "religious silence" for a few moments, then declaim neatly formed rhymes on whatever was proposed.

This talented child was born in 1825, the daughter of a Neapolitan bookseller and an ambitious mother who very early taught her to read (using the "look-see" method, not phonetics); at five Giannina composed her first little poem and cried out, "Oh, mother, I have become a poet." A few years later the family found that they could always collect a crowd by letting their daughter recite Dante, so they began to schedule public appearances for her—against her wishes, for they had to trick or cajole her into performing. At this time her mother would even lend her out to groups of strolling beggars, for a price.

At school she won a prize and was taken to meet the King. When he asked her what she wanted most in the world, she replied, "a chance to

---

*Dora d'Istria, a Wallachian whose proper name was Elena Ghika, married to a Russian prince in 1849, was considered by Greco and others as the prototype of the new woman. Educated at home, she later traveled on long voyages to the East, especially hoping to find out how women lived in other cultures and how to speed enlightenment their way. The list of her books covers twenty pages of Greco's text, and includes treatises on Rumanian popular songs, studies in the Indian epic, the *Mahabharata*, a discussion of monastic life in the Eastern church, one on zoological mythology, studies in political economy especially dealing with agriculture, a discussion of Austrian propaganda in the Danubian countries, a description of women in the Orient, historical studies on the Albigenses and on church-state relations in the fourth century—all this among essays on all phases of the woman question, polemics against war, and a few souvenirs and fiction pieces thrown in for good measure.

An interesting study could be made of the European women of great wealth who could only find the freedom to do what they wanted in the East: such women as Jane Digby, Dora d'Istria, and Cristina Belgiojoso, and doubtless others. In the East the restricting conventions of western Europe on life did not obtain, and the eastern rules did not apply to such eccentric foreigners. Though these women had unusual opportunities, they may have expressed very widespread wishes. Lesley Blanch has almost written the book I have in mind in *The Wilder Shores of Life*, but she does not mention Dora d'Istria, who may be the most interesting character of all.

†The extemporizer-declaimer had a long vogue in Italy, undoubtedly related to the national love of extempore theatre in the Commedia Arte. Mme de Staël had met such a woman on her trip to Italy, observed her sibylline trances, and explained that she valued the art form because it gave an opportunity to see into the imagination of "the people."

study," so he arranged a scholarship at what was reputed to be an excellent convent school. Alas, it proved disastrous. The child could not adapt to the rigid routines, while her gift of composition languished: "The caged bird is mute."[13] The teachers could hardly wait to get rid of her, and used a cholera epidemic as an excuse to send her home. Here she began to write again, but was cautious enough to try to keep her mother from finding out by hiding the manuscript under her mattress. Giannina was betrayed by a sister, and the poems were taken by her mother to a professor who left comments in the margin. Subsequently she was tutored by this man and others in the rules of grammar and composition, with other sessions to provide her with general culture. In order to pay for these lessons Giannina's mother used to exhaust herself going from house to house giving lessons to less brilliant students. Not atypically, the family, composed of twelve brothers and sisters, hoped to develop her talents and live on her income. Building her reputation was slow; there was one dreadful day when they hired a hall and absolutely nobody came, so they went out into the streets and pulled in an audience for a free performance. Eventually, however, she became the most widely known and popular feminine personality in all Italy.

It seems that she never did learn to enjoy giving recitals, though she was very clever at it. Once, when the audience proposed something indecent as the subject for her to improvise on, she turned the occasion into a triumph by shaming them, to the point that the repentant listeners took up a collection. But under the regime of close supervision and intense exploitation, it was difficult for the girl to grow up. At a New Year's Eve reception at the Maffei salon in 1859, she improvised stirringly about the Italian struggle for nationhood, and right afterward climbed into her mother's lap and broke into tears.[14] Emilia Peruzzi once called this mother a disaster—"*una vera calamità*"—and suggested to Giannina that it would be well for her to marry far away from home.[15] Grazia Mancini felt that though she showed "genius" and facility, she was timid and reserved and obviously under the thumb of her family. When the elder Millis died, Giannina gave up performing and turned to her own interests, teaching history and morals at a girls' boarding school in Rome, where, after she was fifty, she married one of the professors.

Meanwhile, the question of opening, or reopening, the universities to women became acute. In July of 1870 Salvatore Morelli, who had sought election to the Italian Parliament solely to advance women's causes, made a motion that women should be freely admitted to both *lycées* and universities. He was voted down, with the lame excuse that no law excluded them if properly prepared, but that few girls had this preparation and that there was scattered opposition among the faculty.[16] A couple of years later, a trickle of girls started to attend the University of Turin, and by the 1880s they were admitted more freely. In fact, Lily Braun thought she noticed at this time that it was far easier for them to be accepted as equals, both as students and as teaching assistants, than in France or Germany.[17] If this was so, it was probably because of the ancient tradition of women in university life.

The first woman to get an Italian medical degree was a Russian named Anna Kuliscioff,* who completed her studies in 1887 but was not allowed to practice; the first Italian was Velleda Farné. The first diploma in law was awarded to Lydia Poët in 1897.[18]

But surely the most distinguished woman graduate of the nineteenth century was Maria Montessori. This enterprising young woman, born in 1870, was determined to go to medical school in Rome, a faculty that had not yet been breached. Having graduated from one of the new technical high schools established during the 1880s, she found no difficulty in getting admitted to the fields of mathematics and science, but after she got her diploma in 1892, and was theoretically eligible for medical studies, she met obstacles: as in other countries, the sexual norms of the period made admission into medical programs especially difficult. Montessori had already announced her intention to the professor of clinical medicine, Guido Bacelli, a man who had used his membership in the Chamber of Deputies to institute widespread educational reforms, but for whom getting a woman into anatomical dissection rooms was too much of a reform. He flatly refused her. No one knows exactly how she got in but years later she ascribed her eventual acceptance to the personal intervention of Pope Leo XIII.†[19]

During her studies, Montessori was warmly supported by her liberal mother, though her stricter father strongly disapproved; even he was softened, however, when she won a prize with a handsome stipend. From the viewpoint of the university, the proprieties were observed by having her go alone into the dark dissecting rooms after hours, when the male students had left. She was also escorted through the streets of Rome each day on her way to lectures, often by her father, so that her reputation would be unimpeached.

In 1896 she won her degree, having given the lecture that each senior student was required to make to the class, and having defended orally before the professors her research on delusions of persecution. By this time she was a public figure and was almost immediately chosen as a delegate from Italy to the international women's congress being held in Berlin that year.

As is well known, her medical work in the slums brought her into contact with a number of retarded and emotionally disturbed children,

---

*Anna Kuliscioff became the leading socialist woman in Italy. She never got on with Anna Mozzoni, who even in her slide to the left put feminism first. Kuliscioff favored protective legislation for women and children, for example, whereas Mozzoni considered this paternalistic. Yet Kuliscioff could not stand the sort of sentimental maternalism expressed in Ada Negri's popular poem *Maternitá*.

†Her biographer, Rita Kramer, questions the accuracy of this memory and thinks that the Pope may merely have approved the decision after the fact, along with a general endorsement of the profession of medicine for women (Kramer, 38).

and eventually led her away from the field of medicine into pedagogy; here she effected a complete and permanent revolution in theory and practice. Her vision for her sex was that women would be freed by technology from slavish domestic work and would then be able to devote themselves to the scientific study of the needs of children, thus fulfilling their maternal tasks on a higher plane. (It is interesting that she wanted to be called a "*medico*," like a male doctor, and rejected early the feminine form, "*medichessa*.") She shared the hope (also uttered at the exposition of women's work at Florence in 1889) that machines would soon take over most routine household work, and day-care centers would free both working-class and middle-class women to work outside the home. She felt that while previous centuries had boasted a few learned, and many ignorant, women, now culture could be widely diffused among the whole sex.

Like Anna Maria Mozzoni, Maria Montessori had a child out of wedlock, and though at first she sent him away in secrecy, she later brought him home, gave him her name and made him into a leading propagandist for her educational theories around the world. She and the child's father, Dr. Montesano, seem to have agreed that while they did not wish to marry each other, neither of them would marry anyone else; but Montesano broke this promise, causing much pain to his former partner.[20] Neither she nor Mozzoni seems to have lost public respect for their unmarried parenthood, though it is hard to imagine a leading public figure of the northern countries, such as Helene Lange or Dr. Garrett Anderson, getting away with an illegitimate baby. Italy, with its long tradition of sexual freedom, was more hospitable. Montessori went on to enjoy a professorial chair at Rome and worldwide acclaim as her methods became famous.

∽ In a way it was harder to set up girls' preparatory schools than to open the universities: the few universities enjoyed prestige in the cities where they were situated and had liberal traditions, while the first small secular schools quickly became subject to local attack. Caterina Ferrucci, a classicist by profession and a member of an academy, started a girls' school in Genoa, but the Church hierarchy spread word that she gave too little time to religion and indeed gave her students a rationalistic outlook, and the school soon sank under this pressure.[21] Hers was one case out of many. Such church influence on schools led many wealthy girls to prefer working under a private tutor.[22]

But if clerical opposition delayed secondary education for middle-class girls, the new government gave a great push to primary instruction, now seen as an essential means of forging a modern united state. Women of the previous generation had been the mothers of heroes, it was said, and the next ones would become workers and teachers with no loss of heroism.[23] Even though the constitution-makers of the Kingdom of Italy were not favorable to women's rights, a sharp turn to the left in the mid-seventies produced an impulse for educational reform as the nation confronted its 75 percent illiteracy rate. Before unification, compulsory schooling had been spotty and laxly enforced, but in 1877 a new law set up free non-denominational schools for both sexes in every commune. These were to provide four years of coeducational elementary work and, in separate classrooms, seven or eight years of secondary work leading to university admission. In general the administration aimed to copy France, though the laws were not so well enforced at first, and the Minister of Public Instruction, Cesare Correnti, explained that the new high schools for girls were not to be truly "high," but more suited to the temperament of women, tailored to teach them how to carry out the elementary education of their own young children.[24] This statement probably placated some alarmed fathers, but it infuriated ambitious girls.

As in France and Germany, normal schools became a second path to higher education for girls to whom the universities were unattainable. The need for their graduates was insatiable for a while, and young women flocked to them. As early as 1866 Anna Maria Mozzoni commented that the girls' normal schools were overflowing because they provided the only way for most young women to continue their education beyond the elementary level, while teachers' academies for boys lacked students.[25] After 1870 even greater numbers of girls found the courage to attend these schools and then to spread out into every corner of the country, where the progressive lay government hoped they would compete for the influence hitherto wielded by the parish priest.[26] By 1894 there were thirty-seven thousand women in elementary teaching, and six thousand more in infant schools.[27]

These women were a new social breed. In one way they were heroines; in another, social climbers, for teaching was a good way for lower-middle-class girls to gain entrance into a profession; in still a third way, they were seekers for security in a world where husbands and dowries were less forthcoming than earlier.

Certainly the ideals of the organizers of schools were high, and to implement the system of normal schools, the government enlisted the aid of Italy's most distinguished literary women. Thus it assigned Giulia Molino Colombini, the poet whose work had inspired Victor Emmanuel, to plan a curriculum that would make the new teachers loved as well as respected.[28]

They put the direction of a *lycée* in Rome in the charge of Erminia Fusinato-Fuà, another long-time patriot and poet, and, on Oscar Greco's scale, Italy's third most distinguished woman. Born into a doctor's family, she became a housekeeper for her sisters when her mother died, and at ten she used to compose a daily set of verses to carry to her father along with his coffee.[29] Later on she became a conspirator and married Arnaldo Fusinato for love. When in 1874 the idea of a Society of Science, Letters, and Ethics for women was broached, she became the first president, acting under the Princess (and future Queen) Margherita, who held the honorary title.[30] This organization set up lectures by first-rate professors to eager throngs of listeners, functioning something like the *Viktorialyceum* in Berlin. To her students-in-training Erminia outlined her theory of the feminine role—that of a mother in school, a teacher at home; she hoped that teachers would so be so much admired that pupils from underprivileged homes would acquire good manners unconsciously. Her last appointment was as Inspector-General of girls' schools for the state; she and Giannina Milli both received this assignment from Cesare Correnti.

Another poet-schoolteacher, Ada Negri, represented the new generation for whom teaching was not so much a means of social service or self-expression as a career to which a poor girl could aspire. Her beguiling autobiography about her working-class childhood ends with her appointment as the mistress of a primary school in a tiny north Italian mountain hamlet. Two years later her first book of poems, mostly about the hardships of factory workers and peasants, astonished the world with its sincerity and pathos.[31] The publicity led to her transfer to a bigger city school, and then to a normal school in Milan, and eventually she married a rich factory owner with whose help she is said to have put many benevolent ideas into practice. Her later poems glorified motherhood.

To the normal school students it was preached that their office was to advance civilization, that their work was a true vocation. They ought not to expect to marry. (A person whose childhood wish had been to be a mother might be fit to become a decorator, machinist, or telegraphist, but a *true teacher* was dedicated to celibacy from birth.)[32] Turning away from personal concerns, they should be trained to spread rationality and secular "progress." This was the nation's answer to the Church. A hint as to how well the teachers performed may be caught in the remarks of an outraged Frenchman in 1896: "The real and most dangerous agents of rural socialism are the primary teachers."[33]

On the other hand, the ideas of the leaders could not always meet the needs of the masses of poor girls who wanted to move into the profession. One of Matilde Serao's most moving tales ("*Scuola normale femminile*") described the normal school in Naples where she was a student on her own way up the ladder, during the 1870s. A hundred and sixty girls were crowded into an ancient Jesuit convent, leaky and inconvenient, with a faculty still largely recruited from clerics left over from the previous regime. Their methods of teaching stressed memory rather than comprehension, while spontaneity either by a teacher or by a girl was felt to be threatening. The girls were poor, mostly decent, struggling against poverty, illness, loneliness, worries at home, bad food, insufficient sleep, overwork, bad eyesight, and constant worry about the examination that would confront them at the end of their course. Serao presents the mass of girls as a sea of emotionality, jealousy, licit and illicit crushes, exhaustion, and boredom. In a final chapter she described her senior classmates three years after graduation. Only one, the ugliest and brightest girl, had been able to get a good teaching position where she was able to introduce somewhat better methods of instruction.

Matilde Serao did not continue in teaching but became the outstanding woman novelist of the next quarter-century.[34] She was also the first professional woman journalist and director of a daily paper. Born in Greece in 1856, she moved to Naples as a child and there attended the ordinary schools and the girls' normal school. After this, because she needed to earn money more quickly than a schoolteacher's pay would allow, she took the three-month course of a telegraphist. In her spare time she began writing her first sketches, which were published anonymously in a Neapolitan paper.[35] She said of herself that she pushed ahead in life as if she were a man, paying no attention to the weakness of her sex, cutting short her curly hair, and occasionally dressing as a boy. As her interest in literature grew, she found Naples too provincial and moved to Rome, where she became part of a famous group of young writers, among them D'Annunzio. She married one of his friends, Eduardo Scarfoglio, with whom she founded a paper. Though it was not immediately successful in Rome after they moved to Naples it became the best and most famous daily in southern Italy, and it was still under their direction at the time of the First World War.

Conditions like those Serao had described in the normal schools of the seventies account for the disapproval expressed by Maria Montessori when she began to look at ordinary elementary classrooms. It was this that led to her radical system of studying children individually and letting them move ahead actively, at their own pace, using special materials that she designed herself.

∽ The question of work other than teaching was not totally neglected in Italy. Although paid jobs were not common by modern standards among middle-class Italian wives, there were few signs of the sort of horror of professionalism that one runs into in England and Germany. Theodore Stanton noticed that the language had feminine forms for various professions—*autrice, dottoressa, pittrice*—which were lacking in other tongues. By 1897, according to Emilia Mariani, the proportion of working wives was higher in Italy than in any other country. (Forty-one percent, she declared, though the statistic is not clearly defined and surely includes the working-class contingent.)[36]

The many advantages that would accrue if wives worked outside the home were laid out in one of the lectures given at the Women's Exposition held at Florence in 1889. It was explained that husbands would be happier with wives who were kept busy and were therefore less seducible; that children cared for in schools and nurseries would get better attention, while at the same time they would feel pride in their mother's accomplishments; that parents who prepared their daughters for a profession could take satisfaction that it was as good as a dowry if they married and a way of making life content if they did not; that the girls themselves, thus prepared, would be free to marry for love because the dreadful need to have a man would be eliminated, that widows would be prepared to support their children.[37] What is remarkable about this enthusiastic presentation is that nowhere does it mention a sense of self-fulfillment as one of the advantages of employment. Rare indeed, apparently, was the parent like the sculptor Giovanni Dupré, who took his young daughter Amalia into his studio simply because he noted the great personal satisfaction she received.[38] (Her works became well known and were cited by those who wanted to prove that women could succeed in the arts.)

ᜂ Side by side with the increasing number of "new nineteenth-century women" was the mass of "asiatic or medieval women" turned out by old-fashioned convent schools. Lady Morgan, who in 1821 had admired the learned ladies she met so very much, found the average Italian woman exceptionally badly educated. Although Ginevra Cano-nici furiously retorted that the reason Italian ladies failed to shine before this foreign visitor was that they were naturally modest, and that English-speaking persons rarely understood Italian very well, she could offer only sixteenth- and seventeenth-century examples to refute Lady Morgan's criticism of nineteenth-century education.[39]

There are several reasons for the low educational standard, not least of which was the deliberate policy of the occupying powers to discourage liberal studies. For this purpose the Roman church could almost be classed as an occupying power; certainly before 1870 nearly all girls' education was carried on within convents—the Sacred Heart or Carmelites for the rich, the Sisters of Charity for the poor, both groups imbued with a spirit of reaction that caused feminists to despair.[40] Malvina Frank (number two in Greco's reckoning), who was born in Venice and educated until the age of fourteen at the "Imperial College," an institution run by the Austrian government, criticized her education bitterly.* As she put it, "I always took all the prizes, and I did not know anything fundamental, nothing well, I was not satisfied at anything, and was not even deceived by the prizes."[41] After leaving school, according to both Italian and foreign observers, Italian ladies were not so fond of reading as their northern sisters. Anna Maria Mozzoni believed that for

*Malvina was much interested in a college for women recently incorporated by governmental decree in Nova-Yorck at Pough-Keepsic on the Hudson by one Matteo Vassar, a small self-made merchant. The institution, she believed, was united with the state University (Frank, *Fidenzate*, 41 and *Mogle*, 487). She also mentioned Oberlin, which had been graduating women for thirty years when she wrote. Oscar Greco mentioned the additional fact, which pleased him very much, that the best Greek scholar at the University of Michigan was a woman (Greco, 10).

German and English women a place to read in the home was a necessity, but for Italians, at best a luxury[42]—and even when they did read, as Stendhal sardonically noted, they missed the point.[43] They might smuggle in Voltaire to read, yet the next day shed tears while kissing a reliquary.

Another factor was the early age at which Italian girls married. Princess Belgiojoso vehemently urged a more stringent education for women; yet she felt that once married, very few wives would be permitted by their husbands to continue with a program of study. Then she traced the sad results of this attitude: women who turned their children off by their ignorance and lost their husbands' love when beauty and health were gone.[44] At this point there was nothing left for them to do, she said, but return to the Church and find a new mission in converting their husbands and sons. Even if they failed in this, they could still feel heroic in their resignation.

It was also a common apprehension, in Italy as elsewhere, that genius of any sort, but particularly in scientific fields, would repel husbands. It was remembered that Corinne, the great model of feminine talent, had had difficulty holding on to a lover, while as late as 1889 a lecturer at the Florence Exposition felt that women scientists would have to be vestals (you wouldn't want one around the house, but then she wouldn't want a man, either). The speaker hesitantly guessed that never would many women become scientists. (Princess Belgiojoso, on the other hand, believed that men secretly admired intellectual talent in a woman.)

Although in many countries women's passage from home to public life was through involvement as volunteers in personal charity, in Italy this path opened up later than elsewhere. "They have no habits of country life," complained Frances Power Cobbe, nor of the duties that arise "so naturally" in taking care of their dependents, nor, in cities, did they have the custom of visiting hospitals or orphanages.[45] The nobility might pay for peasants' daughters' dowries,[46] or even "paddle around among the poor with baskets of cakes," as Lady Morgan described it,[47] and religious sisterhoods might welcome processions of poor pilgrims at Rome: but the English women, at least, had the feeling that their motivation was basically egoistic, and that Italian women did not really involve themselves generously. Miss Cobbe, who even in Italy kept up her good custom of visiting hospitals carrying supplies of food and coffee, once asked a nursing sister if the patients had no Italian visitors. Oh, yes, was the response, Princess So-and-so will come, Countess So-and-so; they may visit once a week, or once a month, and may even comb the hair of the sick in order to get credit for themselves in heaven, but they do not bring supplies, no.*[48]

*The contribution of the various religious orders, male and female, should not be ignored. During the cholera epidemics, the only service to carry the sick to the hospitals, as well as carry the dead away, was provided by the Misericordia, a penitential society of men of all classes from artisans to noblemen, who hid their identities behind friars' habits and

Yet there was always a group of enlightened women among the class that has been described as living more like the English than most other continentals. Massimo d'Azeglio told how much he admired his brother, Roberto, and sister-in-law, Costanza, for their devotion to the poor and the hours they spent in teaching, often going back to the schoolroom after dinner.[49] Costanza described her daily schedule in 1843. Every morning at nine she went to teach in her school. At ten she returned home for tea, then she went back to the school until a quarter past eleven, at which time she heard mass. After that she went to read to her old father. By 1850 she was on the board of the newly formed public school for poor girls, though she commented that it was two generations late in starting.[50]

Anyone with open eyes could see much that needed to be done, as did Grazia Mancini, whose diary as a young girl is full of insight. In 1861 she left her home in progressive Turin to visit her grandmother in Naples, and was disgusted at the dirty dishes, the corners never swept, the disease, the sad love songs of the poorer areas; and she cried out to the women of Italy to change all this.[51] Little had been accomplished by 1889, when discussions of women's work were held in connection with the Exposition at Florence.[52] One of the recommendations there was for Italian women to imitate the English and grapple with poverty. Indeed, it was often foreign women who pointed the way. Englishwomen, Russians, Poles, and Americans who happened to marry Italians brought in fresh ideas. Grazia Mancini met a Swiss woman in Turin in 1857 whose accomplishments were so great that Grazia felt that a mere thousand Italian women doing as much could eradicate poverty, or at least the worst misery, from the peninsula.[53]

Great disasters, such as wars or epidemics, would, of course, force a certain amount of involvement by all classes. The admirable amateur devotion shown by women on the battlefield has been described, but even behind the front, women of all classes—countesses, merchants' wives, and working-class women as well—gathered together to meet the emergency.[54] Grazia Mancini worked with such a committee in 1859, making bandages all day.[55] After the battle for Palermo was over, Garibaldi suggested to his lady helpers that they turn their attention to relieving the hunger of orphans, for he told them that four-fifths of the children in a local asylum were dying for lack of nourishment.[56] He left it up to their generous hearts to figure out what to do about it, and it took a while for his advice to be adopted on any large scale.

---

masks (Somerville, 309). Ordinarily hospital nursing was carried out by nuns. There was a running battle between the religious sisters and the medical students of Siena, caused partly by the laxity of student morals. In the springtime of 1848, it was easy for the students to define their hostility as a defense of liberalism, and they actually got the sisters expelled, but the hospital deteriorated so badly in the course of a few months that it had to recall them (Jameson, *Sisters*, 88).

This sort of work, though often useful in getting ladies off their balconies, was insufficient to meet the growing need. Private charity simply could never solve the problems of Italy, as even the young Grazia Mancini concluded, and the slow changeover from private charity to public welfare had developed quite strong roots by 1900. Instead of carrying cakes to the poor, the idea arose of setting up public kitchens; combing the hair of a patient was replaced by enforcing public health measures. If charity were only well organized, women, and especially ladies, who had so much time on their hands, could help much more usefully. It would take a great number of them to teach the poor cleanliness and efficiency and to demonstrate to them the principles of family love.

So hospitals and blind schools and old folks' homes and outdoor hostels for rickety or tubercular children proliferated, though it was noted that some of the old folks preferred a precarious liberty to being shut up where they had no liquor.[57]

The most renowned practitioner of the new charity was undoubtedly Laura Solera Mantegazza, mother of the well-known anthropologist Paolo Mantegazza. Her adoring son wrote in his memoir of her love of friends and children, of study, of Italy; though typically, he made almost no mention of his father, her husband. Her idealism was kindled when she turned her home into a hospital for Garibaldi's wounded, while her own family slept on straw for two months. One time she went personally to the battlefield to rescue the wounded, shaming her servants into accompanying her.[58]

After this crisis was over, her long career of setting up institutions to meet various human needs began. Her first venture, in 1850, was an establishment where working mothers could leave their infants, close to the places of work so that the women could come and nurse them. While academic observers believed that working-class mothers did not really want to suckle their young, it turned out that half of them did. The institutions Signora Mantegazza set up cut down on the previously high rate of child abandonment, and in the course of fifty years, thirty-five thousand babies want through her centers.

Her next venture was a school for illiterate adults, where she herself did part of the teaching. Like Maria Montessori later, she cut out her own letters for the students to copy. After this, she founded various technical and vocational schools for young women so that they might have "a less humiliating destiny." Her hope was that real work would supply real satisfaction, and the girls would have less need to withdraw into adolescent fantasies.

She would do anything to raise money for her projects. She wrote letters, printed brochures, rang doorbells, prayed, went back again and again to solicit from donors, and ran fairs. She would never accept any money for herself and hated public recognition, but she was ardently committed to bringing benefits, both material and psychological, to less fortunate members of her own sex.

Such women carried the earlier tradition of philanthropic work a step farther. Admirers of the women's involvement felt that they were really defending the holiest of women's rights, the right to show what they could do by expanding their "maternal" energies. Furthermore, the work of actually founding, raising money for, organizing, and running institutions brought even convent-educated women into greater contact with the outside world, developing skills far beyond those of most earlier charitable ladies.

By 1900 Italian women were serving everywhere on boards and staffs of hospitals, orphanages, and schools.*[59] They proved the assertions of earlier feminists that women could work at executive and administrative levels that had once been considered male domains.

ᴄᴐ Thus it seems that Italian women tended to fall into extreme categories. Some were heiresses to a long tradition of scholarship and personal involvement at the very highest levels. Others, the majority, were less exposed to modern ideas than those of other nationalities. Their women's movement was small and ineffective because of the inertia of the mass; yet its leaders were committed socialists, somewhat like their Latin co-workers, the French, and farther ahead of their time than the English suffragettes or the German *Bund*.

---

*The first woman school inspector, Felicita Morandi, was appointed in 1867 and spent thirty years in the service. By the time of her retirement, there were twelve such women, inspecting all institutions for educating girls, up and down the peninsula. Matilde Serao made fun of the ones that came to visit her normal school, presenting them as society ladies over whose eyes the wool was easily pulled, but doubtless there were good ones as well as bad.

⌁29.

"The *Feme Covert*"

"I want to know if a thing can be legally right and morally wrong," Ideala answered.

"Of course not," the Bishop rashly asserted.

"That depends," the lawyer said cautiously.

"If I sign a contract," Ideala explained, "and found out afterwards that those who induced me to become a party to it had kept me in ignorance of the most important clause in it, so that I really did not know to what I was committing myself, would you call that a moral contract?"

"I should say that people had not dealt uprightly with you," the Bishop answered; "but there might be nothing in the clause to which you could object."

"But suppose there *was* something in the clause to which I very strongly objected, something of which my conscience disapproved, something that was repugnant to my whole moral nature; and suppose I was forced by law to fulfil it nevertheless, should you say that was a moral contract? Should you not say that in acting against my conscience I acted immorally?"

We all fell into the trap and looked an encouraging assent.

"And in that case," she continued, "I suppose my duty would be to evade the law, and act on my own conscience?"

The Bishop looked puzzled.

"I should only be doing what the early martyrs had to do," she added.

"That is true," he rejoined, with evident relief.

"But I don't see what particular contract you are thinking of," said the lawyer.

"The marriage contract," Ideala answered, calmly.

Sarah Grand, 1893

Although the English women's movement was, in the end, the most successful in Europe, Englishwomen did not begin the nineteenth century in an advanced position.

When Flora Tristan visited the island in 1839, she got a most dismal impression. She felt that in no part of the world with which she was familiar did women have less freedom, or were they under a more atrocious domestic despotism, and she attributed this largely to the laws, and particularly to the fact that they had no legal right to an inheritance. Because of that, she felt, their education was neglected and their lives became monotonous, sterile, and sad. She was particularly shocked that at a time when Britain was ruled by a queen, pretending to represent the whole nation, women were not even allowed in the visitors' gallery in Parliament.*

Blackstone's basic position regarding women in English law was quoted in Chapter 10. After explaining that a married couple were considered as "one person," the legal commentator went on to say: "But though our law in general considers man and wife as one person, yet there are some instances in which she is separately considered, as inferior to him, and acting by his compulsion."

When feminist issues began to be debated in Parliament, in 1866, advocates of the rights of women put the question why the word "man" should not be considered a generic term, embracing both sexes, as in the Magna Carta—"No free man shall be taken or imprisoned . . . ."[1] Actually Blackstone, unconscious of the inconsistency, explained the rights of an Englishman as including "free use and enjoyment of all his acquisitions, without any control or diminution, save only the laws of the land," and again, "confinement of any person in any wise is imprisonment." Unmarried women were included in the freedoms accorded Englishmen, but a wife lost all of her rights as a single person, and her husband was civilly responsible for her acts, and even sometimes for her crimes. She could own no personal property, and her rights to inherit real estate were limited to reversion after he died.[2] During most of the period, the man had the right to chastise his wife, and even when he did serious damage, such as causing the loss of an eye, the sentences were usually light. The presumption of her innocence of a crime, even murder, committed in his presence was not abolished until 1925. She could not be convicted of setting fire to her husband's house even if she did it with the motive of revenge.[3] Furthermore, no one could give shelter to a fleeing married woman against her husband's wish unless he had actually turned her out of doors. And this rule was no mere scrap of paper. Mary Vivian Hughes had an aunt who had eloped with a man so brutal that she had to leave him. After that the poor woman supported herself by giving music

---

*Though Flora's view was common among French writers—see Taine, for instance—it was not universal. Jenny Lind, for one, felt that Englishwomen were far better off than women in Sweden, whose laws she found oppressive. She herself had gained her liberty only by a direct appeal to the King. Looking around England, she believed that the laws allowed women there to develop "noble characters."

Flora noticed too the contrast between the numerous women writers of high caliber and the servitude of ordinary women. It shocked her that in the country of Mary Wollstonecraft, none of these writers had taken up the cause of feminism in the vigorous way that Mme de Staël, George Sand, and Mme d'Agoult had in France. Modern critics have reiterated Flora's question and tried to explain why such gifted women as George Eliot and Charlotte Brontë seemed more interested in themes of resignation than of protest.

lessons and fled from lodging to lodging to escape her husband's pursuit. "Victorian times are supposed to have been so settled and happy and care-free, but my recollections hardly tally with this rosy picture," she concluded. "Surely to-day [1934] no woman would endure such humiliations year after year."[4]

An interesting assumption was that a wife had no power to consent to her own seduction, so that the law supposed that she yielded to force.[5] If an unmarried woman was seduced, she had no legal recourse against the man, nor did her father except as he was deprived of her services, so that evidence of some slight service was required for prosecution.[6] The husband of an adulterous wife could collect damages from her lover, but this provision was not reciprocal; a wife had no claim against her husband's mistress.[7]

Mona Caird bitterly remarked that if the marriage contract were made more glaringly absurd, if it were declared that a woman to be legally married had to put out her right eye, no sane person would argue that the contract was just, simply on the ground that she had the choice of remaining single.[8] The existing marriage law was based on exactly the same principle, and there was no constitutional path of redress. As Frances Cobbe complained, even the best men took their cues from the unjust laws and the deconsideration of women was both the cause and the result of these laws.[9]

For many women marriage proved to be a prison with torture, and Caroline Norton, one of the victims, said, "I believe that men have no more notion of what the anguish is than the blind have of colors."[10] The prison analogy could be quite literal. Not only was marriage traditionally indissoluble in England, but the right of a husband to restrain his wife was specifically upheld in the Cochrane case of 1840, discussed in Chapter 11. Mr. Cochrane sued in the Court of Common Pleas and received a judgment that it was within his rights to restrain her person until "she will cheerfully and frankly resolve on performing the contract she has entered into."[11] During the ensuing fifty years, however, sentiment changed, as was shown by a reversal in the *Queen* v. *Jackson* case of 1891. Mr. Jackson's wife, Emily, had gone to live with her sisters while he went on a voyage to New Zealand, and she refused to return to him when he got back. He thereupon kidnaped her with the assistance of two strong young men who pulled her into a carriage as she was leaving church. In the court's judgment, it was inconsistent with the rights of free human creatures to lock a woman up; the opinion declared that the husband had no right to personal chastisement of his wife in England or any other civilized country (though it had been specifically allowed under the Cochrane rule).[12]

The cruelest provision in all of English law was that a mother had no rights over her own children as long as her husband was living. He had the power to take them away from her as soon as they were weaned. A Mrs. Emanuel, who brought her husband a capital sum of £2,000 when she married, and whose marriage settlement had been written to entitle her to a £700 annual income, was persecuted by her husband to make a will in his favor. In order to enforce his point, he sent their six-month-old infant abroad. When she applied to the court for visitation privileges, it was ruled that she had no right to interfere, especially as the child was in good health.[13] It will be remembered that John Keats's widowed mother lost all claims on her minor children when she remarried, and she was unable to sell her first husband's stable to provide for his children.[14] Even a certain Mrs. Greenhill, who obtained an ecclesiastical separation in 1836 from her adulterous husband, found that she was denied access by the state to her three little girls.[15] The court ordered her to be imprisoned for attempting to keep the children with her, and her only recourse was to flee abroad. One of the judges in the case stated that the whole court was ashamed of the decision, but so stood the law, and they must abide by it.[16]

An early martyr to this law was "Miss Weeton," a governess who had prudently saved up her money and at the age of forty-two was persuaded to marry her employer, Aaron Stock, whose aim, as it turned out, was to use her capital to save his bankrupt business. From then on she was kept penniless and was sometimes locked in her room while her husband disported with his mistress; and when she tried to flee, she was forced back into his house by threat of starvation. Their one child, Mary, was sent to a school where the principal was lecherous and his wife alcoholic. In this environment Mary lost both her health and her sweetness; the mother's letters were intercepted, and her persistent efforts to see the child only resulted in her husband's actually having her imprisoned on a false warrant, and threatening to send her to the insane asylum. In 1822 she won a separation agreement. She was not allowed to read it before she signed it, however, and later she found that it granted her only three visits a year with her child, and those only in the presence of the schoolmaster or his wife. Miss Weeton wrote the story of her life for the sake of the daughter she was not allowed to see, and ended it with the pathetic hope that her husband wold not destroy the manuscript.[17] Although she became a devoted feminist, her voice was too small to be heard in those days, and her autobiography was printed only in 1936.

On the subject of divorce and child custody, the woman whose voice carried was Caroline Norton, born a Sheridan and one of the most beautiful and talented women in England. Her marriage to George Norton in 1827 was an affair of high society. It turned out that the Nortons had misled the Sheridans about George's finances, and the couple was in difficulties about money from the start. Luckily Caroline found that she could supplement their income by her literary earnings, and she used to pay for her own and her children's clothes in that way. In 1830 she met Lord Melbourne. She was twenty-two at the time, he was a widower of fifty-one, and for him she began to run a political salon. She used the leverage from this position to seek a political office for her husband, and Melbourne made him a judge in the police court at an annual salary of £1,000—a post that he retained in spite of all that happened subsequently. In 1836 Norton sued Melbourne for alienating his wife's affections, using a drunken coachman as a witness. The evidence was so obviously corrupt that the jury acquitted Melbourne without leaving the box.[18] (In accordance with English procedure, Caroline was not a party to the suit and could not be represented by counsel; only her husband and the Prime Minister had any part in the proceedings.)

Failing to get a divorce for lack of corespondent, George Norton separated from his wife and kept custody of their three children. She was left in acute financial straits and had to live with her brother for a while; what money she earned by writing was always subject to Norton's seizure, if he knew about it, and occasionally he raided her apartment for clothes, books, and jewels. When Lord Melbourne died in 1848, there was a generous bequest to Caroline. She tried to conceal it from her husband, but he ordered her bank books subpoenaed.

The hardest thing of all was the separation from her children. During the Melbourne troubles Norton had ordered them locked up with their nurse, who had orders not to let them see their mother. When she made a futile effort to carry them off, they were secretly shipped to Scotland out of the reach of English law. Even when they were old enough to go to school, back in England, and she drove out to see them, she was met with word that she was not to be admitted. In 1842 one of them was thrown from his pony and died. Caroline, who arrived in time to see him in his coffin, believed that he had suffered from neglect and that his death might have been prevented had she been present earlier.*

But Caroline was a woman to be reckoned with, and she decided to do all in her power to have the law on the custody of children changed. Her 1837 pamphlet, *The Natural Rights of a Mother* complained bitterly that the mother of illegitimate children had access to them, but a married mother had to submit to her husband's will. The effect of her exposé was to get through Parliament an Infants Custody Act in 1839, allowing the Lord Chancellor to grant an innocent mother custody of children up to the age of seven.[19] This Act would have given Caroline access to her children had they been in England, but their Scottish residence would have prevented her even then.)†

In 1855 she composed a second appeal, in the form of a "Letter to

---

*It is ironic that although George Meredith modeled *Diana of the Crossways* on Caroline Norton's history (without giving her any fictional children, it is true), his own separated wife had to be sneaked in by friends and servants to see her son, Arthur (Diane Johnson, 138).

†In Leigh Hunt's *Bluestocking Revels*, in which the god Apollo is supposed to meet the women writers of the day, Caroline Norton is treated thus (Leigh Hunt, 184):

"Mrs. Norton." The god, stepping forward a pace,
Kissed her hand in return, with respect in his face,
. . . .
"Twas a large heart, and loving, that gave us this guide."

the Queen," urging some kind of divorce law and decent property settlement.

> This much I will do, woman though I be. I will put on record—in French, German, English and Italian—what the law for women was in England in the years of civilisation and Christianity, 1855, and the eighteenth year of the reign of a female sovereign! *This* I will do; and others who come after me may do more. The feudal barbarity of the laws between Baron and Feme may vanish from amongst us.[20]

Under existing law neither Mr. nor Mrs. Norton could divorce or remarry. She had received not a farthing from Mr. Norton for three years, although he was the beneficiary of the interest on her inheritance.[21] The government had granted a small pension to her father's children, and Mr. Norton allowed her to keep this, though he was under no compulsion to do so. Once again her pamphlet created sentiment sufficient to get a bill through Parliament. This act (1857) set up a divorce court, for the first time making divorce accessible to people other than wealthy aristocrats, and incidentally providing that a separated wife could keep her own earnings, and a court could order separate maintenance for her, that she might inherit and bequeath her money, and sue and be sued.[22] (Caroline had been injured when an anonymous article had been falsely attributed to her, and she was unable to sue the writer and retrieve her reputation.) Not until 1886 were mothers declared capable of being legal guardians of their children and allowed to appoint someone by will to act with the father for this purpose.

Ironically, the passage of the much-needed divorce bill of 1857 killed for a number of years the chances for a bill for married women's property rights. Members of Parliament could not see the need of doing anything for uninjured wives now that they had made provision, they felt, for those who were really in trouble.[23]

A thoughtful article on married women's property came out in the *Edinburgh Review* in 1857.[24] English law was unique, it found, in making a gift of all a woman's personal property to her husband at marriage and in vesting in him all her subsequent acquisitions.* The ancient right of a widow to a third of her husband's property was found to be now completely extinguished, a fact explained in part by the English law's reliance on individual judges, who tended to favor husbands, rather than on written codes, which provided the norm in most other countries.

Much of the difficulty, the article said, came about because the ancient land laws had usually protected women's rights, even if only to a "jointure," or right to receive income from an entailed property, but there was no such provision in the rules governing intangible property, and the husband regularly took it all.[25] (As for the real property, a widow could get it back if her husband had not dissipated or mismanaged it. He

---

*Some wit suggested amending the marriage vow to read: "With all thy worldly goods I me endow."

would not have been allowed to sell it; in fact, the legal procedures for disposing of it if a couple wished to sell, were so complicated that the accepted procedure was for the would-be purchaser to sue on the grounds that he was the rightful owner, or had rented from the rightful owner. By defending the case ineffectively, the would-be sellers could usually get the property ceded.)[26]

The law when strictly interpreted was so harsh that courts of equity began to treat married women as if they were single to try to save some property for their personal use. Customarily they would require a husband to make some settlement on a separated wife if she had no other means of provision and was not at fault. On the other hand, even if the husband was seriously at fault, as in the case of a man who debauched his step-daughter, the wife-mother was unable to get more than half her own property back through the courts.[27]

A woman's parents might attempt to save her property from her husband by setting up trustees to handle it, but this involved considerable trouble, and the minute the trustees gave her any cash, it immediately became the property of her husband. Money that was earned by a married woman belonged absolutely to her husband.[28] The incident that sent Mrs. Grote rushing to join the women's movement was hearing her stolen watch and purse described in court as the property of her husband.[29] To pay a milliner's bill of £97, Fanny Kemble decided to translate a Dumas play for the English stage. Before her marriage she had been a well-paid actress, but naturally had given up her profession when she married the American Pierce Butler. Alas, she found that there was no way she could pay her own debt.[30]

An American milliner in Paris did so well for her English customers that they persuaded her to move to London; but when her profligate husband turned up, he sold her out and set her adrift with no recourse. Another unfortunate woman did a good business in straw hats; but when her husband sold her property, she had to wait until her son turned twenty-one. Then she could go to work as his "servant" and re-establish her business.*[31]

The *Edinburgh Review* article concluded that in France and Germany, a certain separation of property had not led to marital discord, and it urged that Parliament pass legislation to confer similar rights on Englishwomen. But the legislators were not yet ready for such a drastic step. The person who accomplished for married women's property what Caroline Norton had done for child custody was Barbara Leigh Smith (later Mme Bodichon). Like so many outstanding women of the nineteenth century, she enjoyed a remarkably free and untrammeled girlhood. A

---

*It was possible, at least in London, for a wife to get a legal document entitling her to set up in business on her own, and to enjoy all the rights of a single woman (Josephine Butler, *Woman's Work*, 189). This was exceptional. In general, no woman could make a legal contract, or sue, even if her husband was abroad, or be sued, which meant that she could get no credit.

cousin of Florence Nightingaie, she was the daughter of a rich Unitarian, Leigh Smith, a grocer by trade and a radical member of Parliament, who educated his daughters at home and presented them with allowances of £300 a year and freedom to travel at the age of twenty-one.[32] So she and her friend Bessie Parkes were allowed to chaperone each other on a tour of Belgium, Germany, Austria, and Switzerland on which they carried their own sketching materials and blankets.[33]

In 1856 Barbara undertook to collect petitions for passage of a Married Women's Property Bill. A couple of years after this she and Bessie Parkes founded the *Englishwoman's Journal*, which in turn led to an employment agency for women who desired non-traditional occupations. After her marriage to a French surgeon, Dr. Eugene Bodichon, Barbara lived half the year in Algiers, but her marriage agreement stated that she could pay long annual visits to England, and she by no means gave up her good works.[34]

The failure of her hoped-for bill in 1856 did not discourage her from trying again, and in 1869 another petition went round. In 1870 a law was passed providing that married women might control the money that they earned, and put it in a savings bank. In 1882 another law allowed them to retain possession of the property with which they had entered marriage.

No Englishwoman had suffered more from the old laws about marriage, children, and property than Annie Besant, born in 1847, whose life story was a demonstration of legal barriers at their worst.[35] She married the Reverend Frank Besant after certain hesitations that her mother over-ruled, not wishing the girl to suffer dishonor from a broken promise. As a young wife she began to write, and the first time she received a check for thirty shillings she was so delighted to be able to help (as she thought) with household expenses that she fell on her knees to thank God. But Mr. Besant appropriated the money without even asking her what she would like to have done with it. He had, as Annie said, "very high ideas of a husband's authority and a wife's submission."[36] Annie reacted with hysterics. After two children and a firm determination not to have any more, she underwent a crisis of faith that effectively disqualified her as a clergyman's wife. Except for the humiliation, her husband was probably delighted to see her go. In 1873 the couple arranged a separation agreement according to which Mr. Besant gave her £110 a year (a quarter of his income) and the children were to be divided, he getting the boy and she the girl, Mabel, except for a month every year when they were to be exchanged. She kept her clothes and personal items but no furniture, and she found it impossible to set up living quarters on her income.[37]

Annie found a supportive group of freethinkers who were delighted to use her literary talent to spread their gospel, and she was soon earning money with her pen and on the lecture circuit. One of her causes was population control, so when a bookseller she knew, Henry Cook, was sentenced for selling Knowlton's *Fruits of Philosophy* (which, though it contained specific birth control information, had been selling quietly and unmolested for forty years), Annie persuaded her friend Charles Brad-laugh that the book must be defended. They got out a new edition, advertised it widely, and practically invited arrest. By the time they were arraigned, 133,000 copies had been sold. After a highly publicized trial, they were freed with a small fine, but Annie's troubles were not over. Mr. Besant had become alarmed at the possible harm to his little daughter's morals if she were taught "the physiological facts"[38] contained in the pamphlet. He had already been shocked at Mabel's lack of religious education, and relied on the judicial precedent that had disqualified Shelley as the guardian of his own children because he was an atheist. Annie, conducting her defense herself, admitted that she had removed the New Testament from her child because it contained "coarse passages," but hotly denied that she had communicated any physiological facts. The judge awarded Mabel to her father anyway and sent a messenger to collect the child, "shrieking and struggling, still weak from the fever, and near frantic with fear and passionate resistance," as Annie described the episode to her eager readers.[39] Although the final settlement permitted Annie certain visiting privileges, the children found such visits so upsetting, and Annie found them so expensive and restrictive (she had to pay a chaperone to sit with them, and was not allowed to join them in such activities as sea bathing, which the court alluded to "with suggestiveness"), that she gave up all intercourse until they should reach majority. Her offer to pay for Mabel's education at a first-class school was rejected, and she had to endure the knowledge that her daughter was only getting fifth-rate teaching.[40]

∽ The difficulties attending any organization of women in England to work for their own betterment should be obvious. Only a minority of women were discontented, and all of those who were married had a personal relationship—whether of love, fear, or duty—with their own husbands that could have been a dissuading factor. Even so Barbara Leigh Smith got twenty-four thousand signatures on her petition of 1856—a harbinger of the formidable sex solidarity and organizing power of the future.

≈30.

An English Gallery: Education and Self-Education

Can anything, for example, be more perfectly absurd than to suppose that the care and perpetual solicitude which a mother feels for her children, depends upon her ignorance of Greek and Mathematics; and that she would desert an infant for a quadratic equation?

Sidney Smith, 1810

In view of the almost total lack of facilities to give girls any kind of systematic intellectual training in the early part of the nineteenth century, it is astonishing to find how many bright girls insisted on training themselves—and what marvelous success they had. As Ellen Key wrote in 1909, "Nearly every eminent woman of the last fifty years [she could have gone back a hundred] has had such self-instruction, or was an irregularly instructed girl. Knowledge so acquired . . . has many serious gaps, but it has far more freshness and breadth."[1] On the other hand, no one should imagine that such learning was easy. Helen Taylor told Kate Amberley in 1869 that it took a woman ten to fifteen years longer to educate herself than a man with the benefit of a university course.[2] A few examples will show the effort and the commitment.

Sydney Owenson, Lady Morgan, born in 1777, came home from school having never heard the word "chemistry"; but as soon as she found that there was such a discipline, she went every evening to study it with a neighbor. Hearing of the labors of Pauline Lavoisier, she declared that she would rather be the wife of a man like Lavoisier than any queen.[3] She actually married a doctor who was working with Edward Jenner in smallpox prevention, and though she deliberately gave up studying chemistry because she wanted to remain "every inch a woman,"[4] John Killham calls her the first non-socialist feminist to argue that science and the scientific attitude were the key to men's future.[5]

In 1822, when Elizabeth Grant's Highland family suffered reverses, she decided to try to help out, and to do so she undertook "a plan of study.'''⁶ Unfortunately she does not describe her curriculum in detail, but she was one of the few girls of that early period who admitted financial need as a spur. Though the rest of the women under discussion often became famous and self-supporting, their original motivation was most often simply the desire to learn, or perhaps the wish to keep up with their brothers, who had chances to practice exciting things like Latin.

Thus, though Dr. John Welsh wanted the education of his only daughter, Jane, to be like that of a boy, her parents could not agree on just how to do this, so Jane began secretly to take Latin lessons from a youth of her acquaintance.⁷ She sat up late at night and tied a weight to her ankle in order to wake up early and carry on her studying. When she was only ten, Edward Irving, a Scottish schoolmaster, undertook a strenuous program to form her mind, and after their hours of tutoring he used to set her up on the table and add logic to her other studies.*

Harriet Martineau, who was born in 1802, a year after Jane Welsh, wrote in her old age (ca. 1855) to a schoolgirl concerning her own early life:

> Some circumstances lately led me to look back and see what I did with myself from 16 to 20. The exact number of puddings and custards that I made has escaped my memory; but I liked cooking very well and ironing better. I used to get up at 5, first to make my sister's linen when she was going to be married, and then to try whether I could not write stories and scraps of verse. My Latin prospered then, & I read much French, & taught myself Italian. Translation was a good exercise, I found, & I translated Tacitus into prose and Petrarch into verse, and used to read to my mother from French books, trying to prevent her finding out that it was not printed English. Then I learnt Wordsworth by heart by the bushel & all Moore almost. Then did I take to Hartley, as to a new gospel, & puzzle out metaphysical questions in my own mind all day long. Baxter & Doddrige & Priestley were for Sunday: and music out at all odd times, besides my daily practice. Oh, those were glorious days! & I wish you joy, dear, that they are coming to you. . . .⁸

George Eliot too was a very self-improving girl,⁹ taking up in her early twenties Latin, Greek, singing, piano, German, Italian, and French, as well as sufficient Hebrew to be able to check on Old Testament critics. A less well-known writer, Mary Howitt, and her sister undertook to educate themselves after their tutor proved objectionable by his personal attentions. They borrowed books wherever they could and spent many hours a day and late into the night consuming them. Of her husband and herself Mary wrote, "Knowledge in the broadest sense was the aim of our intellectual efforts. . . ."¹⁰ Dr. Arnold's eldest daughter, Jane, learned Latin and Greek from her father well enough to teach them to one of her younger brothers.¹¹ She married W. E. Forster and had considerable influence on the shape of the Education Bill that he prepared for Parliament in 1867. Eliza Lynn (Mrs. Lynn Linton) attacked

---

*Later, she and Irving fell in love, though she married his friend, Thomas Carlyle.

and learned unaided, between eleven and seventeen, French, Italian, German, and Spanish, all so well that she could read them aloud and translate as she read. She also knew small bits of Latin, Greek, and Hebrew.[12] Dr. Elizabeth Garrett Anderson lived at home from age fifteen to twenty-four, working at Latin and mathematics with her brother's tutor.[13] Likewise, Emily Davies, future founder of Girton College, studied Greek and French by herself at home.[14]

Families often put pressure on studious girls to take things easy, as in the case of the Winkworth sisters, Susanna and Catherine. Their father was willing to let them study art and music but was reluctant for them to take up more solid studies for fear that they would be led to unsafe regions of speculation and would grow out of sympathy with the society in which they had to live.[15] The girls refused to be discouraged, however, especially as it was in the back of their minds that they might have to become self-supporting some day. They lived in Manchester and were lucky to be able to take lessons from William Gaskell, who taught them history, composition, chemistry, Greek, and literature. They also studied German and music "in the highest state of delight and excitement"[16] but were even more pleased to be allowed to take lessons in astronomy and to read the works of Mrs. Somerville. When James Martineau wanted to form a class in composition and grammar for young ladies, the sisters jumped at the chance, and won their father's consent although they had feared that he might keep forbidding all further lessons except painting. They hoped, of course, to live in easy circumstances so that they could pursue these tastes for pleasure, but even if they should have to teach, Susanna could not imagine that her father would want them to be private governesses for lack of fitness for any other, higher form of teaching. "I cannot be easy while I could not get my own living without descending in society"—which would be the case if they should lack a sound and regular education.[17]

And yet their consciences were always examining their conduct. Reading *Alton Locke* made Catherine Winkworth wonder if it was right to do anything except strive to raise up the poor and ignorant, while she felt that her own wish to learn Latin and Greek and do translations was a form of temptation. She gives a good description of the sisters' ambivalence in 1856:

> We girls are better off in our house than in almost any I know, as to time for our own pursuits, for Mamma is not only indulgent, but takes a warm interest in all we do; still it makes us feel all the more how wrong it would be to neglect any of those tiny home duties which look so like idleness, and yet are so essential to the pleasantness of daily life, and it really is marvelous how much time they fill up. As to "becoming blue,"* I should not fear that; in the first place, because it is really nowadays an uncommon piece of

*She meant, of course, "blue" in the old-fashioned sense of "bluestocking" or overly intellectual.

> ignorance *not* to have studied Latin, and . . . [being blue comes from] overestimating the value of study altogether, which may be a clear duty at any given time, but can never be a primary one—at least to women.[18]

Although Elizabeth Haldane came along later in the century, when colleges for women had been well established, the same sort of family expectations still hindered her. She was not supposed to leave her widowed mother for mere intellectual gratification, so she settled for a self-imposed course of study, and at twenty-four she translated Hegel's *History of Philosophy*.[19]

∽ The majority of the women who became famous with no background except what their own determined self-education had given them distinguished themselves in literature; or, less frequently, they took up social subjects; and an honored few worked in the natural sciences. Mrs. Gatty was an early example of the last; she was at heart a scientist, and having discarded her cloaks and shawls and shortened her skirts—to the ankles—she prowled around the coasts of Britain in waterproof boys' boots searching for seaweeds.[20] Her classifications became the standard ones, and she won an independent reputation among botanists.

Certainly the star of English women scientists was Mary Somerville, who, according to Joanna Baillie, did more to change the low estimation in which the capacity of women was usually held "than the whole sisterhood of poetical damsels and novel-writing authors."[21] She proved that women were capable of high achievement in fields of mathematics and physics, but for us looking back today, her life is also a demonstration of the awful neglect of girls' mental life, the resistance to any expression of interest in their gifts, and the physical difficulties of arranging space and time for a woman with this unfamiliar concern. Mary's daughter talks about "the almost intuitive way in which she entered upon studies of which she had scarcely heard the names, living as she did, among persons to whom they were utterly unknown, and who disapproved. . . ."[22]

Mrs. Somerville describes her own childhood in the late eighteenth century as a wild one in the Scottish countryside. At seven she was helping with the chores of shelling peas and feeding poultry, but her seafaring father was shocked at finding such a savage when he came home after a long voyage and sent her to school for one year. She learned nothing there. When she got home, then aged eleven, her mother reproached her with having wasted the money spent for her education. She had not learned, in other words, "to write well and keep accounts, which was all that a woman was expected to know."[23] But she compared her own release from school to that of a wild animal from a cage, for she wandered around the countryside again, combed beaches, robbed birds' nests, and in bad weather read Shakespeare when not held to the task of working a sampler. The family disapproved of too much reading, and though she finally obtained permission for the village schoolmaster to tutor her on winter evenings, he was not to instruct her in the hard subjects like Latin and navigation which he taught the boys in his school.

Luckily she finally met an uncle to whom she was able to confess how much she wanted to learn Latin, and he agreed to read Virgil with her every morning before breakfast. Later on she undertook Greek. Then, at a teaparty, she glanced at a ladies' magazine that included mathematical puzzles between the fashion prints, and for the first time learned of the existence of a subject called algebra. At a painting class she overheard the teacher tell a fellow student that "Euclid" would help with perspective, and though she had no idea what Euclid could be, she never forgot the name. So when her young brother was given a tutor, she asked him to buy her an elementary algebra and geometry the next time he went into Edinburgh. "Now I had got what I so long and earnestly desired," she exclaimed,[24] and after practicing a few demonstrations with the tutor, she took off on her own. Her days were filled to the brim with household duties, making and mending her own dresses, practicing five hours daily on the piano, painting—and then she sat up late in bed with her Euclid. This went on until the servants called it to the attention of the family that Mary was using lots of candles, at which point her father forbade her to study: "or we shall have Mary in a straitjacket one of these days."[25] She had just completed six books of geometry, but now she spent her night hours going over them in memory. Discipline was not so strict when she became adult; at twenty she still spent her days painting, practicing, and sewing, but now she began the habit of rising early, wrapping herself in a blanket because there was no fire, in order to read mathematics, Latin, or Greek until breakfast.

Her first husband had no interest in her ideas, and no admiration for women's brains, but he left her alone for great periods of time while she continued her mathematical studies and took lessons in French. After she was widowed, though she had two young children, she began to read Newton, and for recreation she went on doing mathematical puzzles from a newspaper. By winning a prize in a contest, she came to the attention of the editor, a professor at the University of Edinburgh, and she explained to him how much she would like to complete a course in mathematics and astronomy. He directed her to the proper books, which she was now free to buy. Once she had them in hand, she could hardly believe, she said, "that I possessed such a treasure, when I looked back on the day that I first saw the mysterious word 'Algebra,' and the long course of years in which I had persevered almost without hope."[26] About this time, in 1812, she married her second husband, William Somerville, who admired her ability and did all he could to encourage it, eventually copying manuscripts and correcting proof for her books.

It is nearly impossible to imagine what her days must have been like when her children were small. She had several, by both husbands, and lost some too. Besides managing her house—which she did to perfection—she spent three hours every morning teaching her children. She also visited and received friends in the accepted social pattern of the day, read new books on all subjects, wrote for the press, and still spent much time with her needle. Painting was her favorite recreation, though she was accomplished at the piano also.

Her reputation in mathematics grew, and in 1827 Lord Brougham—a fellow Scot, who in his parliamentary career had a hand in every measure to improve education or advance knowledge—wrote to Mary's father-in-law (not to her), to ask if she would write an account of the "mechanism of the heavens" on behalf of the Society for the Diffusion of Useful Knowledge. Brougham explained that if she were to refuse, this whole part of public education would be left blank, because "no one else can do it."[27] And, he added tactfully no one would need to know that she had written it.

Mrs. Somerville until then had modestly assumed that her learning must be inferior to that taught at universities, but her book was so good that it became an essential textbook for any Cambridge undergraduate studying mathematics or physics. In 1834 she was invited to that university and given various honors and dinners, but naturally it would have seemed unbecoming for her to deliver a public lecture. She was also made an honorary member of the Royal Astronomical Society along with Caroline Herschel.

Her arrangements for writing without breaking her social routine required that she learn how to leave her subject and resume it at once when the interruption ended. In winter she used the drawing room because of its fire, and often had to hide her papers quickly when a visitor was announced. "A man can always command his place of business," she remarked. "A woman is not allowed any such excuse."[28]

When her work on astronomy was completed, she turned to conic sections and then to physical geography. She spent her later years mostly in Italy because of her husband's health. (During her stay there, she could not view the comet of 1843 because the only telescope was at a Jesuit college where no woman was allowed to set foot.)[29] At the age of eighty-nine, writing her memoirs, she described the pleasure she still felt in calculus, and in receiving books on higher algebra sent by Professor Pierce of Harvard. Though she was denied the burial in Westminster Abbey that many Englishmen felt she deserved,[30] she would probably have taken even greater satisfaction in knowing that a women's college at Oxford was named in her honor.

A contemporary of Mrs. Somerville, a woman who was known as "the Mrs. Somerville of the Marine World,"[31] was Janet Taylor. In 1832 she began publishing nautical tables and teaching navigation, nautical mathematics, and astronomy to youths in training as well as to old salts who flocked to her classes. She modestly says of herself that she was the person who awakened the spirit of research in the subject. Her texts were published by order of the Lords Commissioners of the Admiralty, and in recognition of her services she was placed on the government's civil list.[32] She died in 1870.

Mary Kingsley's life provides a poignant example of how a woman could do everything a Victorian lady was supposed to do at home and still have an adventurous and productive career.[33] Her field was the study of the religion, laws, fauna, and trade conditions of Africa. A niece of Charles Kingsley, she was born in 1862 and had to stay at home, doing what was expected of a Victorian daughter until her parents died when she was thirty. Though now free of filial obligations, she continued to keep house for her brother whenever he came home from India, so her African trips had to be planned to get her home in time to set up housekeeping in London before she met his boat. Though conventional in this way, Mary let nothing interfere with her pursuit of information or what she felt were her humanitarian duties once she reached Africa. She used to sleep in native huts rather than the houses of Europeans; when a sick trader needed nursing, she thought nothing of breaking the taboos to sit up at his bedside all night. She died of enteric fever caught while nursing prisoners in the Boer War, but not before she had become such an expert on the still-dark continent of Africa that she lectured before scientific societies and gave testimony before government commissions.

Unfortunately it is hard to tell how many women were engaged in science at this level. In the 1851 census, among "persons in the learned professions (with their immediate subordinates) either filling public offices or in private practice" were included such job holders as church pew openers.[34] But a serious interest in scientific questions became acceptable for women as their accomplishments became visible and their admission to learned societies became normal. This happened at different times for different disciplines. The National Association for the Promotion of Social Science founded by Lord Brougham admitted them from its inception in 1857, although for a brief period at the beginning, women wishing to present papers had to have them read by a man.[35] Not until 1892 did the Royal Geographical Society admit "well-qualified ladies" (a speaker who referred to *women*, not ladies, was reproved), and they were still so rare that it was felt unsuitable to have them at the annual dinners, where a handful of ladies might suffer while four hundred men smoked.[36]

The women who have been discussed so far in this chapter were first of all private citizens, content to make their contribution to the sum of human knowledge or to add to human betterment by virtue of what they could do through their specialties. They were functioning the way men with such specialties did, in spite of the added difficulty that being female entailed in those days. None of these women protested publicly against domestic subjection, though they managed to evade or by-pass it privately so that they could get on with their work. Though many of them were friendly to the feminist movement of their day, they were not spear-carriers. If one had to name a social gain that emerged from all this private activity, a gain beyond the accumulation of the individual achievements, it would be that society had to recognize the need for facilities to train women's brains, to meet the overwhelming desire of women for colleges where instruction could be easier and opportunities for learning more comprehensive and far-reaching.

ᔉ For women on the continent, obtaining higher education was a matter of breaking into already-existing institutions, all of which were run by their governments. In certain Latin countries single individuals, with no help from any organized women's movement, managed to break down official reluctance, sometimes with the help of extremely highly placed persons, such as the Empress in France and the Pope in Italy. The new policy went against the bureaucratic grain, to be sure, but it did not meet with nearly so much hostility on grounds that it would take women outside their "sphere" as it met in northern countries. In Germany there was considerable feeling that women should not be admitted to universities at all, and it took a united women's movement using mass political tactics to achieve, much later than in the other countries, the entrance they sought.

In England the whole problem was different. The universities were not run by the government, but consisted of residential self-governing colleges. If women were to have them, they would have to build them for themselves. Each of the early colleges for women was founded by a group of people organized for that specific purpose and working against tremendous financial, as well as psychological, obstacles.

Some English feminists blamed the retarded condition of England's education for women on the failure of the reformers of the sixteenth century to dignify the work of unmarried women. In the eighteenth century, when the situation was probably at its worst, Lady Mary Wortley Montagu fumed that if horses could speak, "it would be an established maxim among them that a mare could not be taught to pace."[37] A college for women was even proposed, in 1775, by Mrs. Elizabeth Montagu, who was willing to endow it if only she could get the famous writer of educational tracts, Mrs. Letitia Barbauld,[38] to be the superintendent. But that lady had enough sense (in the view of the period) to refuse: "The thefts of knowledge in our sex are only connived at while carefully concealed, and, if displayed, punished with disgrace. . . ."[39] Mrs. Dugald Stewart long wanted the pleasure of listening to one of her husband's lectures at the University of Edinburgh, but even after the turn of the nineteenth century, no women were permitted to be present.[40]

The first model of a college for girls was imaginary: Tennyson's poem of 1847, *The Princess*. He was said to have intended this work to advance the cause of women's education, but common preconceptions got the better of him, and the poem shows more about how hope could founder than about how to set to work. It is worth a moment's attention in view of its popularity.

At a party someone reads aloud about an active and resourceful medieval heroine and inquires if there are any such women today. A girl among the guests cries out,

> . . . There are thousands now
> Such women, but convention beats them down;
> . . . You men have done it—how I hate you all!"

Thus is set the tone of sex-hatred, which was, in Tennyson's view, the motivating force behind women's intellectual development:

> . . . "O, I wish
> That I were some great princess, I would build
> Far off from men a college like a man's,
> And I would teach them all that men are taught;"[41]

The girls, she went on, would wander around their enclosed campus in academic gowns of many beautiful hues, but it would be death for any man to look at them. The party thereupon decides to make a game of planning such an institution, which is described in the main body of the poem, using theories "in and out of place." The princess of the tale retreats from the world of men, abandoning a fiancé, and the drama comes from his determination to penetrate the fortress and win his bride back. Disguised as a woman, this prince, with two companions, attempts to matriculate, and manages to go unrecognized for a while until his services are needed to repel the attack of an enemy. He is wounded in the ensuing combat, but luckly the princess has studied medicine, expressly to avoid the need for male doctors in her college community. In nursing the prince back to health she finds her true vocation, that woman

> is not undevelopt man,
> But diverse.[42]

Her transformation is further embellished with the sentiment that

> a lusty brace
> Of twins may weed her of her folly.[43]

It was not really a poem to recruit young women to the cause of higher education, although it was sometimes proclaimed as such, but it does show Tennyson's feeling that marriage should be a matter of mutual learning.

About the time *The Princess* was written, two very interesting experiments were being carried out in London, one by men for women, and the other by women for themselves. The origins of Queen's College lay in the Governesses Benevolent Association, a charitable endeavor organized in 1843 to assist impoverished governesses.[44] At first the directors assumed that the chief problem would be to relieve retired governesses, but they quickly ran into an unexpected difficulty: the widespread lack of preparation among women who sought positions and the fact that there was no qualifying standard to attest their competence. Without dropping other purposes, they decided to start classes and prepare some form of certification. In 1848 the college opened, with two hundred eager students and a curriculum of forty-five lectures per week. It was something like the *Viktorialyceum* in Berlin, but more directly practical.

The organizers of the school were F. D. Maurice and Charles Kingsley, two Church of England clergymen who were also Christian Socialists. Although it was intended mainly for governesses, Maurice insisted that other women could enter because he observed that practically all women were called upon to do teaching at some point in their lives, either to their own children or among the poor.[45]

Although the lecturers were motivated by the best intentions, they shared the common uncertainty about how far women's brains would take them and how far it was right to push them. It was expected that the students would do best in literary subjects, so Kingsley described his course in *Caedmon, Beowulf,* and the *Edda* as one for training "not cupboards full of 'information' . . . but real informed women," and he was serious enough about this mission to teach them things that "prudery or fanaticism normally forbid."[46] As for other subjects, Maurice explained at the opening, "We are aware that our pupils are not likely to advance far in Mathematics, but we believe that if they learn really what they do learn, they will not have got what is dangerous but what is safe."[47] One of the things that was definitely not safe, in Maurice's opinion, would be the opening up of "our "(that is, male) professions, and he hoped that the college would give a "more healthful" direction to the ambitions of any woman who had toyed with the idea of medicine or law.[48] As late as 1888, Helene Lange explained to her German readers that Queen's did not teach "strict science" but that it followed, with the best of intentions, a careful system of adaptation.[49]

All the lecturers were men at first, but to keep everything above criticism, Maurice engaged some ladies of rank and fashion to act as chaperones to the young girls in class.[50] Though it was still called a college, Queen's finally settled down to providing education at the secondary level. Even so, it assuaged part of the vast hunger of English girls for knowledge and training, opening, as Miss Frances Buss said of her student days there, "a new life."[51]

One of its limitations was its strict Church of England atmosphere. The other London college, Bedford, founded and administered by women themselves, was set up on a non-denominational basis.* Mrs.

*If a story from the 1890s can be taken as a clue, Bedford continued to be far less cautious than Queen's. At that time a Mr. Platt, teaching classics, told his students that Latin could be a valuable corrective to Christianity: it taught how to smite back, instead of turning the other cheek (Mary V. Hughes, *London Home*, 31).

John Reid,* a wealthy widow, arranged for some classes in her own home in 1847 and tried from the first to model them on the work at London's University College, from which she drew some of her professors. In other words, she was after a genuine higher education, though she pretended to be "surprised" by a letter from half a dozen honorable men urging the foundation of a women's college at the university level.[52] Although Mrs. Reid had actually planted the letter, in a form of pious deception, the scheme worked and she was able to set up a governing board with a majority of women. The founder spent every penny she possessed on the college and told Malwida von Meysenbug later that it was impossible to imagine the opposition she had had to contend with.[53]

The first year's enrollment included a number of subsequently distinguished women such as George Eliot (who took Latin), Barbara Bodichon, and Dr. Arnold's young widowed daughter, Mary. The students were so unprepared for college-level work that for fifteen years the school had to run a preparatory course alongside the main curriculum, but as soon as the examinations of the University of London became open to women, in 1878, it qualified its students for degrees from that institution.

ᕙ Independent women's colleges were all very well, but unless women could be taught and examined by the same professors as their brothers, in the universities of highest prestige, Oxford and Cambridge, their educational possibilities were never going to seem equal.

The breach in this academic wall was made first at Cambridge, under the leadership of Miss Emily Davies. She was a friend of Barbara Bodichon, whom she met in 1858, and of Dr. Elizabeth Garrett Anderson, who advised her to try to matriculate at London University.[54] This proposal aroused her interest in higher education for women, but she and her friends decided that the older universities should be opened up first, and it became the dream of her life to found a college where girls could be taught by Cambridge dons. By 1865 regular meetings to consider ways to do this were held by a group of women, including the three mentioned and also Helen Taylor, Jessie Boucherett, Dorothea Beale, and Frances Mary Buss. Of these only Barbara Bodichon commanded any substantial funds, and *Punch* ascribes the foundation of Girton largely to her generosity.†

A public meeting, chaired by the Dean of Canterbury, was called for March, 1868, to encourage sponsorship. At this affair all the public

*Not to be confused with Mrs. Hugo Reid (Marion Kirkland), who had written *A Plea for Women* in 1843 in reply to some snide notices of books about women in the *Edinburgh Review* for April, 1841. Mrs. John Reid's maiden name was Elizabeth Jesser.

†The first really large legacy to Girton was left by Jane Gamble in 1885. This Virginian was courted by a fortune hunter and abducted to Genoa in a well-publicized early kidnaping case (Barbara Stephen, *Girton*, 177).

speaking was left to men. In the end only £2,000 was raised toward their £30,000 goal.[55] Kate Amberley's mother, Lady Stanley, was a contributor, though Kate herself was considered too radical for her name to appear. (She had advocated birth control.) As Miss Shirreff wrote: "Never yet have a company of women been able to scrape together funds for an object specially their own, be it club, or reading-room, or hospital, or, as now, a college."[56] And, as Dr. Garrett Anderson put it, "Women want that which the College will give them so very, very much that those who can help them ought not to allow *any* minor disagreements to take from the duties of allies."[57]

It was an equally hard job to sell parents the idea of letting their daughters enroll. Claims that women could not stand the pace were met with tart common sense. No one urged, said Miss Davies, that girls be denied "cold water, or fresh air, or light, or animal food, lest they grow into boys," and it was silly to worry that the free range of thought would injure the delicacy of the female mind.[58] She feared, though, that parents would resent the fact that college life would be "so infinitely pleasanter . . . than home."[59]

In spite of insufficient funding, they plunged ahead. The plan was to rent a large house at Hitchen, a town near enough to Cambridge that professors could ride out there to teach, but removed from the distracting presence of the university undergraduates. In October, 1869, six students had been collected after eighteen undertook the first screening examination.

Miss Davies thought that one of the amenities the girls would appreciate most was privacy, a rare commodity in large English families, so plans at Hitchin, and later for the new building set up at Girton nearer Cambridge, included a separate bedroom and private sitting room for each student, where she could study alone or receive her friends. The students indeed enjoyed their life: someone described that first group as "the happiest women in England."[60] They took long walks in the country, they found an open air swimming bath, and it was only when they tried "football" on the lawn that the headmistress, supposed to exercise the same controls as a wise mother, called a halt.

The first real scandal, which nearly put an end to the college, came in 1871, when the girls donned male costumes to act scenes from Shakespeare for an audience consisting only of their professors, the mistresses, and the servants.[61] The actors were immediately called down. All Miss Davies' essential conservatism and jealous regard for the reputation of her college welled up in outrage, while the girls became extremely rebellious, feeling that they had the right as grown women to decide these things for themselves. One student, Emily Gibson, wondered if she ought not to leave the college in protest against tyranny, and she was only calmed down by Mme Bodichon, who was called in to compose the differences, and who said afterwards that she had never in all her life seen such a spirit of revolt and "such self-confidence."[62] She managed to win the students' compliance only by stressing the importance of not letting the experiment fail.*

In 1872, when the first three Hitchin girls were ready for the Tripos examination (the honors examination set for Cambridge undergraduates), the University Senate rejected a proposal to let them sit officially, but narrowly averted a vote that would have prevented university examiners from reading their papers privately. Not all professors were willing to do this, but enough readers were found to enable the testing to go forward. The three students, carefully chaperoned into Cambridge, passed that first test triumphantly. Back at Hitchin, when the news got out the girls hung flags and rang the alarm bell until the Hitchin fire engine galloped to the rescue.

Meanwhile, Miss Davies found herself in another important dispute, and here she was in the minority, the question being whether to move into the town of Cambridge, with all its advantages and all its assumed risks. Inconsistently enough, considering her shock at the trousers, Miss Davies believed that a move into a university town would restrict the girls' liberty. An aim of the college, she said, had been "that of giving to women an opportunity of laying out their own lives, in circumstances which may help them to lay them out wisely. Women have plenty of practice in submitting to little rules. We aim to give them the discipline of deciding for themselves."[63] The chance of meeting strange young men, she felt, would only make the women retreat into a shell of conventionality. At the same time she realized that the women tutors and mistresses in the growing college would benefit from the society of cultivated men. Mme Bodichon favored taking the plunge, for she feared the effects of isolation. And so the move was made, after renewed scrapings and scratchings for money, which again proved to be less forthcoming than had been hoped. The college assumed the name of Girton in September, 1873.

Miss Davies, having capitulated on this move, won a final policy dispute by her insistence that the girls take exactly the same curriculum as the university men. Her argument was controversial because male education itself was coming under attack as being rigid, outmoded, and arbitrary. Professor James Bryce (author of *The American Commonwealth*) wanted Girton to be set up from the start "with a higher standard than the contemptibly low one of Oxford and Cambridge."[64] He told Miss Davies that "in our view the course at your new College ought to be a model for men's Colleges to follow, instead of a slavish copy of their faults." It seemed pitiable that women would "have to walk the old worn-out roundabout roads where shorter and much better paved roads might

*The gymnasium outfits required at Girton in 1874 had full trousers to the ankle, covered by a skirt reaching two or three inches below the knee, and long sleeves. Even thus covered up, the young ladies could not be seen outside the gymnasium walls. Sports expanded, however: a bicycle club was started in 1894, a swimming club in 1901, and a boat club in 1906 (Barbara Stephen, *Girton*, 152).

pleasantly lead them to their goal."[65] In the course of the argument, John Seeley, a professor of modern history who had been one of the warmest supporters of the Hitchin experiment, resigned from the executive board of the new college. At Hitchin he had lectured on *Lycidas* and other subjects remote from the classical material tested in the Little Go examinations (the first test meted out to Cambridge undergraduates), so that the girls finally gave up listening to him because of the transcendent importance of passing the examination.*[66]

Miss Davies was adamant, and probably right. She insisted that any new curriculum initiated by women would automatically be branded as inferior, and when the girls passed the university examinations in stunningly high form, she was of course, vindicated.

One indirect result of Miss Davies' intransigence about the curriculum was the foundation of a second women's college, Newnham. Its origins lay in a set of extension lectures organized in 1867 by the North of England Council for Promoting the Higher Education of Women. These were delivered in various cities and were immensely popular.[67] (Professor James Stuart, a lecturer in astronomy, had puzzled over the impropriety of having young ladies to whom he had not been introduced asking him questions, or of his questioning them, and finally solved the difficulty by allowing them to hand up written questions. He examined them through written essays, which he graded conscientiously even though he got three hundred responses instead of the thirty he expected.) In 1869 Professor Henry Sidgwick conceived the idea of organizing lecture courses right in Cambridge; so many women wished to attend that the need was felt for a residence hall.[68] Miss Davies was consulted but refused at that time to budge her girls from Hitchen, and she especially disapproved because the Cambridge professors were trying to get the university to set up a special set of examinations just for women—anathema to her convictions. The Poll, the ordinary Cambridge final examination, was felt to be too easy for the girls, but no one was then sure that they could handle the Tripos. Furthermore, the organizers of Newnham were not going to require Latin and Greek in the course. The special examinations were soon given up, but Newnham College went forward.

For a long time women's admission to lectures and laboratories was kept unofficial, and the university libraries were off limits for them except on the same terms as for the general public.[69] Yet on this informal basis, access continued to grow. By 1873, twenty-two out of thirty-four university professors at Cambridge admitted women to their regular lectures,

---

*Seeley's criticism of the existing university curriculum is noteworthy:

We are discovering that instead of using the Classics to train reasoning power, to form literary taste, to convey political information, and to form habits of observation, all which things they can be made to do in a fashion, the proper way is to teach Logic, English, Political Philosophy, and Physical Science, and to do all these things directly and not indirectly. [Quoted in Barbara Stephen, *Emily Davies*, 197]

and Mr. Philip Main, of St. John's College, even rose early to admit girl students to his laboratory before breakfast.[70]

The key question for the women students at Oxford and Cambridge was whether they should be officially admitted to examinations, and if that was granted, whether they would be given regular degrees. The importance of the question was stated by *Punch*:

> In Arts, if once examiners be ours,
> To take degrees we must have equal powers;
>   The loss of these is as the loss of all.
> It is the little rift within the lute
> That soon will leave the Girton lecturer mute;
>   And, slowly emptying, silence Newnham Hall.[71]

But in 1878 the House of Commons overwhelmingly refused Cambridge University permission to admit women to its official examinations, even if the university wanted to do so.[72]

In 1881, however, women were admitted to the honors examination, and when, in 1887, Agnata Frances Ramsey (later Mrs. Montagu Butler) obtained a grade higher than any man on a paper that would have made her the Senior Classic. Miss Davies used the opportunity to push for the admission of women to university degrees. This plea was repeatedly rejected. By 1896, 525 students had attended Girton, of whom 370 had passed with honors by ordinary Cambridge standards, and 41 had completed work qualifying for the bachelor's degree, but they had to accept degrees, if they wanted them, from Dublin or London universities.[73]

One reason for the reluctance to give women degrees was that male graduates of the two ancient universities were entitled to an extra vote in the parliamentary elections to choose a member of the House of Commons from each. Cambridge compromised by allowing women to vote in the university convocation right after granting official permission to take the honors examinations, but it was not until much later that both Oxford (1919) and Cambridge (1921) gave women the right to titular degrees, caps, and gowns; and at Cambridge this did not include full membership in the university until 1948.*

Meanwhile, the first university in England to grant full degrees to women was London, which had been founded in 1828 to give university degrees to dissenters† and to cover a wider variety of modern subjects than the older universities seemed willing to do. In 1878, by means of a supplementary charter, London opened every degree, honor, and prize

---

*In 1882 and again in 1888, Oxford could not find any examiner in Spanish so well qualified as Mrs. Humphry Ward, who officiated as the first woman examiner of men, setting the papers, and reading and reporting on them (Mrs. H. Ward, *Recollections*, 2: 218).

†To get a degree from Oxford or Cambridge, one was required to take communion in the Church of England. London had no such requirement.

to both sexes on an equal basis.[74] And because it was an examining body for the whole country, it could grant degrees to students who had been trained outside London, like the Oxford and Cambridge women.*

∾ Getting girls prepared for college work was just as important as opening up the universities. In 1841 Dr. Arnold of Rugby wrote that the lack of any way to get girls examined made it difficult to give them intellectual training.[75] He taught Latin to his daughter, Jane, along with her brothers, but in the absence of something like the Degree Examination at a university, there was nothing to "concentrate" her reading, none of the machinery that made things work for boys.*

About sixteen years after Dr. Arnold's meditations, both Oxford and Cambridge set "local examinations" for boys who were not expected to become members of universities—in other words, middle-class boys—in order to set some kind of standard for middle-class schools and to act as a stimulus to them.[76] It seemed reasonable that girls might be declared eligible to take these tests with the same beneficial results. So in 1863 Cambridge agreed to have enough extra copies printed that a few girls might attempt them in an informal way. In all, eighty-four papers were given out for this purpose that year. The permission was given only six weeks before the actual date, so there was not much time to prepare, and the lamentable quality of arithmetic standards showed up in the failure of thirty-four out of forty senior girls, although the rate was somewhat better in the junior test.[77]

By 1865 the Cambridge locals were given in six cities to 126 girl candidates, and this time only 3 failed in arithmetic. Ninety passed in all subjects, and indeed later, when the examinations were regularized, girls turned out to have a somewhat lower failure rate than their brothers.†

Thus was forged the first link between girls and the universities, even though there lingered for years a certain prejudice even among schoolteachers. When, in the 1880s, Mary Vivian Hughes and her best friend told their headmistress that they would like to go out for the Oxford senior local, she assured them that it would be quite beyond their competence; nevertheless, by studying on their own *Macbeth*, Addison, and French, they did pass and became "Associates in Arts" of the University of Oxford.[78]

---

*In 1880 Annie Besant was studying chemistry and botany at London, and was proud of being the only woman in England who had taken honors in botany. Although difficulties arose that prevented her receiving her B.A., these were apparently based on her reputation as an atheist rather than on her sex. Thus she was refused permission to use the Royal Botanical Gardens in Regents Park because the curator felt that his daughters, who used to walk there, might be corrupted by her presence. A professor of chemistry told her flatly that no matter how brilliantly she did on an examination paper, he would never pass her because he considered her immoral (Nethercot, 179).

†Apparently he did not plan to teach Jane Greek, but he believed that girls were especially good at modern languages, so he hoped that Guizot's *History of France* could do for her something of what Aristotle did for boys.

Just about the time the local examinations were opening up, the government first acknowledged its responsibility for women's education. Parliament in 1864 was about to set up a Schools Inquiry Commission to consider the question of middle-class education.[79] Its mandate did not include scrutiny of girls' schools until Miss Davies organized a protest.* Evidence of the "unfathomable ignorance" of girls who had been to some of the so-called best schools, and of the actual incapacity of some of the headmistresses who had written to Cambridge about the local examinations, finally came to the attention of the Commission. Its 1867 report came out with a most unflattering view of the subject. Arithmetic was "always meagre and almost always unintelligent,"† the physical sciences were vulgarized, and there was a near-total lack of physical education.[80] At the same time, no natural ineptitude was found in the female sex; girls of seventeen usually exceeded boys in expressiveness. The Commission blamed parents for not demanding a higher standard of achievement for them.

The first two schools with stringent academic requirements, the North London Collegiate School and Cheltenham Ladies' College, had been founded in the previous decade, and their two headmistresses gave valuable testimony to the Schools Inquiry Commission. Frances Mary Buss of North London Collegiate was the pioneer in creating systematic secondary education, as opposed to the old style of girls' "finishing."

> The terrible sufferings of the women of my own class for want of a good elementary training have more than ever intensified my earnest desire to lighten, ever so little, the misery of women brought up "to be married and taken care of" and left alone in the world destitute. It is impossible for words to express my fixed determination of alleviating this evil.[81]

She had no rules to go by, and luckily could not adopt the methods of the boys' schools for "training character"—namely, corporal punishment and heavy reliance on games—so she had to devise new ways to make learning effective.[82]

Born in 1827 of a schoolteacher mother, Miss Buss was one of the early students at Queen's College.[83] From the age of fourteen she had been teaching in her mother's school, and the only time free for her own education was in the evening; since the buses did not run at those hours, she used to walk to her evening classes night after night. In 1850 she took her diploma and was ready to open (still at first in her own home) the North London Collegiate School, which became a model for all others. It eventually included an upper and a lower division, and special effort was made to attract girls whose families were unable to pay.

The other pioneer was Dorothea Beale, whose own education had

*When Miss Davies received a check for £10 for supervising the girls' examinations, it was the first money ever paid by Cambridge University to any woman for a service not menial (Barbara Stephen, *Emily Davies*, 102).

†Many elementary schools required of girls a lower standard in arithmetic than boys because of the many hours they were required to spend in sewing (Bremner, 47).

been cut short when her Paris finishing school closed during the 1848 revolution.[84] After that she studied and then taught for seven years at Queen's College, and in 1858 she was asked to take over Cheltenham, which had been founded a few years earlier. She was glad to make the change, partly because she felt that women were not sufficiently consulted about the management of Queen's. The governing board of Cheltenham was one of the first to elect men and women to membership on equal terms.

Miss Beale was particularly interested in educating the daughters of professional men, and the school became better known than Miss Buss's perhaps because it catered to a higher social class. The school had a kindergarten attached, and could take a girl right through to London University. It came to number over a thousand students, much the largest girls' school in England, and it was always known for the excellence of its teaching.*

Under the stimuli of the local examinations, the Schools Inquiry Commission, and the examples of Miss Beale and Miss Buss, it was not long before more schools were founded.† Many of them sprang out of the efforts of the Girls Public Day School Company, begun in 1872 largely by the work of Mrs. Maria Grey and her sister Miss Emily Shirreff, who wanted an organization to provide equal access for girls "to the education considered best for human beings."[85] Miss Buss had turned her institution into the first public (that is, non-proprietary) school for girls in 1870, after getting several friends to sign the trust agreement and with financial help from the London Brewers and Clothworkers. The Day School Company went on for years, never failing to pay a 5 percent dividend to its stockholders but plowing any profit beyond that back into the schools.[86] Fifteen schools were founded in its first five years, and before it ceased activity, thirty-four in all had arisen. Although they made a point of being open to various social classes and religious sects, the mixing produced much less difficulty than had been foreseen.[87]

༺ As plans for better schools and even colleges for women began to take shape in the middle of the century, the opposition focused on the horrible physical consequences to be expected.[88] Dr. Edward Clarke of Harvard led the charge, in 1873, by announcing that higher education was

---

*In 1904 I. A. R. Wylie attended it, and remembered playing hockey in ankle-length skirts and being rushed from the field when a class from a boys' school appeared to watch. Miss Beale she recalled as "a marvellous, very deaf old lady who rode her tricycle recklessly through Cheltenham traffic" (I. A. R. Wylie, *My Life*, 116).

†The lack of equal treatment for the heads of boys' and girls' schools is shown in the remuneration given. The average pay of the certified headmaster in 1870 was £94 per year, and by 1895 it had risen to £137. Meanwhile, the certified headmistress earned £57 in 1870, and £87 by 1895 (Bremner, 44).

destroying the reproductive functions; and his argument was picked up in Britain the following year by Dr. Henry Maudesley, who declared in one article, "The price of female intellectual work will be the peril of giving birth to a race of puny and enfeebled children."[89] As a mental specialist Dr. Maudesley was entitled to a hearing, but Dr. Elizabeth Garrett Anderson responded immediately that it was not brain work, but lack of physical development, that injured women, and that what they needed was not less study, but more games and gymnasium work. Reviewing this exchange in 1887, the *Edinburgh Review* commented smartly that there were at that time no broken-down women at Oxford or Cambridge, and it was soon discovered that while university women were less likely to marry than their sisters, when they did, they produced the same number of healthy children.[90]

All through the last decades of the nineteenth century, the impression one gets of the women at Oxford and Cambridge is that they were happy and healthy. Girton made a point of liberality at its table, and the girls believed in exercise—riding, walking, tennis. Many must have lived like Mary Vivian Hughes, who describes her life there in the 1880s as wonderfully free and busy, with long walks, much intellectual companionship, exhilarating dances, and merry cocoa parties.[91]

American colleges were widely used as models of what could be done. In France, Emile de Girardin had cited the experience of Antioch and Oberlin as proof that intelligence had no sex, and disproof of the old notion that men were better at abstract and women at concrete subjects;[92] and Emile Acollas announced, in a ringing defense of female brains, that girls actually did better than boys at Oberlin.[93] When the Amberleys visited America in 1867, they toured Oberlin and also Vassar, which particularly charmed Kate Amberley. (When she got to Boston, she persistently asked all the young girls she met why they did not go to Vassar, only to be told firmly by a young married woman that no society girl would think of going to college, that Vassar was populated exclusively by the daughters of mechanics and ministers.[94])

This line of attack was copied in England, in the fear that women might to to college for some unfashionable purpose, such a making money. Frances Power Cobbe worried about this; she agreed that the competitive examinations introduced an unhealthy element of ulterior motive, which she felt had been absent in her own remembered childhood of pure intellectual desire.[95] Even Catherine Winkworth, hungry as she was for knowledge, was at first repelled by the idea of a college for women, "except for teachers and very exceptionally clever and studious girls," though she got over her dislike and became in 1870 secretary of the Committee to Promote the Higher Education of Women.[96]

The notion that women's nature was very different from men's had a strong hold in England, and a cheap and easy way to discount the whole operation of higher education was satire. Max O'Rell explained that the colleges and girls' public schools had "the object of stripping women of the attributes" that made them attractive—no more kisses on the eyelids, for your wife will wear spectacles.[97] Or, as *Punch* expressed it in 1884:

> The Woman of the Future! She'll be deeply read, that's certain,
> With all the education gained at Newnham or at Girton;
> She'll puzzle men in Algebra with horrible quadratics,
> Dynamics, and the mysteries of higher mathematics;
> Or, if she turn to classic tomes a literary roamer,
> She'll give you bits from Horace or sonorous lines from Homer.
>
> . . . .
>
> O pedants of these later days, who go on undiscerning
> To overload a woman's brain and crown our girls with learning,
> You'll make a woman half a man, the souls of parents vexing,
> To find that all the gentle sex this process is unsexing,
> Leave one or two nice girls before the sex your system smothers,
> Or what on earth will poor men do for sweethearts, wives, and mothers?[98]

As girls continued to win high rank in the examinations and prove that they were not in any way inferior academically to the best men, opposition was stilled. In 1881 Miss C. A. Scott obtained a rank that would have made her, if a man, the eighth Wrangler (the Wranglers were the mathematical honors men at Cambridge), and she was topped by Miss Philippa Fawcett, of Newnham, who in 1890 was declared (unofficially, of course) to be above the Senior Wrangler.[99] It is a credit to the undergraduates that when this fact was announced, they cheered and made way for her to pass down the hall.[100] And even *Punch* redeemed his former jibes:

> Many a male who failed to pass
> Will hear it with flushed face and jaw set,
> But *Mr. Punch* brims high his glass,
> And drinks your health, Miss P. G. Fawcett![101]

℘31.

"Independent, Clever Women"

Cries are heard on every hand that women are conspiring, that women are discontented, that women are idle, that women are overworked, and that women are out of their sphere. God only knows what is the sphere of any human being.

Again, we hear cries that the world is going wrong for want of women; that moral progress cannot be made without their help; that Science wants their delicate perceptions; that Moral Philosophy wants the light of their peculiar point of view; Political Economy, their direction of judgment and sympathy with the commonality; Government, the help of their power of organizing; and Philanthropy, their delicate tact. Hospitals must have them, asserts one; Watches must be made by them, cries another; Workhouses, Prisons, Schools, Reformatories, Penitentiaries, Sanatoriums, are going to rack and ruin for want of them, the Arts and Manufactures invite them.

One great corresponding cry rises from a suffering multitude of women, saying, "We want work."

Barbara Leigh Smith Bodichon, 1857

If a twentieth-century woman wants to justify working outside her home, the obvious excuse is the wish to make money. This answer seems practical, sensible, and irrefutable—no matter what additional drives may be moving her. In the nineteenth century, the need to earn money was so much something to be ashamed of that the justification for working was often couched in terms of the good to be accomplished or the talents to be exercised—no matter how gratifying payment might actually be.

No one can read about these women without realizing what an enormous amount of energy was dammed up in them. "The very thought of doing work is like a draught of desert springs to me,"[1] cries Meredith's Diana, while Charlotte Brontë's *Shirley* includes this dialogue:

"Caroline," demanded Miss Keeldar abruptly, "don't you wish you had a profession—a trade?"

483

"I wish it fifty times a day. As it is, I often wonder what I came into the world for. I long to have something absorbing and compulsory to fill my head and hands, and to occupy my thoughts."[2]

To move from fiction to reality, Florence Nightingale, who until she was thirty suffered more than most from enforced inconsequentiality, wrote that men were irritated with women for not being happy; they must act the farce of having no passions, she fumed, and yet they did have passions, intellect, and a sense of moral activity, but no place in society where any one of these things could be exercised.

Examples abound of women whose talents were wasted, or whose energies turned to destruction—women like Jane Carlyle, who impressed all who met her with her enormous unvented potentiality,[3] or the infamous Madeleine Smith, whose biographer believes she was led to murder for lack of any normal way to exercise her sexual and intellectual powers.[4]

Mrs. Jameson attributed the conversions of many Englishwomen to Roman Catholicism to the possibility offered within its religious communities for service at very high levels.[5] (In the 1830s there were no convents in London; by the 1850s seventeen Roman Catholic religious houses for women had opened, and at the same time there was a revival of sisterhoods within the Anglican Church.)[6] She compared the difficulties under which Englishwomen operated to those confronting a Chinese woman walking with her bound feet. "What God made natural, graceful, and easy is rendered a matter of pain and difficulty."[7]

The psychological barriers that have since been largely swept away are now easy to ridicule, but at the time they were serious hurdles indeed. Unless we take them seriously, it is hard to understand what women who wanted to be useful had to go through.

There was the fact that the ordinary course of a woman's day was splintered into small housekeeping duties and small social duties, such as paying calls. Frances Power Cobbe was a serious writer by the age of thirty-three; yet after running the house for her father, amusing the old man, teaching in the village school two days each week, and attending to every case of illness or sorrow in their two villages, she could find time to write the preface for her book only when a cold kept her from accompanying her father to the theater.[8] It was often observed, in fact, that when summoned for the sort of major crisis that everyone could understand, such as illness or some other disaster, women were at their best, "revived by practical reality," as Miss Nightingale put it.*[9]

---

*It struck Miss Nightingale that it would seem very odd to see men sitting around doing worsted work (Ray Strachey, 400). To change the figure, Augusta Webster deplored the way in which acquaintances could "make tatters of her time" (Webster, 161). (Neither was able to follow the counsel of a certain Englishman who once explained how he got so much done. He said that if you have a bushel basket, and put two or three cannon balls in it, you can then fit some tennis balls in between, then fill up the holes with walnuts, and after that you can still find room to pour in quite a lot of sand. But if you start with sand or walnuts, there will never be room for the cannon balls.

It was all too easy for girls left alone with their imaginations to retreat to fantasy, a vice often regarded as their besetting temptation. Dreaming could become a substitute for action, and the natural psychological defense was apathy.[10]

Then there was the real lack of training, not only in specific educational disciplines, but in the general habit of getting on with one's work. Men—or women—who watched "the confused inanities of a ladies' committee" could find excuse enough for not charging other women with high responsibilities.[11]

One needs to remember also the extreme dependence of these women on men. Men controlled far more of the channels to money, love, and jobs than they do at present, and they were inclined to make snap judgments based on general prejudice rather than try to understand any particular woman's dilemma. It is always unnerving to set another person free. In 1926 Count Keyserling would find that "love" had been destroyed in America by women's independence, and America was widely believed to show the troubled path which Europe was destined to follow.[12]

A major drawback was certainly the squeamishness about money—a feeling that many of the early pioneers had somehow to overcome before they could accomplish anything. Thus Mrs. Jameson describes Miss Nightingale's lack of a need for money as a special grace, "a profound consolation" to those who thought about her service,[13] as if payment would have detracted from the romance or value of her work.

The emotional intensity with which parents, fathers in particular, kept their daughters from earning money indicates that their own self-images were at stake. Though the suffering they caused is incalculable, they seemed never to have considered it. Ethel Smyth's father declared that he would sooner see her "under the sod" than off to Leipzig to study music professionally.[14] When Charlotte Yonge announced to her parents that she was about to publish a novel, they called a family council, largely out of horror that she might make some financial profit.[15] Her books, of course, became enormously successful, and her parents finally became reconciled to her career, so long as her royalties went to a good cause. Asked what she would have done if forbidden to publish, she responded quickly, "Oh, I *must* have written; but I should never have published—at least not for many years."[16] Sophia Jex-Blake's father was indignant that she considered acting like a member of a social class beneath her by accepting a salary for teaching mathematics at one of the new women's colleges in London.*[17]

---

*In an American advice book of 1856, a Mrs. Burgess is represented as saying that it would make her feel good to earn some money, and be better for her health and spirits than living as she had been doing. Mr. Burgess responded predictably that he did not wish to have a slave in his house, soiling her hands with labor. Secretly, however, she began to make caps, earning three hundred dollars, which came in so handy when his business failed that they lived happily ever after by working together (Timothy Arthur, 122). This little tale shows a certain American spirit of enterprise.

The social sanctions that could be applied against ladies who did take money are exemplified in the case of a Quaker, a Mrs. Knowles, who invented a kind of worsted work with which she made a portrait of King George III. The customary *quid pro quo* from the court would have been an elegant jewel, but since her religion forbade jewelry, she was asked what she could accept. She answered, in friendly simplicity, money. The Queen came to the conclusion that she was "no lady," and she was never asked to court again.[18] Most people did not get to court, naturally, but even so sympathetic a person as Mrs. Gaskell looked down on Miss Mulock because the latter was driven to write by economic necessity.*[19] Mrs. Ellis summed up the conventional view for her advice seekers: a man could undertake degrading work and still be a gentleman at home, but a woman who touched "trade" would lose caste in that moment.†[20]

All the pressures against professionalism are exhibited in the case of Harriet Danvers (*A Book With Seven Seals*), as Harriet's sister remembered it.

> Harriet . . . decided to Be, to Do, or to Suffer, as for instance: To be a great singer like Jenny Lind; or a hospital nurse like Sister Dora; to do great things in either profession as the case might be, and, if need be, to suffer the righteous anger of her relations in consequence.
>
> Her mother's frequent lament was, "I cannot conceive how a daughter of mine can dream of dragging our name down to the level of the lower classes!"
>
> "Then I must change it," Hetty would retort. "I suppose if I don't marry I shall have to earn my living sooner or later. Molly is treading on my heels, and Charlotte and Emily are looming in the background, besides the three boys to educate and send to college."
>
> "Harriet, though you are my child, it grieves me to say that you always had a disposition to be vulgar," said Mrs. Danvers in a tone of resignation. "I cannot imagine where you get such ideas. It must be from your associates in the parish."
>
> . . . "Well, then, may I try for a Scholarship at the Academy of Music?" asked Hetty eagerly. "If I get one it would probably cover the expenses of my training."
>
> Her father smiled and said, "That depends on what it would lead to—if you got one."
>
> "It would mean free training for the profession," replied Harriet promptly.
>
> "That I will never consent to!" declared Mrs. Danvers with decision.
>
> "Well then, may I go and be trained at a hospital for a nurse?" sighed Hetty. "That would cost nothing, and I must do something in the world."

*In the conversation quoted above between Shirley and Caroline in the Brontë novel, the girls go on to consider whether work would make a woman "coarse," a favorite adjective of the period. Caroline retorted that if a woman was not to be married, it mattered little if she was elegant, only if she was neat and clean.

†Compare the remark in the *Encyclopaedia of the Social Sciences* in the article on "Gentlemen": "The sentiments attaching to occupation are very violent" (6:617). Arthur Livingston, the author, was talking about how no gentleman worked for a living, but the violence seems to have been redoubled when women's occupations were under consideration.

"It would be worse still," said her mother, "You must be content to stay at home like other girls, and help me with the younger ones until you are old enough to marry. There is nursing to be done, and music to teach here, besides the necessity of setting your sisters a good example."

"Oh, Papa!" cried Hetty in desperation. "Why mayn't I go out and do something? There are such limitations at home, and I don't want to be married: I want to be free to do as I please with my life."

The Parson paused before he replied, and ladled out another wineglass of toddy. Then he said, "Well, at any rate I see no harm in your trying for a scholarship if you want to," adding with his humorous smile, "It's ten to one you won't get it."

His wife moaned in despair. "It is always the way: I have no voice in the matter!"

"That depends, my dear," said her husband. "Let her get the scholarship first."

. . . And she did get it. . . .

Harriet had more than her share of assurance to carry her through the world, and she came home radiant to dinner.

Some days later the Scholarship was offered to her on condition that her voice should be trained for professional singing.

The same evening Mr. Danvers called Hetty down to his den for a talk.

"Papa, you won't let mamma stand in the way, will you?" she began eagerly. "I should just love to be a public singer! Think of the money I could earn, and the good I could do with it! Send the boys to college and be off your hands myself."

"Yes, my dear Pussy, that sounds all very well to look forward to," said her father presently as he drew long puffs at his pipe, "but there are other things to be taken into consideration, you know. Mamma and I would not like our daughters to earn their own living, and we trust that it may never be necessary for them to do so."[21]

∽ In spite of the delicacy of their feelings, British women were roused out of their prudery about money by the constantly growing numbers of them who needed self-support. Sufficient financial pressure made even hardheaded fathers compromise their principles. Already in 1857 John Duguid Milne had voiced the opinion that unmarried women should be treated socially just like men,[22] and William Lovett, the labor leader, advocated that women without husbands should be completely free to earn their living in any business they chose.[23] But public opinion became agitated when the census figures of 1851 were interpreted as meaning that England supported a surplus of half a million women, or, as it was often put, one out of three marriageable girls was "doomed" to remain unwed.*[24] Articles began to appear with titles like "My Life and What Shall I Do With It? By an Old Maid," and both women and their families began to wonder if there might not be more ways for them to support

*The introduction to the British census of 1851 listed 10,386,048 males to 10,735,919 females. Counting the soldiers and sailors away from home, the census-takers figured on an excess of females of 512,361. This was the figure picked up by the feminists who were eager to prove the need to do something to help these women.

themselves than by becoming governesses, as twenty-five thousand had already done. In 1855 Anna Jameson studied the census figures and startled the country with the information that three-fourths of the unmarried women in it already lived on their own earnings,[25] and as the early feminists plowed into the facts, they found that an even greater number of wives were supporting husbands, though this style of living had not penetrated the class that was likely to be reading about it. Augusta Webster explained how they took the news:

> The fact that the matrimonial means of livelihood is, in these days, only open to two women out of three, though now pretty generally known, is still only known like such an outside-our-sphere matter as the distance of the sun from the earth, no calculation or miscalculation about which affects our ideas on the household window-blinds.[26]

But the 1861 census made things look even worse, finding 1,537,314 unmarried women over twenty, and 756,438 widows. Even the *Times* came out, on May 28, 1870 in favor of education and jobs for unmarried women.[27]

By the 1880s work before marriage came to be seen as respectable in certain circumstances, but it took a world war to make work after marriage equally so. "Prosperity" for women had been defined in 1868 by Jessie Boucherett as the ability of an unmarried woman to get "an honest livelihood in an ordinary day's work of twelve hours," and of a married one to be supported by a husband without being called upon to work outside her own house.[28] The feeling that "married life is a woman's profession" hung on, even after the corollary that an old maid has "failed in business" had been done away with.[29] Frances Power Cobbe hinted delicately that while it would be undesirable for a woman to pursue her premarital profession during marriage, it might provide a resource should she become a widow,[30] but the more common view was that the care of ten children would be more pressing and more interesting.[31] However distinguished a young woman's performance, like that of Miss Ramsey, who won the highest honors in the classical Tripos at Cambridge and afterward received an appointment as tutor at Girton, it seemed to everybody a matter of course that she would be "lost to Girton" by her 1889 marriage.[32]

Yet married women suffered from the same hunger for the satisfactions that only work can give. Miss Davies noticed how often wives applied for jobs as the secretary to some charity, giving loneliness and want of enough to do as their reasons.*[33]

Of course, women had commonly felt a certain pride in other women who had coped with financial problems better than members of

---

*Dr. Drysdale observed that among the lower classes, where there was less enforced leisure and women were more able to help their husbands at work, the women were more dignified and independent than their social superiors, and their children did not suffer so much from hovering closeness.

their sex were supposed to do. Their numbers were not few. Mary Howitt remembered from her girlhood a "poor Miss Grace," a lady in reduced circumstances who introduced the manufacture of a kind of lacework and became "one of the earliest of that race of independent, clever women who have given a marked character to the present century."[34] One thinks of the Taylor family of Ongar, where "the delightful Jane Taylor and her sisters" paid their share of the family expenses by engraving,[35] or of the two orphaned sisters described by Henry Craik, who chose to take over their father's business instead of going out in the expected path as governesses.[36] They managed to keep the books, hire agents, and maintain their mother in ease. Then there was Maria Edgeworth, who for sixty years collected the rents and oversaw land improvements and the building of new cottages on her father's estate, though it had been left, in accordance with the custom of the day, to an improvident brother. She did this while maintaining a deferential attitude toward the titular heads of the family. In 1852 Augusta Witherspoon, a friend of the Cloughs, was thirty years ahead of her time in deciding to earn her own "portion" by teaching for a year or two to make up the sum needed to marry.

In her novel *Cranford*, Mrs. Gaskell sums up the pathos and the heroism with which Miss Matty, having lost her fortune in a bank failure, faces the world. She is too ignorant to teach, she cannot spell, or even sew, but her friends arrange for her to sell tea in a small shop, everyone silently helping, while she pays off in gold the notes of the bank of which she was a stockholder.[37]

∽ At first every foray had to be an individual one; every woman who wished to break through the barriers had to find her own way to do it, the weak spot in the defense, the strong spot in her character, to seize what advantages she could, and then perhaps to lend a hand to her struggling sisters.

The first work that pulled them out of their homes was often charity. However dubious the results measured by actual amelioration of conditions, the effort was certainly bracing to the individuals who performed it, for it opened their eyes to social conditions, expanded their interests, and eventually made them perceive the need for more knowledge. This led to opening a crack in the door to higher education and, as they acquired expertise, to insisting that women should be listened to in the discussion of public affairs. One reason that charitable work was so easy to slip into was that, at first at least, it did not involve the lady in money-grubbing activities.

The push toward philanthropy was started by early advisers like Hannah More. Her invaluable *Coelebs* expounds the proper attitude for a lady, though inadvertently admitting that even in 1809 some women were wondering why they were excluded from male professions. Mrs. Stanley explains to Coelebs, her expected son-in-law, as she takes him on her rounds, "I have often heard it regretted that ladies have no stated employment, no profession. It is a mistake. *Charity is the calling of a lady; the care of the poor is her profession.* Men have little time or taste for details."[38] And she goes on to decry the attitudes of those who will not meet disease and dirt head-on, or who satisfy their need to help the poor by buying flowers at a charity bazaar.

The sort of visiting she recommended could be organized. For example, in 1853 Catherine Winkworth's parish was divided among the ladies in such a way that Catherine and her sister were assigned forty houses, and they called at each house once a week, lending out church literature and collecting money for a Provident Club. One of Catherine's beneficiaries, a weaver, remarked, "Well, I have always wondered what ladies was made for; I thought them such useless beings; but now I've found out they're the best of good company. . . . I'd liefer hear her talk even than to to the public house!"[39] Once she had to persuade a couple with seven children to marry, and she noted with satisfaction that after this step was taken, their house became cleaner and more respectable.

Apart from visiting cottages, a much-approved and widely pursued activity was running Sunday schools. Credit for this idea too goes largely to Hannah More. Hannah More herself was not without courage; she was persecuted at first as much for her wish to teach the poor to read as for supporting William Wilberforce in his anti-slavery campaign and his unpatriotic wish to make peace with France.[40] By the 1820s there were sixty-two thousand Sunday school teachers in England.[41] Girls like Charlotte Yonge took up the activity eagerly. Charlotte's mother had started a school in 1826, rehabilitating a building and engaging an old servant to teach reading and arithmetic. Charlotte was early assigned to teach the catechism and kept up the work for over seventy years.[42]

Prince Pückler has a beautiful picture of a birthday party at Cobham Hall, with supper on the lawn for all the tenants, and fifty little girls from her ladyship's school, dressed in white, who marched in for tea and cakes.[43] Or again, Lady Shelley talks of taking her daughter to the village school on daily visits, and how good the experience was for her.[44] It may even had helped the scholars. Baring-Gould testified that he had seen rude country bumpkins humanized by attending night school conducted by the rector's daughter.[45]

Such work was harder to do in the cities, of course, though Mrs. Gaskell was said to be a skillful teacher of both boys and girls in Sunday and day schools in Manchester,[46] while Kate Amberley in her first year of marriage took on a class of sixteen factory girls in Gloucester, whom she instructed about the value of fresh air and the harm of tight lacing. Meanwhile, Lord Amberley taught the young men of the area, and together the Amberleys planned to open a public library.[47]

It was natural for such eager almsgivers to want to improve their techniques and learn from the experience of others; nor did they lack for teachers. The general tone is well set out by Charles Kingsley in an 1855 lecture precisely on the subject of women's work in a country parish. The first duty, as he saw it, after that to their own family, was to their domestic servants. The difficulty in this approach was that it might be harder to remain friendly with a person one saw every day than with a distant poor family; and ladies might fear that the servants would take liberties if one got too personal, but Kingsley assured them that this could be avoided by a high standard of self-restraint. After her own household, a lady's next concern should be with her husband's workmen or tenants. Such problems as drainage or sound roofing could only be tackled with the help of the men in the family, of course, but if they proved recalcitrant, Kingsley's advice was that the ladies should go on strike: "If you will not new-roof that cottage, if you will not make that drain, I will. I will not buy a new dress till it is done." But, he went on, what do you do if you want the enjoyment of doing good with your own hands? One easy first step would be to start a club, a particularly suitable activity for unmarried daughters, who would get good training in management with less undesirable contact than was involved in home visiting; that had best be left to mature married women. As for schools, these should be the crown of your labors, the best activity of all—and by all means, let ladies take on the job of teaching *boys*, for only from a lady could they learn courtesy and gentleness.[48]

It seems as if the tenants or pupils would also be heavily steeped in deference. On almost every page ladies are advised not to let down the bars completely, while seeming to act as a sister. (In visiting a tenant, do not let her stand in your presence; on the other hand, never take her for a ride in your carriage.) The attitude prescribed and the deference expected are caught in an episode from *A Book With Seven Seals*, where the two little girls' grandmother takes them out for indoctrination. This gracious lady is carrying bottles of once-used tea leaves to the village needy. Harriet supposes that their grateful recipients will use them to lay the dust when sweeping the floor. Mrs. Jackson quickly disembarrasses her of this idea.

> "My dears," said Mrs. Jackson, "they are too precious to be wasted for that purpose. With tea at the price it is, I find that very few of the poor people can afford to buy it; and some are thankful to receive what we have already made use of, which is better than having none at all."
>
> "But don't you ever give them any real tea, Grandmamma?" enquired Harriet.
>
> "No, my child," replied Mrs. Jackson, "it would not be right to encourage the working classes to indulge in luxuries which are beyond their means. It would only make them discontented with their lot."

As they proceed on their mission, they meet with a group of children playing a noisy game, who stop and stare at Hetty and Mary Anne, thereby incurring the advice of Mrs. Jackson.

> "The first thing you should be taught at school, is to curtsey to your betters," said Mrs. Jackson. "Now let these young ladies see if you have learned to do so, for if not, you have certainly come home fools."

The three older girls proceeded solemnly to bob up and down.

"That is right. Now show your little sisters how to behave to ladies when you see them—so—like good children," said the old lady.

One more aspect of their good deeds is shown in the next visit.

Mrs. Billings was gossiping with a neighbour at her gate. She invited the ladies to walk in; but Mrs. Jackson was not in the habit of entering the cottages she visited. A few words in season, exchanged outside, on the important questions of health, cleanliness and Godliness, as the case demanded, and a request that the pickle-bottle might be returned when empty, for further favors, sufficed for the occasion.

"Mrs. Billings is a born grumbler," she remarked, as she wended her way to Miss Tinkler a few doors further on. "She is never satisfied with the weather or her condition in life, and is seldom grateful for what she receives."

Mrs. Billings had declined the tea-leaves with thanks, having been presented with a quarter-pound packet of real tea the day before by the Rector's lady.[49]

In ways like this, voluntary social service came to seem one of the pillars of a stable social system;[50] it was what kept the upper class from becoming parasitic. No one worried in the early days if it kept the lower class parasitic, but slowly the practitioners of charity began to develop a set of new insights. Lucy Aiken was one of the first to point out that "a positive demand for misery was created by the incessant eagerness manifested to relieve it,"[51] and others noticed that coercing virtue in the recipients of philanthropy deprived them of the moral experience of combatting sin unaided. (Such coercion could start very young; thus Dickens in *Bleak House* shows us a five-year-old who had to give all his allowance to the Infant Bonds of Joy.) Certain girls reported to Mrs. Ellis that their schools did not really teach, and that their benevolence did not really seem to relive misery.*[52] They began to get an inkling of the fact that because they stood so determinedly outside the industrial system, their labors did not do much to change conditions within it.[53]

A certain impetus was given to this critique of charity by political economists who preached that all philanthropy was evil because it somehow jiggled the invisible hand that would otherwise distribute money exactly where it ought to go. Harriet Martineau was a famous exponent of this point of view and preached to her readers that it might be all right to give money for *education*, because that enabled people to rise on their own, and for the sort of hospitals that took care of *accidents*, which could

---

*Millicent Fawcett's moment of revolt came when she overheard two clergymen's wives at a bazaar. "What do you find that sells best?" "Oh, things that are really useful, such as butterflies for the hair" (Fawcett, 117). The general lack of effectiveness in early English charitable work was noticed by the Italian Olimpia Savio-Rossi, who attributed it to the absence of large-scale, full-time organizations run by experienced Sisters of Charity (Savio, *Studii . . . la Donna*).

occur regardless of merit; but to relieve the merely sick would interfere with nature's wish to winnow the race, and simple handouts of relief were the worst charity of all. Poverty was seen at mid-century as part of the natural law, instead of being the will of God, as it had a few years earlier. Later still it would come to seem a national disgrace, but this would require far different means of relief. Beatrice Webb delivered the judgment that charity is twice cursed; it curseth him that gives and him that takes. She also observed that the 1850s were the years in which the great change was made from missionary work to more professional endeavor.[54]

The new type of social work was professional in the sense that its practitioners studied their problem, evaluated its effects, and then formed organizations, hired office space, distributed literature, raised money, and wrote papers about their work; but for a long time it was not professional in that most of the workers remained unpaid volunteers.

One of the first of these new philanthropists was Mary Carpenter, who began working with the poor children of Bristol and who coined two memorable phrases: "juvenile delinquency," which is still current, and "ragged schools," which today sounds, to say the least, quaint.[55] She opened her first such school in 1846, and soon was writing scholarly articles on the prevention of delinquency and delivering evidence to parliamentary commissions.

Another early pioneer was Caroline Chisholm, who assumed the task of encouraging women to emigrate to the colonies.[56] This was supposed to relieve the surplus of single women in England and provide wives for the young men who had gone out to Canada or Australia. Caroline was so certain of what she wanted to do that when Archibald Chisholm proposed to her, she made him take a month to decide whether he really wanted to take on a wife who guaranteed that she would not take care of her domestic affairs until her public duties had been attended to. He took the chance and supported her efforts, even when she took long voyages to the wildest parts of Australia to escort parties of girls, staying until the last girl had found a home. (Dickens is said to have modeled Mrs. Jellyby on Caroline Chisholm, whose neglect of her home duties disgusted him.)

Literally hundreds of private agencies for charity existed in the Britain of the 1850s, not all of which, of course, typified the kind of enlightened approach that Mary Carpenter and her sort were beginning to organize. But they went into every kind of problem, kindness to animals, reform of workhouses, creation of jobs, training for jobs, rehabilitation of prostitutes, improved housing. No one who wanted a cause could lack one to her taste, and they all led inexorably to the need for public action of a kind that no group of mere volunteers could provide.

Among this group of women the most notable was Josephine Butler, who led a crusade against official regulation of prostitution. She was fortunate in her antecedents, birth, upbringing, education, marriage, family, and friends. She could have chosen to do nothing all her life instead of embarking on a career that subjected her to exhaustion, abuse, and misunderstanding.[57] As one of eight children in a home where the girls were considered as able as the boys were to ride a horse or to carry on intellectual conversation with the parents' guests, she read the Parliamentary Blue Books, official reports on social problems, with her father and then walked around the countryside with him to study poverty at first hand.[58] Her adolescence was stormy, like many an idealistic girl's, full of horror at the evils of the world and self-reproach that she could do so little about them, but she became more realistic when she married George Butler, a clergyman and teacher, profoundly suited to her, and one who appreciated and supported her intense feelings and radical plans. In the early days when they were living at Oxford, she helped him prepare an edition of Chaucer and became the first woman admitted to the Bodleian. Her natural feminism was shocked, however, to realize that this permission was controversial and conceded grudgingly. At Oxford, too, she read Mrs. Gaskell's *Ruth*, defending the book against a lecturer who stated that he would not let his own mother read such a story of a fallen woman.

Not only in this novel but also in life, the rank double standard troubled her, and she began to seek out women penalized by the system, taking one convicted of infanticide from prison and training her as a house servant. She appalled the sanctimonious Dr. Jowett by quoting Blake when he commented that she "takes an interest in a class of sinners whom she had better have left to themselves."[59] By 1860 Josephine was glad to escape from Oxford's heavily masculine society to the freer air of Liverpool, where her husband headed a school. The loss of a child gave her the impetus, as it did to so many women of her time, to move outward. She found the need to help people whose pain was deeper than her own.

A natural place to hunt for suffering was in the women's prisons, and fortunately her cousin was trying to organize missions there. She introduced Josephine to some inmates who were engaged in picking oakum. Silently Josephine sat on the floor beside them and began picking too. Then she began to read the Bible aloud and to lead them in prayer.

Even though her husband was the headmaster of a school, Mrs. Butler did not shrink from taking sick prostitutes into her own home to nurse them, and it was remarked that Mr. Butler met them at the door as if they were ladies and offered them his arm to escort them to their rooms.

In 1864 a law was passed requiring the medical inspection and licensing of prostitutes in certain towns frequented by the Royal Navy. Police, doctors, and military men had long favored such a law, and one had been scheduled during the early years of Victoria's reign until Her Majesty's ministers realized that they could not bring such a bill to their young sovereign for signature.[60] Later on Prince Albert was known to disapprove of the bill, but it was finally passed after his death. This so-called Contagious Diseases Act allowed a judge or policeman to declare a person to be a prostitute without any evidence. Mrs. Butler realized that her life's calling would be to resist that, though at first she tried to work on less controversial issues such as higher education for women. Suffering from self-doubt and afraid of the opposition she would arouse, she finally went to Mr. Butler and told him that she *must* go out into the streets and cry aloud, or else her heart would break, to which his response was a simple "God bless you."[61] Although his life was never free of anxiety about his wife, he endured it all silently; as for her, she found getting into her work a joyful relief after the period of waiting and wondering. And after fifteen years of struggle, the obnoxious law was repealed in 1883.

Although many reformers were opposed to prostitution, Josephine Butler was notable for her compassion for the women themselves. It seems that Miss Martineau did not want to provide for the "animality of men," and Miss Nightingale was opposed to the law on the grounds of its medical uselessness.[62] Mrs. Butler, who actually went into a soldier's brothel and observed the hundred girls sitting around dully, was moved by outrage at the injustice to the victims.

After writing to every member of Parliament and getting only half a dozen faintly sympathetic responses, Josephine went out among the working people, whose daughters became prostitutes, and there she found her natural helpers. "The awful abundance of compassion . . . makes me fierce,"[63] she said. Her self-imposed schedule was formidable. In 1872 she attended ninety-nine meetings, traveling around England on third-class carriages. She was rebuked at a church Congress by the Archbishop of York for trying to discuss what came to be called "The Cause" and was forbidden by her old antagonist Benjamin Jowett to address university men at Oxford.[64] But what seemed to her most illogical was that ladies should be kept from knowing about the laws passed by men concerning their weaker sisters, because she believed that it was women's blindness that condemned so many to the life of shame.* In 1869 a petition signed by over two thousand women, including Florence Nightingale, Harriet Martineau, Mary Carpenter, and a number of Quakers, was said to have greatly embarrassed Parliament.[65]

Mrs. Butler's program involved setting up voluntary hospitals, teaching women of her own class that there was no impassable gulf

---

*The force of the Victorian conscience should not be underestimated. Sometimes it required facing very disagreeable facts. Mrs. George Moberly, wife of the Bishop of Salisbury, was asked to conduct a meeting about the Contagious Diseases Act: "Perhaps no living person had ever been more averse to approaching such a subject. Sensitive in the highest degree to the hatefulness of women knowing enough of the subject to be able to carry out organized help, and keenly distressed to think that in order to lessen the terrible evil an association would have to be formed involving talk about it." Yet, her religious feeling overcame her almost overwhelming prejudice, and in 1881 she called a meeting of local ladies and they started a shelter for girls. A few years later Mrs. Moberly thanked God for the great work that "*only* pure minded women could do" (Moberly, 297).

between them and the unfortunates they were helping, and getting laws punishing both sexes equally in solicitation cases. She was not concerned merely with kindness and justice, but had a still more forward-looking interest in constitutional issues of privacy and regulation. She often found it much harder to explain this aspect of her work than the moral issues, but she and John Stuart Mill, who assisted her, felt that they were really defending the English constitutional right not to be arrested without cause.[66]

Naturally she and her followers met many rough moments. In 1869 there was a riot in Glasgow when she tried to speak, and medical school professors incited their students to break up the meeting. At another time a Cambridge professor speaking for her cause had chairs and benches hurled at him and was covered with mud, flour, and "more unpleasant things." At Colchester an innkeeper was told that his inn would be set on fire if he did not get her out of there. At one meeting place, a hayloft (reached through a trap door for want of any better access), they found the floor strewn with cayenne pepper. As they tried to damp it down, someone set fire to the hay bales below and a few of their persecutors climbed the ladder and began to paw the women, while threatening to throw their male defender out the window. Even when the police came—belatedly—they looked on cynically without stopping the disorder. Nineteenth-century crowd violence started before the suffragettes appeared, and it was not limited to attacking the lower classes.

Carrying her crusade abroad, she met with more politeness but even less official sympathy. Regulation of prostitution had long been carried on in most continental countries, and though the Paris police accorded her an interview, she came to the conclusion that they were sadistic and corrupt. Slowly she built up a network of private citizens who admired her courage and wanted to clean up this social evil in their own countries. A series of international conferences was organized and provided an opportunity for men and women of different religions, nationalities, and classes to meet. At one of these George Butler made a speech on the value of holding women as the complete equals of men, and sometimes as their guides in moral matters. Josephine wrote, "He said all this . . . his hand on my chair, and standing over me like a guardian angel. They saw in his face and manner, a noble honesty and humility which does not particularly characterize men of the German race in their relations to women."[67]

Octavia Hill chose to work on the question of low-income housing.[68] She had begun teaching in her mother's ragged school at the age of thirteen; later on she studied art with John Ruskin and came into contact with the Christian Socialists who surrounded F. D. Maurice. In 1864 she began her successful venture of buying (with money loaned by Ruskin) apartment houses that she rehabilitated and managed so that the tenants got plain but decent housing, with personal supervision and encouragement in a healthy way of life. It was important to Octavia that the project, which eventually became quite large, should be on a financially sound basis, and that a group of women be trained in the fine art of managing the complexes so as to bolster the tenants' self-respect.

Few young women had the advantages that accrued to Angela Burdett-Coutts, the heiress of a fortune that made her the richest woman in England.[69] She spent her money with great seriousness, trying to get the best advice (much of it from Charles Dickens) so that she would do the most good and the least harm. Besides giving large sums to education and the Church, she set up a home for fallen women in 1846, relieved famine in Ireland, and helped start programs for the prevention of cruelty to children and animals. Yet even though Dickens wrote to the inmates of her hostel as if they were his sisters, Angela knew how to maintain her Victorian distance. She possessed "the faculty of winning obedience without effort; and the gift of erecting impassable yet imperceptible barriers against familiarity."[70]

Beatrice Webb, coming along half a century later, showed how the ancient pattern of expectations concerning daughters could be used by one who was determined to become consequential. She decided to use the extra freedom that society was prepared to give its leisured young women to carve out a professional career of research into social problems.[71] If she had been a man, she would have been expected to pick some profitable profession. For her, being a woman was a distinct advantage, partly because with so few in the field she had a certain scarcity value. Concerned with her own work and ambitions, she was hostile for years to woman suffrage.*

The goal she set herself was to discover the causes of poverty. Although slumming was fashionable among people of her class, Beatrice went further and actually got a job finishing trousers in a sweatshop, living among workers at the time. She turned out to be so bad at sewing that she would have been quickly fired except that she was recognized, even incognito, as having the requisite force of character to act as forewoman.[72] When she wrote about this episode in "Pages from a Work-Girl's Diary," she pretended that her stint had lasted all of three weeks and even altered her text in order to give this impression, but the real episode as a wage slave had lasted only a few days.[73] Most of her work was among parliamentary papers and books, or in making surveys that did not involve impersonation.

Though her family tolerated and was even proud of her increasing professionalism, they could not resist expressing strong disapproval of her proposed marriage to Sidney Webb, the son of a hairdresser who had

---

*On the other hand in her twenties she dreamed of a "ruling caste" of single women in public life who would seek a masculine reward for masculine qualities: . . . it will be needful for women with strong natures to remain celibate; so that the special force of womanhood—mother feeling—may be forced into public work (Muggeridge and Adam, 109).

won top honors on the open examination for the British Civil Service. Richard Potter, her father, would have been willing to take his brilliant daughter as a business partner if she did not marry—though certainly not if she did—but he proved unwilling to let her marry a socialist of unsatisfactory class background. So they had to wait for Mr. Potter's death to be married. Their subsequent joint career, including setting up the London School of Economics and serving on several Royal Commissions, is well known. Beatrice was particularly renowned for writing the minority report for the Royal Commission on the Poor Law of 1905, one indication of how far women had come by that time.

ᴄᴏ The feeling about women's taking part in public affairs had changed in the years since Mary Carpenter and Florence Nightingale were not allowed to testify in person before Parliamentary Commissions. The situation began to seem absurd when the World Anti-Slavery Convention, held in London in 1840, refused to seat four women delegates from America. Women insisted that they were in closer touch with human suffering than men, and so they were determined to make their voices heard before Parliament and the public, not flinching from hard issues like education, poverty, and prostitution.

An incident showing how sentiments had changed occurred at a meeting of churchwomen presided over by the wife of the Bishop of London. When the Contagious Diseases Act came up for discussion, she demanded that all the young women, married and unmarried, leave the room. No one stood up, whereupon Mrs. Sheldon Ames congratulated them on their common sense.[74]

Elizabeth Chapman imagined how a man who had been in Australia for ten years would react if he returned to England around 1885. She thought he would be more astonished at the change in women's situation than in all the improvements wrought by science; he would discover that girls now went to high schools, and got university degrees, and even went into brothels to rescue the inmates.[75]

The special quality that women felt they were able to bring to public questions was compassion for individuals. They were determined to break down the huge, impersonal institutions created by the male sex in its theoretical wisdom. They watched male-run institutions for the poor, the sick, the young, the delinquent, functioning under the assumption that reform could be achieved en masse. But one cannot learn to cook, or be a nurse, in the huge institution, declared Frances Power Cobbe.[76] Mrs. Butler argued in 1869 that if large-scale reform and centralization were carried to extremes, "the last state of our poor will be worse than the first."[77] We need homes, not asylums, she added, and while admitting that much feminine philanthropy had failed, she was sure that the masculine would fail also unless women's insights were combined with it.

It might be pointed out that many of these philanthropic volunteers were disliked by the official feminists, who charged them with caring more about their own causes than about the political rights of women.[78] Harriet Martineau, for example, objected to the way in which Caroline Norton used her journalistic talent to change the laws of child custody because she felt that Caroline acted from purely personal motives and not from "principle." Another source of reproach was that these charity-minded women were all dependent on some man for their income, they all had leisure provided by servants, and therefore they seemed to be not in the same class with the hard-working, independent, and truly professional women who were coming along at the same time. Yet just because of their position as ladies and their indifference to money, a whole generation had a certain kind of freedom that was never to be enjoyed in quite the same way again.

Let Emile Boutmy, speaking from France in 1904, have the final word on the subject:

> Our young girls in France would consider it inconsistent with their rank, and with the reserve becoming to their sex, if they sought for masculine or arduous occupations outside their own homes. In England they are daunted neither by the difficulty of establishing and organizing a charity mission, nor by the amount of time and perseverance inevitable in a work of social relief, entailing incessant inquiry, nor by the repugnant duties which fall to the lot of a nurse in a hospital. . . .[79]

I trust that this short expedition into the volunteer work of English-women will disabuse those who imagine that it amounted only to what men "allowed" women to do, and what did not threaten male supremacy. To me the point seems to be that women learned so much from their permitted experimentation that they ended with not only a valuable social contribution, but precisely one that did threaten men. By exploiting the possibilities of their peculiar situation, some women at least became such experts in all fields of welfare that they insisted on getting their hands on the controls, and they could not very well be denied.[80] Thus they came to sit on hospital boards, poor-law investigations, and county councils. Compared with their contemporaries of other nations, they showed up very well. In 1867 Professor Franz von Holtzendorff told German women that they were far behind, and he named nine English-women active in public affairs and used to the lecture platforms who had no analogues in Germany; and the ones he named (from Elizabeth Fry to Florence Nightingale) were all women who had won recognition for their unpaid efforts to reform social evils.[81]

∾32.

Englishwomen in the Professions

I am often tossed in my mind whether a life in which I neither write books nor visit the poor is rightly arranged for a woman who is not married nor an invalid.

Catherine Winkworth, 1874

Prior to the opening up of a wide range of new professions to women, there was profound consideration of the single one that had traditionally been open to ladies in pecuniary need—teaching. It was assumed by all, during the first fifty years of our period, that a single woman left alone and without resources would seek a position as governess, while widows with families to support, or sometimes a group of sisters, might open their own small school.* The system failed in providing either good teachers or sufficient income, and by the 1840s its flaws pressed upon public attention.

Part of the concept of the new domesticity had been the education of girls at home, a strong motif in theoretical and practical books of advice in the early part of the nineteenth century so that middle-class and upper-class families created a great demand for private governesses.[1] Unfortunately it was not so great as the supply. The necessary result of overcrowding was underpayment. In 1851 there were about twenty-five thousand governesses in England, at an average annual salary of £30 or £40, with £100 as the upper limit.[2] One of the first great shocks to public opinion was the discovery of how many of them were supporting other people. Instead of being lonely spinsters, all too many were charged with heavy family responsibilities.[3] George Butler, in an essay on education as

---

*Such schools could be very small indeed, like the one started by Anne Jemima Clough in 1841 against considerable family opposition. She took in three or four pupils, never more than six, over a four-year period (B. A. Clough, 21). Teaching in one's own home seems to have been an attractive alternative to becoming a private governess. Doubtless hundreds of such schools were set up. Browning's aunts kept one, as did Harriet Martineau's sister, the Rossettis, and Edith Nesbit's mother. We know of these because of their distinguished connections, but there must have been many more that left no trace in history (Arthur Clough, 21; Barbara Stephen, *Emily Davies*, 56; Shaen, 58; Doris Moore, 6).

a career for women, cited a number of pathetic examples, of which the following is typical: "Miss Eliza Bellars has been teaching more than thirty years; gave all she could spare from her salaries to her parents, and when keeping a school with a sister made a home for them, and helped two brothers and their families."[4]

Another reason for the overcrowding of the profession was the upsurge of girls from tradesmen's families who hoped to raise their social status by taking positions in genteel families. Lady Eastlake pointed out in the *Quarterly Review* for 1848 that such girls would always remain "underbred," and apparently the social level from which governesses were drawn continued to decline in the next thirty years because Augusta Webster complained in 1879 that the standard for domestic servants had been depressed simultaneously, as girls who would have made capable domestics had turned into incapable governesses.[5]

As social consciences became more sensitive, in the forties and fifties, people started to concern themselves about psychological as well as financial pressures. It was pointed out that the life of a governess was always lonely, that they were strangers in the houses where they lived, neither full social equals nor yet servants. "There is no other class which so cruelly requires its members to be in birth, mind and manners above their station, in order to fit them for their station."[6] The *Edinburgh Review* startled its readers in 1859 by reporting that the largest class of women patients in lunatic asylums were governesses.*[7]

One early governess wrote a long story of her life[8] that makes vivid some of the conditions under which these women lived. "Miss Weeton," whose cruel treatment as a wife and mother has already been recounted, began her "life of slavery" at the age of eleven, helping her widowed mother run a school. Her day was nine hours long, hours of cooking, cleaning, nursing sick members of her family, and managing the children. Often she had to go without a meal in order to help pay off the family debt and put her brother through a good school. In 1808, surviving twenty years of this life, she found herself alone, with a tiny income and freedom to choose her future. After her experience of teaching in a school, she felt that being a live-in governess might be an improvement, especially as she was dotingly fond of children, but the position she took in 1812 made her very little better off than before. She was responsible for five children under seven for thirteen hours a day, and found that she had to rise at six if she wanted to get anything done for herself, like sewing or writing. The youngsters had been badly spoilt, but the parents let her use her own

*As a corrective to the widely accepted picture of the persecuted and colorless governess, Lady Cardigan protested that none of her friends had ones of that type. She remembered clever, sensible women who were treated as ladies, though they had tact enough not to become too familiar. Instead they formed their own society and would often take their pupils along to spend delightful evenings among cheerful, smiling young women who seemed to be having a thoroughly good time (Adeline, 21). Perhaps at the period she spoke of, the employers' consciousness had been raised by books like *Jane Eyre* and the *Edinburgh Review* article.

methods of discipline, and she went slowly to work to make them socially aware. She found, for example, that the seven-year-old had no sense of common modesty because she had been washed naked so as to inure her to the cold. What really shocked Miss Weeton's sensibility was the apathy with which the parents regarded their children's progress, never taking any interest in what the children were learning; even when the governess decided to make a report every Saturday she could hardly get them to listen, and she felt that they would not have cared if the children had been indoctrinated with atheism or other wicked ideas.

By the 1840s, after such conditions had been ventilated in the press, some kind of public action seemed required. One obvious need was for better training and testing of candidates. There had been no standards at all, but if governessing were to become a true profession, explained Maria Edgeworth, this would create a strong motive for moral and intellectual improvement.[9] Some of the institutions that accomplished this change have been described in an earlier chapter.

Meanwhile, the Governesses Benevolent Association, founded in 1843, attempted to gather funds for the relief of the most pressing hardship cases, but was stymied by the extent of the need, which could never be met by the resources available. By 1848 the Association had distributed £783 among 333 cases of temporary difficulty and provided pensions for thirty-two aged women.[10] A Provident Fund was set up to invest savings, and an employment agency found positions for 807. Although the fund grew with the years, and the relief offered expanded, they could never keep up with the demand. The only way to change these circumstances was to open up well-run schools for girls, and to find alternative professions for able women.*

ᏦᏏ Another form of remunerative work that had always been available, albeit only to women with a certain talent, was writing. Literary work was the easiest way for them to make money and had many accessory advantages: it was the most private of the arts, requiring no extra equipment or space beyond what was already there in an ordinary home and only the sort of special training that a woman could acquire by herself, and it was sufficiently inconspicuous for women to continue when married. It is well known how many female writers protected their anonymity by adopting male pseudonyms and then vigorously denying— often to close friends—that they had written the books they were asked about. (Charlotte Brontë, Elizabeth Gaskell, and George Eliot are among those guilty of this particular white lie.)[11] Even so, the difficulties were often formidable. Though many of them had the protection of the

---

*Miss Martineau's 1859 essay on female industry quoted from one of the Association's reports on the 120 applications it received for three annuities of £20 each. All the applicants were over fifty, 49 were over sixty, 99 were unmarried, and 83 possessed absolutely no income ("Female Industry," 330).

walls of their home, within those walls were often no special places set aside for writing. Thus Mary Howitt, who had some ambition to be "distinguished in [her] day,"[12] had to write in the dining room amid constant interruptions, but she remarked philosophically, "I can bear interruptions better than either William or Anna Mary," both of whom were also trying to write. "It would drive them mad; the poor mother of a family learns to be patient. . . ."[13] Still, with all the interference, Flora Tristan believed that more Englishwomen than French took up writing because their lesser involvement in household duties gave them an advantage in leisure time.

Women with less talent, or greater financial need, or more courage about breaking the social taboos against self-support and living away from home, became journalists. Harriet Martineau was the most distinguished of these pioneers.

Born in 1802, she was the first woman who wrote under her own name at journalistic hack work solely to make money. After an unhappy youth, having lost her hearing as a small child, she watched her father, brother, and fiancé die before she was twenty-four. Her mother's affairs were left in such bad hands that the family lost everything; Harriet says that the debacle left her with precisely one shilling in her pocketbook, but she was nevertheless delighted: "In a very short time, my two sisters at home and I began to feel the blessing of a wholly new freedom. I, who had been obliged to write before breakfast, or in some private way, had henceforth liberty to do my own work in my own way; for we had lost our gentility."[14] All of her sisters went on to win friends, independence, and reputation; her sister Rachel became a headmistress. For Harriet, whose deafness precluded teaching as an occupation, writing came naturally, and the obvious place for her to get assignments was in London, but her unhappy mother, who had not thrown off quite so much of her background, was horrified and delayed Harriet's departure for a long time. (Later the daughter wondered at her own capitulation, especially when she remembered that she had never meant anything "so disreputable" as going into lodgings like a man; she had intended to board in a family.) When she was twenty-nine her need to move to London was so pressing that she simply packed up, and because her brother James gave approval, their mother's horror softened. Once there, she adopted a brutal schedule, allowing herself only five and a half hours of sleep a night, attending no parties, and paying no calls (a sure sign of lack of gentility). In fact, life in London was so hard for writers of either sex in those days that a clergyman told her that he did not know any writer free from the habit of using stimulants, and that most people would not believe the amount of opium that was taken to relieve the wear and tear of writing.[15]

Her subject at first was economics because she had been impressed with the work of Malthus, little imagining how furious would be the criticism of a woman writer who preached the gospel of population control. Since she believed that he was "pure and benevolent" she was completely unprepared for the low-minded and foul-mouthed attack by popular writers on "a woman whom they knew to be innocent of even comprehending their imputations."[16] For ten years, she said, she had to put up with indecent jests at her expense while she defended Malthus' compassion for hungry children and the casualties of the fearful infant mortality rate. (Malthus himself thanked her for her article on the blessedness of domestic life.)

She got a little house in London and finally brought her mother to live with her, saying, "I am now as much a citizen of the world as any professional *son* of yours could be."[17] When Guizot was Minister of Education in France, under Louis Philippe, he devoted the opening article of a new periodical to Harriet Martineau as the only woman in history who ever substantially affected legislation other than through some man. Her great contribution was the popularization of the then-new truths of economic liberalism, of which her insistence that unmarried women should have free access to the job market was only one element. She was also a passionate advocate of the abolition of slavery.

Today her liberalism seems oddly spotty. She was in favor of women doing responsible things like becoming doctors, but not much in favor of abstract rights for women as a class. She wanted population control, but was against "meddlesome" legislation concerning factory women and labor because of her thoroughly laissez-faire views. She was against slavery, but against welfare too, thinking (as someone said about her) that the best charity was a matter of telling the poor the truths of economics. Mary Howitt made fun of her for being so very happy (not believing in God, she had no one to domineer over her)[18] while Carlyle felt that she was "totally inadequate to grapple with deep spiritual and social questions."[19] What she was supposed to lack was just what men usually expected in women—intuition about feelings and warm human sympathy. She was indeed a "strong-minded woman," living a rather heroic life and one that gave to certain people, at least, a new sense of what a woman could accomplish.

More diffident women than Harriet could sometimes find a source of income in translation. Even George Eliot began her literary career that way, in giving Strauss and Feuerbach to English readers, while Susanna Winkworth rendered *German Love* and Sarah Austin an anonymous translation of the travels of Prince Pückler-Muskau. Augusta Webster translated from the Greek.

Of course, many women were not satisfied with either journalism or translation but longed to express their own creativity. An early and highly professional woman writer was Sydney, Lady Morgan. As the daughter of an Irish actor who was constantly in difficult straits, Sydney determined to earn her own living as early as possible.* Although her father was eager to keep her in school, she refused to go, and, probably in

*She was born sometime during the 1780s but because of her reluctance to divulge her age, her actual birth date is uncertain.

her early teens, got herself a job taking care of the daughter of a school-mistress who agreed in return to educate Sydney's younger sister. By 1805 she had composed the first of several novels and decided to take the manuscript personally to London and negotiate with a publisher face to face,[20] although people less interested than she in the almighty pound felt that her financial discussions were ungenteel. She kept on bargaining all her life, however. Her sharp, possibly oversharp, observations on foreign travel have been widely quoted.* Harriet Martineau could not stand her flamboyance and her vanity, which in Harriet's opinion would tend to discredit the accomplishments of all literary women. But Lady Morgan herself was always much interested in the position of women as she observed it around the world, and she eventually composed a historical work called *Woman and Her Master*.† In recognition of her achieve-ments, Melbourne granted her a pension of £300 in 1837.

Forty years after Lady Morgan launched herself in London, another young woman, Eliza Lynn Linton, arrived in the city, settled down in a private boarding house near the British Museum (proving that such independence was possible in those days), and went to the reading room daily to study and plan for her novels.[21] Her potboilers were successful, and she also had the distinction of being the first woman newspaper writer to draw a fixed salary.[22] (Harriet Martineau was paid by the article.) When she married, rather late, in 1858, she was able to furnish her husband's home out of her own earnings. He had been an impractical, radical widower who never supported his family, and though Eliza was able to introduce some order into the household, and sent his boys promptly off to school, she found that running a home cut seriously into her time for writing.

It became gradually more acceptable, though not physically easier, for women to work hard and professionally at literature.‡ No one could have worked harder than Alice Meynell, who with her husband edited a journal in the 1880s, both of them composing editorials and reviews and reading proof. She almost gave up poetry, for which she was gifted, in the steady grind of the office.[23]

The really great women novelists and poets, of course, were some-what set apart. They worked at home, as a rule, and usually not purely for money. Mrs. Gaskell was driven into writing by the death of her only son at the age of one and a half.[24] Her grief was so prostrating that her husband suggested that she take up writing as an occupation, and later

---

*When she switched publishers between the first and second editions of her notes on France, the first publisher took revenge by advertising her earlier volumes as "Lady Morgan at half price," which gratified the many enemies made by her sharp tongue.

†The editor of her memoirs, in 1863, took pains to tell her readers that there was "nothing American or strong-minded in *Woman and Her Master*. It is in contrast to the *Rights of Women* tone. . . " (Morgan, *Memoirs*, 3,219).

‡Jessie White Mario became the first woman foreign correspondent in 1856, when she persuaded the *Daily News* to appoint her to cover affairs in Italy (Ridley, 376).

she came to feel that her experience of motherhood and life had made her a much better writer than she would otherwise have been. A woman of talent, she explained, could not drop her domestic duties as an equally talented man could, but at the same time she must not shrink from the added responsibilities of authorship. "She must not hide her gift in a napkin; it was meant for the use and service of others." Charlotte Brontë had as great a sense of mission for herself and her sisters, as she wrote in 1841: "I want us *all* to get on. I know we have the talents, and I want these to be turned to account."[25]

The problem of the woman artist was set out by Elizabeth Barrett Browning in a long narrative poem, *Aurora Leigh* (1856). Its title character, like Corinne, is nurtured in Italy, but when she is thirteen her father dies and she is sent to a rather prissy aunt in England. Here she receives all the stereotyped advice and tiresome insistence on female passivity that must have oppressed so many girls.

> I read a score of books on womanhood
> To prove, if women do not think at all,
> They may teach thinking [to a maiden aunt
> Or else the author]—books that boldly assert
> Their right of comprehending husband's talk
> When not too deep, and even of answering
> With pretty "may it please you," or "so it is,"—
> . . . .
> They must never say "no" when the world says "ay. . . ."[26]

Free at twenty, Aurora has to make the fatal choice between love and self-fulfillment as an artist. Her first step is to reject the marriage proposal of her cousin Romney, who has very high ideals of helping mankind, but in impersonal ways, by "formal universals" typical of the male intellect. Her answer to him: "I too have my vocation,—work to do." She explains to him that he is wrong to see woman merely as the complement to man:

> every creature, female as the male,
> Stands single in responsible act and thought. . . .[27]

Later on, after several years of taking care of Romney's bastard child, whom she has adopted along with its mother, she learns to be less uncompromising about her art, asking herself if she had been wrong in pleading for independence, "passioned to exalt the artist's instinct in me at the cost of putting down the woman's."[28] She comes to feel "all that strain of sexual passion, which devours the flesh in a sacrament of souls."[29] When Romney comes back into her life, having learned his own lessons, she accepts him with the conventional conclusion: "Art is much, but love is more."*

*Like Robert Schumann, another husband of a woman of genius, Robert Browning never portrayed a creative woman in his own work. One must judge them singularly blind to what was in front of their faces (W. S. Johnson, 249).

On the whole, English women writers had a narrower sweep than some of their continental, particularly their Latin, contemporaries.[30] Though many of them were first-rate in their own sphere of portraying personal relations, domestic problems, and identity crises, they did not regularly turn out essays and works of history and philosophy, such as came from the pens of Mme de Staël, Hortense Allart, Mme d'Agoult, Cristina Belgiojoso, Jenny d'Héricourt, or Dora d'Istria, most of whom also tried their hand at fiction. Virginia Woolf once compared George Eliot with Tolstoy, whose superior breadth and vigor she attributed to his being able to live as a soldier and among all classes of people.[31] In some degree women of the Latin races enjoyed this more extensive and varied experience, particularly in sexual relationships. Perhaps also their cultures were more given to thinking in abstractions. English individualism and English concreteness carried over into Englishwomen's writing.

Women whose gifts were in arts other than literature had on the whole a much harder time. As Ethel Smyth said of her father, "We knew no artists, and to him the word simply meant people who are out to break the Ten Commandments." Ethel, a composer, was the most talented English woman musician of the nineteenth century, but she had to wage a terrible campaign to get to Leipzig for training. She announced to her family that she intended to go there instead of being presented at court, but the argument, which began at the dinner table, became so terrific that she realized she would have to carry on a sort of political warfare by deliberately breaking taboos until her family felt disgraced.[32] The means she chose were to borrow five shillings from local tradesmen, then ride third class to London, take an omnibus to the concert hall, and there listen to her heart's content to Joachim or Clara Schumann. Any of these things alone would bring opprobrium; together they finally persuaded her family to let her go: ". . . on July 26, 1877, . . . I was packed off, on trial, and in deep disgrace, but too madly happy to mind about that, to the haven of my seven years' longing."[*][33]

Later, when she showed one of her choral pieces to a famous conductor, his first reaction was that he would not have believed that it had been written by a woman. When Ethel retorted that a week afterward he *still* would not believe it, he admitted that she was right.[34] Ethel became a great supporter of the Votes for Women movement, wore their colors of purple, green, and white on her plain, mannish clothes, and composed the "March of the Women," which became the theme song of the suffragettes.[35]

A woman who did not suffer from her family's unwillingness to let

[*]In her autobiography she tells of her later liberated style. On one trip in the spring of 1884, she walked across the Apennines alone, carrying only a camel's-hair cape, a comb, a toothbrush and soap, a stick, a map, and a revolver, with her money sewn into the hems of her clothing, She slept in monasteries or small inns, and twice slept out of doors. She made friends on the way with a monk and with an Italian baron who shared a picnic with her (Smyth, 2: 93).

her become an artist but rather from the general inequality in financial matters that was inflicted on English girls and women was Fanny Kemble, the best-known actress of mid-century.[36] She belonged to an old theatrical family, being the niece of the famous Mrs. Siddons. Still, it was not at first contemplated that she should join her father on the stage, and her own early hopes were centered on a literary career. But her father's reluctance to see her on the boards evaporated under his need to send £300 a year to his son, James—out of an income of £800—and so Fanny's earnings were needed. She had previously enjoyed an allowance of £20 a year, out of which she bought gloves and shoes, and her salary of thirty guineas a week delighted her because it meant that she no longer had to wear faded, turned, and dyed clothing. But when she made an extra sum by writing a play, the family impounded it to pay for James's army commission. She continued to act until she married the American Pierce Butler, but no one, not even she, could imagine her returning to her profession after that event, even though she had no children and the marriage proved miserably unhappy. In this matter, English custom was far different from the German or even the Italian, where married actresses and singers continued to keep on with their work and to enjoy great respect; indeed, in the south of Italy they might lose less respectability for having lovers than an Englishwoman might lose by performing at all.

A possible exception was Clara Novello, an English singer who was always attended at her operatic performances by her mother.[37] Just before 1848 she married an Italian count, perhaps because a foreign husband would not share the prejudice against the combination of marriage with a career. Though within a few years they had to return to England for political reasons, with no means of support but her profession, she was said to manage so well that her public duties never interfered with her care of four children or her making a home for her husband.*

It is obvious that even though the great women artists won a certain success, a woman of less talent or energy might be totally thwarted by the climate of feeling surrounding what women should do with their lives. As Harriet Martineau put it succinctly:

> A Jenny Lind cannot be stopped in her singing, nor a Siddons in her dramatic career, nor a Currer Bell in her authorship, by any opposition of fortune; but none of us can tell how many women of less force and lower genius may have been kept useless and rendered unhappy, to our misfortune as much as their own.[38]

---

*Although Jenny Lind, the Swedish Nightingale, was the idol of western Europe, she herself told Catherine Winkworth that she was "crushed by her gift" and was never satisfied until she had given up the operatic stage and limited herself to appearing in oratorios and performances that would prove "that an artist's life, even a woman's, might be a true Christian life" (Shaen, 227). Her complete retirement from secular performances coincided more or less with her marriage, though the psychological pressures of religion and respectablility had clearly affected her earlier.

(She was wrong here about Jenny Lind, and it is interesting that she mentioned Mrs. Siddons rather than Fanny Kemble, whom she happened to detest.*)

⌇ A particularly controversial field for women was medicine, which they had formerly practiced and which had been taken out of their hands. There had been a tradition of women performing medical services, particularly as midwives, throughout the eighteenth century, but by the mid-nineteenth all such work was firmly in the hands of men, who explained that midwives lacked "science." This explanation does not cover why women were forbidden to acquire science, but it was the standard one.

The extraordinary exception was "Dr. James Barry," a woman who served in the British army as a medical officer from 1813 until 1859.[39] Although foreign universities in the eighteenth century had turned out a few women physicians, there was no hope that a British one would do so knowingly. Those responsible for the little girl who became Dr. Barry noticed her unusual intelligence and decided that the only way to train her for a profession commensurate with her ability would be for her to dress as a boy and enter the University of Edinburgh. She was probably the illegitimate child of a member of a powerful family, but her origins are obscure. In 1809, at the ripe age of ten, she matriculated, to graduate three years later. Then her unknown friends apparently got her a commission in the army, and in 1816 she was sent to Capetown. With three-inch-thick soles, padded shoulders, and a visible penchant for dancing with the prettiest girls at military balls, she maintained a lifelong pose. Her military record is that of a brilliant physician but a controversial officer; she insisted on strict hygienic measures in army hospitals and was impatient of stupidity wherever she found it. She rose to be Inspector General of the army medical department, and her sex was disclosed only when an attendant laid out her body after death. Incidentally, she showed signs of having borne a child.

Dr. Barry was still practicing as a man when Jessie White Mario applied to the medical faculties at London in 1855, saying that she could produce all the certificates of character and capacity that would have been required of a male applicant. She was rejected out of hand with no reasons given.[40] It was ten years later that the door opened for the first time, for Elizabeth Garrett Anderson, then closed again momentarily until it was forced open for good.

Elizabeth Garrett's father was a self-made man who had the peculiarity of wishing to educate his daughters as thoroughly as his sons. He

*Harriet had very little feeling for the arts and sensuous expression, but in Fanny she saw an "incurable vulgarity," and she tells us that she found Fanny's American journal (largely about the treatment of slaves on Mr. Butler's plantations) so outrageous that she induced her to delete thirty pages of it (Martineau, 1: 364).

sent Elizabeth to boarding school, and later, after he got over his first shock at her intention of studying medicine, he backed her up and provided everything that money could supply to smooth her difficult path. (Her mother, meanwhile, sobbed her heart out at "the disgrace.")

Elizabeth Garrett conceived the idea from Dr. Elizabeth Blackwell, the first modern woman physician, American-trained, whom she met through Barbara Bodichon. Dr. Blackwell had written an article for the *Englishwoman's Journal* outlining a four-year medical course for women, and she came to England to deliver lectures on the subject in 1858. Fired up by her example, Elizabeth Garrett started training at the Middlesex Hospital on August 1, 1860. From then on, she had to dodge from place to place, persuading one doctor to instruct her in a particular branch, then moving elsewhere to pick up another part of the needed knowledge. At some medical schools she was not allowed to pay fees, lest this establish her as a regular student; at others, the students among whom she sat showed their spite, especially when she knew answers that they did not. The students at the Middlesex Hospital petitioned their faculty in 1861 not to allow her to return on the grounds that they were subject to ridicule from other schools for sharing their benches with a woman, and that lecturers might soft-pedal certain subjects in the presence of a lady.

There were at that time several licensing boards for different aspects of medicine, all of whose Latin charters except one used the word *"vir"* (man) to refer to the candidate. But in the charter for the Apothecaries' Hall, the word was *"homo"* (human being). After Elizabeth had come out ahead of the seven male candidates of her year, Mr. Garrett threatened to sue the Apothecaries if they refused to examine his daughter, and through this narrow loophole she emerged in 1866 with a certificate entitling her to hang out her shingle in London. That same year, when French universities were opened to women, she went to Paris to obtain competence in additional specialties. There, in March of 1869, she took her orals before three examiners in full academic regalia, and students who had packed the galleries. Her success is said to have pleased the Empress.

Back in London, in full practice at the age of thirty-four, she became engaged to James Skelton Anderson, insisting on the right to continue her career. As she wrote to her sister, "The woman question will never be solved in any complete way so long as marriage is thought to be incompatible with freedom and with an independent career."*[41] She

---

*Frances Power Cobbe had at first imagined that the Andersons' marriage must "put an end, necessarily, to her further projects of public work." Her regret at this presumed solution was expressed in a verse (*Life*, 2: 426):

"Oh, stay!"—a lover cried "Oh, rest
Thy much-learned head upon this breast;
Give up ambition! Be my bride!"
—Alas! *no* clarion voice replied,
Excelsior!

worked right through three pregnancies, operating and lecturing and trying to keep her private life unobtrusive, though when the health of one of her children required a long cruise, she gave up her work temporarily, winning widespread popular approval thereby.

Among her patients were Lady Amberley and Josephine Butler. The latter expressed the enormous satisfaction she derived from getting medical attention from a member of her own sex, breaking the "wicked custom" of male physicians. "I was able to *tell* her so much more than I ever could or would tell any *man*."[42]

Her remark reflects the running controversy that for years balanced the impropriety of having women in the dissecting room against the impropriety of having women patients examined by male physicians. Sir William Jenner, the Queen's doctor, voted against admitting women to London University in 1877, saying that he had but one daughter, and he would prefer to see her body "upon the benches of the dissecting room than pursuing the course of study necessary to entitle her to take a medical degree."[43] On the other hand, once a few women had met the challenge, they were able to protect the modesty of hundreds of grateful patients. Elizabeth Blackwell had been led into medical studies when a woman friend of hers, ill with a painful disease, remarked that the worst sufferings would have been avoided if she could have had a woman doctor. Mrs. Menzies exploded that her London physician could not "forget that he is not a vet" in referring to her anatomy,[44] while Kingsley felt it a disgrace that a man should have the right of trying to interpret a hundred women's secrets.[45] F. W. Newman (1869) brought out in print what may have been a common hidden fear—that male doctors were guilty of "impure handling of women." He favored women doctors, but hardly for liberal reasons.*[46]

As early as 1859, Elizabeth Blackwell was hoping to found a hospital for women and children staffed by women physicians, where women students could train; but though 1864 saw the establishment of something called the "Ladies Medical College," this was intended only for midwives.[47] Miss Nightingale sniffed at it because it did not even pretend to train women to handle abnormal deliveries.

Meanwhile, the little loophole through which Miss Garrett had slipped—the Apothecaries' board—was legally closed, to make clear the hope of the authorities that there would be no more women doctors in

---

*This attitude was still strong as late as 1909, when a burst of correspondence in the *Manchester Guardian* on the subject of women doctors included a note from an ex-nurse saying that she had watched dozens of women endure severe suffering because they did not want the embarrassment of being examined by a male doctor, and a letter by a woman who signed herself "Head Mistress" who would "like to say that many women have told me they would certainly, if it were possible, have a woman surgeon in case of need. I know several ladies who went from Devonshire to London purposely to consult women doctors, as they did not wish to consult men doctors about, or be attended by them for, internal trouble. . . . Two friends from Westmoreland said to me only the other day, 'What a comfort it is to think there is now a lady surgeon in the North of England' " (*Manchester Guardian* Dec. 6, 15, 17, 22, 1909).

England. The person who really opened up the medical schools was Sophia Jex-Blake, who got herself and four other women admitted at Edinburgh in 1869.[48] Their passage was stormy. Although a female presence was said to have improved the gentlemanly behavior of the students at Geneva, New York, where Dr. Blackwell had studied, things turned out quite the opposite at Edinburgh. During a riot in 1870, a sheep was pushed into the classroom on the grounds that inferior animals were no longer excluded.[49] After this the men used their medical vocabulary to hurl insults at the women,[50] but the women were all the more determined to finish their studies in order to protect women patients from doctors such as these. Though a Miss Pechey had earned the right to a particular scholarship, by high grades, it was awarded to a man instead, and ten days before the first professional examination the young women were told that they would not be allowed to take it. They appealed to the courts but lost their case, and those who still had stomach for the study completed their degrees at Bern.[51] Miss Jex-Blake did not get her degree until 1877, though she achieved some useful administrative work in setting up a medical school in the meantime.

In 1875 the Midwifery Board of Examiners all resigned rather than examine women medical students,[52] but very shortly thereafter Parliament relented and passed a law that women could be admitted to British medical schools; and that battle was over.

On the whole there was less resistance to the idea of nursing as a profession, and what prejudice there was among upper-class mothers was not so much that it was an *unfeminine* thing for their daughters to do as that it was unsuitable for a *lady*—an idea spread about in England after the religious orders had been closed. As we have seen, the tradition of high-grade hospital management had never been given up in Catholic countries, and the French soldiers in the Crimea were well taken care of by Sisters of Charity. But in England no respectable woman wanted to do this work, and if one hired a nurse, one could count on little science and little common decency. When Florence Nightingale asserted that nursing was to be her vocation, her family reacted "as if I had wanted to be a kitchen-maid."[53] Later on she admitted that it was even worse than that, inasmuch as no respectable maid would associate with the surgeons and nurses in existing hospitals, which, of course, were mainly for the poor.[54]

Miss Nightingale's luminous example changed all this, both through the glamorized figure of the Lady with the Lamp and through her close association with members of the British government. "Thousands of women," declared her earliest biographer, "are, in consequence of Florence Nightingale's career, born free; but it was at a great price, and after long and weary struggles, that she herself attained such freedom."[55]

Her struggles began as soon as she realized that her exceptional energy and competence could be given no outlet under the customary expectations for women of her class. "For how many long years, I have watched that drawing-room clock and thought it would never reach the ten!"[56] She felt that women were treated like "moons" in their families; "yet the Earth never sees but one side of her; the other side remains forever unknown."[57] At thirty-one she was still treated like a child, and even after the government had commissioned her to go out to Scutari, she had to ask permission of her parents.

One early hope was quickly dashed. It seemed to her that the Church of England should give some opportunity for service, but it "told me to go back and do crochet in my mother's drawing-room, or, if I were tired of that, to marry and look well at the head of my husband's table."[58]

Looking elsewhere for support, she found that Elizabeth Fry, the great Quaker reformer, had set up a nursing school in London in 1840; and in 1848 the St. John's House was founded to train nurses in London's teaching hospitals. But when she finally won permission to take up her career, Florence Nightingale chose to begin her training in Düsseldorf, at Theodor Fliedner's Kaiserswerth.

By 1851, when Florence Nightingale arrived, the Kaiserswerth establishment contained a hospital with a hundred beds, an infant school, a penitentiary for twelve inmates, an orphan asylum, and a normal school.[59] The nursing candidates were called deaconesses, although they took no religious vows; there were 116 of them when she was there, mostly drawn from the peasant class. The Nightingale judgment on all this was balanced: she found a good tone but was dissatisfied that actual training was lacking. She went on to Paris to learn what she could from the Sisters of Charity. Here twenty sisters took care of two hundred orphans, an infant crèche, and a hospital for sick or aged women. Continuing her inspection in Italy, she went on a retreat with some of the nuns.

Having finished her tour of study, she headed for a short time a small nursing home in London. Then the Crimean War broke out, and Sidney Herbert asked her to take charge of the field hospitals. The story of her success is too well known to need repeating. She went with a complement of ten Roman Catholic nurses, eight Anglican sisters, six women from St. John's House, and fourteen from various hospitals around London. Her great success lay not so much in her nursing skills as in her organizing ability—she turned out to be a superb administrator—and her moral authority as a gentlewoman. Under her aegis the common soldiers restrained their bad language, read the books she offered them, and put money away in the savings bank she had set up.

After she returned to England, she wrote treatises on nursing, on hospital administration, and on the reorganization of services for the British army. She opened her own nursing school at St. Thomas's Hospital, but even with her reputation and expertise she was not allowed to testify in person before a parliamentary committee, which plied her instead with written questions.

She steadfastly refused to take money for her work—though the government paid her expenses in the Crimea—but lived on a £500 allowance, only reluctantly increased by her wealthy father after her sister had married and Florence wanted to live in a house of her own.

It was one of Miss Nightingale's purposes to make a better life for women, to give them more choices and more ways to be useful, and she laid great stress on the point that they should do these things *without emotion*.[60] Yet she was far from interested in the jargon of women's rights. One does not want to hear, "How wonderful for a *woman!*" she remarked crisply, adding the advice that one should go straight to do God's work in simplicity.[61]

Doctors were slow to shed their prejudices and for a long time hesitated to call on the trained women for fear of hysterics in the "impertinent femalities."[62] And, according to Mrs. Jameson, it did become fashionable for frivolous and fine ladies to take up nursing after Miss Nightingale's example. Yet things were never so bad again after her achievements.

Though none of her companions in the Crimea turned out to be capable of carrying on her administrative work, Florence Lees (later Mrs. Cravens), whose training had been financed by a fund set up in Miss Nightingale's honor, served in the Franco-Prussian War and afterward set up the Metropolitan and National Nursing Association to educate women as visiting nurses in poor homes. Characteristically, only gentlewomen were accepted for this training, on the grounds that their influence on the moral and sanitary standards of the clients would be the most beneficial.[63]

ᴄᴧ The purpose of this chapter has not been to detail the accomplishments of Englishwomen in the professions but rather to lay out the conditions surrounding their ability to undertake such work and have it accepted by the world at large. Only women who succeeded in making a mark on history have been mentioned. No one can ever know how many mute inglorious George Eliots blushed unseen. Nor have I enumerated all the careers that opened up. For instance, interior decorating became a profession at this time, invented largely by Mrs. Haweis as a way to use lucratively her special knowledge and taste; yet when Agnes Fawcett and Rhoda Garrett started a firm in this field, it was quite as unprecedented as the decision of Agnes's cousin Elizabeth Garrett to turn doctor.[64] It took the same kind of imagination to dream up other new fields of work, and the same sort of opposition was encountered.

When one contemplates the pattern of these Englishwomen's lives, several differences from the patterns of other countries are striking. Absent, for example, was the sense of relief repeatedly voiced by Latin women at the availability of a solid career as a means of escape from a forced marriage. Englishwomen who did not marry were delighted not to be dependent on their fathers and brothers, but the tradition of arranged marriage did not obtain in their country, and so they were spared that last ignominy.

Englishwomen decided what they wanted to do and achieved it mostly by individual determination and effort. In Germany it took a mass movement to open up professions to women job-seekers. In England, the mass movement emerged as a way to attain votes and civil rights, but work was seen rather as a goal in itself, not as a stepping stone to further rights. This can help explain why many extremely accomplished professional women did not support the drive for suffrage and why those who did often did it in a private way, not as a part of the general campaign.

There was considerable resistance to the idea of women's working, particularly married women, perhaps because Englishmen were especially proud of their role as sole supporter of the family. In Latin countries, where women were provided with dowries and accustomed to help with the family enterprise, there was less opposition to letting them move outside the home; and when they did so, they were often already familiar with managerial skills. English widows, it has been remarked, did not expect to carry on the family business alone. French ones did.[65]

Among the advantages of the English should probably be included the fact that, as individualists, they were less easily discouraged by disapproval. From girlhood they were more used to making decisions for themselves than the unmarried women of other countries, and so when they found a vocation, they were not to be held back even by seemingly insuperable obstacles.

ᴄᴏ33.

An Irrepressible Army

Mr. Mill presented to the Commons a petition signed by 21,757 women, who asked for the Franchise. The first signature was that of Mrs. Somerville, Mechanist of the Heavens; the second that of Miss Florence Nightingale, Healer on Earth. Right or wrong, the request ought to have been granted to such petitioners.

Punch, 1868

Men no longer need special privileges to protect them against Women; and . . . the sexes should henceforth enjoy equal political rights.

George Bernard Shaw, 1884

Having related several sorts of activity that freed certain English-women from their old social roles and conventions, I must now detail their organized effort to attain equal civil and political rights. In this, chapter I shall deal first with the theory and then with the militant struggle for these rights. The theory began with Mary Wollstonecraft, and climaxed with John Stuart Mill's *Subjection of Women*; the demand for votes began with a few scattered petitions and culminated in a campaign whose violence was unmatched in any other country.

ᴄᴏ Well known as the first great English feminist, Mary Wollstonecraft by her *Vindication of the Rights of Women* (1792) and by her romantically unconventional and unhappy life has become a twentieth-century feminine idol. In the nineteenth century, even so strong an advocate of women's rights as Harriet Martineau called her "a poor victim of passion" who could not do anything to improve the condition of her sex. Miss Martineau believed that the women's cause needed advocates with more "self-discipline" and without such doubtful personal inclinations.[1] In her way, of course, Mary Wollstonecraft demonstrated extreme self-discipline, having several people dependent on her for support. What made her angry was that it was so difficult for a woman to control her own destiny, to forge her own independence.

A few years after the *Vindication* appeared, the conventional view of woman suffrage was expounded by that hardened old bachelor and earnest reformer Jeremy Bentham, who in his musings on the electorate laid it down that one "cannot presume a sufficient degree of knowledge in women, whom their domestic condition withdraws from the conduct of public affairs; in children . . . ; in those who are deprived by their poverty of the first elements of education."[2] Bentham's disciple James Mill formalzed the doctrine of exclusion by writing an essay on government for the *Encyclopaedia Britannica* in which he declared that, "all those individuals whose interests are indisputably included in those of other individuals, may be struck off from political rights without inconvenience. . . . In this light . . . women may be regarded."[3]

To this dictum there came a very swift and very sharp riposte, but one not at all in the spirit of Mary Wollstonecraft, for in the years between 1792 and 1825 the doctrines of the French utopian socialists had begun to spread, including their belief that changing the whole social structure could meet problems better than merely opening up opportunities to individuals.[4] This rejoinder, entitled *Appeal of One-Half the Human Race, Women, Against the Pretensions of the Other Half, Men*, was signed by William Thompson, a liberal Irish landowner. The introduction makes clear, however, that Thompson owed most of the ideas and a good part of the writing to Mrs. Anna Wheeler (very much as John Stuart Mill credited Harriet Taylor for a major part of *The Subjection of Women*). Thompson describes his collaborator's mind as more comprehensive than Mary Wollstonecraft's; it certainly centered more systematically in the communitarian doctrines that had arisen with the new century.

Mrs. Wheeler is monotonously listed in the literature of feminism as the only radical voice between Mary Wollstonecraft and John Stuart Mill, and she did, of course, make a bold and poignant statement. But in a way she was an anomaly. She represented only the echo of the bustling activity of utopian feminists across the Channel and was hardly a participant in the straight line of British feminist thought. A quotation from Wollstonecraft will make this clear: "every obligation we receive from our fellow-creatures is a new shackle, takes from our native freedom, and debases the mind."[5] Here speaks the native individualist. To a socialist mind, these obligations are not "shackles" but rather helping hands, as symbolized by the Saint-Simonian uniform, which fastened in back just so one would have to ask for help from others.

Born in 1785, the daughter of the Protestant Archbishop of Ireland, Anna Wheeler was married at fifteen to a dipsomaniac and bore six children, four of whom died. Fleeing from her husband, she took refuge in the home of a relative on Guernsey, from whom she hoped to get an inheritance. When she had exploited this man to the limit, she moved on in 1816 to France, where she lived for a while with some kind of socialist group.* She seems to have been a person whose keenly expressed fury

---

*Though the community, at Caen, is often described as a Saint-Simonian one, and this term has been repeated in a succession of books, I have not found any original authority for this designation. Saint-Simon himself, to the best of my knowledge, did not set up communes, and the feminist doctrines for which his followers became famous were not elaborated until after his death in 1825, and hence a few years later than the publication of the *Appeal*. I have asked four scholars who have mentioned this year at Caen, in writing or

enhanced her charisma, but her intimates also suffered by reason of this characteristic. Her daughter, Rosina, who later became the very difficult wife of Edward Bulwer-Lytton, suffered beatings and neglect while her mother pursued ideology.

Carrying this ideology from France back to Ireland, she made a tremendous impression on Thompson, who was quickly persuaded to help her defense of women. In his introductory eulogy, Thompson frankly acknowledged that they looked forward to a society where competition would give way to cooperation, where private property would be unknown, where children would be reared by the whole society and no parent would have any vested interest in his own. He outlined a complete Equal Rights Bill for women that arranged their position in political, occupational, and sexual affairs.

The book put some of the blame for women's dependency on the authoritarian character of the family, as then constituted, but it went on to insist that women's own need for sexual satisfaction magnified this dependency tenfold.[6] On the other hand, women were trained not to ask for sex, or even to seek gratification for themselves in any way, and thus were deprived of the joy of self-determination. The ideal socialist world of the future would do away with all such acts of subordination.

Not expecting Utopia to materialize immediately, however, Thompson urged equal suffrage as a first step toward the improvement of society. Against the usual arguments of his day he mounted a sarcastic attack; if women were weaker, he said, all the more did they need the protection that the ballot box would afford; if they had less muscle, they would necessarily rely more on brain power; and surely men lost as much time in vice and folly as could be charged to women for childbearing and the other functions of their bodies.

Thompson mentioned Fourier and Robert Owen as having formed the thought of himself and his coauthor. Mrs. Wheeler apparently met Fourier in France and, as we have seen, he was the century's seminal thinker on the subject of sexual and economic freedom for women. But she liked even better the ideas of the only British utopian socialist of distinction, Robert Owen. Like Fourier and the other utopians of France, Owen carried on small reforms at home (in Scotland in his case) and sent out a colony to practice his ideas in the New World. Mrs. Wheeler preferred his widely discussed writings to Fourier's because Owen insisted on strict equality, while Fourier permitted some differential income in his phalansteries.[7]

In any case, these socialist ideas became diluted in England. In France the generation touched by them in youth kept alive a vision of social planning that had little appeal in England, with its free enterprise system and strong sense of individualism.[8] Furthermore, the English in

---

discussion, whether they knew any more about it, and none of them could quote an original source.

general were not so willing to countenance the idea of free love, for the slightly incongruous reason that it eliminated the spiritual aspect. The utopians, of course, were trying in their way to eliminate materialism, which they considered tied up with money, while the Anglo-Saxons tended to relegate sex itself to the material plane. Even William Lovett, the labor leader, familiar with the sad effects on wives of drunken or spendthrift husbands, specifically rejected a socialist solution to marital problems, which to him meant loose sexual attitudes and perhaps also a revolting instrusion into personal affairs.[9]

An admiring Frenchman declared that Englishwomen showed their "race" by the care with which they selected only certain of the Fourierist ideals.[10] The word seems odd to us, though it was characteristic of the time. We would more likely credit the acculturation of the middle class, not genetics, but in any case what he was talking about was the English refusal to endorse the abolition of marriage, or communal child care, or even the sovereignty of their own sex, although they became active in such practical tasks as helping poor women find employment as well as in demanding political and social rights for themselves.

Nevertheless, the utopian wave washed over a certain generation of English youth, and because of it, some of England's first class minds retained through life the realization that there was a woman problem. Two of these who specifically acknowledged a particular debt to the French socialists in this regard were Mill and Marx (if we may classify the latter as an English thinker for the moment). Both of these men found the feminist legacy of Fourier and the Saint-Simonians much more important that the social planning aspect. Others in that generation of young Englishmen in the thirties, like Tennyson and Carlyle, remembered their exposure to these thoughts all their lives. Though they came to disagree with them, they nevertheless had been provided with a set of ideals that they could not leave intellectually unattended.*

∽ If so much theorizing about male authority and female brains repelled middle-class women, they could look to one small sect in their own midst that had for two centuries given more than lip service to the principle of sexual equality: the Quakers. Though their practice was not so liberal as their preaching seemed at first glance, they nevertheless provided a useful object lesson and won as much admiration beyond their own membership as the socialist groups had condemnation. Quaker women had always been free to preach like men, whenever the inner light instructed them. They made no vow of obedience in their marriage

*This is often the case with radical ideas that hit a youthful generation; something like it happened to the 1930s cohort, under the influence of Leninist communism. Saint-Simonianism in Germany struck a generation of second-rate poets and writers—second-rate except for Heine, that is. It did not create a tradition for feminism, one possible reason for the slow growth of the women's movement in that country.

services; rather, the partners promised to fulfill reciprocal obligations.[11] Frances Power Cobbe wished that other English couples could learn from them that lack of a "head" need not necessarily lead to family disharmony.[12]

In the first years of the century, Elizabeth Fry became a universal exemplar of this system, stimulating good works among women of many faiths and nationalities. After she passed from the scene, her labor was taken up by Ann Wright,[13] who in 1847 composed the earliest leaflet on woman suffrage.* The subject of sexual equality continued to be argued, and in 1873 the Quaker journal, the *Friend*, carried a debate about it. An introductory letter explained that no other organization allowed women as important a part as the Quakers did, and questioned why women should not be given a similar part in the great society of the world. This point led, rather naturally, to a closer look at how democracy worked within the Friends' group itself. The meetings had always, and proverbially, been divided by sex. They had a Men's Yearly Meeting, the women met separately, and all parties agreed that neither men nor women would have liked a mixed assembly at that time. But some complained over the years that the kinds of questions left to the women's meetings had dwindled in importance. They had once had the authority to spend welfare money on the poor of their own sex, but at a certain point the Society had consolidated its funds, after which male officials distributed all of them. The discussion ended with a paper in which William Pollard urged giving responsibilities of real significance back to the women's meetings. He even thought it possible to institute a few joint sessions.[14] (The 1880s saw part of this platform adopted, and in 1896 the Society instituted regular joint Yearly Meetings and discontinued the separate seating arrangements in local ones.)

In John Stuart Mill, all past theorizing about women's equality and all he could find out about their actual achievement[15] and condition (including Tocqueville's discussion of the near equality of women in America) fused with the influence of the woman he loved, Harriet Taylor. Mrs. Taylor has often been held up as an example of a brilliant woman held down by the conventions applied to her sex, while some students, on the other hand, consider her reputation much overblown in her lover's vision. What Mill said was that they composed *The Subjection of Women* together, and he acknowledged his indebtedness to both her ideas and her judgment.† *The Subjection* became a universal text. Julie Daubié in France, Helene Lange and Hedwig Dohm in Germany, Anna Maria Mozzoni in Italy, all wrote important books on women's emancipation, but none of them embodied quite the lofty logic, the cogent statement of principle that Mill's work attained.

*Which I have not been able to locate.

†Mill said that he and Harriet discussed everything together to the point that he could not distinguish his thought from hers, and he wished that their names could have appeared on the title page together. His estimate of her influence has been questioned.

Although *The Subjection* was written in 1861 and published in 1869, Mill had been thinking about the question all his adult life. In 1832, when he was newly in love with Harriet, he composed for her an essay on marriage and divorce that attacked all the coercive aspects of marriage in law and custom, declaring in the best Saint-Simonian style that "the highest natures" would not wish to be united by any tie but free choice.[16] He was too practical to leave it there, however, for he knew that to make that choice realistically possible, women would need to be educated for self-support. With this advantage they would come to regard unwilling dependence with as much scorn as men were trained to do. On the other hand, if her household services were freely given, a wife could allow her husband to bring in the money for them both. Just because she could support herself, it did not follow that she inevitably would. In fact, Mill considered it undesirable to burden the labor market with the double competition that outside employment for married women would bring, and he believed that wives usually carried the larger share of the bodily and mental exertion required to keep the joint home going.

The program outlined in *The Subjection* merits a close look. Mill opened by stating that the principle hitherto regulating the relation of the sexes was wrong in itself and a chief hindrance to the improvement of mankind. The main idea of the modern world, he declared, was that no one should hold an ascribed place, that all people could raise themselves to limits set only by their own ability, *except women*. Following this, he described the existing laws that held women down and pointed out that the fact that they were not often pushed to extremes in everyday life did not justify keeping them on the books.

The third chapter focused on female capacities. Even though women had never reached supreme genius, in no field had they failed to reach the next-to-highest rank. Possibly, he supposed, they might actually be deficient in originality, even though they seemed more practical and intuitive than men, but perhaps they were deficient only because of the nature of their assigned tasks. In any case, until they had reached full equality in education and job openings, no one could be sure *what* they could accomplish. The next chapter described the benefits that would accrue from their equal treatment. First, justice was a good thing in itself for the state that practiced it; furthermore, the nation would double its pool of mental resources, and the gain in private happiness would prove inestimable. At the time he was writing, he perceived that changes in the relationship between the sexes had already occurred, as men's lives became more domesticated and they were thrown increasingly into the company of their wives. The problem was that women's inferior education often rendered true intimacy impossible. (Incidentally, he thought philanthropy a very poor way for women to gain practical experience.)

The Subjection of Women marked a milestone in the progress of the women's movement. Feminists acclaimed it as their definitive manifesto, and their enemies excoriated it, though they found Mill's lawyer-like logic hard to answer. In James Fitzjames Stephen it roused fury, for he thought that men were meant to govern.[17] Dr. Acton thought he noticed a sudden increase in sexually uncooperative wives, and he laid the blame on Mill's pernicious text.[18] The *Edinburgh Review* picked for its reviewer "a talented lady" who, writing more in pity than in anger, opined that Mill did not compose "in the atmosphere of wedlock" as ordinarily lived, and felt that if he had had such a background he would understand why women were meant to stay home.[19] Meanwhile, it amused Catherine Winkworth to find out how wretchedly oppressed was the sex to which she belonged.[20] But in Mrs. Somerville, who personified much of what Mill hoped for from women, it enlisted warm appreciation,[21] and Mrs. Charles Kingsley, a former opponent of women's rights, professed herself converted in an hour.[22]

Though apparently influenced by his wife not to turn down Mill's argument completely, Charles Kingsley's approach was both unctuous and gingerly. In his two letters to Mill on the subject, written in 1869 and 1870, he expressed the hope that Mill would believe him emancipated from all the forms of prejudice that had been fostered by canon law, but at the same time he felt that "in the face of British narrowness," it would be tactful not to discuss the woman's rights yet. He was particularly distressed that fanatical old maids had taken up the cause, worked into hysteria by "repressed sexual excitement," while "the highest type" of Englishwoman (cultured, thoughtful, brave, prudent, pure, and wise) often rejected it. Women brought up in the shadow of the canon law suffered wrongs "too sacred to be detailed . . . most of all before the press," Kingsley went on, but those who had been conscientious in their slavery could teach the others "a noble freedom."[23] This kind of wide-eyed timidity was harder to respond to than outright opposition, and one may suppose that Mill was disgusted.

Since history and public sentiment often seem to move in pendulum-like swings, we might expect that after Mill had carried to its logical extreme the perhaps typically English individualism of Mary Woll-stonecraft, some other thinker would pick up the thread dropped by the early socialists. Their natural heirs would seem to be the Fabians, but actually feminism never became a central doctrine for these end-of-the-century socialists, as it had been for their earlier counterparts. The original Fabian group of 1882 had indeed considered forming a utopian colony but quickly gave up the idea. The first *Fabian Manifesto*, drafted by Bernard Shaw in 1884, gave lip service to equal rights, but, as we have seen, their leading woman member, Beatrice Webb, had so many other priorities that she was slow to come around to contemplating women's special needs. During the period when H. G. Wells was a Fabian, he was insistent that the group sponsor a new sexual morality, thus carrying forward one central idea of the utopians, and he told his Fabian group that women's discontent created "a huge available source for socialism."[24] The group, however, was not yet ready for Wells's implications, and though he converted Beatrice Webb to woman suffrage, he later withdrew from the society when he could not get her or the rest of the membership to endorse free love. On other feminist demands the Fabians reacted slowly, and they never reached the cutting edge of this particular problem. When they came out for equal rights in 1906, events had run far ahead of them.

⌒ Mill's definitive text on sex equality laid out the theory, but the practical steps toward obtaining the vote remained to be taken. Suffragists could reasonably feel optimistic at first because they had watched so many other reforms being rationally dealt with. Yet shortly after 1870 women perceived that feminist progress had been stalled. The only women to benefit by legislation up to that point were those few who needed the services of the divorce court. And for forty years thereafter, women watched incredulously the slow but steady increase in the violence and irrationality that were turned against them.

The crescendo of brutality, which reached its climax in the pre-war years (but which had offered previews during Mrs. Butler's Contagious Diseases crusade and the Bradlaugh-Besant birth control affair) is hard to explain. It is possible that militant women aroused unconscious male fears in a more disturbing way than did even the rising lower classes. The same men who could see the need, however painful, to extend the franchise to £10 ratepayers or agricultural workers, and to open up schools and universities to wider social classes, stood utterly aghast at the prospective change in character of the female sex. It threatened both their home comforts and their sense of the fitness of their own position as properly in charge of things, and it was peculiarly painful because it hurt the male ego, not only where men could admit the justice of the complaint, but also in places where they felt themselves at their best and highest—in their carefully nurtured sense of responsibility and care for the weak, and in their sexual restraint.

There was impersonal violence at Peterloo and there were frightened barricades against the Chartists, but there was a personal rancor in the burning of the barn where Mrs. Butler was speaking and the tearing off of the clothes of police victims in the suffragette marches. The women's struggle was *sui generis*, and it cannot be integrated into a discussion of the class structure, however valuable that approach has proved to be for social historians analyzing male doings.*

Sometimes it seemed as if the very men most concerned about liberties for their own sex gratuitously sealed all loopholes against the

*The parallel between what happened to women in England and to blacks in America is striking, providing confirmation of the theory that something besides a class conflict was at stake. When the franchise in New York State was based on property qualifications, some black men could vote. When democratic reforms extended the franchise to all white men without question of property, special restrictions were put upon the blacks, as Dixon Ryan Fox has revealed.

other. Women remembered that such a pillar of seventeenth-century liberal principles as Sir Edward Coke, who formulated most of the rules subsequently gathered up in the Petition of Right, had deprived women of their traditional privilege of serving as justices of the peace, quoting scripture to fortify his reasoning. In the nineteenth century the very Reform Act of 1832 that had broadened suffrage for men used for the first time the word "male" in defining the "persons" eligible to vote.[25] The constitutionality of this definition was tested shortly after the act became law when a Miss Mary Smith, of Yorkshire, petitioned the House of Commons for the right to register. Guffaws greeted her request.[26]

In 1838 the *Metropolitan Magazine* published an article calling for the formation of a women's party. This "Outline of the Grievances of Women" was widely attributed to Caroline Norton, although she denied authorship.[27] The advice, however, was acted on, in certain places at least; in 1851 the Sheffield Female Political Association passed the first public resolution in favor of woman suffrage.[28]

Only after 1858, when the *Englishwoman's Journal* was founded, was there a continuing organ to publicize the women's movement, and after that date the pot never ceased to boil. The *Journal*'s editors were interested in everything, from legislation to careers, from the tearing down of stereotypes to the opening up of swimming baths. And their editors and readers were eager to sign petitions for the vote.

With the election of John Stuart Mill in 1865 as M. P. for Westminster, Englishwomen seemed to have found a champion more effective than Léon Richer in France, less sentimental than Salvatore Morelli in Italy, and less likely to cause ideological splits than August Bebel in the Reichstag. Many women friends actively campaigned for Mill, and he promised them that he would introduce a bill for their suffrage if they could get a hundred signatures on a petition. Barbara Bodichon and Jessie Boucherett composed a draft asking for sex-blind enfranchisement of all householders, and obtained 1,499 signatures within three weeks.[29] (This measure would, of course, have excluded married women.) Mill presented it to Parliament on May 7. It did not pass, but it seemed that another good chance would arise when the Second Reform Bill came under debate the following year. About this time the National Society for Women's Suffrage, a loose federation of groups across England, held its first meeting in Manchester with Dr. Richard Pankhurst as its keynote speaker.[30] A second petition was drawn up and signed only by women who possessed all the legal qualifications to vote except for their sex.[31]

In his speech in Parliament on May 20, 1867, animated by the general optimism of the time, Mill explained that adding women to the electorate "could excite no party or class feeling in this House," would not disturb property or "afflict the most timid alarmist with revolutionary terrors." Women, he explained, did not hold mass meetings in the parks (little did he foresee the future!), but "in a silent domestic revolution men and women are, for the first time in history, really each others' companions." This new role in the home meant that women could no longer be kept apart from the interests that involved their husbands. Though Mill's was a very mild-mannered speech, ending with the resolution to strike the word "male" and insert the word "person" in the "Representation of the People Bill" before the House, the amendment failed to pass.

Nevertheless, some women in various parts of England chose to ignore the masculine restriction and tried to register for the next election. In certain localities near Manchester, the officials allowed them to do so, but the decision was reversed at higher levels and the defendants were fined. The women's suffrage societies brought the case to court, where they were represented by Dr. Richard Pankhurst, arguing from history that ancient statutes had permitted women electors. The Court of Common Pleas chose to decide, instead, that centuries of disuse had effectively disfranchised women, and it imposed a fine on those who had attempted to register.[32] (They overlooked the name of one woman, and she actually cast her ballot.)

In the year following this disappointment, however, women gained an important right through an amendment added by Jacob Bright to the Municipal Corporations Bill. It gave them back the franchise in local elections, of which an 1835 bill had deprived them.[33] Soon thereafter they were made eligible for election to school boards and various other local government boards. Mrs. Nassau Senior became the first woman Poor Law Inspector as a result. In 1888 women were permitted to vote for county councils, although the first two women elected to the London County Council were not allowed to take their seats, a prohibition that lasted until 1907. Meanwhile, the privilege of voting for town and county councils was extended to married women in 1894.[34]

Mill lost his seat in 1868, but the momentum in favor of parliamentary suffrage did not immediately dissipate. In 1870 the bill to extend votes to women passed a second reading 124 to 91, only to be killed by the direct intervention of Gladstone, who felt that female suffrage would shake society to its foundations.[35] Though there was probably a majority of members personally favorable to woman suffrage for years after 1870, the government's leaders—first Gladstone, then Herbert Asquith—were so hostile that they laid it upon their party followers as a matter of discipline to vote nay. In any case, no such bill would have passed the House of Lords, and the favorable wave receded, not to rise so high again until the twentieth century.*

*The sentiment of members opposed to woman suffrage was expressed by Mr. Smollett when he complained on April 7, 1875, about having to waste one night every session on this question, "to the detriment of the *real* legislation." He considered the bill on the floor one of the "tinest and puniest measures" it had ever been his fortune to criticize. Mr. Smollett ascribed the agitation to "turbulent women from America" wearing bloomers, and could not resist going on to observe that "the pectoral, abdominal, and fundamental development of the sex looked grotesque in male attire." These dreadful women "entered into any hysterical crusade against the Contagious Disease Act," which should never be discussed by anybody but men. Even some members of Parliament failed to find this speech

The visceral nature of certain objections to woman suffrage remained apparent. When the *Edinburgh Review* had first broached the subject in 1841, it assumed that no one favored the extension of suffrage to married women, since its ability to split households was "too obvious to require discussion," and the ribaldry, calumny, and intimidation at the polling places would be enough to keep nice women, married or single, away.[*36] Herbert Spencer, who was far more esteemed as a social philosopher in his own day than in ours, told his readers that the very salvation of society depended on the absolute separation of the family and the state.[37] Dr. Alexander Walker, in *Woman Physiologically Considered*, made fun of the very idea of letting them sit in Parliament, where the pretty ones would corrupt the whole body, and the prettiest would surely be voted for.[38]

Unlike the issues involved in the Corn Law repeal bill or the education bills or even the Reform bills for men, the issues involved in woman suffrage were one-sided. Mill was right: no party or class interest was at stake, just a gut discomfort at having domestic routines altered. Augusta Webster neatly burlesqued their inability to agree on what would go wrong if women had the vote. It seemed, she declared, that they would either plunge the country into war or sacrifice the honor of the country for peace; they would fall under the yoke of the priesthood and become abject conservatives, or abolish morality and hasten the day of anarchy.

> There are fears that they will make matrimony illegal, suppress cooking, and have the Prime Minister chosen for his good looks and his skill at lawn-tennis. It is also apprehended that they will at once throw off all their present customs, tastes, virtues, and attractions—which, as is well known, are the compensations bestowed on them by nature for the absence of a vote—and will become coarse-featured unmannerly hybrids, men-hating, and hateful to men. They will wear coats and trousers, they will refuse to sew on shirt-buttons, they will leave off *poudre de riz* and auricomiferous waters, they will be Bishops and Judges, and they will break all the commandments.[39]

---

funny. By 1913 opponents of suffrage had become so desperate that they produced their heaviest artillery. Sir Almroth Wright, a physician and Fellow of the Royal Society, brought out *The Unexpurgated Case Against Woman Suffrage*. After attributing dishonesty to Mill and assuring every girl that she could get everything she ever wanted if she would use her sex appeal on the right man, he explained his *ultima ratio*—namely, that a vote was something for which a man traded off his physical force. The possibility of resorting to force was all that validated the vote, he declared, much as gold was presumed to validate paper bank notes. Since women did not have this way of making their votes count, their suffrage would be fraudulent and would vitiate the entire electoral process.

*A suggestion of the nature of English elections was given in 1865: "When a citizen returns home, his clothes torn to pieces, the crown of his hat broken in, his face bleeding and covered with scratches, how is it possible that he should entertain a doubt as to the reality of the share he has taken in the election of his representatives?" (Davesiès, 389).

But Mrs. Webster went on to say that in spite of six parliamentary defeats, the women in favor of suffrage had become an irrepressible army—that no matter what, they would continue.

As women gained self-confidence as speakers, voters began to accept their appearance on political platforms,* and it was not long before the two parties figured out how to make use of their interest. Thus Conservative ladies were gathered into the Primrose League, while Liberals formed the Women's Liberal Federation. This departure from tradition was made easier by the Corrupt Practices Act of 1883, which by cutting down on ribaldry, calumny, and intimidation at the polling places (which had so disturbed the *Edinburgh Review* in 1841) made them more suitable for ladies. Apparently, once the voters could no longer be bought, the parties thought they might as well use women campaigners.†

Many people of both sexes who favored using women in corralling votes were not yet ready to take the big step toward letting them vote themselves. Gladstone told the ladies who were working for his cause in 1879 that the memory would gild their future lives; yet he believed that casting a ballot would trespass upon their delicacy. By 1884 suffragists were convinced that he was a determined enemy of woman suffrage.[40]

The Women's Liberal Federation itself was badly split between a militant faction that wanted to make votes for women the main aim of the organization and the moderates who were willing to wait. By 1892 the militants, led by Rosalind, Countess of Carlisle (a daughter of Lady Stanley of Alderley), gained the majority and instructed the Executive Council to work for the parliamentary franchise.[41] The fact that Mrs. Gladstone did not resign her chairmanship at this point may or may not indicate that her husband's hostility had softened.

The cause had suffered an embarrassing set-back in 1889 when the *Nineteenth Century*, a monthly review, carried "An Appeal Against Female Suffrage" drawn up by Mrs. Humphry Ward and signed by a galaxy of more than a hundred women bearing names of the high distinction.[42] Among the signers were Lady Stanley of Alderley, Beatrice

---

*Two reactions to Kate Amberley's public speaking show how her own family took it. Her aunt wrote: "I have been terribly ashamed of my Goddaughter & think it is a great pity she was not born an American" (Amberley and Amberley, 2: 350). But her mother-in-law wrote:

> I am not in the least disposed to make fun of you—I am strongly for the cause, you feel that speaking for it in public is yr vocation & it is all right you should do so—*One* of yr vocations, I prefer to say—neither the greatest, highest, nor most difficult—but let it by all means have its place in yr life if it takes the form of duty to yr mind. If you never do anything naughtier than presiding & speaking at public meetings, we may well be proud of you—if you never do anything better we may well be ashamed of you! [Ibid., 2: 484]

†The Liberal party professed to believe in votes for women, but feared that most women would vote Conservative. The Conservatives expected to gain some votes, but were passionately opposed on principle (Ray Strachey, 283).

Webb, and the wives of Walter Bagehot, Matthew Arnold, and T. H. Huxley. To these upper-class women, who were used to getting what they wanted in life anyway, the need of their lower-class sisters for the ballot as an instrument for gaining essential reforms seemed far from pressing, and they argued that voting would seem distasteful and ridiculous, and would tend to lower women's moral force. Years later Beatrice Webb recanted and explained what had led her to sign. She admitted that she had always received preferential treatment from editors and that her conservative family background had made her anti-democratic; furthermore, the style of some of the most active suffragists irritated her.[43]

On the other hand, nearly all the women who worked outside their homes favored votes for women, The headmistresses of girls' schools passed a pro-suffrage resolution, and women doctors came out for it by thirty-five to one.[44] And in the same year as the *Nineteenth Century*'s "Appeal," the Woman's Franchise League was formed in the living room of Mrs. Emmeline Pankhurst.

This redoubtable lady undertook her first political activity in company with her husband, Dr. Richard Pankhurst, working for the Married Women's Property Bill of 1880. Shortly thereafter she joined the Manchester Women's Suffrage Committee. A move to London in 1885 expanded and radicalized her views, to the point that she left the Liberal party and signed up with the just-founded Independent Labour party (ILP) in 1893.[45] Unlike the older parties, the ILP did not segregate its women members but let them play a central role. In 1904 they elected her to their executive committee, and they arranged to have a suffrage bill introduced into Parliament.

From then on Mrs. Pankhurst, with her daughter Christabel, dominated the suffrage movement. It is useless to guess whether without her, or if she had been different, votes for women would have come sooner or been delayed longer; she was clearly a person who could not brook opposition, or even disagreement, and her life from 1905 to 1918 was a succession of splits from people with whom she had been friendly. She would doubtless feel that the continued narrowing of her interests and of her base of support represented also a deepening of commitment to a single radical cause, but others would disagree. A list of her cast-offs suggests what her political style was life: in 1905 she split with the so-called constitutional suffragists, led by Millicent Garrett Fawcett* in the National Union of Women's Suffrage Societies, and with all those who wished to work within the system; in 1907 she resigned from the ILP; a year later, as her tendency to dominate increased, a number of women left her organization and formed the Women's Freedom League; in 1912 followed a break with the Pethick-Lawrences, hitherto her right-hand helpers, because they could not approve the move toward violent militancy.† By 1914 she had driven off even her daughter Sylvia, who wanted

*Dr. Elizabeth Garrett Anderson's sister, and the mother of Philippa G. Fawcett.

†Which led to *Punch*'s cartoon of the Budding Suffragette: "I say, . . . are you a Peth or a Pank?" (Graves, 4: 173).

to organize the poor women of London's East End, while her mother would use only an "elite." A year later she virtually abandoned the suffragettes themselves in her unbridled enthusiasm for war recruiting, and finally, in 1918, after women had received the vote, she joined the Conservative party.

When Mrs. Pankhurst founded the Women's Social and Political Union (WSPU) in 1903, she intended to help working-class women, in line with her orientation of the moment. The WSPU retained close, though informal, relations with the ILP, even though the Labour party was divided on the question of woman suffrage. The leader, Kier Hardie, it is true, never wavered in his support of the women's vote, but Philip Snowden, who also served on their executive board, became positively hostile.[46] He preferred to extend the vote to all adult males, believing that votes cast by women would not help labor, but would mainly benefit the middle class. Although the ILP had originally favored a woman suffrage plank, Christabel Pankhurst noticed that their support grew lukewarm. "One gathers that some day, when the Socialists are in power, and have nothing better to do, they will give women votes as a finishing touch to their arrangements, but for the present they profess no interest in the subject."[47] When, in 1907, the ILP formally declared that it would not support any future bill giving women the same voting rights that men possessed at that time, namely with property qualifications—though nearly all woman suffrage bills were drawn up with these terms—the Pankhursts severed their connection with the ILP and at the same time took personal control of the WSPU.* From that time on, all democratic processes within the organization ceased, and the group functioned like a military machine (very much in the way that the Booths managed the Salvation Army).

Through all this Kier Hardie remained consistently on the side of woman suffrage, against his own party and the majority of the House of Commons. It is therefore sad to recall that Mrs. Pankhurst turned even on him, using the excuse that in the months just before World War I he focused his attention exclusively on the reduction of armaments in an effort to maintain peace, and so neglected temporarily to give the woman question the priority the Pankhursts felt it deserved.[48]

Even before the final break with the ILP, the suffragists realized that they would need the backing of some major party in order to gain serious attention for their bills. The Liberals represented the obvious choice, especially as they were expected to return to power shortly. At an important party rally at Manchester in October, 1905, Sir Edward Grey was expounding the policies that his party would support when Christabel Pankhurst and her friend Annie Kenney rose from the audience and inquired whether votes for women would be among them. Sir Edward ignored the interruption, whereupon one of the women jumped on to a chair to repeat her question. The chairman maintained his impassive

*In 1913 the ILP modified its position and said that it would not accept any franchise bill that did not include women (Fawcett, 212).

attitude. (Grey was believed to be personally in favor of votes for women but was not permitted to make it a matter of party principle.) The protesting women were dragged down and hustled out of the hall by police, and Christabel, whose hands were held behind her, spat at a policeman. In court they were sentenced to pay a fine, which they haughtily refused to do, and so they had to spend a few days in prison. This brought a gratifying increment in publicity and public sympathy. "There is no other way whereby we can put forward our claims to political justice," averred Christabel.[49]

When the Liberals won as expected and took control of the government, their top echelons were so divided that they decided to sidestep the issue by letting a woman suffrage bill be introduced, if at all, only through a private member's bill. Everyone knew that such bills, lacking government support, received very slight attention. This policy also meant that at party rallies, questions about suffrage were deemed inappropriate.

So, in 1906, when a delegation representing all the various suffrage societies (and there were several besides the WSPU), carrying the word from 260,000 women and bearing a petition signed by 1,530 women university graduates, waited upon the Prime Minister, Sir Henry Campbell-Bannerman, he answered that while he was not personally opposed to their demand, he was unable to pledge his government to work for it.

Determined to bring their cause somehow to public consideration, the WSPU continued their demonstrations, courted arrest, and valued each flamboyant case as a triumph for women. The other great wing of the suffrage movement, led by Mrs. Fawcett, did not favor militancy but tried always to work constitutionally.

The WSPU's success was such that in 1906–1907 they could chalk up 191 weeks of imprisonment, and the following year, 350. At first the members were treated as "political" prisoners, which meant somewhat better jail conditions than were meted out to criminals, but soon the government ordered them thrown in with the latter. The first of their famous hunger strikes were intended to win back their right to be sent to the political prisoners' quarters.

Mrs. Pankhurst herself was the first hunger striker, and she was set free in less than four days. But as other women began to copy her example, the government clamped down, and soon adopted the policy of forcible feeding by rubber tubes, which is a brutal, dangerous, and conceivably fatal procedure when applied to a resisting victim.

As the campaign heated up, both sides became more violent. The women began a deliberate campaign of destruction, starting with breaking windows in government buildings and then moving into arson, which was estimated to have destroyed half a a million pounds worth of property before it ended.[50] They chained themselves to gallery seats in the House of Commons, painted out house numbers, slashed paintings in museums, and forged tickets of admission to closed party meetings.

Finally one of them threw herself in front of the King's horse and was killed.

Meanwhile, the police escalated their attacks.[51] They pinched the breasts of the women whom they were trying to control, knocked them down, twisted their arms, tore off their clothing, smashed their faces into railings, and hurled foul language such as these ladies had never heard before.

Through it all the women kept coming on, enduring the pain and insult, insisting on their rights—and all with a curious gaiety. I. A. R. Wylie, who occasionally stood guard at night outside the walls within which suffragettes were imprisoned (four women at a time stood in four-hour shifts), described her companions in the movement as "an amazing crowd of duchesses, debutantes, shopgirls, governesses, old ladies, Perfect Ladies, and charwomen who came together under the purple, white and green banner."[52] She added that the WSPU members were "the sanest, most level-headed and light-hearted aggregation I have ever had the luck to meet. I never saw them rattled or out of hand. Their stridency was a matter of policy. They felt that it was time someone shrieked loud enough to wake somnambulists in Whitehall."[53] Or, as a friend of the Pankhursts put it: "The wonderful days . . . can one never pin down on paper the joy and emotions of 1906–14?"[54]

Mrs. Pankhurst's younger daughter, Sylvia, although no less committed to the cause of suffrage, had to smother for a long while her disagreement with her mother's and sister's elitism. Eventually she broke with them, to set up a dissident branch of the WSPU that sought mainly working-class women as members.[55] These were the women who, under intolerable living conditions, most desperately needed the vote. The family split became final in January, 1914, when the three Pankhursts met in Paris, whither Christabel had exiled herself rather than subject herself to almost certain imprisonment. She thought of herself as the general of an army whose leadership was too important to be interrupted. At this, their last meeting, Christabel laid out her program of using only "picked women," the strongest and the most intelligent. These women were "to take their instruction and march in step like an army."[56]

Sylvia was the only Pankhurst to consider World War I a disaster.

In 1911 all branches of the women's movement, militant and constitutional, joined in a huge parade of 40,000 marchers, with a special brigade of 700 ex-prisoners, and pageants representing, among other things, peeresses sitting in the Parliament of Edward III.*

---

*Their high spirits were shown in their announcement of a water carnival on the Serpentine. The Office of Works, as expected, locked the boats together, but the suffragettes simply threw off their wraps, revealed themselves in bathing costume, and swam out to the boats to cut them free. When they came ashore, the police picked them up and took them dripping wet to the police station (E. Sylvia Pankhurst, 547).

All this activity slowly influenced the views of the public, but it seemed only to drive Parliament into a panic. Some believe that Lloyd George, then Chancellor of the Exchequer, turned away from a pro-suffrage position after the heckling he received at a 1911 meeting, and shortly thereafter Mr. McKenna, the Home Secretary, restored forcible feeding, which Winston Churchill had stopped in one of the few humanitarian gestures of the party in power. The women then increased their militancy, began a stepped-up arson campaign by setting fire to a minister's house and attempting to fire the theater where Mr. Asquith, then Prime Minister, was to speak. Parliament could only dig in its heels; whatever the outcome, they announced, they would never give in to civil violence.

In order to keep the hunger strikers from actually dying in prison, with all the unfavorable publicity which that would bring, the government decided on a "cat and mouse" technique of releasing starving women long enough to regain their health, then rearresting them and carrying them back to prison to finish out their sentences.[57] (Many of the hunger strikers, however, had permanently injured their health by their long abstinence and their active resistance to the forced feeding and the violence connected with this revolting procedure.)

By the spring of 1914 all parties had settled into positions from which there could be no retreat. Mrs. Pankhurst entered her tenth hunger strike. Sylvia and some of her partisans decided to outmaneuver the Cat and Mouse Act by undertaking thirst as well as hunger strikes and announcing that in the future they would neither eat nor drink, in or out of prison, until death.[58]

In the end it was Sylvia's delegation of working-class women that was received by Prime Minister Asquith in June, 1914. Their simple stories finally shook his anti-feminist faith. He told them that he was prepared to support a suffrage bill, but within the month he was faced with the catastrophe that wiped out for the time being all thought of woman suffrage.[59]

By this time Emmeline and Christabel Pankhurst had begun to suffer what can only be called hallucinations: the entire male sex was the enemy; white slavers and carriers of venereal disease were responsible for nearly all the ills of the world; and these evils could be lanced only by the surgical technique of women's violence.[60] When war broke out, Christabel's first statement, from France, labeled it "God's vengeance upon the people who had held women in subjection," but soon she decided that Germany was a "male" nation, while little Belgium was a suffragette country.[61] Within a month she was urging all suffragettes to serve in the soldiers' canteens, and soon after she was advocating the extirpation of pacifists and the industrial conscription of women.[62]

When Asquith actually came out for woman suffrage in 1916, stating that women deserved the vote after their heroic contributions to the war service, and, furthermore, would need to be heard in discussions on the post-war readjustments, both Mrs. Pankhurst and Christabel repudiated his speech and declared that they would not want votes for women to take priority over votes for all the soldiers and sailors.[63]

Most of the other suffrage societies also supported the war and dropped their campaigns for the duration, but a few seceders mostly Quakers and socialists, formed the Women's International League for Peace and Freedom, at The Hague. A small group called the United Suffragists continued to concentrate on the issue of woman suffrage and published a paper called *Votes for Women*.[64]

The cause was almost won, with or without their support for the war. In January, 1918, a "Representation of the People Act" enfranchised six million women over thirty, including householders, married women, and university graduates. The age limit was supposed to compensate for Britain's million surplus women by equalizing the votes of the two sexes, but its patent unfairness found redress in 1928 when Parliament made the age limit the same as men's—twenty-one. Before that, in 1919 a Sex Disqualification Removal Act allowed women to be elected to Parliament, to take various other public offices, and to be called to the bar.[65]

Thus both German and English women received the vote right after the war, but in different ways. The German middle class had the vote handed to them by the socialist revolutionaries with whom it had always refused to cooperate, while the English militants earned it by purging themselves in war service. Though their long pre-war campaigns were certainly significant, neither group of women obtained the suffrage directly as a result of their own fight for it.

∽Conclusion:
Individualism and Socialism

I do not want women to have power over men,
but over themselves.

Mary Wollstonecraft

The nineteenth century was a period in which middle-class women acquired both the desire and the power to make personal decisions of a new kind. In other words, they developed individuality. We have Theodor von Hippel's word for it that at the start of the century women were so undifferentiated that a man might as well pick his wife blind-folded, and Georg Simmel's observation a hundred years later that the individualization that they had developed in the meantime was demon-strated by the number of close personal relationships that they formed. Ellen Key noted that in the years before World War I, men's appreciation of women's personality rose rapidly; in earlier times men had been much the more interesting sex, but women were fast catching up.

In many ways the individualization of men had made great strides in the eighteenth century: we think of political man with his right to the pursuit of happiness, and economic man with his attention to private gain, and even personal man, if we accept Karl Weintraub's study of autobiographical styles, which indicates that the ability to regard oneself as a developing personality first appeared in the late eighteenth century. The "new woman" followed this new man during the period covered in the present study.

Her appearance was not, however, a simple matter of women's following men out of the house. Women were held by different bonds, among them babies, sexual laws, and the fact that outside jobs were unavailable. If home is thought of as a place from which women sent men out, the inference is that it was also a place for men to keep women in, and yet I believe that in that limited sphere, women took their first steps toward the kind of autonomy that they have today. The cult of domestic-ity of the early nineteenth century can not be fairly described as a male chauvinist plot; it represented a serious effort to lower the appalling infant mortality rate and in some sense offered women a duty parallel with the work ethic that the industrial system pressed upon men. I hope I have shown in the chapter on housekeeping that home often became a place where women could apply their personal taste, develop administrative abilities, and take responsibility for their children's health and education. This was a step up in itself, but it also generated the first demand for better and more serious schooling for the women. The very limitations provided a stimulus for enlargement: as one nineteenth-century feminist declared, "the obstacle is always generous." Home in those early days was a base to stand on, not a trap, and only later did it threaten to become a stopping place.

As they explored their responsibilities, women came to want money to spend at their own discretion. Money gives access to all sorts of choices, choices that both reveal and develop individual character. So it is not surprising that in every country women strove to change the laws so that they could enjoy this power.

As choices widened, women's more difficult demand came in the selection of careers. Not all women agreed that their single vocation was settled at the moment of their birth, that home was their only legitimate theater. Sometimes they wanted work for the sake of the income it would yield, but often the possession of money from their families gave them freedom to follow their calling. In this way several brand-new professions, such as nursing and social work, were created, jobs that had not previously been done by men, though women, of course, wanted to enter male professions also.

In those three areas of autonomy, home, money and work, progress could be straightforward. It was not easy to become the first woman doctor, but at least the steps to be taken were clear, and the sign of victory definite. It was not so in the last field, the control over their own bodies. Here the issues were tangled, the actors were often at cross-purposes, and there was no observable measure of success. One could not get sexual equality merely by changing a law and forcing one's way into a masculine institution. Sexual autonomy might mean one of several things. Was it the right to marry the man of one's choice? Freedom to find sexual fulfillment elsewhere? Or the right to escape the bondage of the flesh and go after higher things? Or was it only complete when one could limit family size so as to have more time and better health for other enterprises?

Freud distinguished between the glorification of sex as instinct, which he considered to be the attitude of the ancient world, and the glorification of the sexual object (the loved personality), the characteristic, in his view, of modern times. Certainly the predominant sexual wish of nineteenth-century women, including feminists, was to marry the right man, which meant not being forced to marry for financial reasons. This was particularly true in the Latin countries, where marriages had for so long been arranged, and for many women, like Hélène in the Margueritttes' *Femmes nouvelles*, being able to marry the man they loved was all the liberation they wanted. For them the prime reason for holding a job was that it gave them a wider sexual choice. But English and German girls too had a strong feeling about the ideal marriage that they believed their new individuality would facilitate, and its predominant value was a single, equal ethical standard.

Only a minority of women took the opposite path and glorified the sexual instinct rather than the object. Movements with this appeal come to birth periodically, trying to get back to a nature that they conceive as perfect sexual indulgence. The Saint-Simonians in France and the pre-war erotic movement in Munich provide examples of this trend, but they were far from the mainstream of nineteenth-century feminism.

A far greater number of women especially in England and Germany, would have liked to eliminate sex as an instinct. They agreed with John Stuart Mill that nature was "a horrible old harridan" to be resisted at any cost. We could analyze child-rearing patterns and figure out reasons why so many men and women regarded sex as ugly and dangerous, but instead let us try to look at the values in their own terms, not ours. The Victorians and their continental contemporaries thought of themselves as having reached a higher stage of civilization, based on rationality and civility; and the passions, especially the sexual passions, were seen as a holdover from a previous, imperfect period, and extremely interruptive of the things they were trying to do with their brains. A new demand for the idealization of relationships between the sexes ("celibacy is the aristocracy of the future") put tremendous strains on both partners, without their being aware of exactly what was the trouble.

Freud was enough of a child of his century to express this idea in *Civilization and Its Discontents*, even though those living at the time would not often accept him as their spokesman. He declared that civilization depended on sexual repression, which acted like a steam engine relaying power to other areas. To be sure, he thought repression had been carried to an extreme and suggested a lessening of tension, but by no means a complete abandoning of taboos.

Today some of Freud's spiritual descendants want to do away with nearly all repression. The free expression of sexual impulses seems a democratic sort of value, in tune with our desire for equality in all areas (Matthew Arnold pointed out the connection between the average sensual person and the philosophy of the Rights of Man), and high civilization is not such a value. So sex becomes a virtue, repression a sin, and our forefathers of a hundred years ago are seen as either silly or hypocritical.

Of course they did not succeed in what they were trying to do, and their main premise may have been at total variance with the biological facts. (So may ours.) Repression by the means available to them was impossible, and we can review the evidence of their huge amount of prostitution, their many and strange perverse forms of pleasure, their pornography—an endless list.

But still there was this thread of insistence that sex be transformed to a higher value, and some of their efforts were neither silly nor hypocritical. Men who wanted to introduce into the world justice, self-control, social order, and better emotional and spiritual relationships with other people began to be sensitive about justice for the second sex. Naquet, the French divorce reformer, could not understand how so odious a practice as forcing sex on an unwilling victim could continue in an era of civilization, and this sensitivity became one of the ways in which men increased their valuation of women.

There is no doubt that this new valuation, and the new demands that women were making for themselves, created a rising awareness in men who in previous centuries would have treated women as a superficial part of life, to be enjoyed but not taken very seriously. As for women, they were now insisting that they must be more than objects of masculine fancy or accommodation. Men had been able to separate the world of ideas and the world of public action from the world of sexual pleasure. Now women wanted to move into the world of ideas and public action, and they found that when talking with men on this level, sex intruded. Of course women wanted sexual pleasure too, but the priorities were difficult to adjust, and many women felt that if they could just get education and employment, they would let sex go by the board for a while. Then when these two attitudes crossed, men would find that their old liberty to express their needs and desires conflicted with women's new demand for equality (whatever that turned out to mean), and the disagreements were on such a non-verbal level that they were hard to compose.

The ultimate form of women's control over their own sexual lives would have been limitation of the size of their families, but this was not advocated in the nineteenth century with the persistence that the subject deserved. Isolated writers in every country urged birth control with all the arguments that would become commonplace a century later, although many of the theorists, from Malthus to Annie Besant to the Fabians, were more interested in its effect against poverty than in what it would do for women's personal autonomy. But most English people did not like to discuss a subject that might open the floodgates of sensuality, while French feminists did not need to thrust into the limelight a secret that most French wives already possessed.

Every country had its version of the "new woman." She always practiced some combination of the freedoms that have just been alluded to. "The way the old clingingness has been thrown aside is amazing," says Wells in *Ann Veronica* (1909), commenting on the rapidity of the change. In life as well as in late nineteenth-century fiction, women were shown to be self-reliant and independent in judgment; they talked to men as equals and felt with Kate Amberley "a strong inclination to go against the world." Or, like Chiara Maffei, they expressed the wish to belong to themselves alone, to be self-judged. Even critics of the women's movement noticed that feminism was the latest wrinkle of individualism, or, as Ellen Key announced, "practically the greatest egoistic movement of the nineteenth century and the most intense affirmation of the right of the self that history had yet seen."

∽ The question naturally arises why the feminist movement, looking for political allies, failed to team up with the single political party that said it stood for the complete political and economic equality of the sexes. It would seem that feminism and socialism, the two great liberating movements of the nineteenth century, could have cooperated on their over lapping aims more than they did. Instead, the relationship blew hot and cold. In those countries where the women's movement was relatively weak, Italy and France, feminist leaders like Maria Deraismes and Anna Mozzoni finally turned to socialism out of despair, but in England and Germany, where there were large and well-organized middle-class feminist groups, they ostentatiously split with the socialist parties.

Obviously a good part of the reason was the antipathy that many members of the middle class, both men and women, felt toward any idea of social revolution. On the other hand, the women who opened up schools, colleges, and professions, who insisted on civil rights, who organized, marched, and flouted opinion, were too courageous to be turned away from an ideology that promised help; and in fact many of them approached socialist ideas spontaneously, and hopefully. If they were often disappointed in what they found, I think a good part of the reason was that while socialism promised to lift the domination of the masculine sex, it substituted its own kind of group control. Some committed socialist feminists, like Flora Tristan, were willing to assert that individualism was the chief fault of the age, and that association would be its cure, but a far greater number of middle-class feminists were threatened by a party discipline that seemed to undermine the chief accomplishment of their years of struggle for personal autonomy. We remember that Lily Braun was specifically warned by her husband not to develop an individual personality because it would hurt the socialist cause to which they both adhered. When she proved unable to accomplish this act of submission, she found herself quite unwelcome in the tightly organized ranks of the Social Democratic Party. In fact, socialism was unable to satisfy women in any of the four areas where middle-class women were flourishing their triumphs: home, money, work, and love.

In regard to the private household, socialist women were indeed to be freed both from masculine tyranny therein and from household drudgery. Robert Owen hoped that the citizens of his commonwealth would eat at a common table. With the children siphoned off to a communal nursery, he wanted his adults to use the occasion to discuss public affairs with civility. His idea that women could be particularly helped by this socialization is quite touching.*

The persistence of this socialist tenet is shown by Sidney Webb, a good Fabian socialist, who looked around in 1916 and decided that the substitution of the individual human being—man, woman, or child—for the family group was a good thing because it made it easier for the state to meet community needs, presumably on an "individual basis." In other words it would be easier to regiment people who lacked a buffer of group support.

But even socialist women rebelled against this idea at times, while middle-class women were nearly unanimous in saying that they cherished their homes and particularly their close personal relationship with their children. They wanted to keep family life and affection out of the industrial system and the cash nexus, while socialists seemed to value these services only if they were publicly run and paid for.

Though under socialism there would be equal pay for equal work, there would be no private property, so that the fight of middle-class women for laws like the Married Women's Property Act would become irrelevant. I have tried to show what a large factor private income was in allowing hundreds of women to make creative choices in their lives. Here too the socialists seemed to offer a kind of regimentation instead.

Naturally socialists were mainly interested in the conditions of industrial workers, and though they assumed that when they came to power women would make a gigantic leap into all kinds of careers, they lacked concern for the painful efforts of the middle classes to pry open the professions and the doors to higher education one by one.

Though love was to be free under the socialist system, the apparently casual pleasure of the imagined partners sounded depersonalizing to middle-class women who wanted above all fidelity and commitment in this area. When Claire Bazard complained that the Saint-Simonians did not know a thing about the "love of each," "*individual ties are yet to be formed among them*" (emphasis added), she was forecasting a judgment that more than anything else kept women away from socialist love.

∽ The very essence of nineteenth-century feminism was an insistence on individual human values. They did not want to be freed from their ancient legal and personal bonds only to fall under new ones created by the state. This was the point of Josephine Butler's campaign to abolish the unconstitutional law requiring the enforced medical examination of

---

*The fast-food chains of the second part of the twentieth century give women half of the benefits these utopians were seeking; they allow women to escape squalid kitchen chores, but they do not provide access to adult conversation, nor do they free them to pursue professional careers.

prostitutes. These unhappy women were an extreme class, to be sure, but in a way they were a paradigm of the new as well as the old ways in which women could be oppressed. Mrs. Butler was against both forms of oppression, by individual men and by the state, and she would not have separated these causes. She would not have understood, or sympathized with, Brian Harrison's recent criticism that her campaign was "retrogressive" in its fear of state and bureaucratic control, even though he praises her feminism as forward-looking. Mrs. Butler regarded the state and its bureaucracy as a distinctly masculine creation, with no true liberation possible through its impersonal control, and she would have heartily agreed with Virginia Woolf's view that women should not play by men's rules.

The accomplishment of nineteenth-century feminists was to lay the groundwork for women's autonomy and for their cooperation. Of necessity they left the succeeding struggle to their granddaughters.

Appendix:
Demography and Feminism

Steve Hochstadt

The preceding text by Priscilla Robertson examines in detail the family lives and domestic customs of the educated western European elite. The nineteenth-century feminist political movement developed within this social context, staffed mainly by women from the upper and upper middle classes (hereafter referred to, for the sake of simplicity, as the "upper classes"). The traditional patterns of family life, and the feminism that challenged those patterns, were both molded by peculiarly upper-class attributes, such as possession of status and wealth, family connection, and access to education. The purpose of this essay is to outline the unique demography of the European upper classes and to argue that upper-class family structure provided a particularly fruitful ground for the growth of feminist ideology. The development of feminism then encouraged changes in these demographic characteristics, in some cases which were in the opposite direction from the demographic evolution of the rest of the population.

Attempts to trace relationships between birth, marriage, and death, on the one hand, and ideology, on the other, are still rare.* This essay tentatively advances the hypothesis that demographic differences among the classes are a partial explanation for different attitudes toward the position of women. The argument is tentative for two reasons: the speculative nature of links between demographic evidence and political attitudes and the incompleteness of the evidence itself. Some of the important sources for this appendix are investigations of small upper-

I wish to express sincere thanks to those who have helped me with advice and comments on previous drafts: Abbott Gleason, John Knodel, R. Burr Litchfield, Ann-Louise Shapiro, Richard Stites, and Elizabeth H. Tobin.

*Another attempt to relate demography and feminism has been made by Daniel Scott Smith for nineteenth-century America. His argument, however, is based on demographic changes in the entire population, leaving unexplained the class nature of feminism ("Family Limitation, Sexual Control, and Domestic Feminism in Victorian America," *Feminist Studies* 1 [Winter-Spring 1973]: 40–57).

class groups, such as the Genevan bourgeoisie or the English peers,* which may not be representative of the entire social stratum in question. It is obvious that a comparison of these two studies would not necessarily be a valid indicator of the relationship between the English and Swiss upper classes as defined here. Precise international comparisons simply cannot be undertaken with the data on hand.

Because of the problems of comparison and the present scarcity of studies isolating the upper classes, only a few selected aspects of family life will be examined here. Relevance to the text and availability of several sets of data are crucial criteria. These results are suggestive of certain interpretations but do not constitute sufficient proof. Further research, perhaps stimulated by the ideas gathered here, is required for more substantial verification. The comparative study of demography and family psychology is yet in its infancy.

The central topic of the text is the marriage relationship, from courtship through divorce. The marriage patterns that prevailed in the upper classes at the beginning of the nineteenth century were crucially dependent upon the ages of the partners. Parents of daughters were naturally anxious to find a match as soon as possible after the daughter reached marriageable age, both to relieve themselves of the burden of support and to assure the husband that she would still be naive and submissive. The prospective husband should already have shown his suitability through financial success, following a period of educational preparation. This pattern of expectation, common to parents and prospective mates, typically resulted in a wide age difference between husband and wife. The word "wide" is used in a relative sense: the difference of perhaps five to seven years for upper-class marriages was much greater than the average difference for all marriages in the nineteenth century. This age difference, stemming from courtship habits, reinforced the husband's ability to demand submission from his younger bride during the marriage.† Male domination was a natural consequence of demographic structure. The pattern was stable for generations, as psychological and material considerations flowed together to ensure its continuation. This simple demographic fact made it extremely difficult for women to increase their influence over their own lives.

Table 1, representing data drawn from various nations and various times in the nineteenth century, demonstrates both the universality of the

*Louis Henry, *Anciennes familles Genevoises, Etude démographique XVIᵉ–XXᵉ siècle* (Presses Universitaires de France, 1956); T. H. Hollingsworth, "The Demography of the British Peerage," supplement to *Population Studies* 18, no. 2 (November 1964).

†A hint that the age superiority was consciously maintained comes from a famous source: a letter from Thomas Buddenbrooks to his mother about his prospective bride, in the novel by Thomas Mann. He writes, "I hope you see no objection in the fact that Gerda is only three years younger than I!" (Mann, *Buddenbrooks, The Decline of a Family*, trans. H. T. Lowe-Porter [Harmondsworth, England: Penguin Books, 1971], p. 222).

TABLE 1. *Average marriage age by social standing in the nineteenth century*

Place	Social Class	Men	Women	Difference	Date
Bordeaux	Bourgeoisie	33.3	25.4	7.9	1823
	Peuple	29.5	26.8	2.7	
York, England	White collar, professionals	30.4	25.2	5.2	1838–1865
	Laborers	25.4	24.4	1.0	
England	Professionals, upper class	29.8	25.4	4.4	1850–1852
	All marriages	25.6	23.7	1.9	
Italy	Liberal professions	31.8	25.4	6.4	1896
	All marriages	27.7	24.8	2.9	
Copenhagen	Officials, merchants	32.2	26.5	5.7	1878–1882
	Workers	27.5	26.8	0.7	
Rotterdam and	Richest families	30.7	26.0	4.7	1877–1881
Dordrecht	Poorest families	28.2	26.9	1.3	
New Jersey	Professionals	28.2	23.4	4.8	1848–1850
	Laborers	25.1	21.8	3.3	

NOTE: First marriages only in Italy, Copenhagen, England, and New Jersey.
SOURCES: Bordeaux: Guillaume, 271; York: Armstrong, 165; England: Ansell, 46; Italy: Raseri, 159; Copenhagen, Rotterdam, and Dordrecht: Prinzing, "Heiratshäufigkeit," 551; New Jersey: Monahan, 2:283–84.

age difference in the western upper classes and its absence in the majority of the population. In each case, the difference in age between upper-class husband and wife is greater, by a considerable margin, than the difference between lower-class mates. The excess is always caused by a higher *male* age at marriage for the upper class. The female age at marriage does not vary widely between classes, and in three cases is lower for the upper classes. Where available data shows a more detailed gradation of classes, the smoothness of the rise in the male marriage age and the stability of the female age is apparent.* It might also be mentioned that Table 1 shows the difficulties of comparing studies directly. The dates do not match. Four of the data sets come from cities, while the rest deal with larger areas. Each class grouping is unique, and the kinds of marriages counted (first versus all) are not the same. Thus while it can be concluded that upper-class men married later than lower-class men in various parts of Europe, we cannot be sure about the relationship between the marriage ages of French and English men.†

In spite of the deficiencies of the evidence, the situation is clear: in the nineteenth century, the upper-class husband was normally at least five years older than his wife. We do not know how far back into the past this pattern extended. That it was well established by 1700 for the English and Italian nobilities is certain.‡ Scattered French evidence shows that, in some villages in the seventeenth century, the husband-wife age difference was greater as one moved up the social ladder.§ The continuity of this marriage structure was based upon a certain set of social practices, which included female exclusion from higher education, dowries, extremely close parental supervision, and sexual subordination. The movement toward female independence, from both family and husband, broke that social pattern. The "artificial" age differential, which represented this traditional pattern's demographic basis, simultaneously tended to dis-

---

*Friedrich Prinzing, "Heiratshäufigkeit und Heiratsalter nach Stand und Beruf," *Zeitschrift für Socialwissenschaft* 6 (1903): 551, 556; Enrico Raseri, "Sur les variations de taux de natalité et sur l'âge moyen des époux, suivant les conditions économiques," *Bulletin de L'Institut International de Statistique* 11, pt. 1 (1899): 158.

†A further hindrance to comparison between any two groups is the likelihood of dissimilar age distributions in the single population. A population with relatively more single women under twenty, for example, will have more marriages of women under twenty than another population, although the probabilities of marriage at any particular age might be identical for both groups. For a fuller description of the difficulties in calculating and using average age at marriage, see Thomas Monahan, *Pattern of Age at Marriage in the United States,* 2 vols. (Philadelphia: Stephenson Brothers, 1951), 1: 221–36.

‡R. B. Litchfield, "Demographic Characteristics of Florentine Patrician Families, Sixteenth to Nineteenth Centuries," *Journal of Economic History* 29 (June 1969): 199; Hollingsworth, "British Peerage," p. 25.

§Raymond Noel, "L'état de la population de Mostuejouls (Aveyron) en 1690," in *Hommage à Marcel Reinhard: Sur la population française au XVIIIᵉ et au XIXᵉ siècles* (Paris: Société de Démographie Historique, 1973), p. 517; Noel, "La population de la paroisse de Laguiole d'aprés un rencensement de 1691," *Annales de Démographie Historique, 1967,* p. 220.

appear. The broadening of opportunies for women to work or be educated made postponement of marriage for them more likely. A change in psychological and social attitudes was paralleled by demographic change: female marriage age rose for the upper classes in the later nineteenth century. This simple change had a broad effect on the entire family structure, opening more possibilities for a stronger female voice within the home. Demographic change could be both result and cause of growing female independence, accelerating and widening the movement.

A substantial body of data on marriage age is required, spanning the nineteenth century, in order to show this process in detail. Unfortunately, we must presently be satisfied with the barest hint of confirmation provided by the scattered information at our disposal. The only suitably lengthy time series which have been calculated for upper-class groups are presented in Tables 2 and 3. Two tables have been utilized since the first four series extend over a much longer time period. These data are once again not comparable from group to group because the men and women whose marriages have been tabulated were not chosen by the same criteria, nor were the researchers' methods of calculation the same, as is specified in the notes.

Except for the Genevan bourgeoisie, each series in Tables 2 and 3 shows a more or less steady advance of female age at marriage in the nineteenth century. Because of the differing series lengths and the imprecise dating of the series in Table 2, it is not possible to pinpoint the beginning of this trend, or even to say with assurance that it was a nineteenth-century phenomenon. On the other hand, male marriage ages show no particular trend: for five series they are relatively constant, for the Genevan bourgeoisie they drop, and for the English upper-class sample they rise steadily. Clearly the movement in the female age at marriage was not a simple reflection of changing marriage patterns for the entire upper class.

The tabulated age differences present a clear trend toward a smaller gap, with the notable exception of the English upper-class sample in Table 3. This series ends, unfortunately, in 1870, when the progress of the feminist movement was accelerating. The magnitude of the differences is also interesting. For the smaller groups at the very top of the social pyramid (Table 2 and the Bordeaux bourgeoisie in Table 3), differences between 6 and 12 years drop to a range of 4 to 8 years. The broader groups from England and New Jersey, which include a larger portion of the upper middle class, have a difference of between 3 and 5 years, but only for the New Jersey sample does the difference diminish. The increase in the female marriage age in the English professional class is more than offset by a slightly faster increase in the male age.

More corroborative evidence comes from several studies of French families by Catherine Rollet.* She shows that for two of three high

*Catherine Rollet, "Genealogies et démographie," in *Hommage à Marcel Reinhard*, p. 549, table 1.

TABLE 2. *Average marriage age for upper-class groups, 1700–1899*

	English Peers				Genevan Bourgeoisie			Danish Nobility			Milan Patricians		
Date	Men	Women	Difference	Date	Men	Women	Difference	Men	Women	Difference	Men	Women	Difference
1700–1724	30.2	23.5	6.7	1700–1749	31.9	26.3	5.6	30.4	23.4	7.0	33.4	21.2	12.2
1725–1749	29.7	24.2	5.5										
1750–1774	29.6	23.9	5.7	1750–1799	31.5	24.0	7.5	28.5	22.4	6.1	30.8	20.4	10.4
1775–1799	29.2	25.5	3.7										
1800–1824	30.8	25.4	5.4	1800–1849	29.4	22.7	6.7	31.6	24.7	6.9	31.5	22.3	9.2
1825–1849	30.8	25.6	5.2										
1850–1874	31.9	26.2	5.7	1850–1899	29.2	24.7	4.5	30.9	24.7	6.2	32.3	24.4	7.9
1875–1899	30.0	25.7	4.3										

NOTE: Only first marriages tabulated.
SOURCES: England: Hollingsworth, 25; Geneva: Henry, 55; Denmark: Hansen, 17; Milan: Zanetti, 87, table IV, 3.

TABLE 3. *Average marriage age for upper-class groups, 1800–1913*

	English Upper Class				Bordeaux Bourgeoisie				New Jersey Professional Class		
Date	Men	Women	Difference	Date	Men	Women	Difference	Date	Men	Women	Difference
1800	27.9	24.3	3.6								
1810	28.3	24.5	3.8								
1820	28.6	24.7	3.9	1823	33.3	25.4	7.9				
1830	29.0	25.0	4.0								
1840	29.4	25.2	4.2					1848–1850	28.2	23.4	4.8
1850	29.8	25.4	4.4	1853	32.3	26.1	6.2				
1860	30.1	25.6	4.5					1868	27.8	23.0	4.8
1870	30.5	25.9	4.6	1883	32.0	*	—	1880	28.1	24.3	3.8
								1890	28.2	23.9	4.3
								1900	28.0	24.8	3.2
				1913	32.8	27.3	5.5	1911	28.4	25.2	3.2

NOTE: For England and New Jersey only first marriages tabulated.
*The figure given here in the source is clearly an error and is thus omitted.
SOURCES: England: Ansell, 46; Bordeaux: Guillaume, 271; New Jersey: Monahan, 2:283–84.

bourgeois familes, whose genealogies have been traced through the nineteenth century, the average age difference dropped from above 8 years to 5.0 and 3.1, respectively, while the third family lineage showed little change.

A more detailed breakdown of age differences for both the bourgeoisie and the rest of the population in Bordeaux, shown in Table 4, demonstrates the variety of experiences compressed in such an "average." There had always been marriages in which the wife was more than five years older than the husband, but they were rare, only 0.9 percent in 1823 for the bourgeoisie. In 37.4 percent of the 1823 marriages, the man was over ten years older than his wife. Fewer than one-third of the wives married in this year were within five years of their husbands' age. This is a statistical description of the traditional marriage pattern of the upper classes. By 1913, the situation had changed dramatically. Fewer than half of the husbands were five years older. A woman older than her husband was no longer a rarity. That this change was limited to the upper classes is clearly shown by the stability of the distribution of marriages among *le peuple* of Bordeaux. Extreme age differences were uncommon throughout the period. Even in 1913, marriages in the lower class had smaller age gaps than those in the bourgeoisie.

Thus far we have tentatively established that upper-class women were marrying progressively later in the nineteenth century, tending to narrow the large gap between the ages of husband and wife. But if the female age at marriage were rising for *all* classes, this explanation of a growing upper-class feminist consciousness would clearly be inadequate. For the demographic change to be linked to the social-psychological one, they both must be limited to the upper classes. In fact, a striking contrast to the rising upper-class female marriage age is shown in the *downward* trend for both sexes in the rest of the population after 1850. This tendency was noticed even in the nineteenth century: the German statistician

TABLE 4. *Marriages in Bordeaux by social class: percentage of marriages grouped by age difference, 1823 and 1913*

Age Difference	Bourgeoisie (%)		Peuple (%)	
	1823	1913	1823	1913
Woman more than 5 years older	0.9	7.4	7.4	6.0
Age difference less than 5 years	27.8	47.2	59.3	64.2
Man 5–10 years older	33.9	25.6	19.8	19.7
Man more than 10 years older	37.4	19.9	13.4	10.1
Total	100.0	100.0	100.0	100.0

SOURCE: Guillaume, 276.

Friedrich Prinzing collected figures from many European nations in a 1902 article demonstrating the universal drop in male and female marriage ages since 1850.* Some of his findings are gathered in Tables 5 and 6. These numbers all express averages for the entire population of nations or regions; the tendency of the upper-class women shown previously is masked by the much larger numbers of women in the other classes, whose average marriage age was declining. Only for England do Prinzing's figures indicate a rise in female marriage age, coming at the very end of the century. Men's ages, where statistics were available, were also dropping.

Prinzing's work seventy years ago was extraordinarily sophisticated for the time, and his results still stand, although his methods have since been superseded. From 1750 to 1850 there was probably a general stability in marriage ages of both sexes in western Europe for the total population.† The latest studies of individual nations, originating from the Princeton Office of Population Research, by John Knodel on Germany and Etienne van de Walle on France, confirm the slow, steady drop in average age at marriage for females in the latter half of the nineteenth century.‡

The complicated changes in demographic structures that have been traced in the previous pages indicate that demography must take into account the separate evolutions in social and material circumstances of the classes. In the early nineteenth century, as probably in previous centuries, the marriage age for upper-class and professional men was much higher than for those less favored with status and wealth. After about 1850 increased opportunities for upper-class women to pursue a more independent life in universities, in government, and in commerce brought the same pressures to postpone marriage that upper-class men had long experienced. The rise in the average marriage age of upper-class women and the lessening of the age differences within marriage were both result and cause.§ These alterations in marital customs were related

---

*Friedrich Prinzing, "Die Wandlungen der Heiratshäufigkeit und des mittleren Heiratsalters," *Zeitschrift für Socialwissenschaft,* 5 (1902): 661–66.

†Katherine Gaskin compares over forty modern local studies of European marriage age, demonstrating that there are no discernable trends for any nation in this period, in "Age at First Marriage in Europe before 1850: A Summary of Family Reconstitution Data," *Journal of Family History* 3 (1978): 23–36.

‡John Knodel, *The Decline of Fertility in Germany, 1871–1939* (Princeton: Princeton University Press, 1974), p. 70; Etienne van de Walle, *The Female Population of France in the 19th Century* (Princeton: Princeton University Press, 1974), p. 127; for the United States, see Monahan, *Pattern of Age at Marriage,* 2: 283–84.

§The transition from peasant and artisan to industrial modes of production in the nineteenth century allowed lower-class men and women to marry *earlier* than before and set up independent households. Prinzing gives this explanation of the decline in national average marriage age in "Wandlungen," pp. 670–74. See also Louise Tilly, Joan Scott, and Miriam Cohen, "Women's Work and European Fertility Patterns," *Journal of Interdisciplinary History* 3 (1976): 447–76.

TABLE 5. *Average marriage age for all marriages: Europe, 1851–1899*

Dates	France	Belgium	Holland	England	Sweden		Italy	
	Women	Women	Women	Women	Men	Women	Men	Women
1851–1860	26.1*	28.8		25.7				
1861–1870	25.7	28.7		25.6	30.9	28.3		
1871–1880	25.5	28.7		25.7	31.0	28.2	30.1†	25.5†
1881–1885	25.0	28.0	27.4	25.6	30.4‡	27.8‡	29.9	25.1
1886–1890	25.1	27.0	27.2	25.8	30.6§	28.0§	29.5§	24.9§
1891–1895	25.2‖		27.2	26.2				
1896–1899					30.5*	27.4*	29.2	24.9

*1853–1860.
†1872–1880.
‡1882–1886.
§1887–1891.
‖1891–1893.
*1896 only.
SOURCE: Prinzing, "Wandlungen," 664–66.

TABLE 6. *Average marriage age for all marriages:*
Bavaria and Prussia, 1835–1899

Dates	Bavaria		Prussia	
	Men	Women	Men	Women
1835–1860	32.4	29.4		
1862–1868	32.7	29.5		
1867–1869			29.8	27.9
1872–1875	32.3	28.7	29.5	26.9
1876–1880	31.6	28.0	29.6	27.1
1881–1885	30.6	27.6	29.5	26.3
1896–1899			28.9	26.6

SOURCE: Prinzing, "Wandlungen," 661, 663.

to changes in women's perception of themselves. The coincidence of the decline of marital age differences with the rise of feminism was not fortuitous. The emancipation outside the family allowed more equality within marriage between partners of nearly the same age. The pattern of cause and effect was not linear, but circular and reciprocal.

The previous section on marriage age linked a demographic trend with the changing attitudes of women traced in Priscilla Robertson's text. A further examination of the widely disparate familial experiences of women in different social classes after marriage leads to a more fundamental appreciation of the environment of upper-class female concern with their subordinate status. A demographic framework unique to the upper classes may have made these women more cognizant of their sexual inferiority and more determined to do something about it. An attempt will be made here to outline the major class differences in family life and to explain their possible effects on women's consciousness. Demography was not the cause of these class differences, but different demographic structures helped to condition the different responses.*

One of the starkest contrasts between the classes was their differential mortality. Put in simple terms, more children from the upper classes survived childhood, and upper-class people lived longer. The direct causal connection between wealth and health was obvious and effective. The harshness of lower-class life is eloquently displayed in Table 7 which compares the percentage of infant deaths according to the fathers' occupational groups. The percentage of stillbirths follows the same pattern. Over half of the males born to welfare recipients did not each their first birthday, while the mortality rate for male children of military officers and public servants was about 25 percent.

*A caution is in order here concerning the data that will be used to support the argument. No attempt has been made to array data from all the countries concerned for each step in the chain of reasoning. This would not be possible, given the paucity of research on the upper classes as a separate social group.

TABLE 7. *Infant deaths and stillbirths by fathers' occupation: Prussia,* 1877–1888

Occupation of Father	% Deaths in First Year		% Stillborn	
	Male	Female	Male	Female
Welfare recipients	44.0	40.2	7.4	5.1
Servants	35.1	31.2	4.9	4.1
Day laborers	26.8	23.3	4.5	3.7
Pensioners	25.8	22.7	4.2	3.6
Wage workers	24.5	21.0	4.0	3.3
Self-employed	23.3	19.9	4.1	3.4
White collar	22.8	19.3	4.0	3.3
Public servants	21.8	18.7	3.7	3.0
Army officers	20.9	17.8	3.5	2.9

SOURCE: Seutemann, 148–49.

This class differential in the probability of death continued through each year of adult life. The statistician Charles Ansell compiled an interesting table that compared his insurance company's "upper class," the total English population, and the peerage in the first half of the nineteenth century, when infant and child mortality were at a much higher level. His results are contained in Table 8. There is a fairly close correspondence between the figures for the upper class and the peerage, while the proportion of the total population surviving at each age falls much more precipitously. By the age of seventy, the percentage of the upper class still alive, 40.9 percent, is nearly twice as great as that for the total population, 23.8 percent. Another way of expressing the same point is to contrast the average life span of the classes: in Bordeaux during the nineteenth century, the bourgeoisie lived from eleven to twenty years longer than the rest of the inhabitants.* These data are merely illustrative of the well-established fact of class differentials in mortality at all ages, a pattern certainly not confined to the nineteenth century.†

The consequences of the much lower mortality of the upper class should not be underestimated. The immanence of death in daily life can affect the entire psychological perspective of the family. Here, however, the concern is merely with the average life expectancy. The longer life of those in the upper classes resulted in a different structure of family life. In

---

*Pierre Guillaume, *La population de Bordeaux au XIXe siècle* (Paris: Librairie Armand Colin, 1972), p. 143.

†For more data on this point: for Prussia, see Karl Seutemann, *Kindersterblichkeit sozialer Bevölkerungsgruppen insbesondere im preussichen Staate und scinen Provinzein* (Tübingen, 1894), p. 69; for Hamburg, R. E. May, "Zur Frage des Geburtenrückganges," *Schmollers Jahrbuch,* 4 (1916): 1645–84; for Holland, C. A. Verrijn-Stuart, "Natalité, mortinatalité, et mortalité enfantine selon le degré d'aisance dans quelques villes et un nombre de communes rurales dans les Pays-Bas," *Bulletin de L'Institut International de Statistique* 13, pt. 2 (1902); for Geneva, Henry, *Anciennes familles Genevoises,* pp. 157–59.

TABLE 8. *Survivors per 1,000 born for social class groups in England*

Age	Upper Class*	Peerage†	Total Population‡
0	1,000	1,000	1,000
1	920	930	851
2	898	915	797
5	873	899	737
10	850	882	703
20	807	829	663
30	744	753	604
40	682	689	539
50	616	610	464
70	409	352	238

*Compiled by Ansell from data gathered in 1874.
†Calculated from deaths in peerage, 1800–1855.
‡Compiled by Registrar General from deaths, 1838–1854.
SOURCE: Ansell, 71.

particular, it lengthened the number of years a marriage endured intact, before death severed the relationship. The findings of a Prussian study of the 1890 are contained in Table 9. The "higher classes," which included both the upper and upper middle classes, had by far the largest proportion of marriages that lasted more than fifteen years, nearly one-half. At the other end of the social scale, only one-fourth of laborers' marriages had endured for fifteen years, and more than half were less than ten years old. Thus the typical upper-class marriage would be much older than the average working-class marriage.* The same relationship is shown by the 1906 French family statistics that classified people by wage: the higher wage groups had longer marriages.† This occurred in spite of the fact that the upper class married several years later. Therefore, the average upper-class woman spent a longer time in the married state than the rest of her sex. She was far more likely to complete her childbearing years, pass through middle age, and become old. The conditions of her marriage, especially the relationship between husband and wife, took on a greater importance.

Naturally much of any nineteenth-century woman's time was spent in the bearing and raising of children. In this crucial respect, also, a widening gulf separated the classes. It is generally agreed that the upper classes had long had a lower marital fertility than the general populace. The European fertility decline, which was the outstanding demographic

*These figures do not mean that half of all laborers' marriages ended before ten years, since the table contains all existing marriages at one time, including even the most recent.

†Derived from tables published by R. Manschke, "Beruf und Kinderzahl," *Schmollers Jahrbuch* 40 (1916): 1907.

TABLE 9. *Duration of existing marriages by social class: Prussia, 1890s*

Years married	Higher Classes (%)	Hand Workers (%)	Clerks (%)	Lower Employees, Domestics (%)	Laborers (%)
Under 5	17.6	22.2	31.6	30.1	34.2
5–9	17.4	20.2	19.8	19.4	23.7
10–14	15.2	16.4	15.2	14.6	14.7
15–24	25.5	22.8	18.7	19.5	18.3
Over 24	24.3	18.4	14.7	16.4	9.1
Total	100.0	100.0	100.0	100.0	100.0

SOURCE: Seutemann, 91.

TABLE 10. *Completed marital fertility by social class and date of marriage: England, 1851–1886*

Social Group	1851–1861	1861–1871	1871–1881	1881–1886	% Decline
Upper class	6.25	5.93	4.97	4.22	31.5
Total population	7.01	6.73	6.11	5.54	21.0

Note: 'Upper class' includes professionals, capitalists, and managers. Fertility has been standardized for differences in age at marriage between the classes, which were defined by the Registrar General.
SOURCE: Innes, 42.

characteristic of the nineteenth century, was led by the upper classes.* The drop in fertility generally began and accelerated after 1870, except for France and the United States, whose declines may have started as early as 1800.† The lead of the upper classes served to widen the fertility gap between the social classes until well into the twentieth century, when the general fertility decline brought all the classes closer at unprecedented low levels. Table 10 represents data collected in England that clearly show both the general trend toward lower fertility after 1870 and the faster pace of the upper-class drop. The figures are the average number of children per woman married for her entire fertile period, and do not reflect the size of an average family. Between the first two decades, the change was small; it then accelerated through the rest of the century. In this period, the fertility of the English upper class dropped 50 percent faster than that of the general population.‡

A very interesting, if technically flawed, study by Jacques Bertillon just before the turn of the century serves to show the universality of the class differences in fertility at that time. Bertillon calculated the fertility of various districts in Paris, Berlin, London, and Vienna, and ranked

*H. J. Habakkuk, *Population Growth and Economic Development since 1750* (New York: Humanities Press, 1971), chap. 3; Knodel, *Decline of Fertility in Germany*, p. 118–20. The Genevan bourgeoisie was clearly already limiting its fertility by 1700, and the decline was nearly complete by the end of the eighteenth century (see Henry, *Anciennes familles Genevoises*, pp. 81–87). In Bordeaux, the bourgeoisie had lower fertility throughout the nineteenth century than the rest of the population (see Guillaume, *Population de Bordeaux*, tables 112, 115, 116, pp. 301–3). According to Hans Hansen, "Demography of Lineages," p. 20, the Danish nobility's fertility began to drop definitively by 1800 ("Some Aspects of the Demography of Lineages Belonging to Danish High Nobility in the Age of Enlightened Despotism [1660–1848]," unpublished manuscript, 1976, p. 20). For evidence that the upper social class led the decline in the United States, see Xarifa Sallume and Frank W. Notestein, "Trends in the Size of Families Completed Prior to 1910 in Various Social Classes," *American Journal of Sociology* 38 (November 1932): 398–408.

†Ansley Coale, "The Decline of Fertility in Europe from the French Revolution to World War II," in S. J. Behrman, Leslie Corsa, and Ronald Freedman, eds., *Fertility and Family Planning* (Ann Arbor: University of Michigan Press, 1969); Etienne van de Walle, "Marriage and Marital Fertility," *Daedalus* 97 (Spring 1968): 486–501.

‡Virtually identical results were published by T. H. C. Stevenson, in "The Fertility of Various Social Classes in England and Wales from the Middle of the 19th Century to 1911," *Journal of the Royal Statistical Society* 83, pt. 3 (May 1920): 415.

TABLE 11. *Fertility by wealth of district in European cities, 1881–1894: births per 1,000 women aged 15–50*

District Type	Paris, 1889–1893	Berlin, 1886–1894	London, 1881–1890	Vienna, 1881–1890
Very poor	108	157	147	200
Poor	95	129	140	164
Comfortable	72	114	107	155
Very comfortable	65	96	107	153
Rich	53	63	87	107
Very rich	34	47	63	71
City total	79	102	109	153

NOTE: For Vienna only, births per 1,000 married women.
SOURCE: Bertillon, 163–76.

these districts by the wealth of the inhabitants.* Table 11 summarizes Bertillon's calculations. Of primary interest is the smooth progression from low fertility in the richest districts to much higher levels, from two to three times as high, in the poorest districts. The differences among the cities are less noteworthy. The figures for Vienna are inflated because the measure of fertility is not the same as for the other cities: births are compared to married women only. Parisian fertility was, of course, the lowest, as the fertility decline had begun in France at a much earlier date. It is interesting that the class difference in Paris, after almost a century of general fertility decline, was still stronger than in London or Vienna, and just slightly less than in Berlin. As we have noted for England (see Table 10), the general fertility decline throughout Europe served to further divide the classes, at least until its last stages after 1900.†

The major causes of the fertility decline and the specific reasons for the lead of the upper classes are not nearly so important here as the consequences. Married women in the upper classes were altering their traditional way of life in the latter half of the nineteenth century simply by having fewer children. This was accomplished by the lengthening of the average time between births, and, more germane to our theme, a shortening of the total childbearing period. Thus the age at which the upper-class woman had her last child became younger.‡ When this fact is

*The fertility measure does not directly assess class fertility since it is based on residential districts rather than social groups, but his results identify the presence of class differences, even if the precise magnitude remains unknown.

†Data for seven German cities at the turn of the century, with very similar results, are presented in Paul Mombert, *Studien zur Bevölkerungsbewegung in Deutschland* (Karlsruhe: 1907), pp. 149–60); Verrijn-Stuart's data for Dutch communities are also useful (see "Natalité," p. 361).

‡As the fertility of the Genevan bourgeoisie dropped to "modern" low levels in the eighteenth century, the average age of the mother at the birth of her last child fell 7 years, from 38.5 to 31.5 (Henry, *Anciennes familles Genevoises*, pp. 87–93).

combined with the much longer average duration of marriage in the upper classes (Table 9), it is clear that between 1850 and 1900 the upper-class woman was spending many more years in the married state after her childbearing was complete than were other women. Her powerlessness, her worldly uselessness, her lack of education in non-domestic matters, were more apparent and irritating.

The changing demography of the upper classes in the last half of the nineteenth century served to heighten these women's awareness of their position, and perhaps to make it less acceptable. The traditional restriction of women's activities was felt even more keenly by those who never married and thus could not exercise the few functions set aside for their sex. The difficulties of single women are clearly described in the text. Significantly, the proportion of women who never married was probably much higher for the upper class than for the rest of the population.

As John Hajnal clearly showed in a 1965 article, western Europe, in comparison with eastern Europe and Asia, has long been characterized by a relatively high proportion of unmarried men and women, generally more than 10 percent of those who reach the age of fifty.* Statistics are sorely lacking for upper-class groups, so that it is impossible to specify class differences precisely. The only available series are for the English peers and the Genevan bourgeoisie.† For both groups, well over 20 percent of both sexes were still single at fifty years of age in the nineteenth century, and presumably never married. Figures for the total population are available for England, France, and Germany after 1850, and for Denmark and Italy about 1900.‡ The percentage of single women at fifty in all these series is fairly consistent, hovering between 11 percent and 14 percent. The gap between the upper-class figures and the national figures cannot be generalized confidently to the European upper class, but a larger proportion of single women might have been an upper-class characteristic. These spinsters could provide both a source of strength for the feminist movement and an example to married women of what could be accomplished by a woman alone.

Two important conclusions can be drawn from this collection of statistics and tables. The most apparent is that there were stark demographic differences in the nineteenth century between the social classes. They originated in previous centuries but were intensified in the

*John Hajnal, "European Marriage Patterns in Perspective," in D. V. Glass and D. E. C. Eversley, eds., *Population in History* (London: Arnold, 1965), pp. 101–46.

†Hollingsworth, "British Peerage," p. 20; Henry, *Anciennes familles Genevoises*, p. 52.

‡For England: *Census of England and Wales 1911*, vol. 7, House of Commons Sessional Papers 1912–1913, vol. 113, Cmd. 6610, p. 429; France: van de Walle, "Marriage and Marital Fertility," p. 492; Germany: Knodel, *Decline of Fertility in Germany*, p. 70; Italy: Hajnal, "European Marriage Patterns," p. 102; Denmark: Harald Westergaard, "On the Study of Displacements Within a Population," *Journal of the American Statistical Association* 17 (December 1920): 384.

nineteenth, especially after 1850. Not only were the upper classes characterized by different levels of fertility and mortality, but certain demographic changes occurred in opposite directions for different classes, as was clearly shown for female age at marriage. Many of these social differences are still apparent.* The basic facts of life, death, and marriage were class-specific.

Secondly, demography can help us to understand better the class nature of European feminism. The women whose words and actions are carefully traced in the text were not representative of all women, although they often couched their arguments in universal terms. It was not simply that upper-class women led the fight for emancipation. The obvious advantages conferred by wealth, status, and education are a simple explanation of their political leadership. Upper-class women also clashed with working-class women in the nineteenth as well as in the twentieth century over the proper aims for concerted action.† An important cause for upper-class women's concern with purely female rights, in the home, in the marketplace, and in the schools, was their particular demographic structure. Their marriages lasted far longer, while their childbearing years were more quickly ended. More of them remained single and were forced to find a place in a male-dominated world. There was both more opportunity and more need for an upper-class woman to ponder the conditions of her sex and to strive to change them. The psychology of upper-class female activism must be seen in the light of their daily family life, whose outlines can be traced in demographic study. As further research probes more deeply into the social-psychological background of feminism, the nature of this political movement will become clearer.

∽ BIBLIOGRAPHY TO APPENDIX

Alberti, Leon Battista. *The Family in Renaissance Florence.* Trans. Renee Neu Watkins. Columbia, S.C.: University of South Carolina Press, 1969.

Ansell, Charles, Jr. *On the Rate of Mortality at Early Periods of Life, The Age of Marriage, The Number of Children to a Marriage, The Length of a Generation, and Other Statistics of Families in the Upper and Professional Classes.* London: National Life Assurance Society, 1874.

---

*For the continued presence of class differences in marriage age in modern Sweden, see Eva M. Bernhardt, "Trends and Variations in Swedish Fertility—A Cohort Study" (Ph. D. diss., University of Pennsylvania, 1971), published in *Urval* 5 (Statistiska Centralbyran); for the United States, see Monahan, *Pattern of Age at Marriage,* 2: 261–65. Striking mortality differentials still existed in England in 1950, as shown in J. W. B. Douglas, "Social Class Differences in Health and Survival During the First Two Years of Life: The Results of a National Survey," *Population Studies* 5, pt. 1 (July 1951): 35–58.

†The clash of ideologies was present in Russia too (see Richard Stites, *The Women's Liberation Movement in Russia: Feminism, Nihilism, and Bolshevism 1860–1930* [Princeton: Princeton University Press, 1978]).

Armstrong, Alan. *Stability and Change in an English Country Town*. Cambridge: Cambridge University Press, 1974.

Banks, Joseph A. *Prosperity and Parenthood: A Study of Family Planning Among the Victorian Middle Classes*. London: Routledge and Kegan Paul, 1954.

Bernhardt, Eva M. "Trends and Variations in Swedish Fertility—A Cohort Study." Doctoral disertation, University of Pennsylvania, 1971. Reprinted in *Urval* 5 (Statistiska Centralbyran).

Bertillon, Jacques. "La natalité selon le degré d'aisance. Etude, à ce point de vue, de Paris, Londres, Berlin et Vienne." *Bulletin de L'Institut International de Statistique* 11, pt. 1 (1899): 163–76.

Census of England and Wales 1911, vol. 7. House of Commons Sessional Papers, 1912–1913, vol. 113, Cmd. 6610.

Coale, Ansley J. "The Decline of Fertility in Europe from the French Revolution to World War II." In *Fertility and Family Planning*, ed. S. J. Behrman, Leslie Corsa, Jr., and Ronald Freedman, pp. 3–24. Ann Arbor: University of Michigan Press, 1969.

Dangerfield, George. *The Strange Death of Liberal England*. London: Constable, 1936.

Douglas, J. W. B. "Social Class Differences in Health and Survival During the First Two Years of Life; The Results of a National Survey. *Population Studies* 5 (1951): 35–58.

Gaskin, Katherine. "Age at First Marriage in Europe before 1850: A Summary of Family Reconstitution Data." *Journal of Family History* 3 (1978): 23–36.

Guillaume, Pierre. *La population de Bordeaux au XIXe siècle*. Paris: Librairie Armand Colin, 1972.

Habakkuk, H. J. *Population Growth and Economic Development Since 1750*. New York: Humanities Press, 1971.

Hajnal, John. "European Marriage Patterns in Perspective." In *Population in History*, ed. D. V. Glass and D. E. C. Eversley, pp. 101–46. London: Arnold, 1965.

Hansen, Hans Oluf. "Some Aspects of the Demography of Lineages Belonging to Danish High Nobility in the Age of Enlightened Despotism (1660–1848)." Unpublished manuscript. 1976.

Henry, Louis. *Anciennes familles Genevoises, Etude démographique XVIe–XXe siècle*. Paris: Presses Universitaires de France, 1956.

Hollingsworth, T. H. "The Demography of the British Peerage." Supplement to *Population Studies* 18, no. 2 (November 1964).

Humphreys, N. A. "Class Mortality Statistics." *Journal of the Royal Statistical Society* 5 (June 1887).

Innes, John W. *Class Fertility Trends in England and Wales 1876–1934*. Princeton: Princeton University Press, 1938.

Knodel, John. *The Decline of Fertility in Germany, 1871–1939*. Princeton: Princeton University Press, 1974.

Litchfield, R. B. "Demographic Characteristics of Florentine Patrician Families, Sixteenth to Nineteenth Centuries." *Journal of Economic History* 29 (1969): 191–205.

Mann, Thomas. *Buddenbrooks: The Decline of a Family*. Trans. H. T. Lowe-Porter. Harmondsworth: Penguin Books, 1971.

Manschke, R. "Beruf und Kinderzahl." *Schmollers Jahrbuch* 40 (1916): 1867–937.

May, R. E. "Zur Frage des Geburtenrückganges." *Schmollers Jahrbuch* 4 (1916): 1645–84.

Mombert, Paul. *Studien zur Bevölkerungsbewegung in Deutschland*. Karlsruhe: G. Braunsche Hofbuchdruckerei, 1907.

Monahan, Thomas. *The Pattern of Age at Marriage in the United States*. 2 vols. Philadelphia: Stephenson Brothers, 1951.

Noel, Raymond. "L'état de la population de Mostuejouls (Aveyron) en 1690," In *Hommage à Marcel Reinhard: Sur la population française au XVIIIᵉ et au XIXᵉ siècles*, ed. pp. 505–22. Paris: Société de Démographie Historique, 1973.

———. "La population de la paroisse de Laguiole d'aprés un rencensement de 1691." *Annales de Démographie Historique* (1967): 197–223.

Prinzing, Friedrich. "Heiratshäufigkeit und Heiratsalter nach Stand und Beruf." *Zeitschrift für Socialwissenschaft* 6 (1903): 546–59.

———. "Die Wandlungen der Heiratshäufigkeit und des mittleren Heiratsalters." *Zeitschrift für Socialwissenschaft* 5 (1902): 656–74.

Raseri, Enrico. "Sur les variations de taux de natalité et sur l'âge moyen des époux, suivant les conditions économiques." *Bulletin de L'Institut International de Statistique* 11, pt. 1 (1899): 149–62.

Rollet, Catherine. "Genealogies et démographie." In *Hommage à Marcel Reinhard: Sur la population française au XVIIIᵉ et au XIXᵉ siècles*, ed., pp. 547–57. Paris: Société de Démographie Historique, 1973.

Sallume, Xarifa, and Notestein, Frank W. "Trends in the Size of Families Completed Prior to 1910 in Various Social Classes." *American Journal of Sociology* 38 (1932): 398–408.

Seutemann, Karl. *Kindersterblichkeit sozialer Bevölkerungsgruppen insbesondere im preussischen Staate und seinen Provinzen*. Tübingen: Verlag der H. Laupp'schen Buchhandlung, 1894.

Smith, Daniel Scott. "Family Limitation, Sexual Control, and Domestic Feminism in Victorian America." *Feminist Studies* 1 (1973): 40–57.

Stevenson, T. H. C. "The Fertility of Various Social Classes in England and Wales from the Middle of the 19th Century to 1911." *Journal of the Royal Statistical Society* 83, pt. 3 (1920): 401–44.

Stites, Richard. *The Women's Liberation Movement in Russia: Feminism, Nihilism, and Bolshevism 1860–1930*. Princeton: Princeton University Press, 1978.

Tilly, Louise; Scott, Joan; and Cohen, Miriam. "Women's Work and European Fertility Patterns." *Journal of Interdisciplinary History* 3 (1976): 447–76.

van de Walle, Etienne. *The Female Population of France in the 19th Century*. Princeton: Princeton University Press, 1974.

———. "Marriage and Marital Fertility." *Daedalus* 97 (1968): 486–501.

Verrijn-Stuart, C. A. "Natalité, mortinatalité et mortalité enfantine selon le degré d'aisance dans quelques villes et un nombre de communes rurales dans les Pays-Bas." *Bulletin de L'Institut International de Statistique* 13, pt. 2 (1902).

Westergaard, Harald. "On the Study of Displacements Within a Population." *Journal of the American Statistical Association* 17 (1920): 381–401.

Zanetti, Dante E. *La demographia del patriziata milanese nei secoli XVII, XVIII, XIX*. Universita de Pavia, 1972.

∽Notes

The authors' full names and the full titles of the books listed as references can be found in the Bibliography.

INTRODUCTION

1. Otto-Peters, *Frauenleben*, ix.

CHAPTER 1

Besides the books described in the text, I have drawn specially in this chapter on works by Karl Hillebrand and Louis-Aimé Martin. Hillebrand was a Heidelberg student who had to flee Germany after the 1848 uprising in Baden. He lived most of his life in France, where he became well known as a professor and writer on French affairs. Hans Kohn calls him one of the most brilliant and accomplished German essayists, while Sylvaine Marandon, in her study of the image of France, relies on him as "remarkably intelligent."

Martin (1782–1847), though a professor of medieval French literature, won a wide audience for his letters on popular science for women (daguerreotypy, calorie theory, polarization of light) in which he tried to share with them the latest theories, believing that women needed a serious education. His *The Education of Mothers of Families* (1834) was quickly translated and widely spread around English-speaking countries. Though crowned by the French Academy, it was put on the Catholic Index for its anti-clericalism. George Eliot thought the book the most masterly and philosophical treatment of the subject she had ever read.

1. Davidoff, 23
2. Edgeworth and Edgeworth, 2: 296.
3. Martin, 3.
4. Ibid., 2.
5. Quoted in Boltanski, 31.
6. Ruskin, *In Queen's Gardens*, in *Sesame and Lilies*, 87 ff.
7. Key, *Century of the Child*, 3.
8. Immermann, 70–72, and passim.
9. Ibid., 94.
10. Riehl, *Die Familie*, 140, 206.
11. Twellmann, *Quellen*, 205.
12. Berry, *Social Life*, 80, 146.
13. Marandan, 260.
14. Daumard, 325–26.
15. Janet, *Famille*, 249.
16. Ibid., 284.
17. Canonici, 29.
18. Greco, 214.
19. E. P. Thompson, *English Working Class*, 363.
20. Farrar, 219.
21. Sewell, 53.
22. Quoted in Blease, 71.
23. Bulwer-Lytton, 1: 19.
24. Mozley, 2: 20–25.
25. Ibid., 24–25.
26. Hayek, 65, 67.
27. Benjamin, 443.
28. Lukacs, 623.
29. B. A. Clough, 74.

561

CHAPTER 2

The feminist Jenny d'Héricourt noted an advance in Michelet's position on women between his first book, *L'Amour* [*Love*], and his next one on the subject, *La Femme* [*Woman*]. In the former, woman is presented as completely subordinate, whereas in the latter she has advanced to the position of being half of a couple, exercising as well as responding to influence. It may have been Michelet's wife who changed his mind; at least she is believed to have created his interest in natural science, and she was obviously a person of intellectual consequence.

Ernest Legouvé (1807–1903) was the chief French theorist of women's education in his period. Although he was originally a dramatist, he worked out a theory of what was wrong with girls' schooling in a series of lectures at the Collège de France during the Second Republic, and during the Third he rose to become the chief inspector for all public female education. He insisted on tough and serious training, which he hoped would lead to much wider job opportunities for women in the civil service and elsewhere.

The Amberley Papers are Bertrand Russell's compilation of the diaries and letters of his parents from their school days until their early deaths. Since their interests embraced almost everything new that was going on in England in their time, the papers are an invaluable source.

Hippolyte Taine (1828–1893), best known as a literary critic of conservative view, was also an observant traveler whose voyages through France and to Italy and England are full of the most revealing details.

1. Riehl, *Die Familie*, ix.
2. Michelet, *Amour*, 49.
3. Ibid., 50.
4. Legouvé, *Histoire*, 279.
5. Goncourt and Goncourt, *Journal*, October 13, 1855.
6. Ibid., May 21, 1857.
7. Schopenhauer, 64.
8. Showalter and Showalter, 85.
9. Turgéon, 1: 438.
10. Wikoff, 112.
11. Stephens, 125.
12. Muggeridge and Adam, 167, 140.
13. Spencer, *Autobiography*, 62.
14. Amberley and Amberley, 2: 35.
15. Taine, *Life and Letters*, 1: 156.
16. Kemble, *Girlhood*, 447.
17. Proudhon, 3: 258.
18. Ibid., *Onzième étude*.
19. Grépon, 95.
20. Quoted in Bax, 48.
21. Braun, *Frauenfrage*, 203.
22. Stewart, 3: 228.
23. Mill, 257.
24. Meyer, 44.
25. Büchner, *Die Frauen*, 117.
26. Rilke, *Letters to a Young Poet*, 58.
27. Buckle, 1: 55.
28. Geddes, 286.
29. Quoted in Thomson, 61.
30. Héricourt, 122, 124.

CHAPTER 3

Besides the books described in the text, notes on the following may prove helpful. Mrs. Trollope is, of course, best known for her *Domestic Manners of the Americans*, but her report on her life in Paris is equally incisive. Thérèse Blanc, who hid under the pen name of Th. Bentzon, was another traveler to America, sixty years after Mrs. Trollope. She comments on French life, particularly marriage customs, as a foil to what she perceived as the very different manners of the Americans, but she was also the author of a course on "practical morals" for the young girls in the French public schools. Sophie, the Countess of Ségur is best known for her numerous delightful children's stories.

1. Simmel, *Sociology of Georg Simmel*, 138.
2. Betham-Edwards, 80.
3. Frances Trollope, *Paris*, 1: 231.
4. Hamerton, *Round My House*, 362.
5. Kurz, *Jugendland*, 187.
6. Turgéon, 1: 71.
7. Thérèse Blanc, *Causeries*, 35.
8. Pelletier, 4.
9. Henry Moll, 271.
10. Personal communication.
11. Michelet, *Amour*, 68.
12. Turgéon, 1: 68.
13. Sand, *Histoire*, 1: 406 ff.
14. Frederic Marshall, 312.
15. Alletz, 98.
16. Hamerton, *French and English*, 368.
17. Murray, "Courtship," 360.
18. Agoult, *Mes souvenirs*, 193.
19. Delphine de Girardin, 307.
20. Farrar, 167.
21. Hillebrand, *France*, 2.
22. Hamerton, *French and English*, 372.
23. Staffe, 29, and passim.
24. Ibid., 40.
25. Legouvé, *Histoire*, 126.
26. Michelet, *Woman*, 273.
27. Sénevier, passim.
28. Ibid., 157.
29. Ibid., 67.
30. About, 22.
31. Michelet, *Amour*, 384.
32. Berry, *Social Life*, 148.
33. Stephens, 180.
34. Tolédano, 83.
35. Legouvé, *Histoire*, 104.
36. Sand, *Histoire*, 2: 77.
37. Balzac, *Physiology*, 48.
38. Hillebrand, *France*, 1.
39. Demolins, 128 ff.
40. Tolédano, 91.
41. October 1, 1842.
42. Sevrette, 234.
43. Hédouville, 90, 119.
44. Gaskell, "French Life," 585.
45. Daubié, 21.
46. Betham-Edwards, 81.
47. About, 187.
48. Daumard, 357.
49. Aléxandre Ségur, 4, 167.
50. Ariès, *Histoire*, 481.
51. Pelletier, 53.
52. Charrier, 516.

CHAPTER 4

A Book With Seven Seals first appeared anonymously in 1928 and the first half has recently been reissued under the name of Agnes Maud Davies. With the ironic perspective of the old, she describes her childhood in an unequaled series of vignettes showing the social pressures subtly built up against spontaneity and straight thinking. In Augustus Hare's several biographies of Victorian women, the irony is unconscious, since he himself was a firm believer in the code of self-restraint and discipline. The results reveal more than he meant to about the punishing side of life in those days. Frances Power Cobbe devoted the freedom which her life as a comfortable old maid gave her to serve a number of good causes, including university training for women and kindness to animals.

1. Tocqueville, *England*, 88.
2. Tocqueville, *America*, 565.
3. Frances Trollope, *Paris*, 2: 81.
4. Taine, *England*, 72.
5. Tolédano, 73.
6. Wey, 180.
7. Arnstein, 198.
8. Shaen, 102–3.
9. Armytage, 34.
10. Amberley and Amberley, 1: 232–33, 264.
11. Ray Strachey, 411.

12. Ellis, *Wives*, 113.
13. Coventry Patmore, 77.
14. Thomson, 112.
15. Spencer, Sociology, 1: 753.
16. Gornall, 811.
17. Meinertzhagen, 176–93.
18. Magnus, 30, 44.
19. Brodie, 136.
20. A. J. C. Hare, *Solitary Life*, 17.
21. Pearsall, 91.
22. Evans, *Victorians*, 143.
23. Nethercot, 24.
24. Granville-Barker, 59.
25. Stock, 1: 137.
26. Beatrice Webb, 270, 399; Cole, 43.
27. Agnes Maud Davies, 160.
28. Mitford, *Ladies of Alderley*, 91.
29. Hanson and Hanson, *Necessary Evil*, 29.
30. Ann Taylor, *Reciprocal Duties*, 86.
31. E. G. Smith, 281.
32. A. J. C. Hare, *Memorials*, 1: 321.
33. Agnes Maud Davies, 292.
34. Ibid., 292 ff.
35. Enid Bell, *Octavia Hill*, 156.
36. Mack and Armytage, 32.
37. Dunn, 57–58.
38. Chitty, 72.
39. Blake, 260–61.
40. Emily Tennyson, passim.
41. Quoted in McGregor, *Divorce*, 72.
42. Laver, *Victoriana*, 34.
43. Amberley and Amberley, 1: 290 291.
44. Sewell, 11.
45. Swinnerton, 163, 171.
46. Nicoll, 94.
47. Mary Howitt, 1: 173.
48. McGregor, *Divorce*, 15.
49. Brodie, 133 ff.
50. Bulwer-Lytton, 1: 88.
51. Amy Menzies, 13, 111.
52. Cobbe, *Pursuits*, 39 ff.
53. Charles Darwin, 2: 385.
54. Taine, *England*, 74.
55. Blanch, 7.
56. Grey and Shirreff, 20.
57. Pearsall, 33.
58. Henley, 18.
59. E. M. Butler, *Pückler-Muskau*, 62.

CHAPTER 5

A series of English visitors provided a running commentary on German social life, which they often contrasted usefully with what they knew at home. In time they run from Vaughan (1843), through William Howitt (1844), Samuel Laing (though his book was published in 1854, it refers to nothing later than 1844), Henry Mayhew (1865), better known for his studies of the English poor, Marie von Bothmer (1877), who wrote for *Fraser's Magazine*, Sabine Baring-Gould (1879), Cecily Sidgwick (1908), I. A. R. Wylie (1911), who in 1939 repudiated her girlhood admiration of things German in the light of the Second World War, and Thomas Smith, who taught English at the University of Munich until the outbreak of World War I and whose views of Germany were published during the war as anti-German propaganda.

1. Hippel, *Über die Ehe*, 23.
2. Baring-Gould, 1: 159 ff., see also Knodel, "Law."
3. Masur, *Imperial Berlin*, 108.
4. Henry Mayhew, *German Life*, 122.
5. Ibid., 121.
6. Braun, *Frauenfrage*, 164.
7. Thomas Smith, 7.
8. Bothmer, *German Home Life*, 191, 361.
9. Baring-Gould, 1: 143.

10. Gert Richter, 85.
11. Vaughan, 206.
12. Laing, 92, See also Horace Mann, 203, and Sidgwick, 92.
13. Berolzheimer, 104.
14. Monchoux, 371.
15. Baring-Gould, 1: 102.
16. Susanna Winkworth, 149.
17. Shaen, 140.
18. Popert, 254, and passim.
19. Thérèse Blanc, *A la Sirène*, 1887.
20. Heyl, 6.
21. Keyserling, *Book of Marriage*, 247.

22. Thomas Smith, 99.
23. Agoult, *Mes souvenirs*, 21.
24. Blos, 62.
25. Braun, Memoiren, 1: 201.
26. Ibid., 48.
27. Bebel, *Die Frau*, 92.
28. Henry Mayhew, *German Life*, 56.
29. Ibid., 112.
30. I. A. R. Wylie, *The Germans*, 242–43.
31. Ibid., 244–45.

CHAPTER 6

In 1889 at an exposition of women's work in Florence, a series of lectures analyzed all phases of women's lives: homemaking, family life, work, marriage, rights, their position in various arts and sciences. The organizers were obviously trying to get the subject of women's place into public discourse. To a reader of today, the contributors seem quite timid. Nearly every speaker qualified a statement about full equality in some apologetic way, without the boldness of Malvina Frank's treatises of twenty years before. Frank's first book was a manual for the recently affianced bride; the second was more a treatise on the position of women throughout history.

1. Costanza d'Azeglio, 320.
2. Gallenga, 2: 304.
3. Quoted in Moers, "Madame de Staël," 231.
4. Gennari, 139.
5. A. J. C. Hare, *Solitary Life*, 196.
6. Cobbe, *Italics*, 138.
7. Keyserling, *Europe*, 155.
8. Galletti, 112.
9. Duff-Gordon, 206.
10. Massimo d'Azeglio, *Things I Remember*, 120.
11. *Donna italiana: esposizione*, 236.
12. Taine, *Italie*, 1: 289.
13. Pierantoni-Mancini, *Impressioni*, 196.
14. Gretton, 182.
15. Niceforo, 33.
16. Galletti, 170.
17. Origo, 5, 117–19.
18. Costanza d'Azeglio, 12.

19. Magni, passim.
20. Drago, 104.
21. Barbiera, 116.
22. Gallenga, 2: 313.
23. Kemble, *Consolation*, 1: 28.
24. Gretton, 152.
25. Duff-Gordon, 167.
26. Gretton, 157.
27. Duff-Gordon, 151.
28. Rossi, 148.
29. Cobbe, *Italics*, 137 ff.
30. Gallenga, 2: 305.
31. Galletti, 163.
32. Pierantoni-Mancini, *Impressioni*, 346.
33. Magni, 42.
34. Personal communication.
35. Malvina Frank, *Fidenzate*, 124.
36. Ibid., 186.
37. *Donna italiana: esposizione*, 386.

CHAPTER 7

August Debay followed his *Hygiène et physiologie du mariage* of 1848 with the *Philosophie du mariage* the following year. The copy of the former book that I happened to read was from the forty-seventh impression, dated 1853, and by 1888 there had been 172 printings. *Le Livre de la famille* of 1892 purports to be the first general handbook on the family. It contains sections on role definition; important rites of passage like birth, marriage, and death; and hints on education, conduct, and etiquette. It supports a conservative position with a hierarchical family and great differentiation of roles, and in accordance with the growing nationalism in France, it emphasizes at length the importance of producing soldiers for the nation. The young women studied by Amélie Gayraud, described in Chapter 21, adopted the second but not the first of these ideals. Marie Bashkirtseff's *Journal* was called by Laura Marholm one of only two books by women about their interior lives. (The other was Jane Carlyle's diary.) Marie wrote of her intentions in 1875: "I believe there is not yet a photograph, if I may express myself thus, of the whole existence of a woman; of all her thoughts, of all, of all." She was fifteen at the time, and her experience continued to be extremely limited. Gustave Droz (1832–1895), whose best-selling *Monsieur, madame et bébé* was first published in 1866, aims therein to portray a normal young man's growth from bachelorhood into fatherhood. He apologized to his feminine readers who might be shocked at the earlier episodes, but insisted that he was able to become a delightful husband precisely because of the kind of life he had led previously. Luise Otto-Peters' *Frauenleben im deutschen Reich* (1876) describes the changes which had come in women's lives in her lifetime, using her own story as an example. The subtitle describes the contents as memories of the past with attention to the present and future.

1. Clark, 127.
2. See Gathorne-Hardy.
3. Braun, *Memoiren*, 1: 122.
4. Martel de Janville, 18–40, and passim.
5. Debay, *Philosophie*, 63.
6. Panton, 15.
7. Quoted in Smyth, 2: 49.
8. Cobbett, 211.
9. Jesse, 14.
10. Chantepie, 80.
11. Lyttelton, 63.
12. Stendhal, *On Love*, 241.
13. Debay, *Philosophie*, 62.
14. Janet, *La Famille*, 207 ff.
15. Michelet, *Woman*, 102.
16. *Livre de la famille*, 236.
17. Adhémar, *Nouvelle Education*, 155.
18. Passy, *Mère et fille*, 6.
19. Wedekind, 123, 152.
20. Quoted in Rosen, 61.
21. Braun, *Memoiren*, 1: 119.
22. Albert Moll, 262.
23. *Nationale Erziehung*, 214.
24. Maillard, 161.
25. Sunstein, 215.
26. Maxe von Arnim, 141.
27. Forel, 95.
28. Harris, 863.
29. Branca, 70; Carter, 67.
30. Tristan, *Londres*, 307.
31. Annie Besant, *Autobiographical Sketches*, 159.
32. Michelet, *Amour*, 72.
33. Maillard, 139.
34. Christ, 168.
35. Newman, 273.
36. Himmelfarb, 305.
37. Ponsonby, 57.
38. Coventry Patmore, 167.
39. Agoult, *Mes souvenirs*, 220.
40. Chapman, "Marriage Reform," 371.

41. Epton, 104.
42. Edgeworth and Edgeworth, 2: 143.
43. Quinlan, 145.
44. Amberley, 1: 77.
45. Frances Trollope, *Paris*, 1: 224.
46. Ibid., 166.
47. Hopkins, 123.
48. Corvin-Wiersbitzki, *Autobiography*, preface.
49. Mack and Armytage, 46.
50. Ibid., 44.
51. Massimo d'Azeglio, *Things I Remember*, 31.
52. Kleist, 76.
53. Farjeon, 364.
54. Sarah Ellis, *Wives*, 7.
55. Forel, preface.
56. Kemble, *Girlhood*, 57.
57. Ibid., 166–67.
58. Pichler, 3: 79.
59. Eckermann, January 29, 1826.
60. Quoted in Crow. 211.
61. Chapman, *Marriage Questions*, 149.
62. Cobbe, *Life*, 2: 501.
63. Shelley, 1: 48.
64. Petrie, 140.
65. Mayreder, 174.
66. *Die neue Gartenlaube*, 218.
67. Tinayre, *Rebelle*, 96.
68. Mary V. Hughes, *London Girl*, 3.

69. Smyth, 1: 61.
70. Hamerton, *Round My House*, 353.
71. Tolédano, 70.
72. Bashkirtseff, 502.
73. Ibid., 503.
74. Ibid., 733.
75. Pierantoni-Mancini, *Impressioni*, 195.
76. Blouët, *Womankind*, 46.
77. Hillebrand, *France*, 3.
78. Michelet, *Amour*, 117 ff.
79. Dumas, *L'Homme-femme*, 40.
80. Dumas, *Les Femmes qui tuent*, 167.
81. Musset, *Confession*, 50.
82. Tristan, *Femme*, 10.
83. Allart, *La Femme*, 23
84. Decaux, 9: 232.
85. Colette, *Earthly Paradise*, 84.
86. Decaux, 9: 232–33.
87. Saunders, passim.
88. Grépon, 172.
89. Quoted in Nethercot, 28.
90. Amy Menzies, 45.
91. Braun, *Memoiren*, 1: 13.
92. Zweig, 78.
93. Carpenter, 95.
94. Meisel-Hess, 320.
95. Bebel, *Die Frau*, 115.
96. Otto-Peters, 74.
97. Annie Besant, *Autobiographical Sketches*, 164.

Chapter 8

1. Taine, *England*, 95.
2. Ibid., 10.
3. Thomas Hughes, *Oxford*, 132.
4. Coventry Patmore, 91.
5. Amberley and Amberley, 2: 317.
6. William Acton, 1894 ed.
7. Wey, 181.
8. Knowlton, 53.
9. Bristed, 414, 420.
10. J. F. S. Russell, 108.
11. Ibid., 107.
12. Reade, 457.
13. Geddes, 286.
14. Himmelfarb, 283.

15. Hamerton, *Autobiography*, 7.
16. Muggeridge and Adam, 167.
17. Hynes, 114.
18. Key, *Century of the Child*, 11.
19. Hynes, 152.
20. Jameson, *Sisters*, 78.
21. Hynes, 201.
22. A. J. C. Hare, *Memorials*, iv.
23. Carlyle, 103.
24. Daubié, 264.
25. Newman, 284.
26. See Gert Richter.
27. Harris, 1: 3.
28. Comte, 219, and passim.

29. Quoted in Viola Klein, 82.
30. Petrie, 117.
31. Legouvé, *Histoire*, 68–69.
32. A. S. G. Butler, 44.
33. Bristed, 420.
34. Corvin-Wiersbitzki, *Ein Leben*, 191.
35. Berolzheimer, 357.
36. Quoted in Barbara Stephen, *Emily Davies*, 8.
37. Petrie, 95.
38. Lyttelton, 55.
39. Quoted in Diane Johnson, 157.
40. Chapman, *Godiva*, 1, 2.
41. Drysdale, 80–87.
42. Spencer, *Autobiography*, 160.
43. Taine, *England*, 92.
44. Blouët, *John Bull and His Island*, 29.
45. Pelletan, 234.
46. Droz, *Monsieur*, 16–20.
47. Héricourt, 248.
48. Daubié, 19.

49. Chantepie, chapter on courtesans.
50. Benda, *Jeunesse*, passim.
51. Dimnet, 193.
52. Gert Richter, 147.
53. Hellman, 166.
54. Ibid., 208.
55. Ibid., 253.
56. Steinbömer, 39.
57. Borolzheimer, 284.
58. Havelock Ellis, 12.
59. Mayreder, 120.
60. Zahn-Harnack, *Wandlungen*, 120.
61. Ibid., 92.
62. Massimo d'Azeglio, *Things I Remember*, 126, and passim.
63. Ibid., 63.
64. Chierici, 9.
65. Parca, 8, and passim.
66. Mauclair, "La Magie de l'amour," 202.
67. Ibid., 53–60.

CHAPTER 9

For housekeeping manuals in England I have drawn more on Haweis than on the better-known Beeton. For the early part of the century, of course, Cobbett was unique. These can all be compared with Millet-Robinet for France. Otto-Peters' *Frauenleben* gives a fascinating picture of daily life in old-fashioned German households. For essayists on household affairs, see Webster for England and Delphine de Girardin for France. Foreign visitors often had keen eyes for differences in approaches to housekeeping, and of these, Sidgwick, Bothmer, Mayhew, Laing, the Howitts, and Wylie were enlightening about German home life, while the invaluable Hamerton, Marshall, and Hillebrand were useful for French life. I have not given page references for each anecdote from these sources, except for direct quotations or surprising statements.

1. Byron, XIV: 24–25.
2. Banks and Banks, 46.
3. Evans, *Ruskin*, 154.
4. Reid, 64.
5. Spencer, *Autobiography*, 428.
6. Lombroso, 50.
7. Bea Howe, 13.
8. *Saturday Review*, February 15, 1868.
9. Grey and Shirreff, 50.
10. Emily Davies, 100.
11. Hopkins, 316.
12. Shaen, 24.

13. Hopkins, 214.
14. Cobbett, 126, 156, and passim.
15. Symons, 121.
16. Barine, 781.
17. Chitty, 92.
18. Stowe, 2: 22.
19. Arthur Clough, 62.
20. Beeton, preface, chap. 1.
21. Hayek, 66.
22. Twellmann, *Quellen*, 222.
23. Cole, 17.
24. Priestley, 26.
25. Kent, 32.

26. Morgan, *Memoirs*, 3: 135.
27. Sidgwick, 132.
28. Twellmann, *Quellen*, 216.
29. See Bothmer, *German Home Life*; Sidgwick; Henry Mayhew, *German Life*.
30. Laing, 127.
31. Sidgwick, 154; Henry Mayhew, *German Life*, 32; Bothmer, *German Home Life*, 52.
32. Sidgwick, 147.
33. William Howitt, *Rural and Domestic Life*, 97.
34. Bothmer, *German Home Life*, 227–28.
35. Weber, *Max*, 40–41.
36. Anna Mary Howitt, 207.
37. I. A. R. Wylie, *The Germans*, 59.
38. Feuerbach, *Liebenswürdigkeit*, 74.
39. Jameson, quoted in Clara Thomas, 85.
40. Weber, *Max*, 40.
41. Twellmann, *Quellen*, 221.
42. Feuerbach, *Leben in Briefen*, 186.
43. William Howitt, *Rural and Domestic Life*, 94.
44. Weber, *Lebenserinnerungen*, 56.
45. Twellmann, *Quellen*, 103.
46. Heyl, 33, 62.
47. Weber, *Max*, 215.
48. Ibid., 272.
49. Thérèse Blanc, *Causeries*, 23.
50. Delphine de Girardin, 479.
51. Janet, 54.
52. Debay, *Philosophie*, 77.
53. Delphine de Girardin, November 9, 1844.
54. Frederic Marshall, 133, 161.
55. Hillebrand, *Aus und über England*, 258.
56. Gaskell, "French Life," 439.
57. Hédouville, 128; Feuillet, 217.
58. Sénevier, 31.
59. Cate, 93.
60. Curie, 144.
61. Janet, *La Famille*, 55.
62. Hamerton, *Round My House*, 158.
63. Hamerton, *Autobiography*, 266.
64. Boltanski, 23
65. *Census of 1851*, introduction, 7.
66. Olsen, 271.
67. Davidoff, "Mastered for Life," 409.
68. Olsen, 270.
69. Rhodes, 32.
70. Dolléans, 241.
71. Laing, 266.
72. Morgan, *Italy*, 3: 52.
73. Cobbe, *Pursuits*, 166.
74. Desmarie, 38.
75. *Donna italiana:esposizione*, 208.
76. Chierici, 10.
77. *Westminster Review*, 52 (Oct. 1849): 21–22.
78. Webster, 59.
79. Otto, 249.
80. MacKenzie and MacKenzie, 95, 180.
81. Margueritte and Margueritte, 54.
82. Otto-Peters, 144, and passim.
83. Haweis, 111.
84. Berolzheimer, 80.
85. Twellmann, *Quellen*, 224.
86. Webster, 10.

CHAPTER 10

The most informative source about German law as it relates to women is by Carl Bulling, who discussed the applicable provisions of the new Civil Code of 1896 with considerable heat and disapproval, but careful scholarship. For my discussion of the distribution of power among family members I have relied for theoretical background on the work of Robert O. Blood. Louis Larcher, one of the numerous French commentators on England, roused the indignation of *Punch* by denigrating the food, art, welfare system, and drinking habits of the

English. Flora Tristan, who visited England in the 1830s, is discussed at length in Chapter 20. A still later French visitor to Britain, Emile Boutmy, was blind. He prepared for his study of English political psychology by careful reading and preparation of notebooks with categories of questions carefully arranged.

1. Bulling, 4, 63.
2. Blood and Wolfe, 3; see also Lupri, 175–95.
3. Horkheimer, 111.
4. Larcher, 47.
5. Bulling, 59.
6. Spencer, *Social Statics*, 162.
7. *The Daily News*, February 16, 1912.
8. Blouët, *Womankind*, 17.
9. Ewell, 84.
10. Blouët, *Womankind*, 26.
11. Turgéon, 1: 118.
12. Caird, *Morality*, 134.
13. Madariaga, *Englishmen*, 36.
14. Blouët, *John Bull and His Island*, 24.
15. Puech, 100.
16. Elizabeth Haldane, 5; Baring, 27.
17. Cobbett, 184.
18. Fanny Kingsley, *Letters and Life*, 1: 72.
19. Dunn, 162.
20. Berners, 17.
21. Alan and Mary Simpson, *Vassar Miscellany News*, February 7, 1975.
22. *The Oxford Book of Nineteenth Century Verse*, 15.
23. Beatrice Webb, 338.
24. Cramer, 10–30.
25. Morgan, *Memoirs*, 2: 146.
26. Ibid., 3: 99.
27. Sarah Ellis, *Daughters*, 115.
28. Nethercot, 30.
29. Hopkins, 231, 303.
30. Maxwell, 82.
31. Mitford, *Ladies of Alderley*, 265.
32. Longford, 1: 173; 2: 79.
33. Stock, 1: 257.
34. Annan, 71.
35. Symons, 244.
36. Sara Stephen, introduction.
37. Ray Strachey, 275.
38. Blanch, 42.
39. Harold Nicolson, 144.
40. Mary V. Hughes, *London Home*, 176.
41. Mary V. Hughes, *London Girl*, 9.
42. Martineau, "Female Industry," 335.
43. Haweis, 6.
44. Manton, 215.
45. Mothe-Langon, 142–43.
46. Frederic Marshall, 179.
47. Betham-Edwards, 89.
48. Benda, *Jeunesse*, 19.
49. Hamerton, *French and English*, 365.
50. Taine, *England*, 292.
51. Boutmy, 218.
52. Manouvrier, 292.
53. Rhodes, 40.
54. Thérèse Blanc, "Amérique," 296.
55. Manouvrier, 296.
56. Michelet, *Prêtre*, 269.
57. Henry Bulwer-Lytton, 2: 93.
58. Laing, 172.
59. Michelet, *Woman*, 185.
60. Michelet, *Amour*, 105.
61. Daubié, 40.
62. Hillebrand, *France*, 33.
63. Koltsova-Masalskaia, 1: 125.
64. Quoted in Bothmer, *German Home Life*, 230.
65. Bulling, 102.
66. Sidgwick, 153.
67. Henry Mayhew, *German Life*, 75, 132.
68. Troll-Borostyáni, 271–72.
69. Ibid., 260.
70. Bebel, *Die Frau*, 209.
71. Henry Mayhew, *German Life*, 132.
72. Bothmer, *German Home Life*, 230.
73. Weber, *Max*, 163.
74. Mommson, 10, 274.
75. Paulsen, "Die Frau," 405–10.

76. Taine, *France*, 156.
77. Fleischhack, 34.
78. Zahn-Harnack, *Wandlungen*, 25.
79. Heyl, 64.
80. Riehl, *Die Familie*, 264.
81. Hettler, 146.
82. Smyth, 1: 195.
83. Michelet, *Woman*, 208.
84. Greco, 31.
85. Gretton, 24–26.
86. *Feuerbach, Liebenswürdigkeit*, 76.

87. Cookson, 412.
88. Janet, *Famille*, 38.
89. Turgéon, 1: 104.
90. Masur, *Prophets*, 177.
91. Kellett, 227.
92. Hippel, *Über die Ehe*, 161.
93. Hillebrand, *France*, 206.
94. Legouvé, *Histoire*, 156.
95. Turgéon, 1: 95.
96. Quoted in Dahrendorf, 165–67.
97. Ibid., 342–44.

CHAPTER 11

Besides the volumes described in the text (and easily identifiable in the Bibliography), I should like to call my readers' attention to Levin Schücking's *The Puritan Family: A Social Study from the Literary Sources*, a German scholar's remarkably sympathetic interpretation of the English family. No one interested in the subject should omit to read all of the preface to Shaw's *Getting Married*, which shows how that sharp-eyed critic viewed English marriages in 1908.

1. Fanny Kingsley, *Letters and Life*, 2: 73, 74.
2. Schücking, 45–50.
3. Stanley, 1: 283.
4. Ibid., 1: 339.
5. Mary V. Hughes, *London Girl*, 261.
6. Mary Howitt, 1: 228.
7. Magnus, 362.
8. Cobbett, 207.
9. Ibid., 172.
10. Enid Bell, *Josephine Butler*, 195.
11. Petrie, 143.
12. Cobbe, *Pursuits*, 222.
13. Somerville, 326.
14. Manton, 218.
15. Amberley and Amberley, 2: 335.
16. Sewell, dedication.
17. Beatrice Webb, 386.
18. Schücking, 176.
19. Tocqueville, *America*, 573.
20. Mill, 303.
21. Stanley, 1: 73.
22. Marlow, 226.
23. Annan, 62.
24. A. J. C. Hare, *Solitary Life*, 258.
25. Immermann, 71–72.

26. Schücking, 1, 2.
27. Taine, *England*, 91.
28. Chitty, 253.
29. Linton, *Girl*, 228.
30. Hester Burton, 80.
31. Gosse, 241.
32. Milne, 23.
33. Sarah Ellis, *Wives*, passim.
34. Doris Moore, 174.
35. Balzac, *Physiology*, 201.
36. Larcher, 47.
37. Blouët, *Womankind*, 14–15.
38. Paulsen, *Autobiography*, 423.
39. William Acton, 208–10.
40. Ryan, 56, 116.
41. Alexander Walker, 105.
42. Drysdale, 49, 356.
43. Havelock Ellis, 121.
44. Crow, 147.
45. Dowling, 630 ff.
46. Shaw, *Getting Married*, 128.
47. Marlow, 87.
48. Caird, *Westminster Review*, 186–201.
49. Morgan, *Memoirs*, 2: 117.
50. Shaw, *Getting Married*, 128.
51. Crow, 41.
52. Bright, 88.

53. Askwith, 61.
54. Ibid., 33.
55. Brodie, 291.
56. William Acton, 180.
57. Drysdale, 84.
58. William Acton, 194.
59. Ibid., 55.
60. Ibid., 95.
61. Key, *Century of the Child*, 55.
62. Cunnington, 207.
63. William Acton, 140.
64. Routh, 149.
65. Samuel Butler, *Life and Letters*, 2: 127.
66. Ray, 123.
67. Houghton, 129.
68. Arthur Clough, 166.
69. Crow, 202.
70. Shaw, *Getting Married*, 140.
71. Emily Davies, 120.
72. Armitage, 8.
73. Mazzoleni, 243.
74. Mary Howitt, 1:183.
75. Booth-Tucker, 1: 116, and passim.
76. Ibid., 1: 171.
77. Pückler-Muskau, 133.
78. Amberley and Amberley, 2: 325.
79. J. F. S. Russell, 11.
80. Battiscombe, 37.
81. Spain, passim.
82. Mrs. H. Ward, *Recollections*, 2: 10, 15.
83. Schücking, 187.

CHAPTER 12

When the state began to talk about educating girls through the *lycée* stage, it caused Catholic educators to take a hard look at their convent schools. Monsignor Félix Dupanloup (1802–1878), Bishop of Orléans, was the most prolific advocate of upgrading the standards of Catholic education while vigorously opposing any state-administered schooling. Twenty years after his death, the Vicomtesse d'Adhémar challenged her fellow Catholics to create a truly modern education, including higher education, for women, wanting to make Catholic women true citizens of the democracy and still preserve the religious schools. Camille Mauclair composed two long volumes on carnal and spiritual love in 1912 and 1913, although the latter was not to be printed until after the war. His first volume is a searching study of prostitution; his second compares a man's feelings with a prostitute and his feelings with a deeply loved equal partner. Madeleine Pelletier, one of the early woman physicians, was a no-nonsense type, strongly pro-abortion and incidentally the editor of *La Suffragiste*.

1. David Hunt, 176.
2. Séché, 6.
3. Pange, Letter from Mme de Rémusat.
4. Alletz, 164.
5. Staël, *Germany*, 1: 48.
6. Ibid., 3: 236.
7. Herold, 74.
8. Morgan, *La France*, 1: 234.
9. Ladreit de Lacharrière, 5.
10. Alletz, 103.
11. Frances Trollope, *Paris*, 1: 183.
12. Frederic Marshall, 321, 349.
13. Janet, *Famille*, 145.
14. Michelet, *Woman*, 51
15. Michelet, *Amour*, 422.
16. Hillebrand, *Aus und über England*, 277.
17. Lefebre, 9, 20.
18. Tolédano, 124 (quoting Marceline Desbordes-Valmore).
19. Delphine de Girardin, 482.
20. Tinayre, *Femme*, 75.
21. Grépon, 14, 55.
22. Adhémar, *Femme Catholique*, 306.
23. Debay, *Hygiène*, 17, 38, 120, and passim.
24. Mauclair, *Amour Physique*, 20, 87.

25. Michelet, *Woman*, 280.
26. Michelet, *Amour*, 27.
27. Linton, "Domesticity," 435.
28. Michelet, *Amour*, passim.
29. Balzac, *Physiology*, passim.
30. Mauclair, *Magie*, 134.
31. Hillebrand, *Aus und über England*, 289.
32. Zola, 178.
33. Sand, *Histoire*, 4: 291.
34. Decaux, 8: 181, 248.
35. Rémusat, xc.
36. Debay, *Hygiène*, 29.
37. Balzac, *Physiology*, 29.
38. Rhodes, 205.
39. Zola, 317.
40. Pelletier, 5, 24.
41. Quoted in Richer, *La Femme libre*, 173.
42. Debay, *Hygiène*, 169, 177.
43. Michelet, *Amour*, 328.
44. Binkley, 74.
45. Zeldin, "Conflict," 33.
46. Ibid., 303.
47. Harris, 490.
48. Boutmy, 106.
49. Frances Trollope, *Paris*, 1: 233 ff.
50 Michelet, *Amour*, 96, 169.
51. Janet, *Famille*, 44.
52. Coleridge, 249.
53. Michelet, *Amour*, 166–77.
54. Hillebrand, *France*, 33.
55. Martin, 32.

56. Martel de Janville, *Marriage*, passim.
57. Hamerton, *Round My House*, 174.
58. Zeldin, "Conflict," 34.
59. Michelet. *Prêtre*, passim.
60. Abensour, 80.
61. Dumas, *L'Homme-femme*, 162.
62. Ibid., 24.
63. Guérin, 1: April 28, 1835.
64. Puech, 379.
65. Sand, *Histoire*, 3: 328.
66. Adhémar, *Femme catholique*, 210.
67. Dupanloup, *Studious Women*, 26, and passim.
68. Pelleton, 21.
69. Rochard, 645.
70. Hillebrand, *Aus und über England*, 3: 287–88.
71. Janet, *Famille*, 72.
72. Rebière, 111.
73. Blanc and Delhoume, 76–77.
74. Rebière, 222.
75. Curie, 320.
76. Charrier, 520.
77. E. Guizot, 1: 339.
78. Tolédano, 119.
79. F. Guizot.
80. Lemmonier, passim.
81. Ibid., 3–5.
82. Adhémar, *Femme catholique*, 299.

CHAPTER 13

1. Huch, in Keyserling, *Book of Marriage*, 169.
2. Stendhal, *On Love*, 183.
3. Immermann, 84 ff. and passim.
4. Steinhauer, 91.
5. William Howitt, *Rural and Domestic Life*, 95.
6. Billroth, 33.
7. Ibid., 105, 121, 179.
8. Legge, 116.
9. Blos, 84.
10. Kurz, *Mutter*, 12.
11. Mommsen, 38.

12. Henry Mayhew, *German Life*, 130.
13. Twellmann, *Quellen*, 564.
14. Feuerbach, *Leben in Briefen*, 188.
15. Kurz, *Jugenland*, 188.
16. Mayreder, 197.
17. Bebel, *Life*, 195.
18. Helene Lange, *Leben serinnerungen*, 231.
19. Gert Richter, 147.
20. Hellmann, passim.
21. David Mitchell, 68.

22. Hegar, 4, 7.
23. Bebel, *Die Frau*, 119.
24. Caird, "Marriage."
25. Forel, 223.
26. Eckermann, March 28, 1831.
27. Braun, *Memoiren*, 1: 14; and Martin Green, 22.
28. Martin Green, 22, 126.
29. Goepfert, 61.
30. Eckermann, January 2, 1824.
31. Hettler, passim.
32. Ibid., 9.
33. Kleist, passim.
34. Ibid., 79.
35. Ibid., 99.
36. Immermann, 90.
37. William Howitt, *German Experiences*, 175.
38. Ibid., 27.

39. Mayreder, 176.
40. William Howitt, *Rural and Domestic Life*, 94.
41. Freytag, *Erinnerungen*, 341.
42. Fontane, *Kinderjahre*, 79.
43. Gert Richter, 50.
44. Twellmann, *Quellen*, 180, 210.
45. Baring-Gould, 1: 227.
46. Bothmer, *German Home Life*, 229.
47. Lewald, *Für und wider die Frauen*, 132–33.
48. Amalie, *The Uncle*.
49. Weber, *Lebenserinnerungen*, 54–55, and passim.
50. Gerhard, 205, and passim.
51. Heyl, 14.
52. Martin Green, 219.
53. Braun, *Memoiren*, passim.

CHAPTER 14

1. Costanza d'Azeglio, 320.
2. Mozzoni, *Passo*, 20.
3. Mrs. H. Ward, *Recollections*, 2: 114–15.
4. Stendhal, *Journal*, 282.
5. Taine, *Italie*, 2: 271.
6. Desmarie, 131.
7. Drago, 204.
8. Morgan, *Italy*, 2: 227.
9. Canonici, 14.
10. Massimo d'Azeglio, *Things I Remember*, 192.
11. Ibid., 231, 232.
12. Morgan, *Italy*, 1: 257.
13. Stendhal, *Journal*, 282.
14. Massimo d'Azeglio, *Things I Remember*, 121.
15. Taine, *Italie*, 1: 290.
16. Desmarie, 132.
17. Cobbe, *Italy*, 274.
18. Gretton, 62.

19. Mario, "Position of Women."
20. Massimo d'Azeglio, *Things I Remember*, 23.
21. Ibid., 11.
22. Ibid., 128.
23. Ricci, 2: 160.
24. *Donna italiana: esposizione*, 355.
25. Ibid., 208.
26. Robert Browning, ll. 710–24.
27. Shelley, 1: 227.
28. Duff-Gordon, 133.
29. Gretton, 38.
30. Ibid., 179.
31. Cobbe, *Pursuits*, 149.
32. Duff-Gordon, 132–38.
33. Gallenga, 2: 302.
34. "Women of Italy."
35. Mazzoleni, 57.
36. Drago, 84.
37. Mozzoni, *Liberazione*, 154.

CHAPTER 15

For certain biographical facts I have drawn on the following sources, all listed in the Bibliography: for George Eliot, Hanson and Hanson; for Frances Hodgson Burnett, M. Laski; for Sir Charles Dilke, Betty Askwith's life of Lady

Dilke; for E. Nesbit, Doris Langley Moore; for H. G. Wells, his own *Experiment in Autobiography;* for Annie Besant, Nethercot; for Mill, Packe; for Mrs. Haweis, Bea Howe; for Thackeray, Gordon Ray; for Alice Meynell, Viola Meynell Dallyn; for Jane Digby, M. F. Schmidt's *Passion's Child*. I have not given page references to the episodes culled from these books except in the case of direct quotation.

1. Hillebrand, *France*, 18.
2. Balzac, *Physiology*, 1.
3. Legouvé, *Histoire*, 207.
4. Chantepie, 87.
5. Maigron, iii.
6. Ibid., 406.
7. Stendhal, *On Love*, 92.
8. Ibid., 242-43.
9. Mauclair, *Magie*, 129, 132.
10. Hamerton, *French and English*, 214.
11. Alletz, 84.
12. Bulwer-Lytton, 1: 80.
13. Hillebrand, *France*, 35.
14. Tinayre, *Femme*, 195 ff.
15. Hamerton, *French and English*, 218.
16. Staffe, 324.
17. Bulwer, 1: 108.
18. Morgan, *France in 1829–30*, 1: 246.
19. Debay, *Hygiène*, 25.
20. Bourget, *Physiologie*, 52.
21. Lemaitre, 737.
22. Tolédano, 107.
23. Tolédano, 79.
24. Hillebrand, Aus und über England, 280.
25. Frederic Marshall, 328.
26. Hillebrand, *Zeiten*, 3: 283.
27. Alexander Walker, 118.
28. Debay, *Philosophie*, 112.
29. Taine, *England*, 95, 97.
30. Ibid., 82.
31. Arnstein, 188.
32. *Westminster Review*, October, 1864.
33. Sewell, 110.
34. Taine, *England*, 80.
35. Ibid., 56.
36. Ibid., 56.
37. Ibid., 81.
38. Ibid., 98.
39. Blouët, *John Bull and His Island*, 40.
40. Shaw, *Getting Married*, 125.
41. Sunstein, 212.
42. George Meredith, *Diana*, 306.
43. Madariaga, *Englishmen*, 228.
44. Annie Besant, *Marriage*, 19.
45. Packe, passim.
46. Quoted in Coventry Patmore, 254, and passim.
47. Morley, 253.
48. Mrs. H. Ward, *Recollections*, 1: 168 ff.
49. Beatrice Webb, 308; quoted from 1887 diary.
50. William Acton, 1899 edition.
51. Himmelfarb, 291.
52. Alexander Walker, 181.
53. A. J. C. Hare, *Solitary Life*, 298.
54. Harris, 358.
55. Hopkins, 207.
56. Quoted in Muggeridge and Adam, 80.
57. Corvin-Wiersbitzki, *Autobiography*, 1: 31.
58. Radziwill, 149.
59. Bunsen, 240.
60. John Russell, 2: 285.
61. Braun, *Memoiren*, 2: 120.
62. Immermann, 78.
63. Laing, 93.
64. Carlile, 14.
65. Braun, *Memoiren*, 2: 55.
66. Nettl, 16, and passim.
67. Martin Green, 10–17, and passim.
68. Mitzman, 216.
69. Ibid., 286–91.
70. Reventlow, 13–15.
71. Gallenga, 2: 320.
72. Ibid., 2: 318.
73. Heine, *Pictures*, 315.

74. Barbiera, 288.
75. Ibid., 139.
76. Ibid., 284–86.
77. Desmarie, 35.
78. Nievo, 218.
79. Stendhal, *Journal*, 288–93.
80. Drago, 119 ff.

81. Ricci, 1: 161.
82. Engels, 78.
83. Harris, 460.
84. Scheffler, 307.
85. Bullough, 169.
86. Taine, *England*, 31.

CHAPTER 16

For English divorce law and history: McGregor, and also Latey; for French, by all means Naquet, whose treatise on divorce and autobiography are both interesting. Although a doctor of medicine, he was fined and imprisoned under the Second Empire for "corrupting public morals" by his criticism of religion, marriage, and the family, and he did not come into his own until the more anti-clerical Third Republic.

1. Luther; Trench, 17.
2. Steinhauer, 70.
3. Naquet, *Divorce*, 67.
4. Sidgwick, 100.
5. Staël, *Germany*, 3: 241.
6. Bothmer, *German Home Life*, 257.
7. Riehl, *Die Familie*, 203, 217.
8. Baring-Gould, 1: 213, 241.
9. Agoult, *Mes souvenirs*, 186.
10. E. M. Butler, *Pückler-Muskau*, 13.
11. Corvin-Wiersbitzki, *Autobiography*, 1: 34.
12. Maxe von Arnim, 53.
13. Mayhew, *German Life*, 138.
14. Berolzheimer, 92.
15. Legouvé, *Histoire*, 189.
16. Ibid., 208.
17. Saunders, 61, and passim.
18. Héricourt, 203.
19. Giraud, *Essai*, 19.
20. Naquet, *Divorce*, 60.
21. Zeldin, 358.

22. McGregor, *Divorce*, 2.
23. Morgan, *La France*, 1: 241.
24. Geoffrey May, 212.
25. Latey, 57.
26. McGregor, *Divorce*, 17; Latey, 91.
27. Latey, 84.
28. Blease, 151.
29. Burn, 156.
30. Kellett, 232.
31. Kaye, "Outrages," 256.
32. McGregor, *Divorce*, 24.
33. Latey, 93.
34. Blease, 140.
35. Chapman, *Marriage Questions*, 171; "Marriage Reform," passim.
36. J. F. S. Russell, 156–328.
37. Hynes, 191.
38. England, Royal Commission on Divorce, preface.
39. Personal communication.
40. Quoted in Burn, 249.

CHAPTER 17

1. Westermarck, 145–49.
2. Larcher, 38.
3. Davesiès, 252.
4. Kemble, *Girlhood*, 24.
5. Hare, *Edgeworth*, 2: 120.

6. E. Sylvia Pankhurst, 332.
7. Beatrice Webb, 113.
8. Hare, *Solitary Life*, 31.
9. Sidgwick, 68.
10. Frances Trollope, *Paris*, 2: 87.

11. M. E. Smith, 38.
12. Carter, 33, and passim.
13. Bodichon, 15.
14. Packer, 24, 153.
15. Robert Cook, 23.
16. Ann Taylor, *Reciprocal Duties*, 79.
17. Greg, 280.
18. Pückler-Muskau, 425.
19. Frances Trollope, *Paris*, 1: 291.
20. Taine, *England*, 64.
21. Mary Jones, 16; Yonge, 22.
22. Martineau, *Autobiography*, 1: 133.
23. Quoted in Wheatley, 400, 368.
24. Martineau, "Female Industry," 293–326.
25. Edward Cook, 1: 100.
26. Ibid., 1: 100.
27. Cobbe, *Life*, 1: 1, 184, and passim.
28. Cobbe, *Pursuits*, 51–52.
29. Frances Trollope, *Paris*, 1: 285–90.
30. Dumas, *Les Femmes qui tuent*, 107.
31. Pelletier, 7.
32. Betham-Edwards, 98.
33. Hamerton, *Round My House*, 364.
34. Taine, 1: *Life and Letters*, 2.
35. Adam, *Sentiments*, 211.
36. Dimnet, 29.
37. Matthew Arnold, "Guérin," 116.
38. Guérin, 1: 72, and passim.
39. Renan, passim.
40. Ibid., 33.
41. Ibid., 61.
42. Michelet, *Prêtre*, 225.
43. Ibid., 223–28.
44. Adhémar, *Femme catholique*, 311.
45. Milne, 137; see also Koltsova-Masalskaia, 1: 199 and Mary Howitt, 2: 195.

46. Jameson, *Sisters*, 143.
47. Legouvé, *Histoire*, 400.
48. Jameson, *Sisters*, 25.
49. Betham-Edwards, 99.
50. Janet, *Elements of Morals*, 202.
51. Riehl, *Die Familie*, 70.
52. Lewald, *Für und wider die Frauen*, chap. 24.
53. Ibid., chap. 16.
54. Ibid., chap. 2.
55. Twellmann, *Frauenbewegung*, 28.
56. Bebel, *Die Frau*, 135.
57. Meisel-Hess, 19.
58. Knodel, *Decline*, 68.
59. Hartmann, passim.
60. Corvin-Wiersbitzki, *Autobiography*, 2: 57.
61. Bothmer, *German Home Life*, 194.
62. Fremantle, 73.
63. Braun, *Memoiren*, 1: 182.
64. Meinecke, 119.
65. Bunsen, 118, 182.
66. Gretton, 50.
67. Morgan, *Italy*, 2: 227.
68. Ravera, 15.
69. Jameson, *Sisters*, 22, 232.
70. Arrivabene, 2: 63.
71. Ibid., 1: 146.
72. Story, 62.
73. Norton, 44.
74. Greville, 31.
75. Desmarie, 112.
76. Caracciolo, *Memoirs*; see also Drago.
77. Ibid., 45–46.
78. Ibid., 70–71.
79. Ibid., 176.
80. Amberley and Amberley, 2: 420.
81. J. F. S. Russell, 12.
82. Métraux and Mead, 36; Daumard, 357.

CHAPTER 18

Many people discussed the legal position of Frenchwomen either at length or in relation to some other matter. Naturally much of the material overlaps. In addition to the specific references listed below, I have drawn largely from the following sources for general facts and ideas. In the 1848–1849 period, Legouvé was asked by the revolutionary government to consider the position of women, and his pamphlet sums up the law of his day. Debay's *Philosophie du Mariage* studies how marriages were limited by the state of the law. Paul Gide in 1867 issued a study of the legal position of women over the centuries, and two years later Elena M. Koltsova-Masalskaia (Dora d'Istria) brought out her comparative study of women all over the world. In the 1880s Léon Giraud put out several studies on dowry rights and more general matters. At the very end of the century, Paul and Victor Margueritte discussed the "new women" of the day, and at the start of the new century, Charles Turgéon gave the world two scholarly volumes on the history of women's emancipation, individual and social, political and familial. Louis Delzons' essay of 1913 is a paean to the conservative originators of the law, which he saw as being currently undermined by permissive legislation. After the war, in 1920, Charles Lefebvre published a series of lectures explaining French family ideals to American soldiers. Frances Clark made a useful study of the position of Frenchwomen in 1937, which naturally included many facts about earlier times. See also Gabriel Lepointe's 1962 contribution to the Jean Bodin Society's volume *La Femme*, in their series of studies of contemporary institutions.

1. Tolédano, 11.
2. Legouvé, *Histoire*, 126.
3. Delzons, 4, 19.
4. Héricourt, 171.
5. Debay, *Philosophie*, 28.
6. Turgéon, 1: 3.
7. Giraud, *Essai*, 49.
8. Ponteil, *Institutions*, 95.
9. Naquet, *Autobiographie*.
10. Legouvé, *Histoire*, 203–4.
11. Decaux, 8: 195.
12. Dumas, *Les Femmes qui tuent*, 1.
13. Abensour, *Féminisme*, 114.
14. Maillard, 242.
15. Colette, *Claudine*, 110.
16. Chéliga, 281.
17. Lefebvre, 163.
18. Lepointe, 503.
19. Ibid., 108–9.
20. Zeldin, *France*, 291.
21. Spengler, 146 ff.
22. Hillebrand, *France*, 8.
23. Legouvé, *Histoire*, 295.
24. Ibid., 297.
25. Giraud, *Essai*, 102.
26. Lallemand, 156.
27. Legouvé, *Cours*, 39.
28. Bullough, 175.
29. Spengler, 223.
30. Legouvé, *Histoire*, 79, 259.
31. Stanton, 256.
32. Legouvé, *Histoire*, 76.
33. Ibid., 76.
34. Richer, *Code*.
35. Giraud, *Essai*, 46.

CHAPTER 19

There have been numberless studies of French feminism in the years of Louis Philippe and the Second Republic. Among them I have found useful the undated *La Légende de la femme émancipée* by Furmin Maillard. It was intended to show the fatal consequences of emancipation by selected examples of failed or unhappy women: Flora Tristan, for example. It was apparently published in mid-nineteenth century. The only copy I could easily find of Jenny d'Héricourt's tract was an American translation of 1864. This fact might lend plausibility to the rumor of her American teaching position; at least it shows that her works were known, and apparently valued, in America. Suzanne Voilquin's story of her life was published in Paris in 1866 with the author's name given as "Madame Suzanne V. . . . " In 1897 Marya Chéliga made a short, scholarly study of the feminist movement in France, to be followed in 1913 by Léon Abensour's more extensive study of feminism under Louis Philippe. The same writer extended his period of interest in a 1921 volume. Marguerite Thibert's 1926 study of feminism in French socialism from 1830 to 1850 is scholarly, as is Edouard Dolléans's section on feminism for Charles Moulin's centenary volume on the 1848 revolution. For Pauline Roland's life, see Edith Thomas. Alain Decaux's *Histoire des Françaises* in many volumes is popular but informative.

The latest study of the subject is *Histoire du féminisme français* by Maité Albistur and Daniel Armogathe (1977).

1. Legouvé, *Cours*, 11.
2. Rousseau, 468.
3. Twellmann, *Quellen*, 163.
4. Grépon, passim; Turgéon, 1: 20; Abensour, *Histoire*, 11.
5. Braun, *Frauenfrage*, 86.
6. Balde, 334.
7. Maillard, 26.
8. Chesnel de la Charbouclais, passim.
9. Rebière, 117.
10. Abensour, *Féminisme sous Louis-Phillipe*, 184.
11. Ibid., 166.
12. Gérard-Gailly, 16, and passim.
13. Delphine de Girardin, March 23, 1844.
14. Stanton, 242.
15. Decaux, 11, 7.
16. Abensour, *Histoire*, 136.
17. See Thibert, *Féminisme*, 239; Abensour, *Histoire*, 13.
18. Decaux, 8: 236, and passim.
19. Grépon, 93.
20. Abensour, *Féminisme sous Louis-Phillipe*, 45.
21. Ibid., xv.
22. Ibid., 113 ff.
23. Ibid., 41.
24. Ibid., 144.
25. Thibert, *Féminisme*, 253.
26. Dolléans, 248.
27. Abensour, *Féminisme sous Louis-Phillipe*, 135.
28. Bulwer, 2: 99.
29. Abensour, *Féminisme sous Louis-Phillipe*, 213.
30. Poinsot, 7, and passim.
31. Burnand, *1830*, 81.
32. Thibert, *Féminisme*, 93.
33. Koltsova-Masalskaia, 1: 88.
34. Legouvé, *Cours*, 19.
35. Decaux, 9: 7.
36. Ibid., 13.
37. Thibert, *Féminisme*, 164.
38. Dolléans, 249.
39. Decaux, 9: 15.
40. Dolléans, 251.
41. Chéliga, 277; Thibert, *Féminisme*, 88.
42. Chéliga, 277.
43. Maillard, 233.
44. Thibert, *Féminisme*, 99 ff.
45. Talmon, 141.
46. Thibert, *Féminisme*, 35, 78; E. M. Butler, *Saint-Simonian Religion*, 7, 50.
47. Thibert, *Féminisme*, passim; Talmon, 108; E. Thomas, 25.
48. Burnand, *1830*, 106.
49. Bowle, 115.
50. Ridley, 24–26.
51. Voilquin.
52. Thibert, *Féminisme*, 226.
53. Cate, 390.
54. Chéliga, 277.
55. Héricourt, 175.
56. E. Thomas, passim.
57. Thibert, *Apôtre*, 491.
58. Mozzoni, *Liberazione*, 12.
59. Lemmonier, 19.
60. Stanton, 239.
61. Chéliga, 277; Abensour, *Féminisme sous Louis-Philippe*, 196.
62. Thibert, *Féminisme*, 82.
63. Héricourt, preface.
64. Malvina Frank, *Mogli*, 497.

CHAPTER 20

The best sources for the lives of the women under discussion in this chapter are their own autobiographies, which, if not always literally accurate, give in each case a lively sense of how they felt about the world and themselves. George Sand's *Histoire de ma vie*, is the longest, coming out in four volumes in 1879. It is of consuming interest. It is hard to understand why it had to wait until 1978 to be translated, and then twice, by Dan Hofstadter and by Joseph Barry. For checking up on what Sand was really doing, I have relied on Curtis Cate's recent *George Sand: A Biography* (1975). Marie d'Agoult's reminiscences were issued in two parts, her early life under the title *Mes souvenirs*, and her life after meeting Liszt under the title *Mémoires*. Charlotte F. Haldane's *Galley Slaves of Love* recounts the story of her affair with Liszt, and there is background material about her in the life of her daughter by Alice Hunt Sokoloff, *Cosima Wagner: Extraordinary Daughter of Franz Liszt*. Both these last books deal much more with the adventures than with the ideas and thoughts of Daniel Stern. Her first-class intellect is neglected. Flora Tristan tells about her marriage and her trip to Peru and about the origin of her social thought in *Pérégrinations d'une paria* (Paris, 1833, 1834). The very scholarly and thorough study of her life and thought by Jules-L. Puech (1925) adds a great deal of fact and interpretation. *Les Enchantments de Prudence* is Hortense Allart's novel based on her own story. It is touching and simple. Her life as told by André Billy, *Hortense et ses amants* (1961) is a thinner volume than Puech's, but it gives his subject due credit for her many-sidedness. Juliette Adam's story, translated as *The Romance of My Childhood and Youth* (1902) is supplemented by *Mes sentiments et nos idées avant 1870* (1905). Neither is a full autobiography. Winifred Stephens's *Madame Adam* (1917) is formal and uncritical.

1. Tristan, *Pérégrinations*, 1: xxxvi.
2. Maigron, 489.
3. Adam, *Sentiments*, 225.
4. Sand, *Histoire*, 3: 279–80.
5. Ibid., 3: 334, and passim.
6. Seillière, *Portraits*, 28.
7. Ibid., 35–41.
8. Sand, *Histoire*, 3: 441.
9. M. J. Howe, 238.
10. Sand, *Histoire*, 4: 122.
11. Ibid., 4: 55–56.
12. Cate, 75.
13. Adam, *Sentiments*, 209.
14. Stephens, 126.
15. Maigron, 428.
16. Dolléans, 250.
17. Agoult, *Mémoires*, 194.
18. Ibid., 1–4.
19. Ibid., 26–39.
20. Ibid., 40.
21. Ibid., 163.
22. C. F. Haldane, 118, and passim.
23. Sokoloff, 47–50.
24. Ibid., 39, and passim.
25. Agoult, *Mémoires*, 242.
26. Agoult, *Liberté*, passim.
27. Goldsmith, 73; Puech, 355.
28. Eléonore Blanc, 12.
29. Puech, 76.
30. Ibid., 69–70.
31. Ibid., 74.
32. Ibid., 341.
33. Ibid., 344.
34. Tristan, *Union*, 98, and passim.
35. Ibid., 93.
36. Puech, 418.
37. Ibid., 458.
38. Ibid., 121.
39. Maillard, 129.
40. Puech, 163.
41. Ruge, 94.
42. Tristan, *Union*, 9.
43. Eléonore Blanc, 48.
44. Puech, 285.
45. Allart, *Enchantements*, vii–ix.
46. Billy, 156, 269, and passim.

47. Ibid., 32.
48. Ibid., 46.
49. Ibid., 161.
50. Ibid., 8.
51. Ibid., title page.
52. Allart, *Enchantements*, 155.
53. Billy, 105.
54. Ibid., 199.
55. Ibid., 155.
56. Allart, *Enchantements*, 311.
57. Ibid., 174.
58. Adam, *Sentiments*, 171–72, 238.
59. Adam, *Romance*, 226, and
    passim.
60. Ibid., 396.
61. Stephens, 91–93.
62. Ibid., 44, and passim.

63. Ibid., 58.
64. Adam, *Idées*, 24.
65. Stephens, 60.
66. Adam, *Idées*, 97.
67. Stephens, 62.
68. Ibid., 97.
69. Adam, *Sentiments*, 131–36.
70. Stephens, 121.
71. Adam, *Sentiments*, 144.
72. Stephens, 169.
73. Ibid., 124.
74. Adam, *Sentiments*, 251.
75. Ibid., 118, 363.
76. Ibid., 463.
77. Ibid., 464.
78. Stephens, 232.

CHAPTER 21

The outstanding analysis of the condition of Frenchwomen in the nineteenth century is Julie Daubié's prize-winning *La Femme pauvre*. The Lyons Academy had offered a prize for the best essay on the subject of raising women's wages to equal those of men, opening new employments to replace the ones that had been taken from them, but the author discussed far more than this. She outlined a whole philosophy of the status of women based on close study of their actual aconditions. Harvard's copy of this book is inscribed by the author to Emile de Girardin. The source for my remarks on Clemence Royer, apart from her own writing, is a small volume by Milice (1926).

1. Daubié, 2, 237, and passim.
2. Abensour, *Histoire*, 136.
3. Boucherett, "Condition of
   Women."
4. Daubié, 197.
5. Clark, 9.
6. Zeldin, *France*, 351.
7. Lemonnier, 22.
8. Camp, 66.
9. Hartman, 32.
10. Betham-Edwards, 93.
11. Adhémar, *Femme catholique*,
    276.
12. Dinah Craik, 55.
13. Charrier, 242.
14. Milice, 20.
15. Royer, 9, and passim.
16. Mazzoleni, 186.
17. Milice, 73.
18. Quoted by Rebière, 239.

19. Lange and Bäumer, 397.
20. Daubié, 130.
21. Morgan, *France in 1829–30*, 2:
    289 ff.
22. M. E. Smith, 39.
23. Charrier, 141; Ruge, 295;
    Legouvé, *Histoire*, 349.
24. Legouvé, *Histoire*, 423.
25. Decaux, 9: 102.
26. Daubié, dedication.
27. Charrier, 146.
28. Kurtz, 197.
29. Somerville, 345.
30. Mario, "Position of Women."
31. Charrier, 289, and passim.
32. Giraud, *Essai*, 371.
33. Charrier, 291.
34. Twellmann, *Quellen*, 415.
35. Charrier, 292.
36. Ibid., 407.

37. Clark, 55.
38. Charrier, 95, 336.
39. *A la mémoire de Maria Desraismes*, 171.
40. Gayraud, 215.
41. Curie, 149–50.
42. Bashkirtseff, 334.
43. Rhodes, 174.
44. Bashkirtseff, 407.
45. Ibid., 416.
46. Ibid., 634.
47. Charrier, 100.
48. Clark, 124.

49. Legouvé, *Histoire*, 423.
50. Charrier, 114.
51. Clark, 132.
52. Lange and Bäumer, 393.
53. Suran-Mahire, 51.
54. Adhémar, *Femme catholique*, 2: 31, 58.
55. Decaux, 9: 246.
56. Grépon, 33.
57. Gerbod, 36.
58. Pelletier, 9.
59. Gayraud, 3–5.
60. Ibid., 205.

CHAPTER 22

1. Abensour, *Histoire*, passim.
2. Brownell, 220.
3. Agoult, *Mes souvenirs*, ix.
4. Vandam, *Notebook*, 196.
5. Amberley and Amberley, 2: 340.
6. Decaux, 9: 165.
7. Chéliga, 278.
8. Decaux, 9: 166.
9. Lange and Bäumer, 373–77.
10. Charrier, 86.
11. Chéliga, 279.
12. Ibid., 284.
13. Grépon, 95.
14. Lange and Bäumer, 397.
15. Zeldin, *France*, 348.
16. Lange and Bäumer, 363.
17. Dumas, *Les Femmes qui tuent*, 180.
18. Ibid., 95.
19. Emile de Girardin, *Egale de son fils*, 170.
20. Betham-Edwards, 92.
21. Abensour, *Féminisme sous Louis-Philippe*, 207–8.
22. Turgéon, 1: 58, 61.

23. Pelletan, 29.
24. Turgéon, 1: 42.
25. Héricourt, 303.
26. Dolléans, 250.
27. Taine, *France*, 8.
28. Stanton, 271, quoting Léon Giraud.
29. Adhémar, *Femme catholique*, 6.
30. Laya, 34, 38.
31. Ibid., 33.
32. Bureau, 90 (quoting Th. Ruyssen).
33. Turgéon, 1: 230.
34. Ibid., 73.
35. Grépon, 25, 245.
36. Bureau, 90.
37. Abensour, *Féminisme sour Louis-Philippe*, 147.
38. Forel, 519.
39. Turgéon, 1: 81.
40. Pelletier, 26.
41. *Le Neo-Malthusisme*, 29; Pelletier, 38.
42. Yvonne Mitchell, 7.

CHAPTER 23

Every student of the German women's movement must be grateful for Margrit Twellmann's study, which she has enhanced with a superb 570-page collection of sources. Unfortunately she only carries them up to 1889. Helene Lange and Gertrud Bäumer's handbook of the women's movement (1901) includes a volume on the history of the movement in "advanced" countries and carries it up to their publication date. A longer perspective is provided by Agnes von Zahn-Harnack, herself an active participant, who looked back in 1928. In no other country were the writings of the leaders so scholarly or so thorough. Lily Braun's *Die Frauen Frage* (*The Woman's Question*) of 1901 led Helene Lange to call her a "popularizer." Werner Thönnessen's 1969 study deals with the attitude of the Social Democratic party to the woman question, a subject which is carried further by Jean H. Quataert in *Reluctant Feminists in German Social Democracy, 1885–1917* (Princeton: Princeton University Press, 1979). Unfortunately this work came along too late for me to derive full benefit from it. She and I are looking at opposite sides of the same coin, and accordingly have different interpretations, especially of the character of Lily Braun.

1. Lange and Bäumer, 7.
2. Hippel, *Über die Ehe*, 179.
3. Hippel, *Verbesserung*, 12.
4. Hippel, *Über die Ehe*, 51.
5. Ibid., 33.
6. Lange and Bäumer, 13.
7. Rilke, *Letters to a Young Poet.*
8. Lange and Bäumer, 16.
9. Keyserling, *Book of Marriage*, 175 ff.
10. Lewald, *Für und wider die Frauen*, 84.
11. Keyserling, *Book of Marriage*, 187.
12. Lange and Bäumer, 21.
13. Hillebrand, "Caroline Schlegel."
14. G. R. Taylor, *Sex in History*, 197.
15. Keyserling, *Book of Marriage*, 179.
16. E. M. Butler, *Saint-Simonian Religion*, 293.
17. Immermann, 99.
18. Willoughby, 131.
19. Bousset, 50.
20. E. M. Butler, *Saint-Simonian Religion*, 69, 268.
21. Ibid., 117.
22. Key, *Rahel*, 18 ff.
23. Ibid., 20.
24. Arendt, xi.
25. Key, *Rahel*, 100.
26. Ibid., 101–2.
27. Ibid., 108.
28. Ibid., 133.
29. Ibid., 149.
30. Key, 154.
31. Ibid., 160–67.
32. Ibid., 69.
33. Ibid., 173.
34. Ibid., 173–75.
35. Ibid., 72.
36. Ibid., 198.
37. Schmidt-Weissenfels, 33.
38. Willoughby, 126.
39. Steinhauer, 7.
40. Lewald, *Für und wider die Frauen*, 17.
41. Steinhauer, 8.
42. Seillière, "Fanny Lewald," 387.
43. Steinhauer, 11.
44. Lewald, *Gefühltes*, 66, 136.
45. Lange and Bäumer, 43.
46. Lewald, *Für und wider die Frauen*, 95.
47. Steinhauer, 47.
48. Twellmann, *Quellen*, 119.
49. Steinhauer, 48.
50. Koltsova-Masalskaia, 2: 88.
51. Hahn, passim.
52. Blos, 18.
53. Aston, *Emancipation*, passim.
54. Ibid., 47.
55. Twellmann, *Quellen*, 85.
56. Feuerbach, *Leben in Briefen*, 49.
57. Ibid., 102.
58. Fleischhack, 152.
59. C. Winkworth, *Sieveking*, passim.
60. Ibid., 301.
61. Ibid., 27–28.
62. Ibid., 27.
63. Ibid., 284.
64. Ibid., 371.
65. Ibid., 487.
66. Ibid., 42.

67. Lange and Bäumer, 32.
68. Meysenbug, 1: vi.
69. Ibid., 1: 80.
70. Twellmann, *Quellen*, 157.

71. See Prelinger; Braun, *Frauenfrage*, 117.
72. Carr, 271.

CHAPTER 24

I am sorry that this chapter was written before I had the benefit of reading Richard J. Evans, *The Feminist Movement in Germany, 1894–1933*(SAGE Publications, 1976), and I recommend it.

1. Lange and Bäumer, 39.
2. Zahn-Harnack, *Frauenbewegung*, 149.
3. Lange and Bäumer, 35.
4. Zahn-Harnack, *Frauenbewegung*, 17.
5. Twellmann, *Quellen*, 3.
6. Blos, 9.
7. Lange and Bäumer, 34.
8. Twellmann, *Quellen*, 27.
9. Zahn-Harnack, *Wandlungen*, 9.
10. Twellmann, *Quellen*, 2.
11. Ibid., 6.
12. Otto-Peters, 137, and passim.
13. Blos, 13.
14. Twellmann, *Frauenbewegung*, 40.
15. Helene Lange, *Lebenserinnerungen*, 199.
16. Lange and Bäumer, 106.
17. Twellmann, *Frauenbewegung*, 54.
18. Twellmann, *Quellen*, 36, 54.
19. Steinhauer, 81.
20. Twellmann, *Frauenbewegung*, 32.
21. Twellmann, *Quellen*, 471.
22. Twellmann, *Frauenbewegung*, 44.
23. Stanton, 144.
24. Bothmer, *German Home Life*, 169.
25. Lange and Bäumer, 66.
26. Twellmann, *Quellen*, 173.
27. Ibid., 197.
28. Marholm, 23.
29. Twellmann, *Quellen*, 229, 537.
30. Paulsen, "Die Frau," 407.
31. Braun, *Frauenfrage*, 33.
32. Bülow, 12.
33. Zahn-Harnack, *Frauenbewegung*, 46–47.
34. Lange and Bäumer, 140.
35. Paulsen, "Die Frau," 403; Bulling, 110.
36. Thieme, 366.
37. Twellmann, *Quellen*, 214.
38. Bulling, 152.
39. Zahn-Harnack, *Frauenbewegung*, 276 ff.
40. Helene Lange, *Lebenserinnerungen*, 238.
41. Zahn-Harnack, *Wandlungen*, 45.
42. Zahn-Harnack, *Frauenbewegung*, 289.
43. Wilson, 234.
44. Thönnessen, 31.
45. Ibid., 63.
46. Bebel, *Die Frau*, 175.
47. Twellmann, *Quellen*, 535.
48. Weber, *Max*.
49. Simmel, "Tendencies," 167.
50. Lange and Bäumer, 118.
51. Thönnessen, 54.
52. Bülow, 34.
53. Twellmann, *Frauenbewegung*, 63–67, 187.
54. Ibid., 188.
55. Bülow, 34.
56. Braun, *Frauenfrage*, 472.
57. Bülow, 36.
58. Ibid., 34.
59. Kramer, 53.
60. Zahn-Harnack, *Wandlungen*, 46.
61. Braun, *Memoiren*, 1: 313.
62. Ibid., 1: 501.
63. Lange and Bäumer, 121.
64. Braun, *Memoiren*, 1: 545.

65. Ibid., 1: 568.
66. Ibid., 1: 631, and passim; 2: 169 ff.
67. Ibid., 2: 327.
68. Ibid., 2: 405.
69. Twellmann, *Quellen*, 490.
70. Lange and Bäumer, 131.
71. Ibid., 134.
72. Twellmann, *Frauenbewegung*, 207.
73. Twellmann, *Quellen*, 273.

74. Ibid., 555.
75. Twellmann, *Quellen*, 185.
76. Ibid., 177.
77. Dohn, 144; Twellmann, *Quellen*, 177–83, 237–38.
78. Zahn-Harnack, *Wandlungen*, 44.
79. Zahn-Harnack, *Frauenbewegung*, 70.
80. Ibid., 61.
81. I. A. R. Wylie, *The Germans*, 196.

CHAPTER 25

For the life of Sonya Kovalevsky I have used Chapman, *Marriage Questions*, 46–50; Rebière, 159–60; Bebel, *Die Frau und der Sozialismus*, 206; Kirchhoff, 248; and Marholm.

1. Kirchhoff, passim.
2. Ibid., 40.
3. Ibid., 295.
4. Ibid., 273.
5. Ibid., 23.
6. Ibid., 6–7.
7. Ibid., 222.
8. Ibid., 105.
9. Ibid., 216.
10. Ibid., 256.
11. Ibid., 125.
12. Ibid., 193.
13. Ibid., 193.
14. Ibid., 123.
15. Lange and Bäumer, 54.
16. Lewald, Frauen, 40.
17. Bousset, 31–34.
18. Twellmann, *Quellen*, 267.
19. Ibid., 179.
20. Ibid., 297 ff.
21. Helene Lange, *Lebenserinnerungen*, passim.
22. Ibid., 274.
23. Twellmann, *Quellen*, 370.
24. Ibid., 341.
25. Sidgwick, 24.
26. Twellmann, *Quellen*, 343.
27. Sidgwick, 23.
28. Twellmann, *Quellen*, 349.
29. Ibid., 283–85.
30. Ibid., 352, 375.
31. Ibid., 401.

32. Ibid., 88.
33. Braun, *Frauenfrage*, 146.
34. Twellmann, *Frauenbewegung*, 96.
35. Braun, *Frauenfrage*, 183.
36. Friedel, 231.
37. Josephine Butler, *Woman's Work*, 96.
38. Maxe von Arnim, 207.
39. Twellmann, *Quellen*, 400.
40. Ibid., 326.
41. Lewald, *Für und wider die Frauen*, 63.
42. Meyer, 2.
43. Lange and Bäumer, 65; Lewald, *Für und wider die Frauen*, 63.
44. Sidgwick, 21.
45. Bothmer, *German Home Life*, 179,
46. Paulsen, *Autobiography*, 251.
47. Mommsen, 58.
48. Ibid., 48.
49. Twellmann, *Quellen*, 381.
50. Anna Mary Howitt, passim.
51. Twellmann, *Quellen*, 389–94.
52. Bunsen, 61.
53. Lewald, *Für und wider die Frauen*, 89.
54. Zahn-Harnack, *Frauenbewegung*, 182.
55. Lange and Bäumer, 96.
56. Schiemann, 846.

57. Zahn-Harnack, *Wandlungen*, 38.
58. Meinecke, 92.
59. Martin Green, 16.
60. Kirchhoff, 165.

CHAPTER 26

Grete Meisel-Hess, born at Prague in 1879, attended the University of Vienna, wrote novels, and explicated the phase of the women's movement concerned with sexual liberation. She believed that feminism might be dysgenic if women became unwilling to marry, a crisis that she thought could only be resolved by socialism. Wally Zepler's collection of articles from the pre-war *Sozialistischen Monatshriften* is invaluable for understanding the debate within the party on women's role.

1. Simmel, "Tendencies," 166.
2. Engels, passim.
3. Bebel, *Life*, 259.
4. Bebel, *Die Frau*, 178, 336.
5. Lange and Bäumer, 111.
6. Twellmann, *Frauenbewegung*, 143.
7. Zepler, 18.
8. Meisel-Hess, 20.
9. Zepler, 38.
10. Ibid., 63 ff.
11. Braun, *Frauenfrage*, 196.
12. Braun, *Memoiren*, 2: 398.
13. Eckermann, January 10, 1825.
14. Gerhard and Simon, 60.
15. Ibid., 112.
16. Ibid., 170.
17. Ibid., 147.
18. Ibid., 230.
19. Ibid., 240.
20. Ibid., 252.
21. Ibid., 261.
22. Zahn-Harnack, Frauen-bewegung, 74.
23. Twellmann, *Quellen*, 416.
24. Zahn-Harnack, *Wandlungen*, 30.
25. Wolf, 31, 58, and passim.
26. Zahn-Harnack, *Frauenbewegung*, 87.
27. Meisel-Hess, 211.
28. Thönnessen, 69.
29. Bebel, *Die Frau*, 78 and passim.
30. Newman, 272.
31. Zepler, 88.
32. Zahn-Harnack, *Frauenbewegung*, 88.

33. Braun, *Memoiren*, 1: 370.
34. Bothmer, *German Home Life*, 233.
35. Feuerbach, *Liebenswürdigkeit*, 57.
36. Pichler, 3: 37.
37. Mare, 49.
38. Ebner von Eschenbach, 150.
39. Twellmann, *Quellen*, 226.
40. Ibid., 413.
41. Ibid., 397.
42. Baring-Gould, 1: 225.
43. Ibid., 2: 33.
44. Kautsky, 550–53.
45. Fleischhack, 190.
46. Ibid., passim.
47. Schumann, 188 ff.
48. Fay, 117.
49. Koltsova-Masalskaia, 2: 96; Blos, 47 ff.
50. Fontane, *Journeys to England*, 204.
51. Tiburtius, 86.
52. Ibid., 149.
53. Twellmann, *Quellen*, 435.
54. Reichstag, *Verhandlungen*, March 11, 1891.
55. Gerhard and Simon, 278; Maxe von Arnim, 246.
56. Nightingale, *Kaiserswerth*, passim.
57. Twellmann, *Quellen*, 96.
58. Billroth, 368, 426.
59. Otto-Peters, 165.
60. Bischoff, passim.
61. Twellmann, *Quellen*, 437.

62. Zahn-Harnack, *Frauenbewegung*, 280; Helene Lange, *Lebenser-innerungen*, 236.
63. Stein, 3, 4.
64. Bothmer, *German Home Life*, 277.
65. I. A. R. Wylie, *The Germans*, 186.
66. Friedel, 233.
67. Braun, *Memoiren*, 1: 183, 309.
68. Masur, 143.
69. Sidgwick, 294.
70. Zahn-Harnack, *Wandlungen*, 31.
71. Twellmann, *Frauenbewegung*, 222.
72. Weber, *Max*, 516.
73. Twellmann, *Quellen*, 526.
74. Simmel, "Tendencies," 168.

CHAPTER 27

By far the most complete and interesting picture of how Italian women viewed themselves is given by the collection of lectures, under the title of *La donna italiana*, delivered at the Women's Exposition held at Florence in 1889. Nineteen writers discussed everything from the past to the future, from women in the family to women at work, queens, artists, heroines, and teachers. A general air of timidity, however, prevented nearly all the lecturers from coming out in favor of full rights for their sex. For this, one must turn to the prolific writing of Anna Maria Mozzoni. A good selection from her work has been collected and edited recently by Franca Pieroni Bortolotti (1975). Camilla Ravera is a Marxist and deals mostly with the condition of working-class women. Drago's highly popular account of the colorful women of the Risorgimento is useful mainly as a checklist of women who made a name for themselves.

1. November, 25, 1869.
2. Morgan, *Italy*, 2: 206.
3. Quoted in *Donna italiana: esposizione*, 381.
4. Drago, 19.
5. Quoted in *Donna italiana: esposizione*, 154.
6. Niceforo, 55–56.
7. Drago, 11.
8. Pieroni, 36.
9. Drago, 35.
10. Gattey, 4 ff.
11. Drago, 140.
12. Ibid., 291.
13. Mazzini, 125.
14. Drago, 67.
15. Amy Menzies, 59; Drago, 112; A. J. C. Hare, *The Years with Mother*, 206.
16. Arrivabene, 2: 64.
17. Drago, 290.
18. Treves. 183.
19. Drago, 19.
20. Arrivabene, 2: 37.
21. Mariani, 489.
22. Magni, passim; Drago, 105.
23. Ricci, 2: 110.
24. Barbiera, 263.
25. Berti, Le donne, 109.
26. Ibid., 120.
27. Ravera, 8.
28. Barbiera, 1 ff.
29. Visconti, 31.
30. Malvina Frank, *Mogli*, 4.
31. Barbiera, 168, 338.
32. Lefebvre, 81.
33. Pierantoni-Mancini, 41.
34. Malvina Frank, *Mogli*, 322; Mariani, 480.
35. Malvina Frank, *Mogli*, 356.
36. Mariani, 488.
37. Stanton, 317.
38. Pieroni, 104.
39. Mariani, 481.
40. Malvina Frank, *Mogli*, 327.
41. Malvina Frank, *Fidenzate*, 19.
42. Lange and Bäumer, 414.
43. Pieroni, 144 ff.

44. Ibid., 101.
45. Ibid., 99.
46. Mozzoni, *Donna*, vii.
47. Mozzoni, *Liberazione*, 61; Pieroni, 61.
48. Cobbe, *Italics*, 244.
49. Pieroni, 82.
50. Ibid., 33.
51. Lange and Bäumer, 421.
52. *Free Religious Index*, May 19, 1881, 560–61.

53. Mozzoni, *Liberazione*, 15, passim.
54. Pieroni, 241.
55. Lange and Bäumer, 420.
56. Malvina Frank, *Mogli*, 355.
57. Stanton, 313.
58. Pieroni; 117–18.
59. Mariani, 490.
60. Pieroni, 125.
61. Lange and Bäumer, 419.
62. Pieroni, 126.
63. Mariani, 483.

CHAPTER 28

1. Koltsova-Masalskaia, 1: 254 ff.
2. Stanton, 312.
3. Lange and Bäumer, 412.
4. Kirchhoff, 245; also *Donna italiana: esposizione*, 278.
5. Assing, 252.
6. Josephine Butler, *Woman's Work*, 95.
7. Rossi, 150.
8. Morgan, *Italy*, 2, 24–25; *Donna italiana: esposizione*, 277.
9. Norton, 59.
10. Gennari, 135.
11. Moers, "Mme de Staël," 225.
12. Drago, 252 ff.
13. Ibid., 254.
14. Barbiera, 239.
15. Peruzzi, 509.
16. Malvina Frank, *Mogli*, 419.
17. Braun, *Frauenfrage*, 140.
18. Pieroni, 123; Mariani, 493.
19. Kramer, passim.
20. Ibid., 93.
21. Berti, "Le donne," 110.
22. Villari, 123.
23. Pieroni, 41.
24. Greco, 5.
25. Mozzoni, *Passo*, 19.
26. Greco, 14.
27. Pieroni, 124; Mariani, 482.
28. Mariani, 485.
29. Berti, "Le donne," 130.
30. Chierici, 13, and passim.
31. Bazin, 57–64.
32. *Donna italiana: esposizione*, 420.

33. Bazin, 5.
34. Wilkins and Altrocchi, introduction.
35. Gisolfi, 14.
36. Mariani, 482.
37. *Donna italiana: esposizione*, passim.
38. Dupré, 371.
39. Canonici, 7.
40. Mozzoni, *Passo*, 21.
41. Greco, 211.
42. Mozzoni, *Passo*, 39.
43. Stendhal, *Journal*, 43.
44. Belgiojoso, passim.
45. Cobbe, *Pursuits*, 156.
46. *Donna italiana: esposizione*, 208.
47. Morgan, *Italy*, 1: 282.
48. Cobbe, *Life*, 1: 294.
49. Massimo d'Azeglio, *Things I Remember*, 306.
50. Costanza d'Azeglio, 57, 397.
51. Pierantoni-Mancini, *Impressioni*, 198, 228.
52. *Donna italiana: esposizione*, 259, 261.
53. Pierantoni-Mancini, *Impressioni*, 54.
54. Arrivabene, 1: 135.
55. Pierantoni-Mancini, *Impressioni*, 82.
56. Arrivabene, 2: 51.
57. Bruni, 175.
58. Mantegazza, 8, and passim.
59. Lange and Bäumer, 421.

CHAPTER 29

1. Annie Besant, *Marriage*, 6.
2. Barbara Leigh Smith, 6.
3. Annie Besant, *Marriage*, 8.
4. Mary V. Hughes, *London Child*, 99.
5. Gide, 287.
6. Barbara Leigh Smith, 4.
7. Annie Besant, *Marriage*, 9.
8. Caird, 117.
9. Cobbe, *Life*, 1: 154.
10. Ray Strachey, 39.
11. Dowling.
12. A. P. Stone, 671.
13. Alexander Walker, 160.
14. Amanda Ellis, 275.
15. Alexander Walker, 161.
16. Ray Strachey, 38.
17. Stock, passim.
18. Marreco, passim.
19. Blease, 129.
20. Quoted in Ray Strachey, 74.
21. Kaye, "Outrages," 536.
22. McGregor, *Divorce*, 17.
23. Crow, 157.
24. *Edinburgh Review*, January, 1857, 102.
25. Gornall, 806.
26. Gide, 289.
27. Alexander Walker, 155.
28. Annie Besant, *Marriage*, 11.
29. Fawcett, 61.
30. Driver, 125.
31. *Edinburgh Review*, January, 1857, 195.
32. Manton, 47.
33. Hester Burton, 30.
34. Barbara Stephen, *Girton*, 4.
35. Nethercot, passim.
36. Ibid., 30.
37. Annie Besant, *Autobiographical Sketches*, 75.
38. Nethercot, 134.
39. Ibid., 136, 137.
40. Annie Besant, *Autobiographical Sketches*, 167.

CHAPTER 30

1. Key, *Century of the Child*, 205.
2. Amberley and Amberley, 2: 312.
3. Morgan, *Memoirs*, 1: 113.
4. Ibid., 202–3.
5. Killham, 122.
6. Elizabeth G. Smith, 356.
7. Hanson and Hanson, *Necessary Evil*, 6.
8. Quoted in Wheatley, 152.
9. Hanson and Hanson, *Necessary Evil*, 36.
10. Mary Howitt, 1: 95.
11. Mrs. H. Ward, *Recollections*, 1: 45.
12. Layard, 27.
13. Manton, 37.
14. Barbara Stephen, *Emily Davies*, 31.
15. Shaen, 13.
16. Ibid., 11.
17. Ibid., 19.
18. Quoted in Shaen, 158.
19. Elizabeth Haldane, 120, and passim.
20. Maxwell, 91.
21. Somerville, 266, and passim.
22. Ibid., 2.
23. Ibid., 24.
24. Ibid., 53.
25. Bremner, 10.
26. Somerville, 80.
27. Ibid., 169.
28. Ibid., 163.
29. Martineau, *Autobiography*, 1: 358.
30. Cobbe, *Life*, 2: 351.
31. Mozans, *Women in Science*.
32. Jameson, *Sisters*, 45.
33. Howard, passim.
34. Milne, 212.
35. Ray Strachey, 87.
36. Middleton, 11.
37. Bremner, 9–10.
38. Blease, 77.

39. Grisewood, 255.
40. Hare, *Edgeworth*, 1: 135.
41. Tennyson, *Princess*, Prologue, 11, 127–30, 133–36.
42. Ibid., Part VII, 11, 259–60.
43. Ibid., Part V, 11, 453–54.
44. Alice Zimmern, 20 ff. and passim; Bremner, passim.
45. Grisewood, 256.
46. Fanny Kingsley, 1: 128–29.
47. Ray Strachey, 61.
48. Maurice, 13.
49. Helene Lange, *Education*, 9.
50. Grisewood, 257.
51. Stanton, 33.
52. Helene Lange, *Education*, 9.
53. Meysenbug, 3: 102.
54. Barbara Stephen, *Emily Davies*, passim.
55. Barbara Stephen, *Girton*, 21.
56. Alice Zimmern, 107.
57. Manton, 224.
58. Emily Davies, 168.
59. Barbara Stephen, *Girton*, 174.
60. Barbara Stephen, *Emily Davies*, 223.
61. Stephen, *Girton*, 47.
62. Stephen, *Emily Davies*, 164.
63. Ibid., 252.
64. Barbara Stephen, *Girton*, 16.
65. Kamm, *Hope*, 252.
66. Barbara Stephen, *Girton*, 35.
67. See Bremner; Ray Strachey; Petrie.
68. B. A. Clough, 147.
69. Barbara Stephen, *Girton*, 74, and passim.
70. Ray Strachey, 249.

71. Graves, 3: 117.
72. Webster, 89.
73. Pratt, 81.
74. Pratt, 86; Bremner, 140.
75. Stanley, 2: 215.
76. Alice Zimmern, 40 ff; Dibelius, 422.
77. See Pratt; Alice Zimmern; Stanton.
78. Mary V. Hughes, *London Girl*, 7.
79. Alice Zimmern, 42.
80. Ibid., 45.
81. Ray Strachey, 127.
82. Mary V. Hughes, *London Girl*, 45.
83. Kamm, *Buss*, passim.
84. See Carew; Ray Strachey.
85. Pratt, 74.
86. Bremner, 114–15.
87. Banks, 191.
88. Showalter and Showalter, 86.
89. *Edinburgh Review*, July, 1887, 94.
90. Banks and Banks, 121.
91. Mary V. Hughes, *London Girl*, 141–47.
92. E. Girardin, *Égale*, 122.
93. Acollas, 77.
94. Amberley and Amberley, 2: 111–12.
95. Cobbe, *Life*, 1: 65.
96. Shaen, 260.
97. Blouët, *Womankind*, 77.
98. Graves, 3: 119.
99. Bremner, 134.
100. Fawcett, 139.
101. Graves, 3: 122.

CHAPTER 31

Three books by women, coming out in the late 1850s or 1860s, called attention to what women could do. Anna Jameson was particularly impressed with the work of nuns, and her *Sisters of charity* was really a call to Englishwomen to go and do likewise. Frances Power Cobbe's *Essays on the Pursuits of Women* and the volume edited by Josephine Butler called *Woman's Work and Woman's Culture* both explored with encouraging detail the kinds of opportunities that were just opening up.

1. Meredith, *Diana*, 368.
2. Brontë, *Shirley*, 178.

3. Hardwick, 174.
4. Jesse, 6.

5. Jameson, *Sisters*, 57.
6. Priestley, 122.
7. Jameson, *Sisters*, 18.
8. Cobbe, *Life*, 1: 98.
9. Quoted in Barbara Stephen, *Emily Davies*, 11.
10. Ibid., 186.
11. Henry Craik, 13.
12. Keyserling, *Europe*, 66–67.
13. Jameson, *Sisters*, 136 n.
14. Smyth, 1: 124.
15. Granville-Barker, 57.
16. Coleridge, 153.
17. Peterson, 9.
18. Farrar, 30.
19. Hopkins, 100.
20. Sarah Ellis, *Women*, 104.
21. Agnes Maud Davies, 190 ff.
22. Milne, 121.
23. Lovett, 431.
24. Jameson, *Sisters*, 40.
25. Basch, 105.
26. Webster, 97.
27. Rosen, 3.
28. Boucherett, 99.
29. *Saturday Review*, 1859, quoted in Banks and Banks, 42–43.
30. Cobbe, *Pursuits*, 68.
31. Lawrenny, 319.
32. Helene Lange, *Education*, 32.
33. Emily Davies, 110.
34. Mary Howitt, 1: 60.
35. *Edinburgh Review*, April, 1859, 333.
36. Henry Craik, 32.
37. Gaskell, *Cranford*, 237.
38. More, *Coelebs*, 173.
39. Shaen, 96–97.
40. Yonge, 153.
41. Quinlan, 164.
42. Coleridge, 48.
43. Pückler-Muskau, 263.
44. Shelley, 2: 217.
45. Baring-Gould, 2: 341.
46. Hopkins, 302.
47. Amberley and Amberley, 1: 387, 390.
48. Charles Kingsley, *Sanitary Lectures*, 3 ff.
49. Agnes Maud Davies, 57.
50. Cole, 23.
51. Channing and Aikin, Aikin to Channing, September 16, 1831.
52. Sarah Ellis, *Daughters*, 123.
53. Milne, 41.
54. Cole, 26.
55. Thomson, 16; Ray Strachey, 83.
56. Pratt, 47.
57. A. S. G. Butler, 30.
58. Petrie, 26 ff.
59. Ibid., 40.
60. Josephine Butler, *Great Crusade*, 2.
61. Ibid., 8.
62. A. S. G. Butler, 70.
63. Petrie, 96.
64. A. S. G. Butler, 77.
65. Ramelson, 116.
66. Josephine Butler, *Great Crusade*, 40.
67. Enid Bell, *Josephine Butler*, 134.
68. Enid Bell, *Octavia Hill*, passim.
69. Osborne, passim.
70. Ibid., 13.
71. Crow, 322.
72. Cole, 31.
73. Muggeridge and Adam, 113.
74. A. S. G. Butler, 79.
75. Chapman, *Godiva*, 55.
76. Cobbe, *Life*, 1: 299.
77. Josephine Butler, *Woman's Work*, xxxvii.
78. Muggeridge and Adam, 116.
79. Boutmy, 13.
80. Crow, 140.
81. Twellmann, *Quellen*, 160.

CHAPTER 32

Ray Strachey's *Struggle* is a classic history of "the stirring story of woman's advance in England," and includes for good measure Florence Nightingale's *Cassandra*, a previously unpublished manuscript about her thoughts and feelings as she tried to work out her destiny. The works of Enid Moberly Bell tell much about the individual lives of English pioneers, and her book *Storming the Citadel* tells of their break into medicine. The material about Elizabeth Garrett Anderson is taken either from Bell, or from Jo Manton's biography.

1. Milne, 129.
2. Thomson, 39 ff.
3. Martineau, "Female Industry," 371.
4. Josephine Butler, *Woman's Work*, 60 n.
5. Webster, 54.
6. Quoted in Thomson, 41.
7. *Edinburgh Review*, April 1859, 307.
8. Stock, passim.
9. Edgeworth and Edgeworth, 2: 141.
10. *Quarterly Review*, 86. (1880.)
11. Hopkins, 209.
12. Mary Howitt, 1: 229.
13. Ibid., 2: 46.
14. Martineau, *Autobiography*, 1: 142.
15. Ibid., 1: 193.
16. Ibid., 1: 206.
17. Wheatley, 94.
18. Mary Howitt, 2: 69.
19. Symons, 165.
20. Morgan, *Memoirs*, 1: 222.
21. Layard, 50.
22. Crow, 192.
23. Dallyn, 60.
24. Hopkins, 66.
25. Gaskell, *Brontë*, 219.
26. E. B. Browning, 358.
27. Ibid., 373.
28. Ibid., 419.
29. Ibid., 500.
30. Woolf, *Collected Essays*, 2: 143.
31. Ibid., 2: 144.
32. Smyth, 1: 131.
33. Ibid., 1: 134.
34. Ibid., 1: 268.
35. E. Sylvia Pankhurst, 377.
36. Kemble, *Girlhood*, passim.
37. Farrar, 250.
38. Martineau, "Female Industry," 333.
39. Rose, passim.
40. Daniels, 41.
41. Manton, 213.
42. Petrie, 65.
43. *Scientific American*, February, 1878.
44. Amy Menzies, 135.
45. Fanny Kingsley, 2: 194.
46. Newman, 279.
47. Donnison, 230.
48. Enid Bell, *Citadel*, passim.
49. Pratt, 111.
50. Ray Strachey, 179.
51. Ibid., 254 ff.
52. Ibid., 254.
53. Lytton Strachey, 21.
54. Pratt, 119.
55. Edward Cook, 1: 23.
56. Ibid., 1: 106.
57. Ibid., 1: 59.
58. Ibid., 1: 57.
59. Nightingale, *Kaiserswerth*, passim.
60. Cunnington, 194.
61. Nightingale, *Writing*, 215.
62. Jameson, *Sisters*, 55.
63. Ramelson, 40.
64. Fawcett, 49.
65. Blouët, *Womankind*, 89.

CHAPTER 33

A useful and interesting book is John Killham's *Tennyson and "The Princess,"* which traces the Saint-Simonian influence in English thought in far greater depth than the title indicates. Richard Pankhurst's essay on the subject, "Saint-Simonism in England," is rather carelessly edited and not nearly so rich in detail as Killham's volume.

For the campaign for the vote, Sylvia Pankhurst's *The Suffragette Movement* tells mainly the story of her own family's involvement. It is very full and somewhat confusing. It should be compared with the autobiography of Millicent Garrett Fawcett, the leader of the other half of the suffrage movement, and with Andrew Rosen's *Rise Up, Women!* which corrects Sylvia Pankhurst through careful research into comtemporary documents. Let me call attention also to George Dangerfield's singularly insightful *The Strange Death of Liberal England*, which puts the suffrage campaign in place beside other critical issues of the pre-war period and gives them all contextual meaning.

1. Martineau, *Autobiography*, 1: 400.
2. Bentham, 1: 103.
3. Quoted in Killham, 68.
4. Ramelson, 60; Sadleir, 68–72.
5. Quoted in Woolf, 3: 194.
6. William Thompson, 62.
7. Ibid., 204.
8. R. Pankhurst, 500, and passim.
9. Lovett, 430.
10. Davesiès, 246.
11. Josephine Butler, *Woman's Work*, xlv.
12. Ibid., 25.
13. Ramelson, 71.
14. Isichei.
15. Packe, 202.
16. Hayek, 60–65.
17. Lippincott, 152; see also J. F. Stephen, passim.
18. William Acton, 140.
19. *Edinburgh Review*, October, 1869, 589.
20. Shoen, 269.
21. Somerville, 344.
22. Packe, 493.
23. Fanny Kingsley, 2: 178.
24. MacKenzie and MacKenzie, 334.
25. Ramelson, 63.
26. Ibid., 72.
27. Killham, 142.
28. Blease, 120.
29. Packe, 450; Rosen, 6; Ramelson, 74.
30. Rosen, 7.
31. Blease, 211.
32. See E. Sylvia Pankhurst, 43; Rosen, 14.
33. Ramelson, 82; Strachey, 305.
34. Rosen, 25. See also Blease.
35. Parliamentary Debates, April 7, 1875.
36. *Edinburgh Review*, April, 1841.
37. Spencer, *Principles* I, 758.
38. Alexander Walker, 83.
39. Webster, 273.
40. Fawcett, 112.
41. Marlow, 268.
42. Ramelson, 88; Houghton, 352.
43. Beatrice Webb, 341.
44. Blease, 262.
45. Rosen, 18.
46. See E. Sylvia Pankhurst; Rosen.
47. Quoted in Rosen, 27.
48. Rosen, 70; E. Sylvia Pankhurst, 511.
49. Wingfield, *Aftermath*, 311; E. Sylvia Pankhurst, 189–90.
50. E. Sylvia Pankhurst, 439.
51. See Dangerfield, *Death*; Blease; E. Sylvia Pankhurst.
52. I. A. R. Wylie, *Life*, 167.
53. Ibid., 167–78.
54. Quoted in E. Sylvia Pankhurst, 312.
55. E. Sylvia Pankhurst; Rosen.
56. Dangerfield, *Death*, 369.
57. Ray Strachey, 330.
58. David Mitchell, 45.
59. Dangerfield, *Death*, 382.
60. Rosen, 195.
61. Ibid., 247.
62. Ibid., 251.
63. E. Sylvia Pankhurst, 600.
64. Ibid., 593.
65. Charrier, 456.

ᗱᗷibliography

A la mémoire de Maria Deraismes le 6 février 1895, anniversaire de sa mort. Paris, [1895].

Abensour, Léon. *Le Féminisme sous le règne de Louis-Philippe et en 1848.* 2d ed. Paris, 1913.

———. *Histoire générale du féminisme: Des origines à nos jours.* Paris, 1921.

About, Edmond. *Les Mariages de Paris.* Paris, 1856.

Acland, Eleanor. *Good-bye for the Present: The Story of Two Childhoods: Milly: 1878–1888 and Ellen: 1913–1924.* New York: Macmillan, 1935.

Acollas, Emile. *Le Mariage: Son passé, son présent, son avenir.* Paris, 1880.

Acomb, Eveleyn, and Brown, Marvin, eds. *French Society and Culture Since the Old Regime.* The Eleutherian Mills Colloquium, 1964, of the Society for French Historical Studies and the Société d'histoire moderne. New York: Holt, 1966.

Acton, Lord John. *Essays on Freedom and Power.* Ed. Gertrude Himmelfarb. Boston: Beacon Press, 1948.

———. "George Eliot's 'Life.' " *Nineteenth Century* 17 (1885): 464–85.

Acton, William, Dr. *Functions and Disorders of the Reproductive Organs in Childhood, Youth, Adult Age, and Advanced Life: Considered in Their Physiological, Social, and Moral Relations.* London, 1857.

Adam, Mme Juliette Lambert LaMessine. *Idées antiproudhoniennes sur l'amour, la femme et le mariage.* Paris, 1858.

———. *Mes sentiments et nos idées avant 1870.* Paris, 1905.

———. *The Romance of My Childhood and Youth.* New York, 1902.

Adams, William Edwin. *Memoirs of a Social Atom.* 2 vols. London, 1903.

Adeline Louise, Countess of Cardigan and Lancaster. *My Recollections.* New York, 1909.

Adelmann, Helene. *Aus meiner Kinderzeit.* Berlin, 1892.

Adhémar, Marie Blanche Angeline Verdet, Vicomtesse d'. *La Femme catholique et la démocratie française.* Paris, 1900.

———. *Nouvelle éducation de la femme dans les classes cultivées.* 1896. 2d ed. Paris, 1897.

Agoult, Comtesse Marie Catherine Sophie d' [Daniel Stern]. *Essai sur la liberté considérée comme principe et fin de l'activité humaine.* 1847. New ed. Paris, 1963.

———. *Mémoires: 1833–1854.* 8th ed. Paris, 1927.

———. *Mes souvenirs: 1806–1833.* Paris, 1877.

Aicard, Jean. *L'âme d'un enfant.* 1897. New ed. Paris, 1912.

Albistur, Maité, and Armogathe, Daniel. *Histoire du féminisme français.* 2 vols. Paris, 1977.

Allart de Méritens, Hortense. *Les Enchantements de Prudence...*avec Préface de George Sand. 1872. New ed. Paris, 1877.

595

————. *La Femme et la démocratie de nos temps*. Paris, 1836.

Allem, Maurice [pseud.]. *La Vie quotidienne sous le Second Empire*. Paris: Hachette, 1948.

Allen, Grant. *The Woman Who Did*. Boston and London, 1895.

Alletz, Edouard. *De la démocratie nouvelle: ou, Des moeurs et de la puissance des classes moyennes en France*. Vol. 1. 2d ed. Paris, 1838.

Amalie, Princess of Saxony. *Social Life in Germany: Illustrated in the Acted Dramas of Her Royal Highness the Princess Amelia of Saxony*. Trans. Mrs. Jameson. 2 vols. London, 1840.

Amberley, John Russell, and Amberley, Katherine Louisa. *The Amberley Papers: The Letters and Diaries of Lord and Lady Amberley*. Ed. Bertrand and Patricia Russell. 2 vols. London: Hogarth, 1937.

Amicis, Edmondo de. *Ai ragazzi: Discorsi*. Milan, 1895.

————. *Cuore, an Italian Schoolboy's Journal: A Book for Boys*. Trans. from 39th Italian ed. by Isabel F. Hapgood. New York, 1887.

Ancelot, Mme Marguerite Louise Virginie Chardon. *Marie: ou, Les Trois Epoques*. Paris, 1836.

Anderson, Robert. "Secondary Education in Mid-Nineteenth Century France: Some Social Aspects." *Past & Present*, no. 53 (Nov. 1971): 121–46.

Andreas-Salomé, Lou. "Der Mensch als Weib." *Neue Deutsche Rundschau* 10 (1899): 225–43.

Annan, Noel Gilroy. *Leslie Stephen: His Thought and Character in Relation to his Time*. Cambridge: Harvard University Press, 1952.

Appleman, P.: Madden, W. A.; and Wolfe, M., eds. *1859: Entering an Age of Crisis*. Bloomington: Indiana University Press, 1959.

Arendt, Hannah. *Rahel Varnhagen: The Life of a Jewess*. Trans. Richard and Clara Winston. London: Leo Baeck, 1958.

Ariès, Philippe. *Centuries of Childhood: A Social History of Family Life*. Trans. Robert Baldick. New York: Knopf, 1962.

————. *Histoire des populations françaises et de leurs attitudes devant la vie depuis le XVIIIᵉ siècle*. Paris: Self, 1948.

————. "Sur les origines de la contraception en France." *Population* (Paris) 8 (1953): 465–72.

Armitage, Doris Mary, ed. *The Taylors of Ongar: Portrait of an English Family*. Cambridge: Heffer, 1939.

Armytage, W. H. G. *Heavens Below: Utopian Experiment in England, 1560–1960*. Toronto: University of Toronto Press, 1961.

Arnim, Freiherr Ludwig Achim von. *Deutscher Geist: Ein Lesebuch*. Vol. 1. Suhr Kamp, 1953.

Arnim, Maxe von [later Gräfin von Oriola]. *Maxe von Arnim, Tochter Bettinas, Gräfin von Oriola, 1884–1894: Ein Lebens- und Zeitbild aus alten Quellen geschöpft*. Ed. Johannes Werner. Leipzig: Koehler & Amelang, 1937.

Arnold, Matthew. *A French Eton: or, Middle-Class Education and the State, and Schools and Universities in France, 1864, 1868*. London, 1892.

————. "Maurice de Guérin" and "Eugénie de Guérin." In *Essays in Criticism*. 2d ed. London, 1869.

————. *Schools and Universities on the Continent*. London, 1868.

Arnold, Thomas. *Sermons*. 3 vols. 3d ed. London, 1844.

Arnstein, Walter, ed. and trans. "A German View of English Society: 1851." *Victorian Studies* 16 (1972): 183–203.

Arrivabene, Count Carlo. *Italy under Victor Emmanuel: A Personal Narrative*. 2 vols. London, 1862.

Arthur, Arnold. "The Political Enfranchisement of Women." *Fortnightly Review*, n. s. 11 (1872): 204–14.

Arthur, Timothy Shaw, ed. *The Wedding Guest: A Friend of the Bride and Bridegroom.* Philadelphia, 1856.

Askwith, Betty. *Lady Dilke: A Biography.* London: Chatto, 1969.

Asquith, Margot, ed. *Myself When Young: By Famous Women of To-Day.* London: Frederich Muller, 1938.

Assing, Ludmilla. "La posizione sociale della donna." *Giornale d'Igiene e Medicina Preventiva*, Aug. 16, 1866, pp. 247–356.

Aston, Louise. *Aus dem Leben einer Frau.* Hamburg, 1847.

――――. *Meine Emancipation, Verweisung und Rechtfertigung.* Brussels, 1846.

Auden, W. H. "One of the Family." Essay on *Max*, biography of Max Beerbohm, Lord David Cecil. *New Yorker*, Oct. 23, 1965. pp. 227–44.

Auerbach, Berthold. *Die Frau Professorin, 1846.* Gesammelte Schriften, vol. 3. Stuttgart, 1857.

――――. *Der gebildete Bürger: Buch für der denkenden Mittelstand.* Carlsruhe, 1843.

Ausubel, Herman. *The Late Victorians: A Short History.* New York: Van Nostrand, 1955.

Azeglio, Marchesa Costanza Alfieri d'. *Souvenirs historiques de la Marquise . . . née Alfieri, tirés de sa correspondance avec son fils Emmanuel . . . de 1835 à 1861.* Turin, 1884.

Azeglio, Marchese Massimo Tapparelli d'. *Lettere a sua moglie Luisa Blondel.* 2d ed. Milan, 1870.

――――. *Things I Remember.* 1862. Trans. E. R. Vincent. London: Oxford University Press. 1966.

Baines, Edward, Jr. *The Social, Educational and Religious State of the Manufacturing Districts . . . In Two Letters to the Right Hon. Sir Robt. Peel, Bart.* London, 1843.

Bainton, Roland. *Women of the Reformation in Germany and Italy.* Minneapolis: Ausburg, 1971.

Bakan, David. *Slaughter of the Innocents.* San Francisco: Jossey-Bass, 1971.

Balde, Jean. "Napoléon et l'éducation des filles." *Review Hebdomadaire*, (1921): 333–51.

Balfour, Michael. *The Kaiser and His Times.* Boston: Houghton Mifflin, 1964.

Balzac, Honoré de. *Béatrix. 1839.* Trans. Katharine Prescott Wormeley. Boston, 1895.

――――. *The Physiology of Marriage.* 1829. London: privately printed, 1914.

Banks, Joseph Ambrose. *Prosperity and Parenthood: A Study of Family Planning Among the Victorian Middle Classes.* London: Routledge, 1954.

Banks, Joseph Ambrose, and Banks, Olive. *Feminism and Family Planning in Victorian England.* Liverpool: Liverpool University Press, 1964.

Barbiera, Raffaello, *Il salotto della Contessa Maffei e la società milanese (1834–1886).* Milan, 1895.

Barine, Arvède. "La Femme d'un grand homme: Madame Carlyle." *Revue des Deux Mondes* (1884): 767–96.

Baring, Maurice. *The Puppet Show of Memory.* London, 1922.

Baring-Gould, Sabine. M. A., Rev. *Germany: Present and Past.* 2 vols. London, 1879.

Barrie, James M. *Margaret Ogilvy.* New York, 1896.

Basch, Françoise. *Relative Creatures: Victorian Women in Society and the Novel.* New York: Schocken, 1974.

Bashkirtseff, Marie. *Journal of Marie Bashkirtseff.* Trans. A. D. Hall, Chicago, 1890.

Bastide, Stuart. *La Question des tours.* Rodet, 1878.

Battiscombe, Georgina. *Mrs. Gladstone: The Portrait of a Marriage.* London: Constable, 1956.

Bax, Ernest Belfort. *The Fraud of Feminism.* London, 1913.

———. *Outspoken Essays on Social Subjects.* London, 1897.

———. *Reminiscences and Reflections of a Mid and Late Victorian.* London, 1918.

Bayle-Mouillard, Elisabeth [Mme Elisabeth Celnart]. *Manuel complet de la maîtresse de maison et de la parfaite ménagère.* 3d ed. Paris, 1834.

———. *Manuel des dames: ou, L'Art de l'élégance.* 2d ed. Paris, 1833.

———. *Manuel des nourrices.* Paris, 1834.

Bazin, René. *The Italians of To-Day.* 1897. Trans. William Marchant. New York: Holt, 1908.

Beaumont, Joseph. *Memoirs of Mrs. Mary Tatham, Late of Nottingham.* London, 1838.

Bebel, August. *Die Frau und der Sozialismus (Die Frau in der Vergangenheit, Gegenwart und Zukunft).* 10th ed. Stuttgart, 1891.

———. *My Life.* London, 1912.

Becker, Howard. *German Youth: Bond or Free.* International Library of Sociology and Social Reconstruction, ed. Karl Mannheim. London: K. Paul, Trench, Trubner, 1946.

Beeton, Isabella, ed. *The Book of Household Management.* 1861. Facsimile rpt. London: Cape, 1968.

Belgiojoso, Cristina. "Della presente condizione delle donne e del loro avvenire." *Nuovo Antologia di Scienze, Lettere ed Arti* (Jan. 1866): 96–113.

Bell, Daniel. "Charles Fourier: Prophet of Eupsychia." *American Scholar* 38 (1969): 41–58.

Bell, Enid Moberly. *Josephine Butler: Flame of Fire.* London: Constable, 1963.

——— *Octavia Hill: A Biography.* London: Constable, 1942.

———. *Storming the Citadel: The Rise of the Woman Doctor.* London: Constable, 1953.

Benda, Julien. *La Jeunesse d'un clerc.* Paris: Gallimard, 1936.

———. *La Trahison des clercs.* 1927. Paris: Club Français du livre, 1958.

Benedek, Therese. "Parenthood as a Developmental Phase." *Journal of the American Psychoanalytic Association* 7 (1959): 389–417.

Benet, Mary Kathleen. *Writers in Love.* New York: Macmillan, 1977.

Benjamin, Walter. "Paris, Capital of the 19th Century." 1927. Trans. Suzanne Ruta. *Dissent* (1970): 439–47.

Bennett, Arnold. *Whom God Hath Joined.* London, 1906.

Bennett, Daphne. *Vicky: Princess Royal of England and German Empress.* New York: St. Martin's, 1971.

Benson, Arthur Christopher. *Alfred Tennyson.* 1904. 2d ed. New York, 1907.

Benson, Edward Frederic. *Our Family Affairs: 1867–1896.* New York, 1921.

Bentham, Jeremy. *Theory of Legislation.* Boston, 1840.

Bentley, Phyllis. *The Brontës.* London: Home & Van Thal, 1947.

Berger, Peter L. "The Liberal as the Fall Guy." *Center Magazine* 5, no. 4 (July–Aug. 1972): 38–47.

———. "'Sincerity' and 'Authenticity' in Modern Society." *Public Interest*, no. 31 (Spring 1973), pp. 81–90.

Berners, Lord Gerald. *First Childhood.* London: Constable, 1934.

Berolzheimer, Fritz. *Moral und Gesellschaft des 20 Jahrhunderts*. Munich: Reinhardt, 1914.

Berry, Mary. *Extracts of the Journals and Correspondences of Miss Berry from the Year 1783 to 1852*. Ed. Lady Theresa Lewis. 3 vols. London, 1865.

———. *Social Life in England and France, from the French Revolution in 1789, to that of July, 1830*. London, 1831.

Berti, Domenico. "Le donne italiene del Risorgimento." In *Scritti varii*, vol. 2. Turin, 1892.

———. "Per la scuola normale femminile di Torino." In *Scritti varii*, vol. 2. Turin, 1892.

Besant, Annie Wood. *Autobiographical Sketches*. London, 1885.

———. *The Law of Population: Its Consequences, and Its Bearing upon Human Conduct and Morals*. London, [1870].

———. *Marriage: As It Was, as It Is, and as It Should Be: With a Sketch of the Life of Mrs. Besant*. [Chicago, ca. 1878].

[Besant, Walter]. *The Revolt of Man*. Edinburgh, 1882.

Best, Geoffrey. *Mid-Victorian Britain: 1851–1875*. New York: Schocken Books, 1972.

Betham-Edwards, Matilda. *Home Life in France*. 1905. 6th ed. London, 1913.

Biedermann, Karl. *Deutsche Volks- und Kulturgeschichte für Schule und Haus*. Wiesbaden, 1885.

Billroth, Theodor. *Briefe*. Ed. Georg Fischer. 1895. 5th ed. Hanover and Leipzig, 1899.

Billy, André. *Hortense et ses amants Chateaubriand, Sainte-Beuve, etc*. Paris: Flammarion, 1961.

Binkley, Robert C. *Realism and Nationalism: 1852–1871*. The Rise of Modern Europe, ed. W. L. Langer. New York and London: Harper, 1935.

Bischoff, Charitas. *The Hard Road: The Life Story of Amalie Dietrich, Naturalist, 1821–1891*. Trans. A. Liddell Geddie. London: Martin Hopkinson, 1931.

Bitzius, Albert. [Jérémias Gotthelf]. *Les Joies et les souffrances d' un maître d'école*. Ed. and trans. Max Buchon. 2 vols. Neuchatel, 1859.

Blackwell, Elizabeth, M. D. *The Laws of Life: With Special Reference to the Physical Education of Girls*. New York, 1852.

Blake, Mrs. Warrenne [Alice Elizabeth Blake], ed. *Memoirs of a Vanished Generation: 1813–1855*. London and New York. 1909.

Blanc. Edmond, and Delhoume, Léon. *La Vie émouvante et noble de Gay-Lussac*. Paris: Gauthier-Villars, 1950.

Blanc, Eléonore. *Biographie de Flora Tristan*. Lyon, 1845.

Blanc, Thérèse [Th. Bentzon]. *Causeries de morale pratique*. With Mlle A. Chevalier. Paris, 1899.

———. *Emancipée*. Paris, 1887.

———. *A la sirène*. Paris, 1887.

———. "La Vie de famille en Amérique." In *Choses et gens d'Amérique*. Paris, 1898.

Blanch, Lesley. *The Wilder Shores of Love*. New York: Simon and Shuster, 1954.

Blease, Walter Lyon. *The Emancipation of English Women*. 1910. Rev. ed. London: Nutt, 1913.

Bloch, Iwan. *Sexual Life in England: Past and Present*. 1908. Trans. M. Eden Paul. London: Heinemann, 1938.

Blood, Robert O. "The Measurement and Basis of Family Power: A Rejoinder." *Marriage and Family Living* 25 (1963): 475–77.

Blood, Robert O., Jr., and Wolfe, Donald M. *Husbands and Wives: The Dynamics of Married Living.* New York: Free Press of Glencoe, 1960.

Blos, Anna. *Frauen der deutschen Revolution, 1848: Zehn Lebensbilder und ein Vorwort.* Dresden: Kaden, 1928.

Blouët, Paul [Max O'Rell]. *John Bull and His Island.* Authorized trans. by . New York: 1884.

———. *John Bull's Womankind.* London: 1884.

Blum, Léon. *Marriage.* Trans. W. B. Wells. Philadelphia: Lippincott, 1937.

Böhme, Margarete, ed. *Tagebuch einer Verlorenen: Von einer Toten.* 37th thousand. Berlin, 1905.

Bois, Jules. *Le Couple futur.* Paris: Librairie des Annales, 1912.

Boltanski, Luc. *Prime education et morale de classe.* Paris: Mouton, 1969.

Bonnerive, Georges de [Georges de Lys]. *Officier et soldat.* Paris, 1897.

Booth-Tucker, Frederick de Lautour. *The Life of Catherine Booth, the Mother of the Salvation Army.* 2 vols. New York, 1892.

Born, Stephan. *Erinnerungen eines Achtundvierzigers.* Leipzig, 1898.

Bosanquet, Mrs. Helen Dendy. *The Strength of the People.* New York and London, 1902.

[Bothmer, Gräfin Marie von]. "Female Education in Germany." *Cornhill Magazine* 15 (1867): 354–65.

———. *German Home Life.* 3d ed. London, 1877. Reprinted from *Frazer's Magazine.*

Boucherett, Jessie. "The Condition of Women in France." *Contemporary Review* 5 (1867): 98–113.

Boulay de la Meurthe, Alfred. *Rapport sur la troisième édition du "Manuel des écoles élémentaires" d'enseignement mutuel, par M. Sarazin; et sur le "Manuel pour les écoles primaires communales de jeunes filles," par Mlle Sauvan; fait au conseil de la Société pour l'instruction élémentaire.* Paris, 1840.

Boulding, Kenneth. *The Meaning of the Twentieth Century.* New York: Harper, 1964.

Bourget, Paul, ed. *Physiologie de l'amour moderne: Fragments posthumes d'un ouvrage de Claude Larcher.* Paris, 1891.

———. *Voyageuses.* Paris, 1897.

Bousset, Alice. *Zwei Vorkämpferin für Frauenbildung: Luise Büchner, Marie Calm.* Hamburg, 1893.

Boutmy, Emile. *The English People: A Study of Their Political Psychology.* Trans. E. English. New York and London, 1904.

Bowle, John. *Politics and Opinion in the Nineteenth Century.* New York: Oxford University Press, 1954.

Bradley, Edward [Cuthbert Bede]. *The Adventures of Mr. Verdant Green.* 3 vols. (*An Oxford Freshman; An Oxford Undergraduate Married and Done For*). London, 1857.

Brailsford, Henry Noel. *Shelley, Godwin and Their Circle.* New York, 1913.

Bramsted, Ernest K. *Aristocracy and the Middle-Classes in Germany: Social Types in German Literature, 1830–1900.* 1937. Rev. ed. Chicago: University of Chicago Press, 1964.

Branca, Patricia. *Silent Sisterhood: Middle Class Women in the Victorian Home.* Pittsburgh: Carnegie-Mellon University Press, 1975.

Braun, Lily von Giżycki. *Die Emanzipation der Kinder: Einer Rede an die Schuljugend.* Munich, 1911.

———. *Die Frauenfrage: Ihre geschichtliche Entwicklung und wirtschaftliche Seite.* Leipzig, 1901.

———. *Memoiren einer Sozialistin.* 2 vols. Munich, 1909.

Bremner, Christina Sinclair. *Education of Girls and Women in Great Britain.* London, 1897.

Brialmont, Général Alexis Henri. *De l'accroissement de la population et de ses effects dans l'avenir: Discours prononcé dans la séance publique de la classe des sciences de l'Academie Royale de Belgique, le 16 decembre 1896.* Paris, 1903.

Brieux, Eugène. *La Femme seule: Comédie en trois actes.* Paris, 1913.

———. *Les Remplaçantes.* Paris, 1902.

Briggs, Asa. *Victorian People: A Reassessment of Persons and Themes, 1851–67.* Chicago: University of Chicago Press, 1955.

Bright, Mary Chavelita Dunne [George Egerton]. *Keynotes.* Boston and London, 1893.

Bristed, Charles Astor. *Five Years at an English University.* 1852. 3d rev. ed. New York, 1874.

Brochard, André. *The Young Mother's Guide on the Care and Education of the Infant.* Authorized trans., with notes, by "an English Physician." London, 1874.

Brodie, Fawn M. *The Devil Drives: A Life of Sir Richard Burton.* New York: Norton, 1967.

Brontë, Charlotte. *The Professor.* 1857. Boston, 1891.

———. *Shirley.* 1849. Boston, 1891.

———. *Villette.* 1853. Boston, 1891.

Brooke, Michael Z. *Le Play, Engineer and Social Scientist: The Life and Work of Frédéric Le Play.*, London: Longmans, 1970.

Brown, James Baldwin. *Young Men and Maidens.* London, 1871.

Brownell, William Crary. *French Traits: An Essay in Comparative Criticism.* 1888. Rpt. ed. New York, 1902.

Browning, Elizabeth Barrett. "Aurora Leigh." 1857. In *The Poetical Works of Elizabeth Barrett Browning.* New York, 1897.

Browning, Robert. *The Ring and the Book.* New York, 1898.

Bruni, Oreste. *La nostra redenzione morale: Libro offerto al popolo italiano.* Castello, 1886.

Brunschwig, Henry. *La Crise de l'état prussien à la fin du XVIIIe siècle et la genècle et la genèse de la mentalité romantique.* Paris: Presses Universitaires de France, 1947.

Buchan, William, M. D. *Domestic Medicine: or, A Treatise on the Prevention and Cure of Diseases, by Regimen and Simple Medicines.* 1769. 22d rev. and enl. ed. Exeter, England, 1838.

Büchner, Luise. *Aus dem Leben: Erzählungen aus Heimath und Fremde.* Leipzig, 1861.

———. *Die Frauen und ihr Beruf: Ein Buch der weiblichen Erziehung.* Frankfurt am Main, 1856.

Buckle, Henry Thomas. "The Influence of Women on the Progress of Knowledge." In *The Miscellaneous and Posthumous Works of Henry Thomas Buckle,* vol. 1, ed. Grant Allen. London, 1885.

Buisson, Eugène. *L'Homme, la famille et la société considérés dans leurs rapports avec le progrès moral de l'humanité.* 3 vols. Paris, 1857.

Bulling, Carl. *Die deutsche Frau und das bürgerliche Gesetzbuch.* Berlin, 1896.
Bullough, Vern. *The History of Prostitution.* New Hyde Park, N. Y.: University Books, 1964.
Bülow von Dennewitz, Gräfin Gertrud. *Die deutschen Frauen und der Bismarckkultus von Gräfin Gisela von Streitberg.* Leipzig, 1894.
Bulwer, William Henry Lytton Earle, Baron Dalling and Bulwer [Bulwer, Henry Lytton]. *France: Social, Literary, Political.* 2 vols. New York, 1834.
Bunsen, Marie von. *The World I Used to Know: 1860–1912.* Ed. and trans. Oakley Williams. London: Butterworth, 1930.
Bureau, Paul. *Towards Moral Bankruptcy.* Trans. Mary Scharlieb. London: Constable, 1925.
Burn, William Lawrence. *The Age of Equipoise: Study of the Mid-Victorian Generation.* London: Allen and Unwin, 1964.
Burnand, Robert. *La Vie quotidienne en France de 1870 à 1900.* Paris: Hachette, 1947.
————. *La Vie quotidienne en France en 1830.* Paris: Hatchette, 1943.
Burnett, John. *Plenty and Want: A Social History of Diet in England from 1815 to the Present Day.* London: Nelson, 1966.
Burton, Elizabeth. *The Pageant of Early Victorian England: 1837–1861.* New York: Scribner, 1972.
Burton, Hester. *Barbara Bodichon: 1827–1891.* London: J. Murray, 1949.
Butler, Arthur Stanley George. *Portrait of Josephine Butler.* London: Faber and Faber, 1954.
Butler, Eliza Marian. *The Saint-Simonian Religion in Germany: A Study of the Young German Movement.* Cambridge: The University Press, 1926.
————. *The Tempestuous Prince: Hermann Pückler-Muskau.* London: Longmans, 1929.
Butler, Josephine E. *Memoir of John Grey of Dilston.* 1867. Rev. ed. London, 1874.
————. *Personal Reminiscences of a Great Crusade.* 1896. 2d ed. London, 1898.
————, ed. *Woman's Work and Woman's Culture: Series of Essays.* London, 1869.
Butler, Marilyn. *Maria Edgeworth: A Literary Biography.* Oxford: Clarendon Press, 1972.
Butler, Samuel. *Alps and Sanctuaries of Piedmont and the Canton Ticino.* London, 1881.
————. *The Life and Letters of Dr. Samuel Butler, Head-master of Shrewsbury School 1798–1836, and Afterwards Bishop of Lichfield in so far as They Illustrate the Scholastic, Religious, and Social Life of England, 1790–1840.* 2 vols. London, 1896.
————. *The Way of All Flesh.* 1903. New York: Modern Library, 1950.
Byrnes, Robert F. *Antisemitism in Modern France.* Vol. 1: *Prologue to the Dreyfus Affair.* New Brunswick, N. J.: Rutgers University Press, 1950.
Byron, George Gordon, Lord. *Don Juan.* 1819–1824. Ed. L. A. Marchand. Boston: Houghton Mifflin, Riverside Edition, 1958.
Cabet, Etienne. *La Femme: Son malheureux sort dans la société actuelle, son bonheur dans la communauté.* 1844. 9th ed. Paris, 1848.
————. *Voyage en Icarie: Roman philosophique et social.* 2d ed. Paris, 1842.
Caird, Alice Mona. "Marriage." *Westminster Review* 130 (1888): 186–201.

————. *The Morality of Marriage, and Other Essays on the Status and Destiny of Woman.* London, 1897.

Camp, Wesley D. *Marriage and the Family in France Since the Revolution: An Essay in the History of Population.* New York: Bookman Associates, 1961.

Canonici-Fachini, Ginevra. *Prospetto biographico delle donne italiane dal secolo decimoquarto fino a' giorni nostri . . . Con una riposte a Lady Morgan.* Venice, 1824.

Caracciolo, Enrichetta. *Memoirs of Henrietta Caracciolo, of Forino, of the ex-Benedictine Nun.* 1864. Trans. 3d ed. London, 1865.

————. *Le memorie di una monaca napoletana.* Intro. Nino Sansone. Milan: Giordano, 1964.

Carew, Dorothea P. *Many Years, Many Girls: The History of a School, 1862–1942.* Dublin: Browne and Nolan, 1967.

Carlile, Richard. *Every Woman's Book: or, What is Love?* 4th ed. London, 1826.

Carlyle, Thomas. *Sartor Resartus.* 1835. Ed. Charles F. Harrold. New York: Odyssey, 1937.

Caron, M. "Les Demi-services dans l'enseignement féminin." *Revue Universitaire* (Paris) 27, pt. 1 (1918): 352–55.

Carpenter, Edward. *My Days and Dreams: Being Autobiographical Notes.* London, 1916.

Carr, Edward Hallett. *The Romantic Exiles: A Nineteenth Century Portrait Gallery.* New York: Frederick A. Stokes, 1933.

Carroll, Berenice A., ed. *Liberating Women's History: Theoretical and Critical Essays.* Urbana: University of Illinois Press, 1976.

Carter, Robert B., Dr. *On the Pathology and Treatment of Hysteria.* London, 1853.

Cate, Curtis. *George Sand: A Biography.* Boston: Houghton Mifflin, 1975.

Cater, Harold Dean, ed. "Henry Adams Reports on a German Gymnasium." *American Historical Review* 53 (1947): 59–74.

Cazamian, Louis. *L'Ame anglaise.* Paris: Boivin, 1927.

————. *Le Roman social en Angleterre: 1830–50.* Paris, 1903.

The Census of Great Britain in 1851. London, 1854.

Chambers, William. *Memoir of Robert Chambers: With Autobiographical Reminiscences of William Chambers.* 5th ed. Edinburgh and London, 1872.

Channing, William E., and Aikin, Lucy. *The Correspondence of William Ellery Channing, D.D., and Lucy Aikin, from 1826 to 1842.* Ed. Anna Letitia Aikin Le Breton. Boston, 1874.

Chantepie, Edouard. *La Figure féminine au XIXᵉ siècle.* Paris, 1861.

Chapman, Elizabeth Rachel. *Marriage Questions in Modern Fiction, and Other Essays on Kindred Subjects.* London and New York, 1897.

————. "Marriage Rejection and Marriage Reform." *Westminster Review* 130 (1888): 358–77.

————. *The New Godiva and Other Studies in Social Questions.* London, 1885.

Charrier, Edmée. *L'Evolution intellectuelle féminine.* Paris: A. Mechelinck, 1931.

Chasles, Philarète. *Etudes sur l'Allemagne au XIXᵉ siècle.* Paris, 1861.

————. *Notabilities in France and England: With an Autobiography.* New York, 1853.

Chastenet, Jacques. *La Vie quotidienne en Angleterre au début du règne de Victoria, 1837–1851.* Paris: Hachette, 1961.

Chauvin, Jeanne. *Des Professions accessibles aux femmes en droit romain et en droit français: Evolution historique de la position economique de la femme dans la société. Thèse pour le Doctorat, presentée et soutenue le samedi 2 juillet 1892 à 2 heures.* Paris, 1892.

Chavasse, Pye Henry. *Advice to a Wife on the Management of Her Own Health.* 1843. 12th ed. Philadelphia, 1877.

Chéliga, Marya. "Le Mouvement féministe en France." *Revue Politique et Parlementaire* 13 (1897): 271–84.

Chesnel de la Charbouclais, Louis Pierre François Adolphe de [Alfred de Montferrand], ed. *Biographie des femmes auteurs contemporaines françaises avec portraits.* Paris, [1836].

Chesterton, Gilbert K. *Robert Browning.* 1903. English Men of Letters. New York: Macmillan, 1908.

———. *William Cobbett.* New York: Dodd, Mead, 1926.

Chierici, Luigi. *Cenno biografico de Erminia Fuà-Fusinato estratto dalla rivista italiana e straniera: L'istruzione secondaria diretta dal Prof. Cav. Oza Giuntini.* Florence, 1876.

Chitty, Susan. *The Beast and the Monk: A Life of Charles Kingsley.* New York: Mason/Charter, 1975.

Christ, Lena. *Erinnerungen einer Überflüssigen.* 1911. Rpt. ed. Munich: Süddeütscher Verlag, 1970.

Christie, Octavius F. *The Transition from Aristocracy, 1832–1867: An Account of the Passing of the Reform Bill, the Causes Which Led Up to It, and Its Far-Reaching Consequences on the Life and Manners of All Grades of Society.* New York and London: Putnam, 1928.

Clark, Frances I. *The Position of Women in Contemporary France.* London: P. S. King, 1937.

Cloete, Stuart. *A Victorian Son: An Autobiography, 1897–1922.* London: Collins, 1972.

Clough, Arthur Hugh. *Poems.* Ed. H. F. Lowry, A. L. P. Norrington, and F. L. Mulhauser. Oxford: Clarendon Press, 1951.

Clough, Blanche Athena. *A Memoir of Anne Jemima Clough.* London, 1897.

Cobbe, Frances Power. *Essays on the Pursuits of Women.* London, 1863.

———. *Italics: Brief Notes on Politics, People, and Places in Italy in 1864.* London, 1864.

———. *Life of Frances Power Cobbe by Herself.* 2 vols. Boston, 1895.

Cobbett, William. *Advice to Young Men and (Incidentally) to Young Women in the Middle and Higher Ranks of Life: In a Series of Letters Addressed to a Youth, a Bachelor, a Lover, a Husband, a Father, a Citizen or a Subject.* 1829. Rpt. ed. London, 1926.

Cöhn, Clara [Clara Viebig]. *Das tägliche Brot.* 2 vols. Berlin, 1904.

Colby, Vineta. *Yesterday's Woman: Domestic Realism in the English Novel.* Princeton: Princeton University Press, 1974.

Cole, Margaret, *Beatrice Webb.* New York: Harcourt, 1946.

Coleridge, Christabel. *Charlotte Mary Yonge: Her Life and Letters.* London, 1903.

Colette, Sidonie Gabrielle. *Claudine à l'école.* 1900. Rpt. ed. Paris: A. Michel, [1929].

———. *Earthly Paradise: An Autobiography.* Ed. Robert Phelps. Trans. Herman Briffault. New York: Farrar, 1966.

Collingwood, Stuart Dodgson. *The Life and Letters of Lewis Carroll.* New York, 1899.

Comfort, Alexander. *The Anxiety Makers: Some Curious Preoccupations of the Medical Profession.* Rpt. ed. New York: Dell, 1969.

Cominos, Peter C. "Late-Victorian Sexual Respectability and the Social System." *International Review of Social History* 8 (1963): 18–48, 216–50.

Comte, Auguste. *The Catechism of Positive Religion.* 1852. Trans. Richard Congreve. 3d rev. ed. 1891. Rpt. ed. Clifton, N.J.: A. M. Kelley, 1973.

Conscience, Hendrik. *La Fille de l'épicier.* Paris, 1860.

Constant de Rebeque, Benjamin. *Le Cahier rouge: Ma vie (1767–1787).* 1831. Oeuvres de Benjamin Constant, ed. A. Roulin. Paris: Librairie Gallimard, 1957.

Conway, Jill. "Stereotypes of Femininity in a Theory of Sexual Evolution." *Victorian Studies* 14 (1970): 47–62.

———. "Women Reformers and American Culture: 1870–1930." *Journal of Social History* 5 (1971): 164–77.

Cook, Sir Edward. *The Life of Florence Nightingale.* 2 vols. London, 1913.

Cook, Robert C. "Malthus in Retrospect: The Stork Visits Dorking—1766." *Population Bulletin* (Washington, D.C.) 22 (Feb. 1966): 1–5.

Cookson, Montague. "The Morality of Married Life." *Fortnightly Review,* n.s. 12 (1872): 397–412.

Corelli, Marie. *Boy: A Sketch.* Philadelphia, 1900.

———. *The Mighty Atom.* Philadelphia, 1896.

Corey, Lewis. "Marquis de Sade: The Cult of Despotism." *Antioch Review* 26 (Spring 1966): 17–31.

Corvin-Wiersbitzki, Otto J. B. von. *Ein Leben voller Abenteuer.* Ed. Hermann Wendel. Frankfort: Societätsdruckerei, 1924.

———. *A Life of Adventure: An Autobiography.* 3 vols. London, 1871.

Coulton, George Gordon. *A Victorian Schoolmaster: Henry Hart of Sedbergh.* London: G. Bell, 1923.

Cousin, Victor. *Report on the State of Public Instruction in Prussia, Addressed to . . . Minister of Public Instruction.* 1831. Trans. from 2d French ed. (1833) by Sarah Austin. New York, 1835.

Coveney, Peter. *The Image of Childhood: The Individual and Society, A Study of the Theme in English Literature.* Rev. ed. Harmondsworth: Penguin, 1967.

Craik, Dinah Mulock. *Fair France: Impressions of a Traveller, by the Author of "John Halifax, Gentleman."* New York, 1871.

Craik, Henry. *The State in Its Relation to Education.* London, 1884.

Cramer, Maurice Browning. "A Voice from the Hutchins College: Pluralistic Interpretation of a Poem by Robert Browning." *Journal of General Education* 30 (1978): 10–30.

Crankshaw, Edward. *The Fall of the House of Hapsburg.* New York: Viking, 1963.

Craven, Isabella. *Recollections of a Maiden Aunt.* London, 1858.

Crepax. Adele. *The Emancipation of Women and Its Probable Consequences: With a Letter to the Authoress by the Right Hon. W. E. Gladstone, M.P.* Trans. Ellen Waugh [Ellis Wright]. London, 1893.

Crosland, Margaret. *Colette: A Provincial in Paris.* New York: British Book Centre, 1954.

Crouzet-Ben-Aben, Jeanne-P. "Bulletin de l'enseignement secondaire des jeundes filles." *Revue Universitaire* (Paris), pt. 1 (1917): 134–40; pt. 2 (1919): 379–84.

Crow, Duncan. *The Victorian Woman.* London: Allen and Unwin, 1971.

Cruse, Amy. *The Victorians and Their Books.* London: Allen and Unwin, 1935.

Cunnington, Cecil Willett. *Feminine Attitudes in the Nineteenth Century.* New York: Macmillan, 1936.

Curie, Eve. *Mme Curie: A Biography.* Trans. Vincent Sheean. New York: Literary Guild of America, 1937.

Curtius, Ernst Robert. *Die französische Kultur: Eine Einführung in Frankreich.* Berlin and Stuttgart: Deutsche Verlags-Anstalt, 1930.

Dahrendorf, Ralf. *Gesellschaft und Demokratie in Deutschland.* Munich: Piper, 1965.

Dallyn, Mrs. Viola Meynell. *Alice Meynell: A Memoir.* New York: Scribner's, 1929.

Dangerfield, George. *The Strange Death of Liberal England.* 1935. Rpt. ed. New York: Capricorn Books, 1961.

———. *Victoria's Heir: The Education of a Prince.* New York: Harcourt, 1941.

Daniels, Elizabeth Adams. *Jessie White Mario: Risorgimento Revolutionary.* Athens, Ohio: Ohio University Press, 1972.

Darwin, Charles. *The Descent of Man and Selection in Relation to Sex.* Vol. 2. New York, 1871.

Darwin, Erasmus. *A Plan for the Conduct of Female Education in Boarding Schools.* London, 1797.

Daubié, Julie Victoire. *La Femme pauvre au XIXᵉ siècle.* Paris, 1866.

Daudet, Alphonse. *Fromont jeune et Risler aîné: Moeurs parisiennes.* 1874. Rpt. ed. Paris, 1880.

Daumard, Adeline. *La Bourgeoisie parisienne de 1815 à 1848.* Paris: S.E.V.-P.E.N., 1963.

Davesiès de Pontès, Lucien. *Social Reform in England.* Trans. Mme Lucien Davesiès de Pontès. London, 1866.

Davey, Richard P. Boyle. "Woman's Life in Old Italy." *National Review.* Rpt. in *Littell's Living Age,* 5th ser., 76: 451–63.

Davidoff, Lenore. *The Best Circles: Women and Society in Victorian England.* Totowa, N.J.: Rowman and Littlefield, 1973.

———. "Mastered for Life: Servant and Wife in Victorian and Edwardian England." *Journal of Social History* 7 (1974): 406–28.

Davies, Agnes Maud. *A Book with Seven Seals.* London: Cayme Press, 1928.

Davies, Emily. *The Higher Education of Women.* London and New York, 1866.

Debay, August. *Hygiène et physiologie du mariage.* 1848. Rpt. ed. Paris, 1853.

———. *Philosophie du mariage.* Paris, 1849.

Decaux, Alain. *Histoire des Françaises.* 10 vols. Paris: Rombaldi, 1973–74.

Defert, Louis. *L'Enfant et l'adolescent dans la société moderne.* Paris, [1897].

Delaisi, Francis. *Political Myths and Economic Realities.* London: Williams and Norgate, 1925.

De La Mare, Walter. *Early One Morning in the Spring: Chapters on Children and on Childhood as It Is Revealed in Particular in Early Memories and in Early Writings.* New York: Macmillan, 1935.

De Luna, Frederick A. *The French Republic under Cavaignac: 1848.* Princeton: Princeton University Press, 1969.

Delzons, Louis. *La Famille française et son évolution.* Paris: A. Colin, 1913.

Demeter, Karl. *The German Officer-Corps in Society and State: 1650–1945.* Trans. Angus Malcolm. New York: Praeger, 1965.

Demogeot, Jacques, and Montucci, Henri. *De l'enseignement secondaire en Angleterre et en Ecosse: Rapport adressé à son exc. M. le ministre de l'instruction publique.* Paris, 1868.

Demolins, Edmond. *A quoi tient la supériorité des Anglo-Saxons?* Paris, 1897.

Demos, John. "The American Family in Past Time." *American Scholar* 43 (1974): 422–46.

Déroin, Jeanne. *Almanach des femmes pour 1854.* London, 1854. Troisème année.

———. *Women's Almanack for 1853 in the English and French Languages.* London, 1853.

Desbordes-Valmore, Marceline. *Corréspondance intime.* 2 vols. Paris, 1896.

———. *Livre des mères et des enfants.* Lyon, 1840.

Desmarie, Paul. *Moeurs italiennes.* Paris, 1860.

Desofi, Nancy. "Feminism in Italy: A Prospective." *Women and Literature* (1974): 20–26.

Deville, M. H. Sainte-Claire. "L'Internal dans l'éducation." *La Revue Scientifique* 8–9, no. 10 (Sept. 2, 1871): 218–22.

Dibelius, Wilhelm. *England.* Trans. Mary Agnes Hamilton, New York: Harper, 1930.

Dickens, Charles. *Bleak House.* 1853. New York: New American Library, Signet Books, 1964.

———. *Pictures from Italy.* 1846. Ed. Paroissien. London: Deutsch, 1973.

Dictionaire de pédagogie et d'instruction primaire. Ed. Ferdinand Buisson. Paris, 1882–1893.

Didon, Abbé Henri. *Les Allemands.* Paris, 1884.

Dimnet, Ernest. *My Old World.* New York: Simon and Schuster, 1935.

Disraeli, Benjamin. *Sybil: or, The Two Nations.* 1845. Rpt. ed. London: Th. Nelson, 1957.

Dohm, Hedwig. *Der Frauen Natur und Recht: Zur Frauenfrage, Zwei Abhandlungen über Eigenschaften und Stimmrecht der Frauen.* Berlin, 1876.

Doin, Guillaume-Tell, and Charton, Edouard. *Lettres sur Paris.* Paris, 1830.

Dolléans, Edouard. "Droit au travail et à l'éducation nationale." In *1848: Le Livre de centenaire,* ed. Charles Moulin, pp. 239–56. Paris: Editions Atlas, 1948.

Donelson, Andrew Jackson. "Documents: The American Minister in Berlin, on the Revolution of March, 1848." *American Historical Review* 23 (1918): 355–73.

La donna italiana: Descritta da scrittrici italiane in una serie di conferenze tenute all' esposizione Beatrice in Firenze. Florence, 1890.

La Donna Italiana: Giornale Politico-Letterario. Rome, 1848.

Donnison, Jean. "Medical Women and Lady Midwives: A Case Study of Medical and Feminist Politics." *Women's Studies* 3 (1976): 229–50.

Dowling, Alfred. *Reports of Cases Argued and Determined in the Queen's Bench Practice Court . . . From Michaelmas Term 1839 to Michaelmas Term 1840.* London, 1841.

Drago, Antonietta. *Donne e amori del Risorgimento.* Milan: Palazzi, 1960.

Driver, Leota S. *Fanny Kemble.* Chapel Hill: University of North Carolina Press, 1933.

Droz, Gustave. *L'Enfant.* Paris, 1885.

———. *Monsieur, madame et bébé.* Paris, 1866.

Drysdale, George. *The Elements of Social Science: or Physical, Sexual and Natural Religion, An Exposition of the True Cause and Only Cure of the Three Primary Social Evils: Poverty, Prostitution, and Celibacy, By a Doctor of Medicine.* 29th ed. London, 1892.

Duff-Gordon, Lina [Mrs. Aubrey Waterfield]. *Home Life in Italy: Letters from the Apennines.* 1908. 2d ed. London, 1909.

Dumas, Alexandre, fils. *Les Femmes qui tuent et les femmes qui votent.* 1880. 21st ed. Paris, 1881.

———. *L'Homme-femme, reponse à M. Henri d'Ideville.* Paris, 1872.

Dunbar, Janet. *The Early Victorian Woman: Some Aspects of Her Life (1837–57).* London: Harrap, 1953.

Dunn, Waldo Hilary. *James Anthony Froude: A Biography.* Vol. 1: *1818–1856.* Oxford: Clarendon Press, 1961.

Dupanloup, Félix, Bishop of Orléans. *Discours de Mgr. l'Evêque d'Orléans à l'assemblée nationale sur le conseil superiéure de l'instruction publique.* Paris, 1873.

———. *Discours prononcés par Mgr. L'Evêque d'Orléans à l'assemblée nationale . . . sur la liberté de l'enseignement superieur.* Paris, 1874.

———. *Du nouveau projet de loi sur la liberté d'enseignement.* Paris, 1847.

———. *La Liberté de l'enseignement supérieur.* Paris, 1868.

———. *M. Duruy et l'éducation des filles: Lettre de Mgr. l'Evêque d'Orléans.* Paris, 1867.

———. *Seconde lettre de M. l'Evêque de'Orléans aux supérieurs et professeurs de ses petits séminaires.* Paris, 1873.

———. *Seconde lettre de Mgr. l'Evêque d'Orléans sur M. Duruy et l'éducation des filles.* Paris, 1867.

———. *Studious Women.* Trans. R. M. Phillimore. Boston, 1869.

Dupeux. Georges. *La Société française: 1789–1960.* Paris: Colin, 1964.

Dupré, Giovanni. *Thoughts on Art and Autobiographical Memoirs.* Trans. E. M. Peruzzi. Edinburgh, 1884.

Ebner von Eschenbach, Marie. *Meine Kinderjahre: Biographische Skizzen.* Berlin, 1906.

Eckermann, Johann Peter. *Conversations of Goethe with Eckermann and Soret.* Trans. John Oxenford. 1874. Rpt. ed. London, 1909.

Eden, Emily. *The Semi-Attached Couple.* 1860. New York: Stokes, [1928].

Edgeworth, Maria, and Edgeworth, Richard Lovell. *Practical Education.* 1798. 2 vols. New York, 1801.

Edinburgh Review. *Woman: Her Influence, Rights, and Wrongs, Education and Labor. A Collection of Articles Thereon Which Appeared in the Edinburgh Review from 1810–1910.* Cleveland, 1914.

Egron, Adrien C. *Le Livre de l'ouvrier: Ses devoirs envers la société, la famille, et lui-même.* Paris, 1844.

Eliot, George. *Adam Bede.* 1859. Personal Edition of George Eliot's Works. New York: Doubleday, 1901–4.

———. *Middlemarch.* 2 vols. 1873. Personal Edition of George Eliot's Works. New York, 1901–4.

Ellis, Amanda M. *Rebels and Conservatives: Dorothy and William Wordsworth and Their Circle.* Bloomington: Indiana University Press, 1967.

Ellis, Havelock. *Little Essays of Love and Virtue.* New York, 1922.

Ellis, Mrs. Sarah Stickney. *The Daughters of England: Their Position in Society, Character, and Responsibilities.* Mrs. Ellis' Works, Uniform Edition. New York, 1844.

———. *The Mothers of England: Their Influence and Responsibility.* Mrs. Ellis' Works, Uniform Edition. New York, 1844.

————. *The Wives of England: Their Relative Duties, Domestic Influence, and Social Obligations.* Mrs. Ellis' Works, Uniform Edition. New York, 1844.

————. *The Women of England: Their Social Duties and Domestic Habits.* Mrs. Ellis' Works, Uniform Edition, New York, 1844.

Emerson, Ralph Waldo. *English Traits.* 1856. Works, vol. 2. New York: Charles C. Bigelow.

Engels, Friedrich. *L'Origine de la famille, de la propriété privée, et de l'état.* Trans. A. M. Desrousseaux [Bracke]. Oeuvres Complètes. Paris: Costes, 1936.

England. Royal Commission on Divorce and Matrimonial Causes. *The Divorce Commission: The Majority and Minority Reports Summarised.* London, 1912. Pref. Hon. Lord Guthrie and Sir Lewis T. Dibdin.

Englishwoman's Domestic Magazine. Vols. 4–6 (1868–69).

Epton, Nina Consuelo. *Victoria and Her Daughters.* New York: Norton, 1971.

Esquiros, Adèle. *L'Amour.* Paris, 1860.

Eulenburg-Hertefeld, Fürst Philipp zu. *Aus 50 Jahren: Erinnerungen, Tagebücher und Briefe aus dem Nachlass des Fürsten.* 2d ed. Berlin: Pactel, 1925.

Evans, Joan. *John Ruskin.* London: Cape, 1954.

————, ed. *The Victorians.* London: Cambridge University Press, 1966.

Ewell, Marshall D. *Blackstone's Commentaries: For the Use of Students at Law and the General Reader; Obsolete and Unimportant Matter Being Eliminated.* Boston, 1882.

Ewing, Juliana Horatia. *Six to Sixteen: A Story for Girls.* Rev. ed. London, 1886.

Fairlie, Henry. "On the Humanity of Women." *Public Interest,* no. 23 (Spring 1971): 16–32.

Farjeon, Eleanor. *A Nursery in the Nineties.* London: Gollancz, 1935.

Farrar, Mrs. John [Eliza Ware Rotch]. *Recollections of Seventy Years.* Boston, 1866.

Fawcett, Millicent Garrett. *What I Remember.* London: Fisher Unwin, 1924.

Fay, Amy. *Music-Study in Germany in the Nineteenth Century. From the Home Correspondence of Amy Fay.* 1880. Rpt. ed. New York: Dillon, 1965.

Females of the Present Day, Considered as to Their Influence on Society, etc., by a Country Lady. London, 1831.

La Femme, pt. 2. *Recueils de la Société Jean Bodin pour l'histoire comparative des institutions* 12 (1962).

Fénelon, François de Salignac de la Mothe-. *Fénelon on Education. A Translation of "Traité de l'éducation des filles" and other documents.* Ed. H. C. Barnard. Cambridge: Cambridge University Press, 1966.

Feuerbach, Henriette. *Gedanken über die Liebenswürdigkeit der Frauen: Ein kleine Bietrag zur weiblichen Charactistik von einem Frauenzimmer.* Nuremberg, 1839.

————. *Henriette Feuerbach: Ihr Leben in ihren Briefen.* Ed. Hermann Uhde-Bernaÿs. Berlin, 1912.

Feuillet, Mme Octave [Valérie]. *Quelques années de ma vie.* Paris, 1894.

Fido, Martin. *Oscar Wilde.* New York: Viking, 1973.

Field, James Alfred. *Essays on Population and Other Papers.* Ed. Helen Fisher Hohman. Chicago: University of Chicago Press, 1931.

Fisher, John. *Eighteen Fifteen: An End and a Beginning.* New York: Harper, 1963.

Flaubert, Gustave. *Madame Bovary.* Paris, 1857.

Fleischhack, Marianne. *Ich suche eine Tür ins Leben: Drei Lebensbilder.* Berlin: Evangelische Verlagsanstalt, 1968.

Flex, Walter. *Der Wanderer zwischen beiden Welten: Ein Kriegserlebnis.* Munich: Beck, 1938.

Fontane, Theodor. *Irrungen Wirrungen.* Berlin, [1888].

————. *Journeys to England in Victoria's Early Days: 1844–1859.* Trans. Dorothy Harrison. London: Massie, 1939.

————. *Meine Kinderjahre.* Sämtliche Werk, vol. 14. Munich: Nymphenburger Verlagshandlung, 1961.

Forel, Auguste. *The Sexual Question: A Scientific, Psychological, Hygienic, and Sociological Study.* Adapted from 2d German ed., rev. and enl., by C. F. Marshall. Brooklyn: Physician's and Surgeon's Book Co., 1937.

Fouillée, Mme Alfred [G. Bruno]. *Les Enfants patriotes.* Boston, 1893.

Fox, Elton. *Two Homes: By a Grandson.* Plymouth, England: W. Brendon, 1925.

François-Poncet, André. *Ce que pense la jeunesse allemande.* Paris, 1913.

Frank, Johann Peter. *Seine Selbstbiographie.* Ed. Erna Lesky. Bern and Stuttgart: Huber, 1969.

Frank, Malvina. *Le fidenzate: Saggio sulla educazione della donna.* Treviso. 1869.

————. *Mogli e Mariti.* Venice, 1872.

Frankel, Charles. "Shifting Currents in French Education." *Columbia Forum,* 13, no. 2 (Summer 1970): 11–16.

Frapié, Léon. *La Maternelle.* Paris, 1908.

Fremantle, Anne. *The Three-Cornered Heart.* New York: Viking, 1970.

Freytag, Gustav. *Debit and Credit [Soll und Haben].* Trans. "L. C. C. " New York, 1858.

————. "Die Erhebung von 1813." In *Bilder aus der deutschen Vergangenheit,* vol. 5. Leipzig, n.d.

————. *Erinnerungen aus meinem Leben.* Leipzig, 1887.

Friedel, Victor Henri. *The German School as a War Nursery.* Trans. S. E. Simpson. New York, 1918.

The Friend, A Monthly Journal: A Religious, Literary and Miscellaneous Journal. London: Society of Friends (Jan.–Dec. 1873).

Fromentin, Eugène. *Dominique.* Paris, 1862.

Fromm, Erich. *The Fear of Freedom.* London: K. Paul, Trench, 1942.

Froude, James Anthony. *The Nemesis of Faith.* 1849. Rpt. ed. Chicago, 1879.

Fuchs, Eduard, and Kind, Alfred. *Die Weiberherrschaft in der Geschichte der Menschheit.* Munich, 1914.

Gagnon, Paul A. *France Since 1789.* New York: Harper, 1964.

Galbraith, John Kenneth. "The Economics of the American Housewife." *Atlantic* 232, no. 2 (Aug. 1973): 78–83.

Gallenga, Antonio [L. Mariotti]. *Italy Past and Present.* 2 vols. London, 1848.

Galletti di Cadilhac, Mme [The Hon. Margaret Collier]. *Our Home by the Adriatic.* 2d ed. London, 1886.

Gardiner, Dorothy. *English Girlhood at School: A Study of Women's Education Through Twelve Centuries.* London: Oxford University Press, 1929.

Garnett, Martha. *Samuel Butler and His Family Relations.* London: Dent, 1926.

Gaskell, Mrs. Elizabeth Cleghorn. *Cranford.* 1853. New York, 1892.

————. "French Life." *Fraser's Magazine* 69 (1864): 435–49, 575–85, 739–52.

————. *Life of Charlotte Brontë.* 1857. Condensed by T. M. C. Boston, 1891.

————. *Ruth.* 1853. New York, 1892.

————. *Wives and Daughters.* 1866. New York, 1892.

Gathorne-Hardy, Jonathan. *The Rise and Fall of the British Nanny.* London: Hodder and Stoughton, 1972.

Gattey, Charles Nielson. *A Bird of Curious Plumage: Princess Cristina di Belgio-joso, 1805–1871.* London: Constable, 1971.

Gauguin, Paul. *Lettres à George-Daniel de Monfreid.* Paris, 1918.

Gaunt, William. *The Pre-Raphaelite Tragedy.* London: Cape, 1942.

Gayraud, Amélie. *Les Jeunes Filles d'aujourd'hui.* Paris: G. Oudin, 1914.

Geddes, Patrick, and Thomson, J. Arthur. *The Evolution of Sex.* New York: Scribner, [1889].

Gennari, Geneviève. *Le Premier Voyage de Madame de Staël en Italie et la genèse de "Corinne."* Paris: Boivin, 1947.

Gérard-Gailly, Emile. *Les Véhémences de Louise Colet.* Paris: Mercure de France, 1934.

Gerbod, Paul. *La vie quotidienne dans les lycées et les collèges au XIXe siècle.* Paris: Hachette, 1968.

Gerhard, Adele, and Simon, Helene. *Mutterschaft und geistige Arbeit: Eine psychologische und soziologische Studie, auf Grundlage einer internationalen Erhebung mit Berücksichtigung der geschichtlichen Entwicklung.* 2d ed. Berlin, 1908.

Gerhard, Melitta. *Das Werk Adele Gerhards als Ausdruck einer Wendezeit, Mit einem Anhang: Adele Gerhard, Das Bild meines Lebens.* Berne: Francke, 1963.

Gerlach, Hellmuth von. *Von Rechts nach Links.* Zurich: Europa-verlag, 1937.

Gide, Paul. *Etude sur la condition privée de la femme dans le droit ancien et moderne.* Paris, 1867.

Gillis, John R. "Aristocracy and Bureaucracy in Nineteenth-Century Prussia." *Past & Present,* no. 41 (Dec. 1968): 105–29.

Gilmour, Robin. "The Gradgrind School: Political Economy in the Classroom." *Victorian Studies* 11 (1967): 207–24.

Girardin, Delphine Gay de. *Lettres parisiennes: 1840–1848.* Oeuvres Complètes de Madame Emile de Girardin née Delphine Gay, vol. 5. Paris, 1860–61.

Girardin, Emile de. *L'Égale de l'homme: Lettre à M. Alexandre Dumas fils.* 3d ed. Paris, 1881.

————. *L'Égale de son fils.* Paris, 1872.

Giraud, Léon. *Des droits de la femme mariée sous le régime de la communauté relativement à l'aliénation de l'un de ses biens faite par le mari sans son consentment.* Paris, 1887.

————. *Draigu: Le Roman de la famme chrétienne.* Paris, 1880.

————. *Essai sur la condition des femmes en Europe et en Amérique.* Paris, 1882.

————. *Etudes et pamphlets. Familia.* Grenoble, 1874.

Gisolfi, Anthony M. *The Essential Matilde Serao.* New York: Las Americas, 1968.

Gissing, George. *The Odd Women.* 1893. New ed. London, 1894.

Giusti, Giuseppe. *Vita di Giuseppe Giusti scritta da lui medesimo.* Ed. Guido Biagi. 1896. Florence, 1898.

Gleim, Betty. *Erziehung und Unterricht des weiblichen Geschlechts: Ein Buch für Eltern und Erzieher.* 2 vols. Leipzig, 1810.

Goepfert, Günter. *Das Schicksal der Lena Christ.* Munich: Süddeutscher, 1971.

Goethals, George W. "Factors Affecting Permissive and Nonpermissive Rules Regarding Premarital Sex." *Studies in the Sociology of Sex,* ed. James M. Henslin, pp. 9–26. New York: Appleton-Century, 1971.

Goldsmith, Margaret. *Seven Women Against the World.* London: Methuen, 1935.

Goncourt, Edmond de, and Goncourt, Jules de. *La Femme au dix-huitieme siècle.* Rev. ed. Paris, 1877.

―――. *Germinie Lacerteux.* 2d ed. Paris, 1865.

―――. *Pages from the Goncourt Journal.* Ed. and trans. Robert Baldick. London and New York: Oxford University Press, 1962.

Gorer, Geoffrey. *Exploring English Character.* London: Cresset, 1955.

Gornall, J. F. G. "Marriage and Property in Jane Austen's Novels." *History Today* 17 (1967): 805–11.

Gosse, Edmund. *Father and Son: Biographical Recollections.* 1907. New York, 1908.

Grabar, Terry H. " 'Scientific' Education and Richard Feveral." *Victorian Studies* 14 (1970): 129–41.

Graf, Alfred. *Schülerjahre: Erlebnisse und Urteile namhafter Zeitgenossen.* Berlin, 1912.

Granville-Barker, Harley, ed. *The Eighteen-Seventies: Essays by Fellows of the Royal Society of Literature.* New York: Macmillan, 1929.

Graves, Charles L. *Mr. Punch's History of Modern England.* 4 vols. New York: Stokes, 1922.

Greco, Oscar. *Bibliografia femminile italiano del XIXe secolo.* Venice, 1875.

Green, Martin. *The von Richthofen Sisters: The Triumphant and the Tragic Modes of Love, Else and Frieda von Richthofen, Otto Gross, Max Weber, and D. H. Lawrence in the Years 1870–1970.* New York: Basic Books, 1974.

Green, Roger Lancelyn. *Mrs. Molesworth.* Bodley Head Monographs. London: Bodley Head, 1961.

Greenacre, Phyllis. *The Quest for the Father: A Study of the Darwin-Butler Controversy as a Contribution to the Understanding of the Creative Individual.* Freud Anniversary Lecture Series of the New York Psychoanalytic Institute. New York: International Universities Press, 1963.

[Greenwell, Dora.] "Our Single Women." Reviews of *My Life, and What Shall I Do with It?* by an Old Maid; *The Afternoon of Single Life; Sisters of Charity and the Communion of Labour,* by Mrs. Jameson; *Hospitals and Sisterhoods; Thoughts on Some Questions Relating to Women,* by the *Englishwoman's Journal* Office; *Transactions* of the National Association for the Promotion of Social Sciences; *L'Ouevrière,* by Jules Simon. *North British Review* 36 (Feb. 1862): 62–87.

Greg, William R. *Literary and Social Judgments.* 1873. Rpt. ed. New York, 1876.

Grépon, Marguerite. *Pour une introduction à une histoire de l'amour.* Paris: J. Vigneau, 1946.

Gretton, Mrs. G. *The Englishwoman in Italy: Impressions of Life in the Roman States and Sardinia During a Ten Year Residence.* London, [1860].

Greville, Charles C. F. *The Great World: Portraits and Scenes from Greville's Memoirs, 1814–1860.* Ed. Louis Kronenberger. New York: Doubleday, 1963.

Grey, Maria, and Shirreff, Emily. *Thoughts on Self-Culture: Addressed to Women.* Boston, 1851.

Griewank, Karl. *Deutsche Studenten und Universitäten in der Revolution von 1848.* Weimar: Böhlaus, 1949.

Grisewood, H., ed. *Ideas and Beliefs of the Victorians: An Historic Revaluation of the Victorian Age*. London: Sylvan Press, 1949.

Gross, Harvey. "Reopening the Case of Wagner." *American Scholar* 38 (1968–69): 114–26.

Guérin, Eugénie de. *Journal*. Ed. G. S. Trebutien. 2 vols. New York, 1893.

Guerrier, Paul. *Etude sur les restrictions et déchéance de la puissance paternelle*. Université de France, Faculté de droit de Dijon. Dijon, 1895.

Guizot, Elisabeth Charlotte P. de. *Lettres de famille sur l'éducation*. 2 vols. 4th ed. Paris, 1852.

Guizot, François-Pierre-Guillaume. *L'Amour dans le mariage: Etude historique*. Paris, 1855.

Hagen, Everett E. *On the Theory of Social Change*. London: Tavistock, 1959.

Hahn, Karl-Heinz. *Bettina von Arnim in ihrem Verhältnis zu Staat und Politik*. Weimar: Böhlaus, 1959.

Hahn-Hahn, Countess Ida. *Society: or, High Life in Germany*. 1831. London, 1854.

Haines, George, IV. *Essays on German Influence upon English Education and Science: 1850–1919*. Connecticut College Monograph, no. 9. New London: Connecticut College, 1969.

———. *German Influence upon English Education and Science: 1800–1866*. Connecticut College Monograph, no. 6. New London: Connecticut College, 1957.

Hajnal, J. "The European Marriage Pattern in Perspective." In *Population in History*, ed. D. V. Glass and D. E. C. Eversley. London: Arnold, 1965.

Haldane, Charlotte Franken. *The Galley Slaves of Love: The Story of Marie d'Agoult and Franz Liszt*. London: Harvill, 1957.

Haldane, Elizabeth Sanderson. *From One Century to Another: The Reminiscences of Elizabeth S. Haldane*. London: Maclehose, 1937.

Hamerton, Philip Gilbert. *An Autobiography: 1834–1858, and A Memoir by His Wife, 1858–1894*. Boston, 1897.

———. *French and English: A Comparison*. Boston, 1889.

———. *Round My House: Notes of Rural Life in France in Peace and War*. London, 1876.

Hannay, Prudence. "Emily Eden as a Letter-Writer." *History Today* 21 (1971): 491–501.

Hanson, Lawrence, and Hanson, Elizabeth. *Marion Evans and George Eliot: A Biography*. London: Oxford University Press, 1952.

———. *Necessary Evil: The Life of Jane Welsh Carlyle*. London: Constable, 1952.

Hardwick, Elizabeth. *Seduction and Betrayal: Women and Literature*. New York: Random, 1974.

Hare, Augustus J. C. *In My Solitary Life: Being an Abridgement of the Last Three Volumes of "The Story of My Life."* 1900. Ed. Malcolm Barnes. London: Allen and Unwin, 1953.

———. *Memorials of a Quiet Life*. 1872. 2 vols. in 1. Rpt. of 9th ed. New York: Routledge, n.d.

———. *The Years with Mother: Being an Abridgement of the First Three Volumes of "The Story of My Life."* 1896. Ed. Malcolm Barnes. London: Allen and Unwin, 1952.

———, ed. *The Life and Letters of Maria Edgeworth*. 2 vols. London, 1894.

Hare, E. H. "Masturbatory Insanity: The History of an Idea." *Journal of Medical Science* (Britain) 108 (1962).

Harkort, Friedrich. *Bemerkungen über die Hindernisse der Civilisation und Emanzipation untern Klassen.* 1844. Frankfurt, 1919.

Harrington, Michael. *The Accidental Century.* New York: Macmillan, 1965.

Harris, Frank. *My Life and Loves.* 1922–27. 5 vols. Ed. John F. Gallagher. New York: Grove Press, 1963.

Harrison, Brian. "Religion and Recreation in Nineteenth-Century England." *Past & Present*, no. 38 (Dec. 1967): 98–125.

———. "Underneath the Victorians." Review of *The Other Victorians. Victorian Studies* 10 (1967): 239–62.

Hartman, Mary S. *Victorian Murderesses: A True History of Thirteen Respectable French and English Women Accused of Unspeakable Crimes.* New York: Schocken Books, 1977.

Hartman, Mary S. and Banner, Lois, eds. *Clio's Consciousness Raised: New Perspectives on the History of Women.* New York: Harper, 1974.

Hartmann, Eduard von. "Die Jungfernfrage." In *Tagesfragen*, pp. 99–132. Leipzig, 1896.

Harwood, George. *The Coming Democracy.* London, 1882.

Haweis, Mary Eliza. *The Art of Housekeeping: A Bridal Garland.* London, 1889.

Hawthorne, Nathaniel, *Passages from the French and Italian Note-Books.* 1871. Hawthorne's Works, vols. 19 and 20. Boston, 1876.

Hawtrey, Stephen. *A Narrative-Essay on a Liberal Education, Chiefly Embodied in the Account of an Attempt to Give a Liberal Education to Children of the Working Class.* London, 1868.

———. *Reminiscences of a French Eton.* London, 1867.

Hayek, Frederick August. *John Stuart Mill and Harriet Taylor: Their Correspondence and Subsequent Marriage.* Chicago: University of Chicago Press, 1951.

Hayes, Carlton J. H. *A Generation of Materialism: 1871–1900.* New York: Harper, 1941.

Hédouville, Marthe de. *La Comtesse de Ségur et les siens.* Paris: Editions du Conquistador, 1953.

Hegar, Alfred. *Der Geschlechtstrieb: Eine social-medicische Studie.* Stuttgart, 1894.

Heilbrun, Carolyn G. "Victoria and Elizabeth: The Feminine Mistake." *Columbia Forum*, n.s. 1 (Winter 1971): 12–17.

Heine, Heinrich. *Germany.* Works, vol. 5. Trans. Charles Godfrey Leland. London, 1892.

———. *Memoirs.* Works, 2 vols. Ed. Gustav Karpeles. Trans. Gilbert Cannan. New York, 1910.

———. *Pictures of Travel.* Trans. Charles Godfrey Leland. 9th rev. ed. Philadelphia, 1882.

Heller, Erich. "The Importance of Nietzsche: On the Modern German Mind." *Encounter* 22, no. 4 (Apr. 1964): 59–66.

Hellmann, Roderich. *Über Geschlechtsfreiheit: Ein philosophischer Versuch zur Erhöhung des menschlichen Glückes.* Berlin, 1878.

Helm, Clementine [later Beyrich]. *Backfischchens Leiden und Freuden: Eine Erzählung für junge Mädchen.* 18th ed. Leipzig, 1881.

Helmrich, Volkmar. *Mutter und Kind: Leichtverständliche Anweisung . . . eine Hülfsbuch für Mutter.* Weimar, 1891.

Henderson, Mrs. *The Young Wife's Own Book: Her Domestic Duties and Social Habits.* Glasgow, 1857.

Henley, Lady Dorothy. *Rosalind Howard: Countess of Carlisle, by Her Daughter.* London: Hogarth, 1959.

Herbertson, Dorothy. *The Life of Frederic Le Play.* Ed. Victor Branford and Alexander Farquharson. Ledburg, England: Le Play House Press, 1950.

Héricourt, Jenny P. d'. *A Woman's Philosophy of Woman: or, Woman Affranchised: An Answer to Michelet, Proudhon, Girardin, Comte, and Other Modern Innovators.* 1860. Trans. from the last Paris ed. New York, 1864.

Herold, J. Christopher. *Mistress to an Age: A Life of Madame de Staël.* 1958. New York: Time, 1964.

Hervieu, Paul. *La Course de flambeau.* Paris: A. Lemerre, 1901.

Hettler, Hermann. *Karoline von Humboldt: Das Lebensbild einer deutschen Frau aus ihren Briefen gestaltet.* Leipzig: Koehler and Amelang, 1933.

Heyl, Hedwig. *Aus meinem Leben.* Berlin, 1925.

Hicks, Phyllis D. *A Quest of Ladies: The Story of a Warwickshire School.* Birmingham, England: Frank Juckes, 1950.

Hillebrand, Karl. *Aus und über England.* Zeiten, Völker und Menschen, vol. 3. Berlin, 1876.

———. "Caroline Schlegel." *Fortnightly Review,* n.s. 11 (1872): 408–27, 549–76.

———. *France and the French in the Second Half of the Nineteenth Century.* Trans. from 3d German ed. London, 1881.

Hillern, Wilhelmine von. *Only a Girl: or, A Physician for the Soul, A Romance.* Trans. Mrs. A. L. Wister, Philadelphia. 1870.

Himes, Norman. *Medical History of Contraception.* 1934. Rev. ed. New York: Gamut, 1963.

Himmelfarb, Gertrude. *Victorian Minds.* New York: Knopf, 1968.

Hippel, Theodor von. *Über die bürgerliche Verbesserung der Weiber.* 1772. Sämmtliche Werke, vol. 6. Berlin, 1828.

———. *Über die Ehe.* 1774. Sämmtliche Werke, vol. 5. Berlin, 1828.

Hirsch, Anton. *Die Frau in der bildenden Kunst: Ein kunstgeschichtliches Hausbuch.* Stuttgart, 1905.

Hobsbawm, E. J. *The Age of Revolution: 1789–1848.* Cleveland: World, 1962.

Hodge, Jane Aiken. *Only a Novel: The Double Life of Jane Austen.* New York: Fawcett, 1972.

Hofstadter, Beatrice. "Popular Culture and the Romantic Heroine." *American Scholar* 30 (1961): 98–116.

Holcombe, Lee. *Victorian Ladies at Work: Middle-Class Working Women in England and Wales, 1850–1914.* Hamden, Conn.: Archon Books, 1973.

Holt, Lee Elbert. *Samuel Butler.* New York: Twayne, 1964.

Holton, Gerald. "On Trying to Understand Scientific Genius." *American Scholar* 41 (1972): 95–110.

Hood, Thomas. *Up the Rhine.* London, 1840.

Hopkins, Annette Brown. *Elizabeth Gaskell: Her Life and Work.* London: Lehmann, 1952.

Horkheimer, Max. "Authority and the Family." 1932. In *Critical Theory: Selected Essays,* trans. Matthew J. O'Connell, pp. 97–128. New York: Herder and Herder, 1972.

Horn, Klaus. *Dressur oder Erziehung: Schlagrituale und ihre gesellschaftliche Funktion.* Frankfurt am Main: Suhrkamp, 1967.

Houghton, Walter E. *The Victorian Frame of Mind: 1830–1870.* New Haven: Yale University Press for Wellesley College, 1957.

Housden, Leslie George. *The Prevention of Cruelty to Children.* New York: Philosophical Library, 1956.

How to Woo; How to Win; and How to Get Married: Being the True Philosophy of Love, Courtship, and Marriage. Glasgow, 1856.

How to Woo: or, The Etiquette of Courtship and Marriage. London, [1879].

How to Woo, When and to Whom. London, 1855.

Howard, Cecil. *Mary Kingsley.* London: Hutchinson, 1957.

Howe, Bea. *Arbiter of Elegance.* London: Harvill, 1967.

Howe, Irving. "Living with Kampf and Schlaff: Literary Tradition and Mass Education." *American Scholar* 43 (1974): 107–12.

Howe, Marie Jenney. *George Sand: The Search for Love.* New York: John Day, 1927.

Howitt, Anna Mary [later Watts]. *An Art-Student in Munich.* Boston, 1854.

Howitt, Mary. *Mary Howitt: An Autobiography Edited by Her Daughter, Margaret Howitt.* 2 vols. Boston and New York, 1889.

Howitt, William. *German Experiences: Addressed to the English, Both Stayers at Home, and Goers Abroad.* 3d ed. London, 1844.

———. *The Rural and Domestic Life of Germany: With Characteristic Sketches of the Cities and Scenery, Collected in a General Tour, and During a Residence in the Country in the Years 1840, 41 and 42.* Philadelphia, 1843.

———. *The Student-Life of Germany By William Howitt: From the Unpublished Ms. of Dr. Cornelius.* Philadelphia, 1842.

Huart, Adrien. *Le Nouvelle vie militaire.* Paris, [1877].

Huber, Victor Aimé. *The English Universities.* Ed. and trans. Francis W. Newman. 2. London, 1843.

———. *Reisebriefe aus Belgien Frankreich und England im Sommer 1854.* 2 vols. Hamburg, 1855.

Hudson, John Corrie. *The Parent's Handbook: or, Guide to the Choice of Professions, Employment and Situations, Containing Useful and Practical Information of the Subject of Placing Out Young Men, and of Educating Them with a View to Particular Occupations.* London, 1842.

Hughes, Emrys. *Keir Hardie.* London: Allen and Unwin, 1956.

Hughes, Henry Stuart. *Consciousness and Society: The Reorientation of European Social Thought, 1890–1930.* New York: Knopf, 1958.

Hughes, Mary Vivian. *A London Child of the Seventies.* London: Oxford University Press, 1934.

———. *A London Girl of the Eighties.* London: Oxford University Press, 1936.

———. *A London Home in the Nineties.* London and New York: Oxford University Press, 1937.

Hughes, Thomas. *Tom Brown at Oxford.* 1861. Rpt. ed. Cambridge and London, n.d.

———. *Tom Brown's School Days: By an Old Boy.* London, 1857.

Hugo, Victor. *L'Art d'être grand-père.* 1877. Oeuvres complètes, vol. 8. Paris, 1914.

Hunt, David. *Parents and Children in History: The Psychology of Family Life in Early Modern France.* New York: Basic Books, 1970.

Hunt, Leigh. "Bluestocking Revels: or, The Feast of the Violets." *Monthly Repository*, 1837. Reprinted in *Poetical Works*, ed. H. S. Milford. London: Oxford University Press, 1923.

Huzard, Antoinette de Bergevin [Colette Yver]. *Les Dames du palais*. Paris, 1909.

Hyde, H. Montgomery. *Mr. and Mrs. Beeton*. London: Harrap, 1951.

Hynes, Samuel. *The Edwardian Turn of Mind*. Princeton: Princeton University Press, 1968.

Ideville, Henry d'. *L'Homme qui tue et l'homme qui pardonne*. Paris, 1872.

Immermann, Karl. *Die Jungend vor Fünfundzwanzig Jahren*. 1839. Immermann's Werke, vol. 18: 17–222. Berlin, 1882.

Ingram, S. J., and Rothrock, G. A. "Papa and His Brood." *History Today* 21 (1971): 32-39.

Isherwood, Christopher. *Kathleen and Frank*. London: Methuen, 1971.

Isichei, Elizabeth. *Victorian Quakers*. London: Oxford University Press, 1970.

Jacob, William. *A View of the Agriculture, Manufactures, Statistics and State of Society, of Germany: Taken During a Journey . . . in 1819*. London, 1820.

Jacobi, Mary Putnam. *Life and Letters of Mary Putnam Jacobi*. Ed. Ruth Putnam. New York: Putnam, 1925.

Jameson, Anna Brownell. *Diary of an Ennuyée [A Lady's Diary]*. London, 1826.

————. *Sisters of Charity and the Communion of Labour: Two Lectures on the Social Employment of Women, with a Prefatory Letter to the Right Hon. Lord John Russell*. New ed. London, 1859.

Janet, Paul. "L'education des femmes." *Revue des Deux Mondes* 109 (1883): 48–85.

————. *Elements of Morals: With Special Application of the Moral Law to the Duties of the Individual and of Society and the State*. Trans. Mrs. C. R. Corson. New York, 1884.

————. *La Famille: Leçons de philosophie morale*. 1855. 3d ed. Paris, 1857.

Jardon, Cornelia. *Die Frau in Bebels Utopien*. Minden im Westf., 1892.

Jenkins, Roy. *Victorian Scandal: A Biography of the Right Honourable Gentleman Sir Charles Dilke*. Rev. ed. New York: Chilmark, 1965.

Jesse, F. Tennyson [Mrs. H. M. Harwood], ed. *Trial of Madeleine Smith*. Notable British Trial Series. Edinburgh: Hodge, 1927.

John, Eugenie [E. Marlitt]. *The Old Mam'selle's Secret*. Trans. A. L. Wister. Philadelphia, 1868.

————. *The Second Wife: A Romance*. Trans. A. L. Wister. Philadelphia, 1874.

Johnson, Christopher H. "Communism and the Working Class Before Marx: The Icarian Experience." *American Historical Review* 76 (1971): 642–89.

Johnson, Diane. *The True History of the First Mrs. Meredith and Other Lesser Lives*. New York: Knopf, 1972.

Johnson, Richard. "Educational Policy and Social Control in Early Victorian England." *Past & Present*, no. 49 (Nov. 1970): 96–119.

Johnson, Wendell Stacy. *Sex and Marriage in Victorian Poetry*. Ithaca, N.Y.: Cornell University Press, 1975.

Jones, Arnita A. "From Utopia to Reform." *History Today* 26 (1976): 393–401.

Jones, Ernest. *The Life and Work of Sigmund Freud*. Vol. 1. New York: Basic Books, 1953.

Jones, Mary Gwladys. *Hannah More*. Cambridge: Cambridge University Press, 1952.

Kahler, Erich. *The Tower and the Abyss: An Inquiry into the Transformation of the Individual*. New York: Braziller, 1957.

Kamm, Josephine. *Hope Deferred: Girls' Education in English History*. London: Methuen, 1965.

———. *How Different From Us: A Biography of Miss Buss and Miss Beale.* London: Bodley, 1958.

Karr, Alphonse. *Les Femmes.* Paris, 1853.

Kaufmann, Walter A. *Nietzsche: Philosopher, Psychologist, Antichrist.* Princeton: Princeton University Press, 1950.

Kaulbars, Baron von. "Notes d'un officier russe sur l'Armée allemande." In *Bulletin de la Réunion des Officiers.* Paris, 1877.

Kautsky, Karl. *Erinnerungen und Erörterungen.* The Hague: Mouton, 1960.

Kay, Joseph. *The Social Condition and Education of the People in England and Europe.* 1850. Rpt. ed. New York, 1864.

Kaye, Sir John William. "The Marriage and Divorce Bill." *North British Review* 27 (Aug. 1857): 86–103.

———. "The Non-Existence of Women." *North British Review* 18 (Aug. 1855): 228–302.

———. "Outrages on Women." *North British Review* 25 (May 1856): 233–56.

Kellett, Ernest Edward. *As I Remember.* London: Gollancz, 1936.

Kelly, Thomas. *A History of Adult Education in Great Britain.* Liverpool: Liverpool University Press, 1962.

Kemble, Frances Ann. *Records of a Girlhood.* New York, 1879.

———. *A Year of Consolation.* 2 vols. New York, 1847.

Kent, Christopher. "The Whittington Club: A Bohemian Experiment in Middle Class Social Reform." *Victorian Studies* 18 (1974): 31–55.

Kessen, William. *The Child.* Perspectives in Psychology. New York: Wiley, 1965.

Key, Ellen. *The Century of the Child.* New York, 1909.

———. *Rahel Varnhagen: A Portrait.* Trans. Arthur G. Chater. New York, 1913.

Keyserling, Count Hermann, ed. *The Book of Marriage: A New Interpretation by Twenty-four Leaders of Contemporary Thought.* New York: Harcourt, 1926.

———. *Europe.* Trans. M. Samuel. New York: Harcourt, 1928.

Killham, John. *Tennyson and "The Princess."* London: University of London, Athlone Press, 1958.

Kingsley, Charles. *Alton Locke, Tailor and Poet: An Autobiography.* 1850. New York, 1911.

———. *The Good News of God: Sermons.* 1859. Rpt. ed. London, 1898.

———. *Sanitary and Social Lectures and Essays (1858–69).* 1880. Rpt. ed. London, 1902.

Kingsley, Fanny E., ed. *Charles Kingsley: His Letters and Memories of His Life.* 1877. 2 vols. Leipzig, 1881.

Kipling, Rudyard. "Baa Baa, Black Sheep." 1888. In Burwash Edition of the Complete Works, vol. 3: 281–316. Garden City, N.Y.: Doubleday, Doran, 1941.

———. *The Female of the Species: A Study in Natural History.* Philadelphia, 1911.

———. *Something of Myself: For My Friends Known and Unknown.* New York: Doubleday, 1937.

Kirchhoff, Arthur. *Die akademische Frau: Gutachten hervorragender Universitätsprofessoren, Frauenlehrer und Schriftsteller über die Befähigung der Frau zum wissentschaftlichen Studium und Berufe.* Berlin, 1897.

Kitson Clark, George. *The Making of Victorian England.* Cambridge: Harvard University Press, 1962.

Klein, Josephine. *Samples from English Cultures.* 2 vols. London: Routledge, 1965.

Klein, Viola. *The Feminine Character: History of an Ideology.* 1946. 2d ed. London: K. Paul, Trench, Trübner, 1971.

Kleist, Heinrich von. *Briefe an seine Braut.* Ed. Karl Biedermann. Breslau, 1884.

Knodel, John E. *The Decline of Fertility in Germany: 1871–1939.* Princeton: Princeton University Press, 1974.

———. "Law, Marriage and Illegitimacy in Nineteenth Century Germany." *Population Studies* (London) 20 (March 1967): 279–94.

Knowlton, Charles. *Fruits of Philosophy: or, The Private Companion of Young Married Couples.* New York, 1832.

Kohn, Hans. *The Mind of Germany: The Education of a Nation.* New York: Scribner, 1960.

Koltsova-Masalskaia, Elena Mikhailovna Gihka Kniaginia [Dora d'Istria]. *Des femmes, par une femme.* 2 vols. New ed. Paris, 1869.

Kramer, Rita. *Maria Montessori: A Biography.* New York: Putnam, 1976.

Kügelgen, Wilhelm von. *Jugenderinnerungen eines alten Mannes.* Leipzig: Koehler and Amelang, 1967.

Kuhn, Anne L. *The Mother's Role in Childhood Education: New England Concepts, 1830–1860.* New Haven: Yale University Press, 1947.

Kurtz. Harold. *The Empress Eugénie: 1826–1920.* London: Hamilton, 1964.

Kurz, Isolde. *Aus meinem Jugendland.* Berlin and Stuttgart, 1918.

———. *Meine Mutter.* Tübingen: Wunderlich Verlag, 1926.

Ladreit de Lacharrière, Jacques, ed. *La Correspondance de Chateaubriand avec sa femme.* Paris, 1908.

Laing, Samuel. *Notes of a Traveller on the Social and Political State of France, Prussia, Switzerland, Italy and Other Parts of Europe During the Present Century.* London, 1854.

Lallemand, Léon. *La Question des enfants abandonnés et délaissés au XIXᵉ siècle:* Paris, 1885.

Lamartine, Alphonse de. *Nouvelles Confidences.* 1851. Paris, n.d.

Lange, Dr. *Selbstbekenntnisse: oder, Vierzig Jahre aus dem Leben eines oft gennanten Arztes.* 3 vols. Leipzig, 1854.

Lange, Helene. *Entwicklung und Stand des höheren Mädchenschulwesens in Deutschland.* Berlin, 1893.

———. *Higher Education of Women in Europe.* Trans. and accompanied by comparative statistics by L. R. Klemm. New York, 1890.

———. *Intellektuelle Grenzlinien zwischen Mann und Frau.* Berlin, n.d.

———. *Lebenserinnerungen.* Berlin: Herbig, 1928.

Lange, Helene, and Bäumer, Gertrud. *Handbuch der Frauenbewegung.* Part 1: *Die Geschichte der Frauenbewegung in den Kulturländern.* Berlin, 1901.

Langer, William L. "Checks on Population Growth: 1750–1850." *Scientific American,* 226, no. 2 (Feb. 1972): 92–99.

Laprade, Victor de. *L'Education homicide, plaidoyer pour l'enfance.* New ed. Paris, 1868.

———. *Le Livre d'un père.* Paris, 1876.

Laqueur, Walter Z. *Young Germany: A History of the German Youth Movement.* New York: Basic Books, 1962.

Larcher, Louis-Julien. *Opinion des anciens et des modernes sur l'éducation: ou, Le Livre des instituteurs et des pères de famille.* Paris, 1859.

Lasch, Christopher. "Better Than to Burn: An Historical Note on Marriage." *Columbia Forum*, n.s. 2, no. 4 (Fall 1973): 18–25.

———. *Haven in a Heartless World: The Family Besieged.* Rochester, N.Y.: Basic Books, 1977.

Laski, Marghanita. *Mrs. Ewing, Mrs. Molesworth and Mrs. Hodgson Burnett.* London: A. Barker, 1950.

Laslett, Peter. "The Comparative History of Household and Family." *Journal of Social History* 4 (1970): 75–87.

Latey, William. *The Tide of Divorce.* Harlow: Longmans, 1970.

Laube, Heinrich. *Erinnerungen: 1810–1840.* Heinrich Laube's Gesammelte Werke, ed. H. H. Houben, vol. 1. Leipzig, 1909.

Laver, James. *Manners and Morals in the Age of Optimism: 1848–1914.* New York: Harper, 1966.

———. *Victoriana.* New York: Hawthorne Books, 1967.

Laverque, Léonce de. "L'Agriculture et la population." *Revue des Deux Mondes* 8 (1857): 481–501.

Lavisse, Ernest. *Souvenirs.* Paris, 1912.

Lawrenny, H. "Custom and Sex." *Fortnightly Review*, n.s. 11 (1872): 310–23.

Laya, Alexandre. *Causes célèbres du mariage: au, Les Infortunes conjugales.* Paris, 1883.

Layard, George S. *Mrs. Lynn Linton: Her Life, Letters, and Opinions.* London, 1901.

Lederer, Thomas. *Mutter und Kind: oder, Schwangerschaft, Entbindung, und Wochenbette, mit einem aus der Darstellung ihres natürlichen Verlaufes abgeleiten Unterrichte für Frauen.* Vienna, 1826.

Lefebvre, Charles. *La Famille en France dans le droit et dans les moeurs.* Paris, 1920.

Legge, James Granville. *Rhyme and Revolution in Germany: A Study in German History, Life, Literature and Character, 1813–1850.* London, 1918.

Legouvé, Ernest. *Cours d'histoire morale des femmes.* (Pamphlet.) Paris, 1848.

———. *L'Education d'un père.* Paris, 1856.

———. *Histoire morale des femmes.* 1849. 2d ed. Paris, 1854.

Lemaitre, Jules. "L'Amour selon Michelet." *Revue de Paris*, Oct. 15, 1898, pp. 732–43.

Lemonnier, Charles. *Elisa Lemonnier: Fondatrice de la Société pour l'Enseignement Professionel des Femmes.* 2d ed. Paris, 1874.

Leopardi, Giacomo. *Selected Prose and Poetry.* Ed. and trans. Iris Origo and John Heath-Stubbs. London: Oxford University Press, 1966.

Lepointe, Gabriel. "La Femme au XIXᵉ siècle en France et dans le monde de l'Europe occidentale." In *La Femme*, pt. 2. *Recueils de la Société Jean Bodin* 12 (1962): 499–514.

Leroy-Beaulieu, Paul. *La Question de la population.* Paris: F. Alcan, 1913.

Lewald, Fanny [later Lewald-Stahr]. *Für und wider die Frauen: Vierzehn Briefe.* Berlin, 1870.

———. *Gefühltes and Gedachtes (1838–1888).* Ed. Ludwig Geiger. Leipzig and Dresden, 1900.

Lewes, G. H. "Currer Bell's *Shirley.*" *Edinburgh Review* 91 (Jan. 1850): 153–73.

Liguori, Saint Alfonso M. de. *De Matrimonio.* Bologna, 1935.

Lilge, Frederic. *The Abuse of Learning: The Failure of the German University.* New York: Macmillan, 1948.

Lindsay, Lord Alexander D. *The Modern Democratic State,* New York: Oxford University Press, 1943.

Linton, Elizabeth Lynn. *The Girl of the Period and Other Social Essays.* Vol. 1. London, 1883.

———. "French Domesticity." *Household Words* 9 (1854): 434–38.

Lippincott, Benjamin Evans. *Victorian Critics of Democracy: Carlyle, Ruskin, Arnold, Stephen, Maine, Lecky.* Minneapolis: University of Minnesota Press, 1938.

Livingston, Arthur. "Theory of a Gentleman." *Encyclopedia of the Social Sciences,* ed. Edwin R. A. Seligman, vol. 6: 616–20. New York: Macmillan, 1931–1936.

Le Livre de l'enfance chrétienne: Instructions religieuses d'une mère à ses enfants. 2d ed. Paris, 1841.

Le Livre de la famille: Morale, éducation, économie domestique de hygiène, soin aux enfants. Paris, 1892.

Lochhead, Marion. *The Victorian Household.* London: Murray, 1964.

———. *Young Victorians.* London: Murray, 1959.

Lombroso, Gina. *The Soul of Woman: Reflections on Life [L'anima della donna].* New York: Dutton, 1923.

Longford, Elizabeth. *Wellington.* 2 vols. London: Weidenfeld and Nicolson, 1969.

Lorence, Bogna. "Parents and Children in the Eighteenth Century." Unpublished manuscript.

Lorenz, Konrad. *On Aggression.* Trans. Marjorie H. Wilson. New York: Harcourt, 1966.

Lovett, William. *The Life and Struggles of William Lovett in His Pursuit of Bread, Knowledge, and Freedom: And with Some Short Accounts of the Different Associations He Belonged To, and of the Opinions He Entertained.* London, 1876.

Lowe, David. *From Pit to Parliament: The Story of the Early Life of James Keir Hardie.* London, 1923.

Lowie, Robert H. *The German People: A Social Portrait to 1914.* New York: Farrar and Rinehart, 1945.

———. *Toward Understanding Germany.* Chicago: University of Chicago Press, 1954.

Lübke, Wilhelm. "Die Frauen in der Kunstgeschichte." In *Kunsthistorische Studien,* pp. 141–76. Stuttgart, 1869.

Lukacs, John. "The Bourgeois Interior." *American Scholar* 39 (1970): 616–30.

Lupri, Eugen. "The West German Family Today and Yesterday: A Study in Changing Family Authority Patterns." Doctoral dissertation, University of Wisconsin, 1967.

Luther, Martin. "A Sermon on the Estate of Marriage, 1519." Trans. James Atkinson. Luther's Works, vol. 44, ed. James Atkinson. Philadelphia: Fortress, 1966.

Lynd, Helen Merrell. *England in the Eighteen-Eighties: Toward a Social Basis for Freedom.* New York: Oxford University Press, 1945.

Lyttelton, Edward. *The Training of the Young in the Laws of Sex.* London, 1900.

Lytton, Edward Bulwer-Lytton, 1st Baron. *England and the English.* New York, 1833.

McClelland, Vincent Alan. "The Liberal Training of England's Catholic Youth: William Joseph Petre (1847–93) and Educational Reform." *Victorian Studies* 15 (1972): 257–77.

Maccoby, Eleanor E., and Jacklin, Carol N. *The Psychology of Sex Differences.* Stanford, Cal.: Stanford University Press, 1974.

McDonald, Donald. "The Liberation of Women." *Center Magazine* 5, no. 3 (May–June 1972): 25–42.

McFall, Frances Elizabeth Clarke [Sarah Grand]. *The Heavenly Twins.* New York: 1893.

———. *Ideala.* New York, 1893.

McGregor, Oliver Ross. *Divorce in England: A Centenary Study.* London: Heinemann, 1957.

———. "The Social Position of Women in England, 1850–1914: A Bibliography." *British Journal of Sociology* 6 (1955): 48–60.

Mack, Edward C., and Armytage, W. H. G. *Thomas Hughes: The Life of the Author of "Tom Brown's Schooldays."* London: Benn, 1952.

[Mackenzie, Alexander Slidell]. *The American in England.* 2 vols. New York, 1835.

MacKenzie, Norman, and MacKenzie, Jeanne. *The Fabians.* New York: Simon and Schuster, 1977.

Madariaga, Salvador de. *Englishmen, Frenchmen, Spaniards: An Essay in Comparative Psychology.* London: Oxford University Press, 1931.

———. *Spain.* New York: Scribner's, 1930.

Magni, Maria. *Adelaide Cairoli.* Turin: Società Subalpina editrice, 1943.

Magnus, Sir Philip. *Gladstone: A Biography.* 1954. New York: Dutton, 1964.

Maigron, Louis. *Le Romantisme et les moeurs: Essai d'étude historique et sociale d'après des documents inédits.* Paris, 1910.

Maillard, Firmin. *Le Légende de la femme émancipée:Histoires de femmes pour servir à l'histoire contemporaine.* Paris, n.d.

Mann, Horace. *Report of an Educational Tour in Germany, and Parts of Great Britain and Ireland, Being Part of the 7th Annual Report . . . 1844.* Ed. W. B. Hodgson. London, 1846.

Mann, Thomas. *Buddenbrooks: The Decline of a Family.* Trans. H. T. Lowe-Porter. New York: Modern Library, 1924.

Mann, Tom. *Tom Mann's Memoirs.* London, 1923.

Manouvrier, Léonce Pierre. "Anthropologie des sexes et applications sociales." *Revue Anthropologique* 37 (1927): 285–300.

Mantegazza, Paolo. *La mia mamma.* 1876. Florence, 1886.

Manton, Jo. *Elizabeth Garrett Anderson.* London: Methuen, 1966.

Marandon, Sylvaine. *L'Image de la France dans l'Angleterre victorienne: 1848–1900.* Paris: A. Colin, 1967.

Marbouty, Mme Caroline [Claire Brunne]. *Ange de Spola: Etudes de Femmes.* 2 vols. Paris, 1842.

March, Harold. *The Two Worlds of Marcel Proust.* Philadelphia: University of Pennsylvania Press, 1948.

Marchand, Leslie A. *Byron: A Biography.* 3 vols. New York: Knopf, 1957.

Marcilhacy, Christianne. *Le diocèse d'Orléans sous l'épiscopat de Mgr. Dupanloup: 1849–1878.* Paris: Plon, 1962.

Mare, Margaret, *Annette von Droste-Hülshoff.* Trans. Ursula Prideaux. London: Methuen, 1965.

Margueritte, Paul, and Margueritte, Victor. *Femmes nouvelles.* Paris, 1899.

Marholm, Laura. *Modern Women: An English Rendering of Laura Marholm Hansson's "Das Buch der Frauen," by Hermione Ramsden.* London, 1896.

Mariani, Emilia. *"Le Mouvement féministe en Italy." Revue Politique et Parlementaire* (Paris) 13 (1897): 481–95.

Mario, Jessie White. "On the Position of Women in Italy." *Nation* (New York) 9 (1869): 456–57, 480–82.

———. "Social Equality in Italy." *Nation* (New York) 9 (1869): 267–69.

Marion, Henri. *L'Education des jeunes filles.* (Etudes de psychologie féminine) Paris, 1902.

Marlow, Joyce. *The Oak and the Ivy: An Intimate Biography of William and Catherine Gladstone.* Garden City, N.Y.: Doubleday, 1977.

Marples, Morris. *Romantics at School.* London, Faber, 1967.

Marreco, Alice Acland-Troyte [Alice Acland]. *Caroline Norton.* London: Constable, 1948.

Marshall, Dorothy. *The English Domestic Servant in History.* London: G. Phillip, 1949.

Marshall, Frederic. *French Home Life.* Reprinted from *Blackwood's Magazine.* New York, 1874.

Martel de Janville, Comtesse Sybille de Riquetti de Mirabeau [Gyp]. *Ce que femme veut?* Paris, 1883.

———. *Marriage No Mystery.* London, [1886].

———. *Souvenirs d'une petite fille.* 2 vols. Paris: Colmann-Levy, 1927.

Martin, Louis-Aimé. *The Education of Mothers of Families: or, The Civilisation of the Human Race by Women.* 1834. Trans. from 3d Paris ed. (1842), with remarks by Edwin Lee. London, 1842.

Martineau, Harriet. *Harriet Martineau's Autobiography: With Memorials by Maria Weston Chapman.* 3 vols. London, 1877.

———. "Female Industry." *Edinburgh Review* 109 (Apr. 1859): 293–336.

Marwick, Arthur. *The Deluge: British Society and the First World War.* London: Bodley Head, 1965.

Masur, Gerhard. *Imperial Berlin.* New York: Basic Books, 1971.

———. *Prophets of Yesterday: Studies in European Culture: 1890–1914.* New York: Macmillan, 1961.

Mauclair, Camille. "De l'amour physique." 1913. *Essaies sur l'amour,* vol. 1. Paris: Ollendorf, n.d.

———. "La Magie de l'amour." *Essaies sur l'amour,* vol. 2. Paris: Ollendorf, n.d.

Maurice, F. D. *Lectures to Ladies on Practical Subjects.* 1855. 3d ed., rev. London, 1857.

Maxwell, Christabel. *Mrs. Gatty and Mrs. Ewing.* London: Constable, 1949.

May, Geoffrey. *Social Control of Sex Expression.* New York: W. Morrow, 1931.

May, Gita. *Madame Roland and the Age of Revolution.* New York: Columbia University Press, 1970.

Mayhew, Henry. *German Life and Manners as Seen in Saxony at the Present Day: With an Account of Village Life, Town Life, Fashionable Life, Domestic Life, Married Life, School and University Life etc. of Germany at the Present Time.* 2d ed. London, 1865.

———. *Selections from "London Labour and the London Poor."* Ed. John L. Bradley. London: Oxford University Press, 1966.

Mayhew, Horace, and Mayhew, Augustus. *Whom to Marry and How to Get Married: or, The Adventures of a Lady in Search of a Good Husband.* Illus. George Cruikshank. London, 1847–48.

Mayreder, Rosa. *A Survey of the Woman Problem.* Trans. Herman Scheffauer. London, 1913.

Mazzini, Giuseppe. "Alle donne d'Italia." In *Scritti editi ed mediti de Giuseppe Mazzini*, vol. 55: 121–25. Imola, 1929.

Mazzoleni, Angelo. *La famiglia nei rapporti coll'individuo e colla società.* Milan, 1870.

Meinecke, Friedrich. *Strassburg, Freiburg, Berlin, 1901–1919: Erinnerungen.* Stuttgart: Koehlin, 1949.

Meinertzhagen, Georgina. *From Ploughshare to Parliament: A Short Memoir of the Potters of Tadcaster.* London: Murray, 1908.

Meisel-Hess, Grete. *The Sexual Crisis: A Critique of Our Sex Life.* 1909. Trans. Eden and Cedar Paul. New York, 1917.

Mendenhall, Thomas C.; Henning, Basil D.; and Foord, Archibald S. *The Quest for a Principle of Authority in Europe, 1715–Present: Select Problems in Historical Interpretation.* New York: Holt, 1948.

Menzies, Allan. *Report of Twenty-One Years' Experience of the Dick Bequest . . . Embracing an Exposition of the Parish School.* Edinburgh, 1854.

Menzies, Amy Charlotte Bewicke. *Memories Discreet and Indiscreet: By a Woman of No Importance.* New York, 1917.

Mercier, Charles. *Les Petits-Paris: Considérations sociologiques relatives a l'hygiène infantile.* Paris, 1894.

Meredith, George. *Diana of the Crossways.* 1885. Rev. ed. 1897. New York: Scribner's, 1911.

———. *The Egoist: A Comedy in Narrative.* 1879. New York: Scribner's, 1909.

———. *Modern Love.* 1862. Works of George Meredith, vol. 24. New York: Scribner's, 1910.

Métraux, Rhoda, and Mead, Margaret. *Thèmes de "culture" de la France.* 1924. Trans. Yvonne-Delphée Miroglio. Havre: M. Etaix, 1957.

Meyer, Jürgen Bona. *Zum Bildungskampf unserer Zeit.* Bonn, 1875.

Meysenbug, Malwida von. *Memoiren einer Idealistin.* 3 vols. Berlin and Leipzig, 1900.

Michelet, Jules. *L'Amour.* 1858. 8th ed. Paris, 1873.

———. *Du prêtre, de la femme, de la famille.* Paris, 1845.

———. *Woman [La Femme].* 1860. Trans. J. W. Palmer. New York, 1867.

Middleton, Dorothy. *Victorian Lady Travellers.* New York: Dutton, 1965.

Milice, Albert. *Clemence Royer et sa doctrine de la vie.* Paris, 1926.

Mill, John Stuart. "The Subjection of Women." 1869. In *Liberty and Other Essays.* Macmillan Modern Readers' Series. New York: Macmillan, 1926.

Millet-Robinet, Cora Elisabeth. *Maison rustique des dames.* 1845. 2 vols. 8th ed. Paris, n.d.

Millet-Robinet, Cora, and Allix, Emile. *Le Livre des jeunes mères: La Nourrice et le nourrison.* Paris, 1884.

Millett, Kate. "The Debate over Women: Ruskin versus Mill." *Victorian Studies* 14 (1970): 63–82.

———. *Sexual Politics.* Garden City, N.Y.: Doubleday, 1970.

Milne, John Duguid. *Industrial Employment of Women in the Middle and Lower Ranks.* 1857. Rev. ed. London, 1870.

Minghetti, Marco. *Miei ricordi.* 3 vols. Vol. 1: *1818–1848.* Turin, 1888–90.

Mirbeau, Octave. *Le Journal d'une femme de chambre.* Paris, 1906. (Enormously popular, this book sold over 101,000 copies in the six years after its initial printing in 1900.)

Mitchell, David. *The Fighting Pankhursts: A Study in Tenacity.* New York: Macmillan, 1967.

Mitchell, Hannah. *The Hard Way Up: The Autobiography of Hannah Mitchell, Suffragette and Rebel.* Ed. Geoffrey Mitchell. London: Faber and Faber, 1968.

Mitchell, Yvonne. *Colette: A Taste for Life.* New York: Harcourt, 1976.

Mitford, Nancy, ed. *The Ladies of Alderley: Being the Letters between Maria Josepha, Lady Stanley of Alderley, and her Daughter-In-Law Henrietta Maria Stanley, During the Years 1841–1850.* London: Chapman & Hall, 1938.

————. "St. Cyr: Mme de Maintenon as Educationalist." *History Today* 15 (1965): 3–11.

Mitzman, Arthur. *The Iron Cage: An Historical Interpretation of Max Weber.* New York: Knopf, 1970.

Moberly, Charlotte Anne Elizabeth. *Dulce Domum: George Moberly, His Family and Friends.* London, 1916.

Moers, Ellen. *Literary Women.* Garden City, N.Y.: Doubleday, 1977.

————. "Mme de Staël and the Women of Genius." *American Scholar* 44 (1975): 225–41.

Moffat, Mary Jane, and Painter, Charlotte, eds. *Revelations: Diaries of Women.* New York: Random, 1975.

Mohl, Mary Clark. *Madame Récamier: With a Sketch of the History of Society in France.* London, 1862.

Moll, Albert. *The Sexual Life of the Child.* 1909. Trans. Eden Paul. New York, 1912.

Moll, Henry. *Une Ame de colonial: Lettres du lieutenant-colonel Moll.* Pref. Maurice Barrès. Paris, 1912.

Mommsen, Adelheid. *Theodor Mommsen im Kreise des Seinen.* Berlin: E. Ebering, 1936.

Monchoux, André. "L'Allemagne devant les lettres françaises de 1814, à 1835." Thesis, University of Paris. Toulouse, 1953.

Moore, David Cresap. "Politics of Deference: A Study of the Political Structure, Leadership, and Organization of English Country Constituencies in the Nineteenth Century." Doctoral dissertation, Columbia, 1958.

Moore, Doris Langley-Levy. *E. Nesbit: A Biography.* Rev. and enl. ed. Philadelphia: Chilton Books, 1966.

More, Hannah. *Coelebs in Search of a Wife.* 1809. Works, vol. 2. New York, 1843.

————. *Strictures on the Modern System of Female Education.* 1799. Works, vol. 4. New York, 1835.

Moreau, Henry C. *L'Un ou l'autre.* Paris, 1901.

Morelli, Salvatore. *La Femme et la science: ou, La Solution du problem humain.* Trans. G. Cipri. Brussels, 1862.

Morgan, Lady Sydney Owenson. *La France.* Trans. A.-J.-B. Defauconpret. 2 vols. 3d ed. Paris, 1818.

————. *France in 1829–30.* 2 vols. 2d ed. London, 1831.

————. *Italy.* 3 vols. London, 1821.

————. *Lady Morgan's Memoirs: Autobiography, Diaries and Correspondence.* 3 vols. Ed. W. Hepworth Dixon. Leipzig, 1863.

Morley, Viscount John. *Studies in Conduct.* London, 1867.

Mosse, George L. *The Culture of Western Europe: The Nineteenth and Twentieth Centuries, an Introduction.* Chicago: Rand McNally, 1961.
————. "Mystical Origins of National Socialism." *Journal of the History of Ideas* 22 (1961): 81–96.
Mothe-Langon, Etienne-Léon de la [Marquis Louis Ranier Lanfranchi]. *Voyage à Paris: ou, Esquisses des hommes et des choses dans cette capitale.* Paris, 1830.
Mourey, Gabriel. *Passé le détroit: La Vie et l'art a Londres.* Paris, 1895.
Mozans, H. J. *Women in Science.* London, 1913.
Mozley, James Bowling. "Dr. Arnold." In *Essays, Historical and Theological,* vol. 2: 1–67. London, 1878.
Mozzoni, Anna Maria. *La donna e i suoi rapporti sociali, in occasione della revisione del Codice civile italiano.* Milan, 1864.
————. *La liberazione delle donna.* Ed. Franca Pieroni Bortolotti. Milan: G. Mazzotta, 1975.
————. *Un passo avanti nella cultura femminile: Tesi e progetto.* Milan, 1866.
Muggeridge, Kitty, and Adam, Ruth. *Beatrice Webb: A Life: 1858–1943.* New York: Knopf, 1968.
Mulock, Dinah [later Craik]. *A Woman's Thoughts About Women.* New York, 1858.
Munby, Arthur J. *Munby, Man of Two Worlds: The Life and Diaries of Arthur J. Munby.* Ed. Derek Hudson. London: Murray, 1972.
Murray, F. Greville. "Courtship and Marriage in France." *Westminster Review,* n.s. 51 (1877): 337–83.
————. "Mademoiselle Viviane: The Story of a French Marriage." *Cornhill Magazine* 26 (1872): 313–40.
Musset, Alfred de. *A quoi rêvent les jeunes filles? Comédie en deux actes.* 1832. Rpt. ed. Paris, 1920.
————. *La Confession d'un enfant du siècle.* New ed. Paris, 1884.
Napoleon I. *Letters of Napoleon.* Trans. and ed. J. M. Thompson. Oxford: Blackwell, 1934.
Naquet, Alfred. *Alfred Naquet: Autobiographie.* Paris: Recueil Sirey, 1939.
————. *Le Divorce.* Paris, 1877.
Neale, R. S. "Class and Class-Consciousness in Early Nineteenth-Century England: Three Classes or Five?" *Victorian Studies* 12 (1968): 5–32.
Negri, Ada [later Garlanda]. *Stella mattutina.* Rome and Milan: A. Mondadori, 1921.
Le Neo-Malthusisme, est-il moral? Opinions de . . . [30 people]. Paris, [1909].
Nesbit, Edith [later Bland]. *The Red House.* New York and London, 1902.
Nethercot, Arthur H. *The First Five Lives of Annie Besant.* Chicago: University of Chicago Press, 1960.
Nettl, John Peter. *Rosa Luxemburg.* Abridged ed. New York: Oxford University Press, 1969.
Die Neue Gartenlaube: Die Gartenlaube als Dokument ihrer Zeit. Ed. Magdalene Zimmermann. Munich: Deutscher Taschenbuch-Verlag, 1967.
Neuman, R. P. "Masturbation, Madness, and the Modern Concepts of Childhood and Adolescence." *Journal of Social History* 8 (Spring 1975): 1–27.
————. "The Sexual Question and Social Democracy in Imperial Germany." *Journal of Social History* 7 (Spring 1974): 271–86.
Newby, Percy Howard. *Maria Edgeworth.* English Novelists Series. London: A. Barker, 1950.

Newman, F. W. "Remedies for the Great Social Evil." 1869. In *Miscellanies,* vol. 3: 267–84. Rev. ed. London, 1889.

Niceforo, Nicola [Emilio Del Cerro]. *Giuseppe Mazzini e Giuditta Sidoli.* Turin, 1909.

Nichols, Beverley. *Father Figure: An Uncensored Autobiography.* New York: Simon and Schuster, 1972.

Nicoll, W. Robertson. *The Round of the Clock: The Story of Our Lives from Year to Year.* New York and London: Hodder & Stoughton, [1910].

Nicolson, Harold. *Helen's Tower.* New York: Harcourt, 1938.

Nicolson, Nigel. *Portrait of a Marriage.* New York: Atheneum, 1973.

Niépovié, Gaëtan. *Etudes physiologiques sur les grandes metropoles de l'Europe occidentale.* Paris, 1840.

Nietzsche, Friedrich. *On the Future of Our Educational Institutions.* Trans. J. M. Kennedy. Complete Works, ed. Oscar Levy, vol. 3. New York, 1911.

Nievo, Ippolito. *The Castle of Fratta [Confessioni du'un ottuagenario].* Trans. Lovett F. Edwards. Boston: Houghton Mifflin, 1958.

Nightingale, Florence. *The Institution of Kaiserswerth on the Rhine for the Practical Training of Deaconesses, Under the Direction of the Rev. Pastor Fliedner, Embracing the Support and Care of a Hospital, Infant and Industrial Schools, and a Female Penitentiary.* London, 1851.

———. *Selected Writings.* Comp. Lucy Ridgely Seymer. New York: Macmillan, 1954.

Nisbet, Ada. *Dickens and Ellen Ternan.* Berkeley: University of California Press, 1952.

North, Marianne. *Recollections of a Happy Life: Being the Autobiography of Marianne North.* Ed. Mrs. John Addington Symonds. New York, 1894.

Norton, Charles Eliot. *Notes of Travel and Study in Italy.* 1859. Boston, 1887.

Nourissier, François. *The French.* Trans. Adrienne Foulke. New York: Knopf, 1968.

Noyes, P. H. *Organization and Revolution: Working-Class Associations in the German Revolutions of 1848–1849.* Princeton: Princeton University Press, 1966.

Oastler, Richard, ed. *The Home, Devoted to the Support of Christian and Constitutional Principles* (London). Vols. 1–4 (1851–53).

O'Boyle, Lenore. "The Democratic Left in Germany, 1848." *Journal of Modern History* 33 (1961): 374–83.

———. "The Middle Class in Western Europe: 1815–1858." *American Historical Review* 71 (1966): 826–45.

———. "The Problem of an Excess of Educated Men in Western Europe: 1800–1850." *Journal of Modern History* 42 (1970): 471–95.

Olney, Clarke. "Caroline Norton to Lord Melbourne." *Victorian Studies* 8 (1965): 255–62.

Olsen, Donald J. "Victorian London: Specialization, Segregation, and Privacy." *Victorian Studies* 17 (1974): 265–78.

O'Meara, Kathleen. *Madame Mohl: Her Salon and Her Friends: A Study of Social Life in Paris.* London, 1885.

Origo, Iris. *Leopardi: A Biography.* London: Oxford University Press, 1935.

Ortega y Gasset, José. *On Love: Aspects of a Single Theme.* Trans. Toby Talbot. London: Gollancz, 1959.

———. *The Revolt of the Masses.* 1930. Authorized trans. New York: Norton, 1932.

Osborne, Charles C., ed. *Letters of Charles Dickens to the Baroness Burdett-Coutts*. London: John Murray, 1931.

Otto-Peters, Luise. *Frauenleben im deutschen Reich: Erinnerungen aus der Vergangenheit mit Hinweis auf Gegenwart und Zukunft*. Leipzig, 1876.

Ouvry, Elinor Southwood, comp. *Extracts from Octavia Hill's "Letters to Fellow-Workers": 1864–1911*. London: Adelphi, 1933.

Owen, David. *English Philanthropy: 1660–1960*. Cambridge: Harvard University Press, 1964.

Oxford Book of Nineteenth-Century Verse. Ed. John Hayward. Oxford: Clarendon Press, 1964.

Packe, Michael St. John. *The Life of John Stuart Mill*. London: Secker & Warburg, 1954.

Packer, Lona Mosk. *Christina Rossetti*. Berkeley: University of California Press, 1963.

Pange, Pauline Laure de. *Lettres de Femnies du XIXe siècle: choisies et présentées par la Comtesse Jean de Pange*. Monaco, 1947.

Pankhurst, E. Sylvia. *The Suffragette Movement: An Intimate Account of Persons and Ideals*. London and New York: Longmans Green, 1931. New York: Kraus Reprint, 1971.

Pankhurst, Richard K. "Saint-Simonism in England." *Twentieth Century* 152 (1952): 499–512; 153 (1953): 47–58.

Panton, Jane Ellen. *The Way They Should Go: Hints to Young Parents*. London, 1896.

Parca, Gabriella. *Love Italian Style*. Trans. Allyn Moss and Romano Giachetti. Englewood Cliffs, N.J.: Prentice-Hall, 1966.

Parker, William H. *The Science of Life: or, Self-Preservation, A Medical Treatise on Nervous and Physical Debility, Spermatorrhea, Impotence, and Sterility*. Boston, 1881.

Parkes, Bessie Raynor Belloc. *Remarks on the Education of Girls*. London, 1854.

Passy, Frédéric. *Les Causeries de grand-père*. Paris, 1905.

———.*Entre mère et fille*. Paris, 1907.

The Pathway of Health and Happiness in Six Letters from a Clergyman of the Church of England to Young Men of All Classes. 1873. 2d ed. London, 1895.

Patmore, Coventry. *The Angel in the House*. 1854–62. 4th ed. London, 1866.

Patmore, Derek. *Portrait of My Family: 1783–1896*. New York and London: Harper, 1935.

Paulsen, Friedrich. *An Autobiography*. Trans. and ed. Theodore Lorenz. New York: Columbia University Press, 1938.

———. "Die Frau im Recht der Vergangenheit und der Zukunft." *Preussische Jahrbücher* 132 (1908): 396–413.

Pearsall, Ronald. *The Worm in the Bud: The World of Victorian Sexuality*. London: Weidenfeld & Nicolson, 1969.

Pelletan, Eugène. *La Famille: La Mère*. Paris, 1865.

Pelletier, Madeleine. *L'Emancipation sexuelle de la femme*. Paris, 1911.

Périer, Elie. *Hygiène de l'adolescence*. Paris, 1891.

———. *Livret de famille*. Vol. 1: *Notes sur la santé des enfants (filles)*. Vol. 2: *Notes sur la santé des enfants (garçons)*. Paris, 1897.

———. *La Première Enfance*. Paris, 1891.

Perthes, Clemens Theodor. *Friedrich Perthes Leben nach dessen schriftlichen und mündlichen Mittheilungen*. 3 vols. Gotha, 1861.

Peruzzi, Emilia Toscanelli. *Vita di me.* Ed. Angiolina Toscanelli Avila. Florence: Vallechi, 1934.

Peters, Karl. *England und die Engländer.* Berlin, 1904.

Peterson, M. Jeanne. "The Victorian Governess: Status Incongruence in Family and Society." *Victorian Studies* 14 (1970): 7–26.

Petrie, Glen. *A Singular Iniquity: The Campaigns of Josephine Butler.* London: Macmillan, 1971.

Pfeiffer, Ida. *A Lady's Voyage Round the World: A Selected Translation from the German of Ida Pfeiffer.* Trans. Mrs. Percy Sinnett. New York, 1852.

Pflanze, Otto. "Towards a Psychoanalytic Interpretation of Bismarck." *American Historical Review* 77 (1972): 419–44.

Pichler, Karoline von. *Denkwürdigkeiten aus meinem Leben.* 4 vols. Vienna, 1844.

Pierantoni-Mancini, Grazia. *Impressioni e ricordi: 1856–1864.* Milan, 1908.

———. *Il Manoscritto della nonna: Publicato per cura della nipote, Grazia Mancini Pierantoni.* Milan, 1879.

Pieroni Bortolotti, Franca. *Alle origini del movimento Femminile in Italia: 1848–1892.* Turin: Einaudi, 1963.

Pietremont, Maria. *Le Bonheur au foyer domestique: Livre de lecture courante pour les jeunes filles.* Paris, 1891.

Piggott, William [Hubert Wales]. *The Yoke.* New York, 1908.

Pinero, Arthur W. *The Notorious Mrs. Ebbsmith: A Drama in Four Acts.* Boston, 1895.

Playfair, William. *France as It Is: Not Lady Morgan's France.* 2 vols. London, 1819–20.

Poinsot, Edmond Antoine [George d'Heylli]. *Mme E. de Girardin, Delphine Gay: Sa vie et ses oeuvres.* Paris, 1869.

Ploss, Hermann Heinrich. *Das Kind in Brauch und Sitte der Völker: Anthropologische Studien.* 2 vols. Stuttgart, 1876.

———. *Das Weib in der Natur-und Völkerkunde: Anthropologische Studien.* 2 vols. 2d ed. Leipzig, 1887.

Pollard, Arthur. *Mrs. Gaskell: Novelist and Biographer.* Manchester: Manchester University Press, 1965.

Ponsonby, Arthur. *Decline of Aristocracy.* London, 1912.

Ponteil, Félix. *Les Classes bourgeoises et l'avènement de la démocratie: 1815–1914.* Paris: Michel, 1968.

———. *Les Institutions de la France de 1814 à 1870.* Paris: Presses Universitaires de France, 1966.

Popert, Hermann. *Helmut Harringa.* 12th ed. Dresden, 1912.

Pratt, Edwin A. *Pioneer Women in Victoria's Reign: Being Short Histories of Great Movements.* London, 1897.

Prelinger, Catherine M. "Religious Dessent, Women's Rights, and the Hamburger Hochschule für das weibliche Geschlecht in Mid-Nineteenth Century Germany." *Church History* 45 (1976): 42–56.

Priestley, J. B. *Victoria's Heyday.* New York: Harper, 1972.

Proudhon, P. J. *De la justice dans la révolution et dans l'église: Nouveaux principes de philosophie practique.* 3 vols. Paris, 1858.

"A Prussian Soldier's Notes on the Prussian Army." *Cornhill Magazine* (1868): 221–30.

"Public Schools: Report of the Commission." *Fraser's Magazine* 69 (1864): 655–69.

[Pückler-Muskau, Hermann Ludwig Heinrich von]. *Tour in England, Ireland, and France in the Years 1826, 1827, 1828, and 1829, with Remarks on the Manners and Customs of the Inhabitants, and Anecdotes of Distinguished Public Characters: In a Series of Letters, by a German Prince.* Trans. Sarah Austin. Philadelphia, 1833.

Puech, Jules-L. *La Vie et l'oeuvre de Flora Tristan, 1803–1844: L'Union Ouvrière.* Paris: Rivière, 1925.

Quinlan, Maurice J. *Victorian Prelude: A History of English Manners, 1700–1830.* New York: Columbia University Press, 1941.

Racowitza, Helene von Donniges. *An Autobiography.* Authorized trans. by Cecil Mar. New York, 1910.

Radziwill, Ekaterina Rzewuska [Count Paul Vasili]. *Berlin Society.* Trans. J. Loder. New York: 1884.

Ramelson, Marian. *The Petticoat Rebellion: A Century of Struggle for Women's Rights.* London: Lawrence & Wishart, 1967.

Ravera, Camilla. *La donna italiana dal primo al secondo Risorgimento.* Rome: Edizioni di Cultura Sociale, 1951.

Ray, Gordon N. *The Buried Life: A Study of the Relation Between Thackeray's Fiction and His Personal History.* Cambridge: Harvard University Press, 1952.

Reade, Winwood. *The Martyrdom of Man.* London, 1872. 19th ed. London: K. Paul, Trench, Trübner, 1910.

Rebière, Alphonse. *Les Femmes dans la science: Notes recueillies.* 2d rev. ed. Paris, 1897.

Redinger, Ruby V. *George Eliot: The Emergent Self.* New York: Knopf, 1975.

Reichstag (Germany). *Stenographische Berichte über die Verhandlungen des Deutschen Reichstages: 8b, Sitzung VII legislaturperiode.* Sessim 1890–91.

Reid, Mrs. Hugo [Marion Kirkland]. *Woman: Her Education and Influence.* Intro. Mrs. C. M. Kirkland. New York, 1848.

Reiffenberg, Baron Frédéric Auguste de. *Nouveaux Souvenirs d'Allemagne.* 2 vols. Brussels, 1843.

Reisner, Edward Hartman. *Nationalism and Education Since 1789: A Social and Political History of Modern Education.* 1922. New York, 1927.

Reiss, Hans. *Politisches Denken in der deutschen Romantik.* Munich: Francke, 1966.

Remacle, Bernard-Benoît. *Des Hospices d'enfans trouvés en Europe.* Paris, 1838.

Rémusat, Comtesse Claire de. *Essai sur l'éducation des femmes, 1824: Précédé d'une étude par Octave Gréard.* New ed. Paris, 1903.

Renan, Ernest. *Brother and Sister: A Memoir and the Letters of Ernest and Henriette Renan.* Trans. Lady Mary Loyd [*sic*]. New York, 1896.

Reuter, Gabriele. *Aus guter Familie: Leidensgeschichte eines Mädchens.* 16th ed. Berlin, 1908.

Reventlow, Gräfin Franziska zu. *Tagebücher 1895–1910.* Ed. Else Reventlow. Munich and Vienna: Langen Müller, 1971.

Rhodes, Albert. *The French at Home.* New York, 1875.

Ricci, Raffaello, ed. *Memorie della baronessa Olimpia Savio (1816–89).* 2 vols. Milan, 1911.

Richardson, Joanna. *Princess Mathilde.* London: Weidenfeld & Nicolson, 1969.

Richer, Léon. *Le Code des femmes.* Paris, 1883.

———. *Le Divorce: Projet de loi proposé à la nouvelle assemblée.* Paris, n.d.

———. *La Femme libre.* Paris, 1877.

Richter, Gert, ed. *Belehrendes und erbauliches Lexicon der Sittsamkeit von A bis Z, welches insbesondere Jungfrauen, Braüte und Ehefrauen, aber auch das männliche Geschlecht, über Anstand, Anmut und Würde in Haus und Gesellschaft unterrichtet.* Gütersloh, Bartelsmann, 1974.

Richter, Ludwig. *Der Feierabend:* [Selections from] *Ludwig Richter's "Lebenserinnerungen eines deutschen Malers."* Ed. Johanne Beer. Leipzig, 194.

Ridley, Jasper. *Garibaldi.* New York: Viking, 1976.

Riehl, Wilhelm Heinrich. *Die bürgerliche Gesellschaft.* 5th ed. Stuttgart, 1861.

———. *Die Familie.* 4th imp. Stuttgart, 1856.

Rilke, Rainer Maria. *Letters to a Young Poet.* Trans. M. P. Herter and John Linton. New York: Norton, 1934.

"Rights and Conditions of Women." Reviews of six books: *Woman and Her Master*, by Lady Morgan; *Woman in Her Social and Domestic Character*, by Mrs. John Sandford; *Female Improvement*, by Mrs. John Sandford; *The Women of England . . .*, by Mrs. Ellis; *Woman's Mission; Woman's Rights & Duties . . .*, by a Woman. *Edinburgh Review* 73 (Apr. 1841): 189–209.

Ritchie, Anne Thackeray. Introduction to *Castle Rackrent* and *The Absentee* by Maria Edgeworth. New York, 1895.

Roberts, Ann. "Mothers and Babies: The Wetnurse and Her Employer in Mid-Nineteenth Century England." *Women's Studies* 3 (1976): 279–93.

Robins, Elizabeth. *Votes for Women: A Play in Three Acts.* London: Mills & Boon, n.d.

Robinson, Henry Crabb. *Crabb Robinson in Germany 1800–1805: Extracts from His Correspondence.* Ed. Edith J. Morley. London: Oxford University Press, 1929.

Robiquet, Jean. *Daily Life in France Under Napoleon.* Trans. Violet M. McDonald. New York: Macmillan, 1963.

Rochard, Jules. "L'Education des filles." *Revue des Deux Mondes* 85 (1888): 644–80.

Roland, Marie-Jeanne Philipon. *Mémoires de Madame Roland.* Ed. Paul de Roux. Paris: Mercure de France, 1966.

Rose, June. *The Perfect Gentleman: The Remarkable Life of Dr. James Miranda Barry.* London: Hutchinson, 1977.

Rosen, Andrew. *Rise up, Women! The Militant Campaign of the Women's Social and Political Union: 1903–1914.* London and Boston: Routledge and Kegan Paul, 1974.

Rosenbaum, Robert A. *Earnest Victorians: Six Great Victorians as Portrayed in Their Own Words and Those of Their Contemporaries.* New York: Hawthorn, 1961.

Rosenberg, Arthur. *Democracy and Socialism: A Contribution to the Political History of the Past 150 Years.* New York: Knopf, 1939.

Ross, Janet Duff-Gordon. *Early Days Recalled.* London, 1891.

Rossi, Count Pellegrino. *Cours d'économie politique.* Vol. 4. Paris, 1854.

Rousseau, Jean Jacques. *Emile: ou, De l'éducation.* 1776. Paris, 1874.

Routh, Harold Victor. *Money, Morals and Manners as Revealed in Modern Literature.* London: Nicholson and Watson, 1935.

Rowbotham, Sheila. *Hidden From History: Rediscovering Women in History from the Seventeenth Century to the Present.* New York: Pantheon, 1975.

Royer, Clémence. *Introduction à la philosophie des femmes: Cours donné à Lausanne.* Lausanne, 1859.

Rudin, Stanley. "The Personal Price of National Glory." *Trans-Action* 2 (Sept.–Oct. 1965): 4–9.

Rudolphi, Karoline. *Gemälde weiblicher Erziehung.* 1807. 2 vols. in 1. 4th ed. Heidelberg, 1857.

[Ruffini, Giovanni]. *Lorenzo Benoni: or, Passages in the Life of an Italian.* New York, 1853.

———. *Vincenzo: or Sunken Rocks.* London, 1863.

Ruge, Arnold. *Studien und Erinnerungen aus den Jahren 1843–45.* Vol. 1. Gesammelte Schriften, vol. 5. Mannheim, 1847.

Ruskin, John. *Praeterita: Outlines of Scenes and Thoughts Perhaps Worthy of Memory in My Past Life, 1885–90.* 1900 New ed. London: Hart-Davis, 1949.

———. *Sesame and Lilies, Unto This Last, and the Political Economy of Art.* 1865. London and New York, 1909.

Russell, Bertrand. *German Social Democracy: Six Lectures.* with an Appendix: "Social Democracy and the Woman Question," by Alys Russell. London, 1896.

Russell, John (advocate). *A Tour in Germany, and Some of the Southern Provinces of the Austrian Empire in the Years 1820, 1821, 1822.* 2 vols. Edinburgh, 1824.

Russell, John F. S. (second earl). *My Life and Adventures.* London: Cassell, 1923.

Ryan, Michael. *The Philosophy of Marriage, in Its Social, Moral and Physical Relations.* 3d ed. North London School of Medicine, 1839. Rpt. ed. New York: Arno Press, 1974.

Sadleir, Michael, *Bulwer: A Panorama.* Vol. 1: *Edward and Rosina, 1803–1836.* Boston: Little Brown, 1931.

———. *The Strange Life of Lady Blessington.* Boston: Little Brown, 1933.

St. John, Christopher. *Ethel Smyth: A Biography, with Additional Chapters by V. Sackville-West and Kathleen Dale.* London: Longmans, 1959.

Sand, George. *Convent Life of George Sand: Selections from "Histoire de ma vie," 1854–55.* Trans. Maria Ellery Mackaye. Boston, 1893.

———. *Histoire de ma vie.* 1854–55. New ed. 4 vols. Paris, 1879.

———. *Lélia.* 1833. 2d ed. 2 vols. Paris, 1833.

Sandford, Mrs. John [Elizabeth Sandford]. *Woman in Her Social and Domestic Character.* 1831. 6th Am. ed. Boston, 1843.

Saunders, Edith. *The Mystery of Marie Lafarge.* London: Clerke & Cockeran, 1951.

Saveth, Edward N., ed. *American History and the Social Sciences.* New York: Free Press, 1964.

Savio-Rossi, Olimpia. "Studii su l'Inghilterra." In 3 parts: "Il pauperismo," "Le prigioni," "La donna." *Rivista Contemporanea Nazionale Italiana* 44 (March 1866): 260–81; 45 (April 1866): 3–19; (May 1866): 129–50.

Scheffler, Carl. *Der junge Tobias: Eine Jungend und ihre Umwelt.* Leipzig, 1927.

Schiemann, Elisabeth. "Erinnerungen an meine Berliner Universitätsjahre." Pt. 1: *Aus den Anfängen des Frauenstudiums an der Friedrich-Wilhelms-Universität.* In *Studium Berolinense,* ed. Wilhelm Weischedel, pp. 845–47. Berlin: Walter de Gruyter, 1960.

Schlegel, Friedrich von. *Friedrich Schlegel's "Lucinde" and the Fragments.* Trans. Peter Firchow. Minneapolis: University of Minnesota Press, 1971.

Schmidt, Margaret Fox. *Passion's Child: The Extraordinary Life of Jane Digby.* New York: Harper, 1976.

Schmidt-Weissenfels, Eduard. *Rahel und ihre Zeit*. Leipzig, 1857.

Schopenhauer, Arthur. "On Women." In *Essays of Schopenhauer*. Trans. Mrs. Rudolph Dircks. London, 1897.

Schöpfer, Jean [Claude Anet]. *Notes sur l'amour*. Paris, 1922.

Schorske, Carl E. "Politics in a New Key: An Austrian Triptych." *Journal of Modern History* 39 (1967): 343–86.

Schröder, Rudolf Alexander. *Unser altes Haus: Jugenderinnerungen*. Bremen: Schünemann, n.d.

Schücking, Levin L. *The Puritan Family: A Social Study from the Literary Sources*. 1929. Trans. Brian Battershaw. London: Routledge and Kegan Paul, 1969.

Schumann, Eugenie. *Memoirs of Eugenie Schumann*. Trans. Marie Busch. London: Heinemann, 1927.

Séché, Léon. *Educateurs et moralistes*. Paris, 1893.

Sedgwick, Henry Dwight. *Madame Récamier: The Biography of a Flirt*. Indianapolis: Bobbs-Merrill, 1940.

Ségalas, Anaïs Ménard. *Enfantines: Poésies à ma fille*. Paris, 1844.

Ségur, Alexandre Joseph Pierre de. *Les femmes, leur condition et leur influence dans l'ordre social . . . continuée jusqu'en 1836*. 1803. Rev. and enl. ed. 4 vols. Paris, 1838.

Ségur, Comtesse Sophie de. *La Santé des enfants*. Paris, 1857.

Seillière, Baron Ernest de. "A Propos du centenaire de Fanny Lewald." *Revue Germanique* 7 (1911): 384–99.

———. *Nouveaux Portraits de femmes*. Paris, 1923.

Sénevier, Valentine de Jussieu de. *Les Confidences de Madame de Lamartine à ses filles d'après une correspondance inédite de la mère du poète*. Paris: Poèsie et Critique, 1957.

Serao, Matilde. *Fantasy: A Novel*. 1883. Trans. Henry Harland. New York, 1890.

———. *Fascino muliebre*. Milan, [1900].

———. "Scuola normale femminile." In *Il romanzo della Fanciulla*, pp. 231–96. Milan, 1893.

Sevrette, Mme Jule. *La Jeune Ménagère: Soins domestiques, cuisine, travaux à l'aiguille, notions de droit usuel, hygiène et médicine élémentaire, jardinage*. Paris, 1904.

Sewell, Sarah Ann. *Woman and the Times We Live In*. 2d ed. Manchester, 1869.

Shaen, Margaret J., ed. *Memorials of Two Sisters: Susanna and Catherine Winkworth*. London, 1908.

Shaw, George Bernard. *Getting Married*. 1908. New York: Brentano's, 1911.

———. *A Manifesto*. Fabian Tracts, no. 2.

Shelley, Lady Frances. *The Diary of Frances, Lady Shelley*. Ed. Richard Edgcumbe. 2 vols. London, 1912–13.

Sherfey, Mary Jane. *The Nature and Evolution of Female Sexuality*. New York: Random, 1972.

Shorter, Edward. "Female Emancipation, Birth Control, and Fertility in European History." *American Historical Review* 78 (1973): 605–40.

Showalter, Elaine, and Showalter, English. "Victorian Women and Menstruation." *Victorian Studies* 14 (1970): 83–89.

Sidgwick, Cecily [Mrs. Alfred Sidgwick]. *Home Life in Germany*. 1908. New York, 1912.

Sieburg, Friedrich. *Chateaubriand*. Trans. Violet MacDonald. New York: St. Martin's Press, 1962.

Silber, Käte. *Pestalozzi: The Man and His Work*. London: Routledge, 1960.

Silbermann, Alphons, and Krüger, Udo Michael. *Abseits der Wirklichkeit: Das Frauenbild in deutschen Lesenbüchern: Eine soziologische Untersuchung.* Cologne: Verlag Wissenschaft & Politik, 1971.

Silver, Catherine Bodard. "Salon, Foyer, Bureau: Women and the Professions in France." In *Clio's Consciousness Raised: New Perspectives on the History of Women,* ed. Mary Hartman and Lois W. Banner, pp. 72–85. New York: Harper, 1974.

Simmel, Georg. *The Sociology of Georg Simmel.* Trans. and ed. Kurt H. Wolff. Glencoe, Ill.: Free Press, 1950.

————. "Tendencies in German Life and Thought Since 1870." *International Monthly* 5 (1902): 93–111, 166–84.

Simon, Jules. *La Liberté.* Paris, 1859.

Smith, Barbara Leigh [later Bodichon]. *A Brief Summary, in Plain Language, of the Most Important Laws Concerning Women: Together with a Few Observations Thereon.* London, 1854.

————. *Women and Work.* London, 1857; New York, 1859.

Smith, Elizabeth Grant. *Memoirs of a Highland Lady: The Autobiography of Elizabeth Grant of Rothemurch, Afterwards Mrs. Smith of Baltiboys, 1797–1830.* Ed. Lady Jane Strachey. 1898. London, 1911.

Smith, Goldwin. "The Machinery of Elective Government." *Nineteenth Century* 11 (1882): 126–48.

Smith, Marion Elmina. *Une Anglaise intellectuelle en France sous la Restauration, Miss Mary Clarke.* Paris: Champion, 1927.

Smith, Sidney. "Female Education." *Edinburgh Review* 15 (Jan. 1810): 299–315.

Smith, Thomas F. A. *The Soul of Germany: A Twelve Years Study of the People from Within, 1902–14.* New York: Dover, 1915.

Smyth, Ethel. *Impressions That Remained: Memoirs.* 2 vols. London, 1919.

Sokoloff, Alice Hunt. *Cosima Wagner: Extraordinary Daughter of Franz Liszt.* New York: Dodd, Mead, 1969.

Solly, Henry. *"These Eighty Years": or, The Story of an Unfinished Life.* Vol. 1. London, 1893.

Somerville, Martha. *Personal Recollections . . . of Mary Somerville: With Selections from Her Correspondence.* Boston, 1874.

Soskice, Juliet M. *Chapters from Childhood: Reminiscences of an Artist's Granddaughter.* 1921. Rpt. ed. Wilmington, Del.: Scholarly Resources, 1972.

Spacks, Patricia M. *The Female Imagination.* New York: Knopf, 1975.

Spain, Nancy. *Mrs. Beeton and Her Husband, by Her Great Niece.* London: Collins, 1948.

Spencer, Herbert. *An Autobiography.* Vol. 1. New York, 1904.

————. *The Principles of Sociology.* 3d rev. and enl. ed. 3 vols. New York, 1891.

————. *Social Statics: or, The Conditions Essential to Human Happiness Specified, and the First of Them Developed.* London, 1851.

Spengler, Joseph H. *France Faces Depopulation.* Durham, N.C.: Duke University Press, 1938.

Spindler, George Washington. "Karl Follen: A Biographical Study." Doctoral dissertation, University of Illinois, 1916.

Spitz, René A. "Authority and Masturbation: Some Remarks on a Bibliographical Investigation." *Psychoanalytic Quarterly* 21 (1952): 490–527.

Stadelmann, Rudolf. *Soziale und politische Geschichte der Revolution von 1848.* Munich: Bruckmann, 1948.

Staël, Germaine Anne de. *Corinne: or, Italy.* 1807. Trans. Isabel Hill. Philadelphia, 1854.

———. *Germany: By the Baroness Staël-Holstein*. Trans. 1810. 3 vols. London, 1814.
Staffe, Baronne Blanche Augustine Angèle. *Usages du monde: Règles du savoir-vivre dans la société moderne: Revue et augmentée*. 1889. 134th ed. Paris: Harvard, 1899.
Stanley, Arthur Penrhyn. *The Life and Correspondence of Thomas Arnold, D.D., Late Head-Master of Rugby School, and Regius Professor of Modern History in the University of Oxford*. 10th ed. 2 vols. New York, 1877.
Stanton, Theodore, ed. *The Woman Question in Europe: A Series of Original Essays*. London, 1884.
Stein, Lorenz von. *Die Frau auf dem sozialen Gebiete*. Stuttgart, 1880.
Steinbömer, Gustav [Gustav Hillard]. *Herren und Narren der Welt*. Munich: P. List, 1955.
Steinhauer, Marieluise Dreschsler. *Fanny Lewald, die deutsche George Sand: Ein Kapitel aus der Geschichte des Frauenromans im 19. Jahrhundert*. Charlottenburg: Hoffmann, 1937.
Stendhal [pseud. of Henri Beyle]. *On Love*. 1822. Trans. Vivian B. Holland. New York: Boni & Liveright, 1927.
———. *A Roman Journal (1817)*. Ed. and trans. Haaken Chevalier. New York: Orion Press, 1957.
Stephen, Barbara. *Emily Davies and Girton College*. London: Constable, 1927.
———. *Girton College: 1869–1932*. Cambridge: Cambridge University Press, 1933.
Stephen, James Fitzjames. *Liberty, Equality, Fraternity*. 1873. Ed. R. J. White. London: Cambridge University Press, 1967.
Stephen, Leslie. *The English Utilitarians*. Vol. 3: *John Stuart Mill*. London, 1900.
[Stephen, Sara]. *Anna: or, Passages from the Life of a Daughter at Home*. 1851. 7th ed. London, 1867.
Stephens, Winifred. *Madame Adam (Juliette Lamber): La Grande Française, from Louis Philippe Until 1917*. New York, 1917.
Stevenson, Robert Louis. *Virginibus Puerisque*. 1881. New York: Scribner's Biographical Edition, 1905.
Stewart, Dugald. *The Works of Dugald Stewart*. 7 vols. Cambridge, Mass., 1829.
Stock, Nelly [Miss Weeton]. *Miss Weeton: Journal of a Governess*. Ed. Edward Hall. 2 vols. London: Oxford University Press, 1936, 1939.
Stoessl, Otto. *Das Haus Erath*. Leipzig: Bücherlese-verlag, 1920.
Stone, A. P., ed. London Council of Law Reporting. *The Law Reports of the Incorporated Queen's Bench Division*. Vol. 1. London, 1891.
Stone, Lawrence. "Literacy and Education in England: 1640–1900." *Past & Present*, 42 (Feb. 1969): 69–139.
Story, William Wetmore, *Roba di Roma*. 3d ed. London, 1864.
Stowe, Harriet Beecher. *Sunny Memories of Foreign Lands*. 2 vols. Boston, 1854.
Strachey, Lytton. *Eminent Victorians: Cardinal Manning, Florence Nightingale, Dr. Arnold, General Gordon*. 1918. Garden City, N.Y.: Garden City Publishers, n.d.
Strachey, Ray. *Struggle: The Stirring Story of Woman's Advance in England*. New York: Duffield, 1930.
Strindberg, August. "*Comrades.*" 1888. Trans. Edith and Warren Bland. In *Modern Continental Plays*, ed. S. Marion Tucker. New York, 1929.
Sunstein, Emily. *A Different Face: The Life of Mary Wollstonecraft*. New York: Harper, 1975.

Suran-Mahire, Mme C. "Le Danger des demi-services." *Revue Universitaire* (Paris) 27 (1918): 105–10.

Swiney, Frances. *The Awakening of Women*. London, 1905.

Swinnerton, Frank. *A Galaxy of Fathers*. London: Hutchinson, 1966.

Symons, Julian. *Thomas Carlyle: The Life and Ideas of a Prophet*. London: Gollancz, 1952.

Tactius. "A Treatise on the Situation, Manners, and Inhabitants of Germany." In *The Works of Tacitus*, vol. 2: 286–342. New York, 1858–70.

Taine, Hippolyte, *Journeys Through France: Being Impressions of the Provinces*. New York, 1897.

————. *Life and Letters of H. Taine*. Trans. Mrs. R. L. Devonshire. London, 1902.

————. *Notes on England*. 1872. Trans. Edward Hyams. Fair Lawn, N.J.: Essential Books, 1958.

————. *Voyage en Italie*. 2 vols. 1866. Collection Litterature, vols. 26–27. Paris: Julliard, 1965.

Talmon, Jacob Leib. *Political Messiansim: The Romantic Phase (1800–1848)*. London: Secker & Warburg, 1960.

Tastu, Mme Amable. *Education maternelle: Simples Leçons d'une mère à ses enfants*. Paris, 1836.

Taylor, Ann Hinton (of Ongar). *Maternal Solicitude for a Daughter's Best Interests*. 6th ed. London, 1816.

————. *Practical Hints to Young Females: On the Duties of a Wife, and a Mother, and a Mistress of a Family*. 3d ed. London, 1815.

————. *Reciprocal Duties of Parents and Children*. Boston, 1825.

Taylor, Edmond. *The Fall of the Dynasties: The Collapse of the Old Order, 1905–1922*. Garden City, N.Y.: Doubleday, 1963.

Taylor, Gordon Rattray. *The Angel-Makers: A Study in the Psychological Origins of Historical Change, 1750–1850*. London: Heinemann, 1958.

————. *Sex in History*. New York: Vanguard, 1954.

Taylor, Isaac (of Ongar). *Advice to the Teens: or, Practical Helps Towards the Formation of One's Own Character*. 2d Eng. ed. Boston, 1820.

Taylor, Isaac (of Stanford Rivers). *Ultimate Civilisation, and Other Essays*. London, 1860.

Taylor, William R. "Domesticity in England and America: 1770–1840." Paper read at the Symposium on the Role of Education, 1964.

Tennyson, Alfred Lord. *The Princess: A Medley*. 1847, 1850. In *Poetic and Dramatic Works of Alfred Lord Tennyson*. pp. 115–162. Cambridge ed. New York and Boston, 1898.

Tennyson, Emily. *The Letters of Emily Lady Tennyson*. Ed. James O. Hoge, University Park, Pa.: Pennsylvania State University Press, 1974.

Thackeray, William Makepeace. *The Newcomes: Memoirs of a Most Respectable Family, Edited by Arthur Pendennis, Esq*. 1854–55. Works, Biographical Edition, vol. 7. New York and London, 1899.

————. *The Paris Sketch Book of Mr. M.A. Titmarsh*. 1840. Works, Biographical Edition, vol. 5. New York and London, 1898.

Théry, Augustin François. *Conseils aux mères sur les moyens de diriger et d'instruire leurs filles*. Rev. ed. 2 vols. Paris, 1859.

————. *Cours complet d'éducation pour les filles. Pt. 1: Education élémentaire de quatre ans à dix ans. Pt. 2: Education moyenne de dix ans à seize ans: (1)*

Exercises de mémoire et le lecture. (2) Conseils aux mères sur les moyens. Paris, 1863–64.

Thibert, Marguerite. "Une Apôtre socialiste de 1848: Pauline Roland." *La Revolution de 1848* 21 (1924–25): 478–502; 22 (1925–26): 524–40.

———. *Le Féminisme dans le socialisme française de 1830 à 1850.* Paris: Giard, 1926.

Thieme, Hans. "Die Rechtsstellung der Frau in Deutschland." In *La Femme*, pt. 2. *Recueils de la Société Jean Bodin* 12 (1962): 351–76.

Thoma, Ludwig. *Erinnerungen von Ludwig Thoma.* Munich, 1919.

———. *Die Geschichte seiner Liebe und Ehe, aus Briefen und Erinnerungen.* Ed. Walther Ziersch. Munich: G. Müller, 1928.

Thönnessen, Werner. *Frauenemanzipation: Politik und Literatur der deutschen Sozialdemokratie zur Frauenbewegung: 1863–1933.* Frankfurt: Europäische Verlagsamt, 1969.

Thomas, Clara. *Love and Work Enough: The Life of Anna Jameson.* Toronto: University of Toronto Press, 1967.

Thomas, Edith. *Pauline Roland: Socialisme et féminisme au XIXe siècle.* Paris; Librairie M. Rivère, 1956.

Thompson, Edward Palmer. *The Making of the English Working Class.* New York: Pantheon, 1964.

———. "The Political Education of Henry Mayhew." *Victorian Studies* 11 (1967): 41–62.

Thompson, William. *Appeal of One Half the Human Race, Women, Against the Pretensions of the Other Half, Men.* 1825. Facsimile rpt. New York: Source Book Press, 1970.

Thomson, Patricia. *The Victorian Heroine: A Changing Ideal, 1837–73.* London: Oxford University Press, 1956.

Thornton, Archibald Paton. *The Habit of Authority: Paternalism in British History.* London: Allen & Unwin, 1966.

Thwaite, Ann. *Waiting for the Party: The Life of Frances Hodgson Burnett, 1849–1924.* London: Secker & Warburg, 1974.

Tiburtius, Franziska. *Erinnerungen einer Achtzigjährigen.* Berlin, 1923.

Tiger, Lionel, and Fox, Robin. *The Imperial Animal.* Toronto and Montreal: McClelland and Stewart, 1971.

Tillett, Benjamin. *Memories and Reflections.* London: John Long, 1931.

Tinayre, Marcelle. *La Femme et son secret.* Paris: Flammarion, 1933.

———. *La Rebelle.* Paris, 1905.

Tocqueville, Alexis de. *Democracy in America.* Ed. J. P. Mayer and Max Lerner. Trans. George Lawrence. New York: Harper, 1966.

———. *Journeys to England and Ireland.* Ed. J. P. Mayer. Trans. G. Lawrence and J. P. Mayer. London: Faber and Faber, 1958.

Tolédano, André. *La Vie de famille sous la restauration et la monarchie de Juillet.* Paris: Michel, 1943.

Touzin, Jenny. *La Dévorante.* Paris, 1879.

Toynbee, Arnold. *Experiences.* London and New York: Oxford University Press, 1969.

Trench, Melesina. *Journal Kept During a Visit to Germany in 1799, 1800.* Ed. The Dean of Westminster (Richard Trench). London: privately printed, 1861.

Treves, Guiliana Artom. *The Golden Ring: The Anglo-Florentines, 1847–1862.* Trans. Sylvia Sprigge. London: Longmans, Green, 1956.

Trilling, Lionel. *Matthew Arnold.* New York: Norton, 1939.
Tristan, Flora [later y Moscozo]. *L'Emancipation de la femme: ou, Le Testament de la paria.* Ed. A. Constant. 2d ed. Paris, 1846.
──────.*Pérégrinations d'une paria.* 2 vols. Paris, 1833, 1834.
──────. *Promenades dans Londres.* Paris and London, 1840.
──────. *Union ouvrière.* Paris, 1843.
Troll-Borostyáni, Irma von. *Die Gleichstellung der Geschlechter und die Reform de Jugend-Erziehung: Die Mission unseres Jährhunderts.* 1884. Rpt. ed. Munich, 1913.
Trollope, Anthony. *Doctor Thorne.* 1858. Ed. Algar Thorold. London and New York, 1902.
Trollope, Frances. *Domestic Manners of the Americans.* 1832. Ed. Donald Smalley. New York: Knopf, 1949.
──────. *Paris and the Parisians in 1835.* 3 vols. London, 1836.
Turgéon, Charles. *Le Féminisme français.* Vol. 1: *L'Emancipation individuelle et sociale de la femme.*Vol. 2: *L'Emancipation politique et familiale de la femme.* Paris. 1902.
Twellmann, Margrit. Vol. 1 *Die Deutsche Frauenbewegung: Ihre Anfange und erste Entwicklung: 1843–1889.* Vol. 2 *Quellen. Marburger Abhandlungen zur politschen Wissenschaft,* vol. 17 (1 and 2). Meisenheim am Glan: A. Hain, 1972.
Unger, Friderike Helene. *Julchen Grünthal.* 2 vols. Berlin, 1798.
[Vandam, Albert Dresden]. *An Englishman in Paris.* 2 vols, in 1. New York, 1892.
──────. *My Paris Notebook.* London, 1894.
Vaughan, Robert. *The Age of Great Cities: or, Modern Society Viewed in Its Relation to Intelligence, Morals and Religion.* 2d ed. London, 1843.
Veblen, Thorstein. *Imperial Germany and the Industrial Revolution.* New York and London: Macmillan, 1915.
Venezia, J. C. "The Protection of Equality in French Public Law." In *The Constitutional Protection of Equality: A Comparative Study.* Ed. Tim Roopmans. Leyden, n.d.
Véron, Louis-Désiré. *Mémoires d'un bourgeois de Paris.* 1853–1855. 2 vols. Paris: G. Le Prat, 1945.
Veuillot, Louis. *Les Libres penseurs.* 7th ed. Paris, 1886.
Villari, Luigi. *Italian Life in Town and Country.* New York and London, 1902.
Visconti Venosta, Giovanni. *Memoirs of Youth: Things Seen and Known, 1847–1860.* 3d ed. Trans. William Prall. Boston, 1914.
[Voilquin, Suzanne]. *Souvenirs d'une fille d'un peuple: ou, La Saint-Simonienne en Egypte, 1834–1836. Par Madame Suzanne V . . . .* Paris, 1866.
Walker, Alexander. *Woman Physiologically Considered, as to Mind, Morals, Marriage, Matrimonial Slavery, Infidelity and Divorce.* London, 1834. Am. ed. New York, 1840.
Walker, Patrick Gordon. "The Origins of the Machine Age." *History Today* 26 (1966): 591–600.
Wallas, Graham. *The Life of Francis Place: 1771–1854.* 1898. 3d ed. New York, 1919.
Ward, Mrs. Humphry [Mary Augusta Arnold]. *Robert Elsmere.* London, 1888.
──────. *A Writer's Recollections.* 2 vols. New York and London, 1918.
Ward, John William. "*Uncle Tom's Cabin,* as a Matter of Historical Fact." *Columbia University Forum* 9, no. 1 (Winter 1966): 42–47.

Watkins, Henry George. *Friendly Hints to Female Servants*. London, 1814.
Webb, Beatrice. *My Apprenticeship*. New York: Longmans, Green, 1926.
Webb, Sidney. *The Decline in the Birth-Rate*. Fabian Tract no. 131. London: Fabian Society, 1907.
———. *Towards Social Democracy? A Study of Social Evolution . . . during the Past Three-Quarters of a Century*. Westminster: Fabian Society, 1916.
Weber, Mariannne. *Lebenserinnerungen*. Bremen: J. Storm, 1948.
———. *Max Weber: Ein Lebensbild*. 1926. 2d ed. Heidelberg: L. Schneider, 1950.
Webster, Augusta. *A Housewife's Opinions*. London, 1879.
Wedekind, Frank. *Spring's Awakening: A Tragedy of Childhood*. 1891. Trans. Eric Bentley. Modern Theatre, ed. Eric Bentley, vol. 6. New York: Doubleday, Anchor Books, 1960.
Weininger, Otto. *Sex and Character*. 1903. Auth. trans., from the 6th German ed. London, 1906.
Weitz, Shirley. *Sex Roles: Biological, Psychological and Social Foundations*. New York: Oxford University Press, 1977.
Wells, Herbert George. *Ann Veronica: A Modern Love Story*. London and New York: Harper, 1909.
Weintraub, J. "Autobiography in Historical Consciousness. *Critical Inquiry vol.* 1, no. 4. 821–48.
———. *Experiment in Autobiography: Discoveries and Conclusions of a Very Ordinary Brain (Since 1866)*. New York: Macmillan, 1934.
———. *Story of a Great Schoolmaster*. New York: Macmillan, 1924.
Westermarck, E. A. *The History of Human Marriage*. 1891. 3d ed. London, 1901.
Wey, Francis. *Les Anglais chez eux*. Rev. and enl. ed. Paris, 1856.
"What Is Woman's Work?" *Saturday Review* 25 (Feb. 15, 1868): 197–98.
Wheatley, Vera. *The Life and Work of Harriet Martineau*. London: Secker & Warburg, 1957.
White, R. J. "The Lower Classes in Regency England." *History Today* 8 (1963): 594–604.
Wiese, Ludwig A. *German Letter on English Education*. 1850. Trans. W. D. Arnold. London, 1854.
———. *Über weibliche Erziehung und Bildung*. Berlin, 1865.
Wikoff, Henry. *My Courtship and Its Consequences; and Revelations from the Foreign Office*. London, 1855.
Wilamowitz-Möllendorf, Ulrich von. *Erinnerungen, 1848–1914*. Leipzig: Koehler, 1928.
Wilberforce, Edward. *Social Life in Munich*. London, 1863.
Wilkins, Ernest H., and Altrocchi, Rudolph, eds. *Italian Short Stories*. Heath's Modern Language Series. Boston: Heath, 1912.
Willey, Basil. *Nineteenth Century Studies: Coleridge to Matthew Arnold*. New York: Columbia University Press, 1949.
Williams. Raymond. *Culture and Society: 1780–1950*. 1958. 2d ed. Garden City, N.Y.: Doubleday, 1960.
Willoughby, Leonard Ashley. *The Romantic Movement in Germany*. London and New York: Oxford University Press, 1930.
Wilson, Edmund. *To the Finland Station: A Study in the Writing and Acting of History*. New York: Harcourt, 1940.
Wingfield-Stratford, Esmé. *Those Earnest Victorians*. New York: Morrow, 1930.
———. *The Victorian Aftermath*. New York: Morrow, 1934.

———. *The Victorian Sunset.* New York: Morrow, 1932.
Winkworth, Catherine, ed. *Life of Amelia Wilhelmina Sieveking.* London, 1863.
———. trans. *Life of Pastor Fliedner, of Kaiserswerth.* London, 1867.
Winkworth, Susanna, trans. *German Love: From the Papers of an Alien by Friedrich Max Müller.* London, 1858.
Wishy, Bernard. *The Child and the Republic: The Dawn of Modern American Child Nurture.* Philadelphia: University of Pennsylvania Press, 1968.
Wolf, Julius, *Der Geburtenrückgang: Die Rationalisierung des Sexuallebens in unserer Zeit.* Jena, 1912.
Wolfe, Bertram D. *"Das Kapital* One Hundred Years Later." *Antioch Review* 26 (Winter 1967): 421–41.
Woman's Rights and Duties Considered with Relation to Their Influence on Society and on Her Own Condition: By a Woman. 2 vols. London, 1840.
"The Women of Italy." Review of *La donna saggia ed amabile* by Anna Pepoli (later Sampieri). 3 vols. *Foreign Quarterly Review* 55 (Oct. 1841): 91–115.
Wood, Herbert George. *Frederick Denison Maurice.* Cambridge: At the University Press, 1950.
Woolf, Virginia Stephen. *Collected Essays.* 4 vols. New York: Harcourt, 1966.
———. *A Room of One's Own.* 1929. New York: Harcourt, 1957.
Wright, Sir Almroth E. *The Unexpurgated Case Against Woman Suffrage.* London: Constable, 1913.
Wrigley, Edward Anthony, ed. *Nineteenth-Century Society: Essays in the Use of Quantitive Methods for the Study of Social Data.* Cambridge: At the University Press, 1972.
Wundt, Wilhelm. *Erlebtes und Erkanntes.* Stuttgart, 1920.
Wylie, Ida Alexa Ross. *The Germans.* Indianapolis, 1911.
———. *My Life with George: An Unconventional Autobiography.* New York: Random, 1940.
Wylie, Laurence. "The Traditional Ideal Family." Lecture delivered at Harvard University for Social Relations Course, Ch. 6 in Social Relations 1080, the Social Structure of France.
Yonge, Charlotte M. *Hannah More.* Boston, 1888.
Young, G. M. *Victorian England: Portrait of an Age.* London and New York: Oxford University Press, 1936.
Young, Michael, and Willmott, Peter. *The Symmetrical Family: A Study of Work and Leisure in the London Region.* New York: Pantheon, 1974.
Young, Wayland. *Eros Denied: Sex in Western Society.* New York: Grove Press, 1964.
Zahn-Harnack, Agnes von. *Die Frauenbewegung: Geschichte, Probleme, Ziele.* Berlin: Deutsche Buch-gemeinschaft, 1928.
———. *Wandlungen des Frauenlebens vom 18. Jahrhundert bis zur Gegenwart.* Wege der Völker, vol. 7, no. 3. Berlin: Pädagogischer Verlag, 1951.
Zeldin, Theodore. "The Conflict of Moralities: Confession, Sin and Pleasure in the Nineteenth Century." In *Conflicts in French Society: Anticlericalism, Education and Morals in the Nineteenth Century,* ed. Theodore Zeldin. London: Allen & Uwin, 1970.
Zepler, Wally, ed. *Sozialismus und Frauenfrage.* Berlin: P. Cassirer, 1919.
Zimmern, Alice. *The Renaissance of Girls' Education in England: A Record of Fifty Years' Progress.* London, 1898.

Zimmern, Helen. *Maria Edgeworth*. Boston, 1883.
Zola, Emile. *Germinal*. 1885. Trans. Havelock Ellis. New York: Knopf, 1937.
Zweig, Stefan. *The World of Yesterday: An Autobiography*. New York: Viking, 1943.

ᴄᴏIndex

A

Abensour, Léon, 298

Abortion: in France, 280n; in Germany, 414

About, Edmond, 41; on French marriage, 50

Abuse, sexual: Christ case, 204; Colette case, 350; comments, 167, 174, 286; in England, 125, 247; English law, 163n; in France, 192–93; German law, 163; Goethe on, 163; Hughes on, 455–56; Mayhew on, 163; Musset on, 112–13; Sand on, 113n

Academic Woman, The (Kirchhoff), 390–95

Academies, literary and scientific: English, 468; French, 326–27; Italian, 441; National Association for the Promotion of Social Science, 469; prizes, 284, 333; Royal Geographical Society, 469; Society of Science, Letters, and Ethics, 446–47

Accolas, Emile, 481

Acton, William: on long engagements, 62; on Mill, 179, 522; on sexuality, 176, 228

Adam, Edmond, 322–24

Adam, Juliette (née Lambert), 301–2, 324–25, 344, 370; *Idées anti-proudhoniennes*, 321–22; life, 45, 319–24; on unmarried aunts, 260

Adelmann, Helene, 421n

Adhémar, M. B. A. d', 345n, 348; on confessors, 197; on feminism, 199; on girls' education, 339; on sex education, 99–100

Administration, women in: in England, 498, 513, 514, 525; in France, 327–28; in Germany, 364, 365–66, 398, 406, 423; in Italy, 429, 447, 453

Adultery, laws concerning, 220–40, 277, 286–87. *See also* Marriage, fidelity in; Sex, extramarital

Advice, books of: Ellis, 27, 55, 105; Helm, 75; *Le Livre de la famille*, 46, 99; Rousseau, 12, 94, 98; Rudolphi, 74–75, 77; Staffe, 39n, 42. *See also* Etiquette

Agnesi, Gaetana, 440

Agoult, Marie d' (née Marie de Flavigny, pseud. Daniel Stern), 26, 30, 290, 301–2, 321, 322–23, 324–25; on courtship, 41, 103–4; *Essai sur la liberté*, 308–9; life, 236, 306–9; on women's role, 343–44

Aiken, Lucy, 163n; on charity, 492

Alexander, Cecil Frances, 57

Allart, Hortense (Hortense de Méritens), 222n, 301–2, 324–25, 370, 411n, 441; *La Femme et la démocratie*, 318; life, 236, 287, 315–19; on sexual brutality, 113

Alletz, Edouard, 50; on French adultery, 221; on French domesticity, 186

Allgemeine Deutsche Frauenverein (All-German Women's Alliance, or ADF), 375, 376, 389, 400; L. Braun and, 384

Almanach des femmes, 291

Althaus, Theodor, 367–69

Alton Locke (C. Kingsley), 465–66

Amalie, Grand Duchess of Saxony, 207–8

Serao, 446–48; women's
periodicals, 285–86, 288–90,
376n, 421, 438–39, 461, 524. *See
also names of individual writers*
Wundt, Wilhelm, 393
Wüstenfeld, Emilie, 368
Wylie, Ida Alexa Ross: at Cheltenham, 480n; on German econ-
omizing, 78, 81–82, 141; on
German women, 389, 423; on
WSPU, 531

Y
Yonge, Charlotte: on education in

marriage, 194; life, 485, 490; on
self-censorship, 106
Young Germany, 355, 372
Young Italy, 429
Yver, Colette (Antoinette Huzard),
Les Dames du palais, 336

Z
Zahn-Harnack, Agnes von, 380, 413
Zepler, Wally, 148, 410
Zetkin, Clara, 383, 400
Zola, Emile, *Germinal,* 192, 383
Zweig, Stefan, 22n, 81, 114, 232

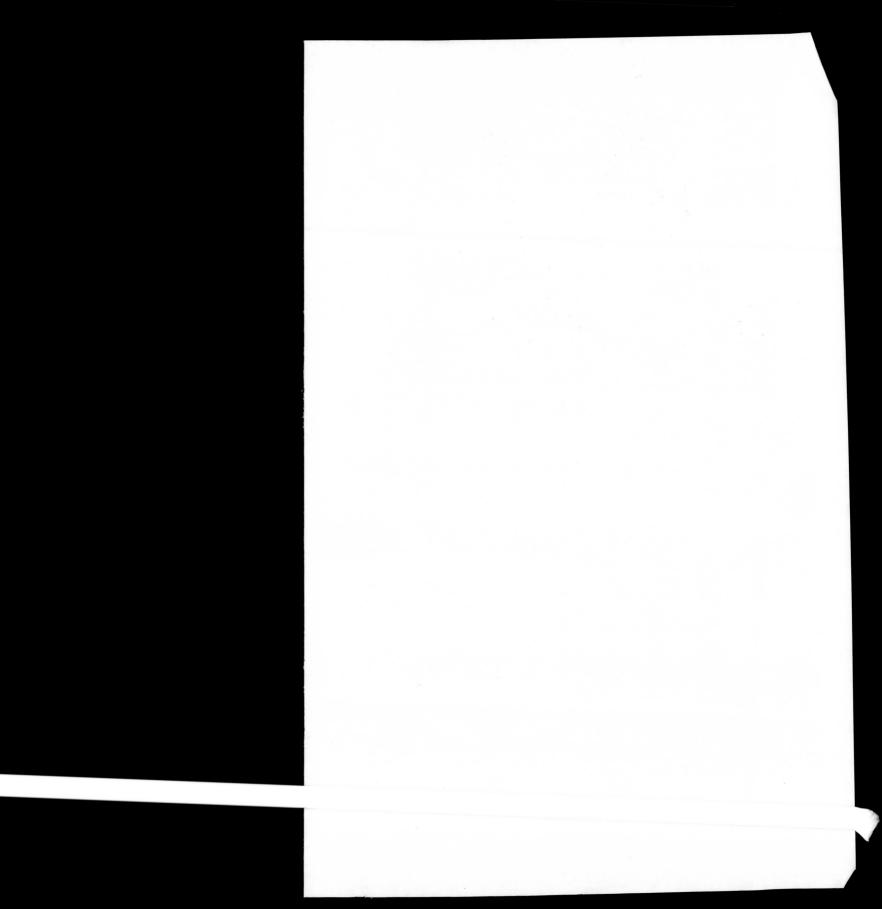